DevSecOps in Oracle Cloud: Securing and Automating Oracle Cloud Infrastructure

Erik Benner, ACED
Ahmed Aboulnaga, ACE Pro
Dhrumil Patel

Pearson

DevSecOps in Oracle Cloud: Securing and Automating Oracle Cloud Infrastructure

Erik Benner, Ahmed Aboulnaga, Dhrumil Patel

Library of Congress Control Number: 2025932599

ISBN-13: 978-0-13-802941-8
ISBN-10: 0-13-802941-5

Director, ITP Product Management
Julie Phifer

Executive Editor
Nancy Davis

Sponsoring Editor
Malobika Chakraborty

Managing Editor
Sandra Schroeder

Development Editor
Ellie Bru

Project Editor
Tonya Simpson

Copy Editor
Chuck Hutchinson

Technical Editor
Jonathan Spindel

Editorial Assistant
Cindy Teeters

Cover Designer
Chuti Prasertsith

Composition
codeMantra

Indexer
Timothy Wright

Proofreader
Jennifer Hinchliffe

Warning and Disclaimer

This book is designed to provide information about implementing traditional and cloud native workloads on Oracle Cloud Infrastructure while leveraging a DevSecOps approach. Every effort has been made to make this book as complete and as accurate as possible, but no warranty or fitness is implied.

The information is provided on an "as is" basis. The authors, Oracle Press, and Pearson shall have neither liability nor responsibility to any person or entity with respect to any loss or damages arising from the information contained in this book or from the use of the discs or programs that may accompany it.

The views expressed in this book are those of the author or authors and do not necessarily reflect the views of Oracle.

Oracle does not make any representations or warranties as to the accuracy, adequacy, or completeness of any information contained in this work, and is not responsible for any errors or omissions.

Feedback Information

At Oracle Press, our goal is to create in-depth technical books of the highest quality and value. Each book is crafted with care and precision, undergoing rigorous development that involves the unique expertise of members from the professional technical community.

Readers' feedback is a natural continuation of this process. If you have any comments regarding how we could improve the quality of this book, or otherwise alter it to better suit your needs, you can contact us through email at feedback@oraclepress.com. Please make sure to include the book title and ISBN in your message.

We greatly appreciate your assistance.

Please contact us with concerns about any potential bias at https://www.pearson.com/report-bias.html.

Trademark Acknowledgments

All terms mentioned in this book that are known to be trademarks or service marks have been appropriately capitalized. Oracle Press or Oracle Corporation cannot attest to the accuracy of this information. Use of a term in this book should not be regarded as affecting the validity of any trademark or service mark.

About the Authors

Erik Benner is the vice president of Enterprise Transformation at Mythics, LLC, and an Oracle ACE Director. He is an expert strategist for both federal, state, and local government, as well as commercial customers across the United States. His customer engagements range from enterprise cloud transformations and data center modernization to large-scale virtualization projects and Oracle Engineered Systems implementations. Erik's passion for volunteering is evident through his role as the president of the Cloud Computing Special Interest Group (SIG), co-chair of the OATUG Oracle Enterprise Manager SIG, and active participation in user groups sitting on various committees. He frequently presents at conferences such as Oracle CloudWorld, Oracle FedForum, East Coast Oracle, ASCEND, and Blueprint4d. Having worked with Oracle and Sun Systems since the mid-'90s, Erik is well-versed in most of the core Oracle technologies, including Oracle Cloud, Oracle Linux, and Oracle Databases.

When not flying to the far points of the country from the Atlanta metro area, he enjoys spending time with his family at their observatory, where the telescopes outnumber the people, or on cloudy nights blowing glass in his private glass studio.

Ahmed Aboulnaga has a professional focus in technical management, architecture, and consulting within Oracle, Java, and cloud technologies, having implemented enterprise solutions for commercial, government, and global customers throughout his career. Ahmed is an Oracle ACE, published author, and frequently presents on new and trending technologies at major conferences. Currently residing in the Washington DC region, Ahmed holds a master's degree in computer science from George Mason University.

Dhrumil Patel is a Solutions Architect at Mythics, LLC. He works closely with the sales and engineering team to provide Oracle Cloud Infrastructure (OCI), thought leadership, and solutioning expertise. He also works with Oracle and internal/external clients to develop highly automated and efficient digital transformation processes and cloud migration processes. Prior to his current role, he held the position of Senior Principal Consultant. He worked with his clients to administer and maintain their on-premises and cloud environments' footprints. Moreover, he has years of experience as a DBA Consultant.

About the Technical Reviewer

Jonathan Spindel: With more than 25 years in the IT industry, Jonathan Spindel is a Senior Principal Solutions Architect and Technical Leader at Bell Integration, a premier provider of digital transformation solutions. His extensive experience spans data center operations and architecture, network operations, AI Infrastructure, RH OpenShift, RH Enterprise Linux, Oracle Linux, and transitional Cloud CSP's Oracle Cloud Infrastructure, AWS, and Azure platforms, supported by multiple certifications in Sales, Solution Engineering, and Cloud Technologies. He also is a published author on Linux and automation and is working on a second book in OpenSource virtualization.

Jonathan is known for his exceptional troubleshooting skills and deep expertise in Oracle Linux, OCI, AWS, and GCP, reflected in his published works, including white papers and a comprehensive book on the subject. As a trusted advisor, he excels in fostering robust client relationships, offering strategic insights on cloud technologies and IT infrastructures, and mentoring peers to drive innovation and achieve business objectives.

Driven by a passion for crafting and delivering tailored solutions, Jonathan translates complex technical challenges into actionable strategies that align with both client goals and organizational needs.

Dedications

Erik: To those who inspired it, everyone who has been up late trying to figure out new and better ways to get things done.

Ahmed: To my father, who encouraged my love of technology and whose voice still guides me to this day.

Dhrumil: To my beloved family. They have supported me throughout this journey, which had ups and downs. Your belief in me has kept me going. This book is dedicated to you all. My words cannot describe my love to you all.

Acknowledgments

Erik: Special thanks to Nancy Davis, executive editor at Pearson, and Ellie Bru, our development editor. You kept pushing us to get a better book and stuck by the team when things slowed down. Thanks to my senior leaders at work, Aaron Cornfeld, Mukund Mohan, Paul Siefert, and Doug Altamura, who encourage me to share my knowledge with others. A special callout to Jennifer Nicholson and the Oracle ACE program for enabling folks to do more. If you want to become an ACE, please feel free to reach out to me or Ahmed. It's a long process, but it's worthwhile. And not least, my co-authors Ahmed and Dhrumil, the other members of the team who worked to get this book done. We hope you learn some new skills and tricks from this book.

Ahmed: Many thanks to my friends and family who continue to support me professionally and personally. Carolin, Ramy, Maya, Walid, Sharif, Pooja, Paul, Mahmoud, Tim, Pradip, Yudhvir, Eric, Michael, and Pat—you have my eternal gratitude. I also want to thank my co-authors Erik, for trusting me enough to extend an invitation to co-author this book, and Dhrumil, for joining us on our journey.

Dhrumil: Special thanks to Erik Benner for his mentorship. Without him, I would never have been part of this journey. Erik Benner and Ahmed Aboulnaga both welcomed me to their team and supported me throughout the process. I would also like to acknowledge Ellie Bru, our development editor, and Nancy Davis, executive editor, for their relentless support through this long process.

Contents at a Glance

Introduction   xxii

1   Introduction to OCI and DevSecOps   1

2   Oracle Cloud Infrastructure—Governance   11

3   Oracle IaaS—Security   37

4   Oracle IaaS—Cloud-Native Technologies   89

5   Oracle IaaS—Network   121

6   Oracle IaaS—Compute   139

7   Oracle IaaS—Storage   165

8   Oracle DBaaS—Databases   183

9   OCI DevOps Service   207

10   Data Safe   225

11   Identity and Access Management   257

12   Operating System Security   293

13   Observability and Management   303

14   Cloud Guard   321

15   An Introduction to Ansible   345

16   Using Ansible in OCI   363

17   Ansible—Installing and Configuring OLAM   383

18   Ansible Full Stack Sample   423

19   Infrastructure as Code   453

20   Terraform API with Examples   461

21   Terraform Sample Use Case   487

**22   Enterprise Manager Cloud Control
       Installation   515**

**23   Using Oracle Enterprise Manager Cloud
       Control   547**

Index   583

Contents

Introduction   xxii

1   Introduction to OCI and DevSecOps   1
What Is DevSecOps?   4
Why DevSecOps?   5
What Makes Up a DevSecOps Team?   6
Benefits of OCI   7
OCI Free Services   9
Summary   10

2   Oracle Cloud Infrastructure—Governance   11
Tenancy Account Management and
Governance   11
        Creating a New Tenancy   12
        Organizational Governance   15
Cloud Advisor   20
        Cost Management   22
        Performance   24
        High Availability   25
        Billing and Budgets   26
        Dashboards   32
Summary   36

3   Oracle IaaS—Security   37
Identity and Access Management (IAM)   37
Security Zones   39
Bastions   44
Threat Intelligence Service   49
Web Application Firewall (WAF)   54
Firewall   65
Vault   80
Audit   84
Summary   87

4   Oracle IaaS—Cloud-Native Technologies   89

Functions   90

    Setting Up the Tenancy   91

    Creating the Application   92

    Setting Up the Linux Host   95

    Creating and Running a Function   104

Streams   107

Events   108

Oracle Kubernetes Engine (OKE)   112

    Docker   113

    Key Terms   113

Summary   119

5   Oracle IaaS—Network   121

Getting Started with OCI Networking   121

    Understanding Concepts and Terminology   121

    Walking Through a Basic Network Architecture Diagram   122

Creating Your First VCN and Subnet   124

    Creating a VCN   124

    Creating a Subnet   125

    Updating the Security List   126

Connecting VCNs Through Local Peering   127

    Creating Local Peering Gateways and Establishing Peering   128

    Adding a New Route Rule to the Route Table   129

    Creating Network Security Groups (NSGs)   130

    Attaching VNIC to the Network Security Group   131

Creating Flow Logs   132

Using Network Path Analyzer   133

Understanding Gateways   136

Securing Your Network   136

Summary   137

6   Oracle IaaS—Compute   139

Building a VM   139

X86 and ARM, AMD vs. Intel... What's the
Scoop?   145

A VM Is More Than a VM; There Are
Options...   147

OS Images and the Marketplace   153

Custom OS Images   160

Summary   163

7   Oracle IaaS—Storage   165

Block Volume   166

Creating and Attaching   166

Configuring Performance   169

Performing a Backup   172

Object Storage   175

File Storage   176

Archive Storage   179

How to Secure Your Storage   179

Summary   181

8   Oracle DBaaS—Databases   183

Oracle's DBaaS Offerings   183

Database as a Base Database
Service   186

Exadata Cloud Service and Exadata
Cloud@Customer   186

Autonomous Database
Services   187

MySQL and MySQL HeatWave   189

NoSQL   190

How to Provision Databases   191

Provisioning Base Database
Service   191

Provisioning the Autonomous
Database Service   196

Provisioning MySQL
Database   199

Provisioning the NoSQL
Database   204

Summary   205

9   OCI DevOps Service   207

Overview of OCI DevOps   208

Deployment Environments   210

Deployment Strategies   210

DevOps Components and Resources   211

How to Create a Working Sample
Project   214

Creating Compute Instances to
Deploy To   215

Granting Permissions to Compute
Instance Run Command
Plug   215

Creating an Artifact Registry to Host
Artifacts   216

Uploading a Script to the Artifact
Registry   216

Creating a Notification Topic   218

Creating a DevOps Project   218

Creating an Environment in the
DevOps Project   218

Adding an Artifact from the
Artifact Registry to the DevOps
Project   219

Adding an Instance Group
Deployment Configuration
Artifact   220

Creating a Deployment
Pipeline   222

Running the Deployment
Pipeline   222

Summary   224

10   Data Safe   225

Security Assessment   225

    User Assessment   228

Data Discovery   230

Data Masking   236

Activity Auditing   241

Alerts   243

How to Add a Database   244

    Registering an Autonomous Database   245

    Registering an Oracle Base Database System   247

    Registering an On-Premises Database   253

Summary   255

11   Identity and Access Management   257

Compartments   257

Users   258

    Database Passwords   258

    API Keys   263

Groups   269

Dynamic Groups   269

Policies   273

Federation   277

Summary   292

12   Operating System Security   293

Oracle Ksplice   293

Oracle Autonomous Linux   296

Vulnerability Scanning Service (VSS)   298

Summary   301

13   Observability and Management   303

OCI Logging Service   303

    Log Format   303

    Log Types   305

    Log Groups   307

Exercise 1: Enabling a Service Log   307

Exercise 2: Creating a Custom Log   311

Oracle Cloud Logging Analytics   313

    Setting Up Logging Analytics for the First Time   313

    Downloading and Installing the Management Agent   317

    Clearing and Resetting Logging Analytics   320

Summary   320

14   Cloud Guard   321

Initial Configuration   322

Recipe Management   331

    Using Detector Recipes   331

    Using Responder Recipes   332

    Accessing Cloud Guard Recipes   332

    Managing Detector Recipes   333

    Managing Responder Recipes   334

Security Zones   338

    Adding a New Security Zone   340

Summary   343

15   An Introduction to Ansible   345

What Is Ansible?   345

What Is OLAM?   346

    Sizing the Deployment   348

OCI Authentication   350

    Getting the OCI Information   350

    Adding the OLAM Credential   353

Collections and Modules   354

    Installing the OCI Collection on Your OCI Development System   354

Playbooks   356

Introduction to YAML   359

Summary   362

16   Using Ansible in OCI   363

Using Ansible   363

Writing Playbooks   363

Sample Playbooks   369

Common OCI Playbooks   374

Summary   382

**17   Ansible—Installing and Configuring
OLAM   383**

Installation   383

Preparing Linux   383

Setting Up PostgreSQL   385

Installing OLAM   387

OLAM Management   392

Resource Management   394

Templates   395

Credentials   399

Projects   401

Inventory   403

Hosts   408

Access Management   410

Organizations   410

Users   412

Teams   414

OLAM Administrative Options   416

Credential Types   416

Notifications   417

Management Jobs   418

Instance Groups   420

Applications   420

Execution Environments   420

Summary   421

18   Ansible Full Stack Sample   423

Ansible in the Real World   423

Planning a Team   423

Creating Users   423

Creating Teams   426

Setting Up an Inventory   439

Summary   451

19   **Infrastructure as Code   453**

The Problem That IaC Solves   454

Introducing Terraform as an IaC Tool   454

Terraform Concepts and Terminology   455

Declarative Approach   457

State File   457

Immutable Infrastructure   457

Plug-ins   458

Terraform and OCI   459

Terraform Best Practices   459

Summary   460

20   **Terraform API with Examples   461**

Setting Up Terraform in OCI   461

Downloading and Installing
Terraform   461

Creating RSA Keys Required for API
Signing   463

Adding a Policy for the User to Read
OCI Resources   465

Exercise 1: Running Terraform for the First
Time   466

Creating a Working
Directory   466

Creating an Initial Terraform
Script   466

Running Terraform Initialize for the
First Time   467

Running terraform plan for the First
Time   468

Running terraform apply for the First
Time   469

Exercise 2: Parameterizing Terraform
Configuration   471

Exercise 3: Understanding the Terraform OCI
Documentation   473

    Updating Terraform Configuration
    from the Terraform OCI
    Documentation   474

    Running the Terraform Script to Create
    and List a Block Volume   478

    Updating a Resource   482

    Parameterizing from Other
    Output   483

    Debugging Errors   484

Summary   485

21   Terraform Sample Use Case   487

Confirming IAM Policies   489

Setting Up Terraform   489

    Applying the Changes   490

Creating a New Compartment   490

    Applying the Changes   491

    Rerunning Terraform Apply with No
    Changes   491

    Rerunning Terraform Apply
    After a Change in Terraform
    Configuration   493

    Rerunning Terraform Apply After a
    Change on the OCI Console   494

Creating a Virtual Cloud Network   494

    Defining a VCN Module   494

    Defining Security Lists and Ingress/
    Egress Rules   495

    Defining the Private and Public
    Subnets   498

    Updating the Outputs File   499

    Applying the Changes   500

Creating a Compute Instance   502

    Applying the Changes   504

Creating an Autonomous Database   505

    Applying the Changes   506

Replicating to a Production
Environment   507

Using Other Terraform Commands   508

Formatting Terraform
Configuration   508

Validating Terraform
Configuration   508

Listing All Resources in the
Terraform State   508

Displaying Details of All Resources
from the Terraform State   509

Viewing the Terraform
Output   510

Destroying Resources   510

Destroying the Entire
Infrastructure   511

Destroying a Single Terraform
Resource   511

Stopping/Starting Instances with
Terraform   511

Summary   512

22   **Enterprise Manager Cloud Control
Installation   515**

Installing and Configuring the Repository
Database   517

Installing and Configuring Oracle Management
Service   522

OPatch   526

Oracle Enterprise Manager 13c
Update 12 for OMS   526

Oracle Enterprise Manager 13c
Release 5 Update 12 for Oracle
Management Agent   527

Installing and Configuring Oracle Analytics
Server   529

Installing JDK   529

Installing FMW
Infrastructure   530

Installing OAS   531

Configuring OAS   532

Integrating OAS with Oracle Enterprise Manager   534

Configuring Security Infrastructure   534

Configuring the Required OAS Datasource   537

Setting OAS Support for Oracle Enterprise Manager-Provided Reports   538

Summary   546

23   Using Oracle Enterprise Manager Cloud Control   547

Setting Up Administrators and Users   551

Monitoring OCI Environments   554

Monitoring OCI Compute Instance   554

Monitoring OCI Autonomous Database   558

Integrating Oracle Enterprise Manager with OCI   564

Setting Up Preferred Credentials   564

Creating an Enterprise Manager Target Group   568

Creating an Oracle Enterprise Manager Super Administrator   569

Creating a Global Named Credential   570

Incorporating Best Practices   578

Monitoring Database Security   579

Patching Oracle Enterprise Manager   579

Sizing Oracle Enterprise Manager   580

Summary   581

Index   583

Introduction

DevSecOps enables individuals and organizations to integrate security seamlessly into the development and deployment processes. Given the increasing frequency and sophistication of cyber threats, it is essential to learn DevSecOps to ensure that security is a proactive and ongoing consideration throughout all stages of software development, rather than merely an afterthought.

By adopting DevSecOps principles, developers, operations teams, and security professionals can collaborate more effectively to identify vulnerabilities early, mitigate risks, and maintain compliance with regulatory standards. Additionally, this approach enhances the ability to respond quickly to security incidents, minimizing potential damage and reducing the costs associated with late-stage security fixes.

As companies adopt faster development cycles and more complex systems, understanding DevSecOps becomes crucial for creating secure, scalable, and resilient applications that meet the demands of modern, high-speed environments.

Implementing Oracle Cloud Infrastructure (OCI) can present several challenges due to its complexity and the wide range of services it offers. The variety of tools and services—including compute, networking, storage, security, and database options—requires a deep understanding of cloud concepts and their integration within the OCI ecosystem. Some architects may assume that OCI is solely focused on Oracle Database, but it actually provides many technologies unrelated to Oracle's Database.

If you want to gain mastery over the different aspects of OCI, hands-on experience is essential. However, gaining this experience can be challenging for learners who may not have access to real-world environments or dedicated training resources. Additionally, staying informed about best practices and optimizing costs within OCI complicates the learning process because it requires a balance between functionality, security, and cost-effectiveness.

This book aims to provide both newcomers to cloud computing and those with experience on other cloud platforms with a comprehensive overview of the core services that OCI offers, along with guidance on effectively utilizing them within a DevSecOps model.

Who Should Read This Book?

This book is intended for developers, DevOps professionals, architects, or anyone interested in understanding the various features of OCI. No prior knowledge of OCI is assumed, although familiarity with general cloud services can be beneficial.

How This Book Is Organized

The book is organized into two parts. The first part (Chapters 1 to 8) focuses on the core Oracle Cloud Infrastructure (OCI) services, helping those new to OCI understand the key differences between OCI and other cloud platforms. The second part (Chapters 9 to 23) delves into using DevOps tools like Ansible and Terraform to deploy and manage solutions within OCI. If you are already familiar with other cloud platforms, you will find value in the introduction to OCI and can easily transition to the more advanced topics and areas of interest covered later in the book.

This book adopts a hands-on approach, featuring step-by-step examples for both Terraform and Ansible. You can utilize this book as a learning tool or as a reference point for implementing specific features.

Book Structure

The book is organized into 23 chapters: Chapters 1–8 drill into core OCI services such as networking, compute, storage, and databases, as well as how many of their most popular features are used. The second part, Chapters 9–23, covers how to use automation with technologies like Ansible, Terraform, and Oracle Enterprise Manager to empower the DevSecOps team to better leverage the power of OCI.

Chapter 1, "Introduction to OCI and DevSecOps": This chapter introduces you to Oracle Cloud Infrastructure. Basic concepts and terminology in OCI are introduced, along with identity and access management. This chapter does not attempt to exhaustively cover OCI at a high level but instead covers the critical basics so that you are familiar with foundational OCI constructs in the chapters that follow. The goal of this chapter is to orient yourself to OCI and is relevant if you have prior experience with other cloud platforms or if you are new to cloud-based development.

Chapter 2, "Oracle Cloud Infrastructure—Governance": This chapter covers how tenancies are organized, showing how multiple tenancies can be organized in a parent/child relationship. The chapter also covers the basics of tracking cloud expenses, plus using budgets, the cost analysis tool, and dashboards.

Chapter 3, "Oracle IaaS—Security": Security is one of the main pillars of the OCI. This chapter covers the Identity and Security services available. It also provides details on how to set up most of these services.

Chapter 4, "Oracle IaaS—Cloud-Native Technologies": Cloud-native technologies include Kubernetes, events, functions, and streams. Functions are an open-source alternative for serverless computing. In this chapter, we show how to set up and call functions. The chapter also shows how to deploy Kubernetes clusters inside OCI, making it easy to maintain large numbers of Docker containers. We also cover events and introduce streams.

Chapter 5, "Oracle IaaS—Network": A robust and reliable network is the backbone of cloud computing. This chapter introduces networking concepts and walks through the setup of your first cloud network.

Chapter 6, "Oracle IaaS—Compute": OCI does compute differently, in a better way, from building more secure compute instances to making the right choice for your workload of AMD, Intel, or Ampere Arm–based computing. This chapter covers how OCI secures compute and allows you to separate the provisioning of CPU and memory, allowing you to optimally deploy IaaS VMs. The chapter also covers custom images and the OCI marketplace, a location for prebuilt images.

Chapter 7, "Oracle IaaS—Storage": OCI offers a number of storage options, each serving a different function. This chapter explains and demonstrates the provisioning of block volumes, object storage, file storage, and archive storage.

Chapter 8, "Oracle DBaaS—Databases": This chapter covers all database options offered as a part of Database as a Service by OCI. It covers different services like Base Database Service, Autonomous Database, MySQL HeatWave, and NoSQL databases.

Chapter 9, "OCI DevOps Service": With OCI DevOps, fully automated CI/CD pipelines can be created. The steps to build, test, and deploy code to OKE, functions, and computer are covered in this chapter.

Chapter 10, "Data Safe": Data Safe is a security and compliance service offered for on-premises and cloud databases. We dive into all features of Data Safe and how to implement them for your database environment.

Chapter 11, "Identity and Access Management": This chapter covers some of the core components of Identity and Access Management (IAM) like User, Group, Compartment, and so on. It also goes into detail on how to configure federation with identity providers like Microsoft Active Directory.

Chapter 12, "Operating System Security": Maintaining a high security posture for your cloud infrastructure is imperative, and this chapter goes over OCI services such as Ksplice, Autonomous Linux, and VSS, which help achieve that.

Chapter 13, "Observability and Management": The OCI Logging Service provides a single pane view to all logging across your OCI infrastructure. In this chapter, we go through the setup, custom logging, and Oracle Cloud Analytics.

Chapter 14, "Cloud Guard": Security is a key area and should never be bolted onto a cloud deployment as an afterthought. This chapter covers Cloud Guard, a free service that allows you to force security on the services running in OCI.

Chapter 15, "An Introduction to Ansible": Ansible is a powerful DevSecOps tool, enabling full-stack automation for the entire lifecycle. This chapter introduces you to OLAM and AWX, which enable enterprise-grade centralized automation, all for the cost of running the server!

Chapter 16, "Using Ansible in OCI": This chapter introduces you to the basics of using Ansible in OCI. It covers authenticating Ansible access to plenty of sample playbooks that can be glued to others to manage your application.

Chapter 17, "Ansible—Installing and Configuring OLAM": This chapter walks you step-by-step through how to install the free OLAM in your cloud environment. It also walks you through each of the features of OLAM.

Chapter 18, "Ansible Full Stack Sample": This final Ansible chapter covers step-by-step how to configure a freshly installed OLAM system to enable end users and development staff to run custom playbooks against an inventory of servers. This chapter combines all the skills you learned in the previous Ansible chapters in the final example.

Chapter 19, "Infrastructure as Code": One tool well-suited for IaC is Terraform. This chapter delves into IaC and Terraform concepts.

Chapter 20, "Terraform API with Examples": This chapter provides multiple step-by-step exercises to demonstrate Terraform usage, including first-time setup, parameterization, and debugging.

Chapter 21, "Terraform Sample Use Case": This chapter takes a diagrammed topology and fully walks through the complete provisioning of this sample architecture using Terraform.

Chapter 22, "Enterprise Manager Cloud Control Installation": Oracle Enterprise Manager is an important and widely used management software. It helps you manage on-premises and cloud deployments. This chapter covers the detailed installation process of Oracle Enterprise Manager and how to integrate Oracle Analytics Server (OAS) for reporting.

Chapter 23, "Using Oracle Enterprise Manager Cloud Control": This chapter covers how to configure Oracle Enterprise Manager to monitor OCI resources. It also goes over integrating it with some of the OCI services like Operation Insight and Logging Analytics and some of the best practices for Oracle Enterprise Manager.

Register Your Product

Register your copy of *DevSecOps in Oracle Cloud: Securing and Automating Oracle Cloud Infrastructure* at informit.com for convenient access to downloads, updates, and corrections as they become available. To start the registration process, go to informit.com/register and log in or create an account. Enter the product ISBN (9780138029418) and click Submit. Once the process is complete, you will find any available content under "Registered Products."

Figure Credits

Cover image: Jullasart somdok/Shutterstock
Figures 3-38, 3-56: Google LLC
Figure 3-57, 11-27–11-41: Microsoft Corporation
Figures 4-5, 4-6, 4-9, 7-2, 7-4, 7-10, 7-12, 12-1, 12-2, 13-9, 13-16, 20-1, 20-5–20-9, 20-14, 20-15, 20-17, 20-19–20-21, 21-2, 21-4–21-6, 21-8–21-14: Linux
Figures 19-3, 20-2, 20-10, and 20-11: HashiCorp
Figure 17-1: Mozilla Corporation

1

Introduction to OCI and DevSecOps

As organizations move to the cloud, there are a few assumptions and challenges that need to be addressed to fully realize the transformation to the cloud and leverage its true benefits.

The most common assumption it that the cloud will save you money. This assumption is true but also false. One of the most common challenges organizations have is overspending in the cloud. This overspending is most commonly caused by two factors: incorrectly sizing the expected resources needed or inefficiently using the resources provisioned. Incorrectly sizing resources is often caused by a lack of understanding of the workload by the architect designing the solution. The second cause of incorrectly sized resources is when the operations team overestimates the needed workload and configures the cloud to provide more than is needed in an effort to eliminate the users complaining about performance problems. Add in the more mundane operational needs for developing and deploying the applications and then mix in the need for security, and you have a cloud project with some serious challenges.

All of these issues can be resolved with your team following a development, security, and operations (DevSecOps) methodology and its related processes. The DevSecOps methodology integrates security practices within the DevOps process. Its goal is to create a culture where security is a shared responsibility throughout the entire IT lifecycle, from initial design through development and operations. The DevSecOps team also benefits from running in a cloud, as Oracle Cloud Infrastructure (OCI) inherently supports the methodology.

OCI, by its nature, enables the DevSecOps methodology. OCI has free and low-cost services in three key areas:

- **Scalability and Flexibility:** OCI offers the scalability and flexibility necessary for DevSecOps practices. Unlike most other cloud service providers (CSPs), OCI's computer service unbundles the compute cores and memory, allowing the administrator to provision exactly what the application needs. Teams can also rapidly provision resources, scale applications, and adjust infrastructure as needed, supporting the quick iteration cycles central to DevSecOps.

- **Automation:** While other CSPs often come with tools and services that facilitate automation, which is a core component of DevSecOps, automated CI/CD pipelines, Infrastructure as Code (IaC), and automated security testing can be implemented more easily using cloud-native tools that are included with OCI for no additional cost. Some examples are Terraform and Ansible, along with Oracle Linux Automation Manager, an AWX-based Ansible manager.
- **Integrated Services:** Cloud providers offer a range of integrated services that support DevSecOps practices, including managed databases, logging, monitoring, and security services. This integration reduces the overhead of setting up and maintaining these services manually. With OCI, many of these services are provided for little to no additional cost and have tight integration into the database.

While OCI is an enabler, your team needs to be aware of some specific challenges. The good news is that OCI already has services and features that address these issues:

- **Shared Responsibility Model:** In cloud environments, security responsibilities are shared between the cloud provider and the customer. DevSecOps teams need to understand and manage their responsibilities, such as securing applications and data while the provider secures the infrastructure. OCI helps solve this issue with its large number of certifications, providing a secure foundation for the cloud workload.
- **Complexity and Visibility:** Managing security in a dynamic cloud environment can be complex. DevSecOps teams need to maintain visibility into their cloud infrastructure and ensure consistent security policies across different services and environments. OCI helps solve this with its Observability and Manageability services, such as Log Analytics, which lets the team analyze, automatically correlate, and alert from almost all events and logs. In this book we will drill down into these areas and more, providing an understanding of how OCI enables a DevSecOps team.

With DevOps, we traditionally follow a basic process of plan, code, build, test, release, deploy, operate, and monitor (see Figure 1-1).

With DevSecOps, we add additional tasks into the process (as seen in Figure 1-2):

- **Scan:** Scan both source code and infrastructure for vulnerabilities. Vulnerabilities can be scanned using the Vulnerability Scanning service.
- **Analyze:** Analyze the results of the scan for vulnerabilities.
- **Remediate:** Patch the vulnerabilities and resolve architectural vulnerabilities. OS patching can be automated by using the OS Management Hub.
- **Threat Management:** Leverage tools like OCI Threat Intelligence or Cloud Guard Threat Detector to gain better insights into how systems are being attacked.

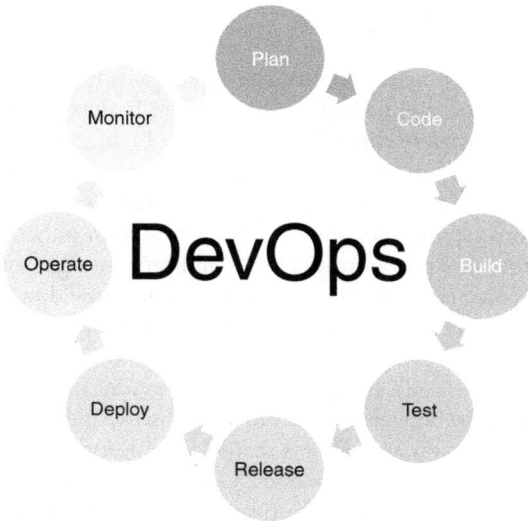

Figure 1-1 DevOps Cycle

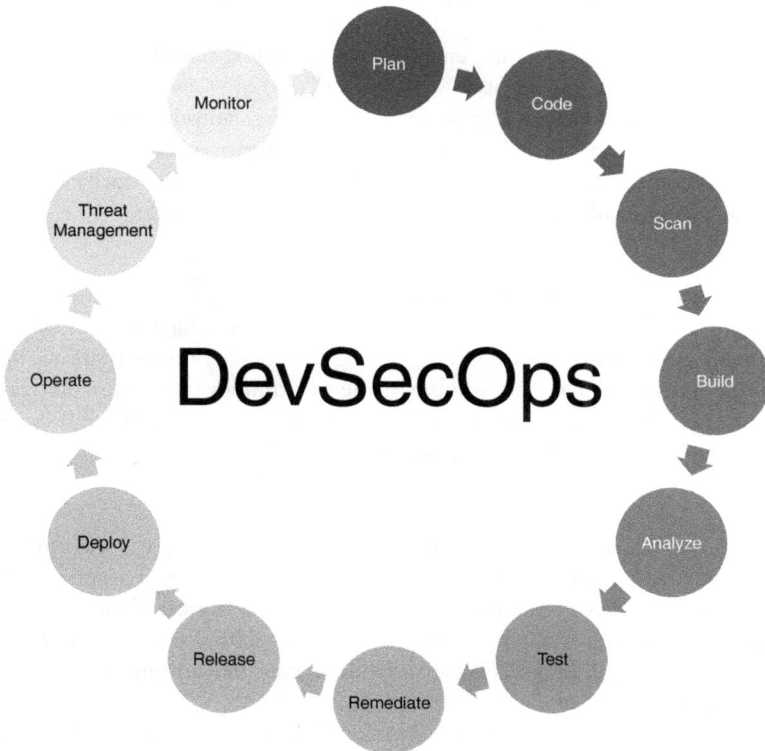

Figure 1-2 DevSecOps Cycle

What Is DevSecOps?

DevSecOps, short for development, security, and operations, is a methodology that integrates security practices within the DevOps process. It aims to foster a culture where security is a shared responsibility throughout the entire IT lifecycle, from initial design through development and operations. In the DevSecOps model, security is considered from the very beginning of the software development lifecycle (SDLC). This approach contrasts with traditional approaches where security was often only considered at the end of the development process. Security checks and processes are automated as much as possible to ensure they are consistently applied and do not slow down the development process. This automation includes automated testing, code analysis, and vulnerability scanning.

While security is a core focus, the regular DevOps model is still followed. This model includes close collaboration between development, security, and operations teams. This collaboration breaks down silos and ensures that security is integrated into all aspects of the development and deployment processes. Continuous monitoring and real-time security analytics help in identifying and mitigating security issues promptly. This process involves constant scanning for vulnerabilities, monitoring application performance, and ensuring compliance with security policies. Security practices are integrated early in the development process ("shifted left"), from the initial design phases through to coding, testing, deployment, and maintenance. This integration is often achieved through practices like securing infrastructure, ensuring secure coding standards, analyzing static code, and testing early-stage security.

One of the key focus areas in DevSecOps is to leverage automation. This is done in almost all aspects of the methodology. The development process automates continuous integration and continuous delivery (CI/CD) pipelines to include security checks, such as static code analysis, vulnerability scanning, and compliance checks.

Note: CI/CD Development or Delivery?

CI/CD empowers teams to quickly and consistently deliver high-quality software by automating the processes of building, testing, and deploying applications. The one bit of confusion often arises from its name: continuous integration/continuous *delivery* or continuous *deployment*. Both "delivery" and "deployment" are commonly used interchangeably, and both terms are correct.

Automation is also used to implement Infrastructure as Code (IaC). IaC practices automate infrastructure provisioning and management, ensuring that security policies are consistently applied across all environments. This approach is most commonly achieved using Ansible, Terraform, or a combination of the two technologies. With OCI, you can also automate IaC by using OCI native technologies, like automatic scaling of the autonomous database service.

Implementing DevSecOps requires adopting a shared responsibility with collaboration between team members. In these cross-functional teams, the development, security, and operations teams collaborate closely, fostering a culture of shared responsibility for security. Each team should designate security champions that help advocate for security best practices and bridge the gap between developers and security experts. Regular feedback loops ensure that security findings are communicated back to development teams for quick resolution and ongoing improvement. Compliance requirements are integrated into the CI/CD pipelines, ensuring that software adheres to regulatory standards. Automated policy enforcement mechanisms ensure that security policies are consistently applied and adhered to across all stages of development and deployment.

Why DevSecOps?

So, you've built a team, coordinated the roles, and elected a security champion. Deployments are fully automated, and many of your operating tasks, like patching, are now automated. And happening on a regular basis. What do you gain?

- **Faster Time-to-Market:** Automation and early security integration reduce delays caused by security issues discovered late in the development process, allowing for faster delivery of features and updates. All of this speed, while increasing your security posture with monitoring and automated security checks, helps in maintaining a robust security posture. By embedding security throughout the SDLC, DevSecOps reduces the risk of vulnerabilities and improves the overall security of applications.
- **Cost Efficiency:** Early detection and mitigation of security issues reduce the costs associated with fixing vulnerabilities later in the lifecycle or after deployment. The automation introduced also enables automatic scaling, using only the resources you need for the workload at the current moment.
- **Improved Compliance:** Automated compliance checks and continuous monitoring help ensure that applications meet regulatory and industry standards, reducing the risk of noncompliance.
- **Increased Collaboration:** A culture of shared responsibility and collaboration between development, security, and operations teams leads to better communication, understanding, and cooperation.
- **Cost Savings:** The effort to identify and address security issues early in the development process is generally more cost-effective than fixing them later in production. Additionally, leveraging cloud-native scaling reduces some of the time needed to develop and maintain control systems, which reduces your cloud spend, since resources that are not needed are no longer being provisioned.
- **Compliance:** Automated compliance checks ensure that applications meet regulatory and policy requirements.

DevSecOps enhances the security, efficiency, and reliability of software delivery. This approach helps organizations deliver secure software faster, more efficiently, and with greater confidence.

What Makes Up a DevSecOps Team?

Understanding the common organizational structure of a DevSecOps team is important to being able to implement the practice. There are traditionally seven different roles on a team, as seen in Table 1-1.

Table 1-1   DevSecOps Team

Role	Skills	Responsibilities
DevSecOps Engineer	Knowledge of security tools, CI/CD pipelines, coding/scripting, cloud security, and container security.	Integrate security practices into the DevOps pipeline, automate security tasks, implement continuous security monitoring, and ensure compliance with security standards.
Security Engineer	Expertise in security testing tools, threat intelligence, incident response, and risk assessment.	Conduct threat modeling, vulnerability assessments, penetration testing, and security audits. Ensure security policies are enforced and updated.
Software Developer	Proficiency in programming languages, understanding of secure coding practices, and familiarity with development frameworks.	Write secure code, follow secure coding standards, and integrate security features into applications.
Operations Engineer	Knowledge of Infrastructure as Code (IaC), configuration management tools, cloud platforms, and system monitoring.	Manage infrastructure, automate deployments, ensure system reliability, and monitor application performance.
Compliance Officer	Understanding of compliance frameworks (e.g., GDPR, HIPAA), audit processes, and regulatory requirements.	Ensure the organization complies with industry standards, regulations, and internal policies. Conduct audits and manage compliance documentation.
Test Engineer	Experience with automated testing frameworks, scripting, and knowledge of testing methodologies.	Implement automated testing, ensure test coverage includes security testing, and validate that security features work as intended.
Product Owner	Strong understanding of product management, security needs, and stakeholder communication.	Define security requirements, prioritize security tasks in the development backlog, and ensure that security is considered in product planning.

Once the team is established, it is important to build and maintain a culture of collaboration. The team must work closely together, breaking down silos between development, security, and operations. Regular communication and collaboration are crucial, especially among developers and other team members who promote security best practices within their teams. This collaboration helps to spread security awareness and practices. Team members should stay updated on the latest security threats, technologies, and best practices through training and continuous education.

Benefits of OCI

Next, let's examine how OCI is different from other clouds. There are several distinct differences where OCI provides operation advantages over other clouds. The first difference is price. OCI generally costs less for each service for the base fees, plus the additional usage metrics. A common example is storage. Now, when comparing price, you must look at not only the cost per gigabyte, but also the performance of the storage. At the time of writing, this is what a sample 1 TB high-performance logical unit numbers (LUNs) can cost between Amazon Web Services (AWS), Azure, and OCI! In Table 1-2, 1 TB volume is compared, using published prices and the maximum performance based on the input/output operations per second (IOPS) available for the service.

Note: Things Change All the Time

CSPs are constantly changing their service offerings. While the information in Table 1-2 is current at the time of writing, the numbers can change.

Table 1-2 Sample Storage Rates

CSP	Max IOPS for the Volume	Cost for the 1 TB Volume, per Month at Maximum Performance	Storage Service Compared
AWS	256,000	$9,799.20	Io2 Block Express
Azure	80,000	$475.70	SSD V2
OCI	300,000	$235.01	OCI Block Storage

This table is also a great example of how some clouds can greatly increase the price based on the performance required. Figure 1-3 shows the breakdown on how AWS io2 storage can rapidly become so expensive.

```
1 volumes x 730 instance hours = 730.00 total instance hours
730.00 instance hours / 730 hours in a month = 1.00 instance months
1,024 GB x 1.00 instance months x 0.125 USD = 128.00 USD (EBS Storage Cost)
EBS Storage Cost: 128.00 USD
Tiered price for: 256,000 iops
32,000 iops x 0.065 USD = 2,080.00 USD
32,000 iops x 0.0455 USD = 1,456.00 USD
192,000 iops x 0.03185 USD = 6,115.20 USD
Total tier cost: 2,080.00 USD + 1,456.00 USD + 6,115.20 USD = 9,651.20 USD (EBS IOPS io2 Cost per instance)
9,651.20 USD x 1.00 instance months = 9,651.20 USD Total IOPS io2 cost
EBS IOPS Cost: 9,651.20 USD
EBS Snapshot Cost: 0 USD
128.00 USD + 9,651.20 USD = 9,779.20 USD (Total EBS cost)
Amazon Elastic Block Storage (EBS) total cost (monthly): 9,779.20 USD
```

Figure 1-3   AWS Io2 Cost Breakdown

There is a significant difference in price. As a rule, OCI will always be less expensive, but more importantly, the OCI price is the same regardless of the region. This means US East and West Coast customers pay the same low price as the US Department of Defense regions pay, or even the US FedRAMPed cloud. The price is the same for international regions. This pricing structure makes it more predictable when budgeting services.

When you are comparing services like this, it is always important to compare the total cost, including, for example, performance, cost with performance, and required dependencies. Additionally, you should look at the service-level agreement (SLA) the CSP provides for performance. If a CSP promises you 120,000 IOPS but has no performance SLA, what happens when you get only 12,000 IOPS? OCI offers SLAs for storage performance. Not all CSPs offer this guarantee!

It's not just storage that costs less. With OCI, the cost to move data within a cloud region is less, as is almost every other service. OCI does not charge for data being moved within a region, and also offers the first 10 terabytes of data transferred between regions (or the Internet) for free.

And it's not just price. Look at compute, where in OCI the CPU and RAM for a virtual machine are not tied together into preconfigured shapes. With other CSPs, you have to buy in preconfigured combinations, often doubling the CPU and RAM in each shape. This approach often limits virtual machines (VMs) to 1, 2, 4, 8, or 16 cores per VM. Each shape, more often than not, fixes the RAM to the shape. So 1 core might have 4 GB RAM, 2 cores gets 8 GB RAM, and so on.

If you need 11 cores, you end up purchasing (and, more importantly, licensing) 16 cores. Also, with RAM tied to the shape, if your VM requires 7 cores and 100 GB of RAM, you are limited to the choice of 64 or 128 GB, and with 64 GB, the shape includes 16 cores. With 128 GB of RAM, you get 32 cores. You end up purchasing 32 cores to the 128 GB of RAM, yet your VM really needs only 7 cores and 100 GB of RAM. Now multiply this amount by 50 VMs for a complex application, and you end up subscribing to a larger percentage of CPU and RAM than is not being used or required, but you still have to pay for them.

Note: What Is a CPU?

Be careful; a CPU is not always the same. Oracle uses an OCPU metric that represents a full core, and the ECPU metric that is approximately one-fourth of a core. Other CSPs often use a vCPU metric, which loosely equates to a single thread per CPU. A CPU thread is a sequence of instructions that a CPU core can execute, serving as the basic unit of CPU utilization. Threads are essential for multitasking, enabling a single core to perform multiple tasks simultaneously. Even then, some CSPs will offer services that equate a CPU to an arbitrary unit of CPU usage that does not align to a core or a thread. This difference can make comparing clouds complicated, so always read the fine print.

With OCI, you can subscribe to a single core at a time and then allocate 1–64 GB of RAM per core. This way, you can use VMs with combinations like 3 cores and 187 GB of RAM, or 32 cores with 32 GB of RAM. The cost is tied to the cores and RAM as separate line items. This model can easily see at least 25 percent less cost, even if the price per hour is the same between CSPs.

There are other differences, such as bandwidth costs, where OCI gives each tenancy 10 TB of free egress traffic. Other CPSs charge for any egress. It's not only egress fees; look carefully at the cost to move data within a CSP region or between regions. Often CSP sales teams do not disclose these rates, which can lead to an unexpected overage in cost. When comparing CSPs, look at all the networking charges, the storage (and the performance charges), as well as how services are allocated to the customer. Often what looks to be low cost can become a larger cost due to how the CSP provisions and prices all their services.

OCI also has an *always-free tier* of service.

OCI Free Services

OCI includes over two dozen always-free services. These are a free tier, which gives you a specific amount of service free every month. This tier is broken into Compute, Storage, Networking, Security Observability and Management, Database, and others.

OCI Compute gives users two free AMD-based VMs, each with one-eighth of an OCPU and 1 GB of RAM. Additionally, you get 3,000 hours of A1 compute and 18,000 GB hours per month of A1 RAM. For A1, this is approximately four cores and 24 GB of RAM free every month.

OCI Storage gives you two free block volumes with up to 200 GB of free space. You also get 20 GB of Object, Object-Infrequent Access, and Object Archival storage free every month. You also receive 50,000 free object storage API requests each month.

Networking starts with 10 TB of egress, a network load balancer (Layer 3/4 support), 10 Mbps load balancer, two service connector hubs, 10 GB of VCN flow logs, two virtual cloud networks, and up to 50 IPsec site-to-site VPN connections.

The Observability and Management free tier includes 1000 tracing events and 10 synthetic monitoring runs of application performance monitoring per hour, 100 emails sent with the email delivery service, 10 GB of logs, monitoring of 1 billion retrieval data points, 500 million ingestion data points, and 1 million HTTPS notifications per month.

Database free services include two autonomous databases with 20 GB storage for each and 133 million reads of NoSQL with 25 GB of storage.

Security gives you five free Bastion hosts for secure accesses, security certificates including five private CAs and 150 private TLC certs, a vault with 20 keys, and 150 vault secrets.

Additionally, developers get up to 744 hours of free APEX (about 1 OCPU). You also receive 100 free cloud dashboards.

You can get a free account at `https://signup.cloud.oracle.com/` You will need a work(ish) email address, a credit card (for personal authentication), and a cell phone (for MFA identity authentication).

Note: Free Has Some Constraints

Normally, you are limited to a single free tier account. You cannot reuse the phone number or email address. Also, email addresses from public email systems like Google, outlook.com, and yahoo.com are not normally approved.

As long as you use the always-free services, OCI is totally free!

Summary

In this chapter you learned what DevSecOps is and some of the benefits. You also learned what makes up a DevSecOps team. Additionally, you also learned a little bit about the OCI differences, as well as the OCI free tier.

Oracle Cloud Infrastructure—Governance

Oracle Cloud Infrastructure (OCI) is not unlike any other cloud. While the terminology might be different, many of the core concepts are the same but have different names. In this chapter, we will review the core administrative features of OCI, including tenancy management and governance, billing and budgeting, dashboards, and Cloud Advisor. It is important for the security side of DevSecOps to understand the options available to isolate the organizations. There are several options to allow for a governance model that fulfills your organizational requirements. The operations team also needs to understand how this is done so that they can align with the same requirements.

Tenancy Account Management and Governance

The *tenancy* is the core OCI organizational unit. It is similar to Amazon Web Services (AWS) accounts or a Microsoft Azure tenant. This is where all OCI resources live within OCI, regardless of the cloud or region, because the tenancy is a global namespace. A *global namespace* is an object that can exist in all regions without an account. When you create your OCI account, you will pick a tenancy name that will be used for all regions within the cloud selected. The tenancy will contain all the services for any region within the cloud, including a cloud subscription assigned to it that sets the rate card (which shows what each cloud service costs) and the billing data for the cloud customer. Tenancies should have at least one compartment per region. A *compartment* is a global namespace where you can add access management policies and cloud resources. The resources include all the technologies used by applications, including the networks, databases, and compute nodes. Since they are a global resource, they can stretch across multiple cloud regions. A *region* is basically a physical data center within the cloud.

Optionally, larger organizations may wish to have multiple tenancies but have them all rolled up into one large unit called a *parent tenancy unit*. This parent tenancy can create child tenancies and share a common cloud subscription. This relationship between the parent tenancy, child tenancy, and compartments can be seen in Figure 2-1.

Organizational Management

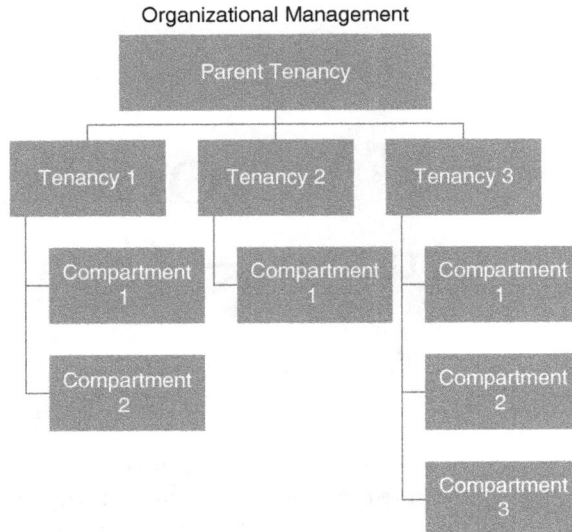

Figure 2-1   Organizational Unit Relationship

Note: You Said Multiple Clouds!

There are multiple independent OCI clouds, mainly broken down into Commercial, US Government, US DOD, UK Government, and US National Security Regions (Secret and Top Secret Workloads). Most customers will use the Commercial cloud that has regions globally. Generally, they all work the same, using the same API, the same web interface, and even the same rates for services. The services available may differ though, due to government approvals required for these clouds.

Creating a New Tenancy

There are two common ways to have a tenancy created. The first is to have the Oracle Sales team or Partner create your tenancy. This is normally done for special tenancies like Government tenancies, where the user must attest that they have a need and the requirement to being a Government cloud. For these tenancies, skip to the confirmation email step described later in the chapter.

The most common way to create your own tenancy is to use the web interface. This approach works well for most customers. You can start this process in several ways, but the easiest is to go to https://cloud.oracle.com and click the **Sign Up** button, as seen in Figure 2-2.

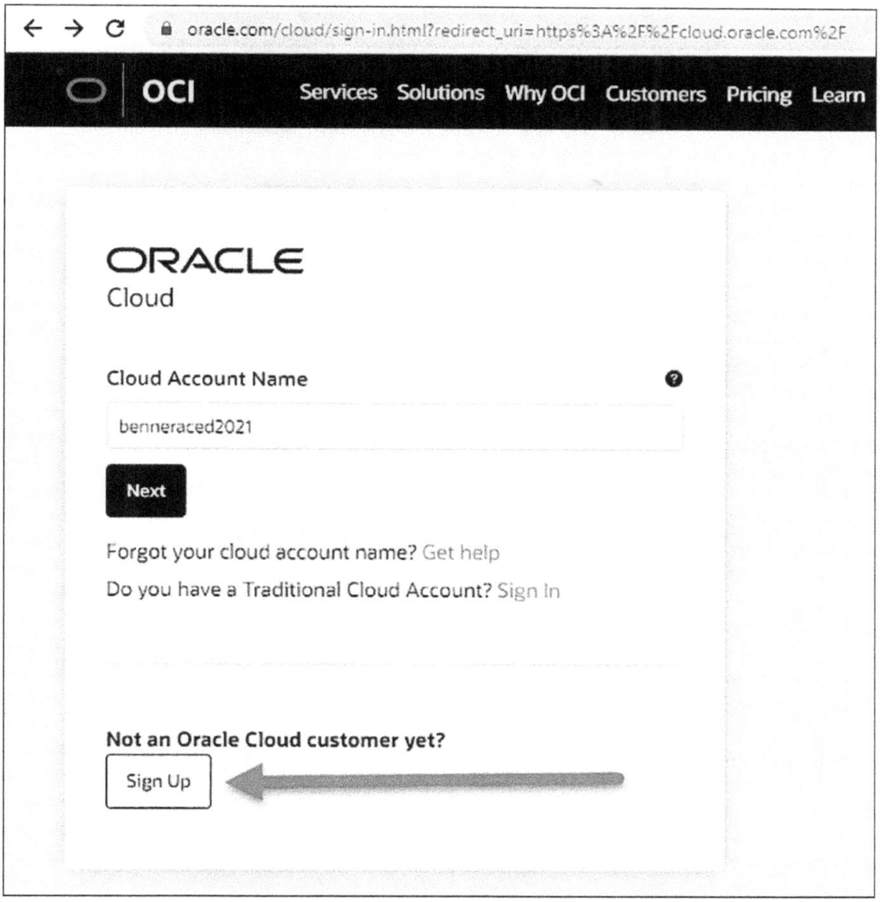

Figure 2-2   OCI Signup

You will be required to put in your name and email address. Next, you will be sent a validation email. You should be in a position to validate that email within 30 minutes. This address will become the primary email address for your tenancy. Once your email is validated, you will be able to set your password, cloud account name, and home region. This step is shown in Figure 2-3.

Next, you will need to provide a mailing address and billing information. The billing information is required, even for the always-free cloud service. Oracle states this information is for verification. Once this information is verified, you can select the **Start My Free Trial** button, as seen in Figure 2-4.

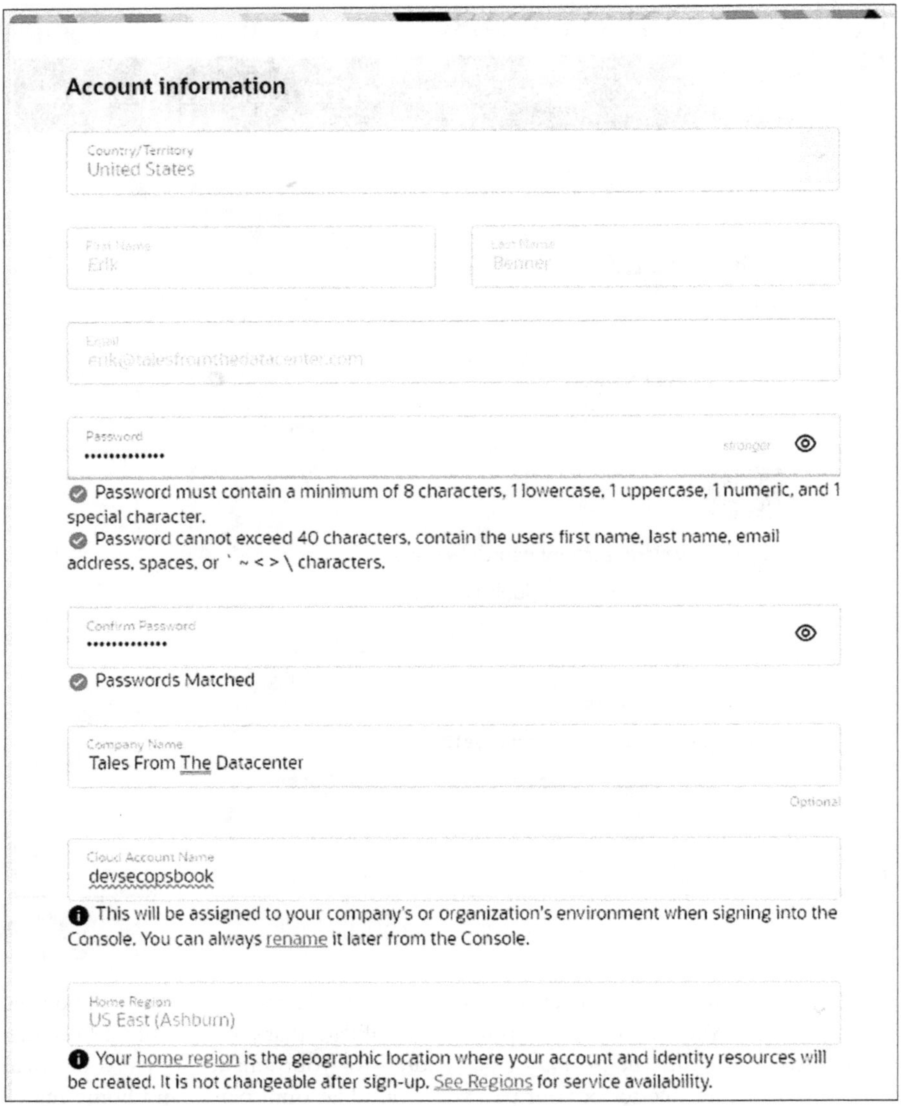

Figure 2-3   OCI Account Creation

Note: Why a Trial Account?

All self-provisioned accounts start off as a free trial. They get access to the always-free services and are pay-as-you-go for other services. You can convert to a discounted paid account through an Oracle Partner or Oracle Sales rep.

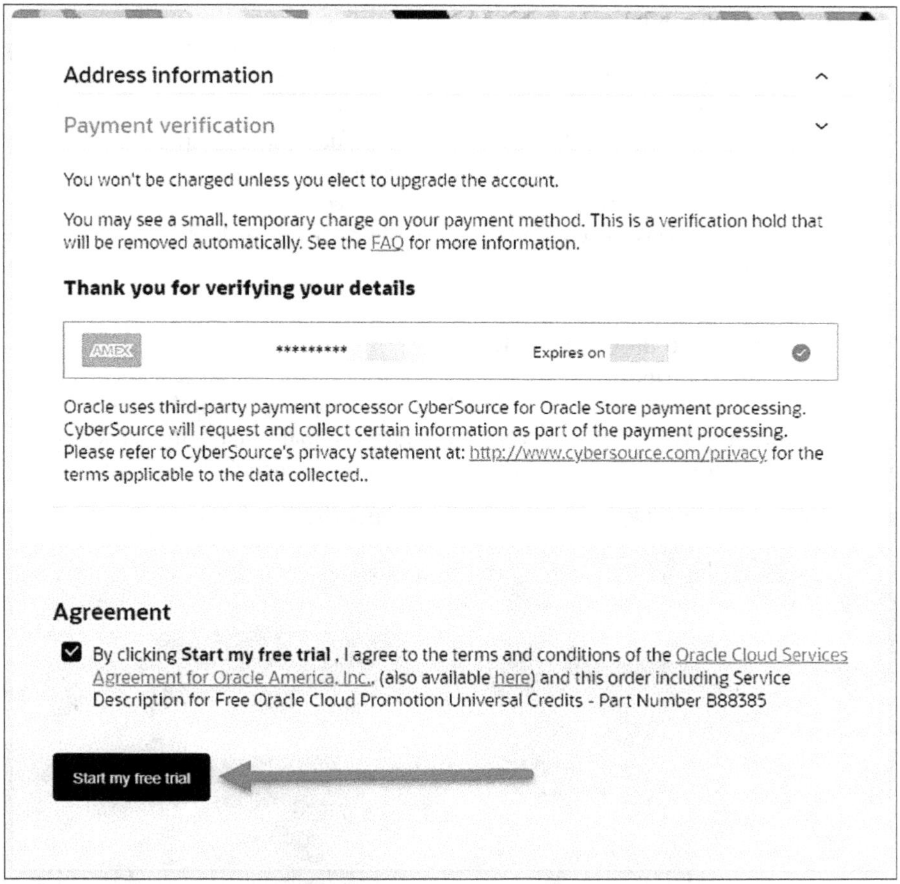

Figure 2-4   Starting the Free Trial

Now the account is provisioned by Oracle. You should receive an email to the admin email address when this process is completed. You can then sign into OCI and start using your services.

Organizational Governance

Larger organizations may want more isolated control between internal organizations. While compartments allow you to isolate access to specific cloud resources like compute, database, and analytics, some cloud abilities are at the tenancy level. To isolate a group of users to their own tenancy but leverage the rate card and subscription of the parent tenancy, you can invite a tenancy into an organization. This way, the parent organization can have financial oversight of the tenancies, while at the same time allowing each individual tenancy to be isolated from its parent with its own access to tenancy-level features like Cloud Advisor.

The parent organization can also establish governance rules that span across all child tenancies, enforcing rules like quota policies, which can limit what resources a tenancy can provision. This ability to limit resources with quotas is important to minimize the impact of a tenancy accidentally subscribing to more expensive cloud services. An example is Oracle Exadata. Although it is a powerful database platform, having a developer provision their own Exadata may be outside of your budget. With quotas, you can limit how many cloud resources that a tenancy or compartment can use. So, you can set the number of Exadatas to zero and limit the Oracle CPUs (OCPUs) for compute to a number like 24.

Inviting a Tenancy into an Organization

To invite an existing tenancy to become a child tenancy, you will need the child tenancy's Oracle Cloud Identifier (OCID). This unique string can be located in the Tenancy Details. You can get the details by going to the main menu and clicking **Governance & Administration > Tenancy Details**, as seen in Figure 2-5.

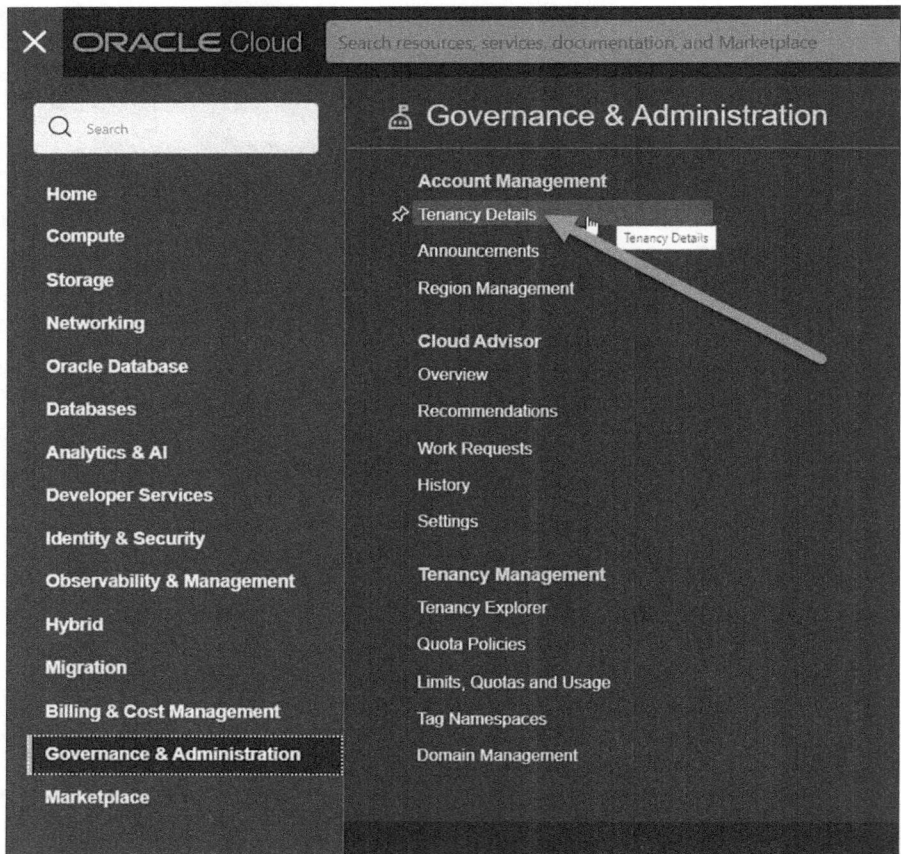

Figure 2-5   Navigating to Tenancy Details

This page will show the details for the tenancy, including your home region, OCID, Customer Support Identifier (CSI), and how long audit logs are kept (see Figure 2-6). The CSI is also an important number because it is required to open a tech support ticket. You also can see the Amazon S3 API compartment, where you can use the S3 API to access object storage. Additionally, you have the SWIFT API Designated Compartment and the Object Storage Namespace. SWIFT is an orchestration technology commonly used by container management technologies like Kubernetes for automating storage actions for disaster recovery, container orchestration, and backups.

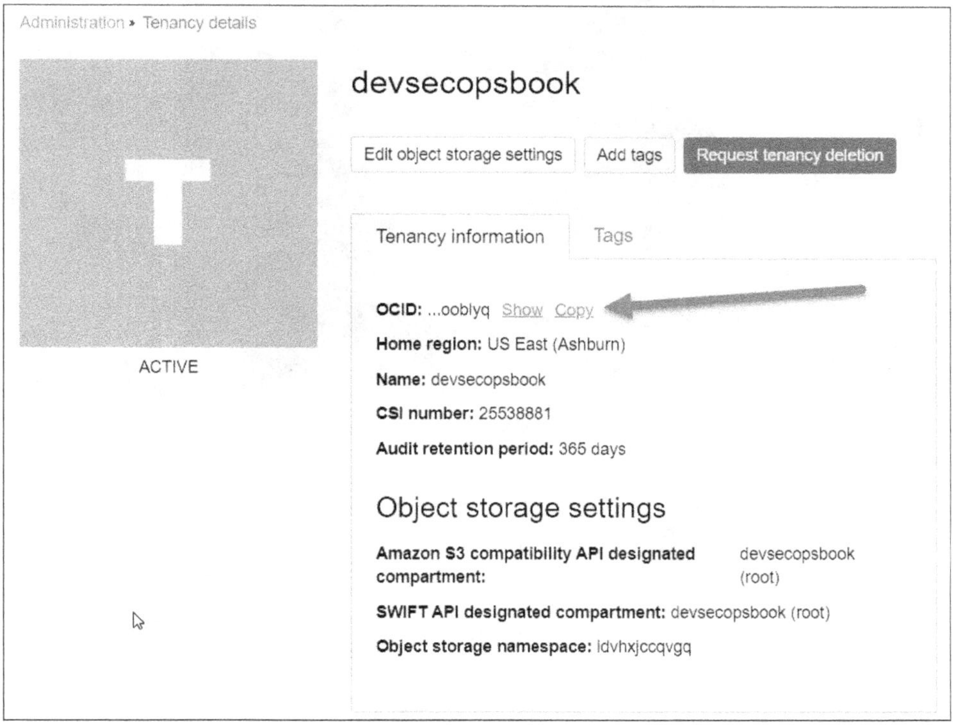

Figure 2-6 Tenancy Details

To copy the OCID, select **Copy**. This should copy the string into your buffer. Optionally, you can select **Show** and display the entire string.

Once you have the OCID, log out of the soon-to-be-child tenancy and log back in to the parent. From the parent tenancy, go to **Governance & Administration > Organizational Management > Tenancies**, as seen in Figure 2-7.

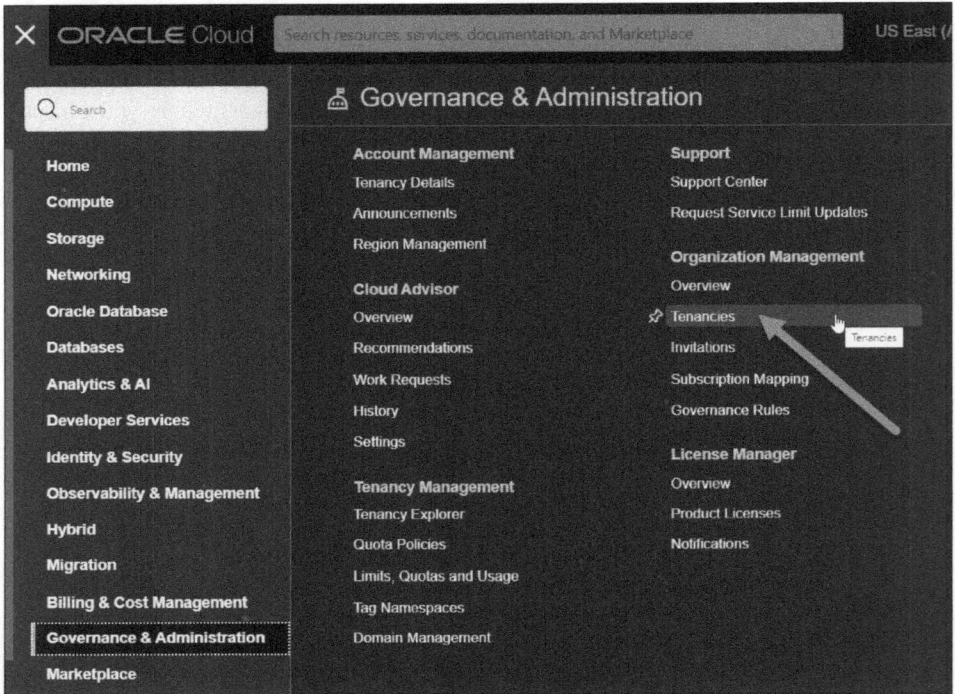

Figure 2-7   Organizational Management Navigation

From the Tenancies page, you can see all the tenancies related to this one. To add a new child tenancy, click **Invite Tenancy**, as seen in Figure 2-8.

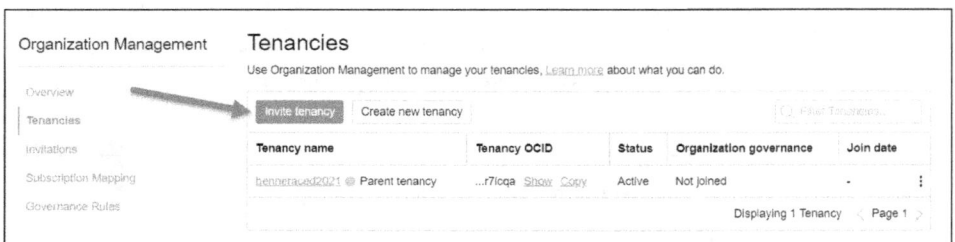

Figure 2-8   Tenancies

From here, you will next invite the tenancy, set up default governance rules, and verify the invitation before sending it.

When you add the tenancy, you will enter the OCID into the OCID field and optionally an email address to send a notification of the invite. This first page is shown in Figure 2-9.

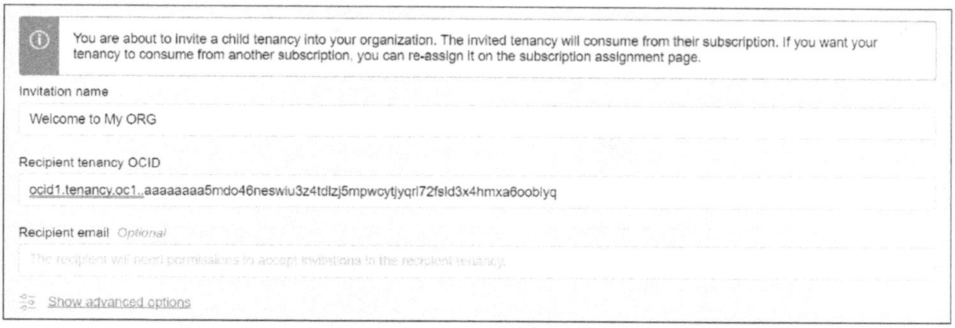

You are about to invite a child tenancy into your organization. The invited tenancy will consume from their subscription. If you want your tenancy to consume from another subscription, you can re-assign it on the subscription assignment page.

Invitation name

Welcome to My ORG

Recipient tenancy OCID

ocid1.tenancy.oc1..aaaaaaaa5mdo46neswiu3z4tdlzj5mpwcytjyqrl72fsld3x4hmxa6ooblyq

Recipient email *Optional*

The recipient will need permissions to accept invitations in the recipient tenancy.

Show advanced options

Figure 2-9   Tenancy Invite, Step 1

On the next page, you have the option to select any mandatory governance rules. You can always add them latter. This is shown in Figure 2-10.

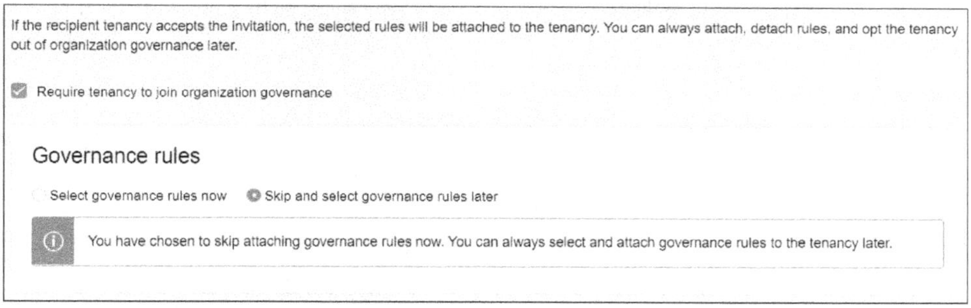

If the recipient tenancy accepts the invitation, the selected rules will be attached to the tenancy. You can always attach, detach rules, and opt the tenancy out of organization governance later.

Require tenancy to join organization governance

Governance rules

Select governance rules now   ● Skip and select governance rules later

You have chosen to skip attaching governance rules now. You can always select and attach governance rules to the tenancy later.

Figure 2-10   Tenancy Invite, Step 2

The last step is a simple verification. Once you have verified the OCID and any initial rules, click **Invite Tenancy**.

Warning: The OCID Should Never Be Shared

Never share the OCID of your tenancy with someone you do not trust. It's the first line of defense in securing your tenancy. The same goes for your CSI number and object storage name space.

Next, log out of the parent tenancy, log back in to the child tenancy, and accept the invitation.

Creating a New Tenancy into an Organization

The easiest way to create a child tenancy is to simply create it from the primary tenancy. You can do this by navigating to **Governance & Administration > Tenancies** and selecting **Invite Tenancy**, as seen in Figure 2-11.

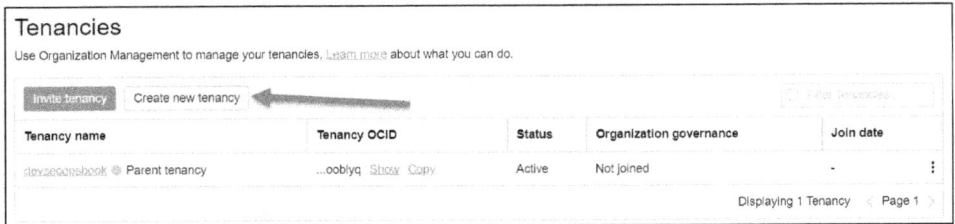

Figure 2-11   Adding a Tenancy

Next, fill out the simple form. Remember, the tenancy name must be unique, and also this new tenancy will have the same rate card and billing invoice as the parent. A sample is shown in Figure 2-12.

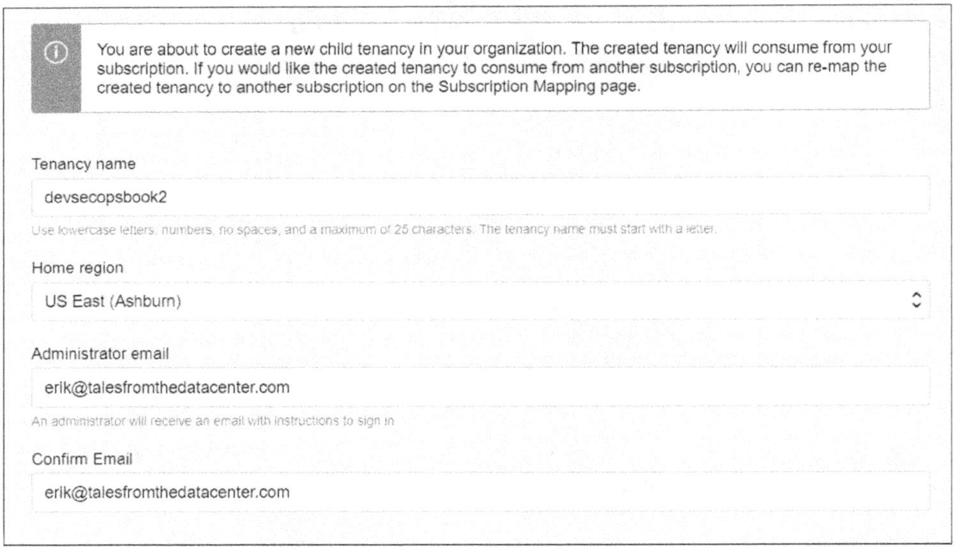

Figure 2-12   New Details

The other steps, like adding in a governance rule and review, are identical to inviting a new tenancy.

Cloud Advisor

There are several challenges when working in a cloud environment. First, there are the security challenges, with many cloud accounts being compromised and data stolen due to an insecure configuration. Most of the large-scale cloud data breaches have been caused by such configurations. Issues like insecure object storage buckets or ports opened up to internal databases from the Internet have compromised large companies like Microsoft, with hundreds of millions of customers having their data stolen (see https://securityboulevard.com/2020/01/microsoft-leaks-250m-customer-details-in-azure-fat-finger-faux-pas/). The reason is that, inherently, most clouds are difficult to secure. This failure to secure clouds has reached such a point that many third-party products have sprung up to help companies address this security issue.

The second most common issue is cloud sprawl—and controlling that sprawl. This situation is often caused by administrators creating resources that were not planned or incompletely deleting resources that are no longer required. An entire new area of operations called *FinOps* has sprung up to help organizations enable financial and cultural management to help control the costs. As with security, many third-party companies are offering paid services to help you manage your cloud spend.

The remaining most common issues revolve around cloud performance and cloud disaster recovery. As with security and FinOps, new companies have been founded to help customers address these issues...for a cost.

Oracle's approach to helping customers combat these issues is with a service called Cloud Advisor. This free service helps you secure your cloud, save money on your cloud spend, and improve high availability and performance. You can navigate to this tool by going to the main menu and selecting **Governance & Administration > Cloud Advisor**, as seen in Figure 2-13.

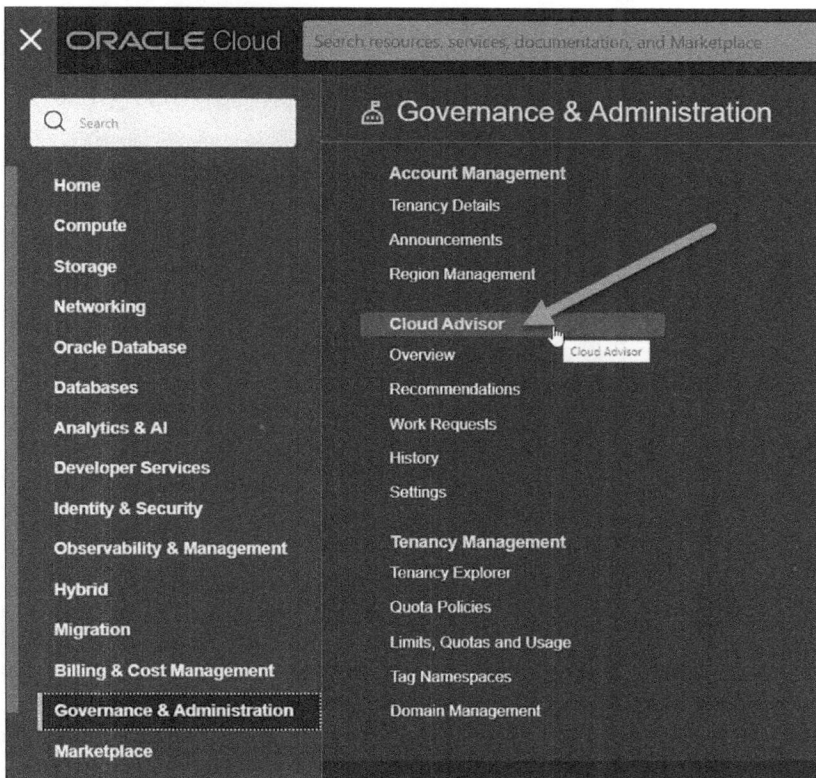

Figure 2-13 Getting to Cloud Advisor

Choosing this option will take you to the main page for Cloud Advisor, showing summaries for cost management, high availability, performance, and security.

Initially, security will not show anything until Cloud Guard is enabled. This service is covered in Chapter 14, "Cloud Guard."

Cost Management

It is not uncommon for most cloud accounts to have some inefficiencies in them. These issues are often caused by the compute and database resources having too much CPU or RAM allocated to the system. Also, storage inefficiencies are not uncomon, often caused by an Ops team member simply forgetting to delete the boot disks when deleting a virtual machine, or by a Dev team member cloning a block volume as part of a development effort and forgetting to delete it when done. With Cloud Advisor, you get a high-level summary of the possible savings identified by OCI when you log in to the Cloud Advisor dashboard, as seen in Figure 2-14.

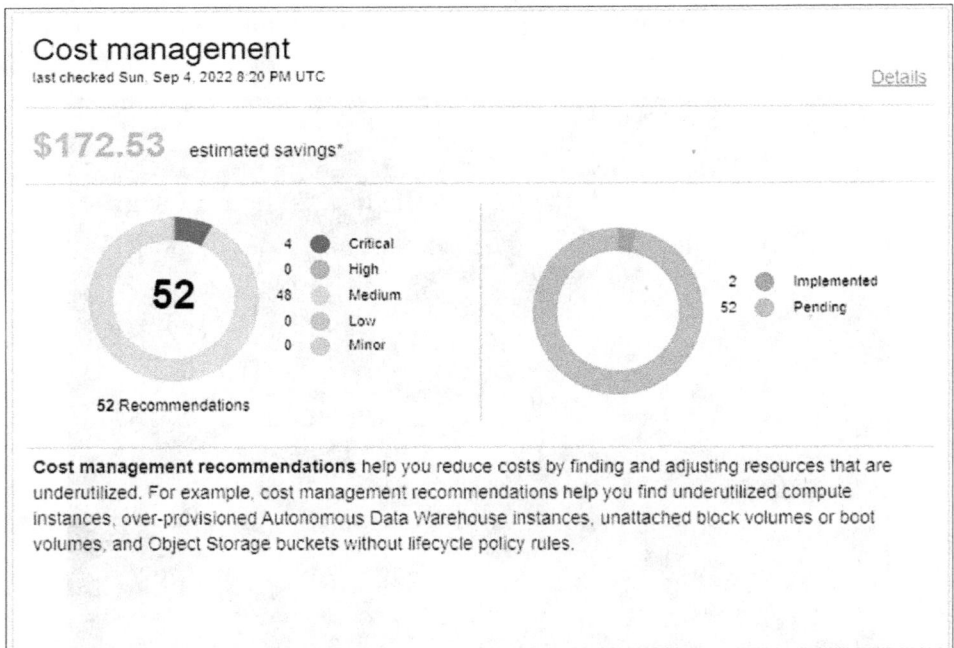

Figure 2-14   Savings Summary

Savings are broken down by the amount of savings per month, from Critical to Minor, and the ranking is based on the overall amount of possible savings. In this example, there is an opportunity for the DevSecOps team to save over $150 a month in the environment. It's not uncommon to see this number even higher, especially with DevSecOps teams that are not checking this amount monthly. While the high level provides a good start to see what the possible savings might be, you can easily drill down to get more details, as seen in Figure 2-15.

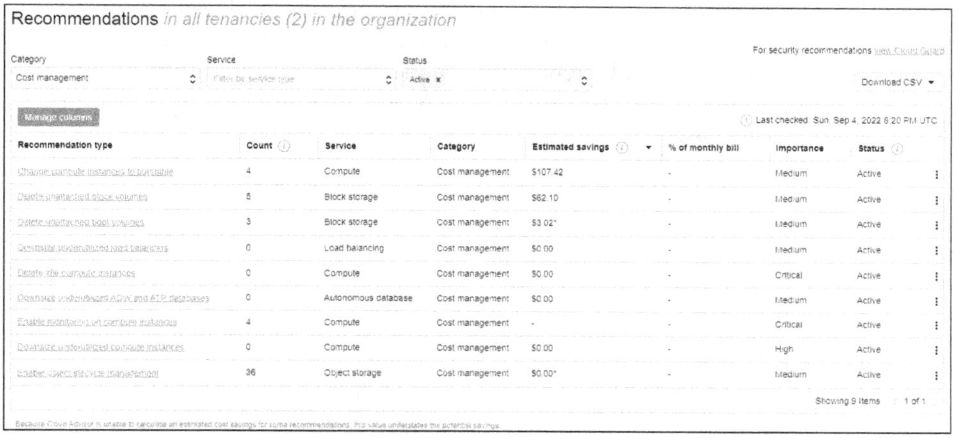

Figure 2-15 Savings Details

On this more detailed page, you can see how the savings are broken down, showing simple changes that can be made to allow for more efficient operations and usage of cloud resources. The number one savings opportunity is to set four of the compute VMs to allow for burstable CPU. In this example, there are several unattached block volumes. You can drill down even more and identify what the volumes are and what tenancy they are in.

Valid cost findings are

- **Delete Idle Compute Instance:** Cloud Advisor identified a compute instance with no workload.
- **Change Compute Instance to Burstable:** This allows a single OCPU E3 instance to dynamically add CPU as needed.
- **Downsize Underutilized Compute:** This identifies compute instances with significantly more CPU allocated than required.
- **Enable Monitoring on Compute Instance:** This identifies compute instances that are not being monitored. If the instance is not being monitored, the other compute-based findings cannot be identified by Cloud Advisor.
- **Delete Unattached Boot Volumes:** This identifies boot volumes that are not being used by any compute instance.
- **Delete Unattached Block Volumes:** This identifies block volumes that are not attached to any compute node.
- **Enable Object Lifecycle Management:** This identifies object storage buckets that are not configured to automatically move infrequently used objects to "infrequent object" storage and older backups to archive storage.
- **Downsize Underutilized Autonomous Databases:** This identifies autonomous databases that have more CPU allocated than is required for the workload.

Performance

Often, moving to the cloud causes performance issues, especially when the cloud offers so many more ways to optimize the environment for performance. It's often difficult for the Ops team to know where there are performance issues and what a solution might be. Cloud Advisor helps with this, by monitoring all the resources and identifying ones with potential performance issues. The Performance widget, as seen in Figure 2-16, shows potential performance issues in the environment.

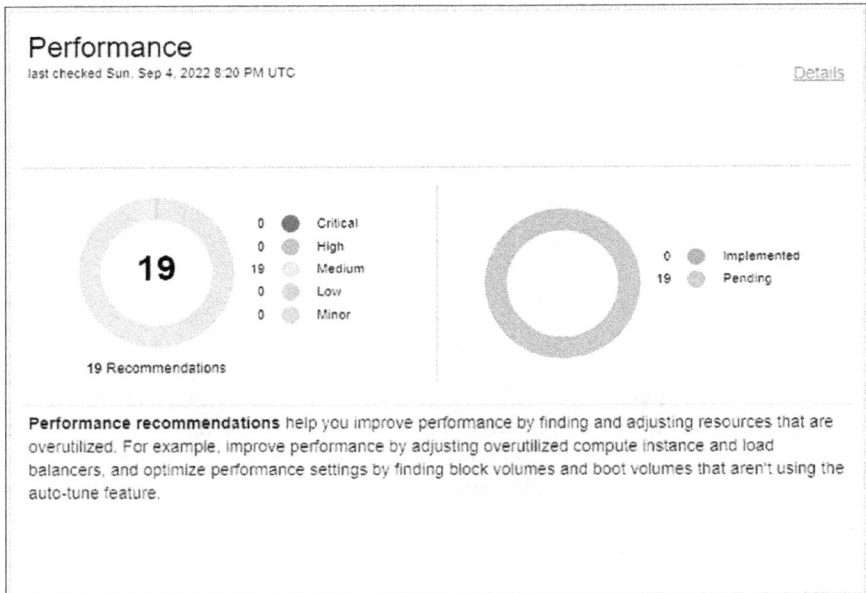

Figure 2-16   Performance Summary

As with the other Cloud Advisor summary, recommendations here are broken into levels from Critical to Minor. A critical performance issue might be a database that is starved for CPU. In this example, no critical issues were identified, but you can easily drill down to see what was seen by clicking **Details**, as shown in Figure 2-17.

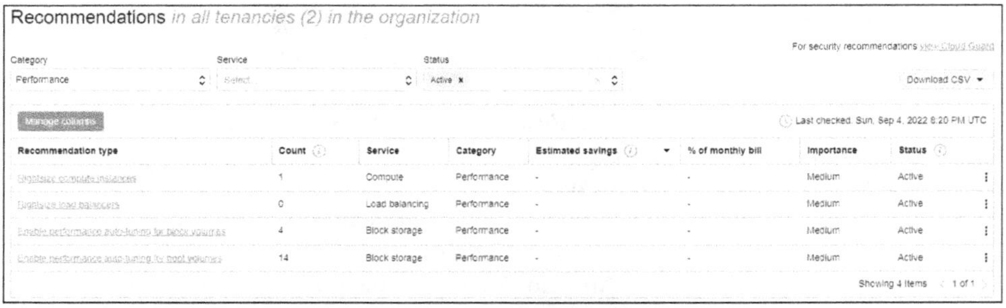

Figure 2-17   Performance Details

From this details page, you can see several identified issues, from compute instances not being sized optimally to storage volumes not leveraging auto-tuning.

Tip: Block Storage Auto-Tiering

Block Storage Auto-Tiering will automatically add volume performance units (VPUs) to volumes when they need the extra I/O. Additionally, block volumes can be automatically set to zero VPUs when detached to save money. See Chapter 7, "Oracle IaaS—Storage," for more information.

Valid performance findings are as follows:

- **Rightsize Load Balancers:** The load balancer does not have enough bandwidth configured.
- **Rightsize Compute Instance:** The compute instance does not have enough CPU or RAM for the workload.
- **Enable Performance Auto-Tuning for Boot Volumes:** This enables the VPUs of a boot volume to shift between low-cost/low-performance to higher-cost/higher-performance as needed.
- **Enable Performance Auto-Tuning for Block Volumes:** This enables the VPUs of a block volume to shift between low-cost/low-performance to higher-cost/higher-performance as needed.

High Availability

High availability (HA) in the cloud is just as important as HA is on-premises! (See Figure 2-18 for a sample summary of HA.) Cloud systems, like any IT system, can fail, so having an appropriate response for both HA and disaster recovery (DR) is still an important task. You might ask, What is the difference between HA and DR? Generally, HA is a failure *within* a region, whereas DR is the failure *of* the region. When you are architecting a cloud solution, these aspects still need to be factored in the plans. The advantage of the cloud is that it makes doing both much easier, with a ton of automation available for both. The Cloud Advisor can automatically identify opportunities to improve the availability of the provisioned resources. This can be something as simple as making sure compute resources behind a load balancer are in different fault domains. As with the other Cloud Advisor services, you can drill down to see what the recommendations are, as seen in Figure 2-19.

In this example, compute nodes are identified as being in the same fault domain. Currently, only the Improve Fault Tolerance finding is supported.

High availability
last checked Sun, Sep 4, 2022 8:20 PM UTC   Details

3

0	Critical
0	High
3	Medium
0	Low
0	Minor

3 Recommendations

2	Implemented
3	Pending

High availability recommendations help you improve system resilience. For example, increase the availability of applications running on Oracle Cloud Infrastructure by using redundant compute nodes in different availability domains to support failover capability and properly leverage fault domains.

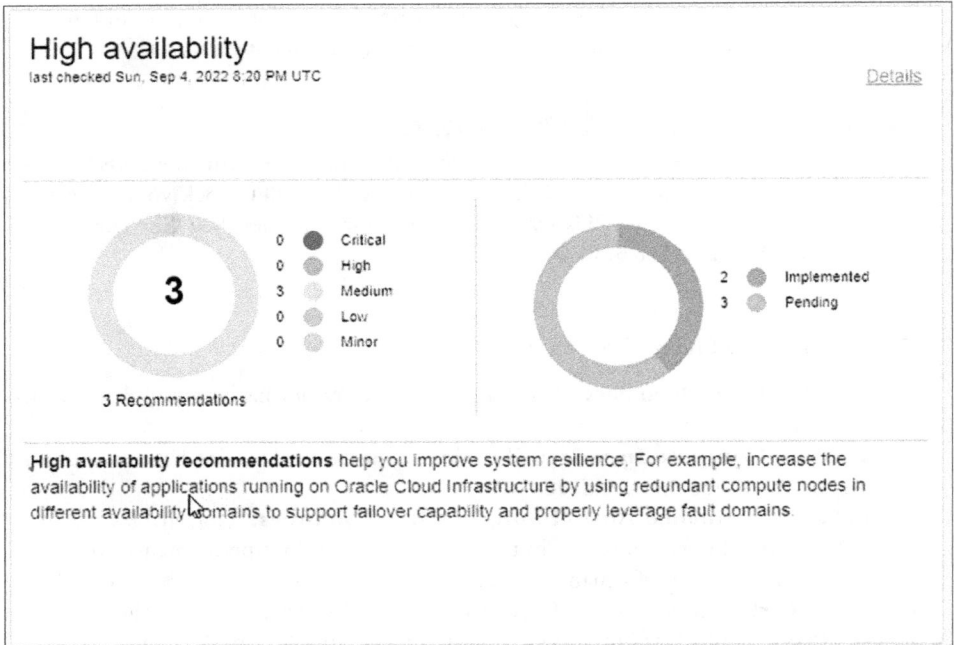

Figure 2-18   HA Summary

Recommendations *in all tenancies (2) in the organization*

For security recommendations use, Cloud Guard

Category	Service	Status	
High availability ⌄	Select... ⌄	Active x ⌄	Download CSV ⌄

Manage columns   ⓘ Last checked: Sun, Sep 4, 2022 8:20 PM UTC

Recommendation type	Count ⓘ	Service	Category	Estimated savings ⓘ	⌄	% of monthly bill	Importance	Status ⓘ	
Improve fault tolerance	3	Compute	High availability	-		-	Medium	Active	⋮

Showing 1 item   ‹ 1 of 1 ›

Figure 2-19   HA Details

Billing and Budgets

One of the challenges with the cloud is understanding where all the expenses are going, as well as tracking the expenses to date to the budgeted amount of funds. OCI makes tracking easy to do with the Billing and Cost Management tools. As with many of the OCI account tools, this free tool lets you explore where costs are going. Several interactive views are available, allowing you to visualize the costs by region, compartments, tags, and services. To access the Cost Management tools, go to the main menu and select **Billing & Cost Management**, as seen in Figure 2-20, and select the appropriate service.

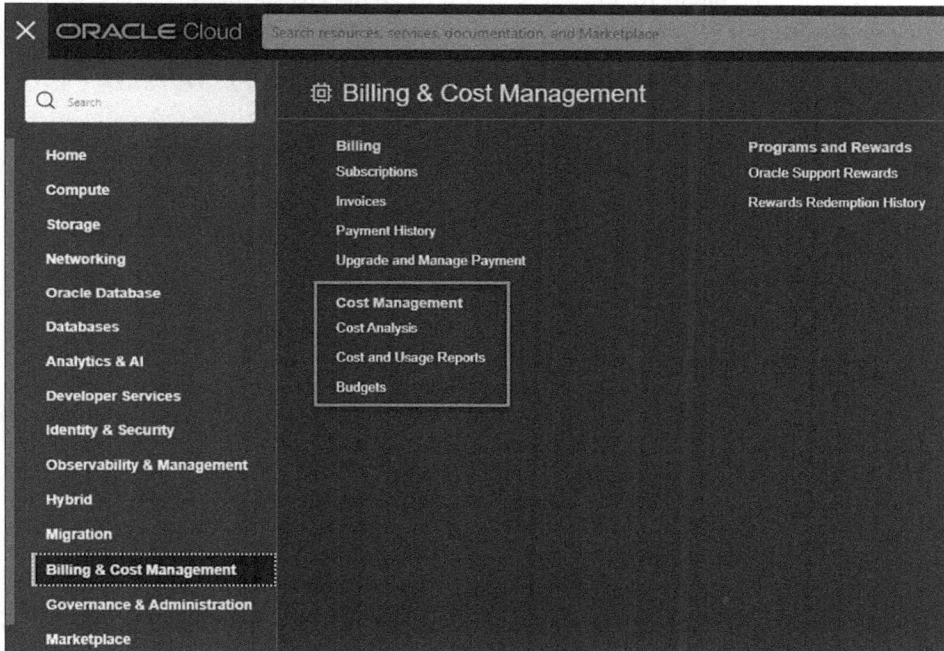

Figure 2-20   Billing & Cost Management Menu

There are three menu options here:

- **Cost Analysis:** Allows graphical free-form visual analysis of the expenses
- **Cost and Usage Reports:** Allows you to download billing data in a CSV format
- **Budgets:** Allows you to set automated budget alerts

The Cost and Usage Reports option is straightforward. Select that option and then select the CSV file you want to download. You can also automate the download of the CSV files via a RestAPI call for importing the data into third-party systems.

The more interesting options are in the Cost Analysis system and the Budgets.

Cost Analysis System

The Cost Analysis system allows you to graphically see where the expenses are going. This page is broken into three sections:

- **Cost Analysis:** Here, you can set the start/stop time, filters, and groupings for the visualizations.
- **Cost Details:** This is where the data is summarized and visualized.
- **Details:** This detailed breakdown can be downloaded into a CSV file.

Cost Analysis Settings

Once a report is built, you can also save it to allow you to rapidly reuse the report.

When setting the report parameters, you first make the change and then click **Apply to Have the Report Rebuilt**. The options, shown in Figure 2-21, are as follows:

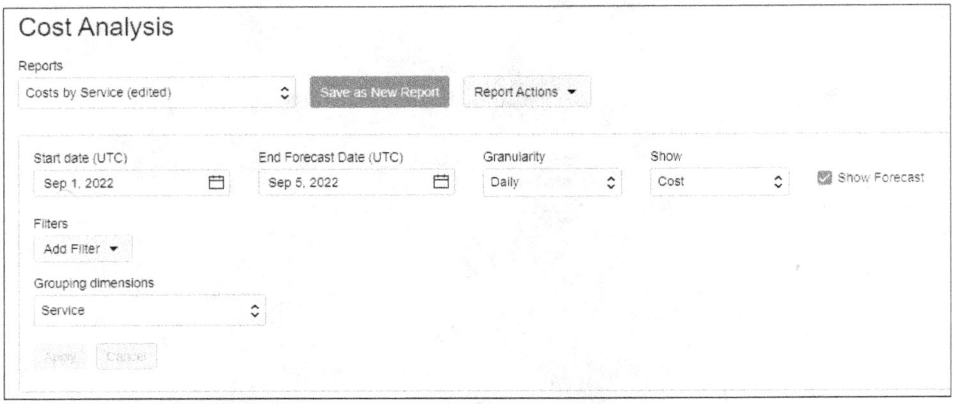

Figure 2-21   Cost Analysis Settings

- **Reports:** The default reports are Costs by Service and Description, Costs by Service and SKU, Costs by Service and Tag, Compute Costs by Compartment, and Monthly Costs. New reports will appear in this drop-down if you save the report.
- **Start and End Dates:** These are the dates you are looking at. It's also helpful to know your billing cycle date if you are estimating a monthly bill.

Tip: Be Careful with the Start/End Dates

The longer the time between the start and end dates, the slower the report will take. Always test reports with smaller windows to speed up things, and then expand to the date range you need.

- **Granularity:** You can choose Monthly or Daily. Daily is helpful for short-term forecasting, but Monthly works well for long-term planning.
- **Show:** You can show cost or usage. Usage is helpful for showing the actual units consumed. This information is also helpful for government customers that use nonmetered billing.
- **Show Forecast:** This option will predict future spend/usage.
- **Filters:** You can filter on many different metrics; the most common are tags and compartments. Tags are helpful because you can assign any resource a custom tag. This capability is helpful to give each application a tag, as well as the different lifecycle tiers such as Production, Development, Test, and Regression.

- **Grouping Dimensions:** This option sets how the resources are grouped in the graphs. The most common are service and compartment.

Cost Analysis

The cost analysis shows the visualized data and, based on the setting, can show a variety of data. An example is shown in Figure 2-22.

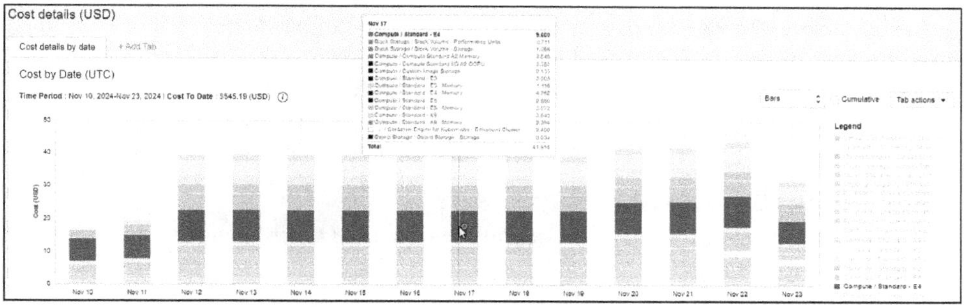

Figure 2-22   Cost Analysis Sample

This example uses the Costs by Service report, for a single calendar month, grouping by the service. You can also mouse over a specific day to see the details of the top resources consumed.

In a second example shown in Figure 2-23, the dates are limited to only a few days, and the grouping is by compartment. This example enables you to see what each compartment is consuming.

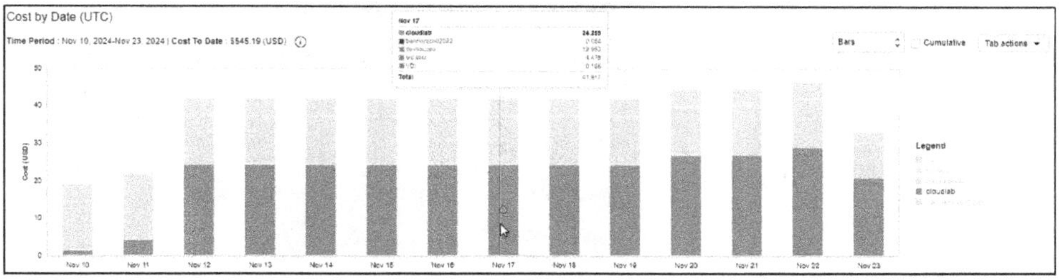

Figure 2-23   Analysis by Compartment

Details

Underneath the graphic are the detailed metrics. This information is helpful when you want to get a detailed report that can be exported into a CSV file. The most common use case is to show usage instead of costs. This information lets you see exactly how much of each SKU is being used based on the dates and filters used in the report. A sample is shown in Figure 2-24.

Date (UTC)	Block Storage / Block Volume - Free (GB Months)	Block Storage / Block volume - Performance Units (GB Months)	Block Storage / Block Volume - Storage (GB Months)	Compute / Standard - A1 (OCPU P
Sep 4, 2022	4.76	23.79	2.38	
Sep 3, 2022	6.01	30.06	3.00	
Sep 2, 2022	6.01	30.06	3.00	
Sep 1, 2022	6.01	30.06	3.00	
Total	22.79	113.94	11.39	

Figure 2-24   Usage Report

In this sample you can see that on September 2, 6 GB of block storage was consumed from the free tier and 30 VPUs for block storage. Additionally, you can scroll to see the other details. With the usage report, you can also click **Tab Actions** and download the data as a CSV file or a PDF.

Tip: Where Did My Graph Go?

When showing usage instead of costs, you see only the Details section. There is no graphic.

Budgets

While the cost analysis system enables you to track detailed usages, you can also track and alert on account spend by creating budgets. You can get to the Budgets under the Cost Management option. Budgets let you track consumption and alert based on actual and predicted spend. You can set the spend by a percentage of the budget or an actual dollar amount.

To create a budget, click **Create Budget** on the Budgets page, as seen in Figure 2-25.

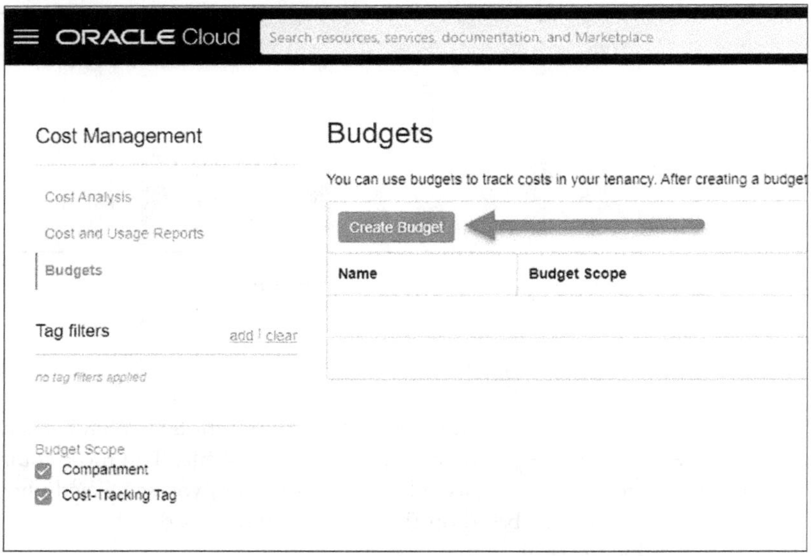

Figure 2-25   Creating a New Budget

Selecting this option will bring up the Create Budget page, with a sample already filled out, as shown in Figure 2-26.

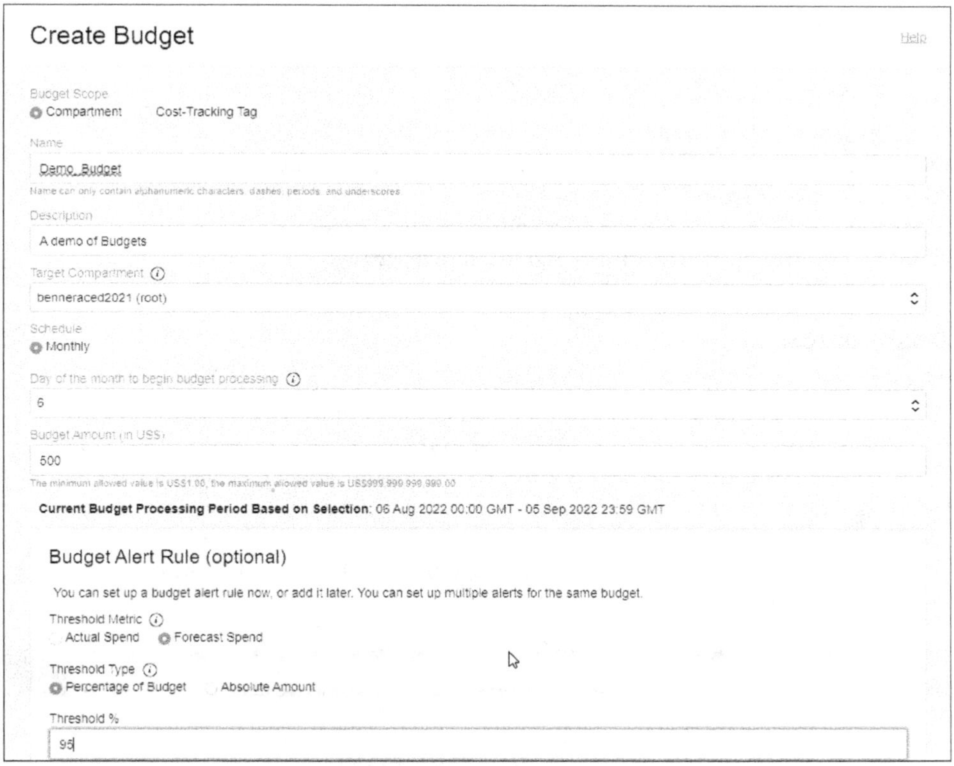

Figure 2-26   Create a Budget

The fields for the budget are

- **Name:** The name of the budget must be all characters, no spaces.
- **Description:** This is your description of the budget.
- **Target Compartment:** This will be the root compartment for your entire tenancy or a subcompartment.
- **Schedule:** This is the timetable; it's set to Monthly. You can then select the day of the month your billing cycle starts.
- **Budget Amount:** This is what you budgeted to spend for the month.
- **Budget Alert Rule:** This section is optional but recommended.
- **Threshold Metric:** You can choose Actual Spend or Forecast Spend. Forecast Spend is helpful when you have some flexibility with your workloads and can identify a possible overage before the billing cycle ends.

- **Threshold Type:** This is either a percentage of your budget or an actual amount of funds spent. Percentage of Budget is useful when combined with Forecast Spend. This setting allows you to alert when the forecasted spend is going to be over 100 percent, or close to 100 percent.
- **Email Recipients:** These are the email addresses of the people receiving the notification from this budget rule.

Then simply select **Create** to set your budget. You also may want to whitelist oraclecloud.com in your email system; this should help prevent the notifications from ending up in your spam folder.

Budgets are a great way of keeping your different DevSecOps teams aware of their cloud spend, helping to prevent any significant overages.

Dashboards

The last feature we will cover in this chapter are the free OCI dashboards. Dashboards are a great way to enable your teams to get a high-level visualized report on system performance, spend, and security customized to the needs of your team. An example is a custom dashboard that is tailored for the FinOps team, showing current and projected spend. Another would be a dashboard customized for the help desk, showing system availability and performance metrics.

Dashboards are available from the main page on the OCI Cloud Console, in a separate Dashboard tab, as shown in Figure 2-27.

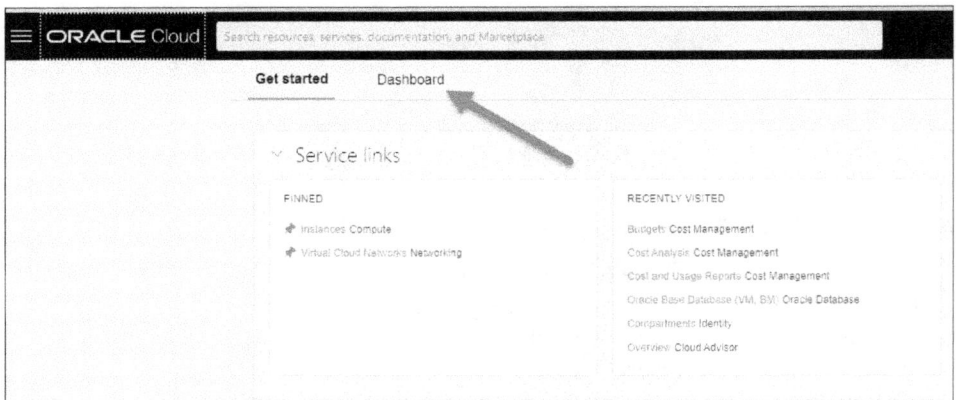

Figure 2-27 Dashboard Tab

The default dashboard (as shown in Figure 2-28) is just a sample. The power of the dashboard is how you can easily modify the dashboard to meet the needs of the teams using them.

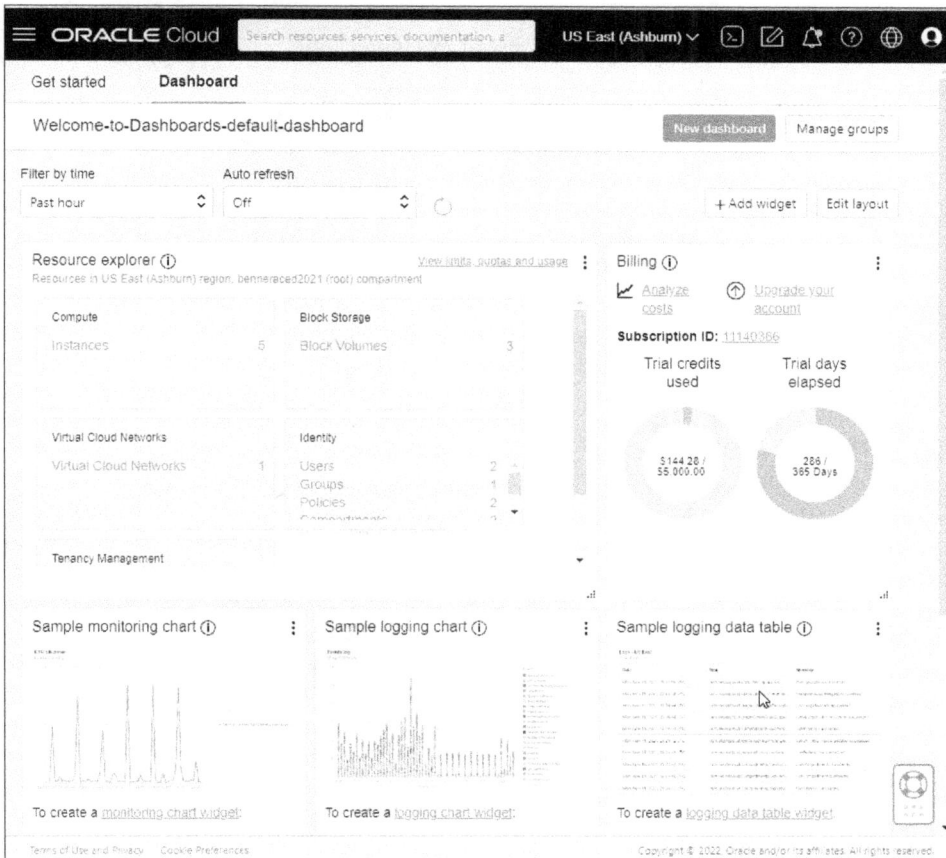

Figure 2-28   Default Dashboard

You can create a new dashboard by selecting **New Dashboard**. You will then be prompted to enter information for the new Dashboard Name, Description, Compartment, and Dashboard Group Name.

The new dashboard starts with a clean slate, where you can then add in widgets that allow you to display statistics from the following areas:

- **Monitoring:** OCI Monitoring services show CPU, RAM, network metrics, and more. You can limit it to a group of systems or to all systems.
- **Resource Explorer:** This shows a summary of all resources.
- **Markdown:** This allows you to add text to the dashboard.
- **Cost Management:** This is similar to the Cost Analysis view.
- **Billing:** This shows a simple graph of the amount of dollars spent.
- **Logging Chart:** This shows the number of log events captured.
- **Logging Data:** This enables you to process and show log data.

For an example, we created a new FinOps Dashboard called FinOps.
You now have a blank dashboard, as shown in Figure 2-29.

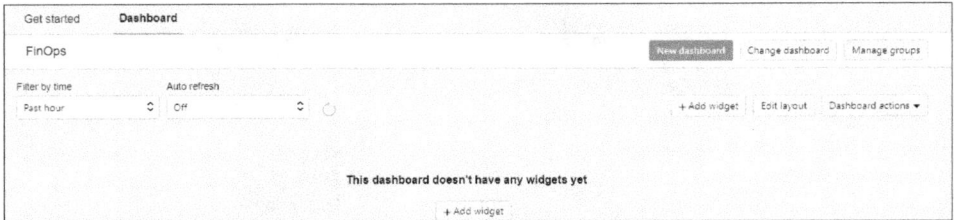

Figure 2-29   Blank Dashboard

To add a new widget, select **+Add Widget** and then, because this is for FinOps,
select **Cost Management**, as shown in Figure 2-30.

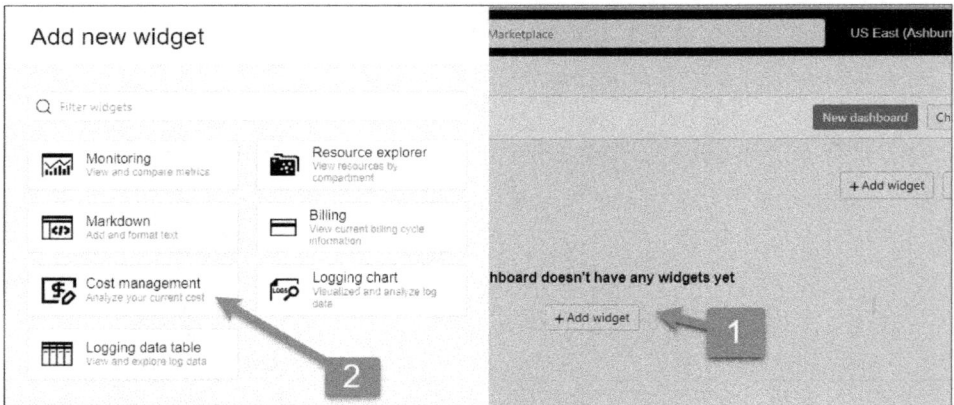

Figure 2-30   Adding a Widget

Selecting this option will then add the default widget to the dashboard. You can then
grab and drag the widget to where you want it, as shown in Figure 2-31.

Most widgets can be modified by selecting the three dots in the upper-right corner of
the widget. What can be modified depends on the widget selected. You also can resize
widgets by grabbing the bottom-right corner and dragging, but keep in mind that some
widgets have minimum and maximum sizes.

When the dashboard is completed, you can save and use it. When viewing a
dashboard, you can set it to automatically refresh or to filter metrics within a specific
recent amount of time. In the sample dashboard shown in Figure 2-32, you can see
the monthly and weekly spend data, as well as tenancy resources consumed, and CPU
utilization metrics for compute nodes.

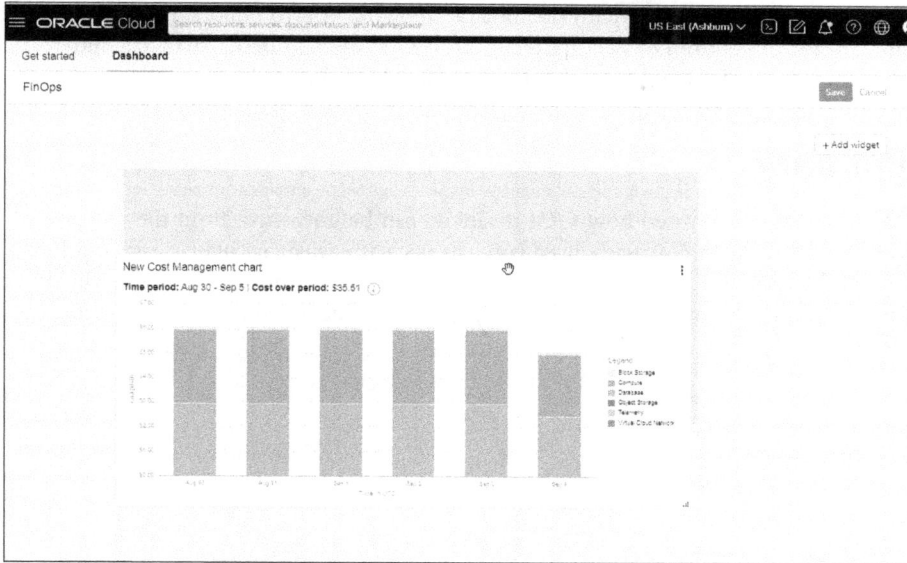

Figure 2-31   Moving a Widget

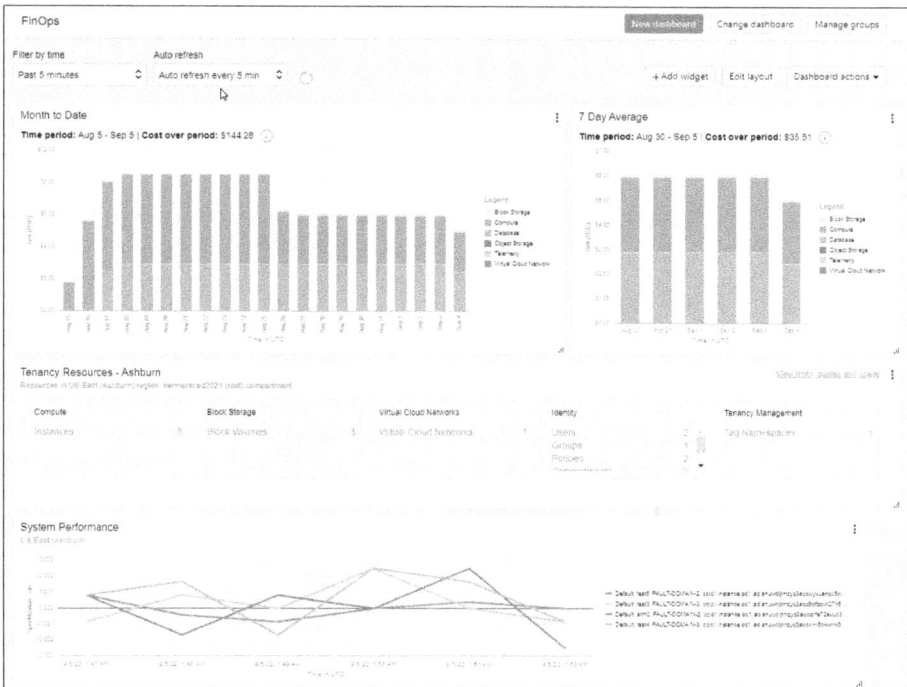

Figure 2-32   FinOps Dashboard

There are a lot of options with dashboards, allowing you to build almost any required dashboard for the entire DevSecOps team, as well as the help desk, financial, and application teams, showing them the data they need for their roles.

Summary

In this chapter, you learned how OCI tenancies can be governed, from the security separation across child tenancies, how you can track the financial operations, and how OCI helps with the challenges of managing performance, availability, and security at a tenancy level. In the next chapter, you will learn more details about OCI security.

Oracle IaaS—Security

Cloud providers allow customers to rent hardware and software resources like compute, storage, and network. These providers manage all or most of the administration, management, and maintenance, depending on the services the customers subscribe to. This type of model is referred to as *Infrastructure as a Service (IaaS)*. We will go over in detail each of these IaaS resources in upcoming chapters.

Oracle Cloud Infrastructure (OCI) enables customers to run their applications, databases, and all critical hardware and software components while maintaining the same level of security standards as on-premises. Oracle manages the network alongside all computing hardware, data centers, and complete infrastructure. Customers are responsible for OS configuration and patching, network configuration, and application patching. Customers get full control of isolation, encryption, access control, security weakness detection, auditing, high availability, and support for third-party security software solutions to keep their environment secure in OCI. Oracle also follows comprehensive security and compliance standards set by third-party vendors. In this chapter, we will review different types of security services offered in OCI.

Identity and Access Management (IAM)

Identity and access management provides access control to all resources in OCI. It helps define who can access what resources with what level of access. These authentication and authorization services allow customers to organize their complete infrastructure footprint fully secured under a single tenancy.

First, let's examine all OCI resources that you can manage under Identity, as shown in Figure 3-1.

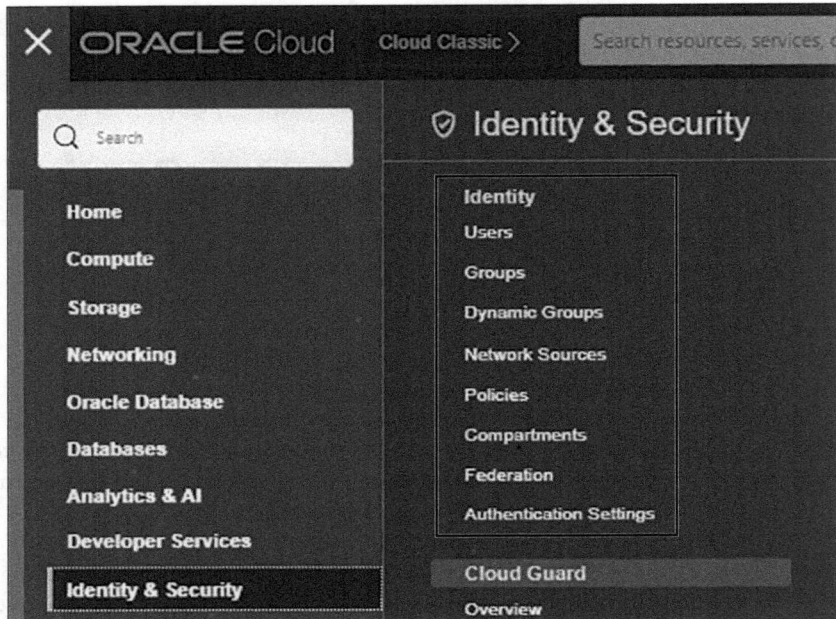

Figure 3-1   Identity & Security Menu

- **Users:** A user is a person, a service account, or a system that needs access to OCI resources. The user will need to be a part of at least one group to have access to any resource. OCI supports multifactor authentication (MFA) and also supports federation with third-party identity providers (IdPs).
- **Groups:** A group contains one or more users requiring similar access to OCI resources. Policies are used to define access privileges for a group.
- **Dynamic Groups:** A dynamic group allows you to create a compute instance as a member by matching a specific rule that you will define at group creation time. This helps instances make API calls to other resources in OCI.
- **Network Sources:** A network source is a collection of IP addresses either from an existing virtual cloud network (VCN) or from public networks.
- **Policies:** A policy defines who can access specific resources in OCI. Policies can include one or more types of rules. These policies are assigned to groups either at the tenancy or compartment level.
- **Compartments:** A compartment is a logical entity within a tenancy to group resources together based on the purpose, organization, or any other reasons. One of the most common scenarios is to separate each division within the organization by compartment, and it also helps to measure usage and billing.

- **Federation:** OCI provides an option to integrate with a third-party identity provider like Active Directory. This federation allows you to manage users and groups within identity providers and authorization in OCI. By default, Oracle provides federation with Oracle Identity Cloud Service.

We will go over all of these and other key concepts with federation examples later in Chapter 11, "Identity and Access Management."

Security Zones

Security zones allow you to create OCI resources that follow strict security guidelines from the very beginning. Security zones can be associated with one or more compartments. They ensure that all resources created are following common security standards and best security practices within these compartments.

These security policies are put together in a *recipe*. OCI has a predefined recipe named the Maximum Security Recipe. It is managed by Oracle and cannot be modified. These policies are for resources like compute, block storage, object storage, file storage, databases, and virtual networks. Any operation that violates any of these policies will be denied. The following are examples of these policies:

- Do not allow users to create public subnets.
- Do not allow users to move a database to a compartment that is not in a security zone.
- Do not allow users to create a block volume without a vault key (encryption).
- Do not allow users to create an instance with an image not approved by Oracle.

Let's go over the process of how to create security zones. Oracle Cloud Guard must be enabled before you move forward. This tool is covered in detail in Chapter 14, "Cloud Guard."

The first step is to log in to your tenancy by going to https://cloud.oracle.com. Click the menu on the top-left corner and then from the main menu click **Identity & Security > Security Zones**, as shown in Figure 3-2.

Let's create a security zone for an oracle-lab compartment using a predefined recipe. To do so, click **Create Security Zone**, as shown in Figure 3-3.

On the next window, select the zone recipe, compartment, and security zone name and description. Then click **Create Security Zone**, as shown in Figure 3-4.

Once the security zone is created, you will find the status on the home page, as shown in Figure 3-5.

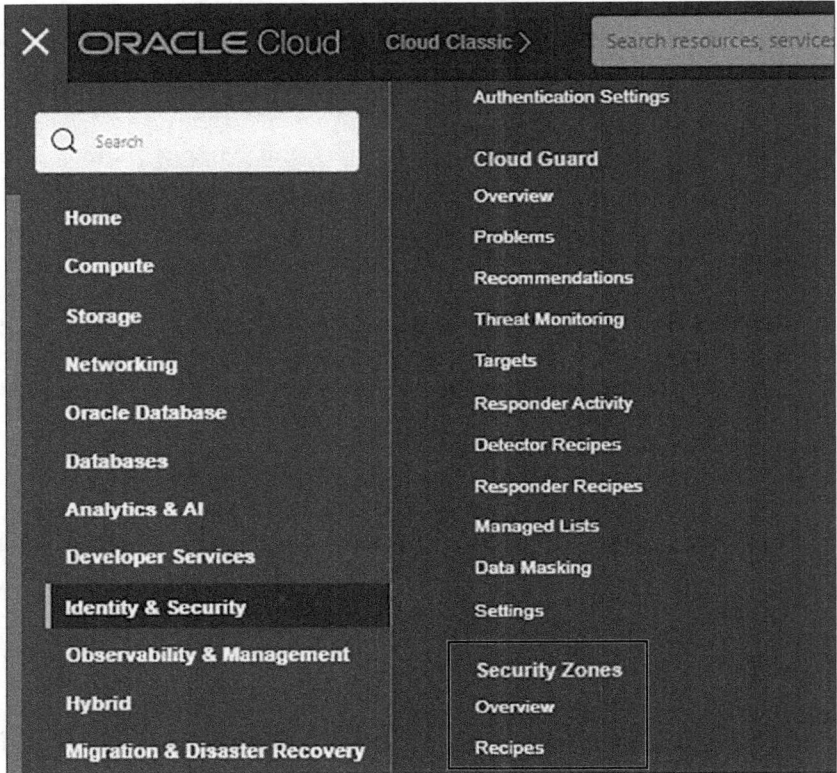

Figure 3-2   Identity & Security Menu

Figure 3-3   Security Zones Home Page

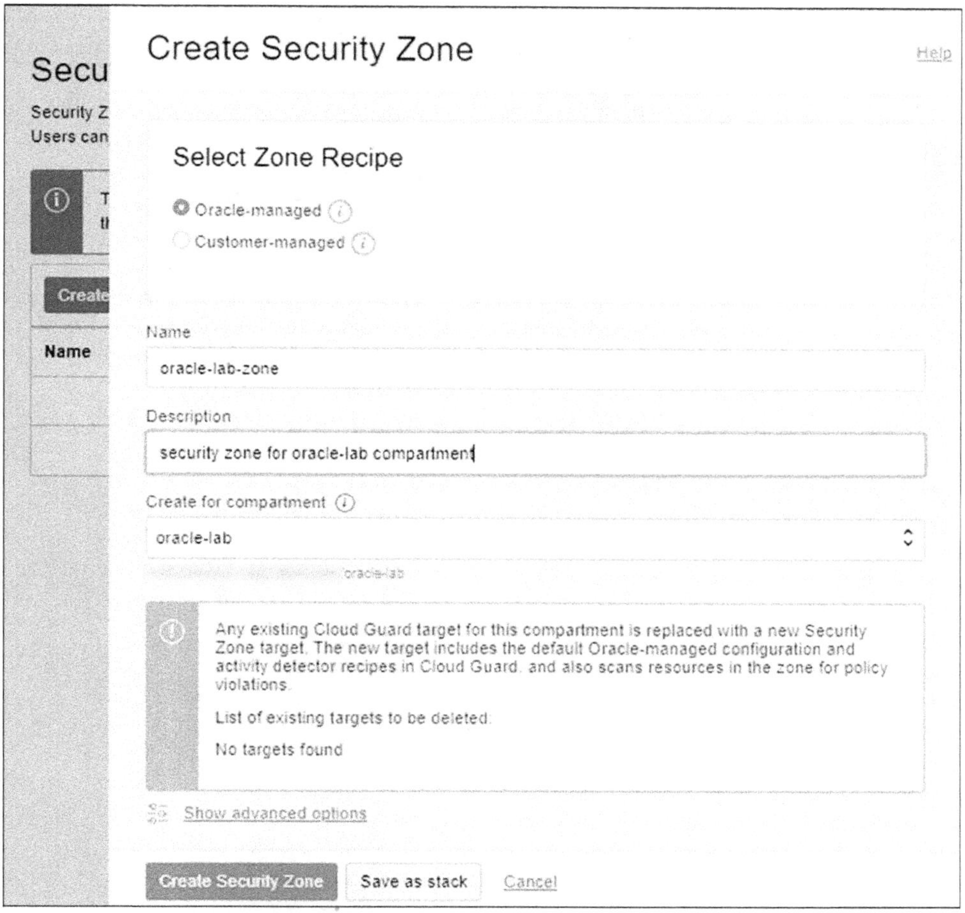

Create Security Zone   Help

Secu

Security Z
Users can

Select Zone Recipe

◉ Oracle-managed ⓘ
◯ Customer-managed ⓘ

Name

oracle-lab-zone

Description

security zone for oracle-lab compartment

Create for compartment ⓘ

oracle-lab   ⌄

oracle-lab

ⓘ Any existing Cloud Guard target for this compartment is replaced with a new Security
    Zone target. The new target includes the default Oracle-managed configuration and
    activity detector recipes in Cloud Guard, and also scans resources in the zone for policy
    violations.

    List of existing targets to be deleted:

    No targets found

⚏ Show advanced options

Create Security Zone   Save as stack   Cancel

Figure 3-4   Create Security Zone

Security Zones

Security Zones automatically enforce security standards and best practices on resources in selected compartments. Users cannot create or update a resource
in a Security Zone if the action violates a Security Zone policy. Learn more

ⓘ The latest Security Zones release includes many significant enhancements and user interface changes. See the release notes for details.

Create Security Zone

Name	Status	Recipe	Created	
oracle-lab-zone	⬤ Active	Maximum Security Recipe - 20200914	Wed, Nov 30, 2022 22:42:31 UTC	⋮

Showing 1 Item   ‹ 1 of 1 ›

Figure 3-5   Security Zone Status

OCI will keep monitoring the oracle-lab compartment for any security violations. All violations will be reported in the detail section of oracle-lab-zone. You can also add any child compartment of oracle-lab to this security zone when desired.

You can create custom recipes by selecting a subset of predefined policies by either policy type or resource type. This capability will be useful if you are seperating resources by compartment, such as all compute instances in one compartment and databases in another compartment. In this scenario, you can create a custom recipe with policies related to a specific resource type and assign it to the appropriate compartment.

To create a custom recipe, click **Recipes** on the left panel, as shown earlier in Figure 3-3. This selection will open a separate window requesting recipe information, as shown in Figure 3-6. Here, provide a recipe name, description, and compartment, and then click **Next**.

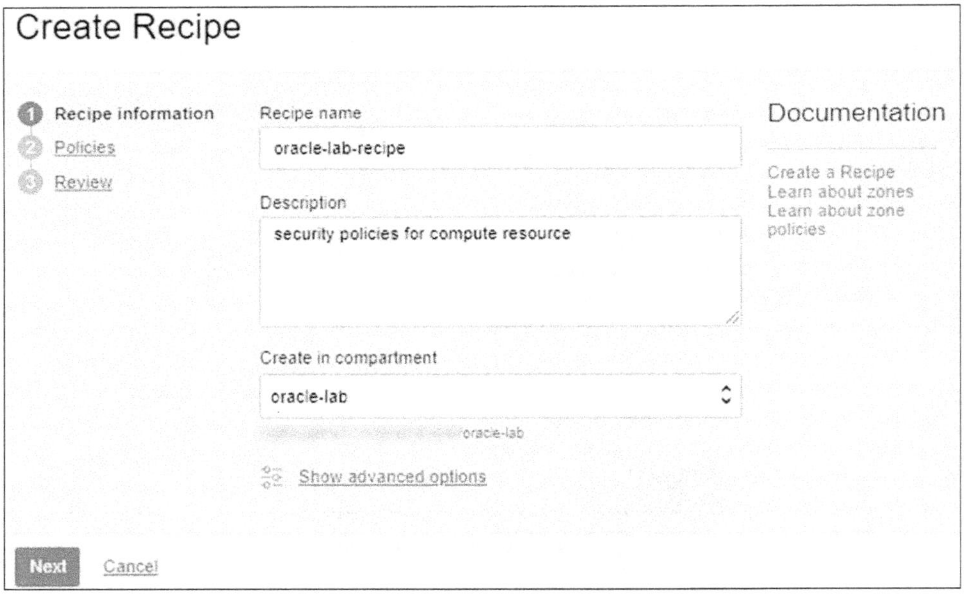

Figure 3-6   Recipe Information

Next, select **COMPUTE** under Resource Type and click **Next**, as shown in Figure 3-7.

Next, review all the information entered so far and click **Create**, as shown in Figure 3-8.

Now this custom recipe can be associated with a security zone. As you have noticed, that security zone service works as a sort of preventive measure for the customer. It prevents any user mistakes and avoids major security issues.

Create Recipe

Recipe information

Policies

Review

Choose the Security Zone policies for this Recipe. Policies restrict user actions to ensure your cloud resources comply with Oracle security best practices.
Learn more

Policy type		Resource type	
All	‎ ⌄	COMPUTE	‎ ⌄

	Name	Type	Resource t
☑	deny_instance_without_sanctioned_image	Use Only Configurations Approved by Oracle	COMPUTE
☑	deny_instance_in_security_zone_in_subnet_not_in_security_zone	Restrict Resource Association	COMPUTE
☑	deny_block_volume_in_security_zone_attach_to_instance_not_in_security_zone	Restrict Resource Association	COMPUTE
☑	deny_block_volume_not_in_security_zone_attach_to_instance_in_security_zone	Restrict Resource Association	COMPUTE
☑	deny_boot_volume_in_security_zone_attach_to_instance_not_in_security_zone	Restrict Resource Association	COMPUTE
☑	deny_boot_volume_not_in_security_zone_attach_to_instance_in_security_zone	Restrict Resource Association	COMPUTE
☑	deny_instance_in_security_zone_launch_from_boot_volume_not_in_security_zone	Restrict Resource Association	COMPUTE
☑	deny_instance_not_in_security_zone_launch_from_boot_volume_in_security_zone	Restrict Resource Association	COMPUTE
☑	deny_instance_in_security_zone_move_to_compartment_not_in_security_zone	Restrict Resource Movement	COMPUTE
☑	deny_instance_not_in_security_zone_move_to_compartment_in_security_zone	Restrict Resource Movement	COMPUTE

Previous **Next** Cancel

Figure 3-7   Policies

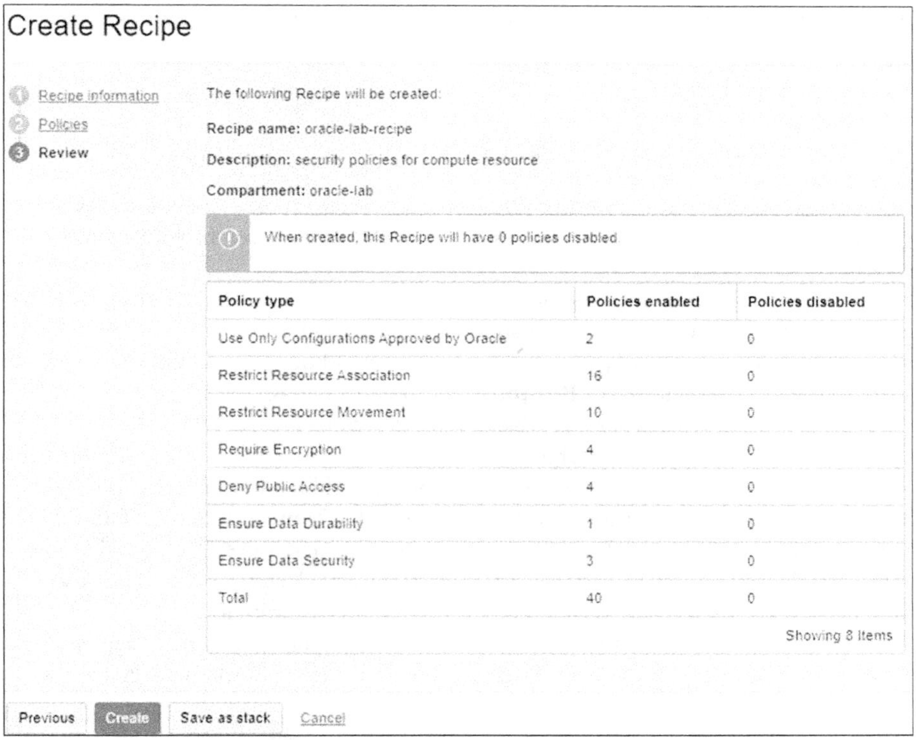

Create Recipe

Recipe information

Policies

Review

The following Recipe will be created:

Recipe name: oracle-lab-recipe

Description: security policies for compute resource

Compartment: oracle-lab

ⓘ When created, this Recipe will have 0 policies disabled.

Policy type	Policies enabled	Policies disabled
Use Only Configurations Approved by Oracle	2	0
Restrict Resource Association	16	0
Restrict Resource Movement	10	0
Require Encryption	4	0
Deny Public Access	4	0
Ensure Data Durability	1	0
Ensure Data Security	3	0
Total	40	0

Showing 8 Items

Previous **Create** Save as stack Cancel

Figure 3-8   Review Information

Bastions

Most customers create critical application servers, database servers, and/or autonomous databases in a private subnet to restrict direct access. Resources like these without public endpoints are not directly accessed from the Internet. So, what will happen when an administrator needs to access these servers to review logs for performance troubleshooting or to perform any maintenance tasks? And how do you access an autonomous database to do any administration work? The answer here is the OCI *bastion* service. It allows you to authorize specific individuals to access these restricted resources. This type of access is only allowed from specific user-defined IPs and only for a limited time.

Bastions provide managed Secure Shell (SSH) and SSH port forwarding session capabilities. Managed SSH sessions allow you to connect to compute instances securely. SSH port forwarding will be useful in case you connect to an autonomous database where you do not have a server to log in to. SSH port forwarding allows access to a specific port on a target autonomous database, so you can connect to the database using SQL Developer.

Setting up a bastion service is an easy process. First, you create a bastion. Next, you create a session on the bastion for either a managed SSH session or an SSH port forwarding session. Now you're ready to connect to a session using your preferred SSH client. There are a few prerequisites before you begin, however:

- Create required IAM policies to use bastion and dependent resources.
- Create a service gateway to access Oracle services without going over the public Internet.
- Enable the bastion plug-in for Oracle Cloud Agent on compute instance.

Bastions are integrated with other OCI resources. You can use an audit to review logs, monitoring services to create alarms and event services to use in your custom development.

Let's create a managed SSH session to access a compute instance for our test scenario. A simple illustration of this scenario is shown in Figure 3-9.

First, log in to your tenancy by going to https://cloud.oracle.com. Go to the menu on the top-left corner and select **Bastions**, as shown in Figure 3-10.

On the home page, click **Create Bastion**, as shown in Figure 3-11.

Now provide a bastion name, target VCN of the target resource, and target subnet that is either the same target as the resource's subnet or other subnet having traffic accepted by the target resource's subnet. Also, provide a Classless Inter-Domain Routing (CIDR) block for the systems connecting to the resource and a session time-to-live (TTL), and then click **Create Bastion**, as shown in Figure 3-12. Here, we have selected a public subnet for bastion so that the ingress rule is added to a private subnet security list.

In a few minutes, a bastion will be created with active status. The next step is to click the bastion name to get to the detail page, as shown in Figure 3-13. Now create the session by clicking **Create Session**.

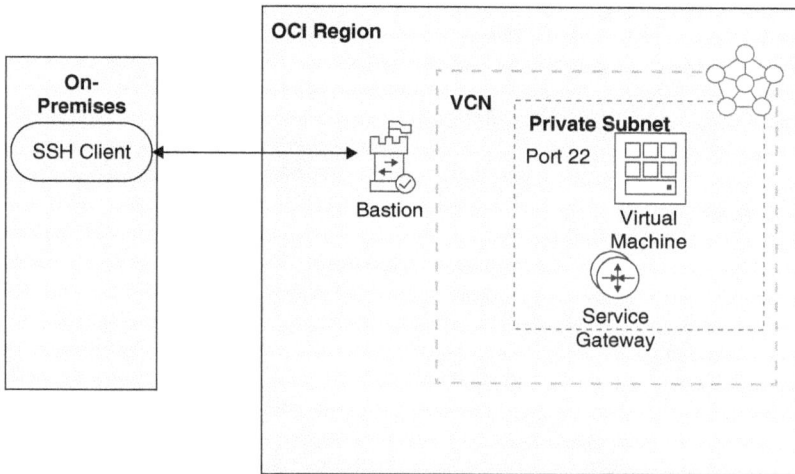

Figure 3-9   Bastion Service

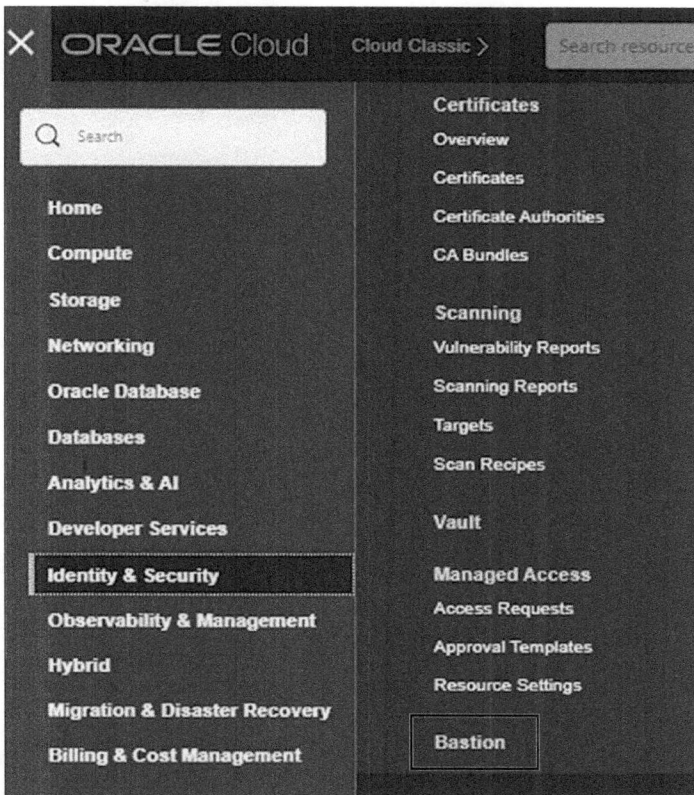

Figure 3-10   Identity & Security Menu

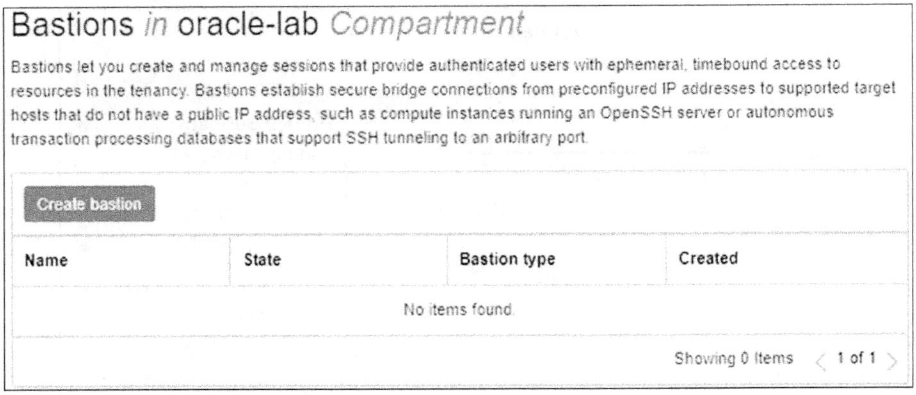

Bastions *in* oracle-lab *Compartment*

Bastions let you create and manage sessions that provide authenticated users with ephemeral, timebound access to resources in the tenancy. Bastions establish secure bridge connections from preconfigured IP addresses to supported target hosts that do not have a public IP address, such as compute instances running an OpenSSH server or autonomous transaction processing databases that support SSH tunneling to an arbitrary port.

Create bastion

Name	State	Bastion type	Created
		No items found.	

Showing 0 Items 〈 1 of 1 〉

Figure 3-11   Bastions Home Page

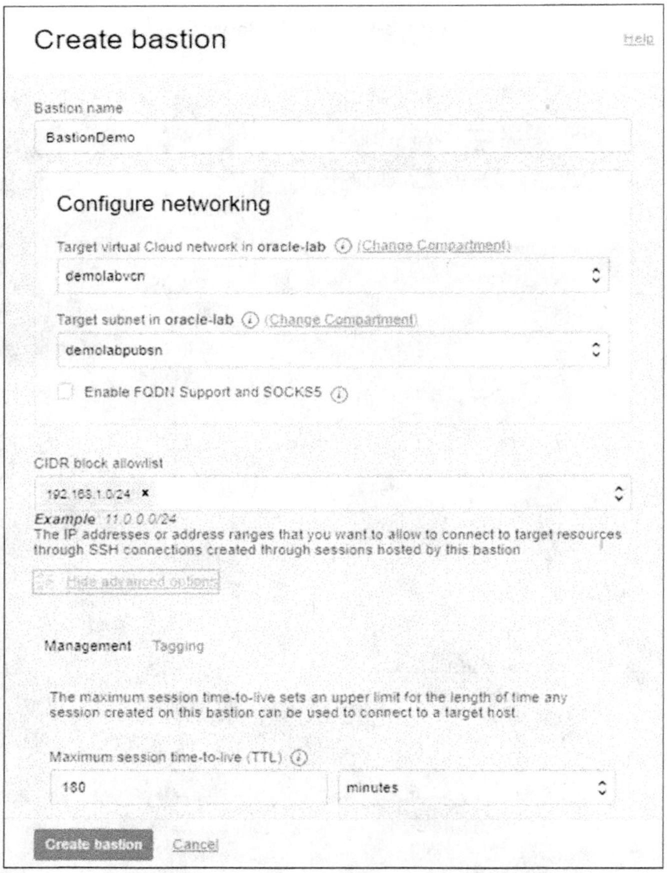

Create bastion   Help

Bastion name

BastionDemo

Configure networking

Target virtual Cloud network in **oracle-lab** ⓘ (Change Compartment)

demolabvcn ⌄

Target subnet in **oracle-lab** ⓘ (Change Compartment)

demolabpubsn ⌄

☐ Enable FQDN Support and SOCKS5 ⓘ

CIDR block allowlist

192.168.1.0/24 ✕

Example 11.0.0.0/24
The IP addresses or address ranges that you want to allow to connect to target resources through SSH connections created through sessions hosted by this bastion.

⌃ Hide advanced options

Management   Tagging

The maximum session time-to-live sets an upper limit for the length of time any session created on this bastion can be used to connect to a target host.

Maximum session time-to-live (TTL) ⓘ

180   minutes ⌄

Create bastion   Cancel

Figure 3-12   Bastion Information

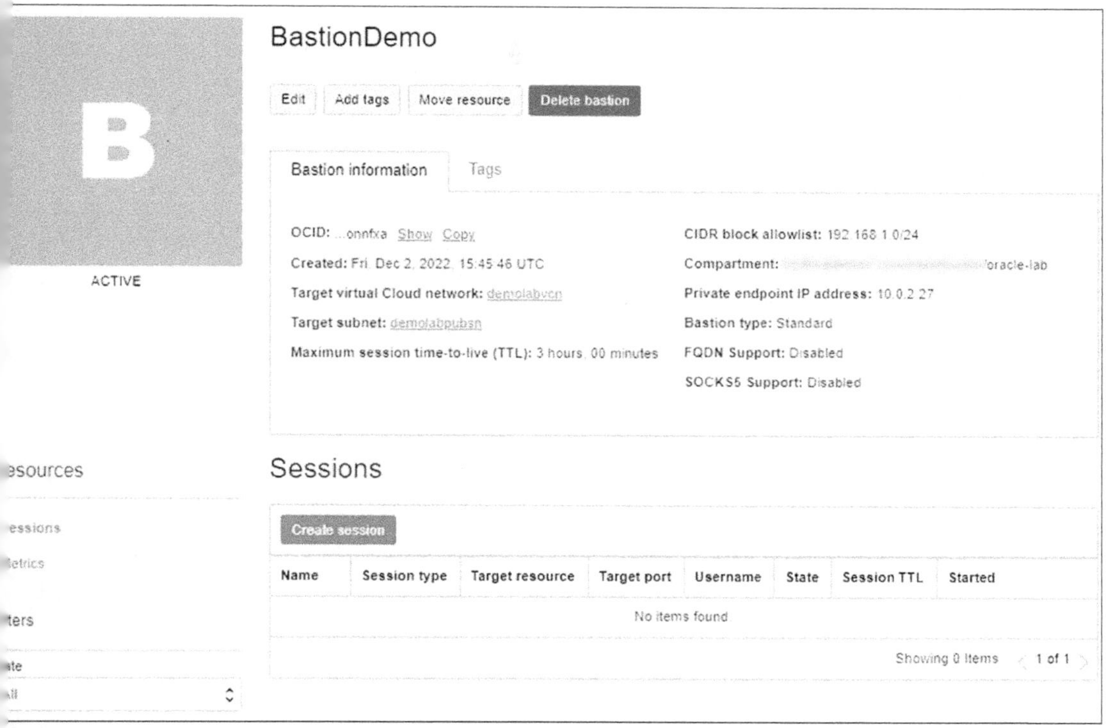

Figure 3-13   Bastion Detail Page

Remember that we're creating a managed SSH session for our test case. Now provide a session type, session name, username to log on to the host, compute instance name, and preferred SSH public key. In the advanced options, you can provide a maximum session time, target port on the compute host, and compute instance IP address, as shown in Figure 3-14.

It will take a minute or so, but once the session is created, you will see the session with the active status. Now click the action menu and then **Copy SSH Command**, as shown in Figure 3-15.

Paste the **ssh** command to Notepad and replace the *<privateKey>* field with the actual location of the private key. Now run this **ssh** command from PowerShell or any PuTTY session. It should look like the session shown in Figure 3-16.

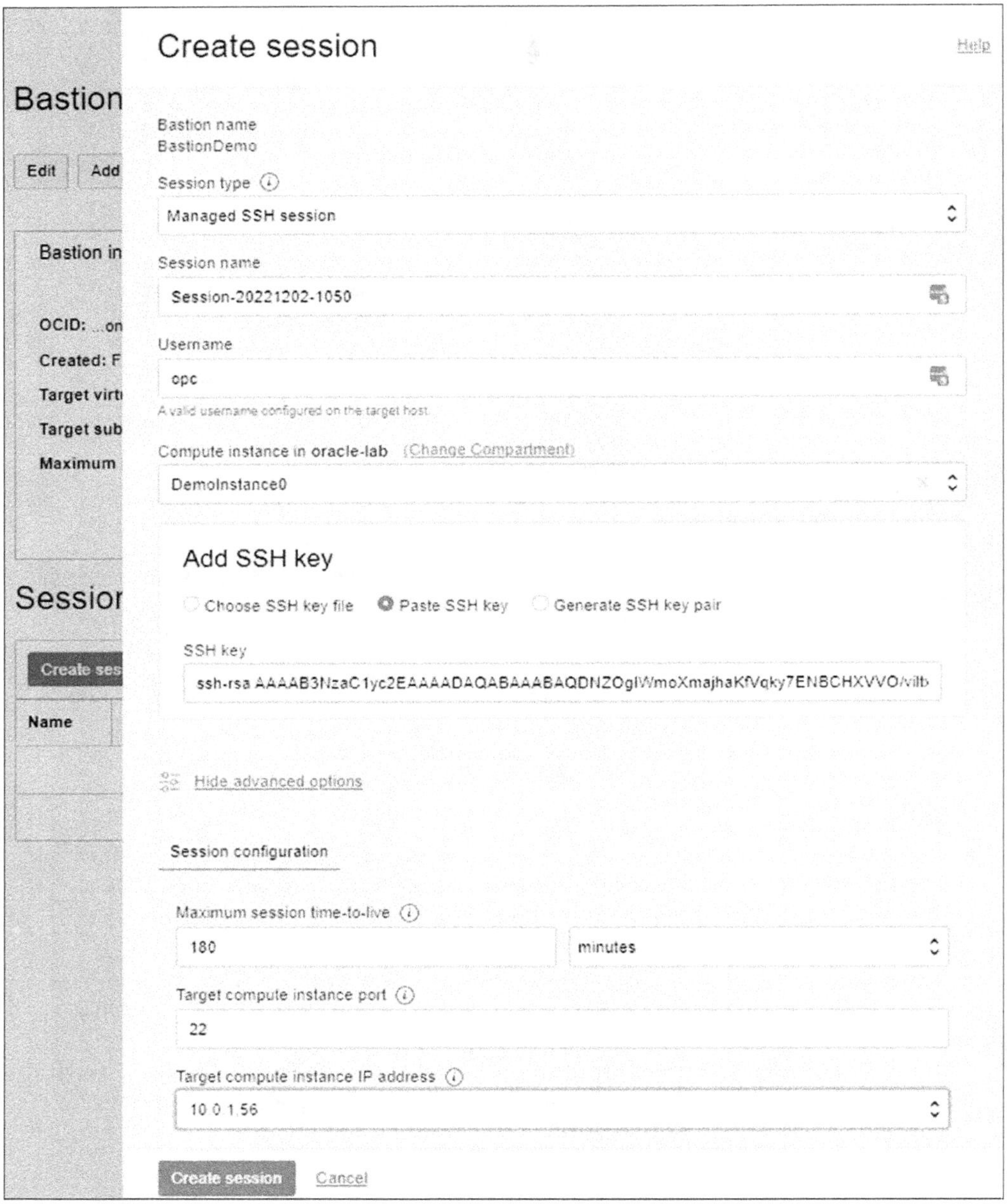

Create session

Help

Bastion

| Edit | Add |

Bastion name
BastionDemo

Session type (i)

| Managed SSH session | ⌄ |

Session name

| Session-20221202-1050 | 🔳 |

Username

| opc | 🔳 |

A valid username configured on the target host.

Compute instance in **oracle-lab**   (Change Compartment)

| DemoInstance0 | ✕ ⌄ |

Add SSH key

○ Choose SSH key file   ● Paste SSH key   ○ Generate SSH key pair

SSH key

| ssh-rsa AAAAB3NzaC1yc2EAAAADAQABAAABAQDNZOglWmoXmajhaKfVqky7ENBCHXVVO/vilb |

⠿ Hide advanced options

Session configuration

Maximum session time-to-live (i)

| 180 | | minutes | ⌄ |

Target compute instance port (i)

| 22 |

Target compute instance IP address (i)

| 10.0.1.56 | ⌄ |

| Create session | Cancel |

Figure 3-14   Session Information

Figure 3-15   Session Action Menu

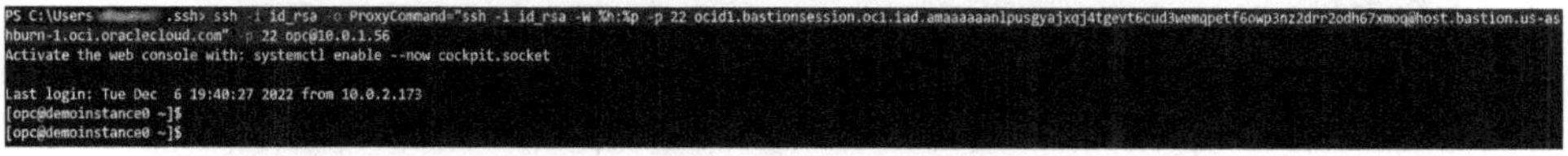

Figure 3-16   Bastion Session Connection

As you can see, it is easy to use bastion, and is very helpful for accessing resources residing in a private subnet.

Threat Intelligence Service

The *Threat Intelligence Service*, as the name suggests, helps protect your environment with known security threats out there. The threat intelligence data is gathered from many different sources, and the service becomes a central hub for it. It is fully integrated with Oracle security products. This data helps detect security threats and prevent it in OCI services.

Let's review how to access the threat indicator database and interpret the information. This database includes data processed by Oracle from open-source feeds, third-party intelligence companies, and other sources that have observed and/or reported this data. You can search the database by using different indicators such as IP addresses, URLs, malware, and domain names.

Log in to a tenancy by going to https://cloud.oracle.com. Go to the menu and click **Identity & Security > Threat Intelligence**, as shown in Figure 3-17.

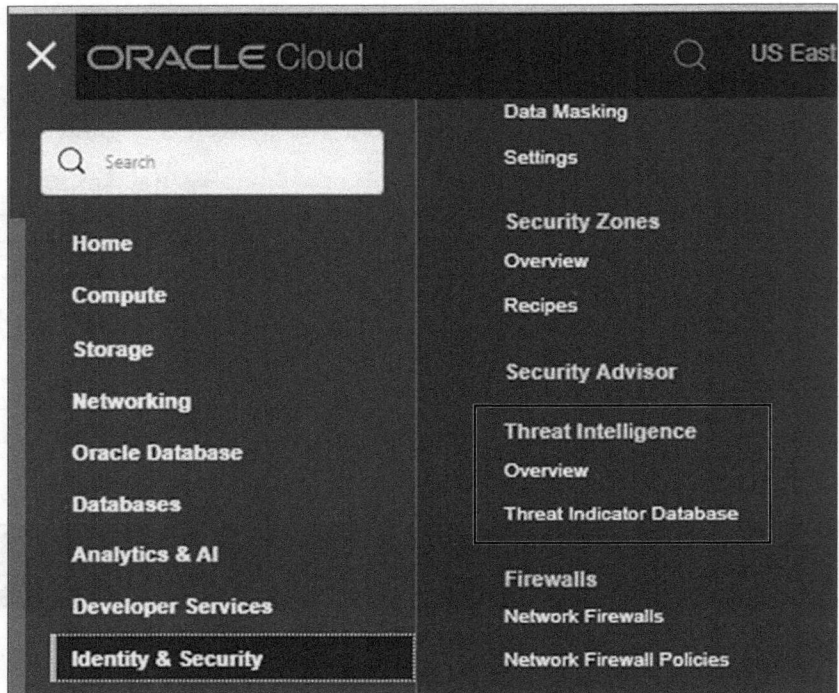

Figure 3-17   Identity & Security Menu

Click **View Threat Indicator Database**, as shown in Figure 3-18.

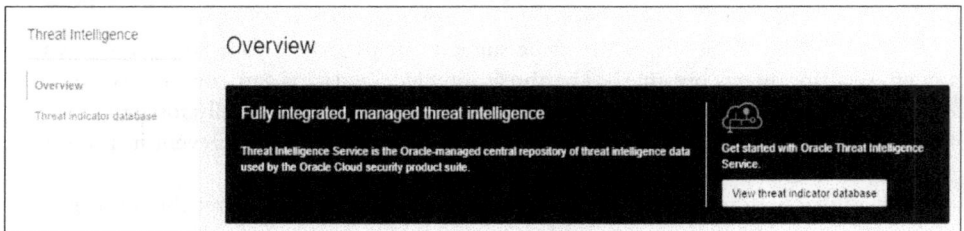

Figure 3-18   Threat Intelligence Home Page

You can search the database for domain name, filename, IP address, malware, MD5 hash, SHA1 hash, SHA256 hash, and threat actor. For this example, select **IP Address** as the search criteria with Date Last Reported as **Last 30 Days** and Confidence Score set as **Higher than 80**. From the search result, select one of the IP addresses, as shown in Figure 3-19.

Search database

Search for
IP address

IP address

Date last reported
Last 30 days

IP address
192.168.1.9

Confidence score
Higher than 80

Search   Reset

Indicator	Type	Threat type	Overall confidence ▲	First reported	Last reported	
103.219.22.63	IP address	Criminal	81	Wed, Nov 30, 2022, 19:11:12 UTC	Sat, Dec 3, 2022, 01:31:13 UTC	⋮
103.8.20.165	IP address	Criminal	81	Wed, Nov 30, 2022, 19:01:19 UTC	Sat, Dec 3, 2022, 01:31:17 UTC	⋮
104.130.169.64	IP address	Criminal	81	Wed, Nov 30, 2022, 19:41:22 UTC	Sat, Dec 3, 2022, 01:36:28 UTC	⋮
104.130.204.251	IP address	Criminal	81	Wed, Nov 30, 2022, 19:56:15 UTC	Sat, Dec 3, 2022, 01:37:56 UTC	⋮
104.219.232.125	IP address	Botnets	81	Wed, Nov 9, 2022, 17:48:25 UTC	Sat, Dec 3, 2022, 02:25:34 UTC	⋮
104.219.233.129	IP address	Botnets	81	Tue, Nov 8, 2022, 17:48:21 UTC	Sat, Dec 3, 2022, 02:22:38 UTC	⋮
104.227.137.34	IP address	Criminal	81	Wed, Nov 30, 2022, 19:11:13 UTC	Sat, Dec 3, 2022, 01:31:09 UTC	⋮

Figure 3-19   Search Threat Indicator Database

IP address 103.219.22.63 is reported by Crowdstrike as a threat with a confidence score of 81, as shown in Figure 3-20. A higher confidence score means the threat is more likely to pose a real risk. This IP only means that the intelligence community is aware of it and that it has been detected in your environment. You can also report any threat as false positive if you are aware of it by creating a service request with Oracle Support.

103.219.22.63

Report false positive

Information

Oracle Threat Intelligence Service indicators are based on data from our sources. Indicators are regularly updated and information displayed here reflects the current state about this data. If this indicator was included as an element in a Cloud Guard problem, you may want to validate the integrity and security of related resources from the impacted environment. The OCI Best Practices Framework provides information and guidance about securing cloud workloads

OCID: mgdynaaq Show Copy
Overall confidence: 81 ⓘ
Last reported: Wed, Nov 30, 2022, 17:16:12 UTC
First reported: Wed, Nov 30, 2022, 17:16:12 UTC

Type: IP address
Most recently reported by: Crowdstrike
For more information on our sources, please visit documentation
Geolocation: Tower Hamlets, Tower Hamlets, United Kingdom of Great Britain and Northern Ireland

Resources

Indicator history

Indicator history

Indicator History provides a record of information relating to this indicator as reported by our threat intelligence source(s). This history does not reflect activity of the indicator in your tenancy.

Last reported	First reported	Threat type	Associated malware	Actor	Reported by
Wed, Nov 30, 2022, 17:16:12 UTC	Wed, Nov 30, 2022, 17:16:12 UTC	Criminal			Crowdstrike

Figure 3-20   Threat Information

Oracle provides out-of-the-box integration of a threat intelligence service with Cloud Guard, which is a useful tool to maintain the security posture of your OCI environment. We will cover only threat intelligence–related sections of the Cloud Guard here.

First, you must enable Cloud Guard if it is not already enabled. Cloud Guard compares audit log data with threat intelligence data to detect any possible threat. For example, any IP address reported in threat intelligence data with a confidence score greater than 80 found interacting with your environment gets reported. You can find all threats detected in the Threat Monitoring section of the Cloud Guard, as shown in Figure 3-21. It will show the last 30-day risk score trend with detailed information.

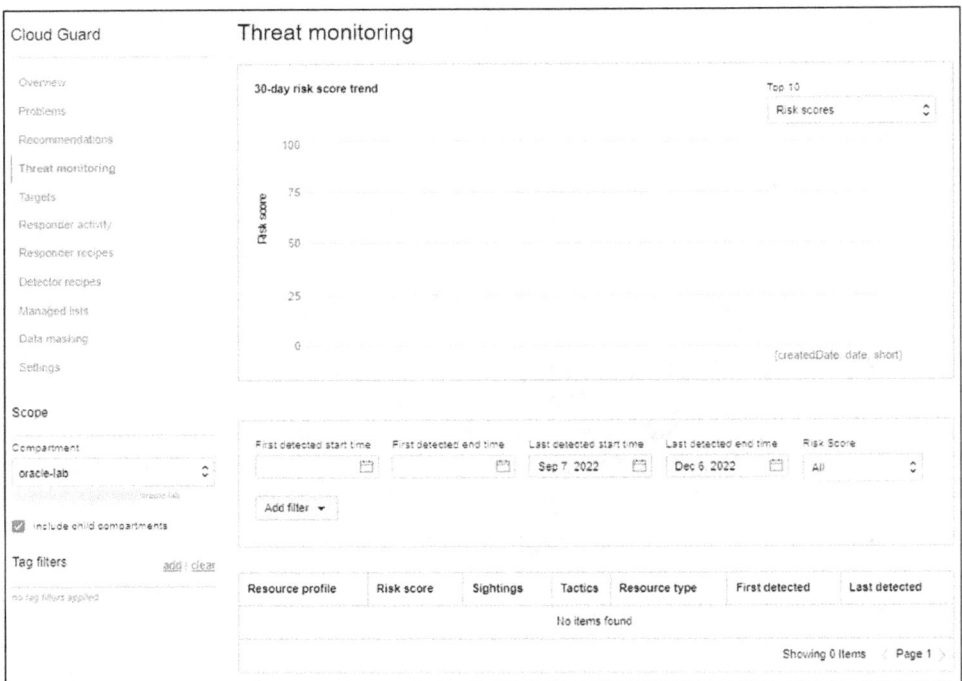

Figure 3-21   Threat Monitoring

Now let's review how different functions of Cloud Guard work together for threat detection. You will first create a threat detector recipe. Oracle provides an out-of-the-box OCI threat detector recipe in the root compartment of your tenancy, as shown in Figure 3-22. You can clone this recipe in any other compartment and modify it if necessary. This threat detector recipe includes a rogue user detector rule to identify any unauthorized access, misuse of privileges, and so on.

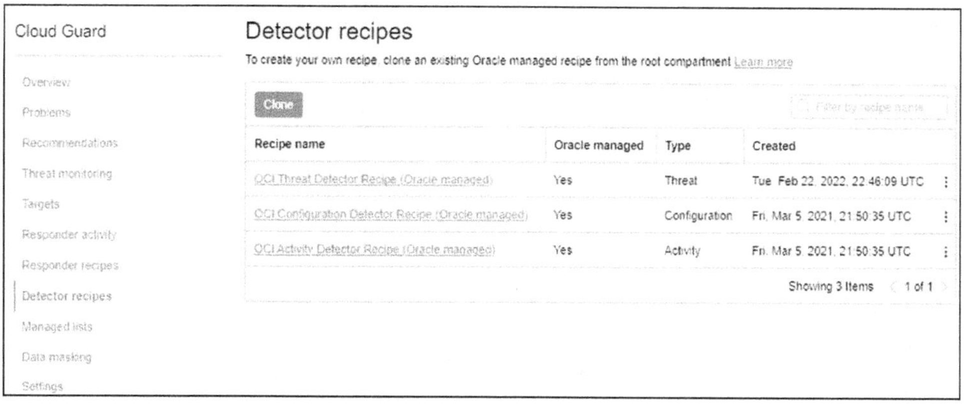

Figure 3-22   Detector Recipe

Next, define a target compartment that you want threat detection to run against by clicking **Create New Target**, as shown in Figure 3-23.

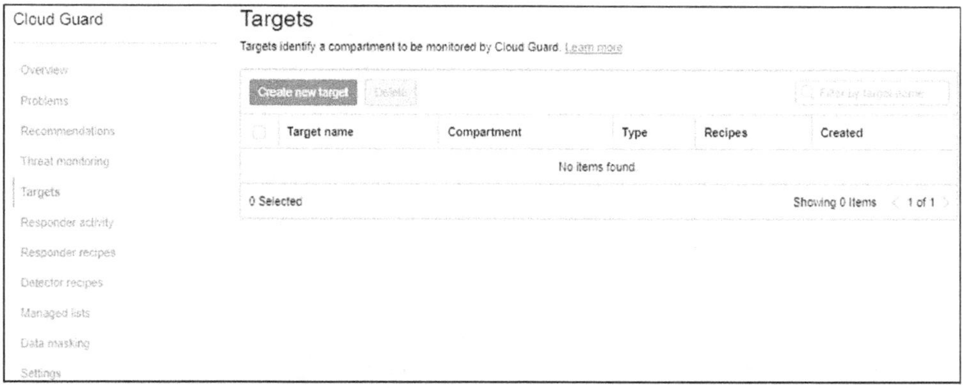

Figure 3-23   Target

Here, provide a target name, select a compartment, and select a configuration detector recipe, threat detector recipe, and activity detector recipe, as shown in Figure 3-24. We have selected Oracle-managed detector recipes here, but you can select custom recipes if required.

Now Cloud Guard will monitor the target compartment against the threat detector recipe and other recipes. Once the threat is identified, it gets reported as a problem. Since we are using an Oracle-managed threat detector policy, the reponse to this policy is to disable the IAM user in the Oracle-managed responder recipe. You can also choose to clone the responder recipe and modify the response.

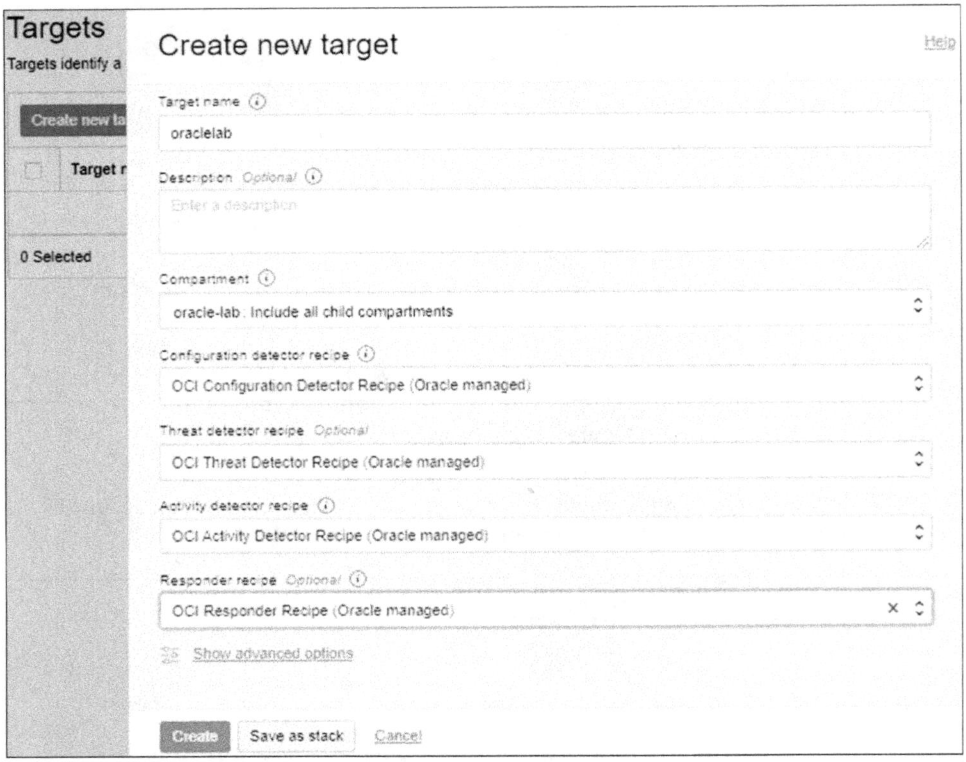

Figure 3-24   Create New Target Window

Web Application Firewall (WAF)

Web Application Firewall is a region-based service. It protects applications from malicious activities, web vulnerabilities, and any other application layer attacks. WAF can be attached to a load balancer or web application domain name.

You will define WAF policies that enable you to specify all rules that can be checked against any incoming application traffic. WAF policies give you the ability to control the request and response by providing access control, set rate limitations by inspecting all incoming HTTP or HTTPS traffic and limiting its frequency, set protection rules to determine what traffic to log, and also allow or block and add firewall resources like the load balancer as an enforcement point.

For access control, rate limiting, and protection rules, you can specify the path, request cookies, request headers, URL query, country/region, source IP, host, and request method as a condition type. Then you can define an appropriate response when conditions have been met. The response can be to perform a check, allow the request, block the request, or complete a custom action. You will also define a default response in case none of these conditions are met.

Access control enables you to specify access rules that will determine the access type based on the response/action defined. Rate limiting limits the request frequency based on the HTTP request properties inspection. Protection capabilities help detect cross-site scripting (XSS) attacks, SQL injection, and other types of malicious attacks. You can also define how to respond to these types of threats.

Log in to your tenancy by going to https://cloud.oracle.com. Go to the menu and click **Identity & Security > Web Application Firewall**, as shown in Figure 3-25.

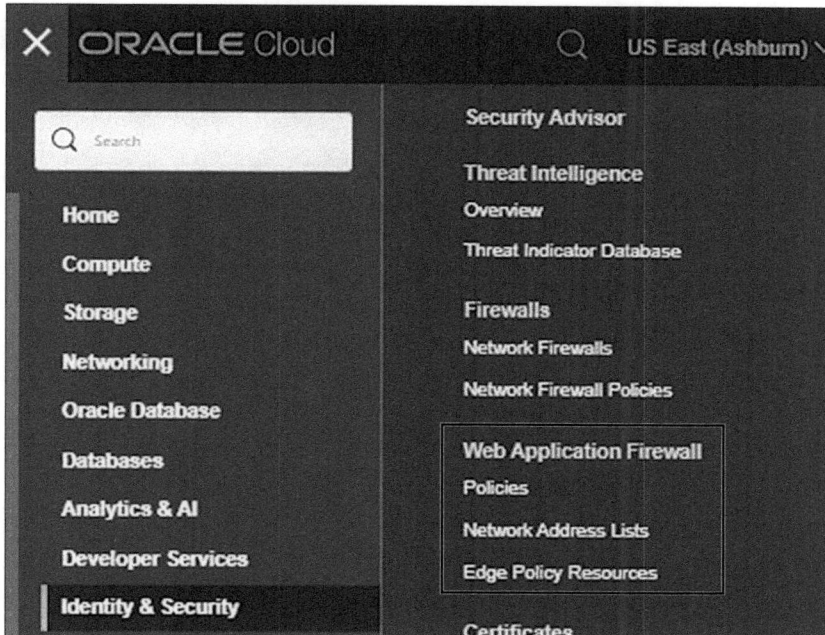

Figure 3-25   Identity & Security Menu

Click **Create WAF Policy**, as shown in Figure 3-26.

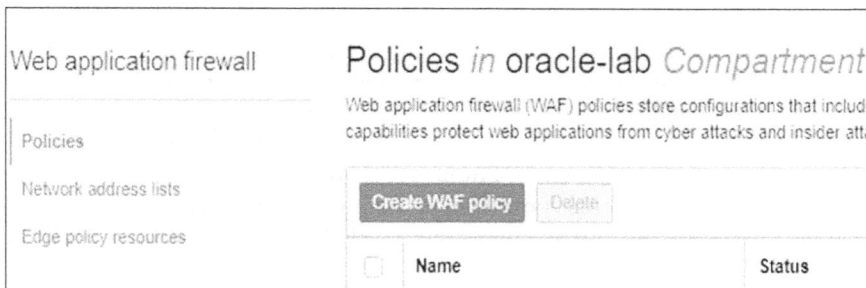

Figure 3-26   WAF Home Page

Next, enter the WAF policy name and compartment; then click **Next**, as shown in Figure 3-27. You can define custom actions here that can also be used for other WAF policies. For our test case, let's use the default actions only.

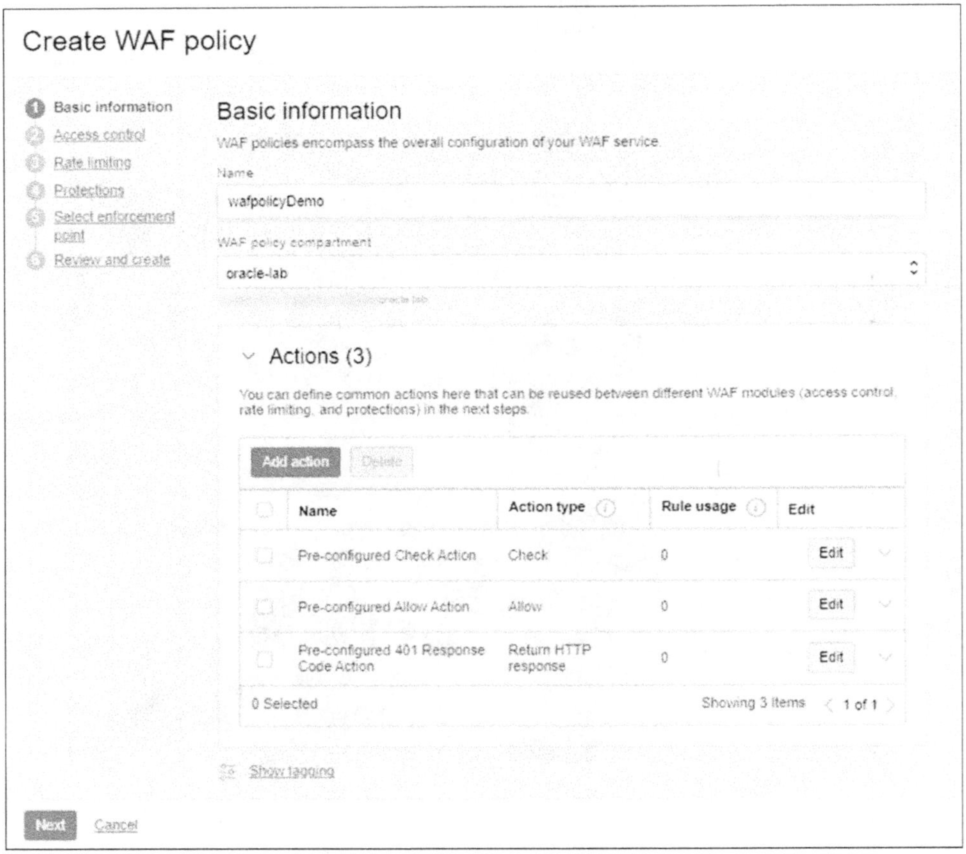

Figure 3-27   WAF Policy Basic Information

Next, you can add an access rule and an appropriate action for it. Click the **Enable Access Control** option and click **Add Access Rule**, as shown in Figure 3-28.

Next, provide a condition type and choose what action to perform. You can provide multiple conditions, and these will be interpreted with the AND operator. For our test case, enter an access rule name, select **Country/Region** as the condition type, and select the condition for all connections coming from the United States. The rule action will be to display the 401 response code. Click **Add Access Rule**, as shown in Figure 3-29.

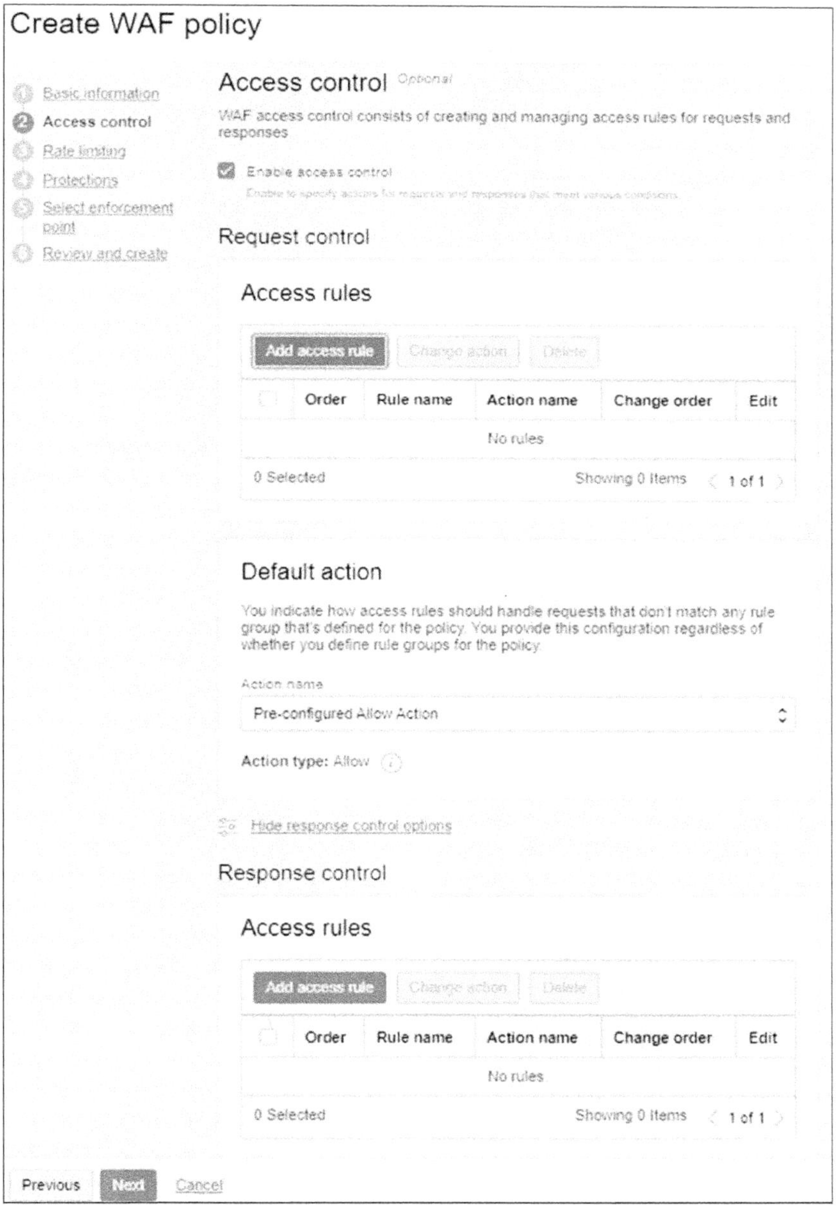

Create WAF policy

1 Basic information
2 Access control
3 Rate limiting
4 Protections
5 Select enforcement point
6 Review and create

Access control *Optional*

WAF access control consists of creating and managing access rules for requests and responses

☑ Enable access control

Enable to specify actions for requests and responses that meet various conditions.

Request control

Access rules

	Order	Rule name	Action name	Change order	Edit
			No rules		

Add access rule   Change action   Delete

0 Selected   Showing 0 Items   < 1 of 1 >

Default action

You indicate how access rules should handle requests that don't match any rule group that's defined for the policy. You provide this configuration regardless of whether you define rule groups for the policy.

Action name

Pre-configured Allow Action   ⇕

Action type: Allow ⓘ

⟳ Hide response control options

Response control

Access rules

	Order	Rule name	Action name	Change order	Edit
			No rules		

Add access rule   Change action   Delete

0 Selected   Showing 0 Items   < 1 of 1 >

Previous   **Next**   Cancel

Figure 3-28   WAF Policy Access Control

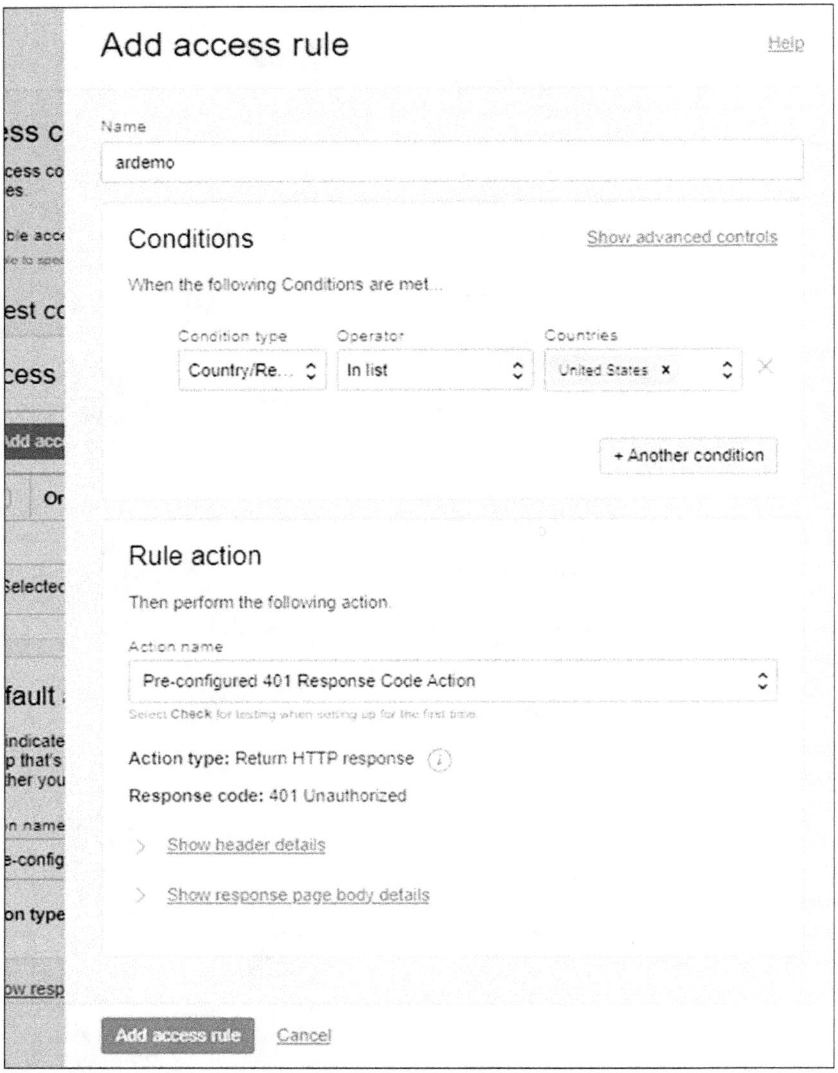

Figure 3-29   Add Access Rule

Review the condition here and click **Next**, as shown in Figure 3-30.

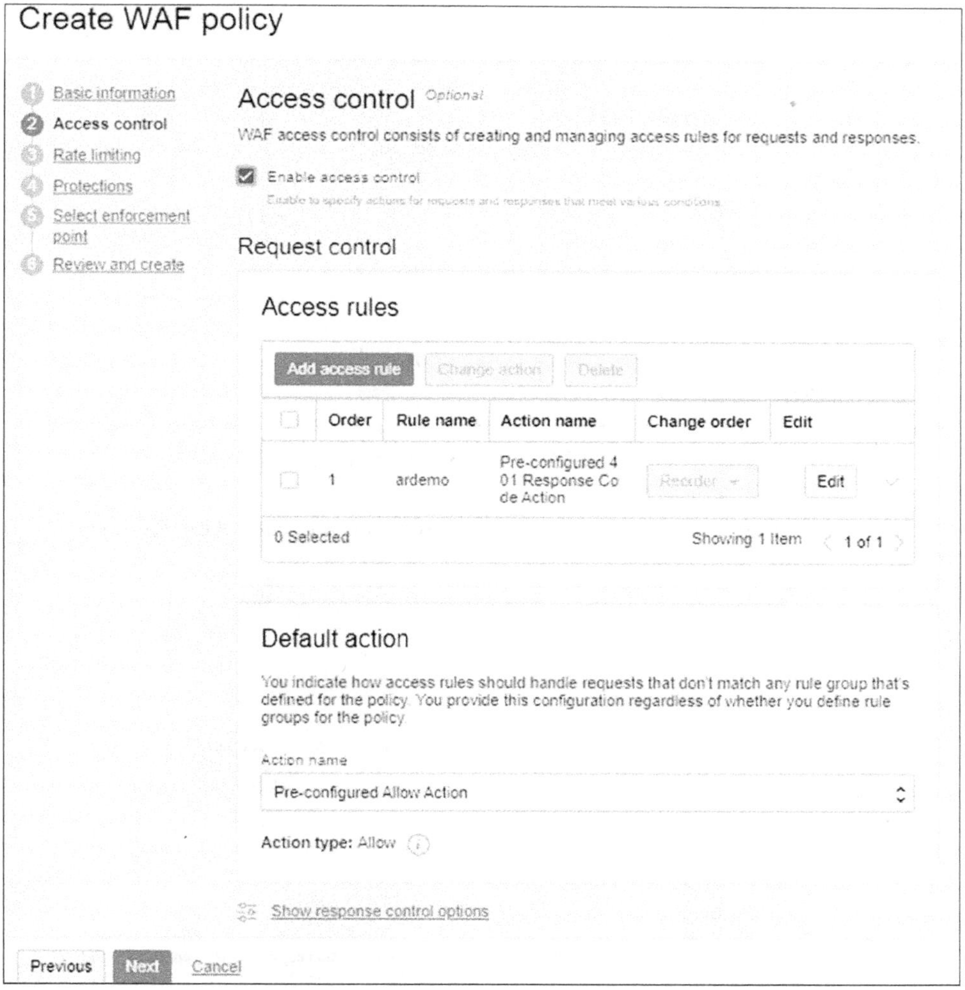

Create WAF policy

1. Basic information
2. **Access control**
3. Rate limiting
4. Protections
5. Select enforcement point
6. Review and create

Access control *Optional*

WAF access control consists of creating and managing access rules for requests and responses.

☑ Enable access control

Enable to specify actions for requests and responses that meet various conditions.

Request control

Access rules

| Add access rule | Change action | Delete |

	Order	Rule name	Action name	Change order	Edit
☐	1	ardemo	Pre-configured 4 01 Response Co de Action	Reorder ⌄	Edit ⌄

| 0 Selected | | Showing 1 Item | 1 of 1 |

Default action

You indicate how access rules should handle requests that don't match any rule group that's defined for the policy. You provide this configuration regardless of whether you define rule groups for the policy.

Action name

| Pre-configured Allow Action | ⌄ |

Action type: Allow ⓘ

⇅ Show response control options

| Previous | **Next** | Cancel |

Figure 3-30 WAF Policy Access Control

Next, you can enable rate limiting and provide a condition type as you provided for the access rule earlier. Based on the condition, a request limit within the specified time will be applied, and a rule action can be defined appropriately. For our test case, let's skip this step. Click **Next**, as shown in Figure 3-31.

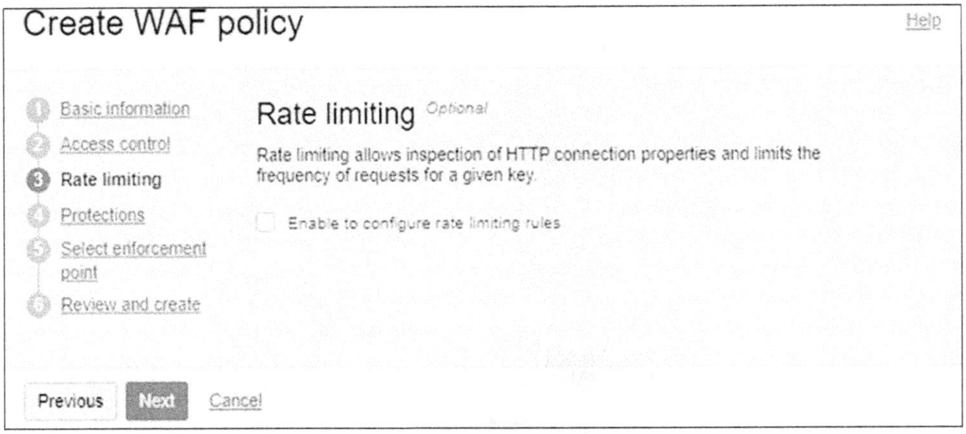

Figure 3-31   WAF Policy Rate Limiting

Next, click **Enable to Configure Protection Rules** and click **Add Request Protection Rule**, as shown in Figure 3-32.

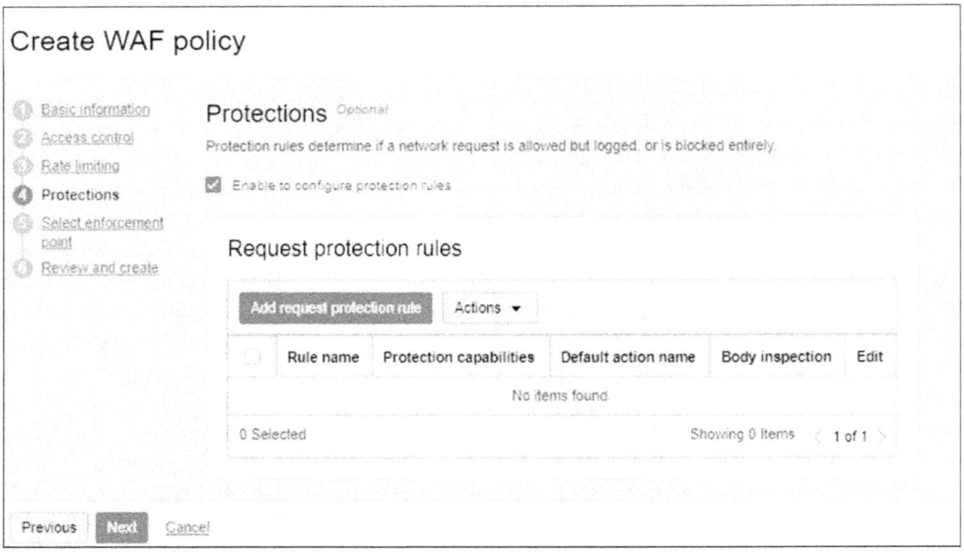

Figure 3-32   WAF Policy Protections

For the protection rule, you can specify the condition type and rule action as we discussed for access rule and rate limiting earlier. For this test case, click **Choose Protection Capabilities**, as shown in Figure 3-33.

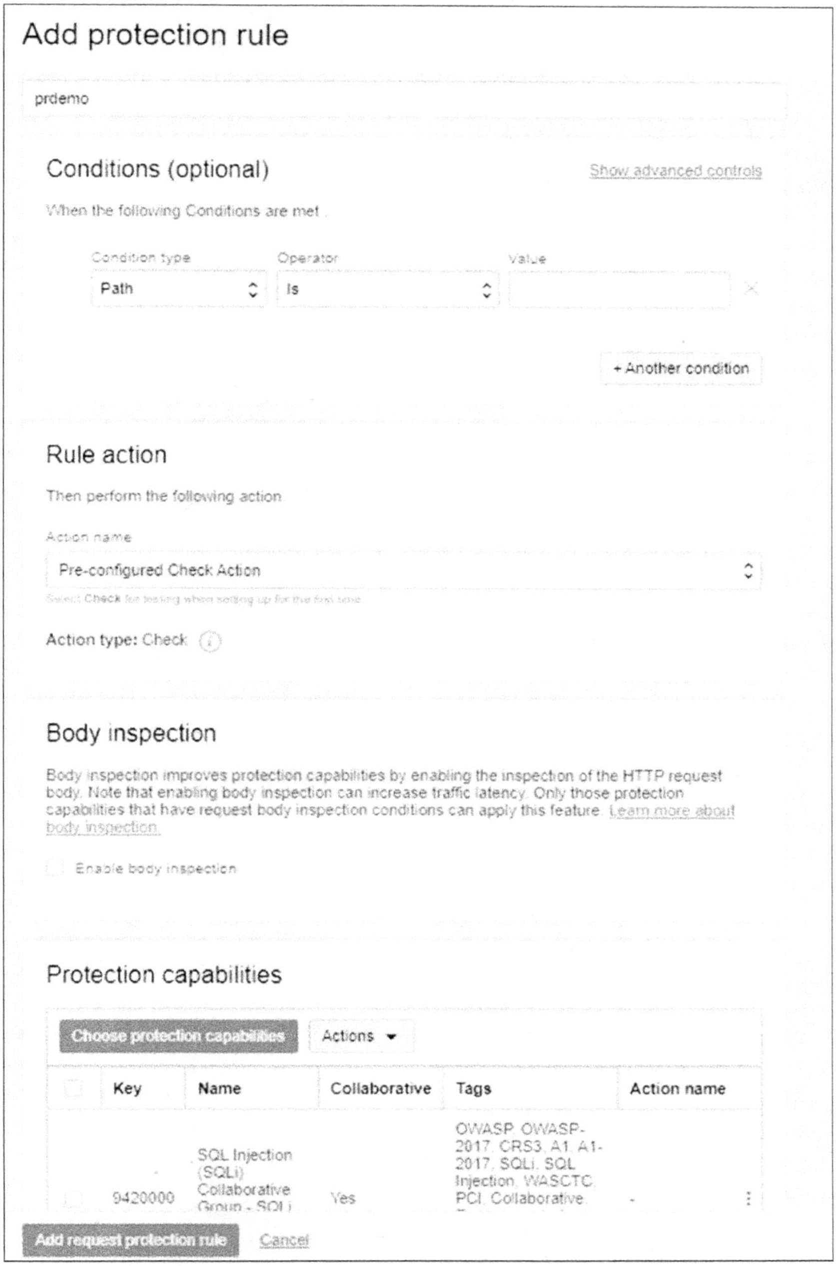

Add protection rule

prdemo

Conditions (optional)

Show advanced controls

When the following Conditions are met

Condition type	Operator	Value
Path	Is	

+ Another condition

Rule action

Then perform the following action

Action name

Pre-configured Check Action

Select Check for testing when setting up for the first time

Action type: Check ⓘ

Body inspection

Body inspection improves protection capabilities by enabling the inspection of the HTTP request body. Note that enabling body inspection can increase traffic latency. Only those protection capabilities that have request body inspection conditions can apply this feature. Learn more about body inspection.

☐ Enable body inspection

Protection capabilities

Choose protection capabilities   Actions ▼

	Key	Name	Collaborative	Tags	Action name
☐	9420000	SQL Injection (SQLi) Collaborative Group - SQLi	Yes	OWASP, OWASP-2017, CRS3, A1, A1-2017, SQLi, SQL Injection, WASCTC, PCI, Collaborative	-

Add request protection rule   Cancel

Figure 3-33   Add a Protection Rule

For this example, we are going to select all recommended XSS attacks and SQL injection protection capabilities provided by Oracle. There are more capabilities provided for you to choose from, however. Here, click **Choose Protection Capabilities**, as shown in Figure 3-34.

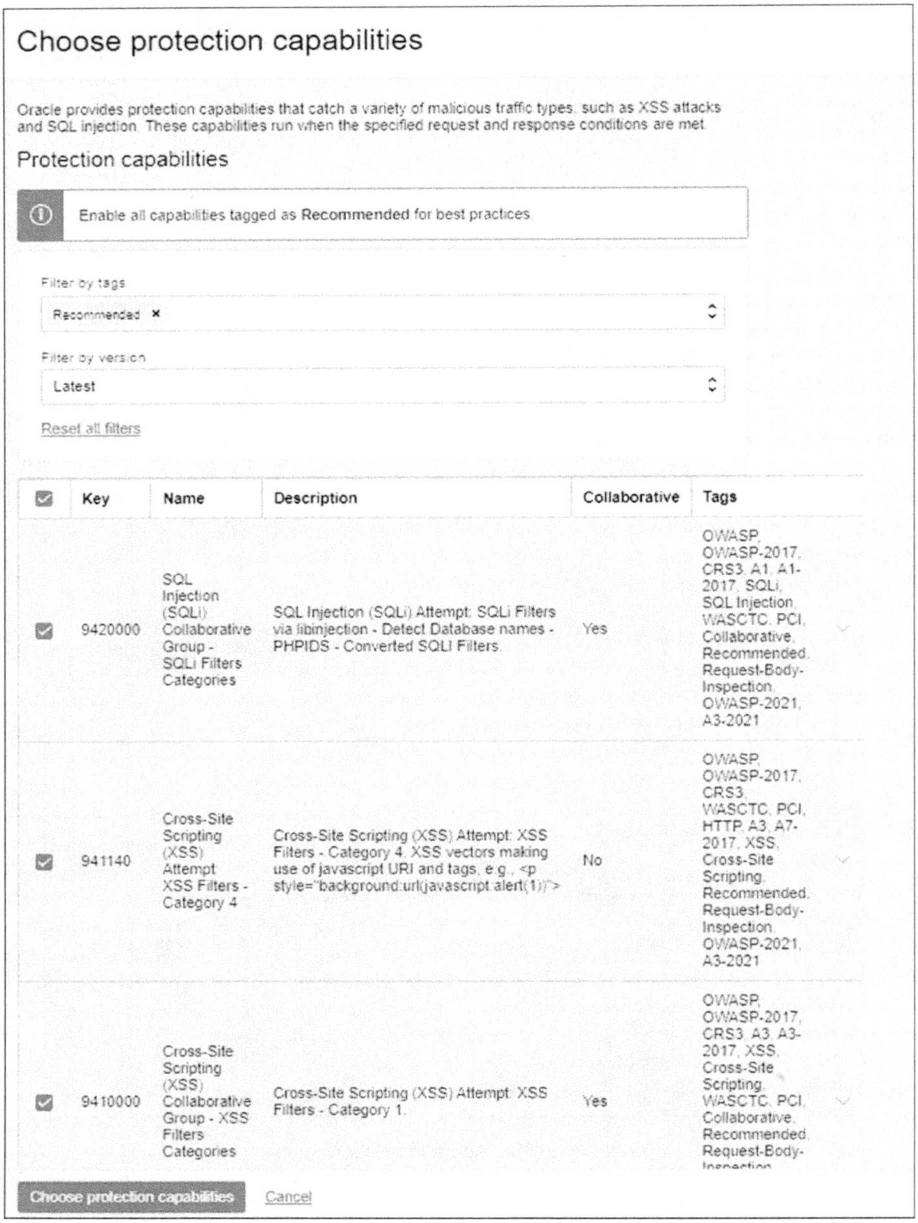

Figure 3-34   Protection Capabilities

Next, review your selection and click **Next**, as shown in Figure 3-35.

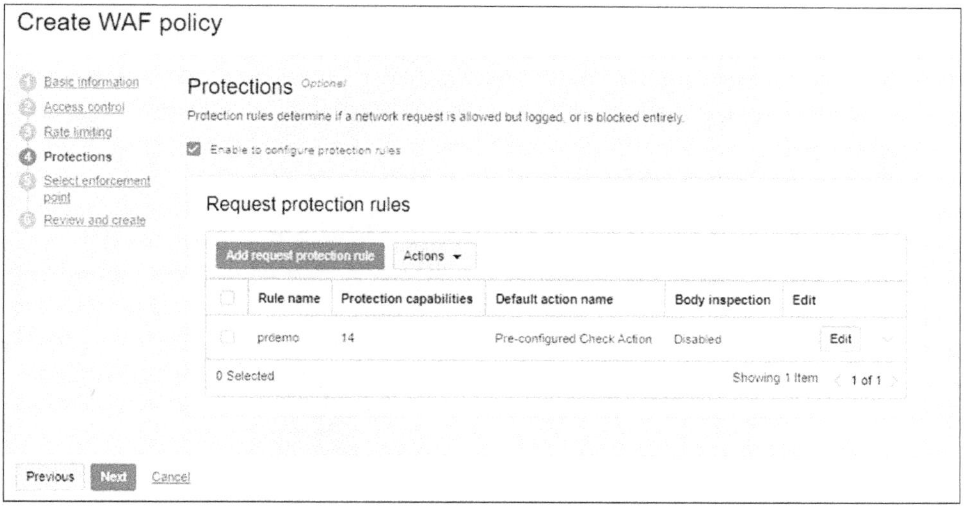

Figure 3-35   WAF Policy Protections with Rule

Next, select the enforcement point where WAF policies will be evaluated. Select the load balancer and click **Next**, as shown in Figure 3-36.

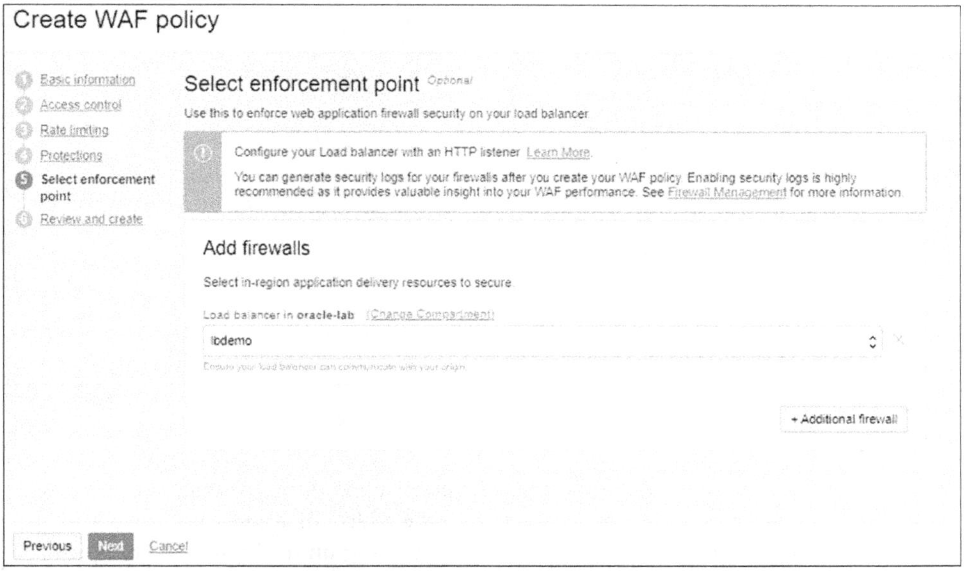

Figure 3-36   WAF Policy Enforcement Point

Now review the information entered so far and click **Create WAF Policy**, as shown in Figure 3-37.

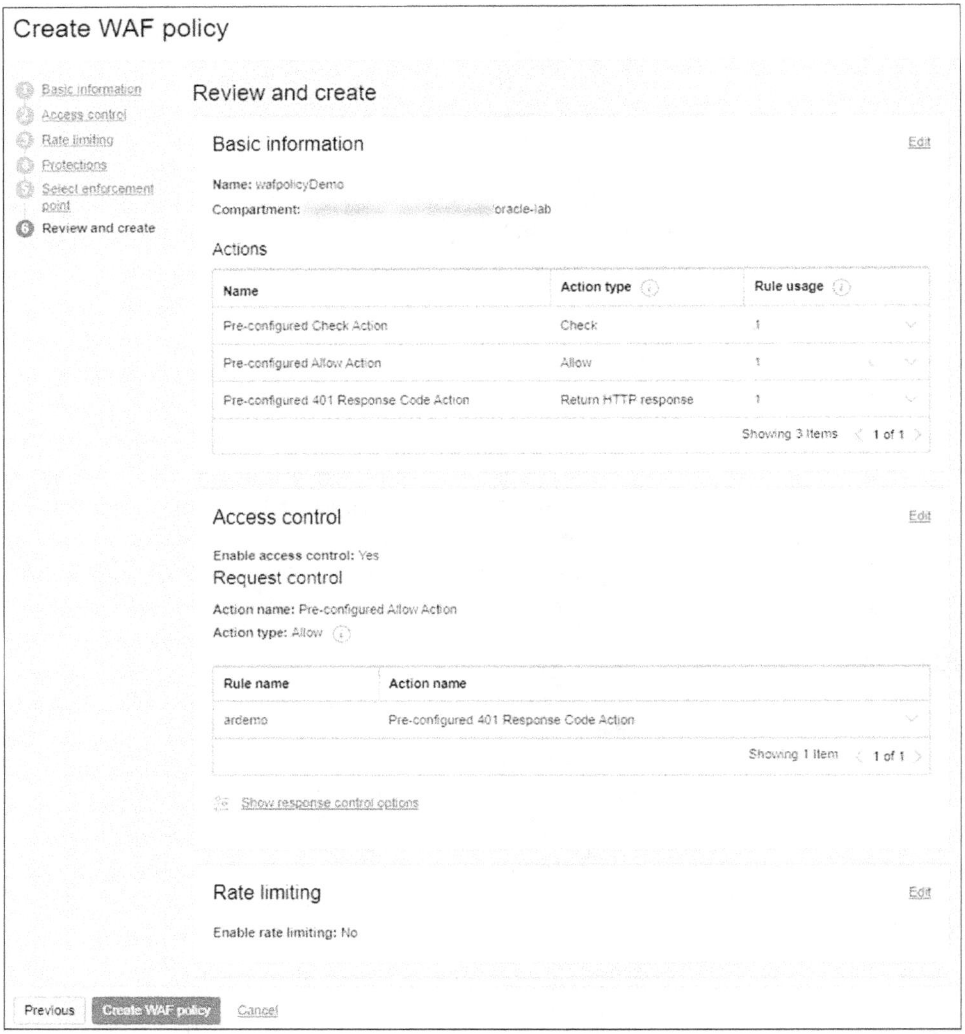

Create WAF policy

- Basic information
- Access control
- Rate limiting
- Protections
- Select enforcement point
- Review and create

Review and create

Basic information   Edit

Name: wafpolicyDemo
Compartment: _____oracle-lab

Actions

Name	Action type	Rule usage
Pre-configured Check Action	Check	1
Pre-configured Allow Action	Allow	1
Pre-configured 401 Response Code Action	Return HTTP response	1

Showing 3 Items ‹ 1 of 1 ›

Access control   Edit

Enable access control: Yes
Request control

Action name: Pre-configured Allow Action
Action type: Allow

Rule name	Action name
ardemo	Pre-configured 401 Response Code Action

Showing 1 Item ‹ 1 of 1 ›

Show response control options

Rate limiting   Edit

Enable rate limiting: No

Previous   Create WAF policy   Cancel

Figure 3-37   WAF Policy Review

In a minute or less, the WAF policy will be created and displayed with the status as active on the policies page. In our test case, we have added an access rule to block all connection coming from the United States. To test it, log on to the site by going to http://<load_balancer_public_ip>, as shown in Figure 3-38.

```
←  →  C   ⚠ Not secure | http://132
                                              🔗  ☆

{"code":"401","message":"Unauthorized"}
```

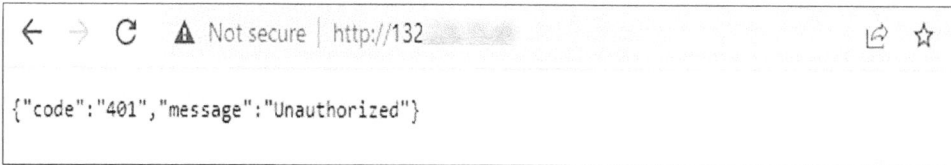

Figure 3-38 WAF Policy Test

Firewall

Oracle has partnered with Palo Alto Networks to provide the OCI native-managed Network Firewall service. This is next generation with the machine learning (ML) firewall service powered by Palo Alto Networks. Oracle has integrated security into the infrastructure and implemented the highest security standards. When it comes to a customer's data, applications, workloads, services, and so on, the customer may need or prefer additional security tools for intrusion prevention and detection, URL filtering, and more. This is where the Network Firewall service can help. The Network Firewall service helps customers to protect their environments according to their custom security standards and compliance policies. These granular security controls allow you to monitor traffic movement in all directions for applications and workflows. Oracle has made it very easy to set up Network Firewall.

The OCI Network Firewall service provides the following security features:

- Stateful network filtering
- Custom URL and FQDN filtering
- Intrusion detection and prevention
- SSL inspection
- Intra-VCN subnet traffic inspection
- Inter-VCN traffic inspection

This service helps protect your environment against security vulnerability exploits, cyber threats, log4j, cryptojacking, ransomware, botnet attacks, and other sophisticated attacks.

Oracle has provided out-of-the-box integration with logging and monitoring services of OCI. So, you can enable logging for firewall policy rules and create alerts based on metrics collected for firewall services. Network Firewall can be deployed in either a distributed network firewall model or a transit network firewall model. In the former model, the network firewall will be created in a dedicated VCN, which is recommended by Oracle, and in the latter model, the network firewall will be created in a Hub VCN and connected to spoke VCNs using a dynamic routing gateway (DRG).

We will use the Network Firewall service to restrict administrator access to a WordPress site originating from a specific IP address CIDR as an example scenario here. Before we begin, you will need to create the required OCI resources as shown in Table 3-1. These resources will be referenced in the network firewall setup.

Table 3-1   OCI Network Resources

Resource Type	Resource Name	Purpose
Compartment	oracle_demo	To create all cloud resources required for the network firewall test
Virtual Cloud Networks	wpmdsvcn	To create all OCI resources like compute instances, network firewalls, and so on
Subnet	wordpress_subnet	To create the compute instance
	firewall_subnet	To create the network firewall
Internet Gateway	internet_gateway	For connectivity to the Internet
Route Tables	WordPressRouteTable	For wordpress_public_subnet
	FWRouteTable	For firewall_subnet
	IGWRouteTable	For IGDemo
Security List	WordPressSL	For wordpress_public_subnet
	FWSL	For firewall_subnet

Let's go over the process of how to set up the network firewall now. First, log in to your tenancy by going to https://cloud.oracle.com. Go to the menu and click **Identity & Security > Firewalls**, as shown in Figure 3-39.

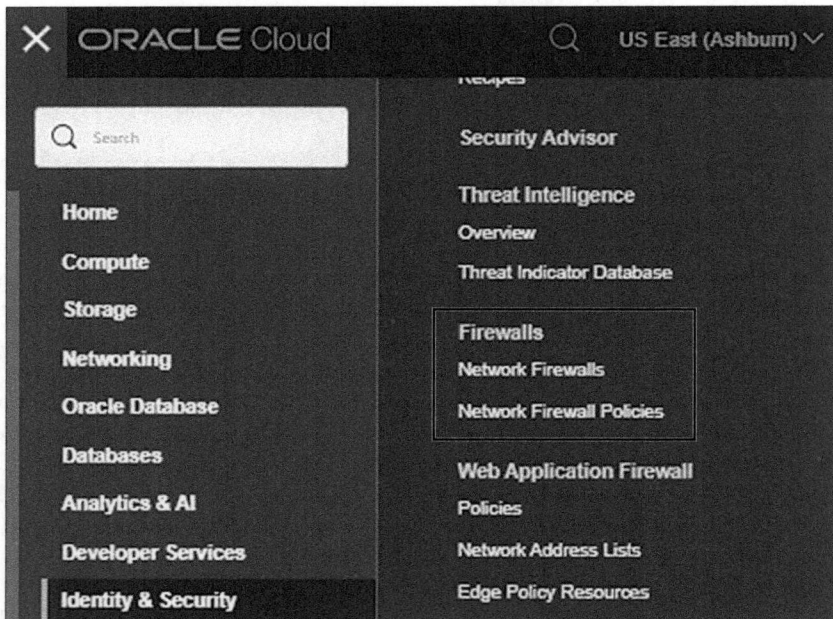

Figure 3-39   Identity & Security Menu

You will need to create network firewall policies before creating a network firewall. You can choose to create a network firewall policy with minimum configuration and then modify it later after the network firewall is created. For our example here, let's go ahead and create the policy with the required configuration. To do so, click **Create Policy**, as shown in Figure 3-40.

Figure 3-40   Network Firewall Policies

Here, provide a policy name and compartment where the policy will be created, as shown in Figure 3-41.

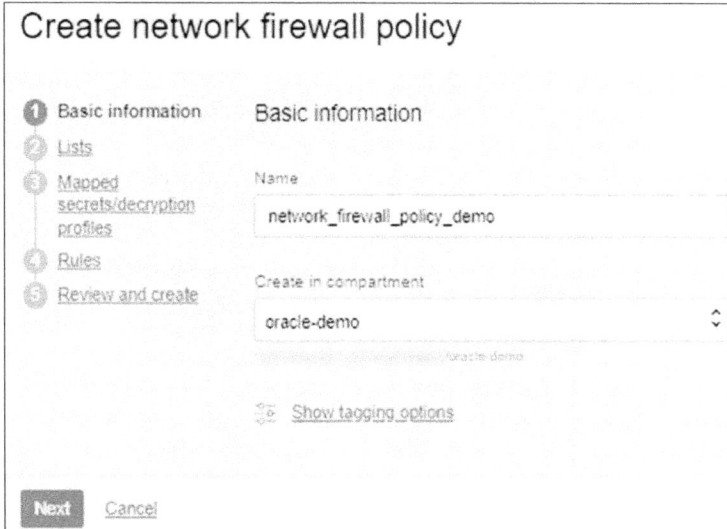

Figure 3-41   Network Firewall Policy Basic Information

Next, create application, URL, and IP address lists. Application lists include the protocol and port range of the applications. URL lists include all application/site URLs. For our example here, we need to create a URL list and an IP address list. Click **Add URL List** first and then **Add IP Address List**, as shown in Figure 3-42. The IP address list provides IP addresses or CIDR ranges. You can create a maximum of 25 lists for each of these categories.

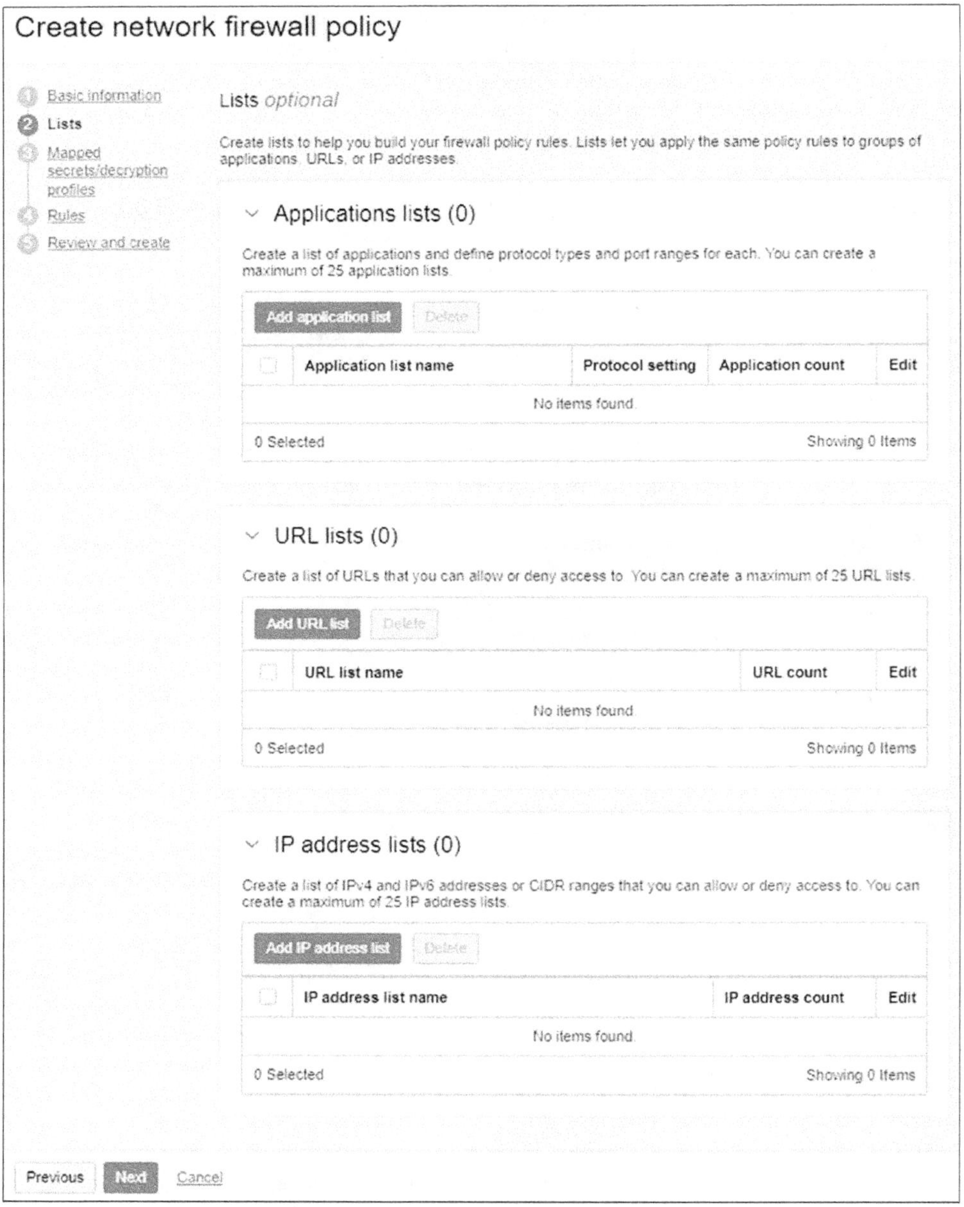

Create network firewall policy

○ Basic information
② Lists
③ Mapped
   secrets/decryption
   profiles
④ Rules
⑤ Review and create

Lists *optional*

Create lists to help you build your firewall policy rules. Lists let you apply the same policy rules to groups of applications, URLs, or IP addresses.

ⴸ Applications lists (0)

Create a list of applications and define protocol types and port ranges for each. You can create a maximum of 25 application lists.

[Add application list] [Delete]

	Application list name	Protocol setting	Application count	Edit
	No items found			
0 Selected				Showing 0 Items

ⴸ URL lists (0)

Create a list of URLs that you can allow or deny access to. You can create a maximum of 25 URL lists.

[Add URL list] [Delete]

	URL list name	URL count	Edit
	No items found		
0 Selected			Showing 0 Items

ⴸ IP address lists (0)

Create a list of IPv4 and IPv6 addresses or CIDR ranges that you can allow or deny access to. You can create a maximum of 25 IP address lists.

[Add IP address list] [Delete]

	IP address list name	IP address count	Edit
	No items found		
0 Selected			Showing 0 Items

[Previous] [Next] Cancel

Figure 3-42   Network Firewall Policy Lists

For our sample scenario, provide a name and URLs; then click **Add URL List**, as shown in Figure 3-43.

For the IP address list, provide a list name and IP addresses; then click **Add IP Address List**, as shown in Figure 3-44.

Figure 3-43   Firewall Network Policy URL List

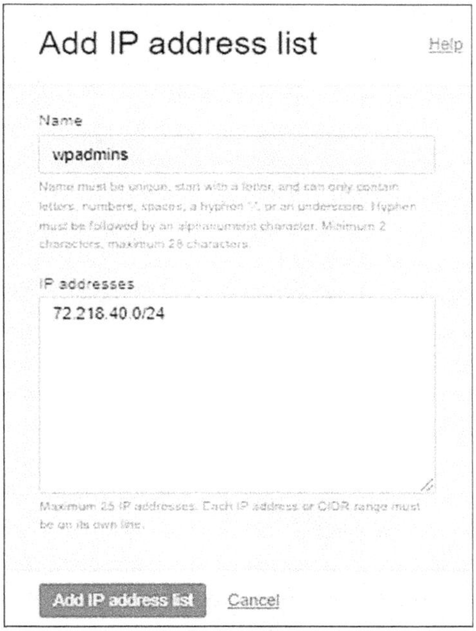

Figure 3-44   Firewall Network Policy IP Address List

Now you can review all lists created previously. You can create more and/or edit or delete the created ones if required. When you're ready, click **Next**, as shown in Figure 3-45.

Create network firewall policy

Lists *optional*

- ① Basic information
- ❷ Lists
- ③ Mapped secrets/decryption profiles
- ④ Rules
- ⑤ Review and create

Create lists to help you build your firewall policy rules. Lists let you apply the same policy rules to groups of applications, URLs, or IP addresses.

⌄ Applications lists (0)

Create a list of applications and define protocol types and port ranges for each. You can create a maximum of 25 application lists.

| Add application list | Delete |

	Application list name	Protocol setting	Application count	Edit
	No items found			

0 Selected   Showing 0 Items

⌄ URL lists (1)

Create a list of URLs that you can allow or deny access to. You can create a maximum of 25 URL lists.

| Add URL list | Delete |

	URL list name ▲	URL count	Edit
	wplogin	1	Edit ⌄

0 Selected   Showing 1 Item

⌄ IP address lists (1)

Create a list of IPv4 and IPv6 addresses or CIDR ranges that you can allow or deny access to. You can create a maximum of 25 IP address lists.

| Add IP address list | Delete |

	IP address list name ▲	IP address count	Edit
	wpadmins	1	Edit ⌄

0 Selected   Showing 1 Item

| Previous | **Next** | Cancel |

Figure 3-45   Network Firewall Policy Lists Review

Next, provide mapped secrets and/or decryption profiles if you are using certification authentication for decryption rules. You can specify a maximum of 25 mapped secrets and decryption profiles each. Mapped secrets allow you to decrypt and inspect traffic with SSL forward proxy or SSL inbound inspection. These secrets will need to be stored in the OCI Vault. Decryption profiles allow you to control inspection checks for server certification, unsupported mode, and failures. We will skip this step for our example, so click **Next**, as shown in Figure 3-46.

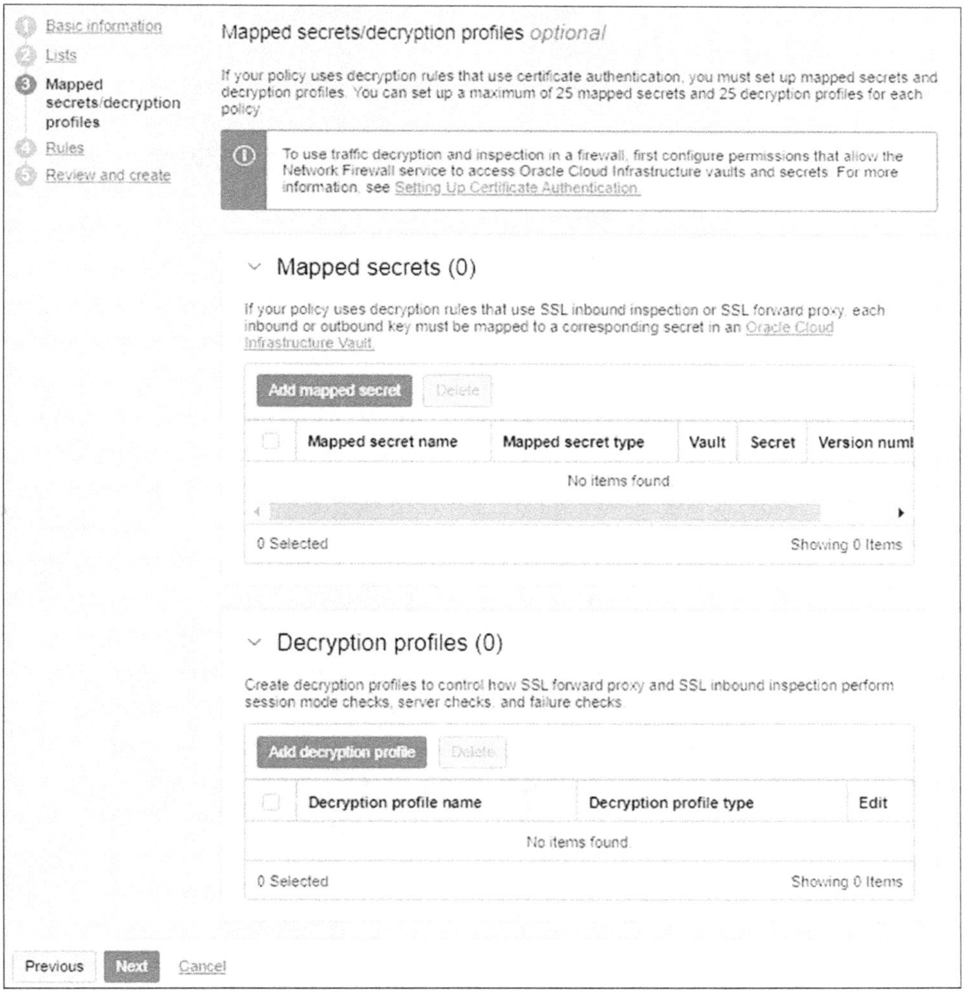

Figure 3-46   Network Firewall Policy Mapped Secrets/Decryption Profiles

Next, set up decryption rules and security rules for the policy. Decryption rules allow you to decrypt traffic with SSL inbound inspection, with SSL forward proxy, or to not decrypt the traffic based on the source and destination IP addresses filter. You will need to have defined the decryption profile and mapped secrets in a previous step to perform decryption. Using security rules, you can allow, reject, or drop traffic and intrusion detection or prevention based on the source IP addresses, destination IP addresses, applications, and URL filters. Decryption rules get evaluated before security rules. A maximum of 50 decryption rules and 50 security rules can be specified. We will skip decryption rules here, so click **Add Security Rule**, as shown in Figure 3-47.

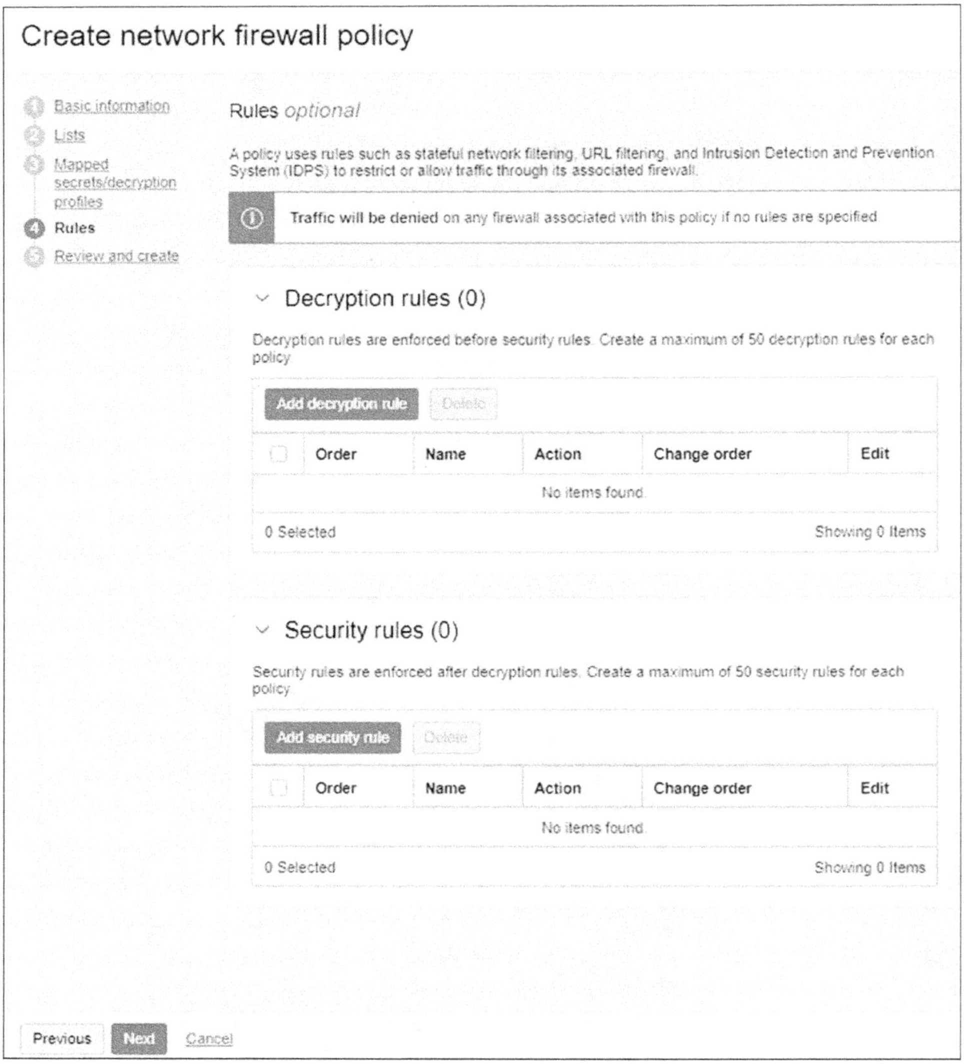

Figure 3-47   Network Firewall Policy Rules

Next, provide a rule name, source IP addresses, destination IP addresses, applications, URLs, and rule actions, as shown in Figure 3-48.

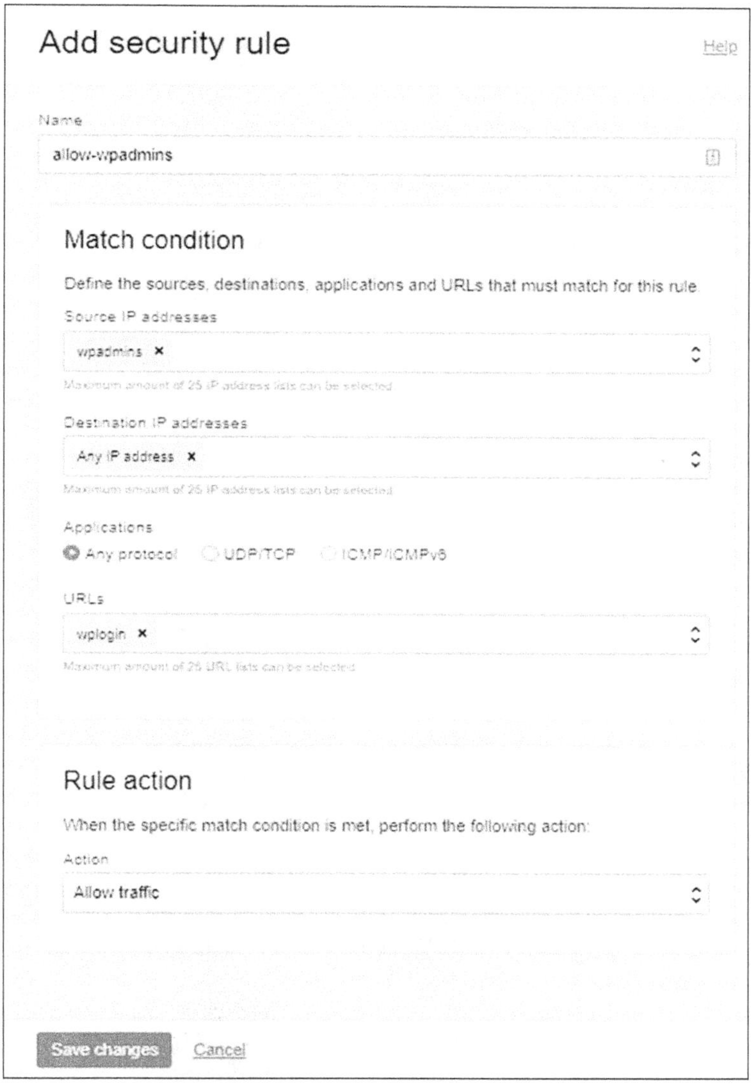

Figure 3-48   Network Firewall Policy Security Rule

Now review the security rule added earlier and click **Next**, as shown in Figure 3-49.

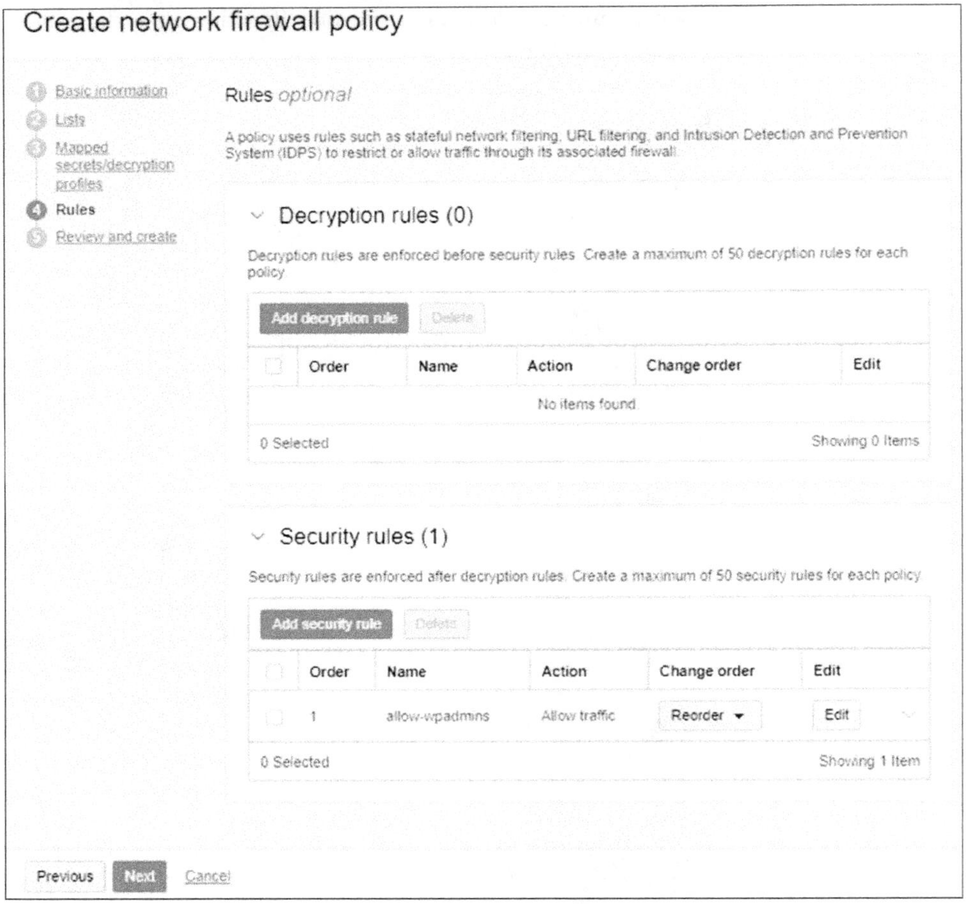

Figure 3-49   Network Firewall Policy Rules Review

You will be presented with all the configuration parameters added so far for the policy. Review the configuration and click **Create Network Firewall Policy**, as shown in Figure 3-50.

Now you're ready to create the network firewall. Go back to the Firewalls home page and click **Create Network Firewall**, as shown in Figure 3-51.

Next, provide a network firewall name, compartment name, VCN, and subnet for network traffic routing and click **Create Network Firewall**, as shown in Figure 3-52.

It will take approximately 30 minutes or more to create the firewall. You will be able to monitor the progress within the work request page. Once the network firewall is created, you will see it listed with an active state, as shown in Figure 3-53.

Now you need to set up route tables and security lists for the subnets containing the network firewall and WordPress server. You will need the network firewall IP for route table configuration, so go to the firewall-demo detail page, as shown in Figure 3-54.

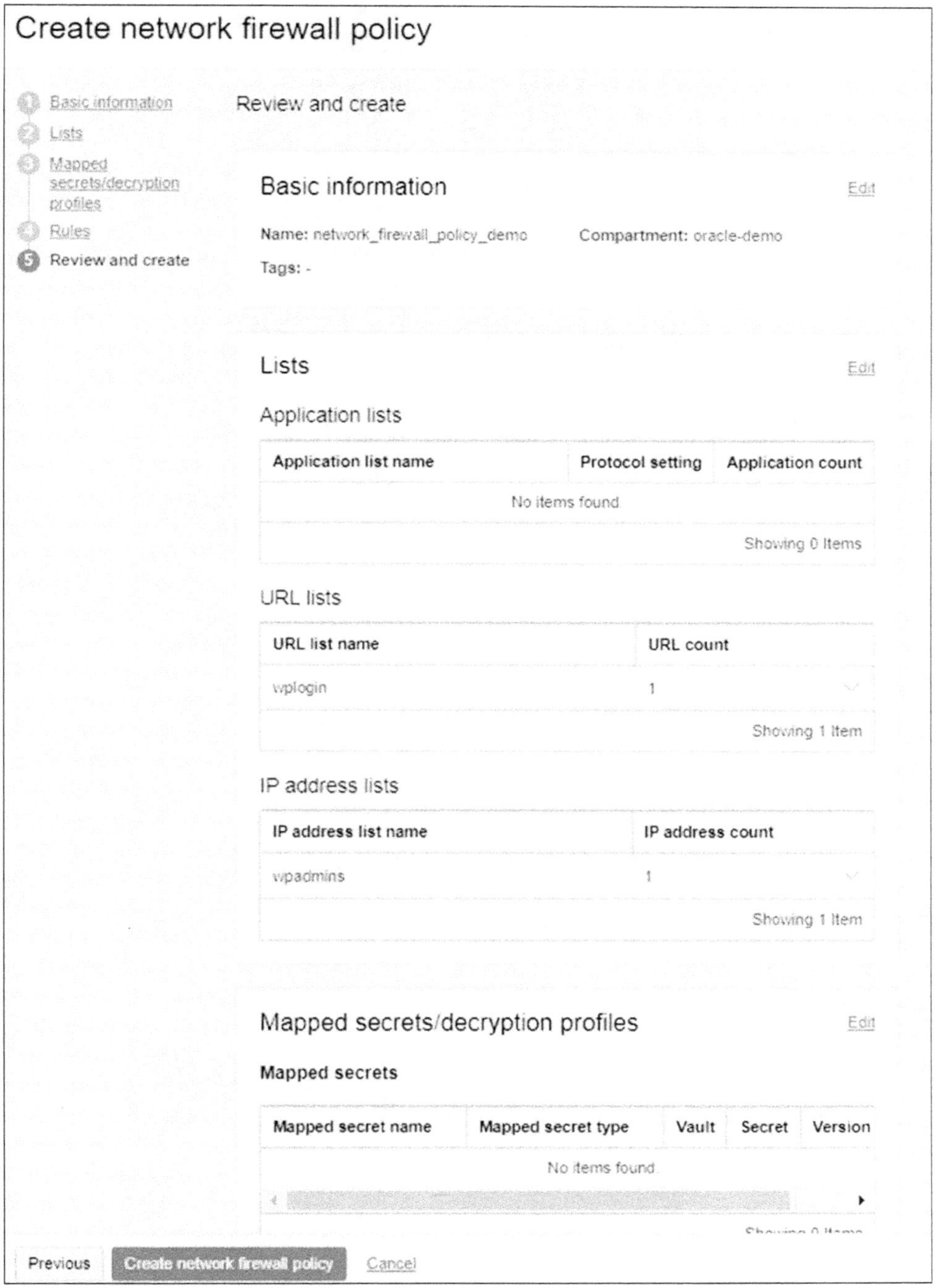

Create network firewall policy

1. Basic information
2. Lists
3. Mapped secrets/decryption profiles
4. Rules
5. Review and create

Review and create

Basic information   Edit

Name: network_firewall_policy_demo   Compartment: oracle-demo

Tags: -

Lists   Edit

Application lists

Application list name	Protocol setting	Application count
No items found		
		Showing 0 Items

URL lists

URL list name	URL count
wplogin	1
	Showing 1 Item

IP address lists

IP address list name	IP address count
wpadmins	1
	Showing 1 Item

Mapped secrets/decryption profiles   Edit

Mapped secrets

Mapped secret name	Mapped secret type	Vault	Secret	Version
No items found				
				Showing 0 Items

Previous   Create network firewall policy   Cancel

Figure 3-50 Review and Create Network Firewall Policy

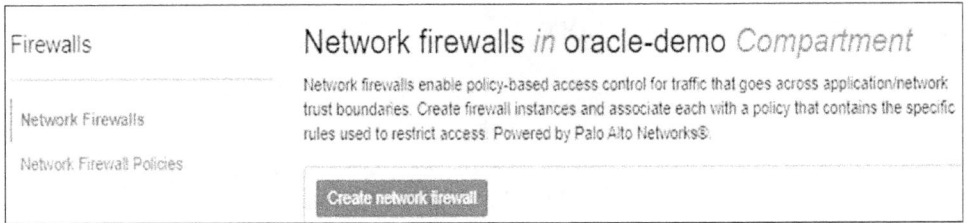

Figure 3-51   Network Firewalls

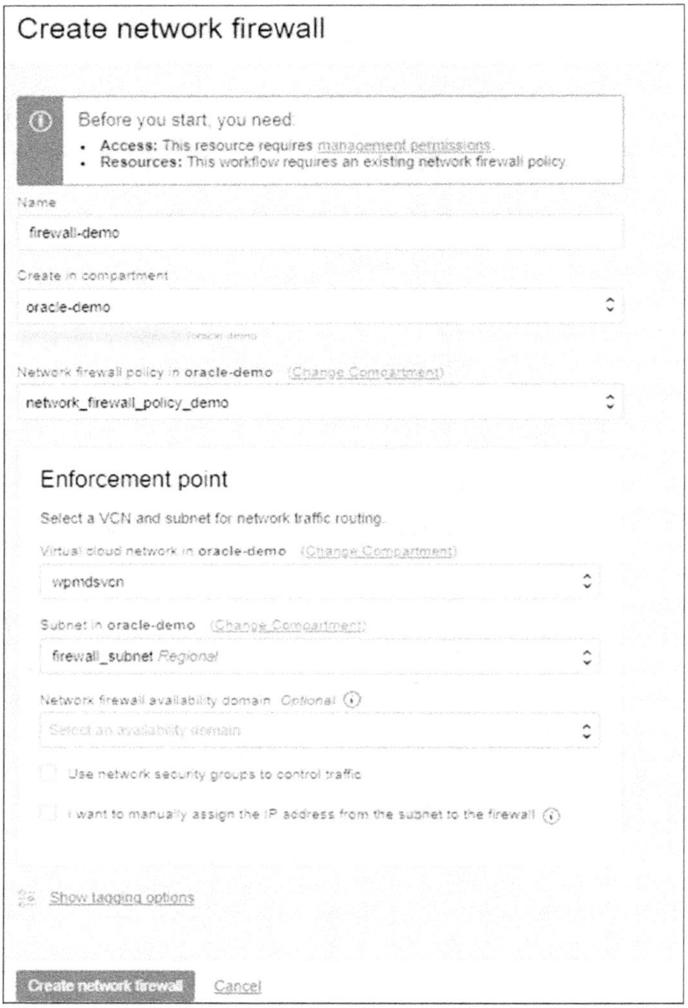

Figure 3-52   Create the Network Firewall

Figure 3-53 Network Firewall State

Figure 3-54 Firewall-demo Information

All traffic coming from and going to the Internet will need to go through the network firewall. Internet traffic will come to the Internet gateway and then will be redirected to the network firewall for inspection based on the network firewall policy rules. All traffic allowed will then go to the WordPress server to acccess the site. A similar process will be followed for the outgoing traffic to the Internet. To achieve this, configure the routing table as shown in Table 3-2.

Table 3-2 Route Table Configuration

Resource Name				
IGWRouteTable	Destination ▲	Target Type	Target	Route Type
	10.0.0.0/16	Private IP	10...	Static
FWRouteTable	Destination ▲	Target Type	Target	Route Type
	0.0.0.0/0	Internet Gateway	internet_gateway	Static
WordPressRouteTable	Destination ▲	Target Type	Target	Route Type
	0.0.0.0/0	Private IP	10...	Static

Now configure the security list *WordPressSL* to allow access to ports 22, 80, and 443 from 0.0.0.0/0 for ingress rules (all traffic coming in) and allow access to all ports on 0.0.0.0/0 for egress rules (all traffic going out). In a similar way, configure the security list *FWSL* to allow access to all ports from 0.0.0.0/0 for ingress rules and allow access to all ports on 0.0.0.0/0 for egress rules. At this point, the network firewall is ready, so let's run some verification tests.

While accessing the WordPress site's URL (http://demo.thetechiewizard.com/wp-login.php) from the desktop with IP address 72.218.40.25 (which belongs to wpadmins IP address CIDR), the network firewall allows the connection, as shown in Figure 3-55.

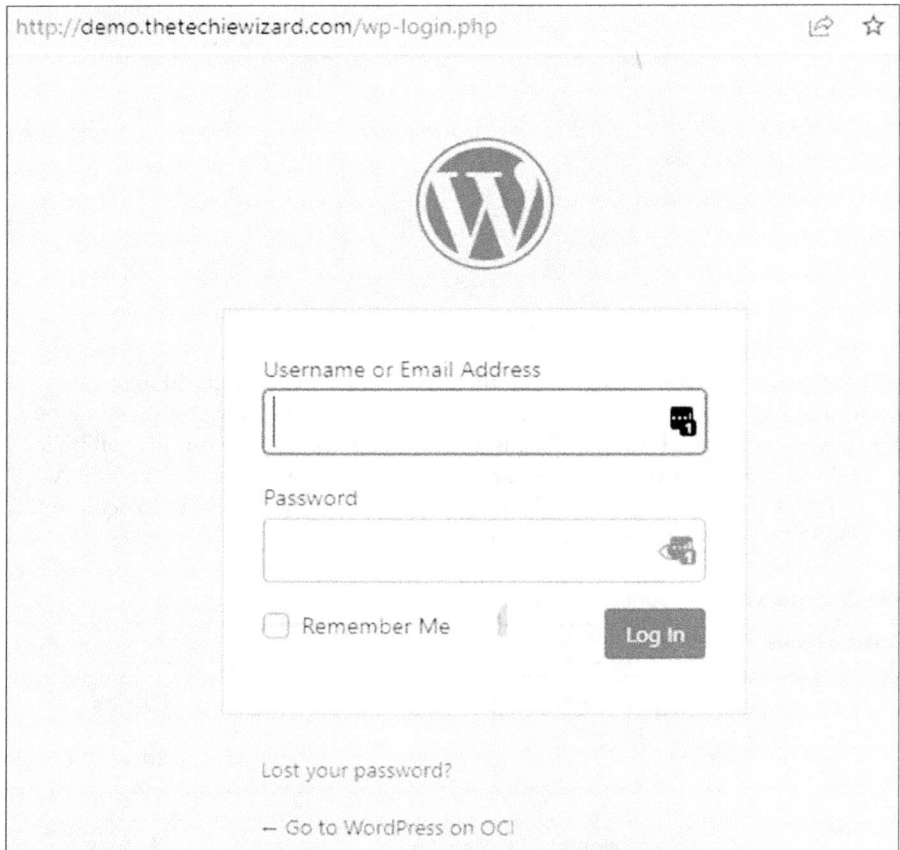

Figure 3-55   Successful Connection

Now trying to access the site from another desktop with IP address 216.5.42.23, we get the error message shown in Figure 3-56.

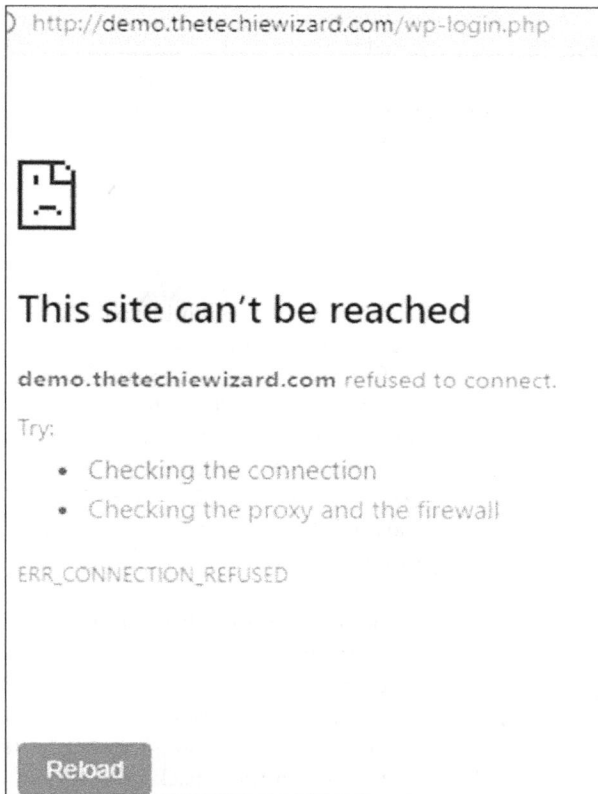

Figure 3-56   Failed Connection

The security list attached to *wordpress_subnet* has an ingress rule to allow access to port 22, but we have not specified any security rule in the network firewall policy for it. So we will get an error while trying to SSH to the WordPress server, as shown in Figure 3-57.

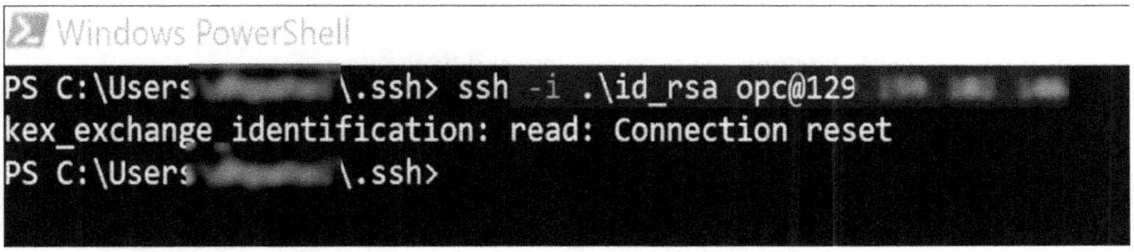

Figure 3-57   SSH Test

The Network Firewall service is integrated with the OCI Login service out-of-the-box. You can enable the logging for all supported rules. Logs can be enabled to view threat logs, traffic logs, or both. OCI will log detail information that passes through the network firewall. Logs are displyed in JSON format. You can filter the logs by time and/or using custom filters. The network firewall can also be monitored using metrics, alarms, and notifications.

Vault

The *Vault* provides a central place for storing encryption keys and secrets. Encryption keys enable you to encrypt data at rest or in transit and to protect your data from unauthorized access. Secrets are certificates, SSH keys, passwords, or authentication tokens used to access other OCI resources. The Vault is integrated with other Oracle resources like database services, object storage, file storage, and more. This makes using the keys and secrets seamless. A simple example is the ADMIN user password of the autonomous database that you can store as a secret in the Vault. The Vault service supports Advanced Encryption Standard (AES), Rivest-Shamir-Adleman (RSA), and the elliptic curve digital signature algorithm (ECDSA) encryption algorithm to store keys and secrets.

Oracle provides you with the option to either store keys on the server or on highly available and durable hardware security modules (HSMs) based on the protection mode. HSMs meet Federal Information Processing Standards (FIPS) 140-2 Security Level 3 security certification. A private vault provides an option to use either multi-tenant partition or a dedicated partition in the HSM. A dedicated partition in the HSM gives you storage isolation with additional functionalities to back up and restore and also provides cross-region replication.

The Vault service gives you choice of software and the HSM as protection mode to store keys. In software protection mode, keys are stored outside the HSM, giving you the ability to export the keys.

Log in to your tenancy by going to https://cloud.oracle.com. Go to the menu and click **Identity & Security > Vault**, as shown in Figure 3-58.

Click **Create Vault**, as shown in Figure 3-59.

Next, provide the name of the vault and click **Create Vault**, as shown in Figure 3-60. You can choose the option to create this as a private vault on a dedicated partition of the HSM. For our test scenario, let's skip it for now.

Once the vault is created, it will be displayed with active status on the Vault home page. Click **demoVault** to get vault information and manage keys and secrets, as shown in Figure 3-61.

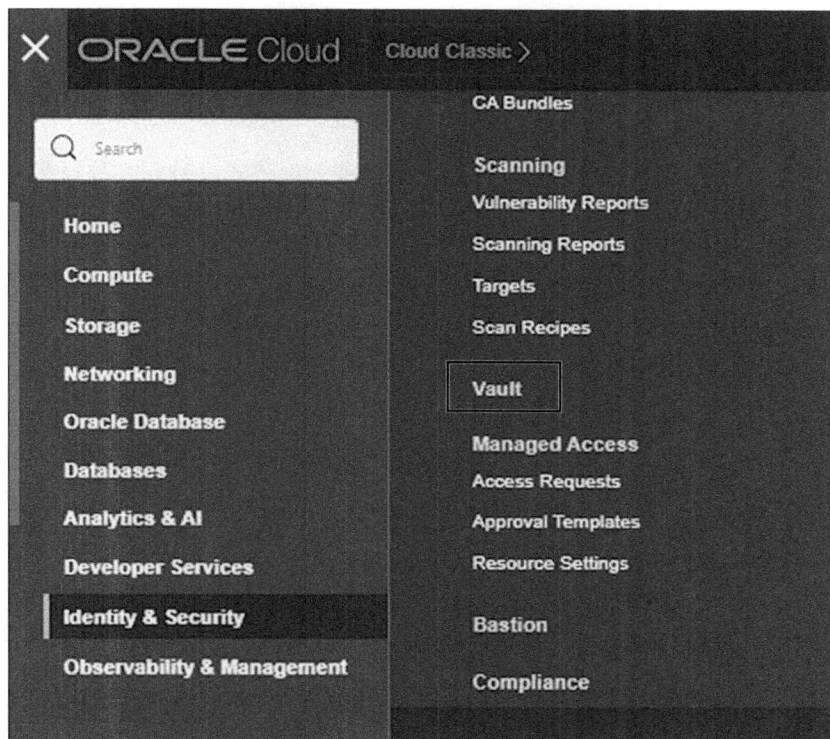

Figure 3-58   Identity & Security Menu

Vaults *in* oracle-lab *Compartment*

Vaults let you centrally manage the encryption keys that protect your data and the secret credentials that you use to securely access resources. Learn more

Create Vault	Restore Vault		
Name	State	Virtual Private	Created
		No items found.	
			Showing 0 Items 〈 1 of 1 〉

Figure 3-59   Vault Home Page

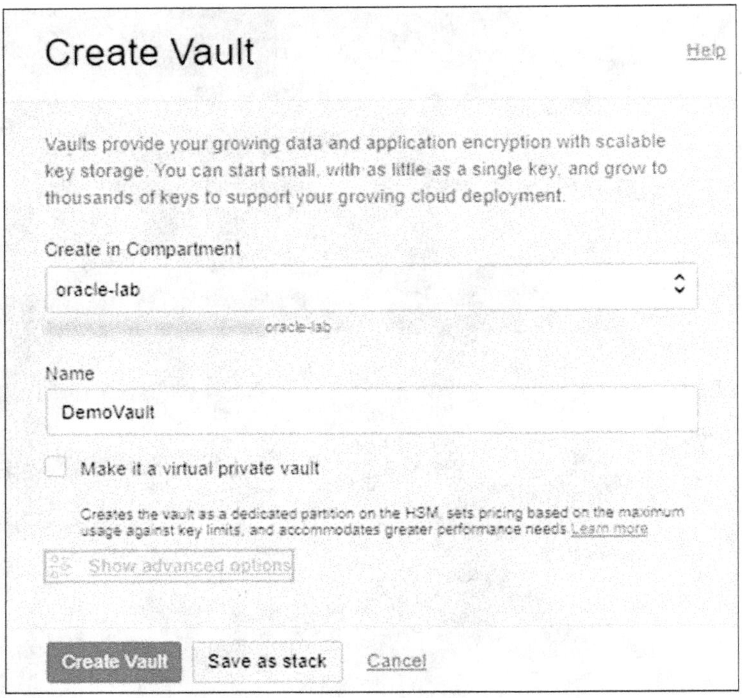

Figure 3-60 Create Vault

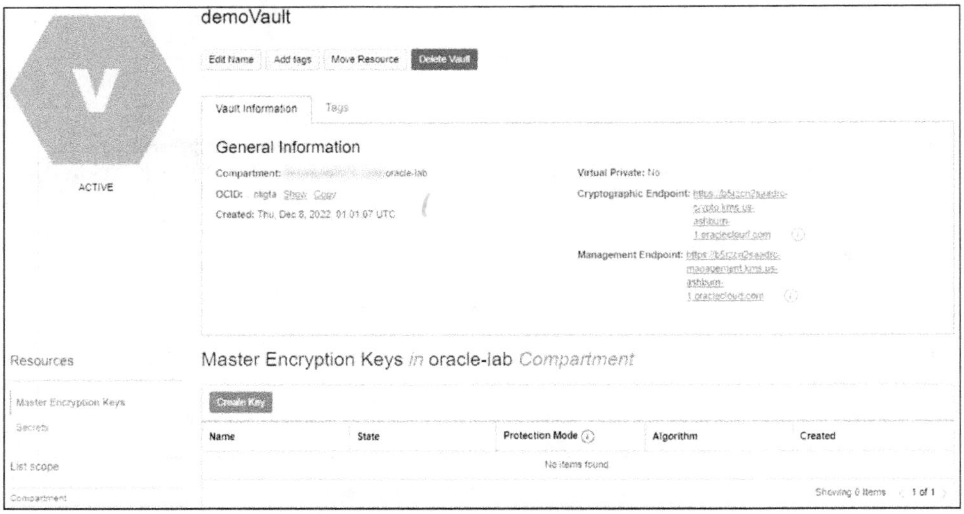

Figure 3-61 Vault Information

The next step is to create the master encryption key. Enter the compartment, protection mode, key name, and encryption algorithm and click **Create Key**, as shown in Figure 3-62. For the protection mode, you can select either **HSM** or **Software**. In HSM mode, the master encryption key is stored and processed on the HSM. In Software mode, the master encryption key is stored and processed on the server. You can also import your own master encryption key by selecting the **Import External Key** option.

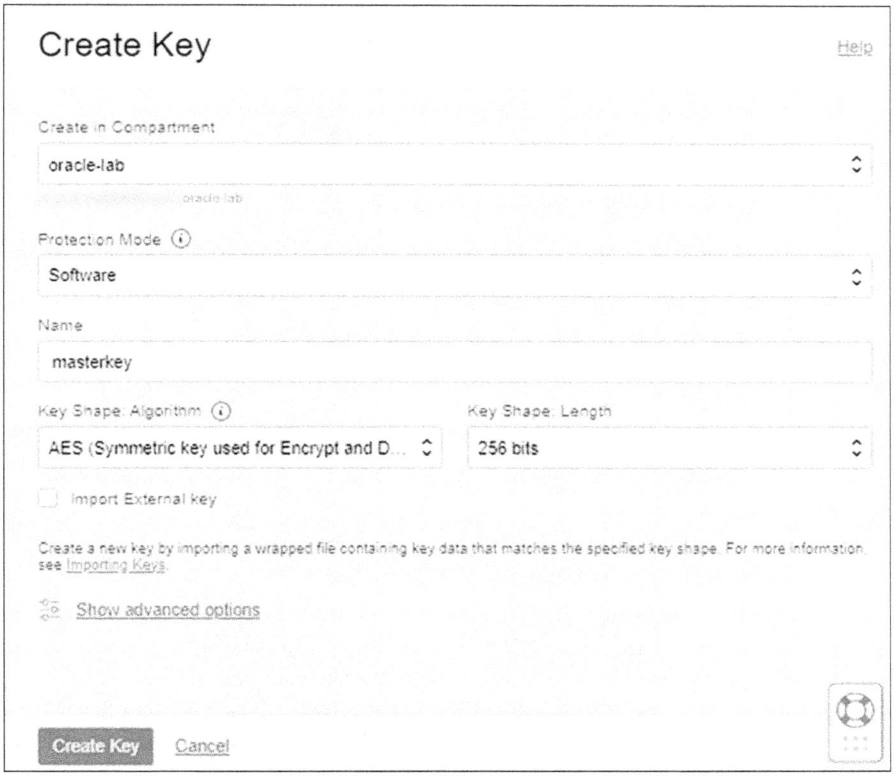

Figure 3-62 Create Key

Next, we will go over creating a secret to store the autonomous database ADMIN password in the vault. To start, go to the Vault details page and select **Secrets** under the Resources section to create a secret. Enter the compartment, secret name, description, encryption key created earlier, and ADMIN user password as secret contents and click **Create Secret**, as shown in Figure 3-63. Secret content will get encoded automatically before sending it to the service.

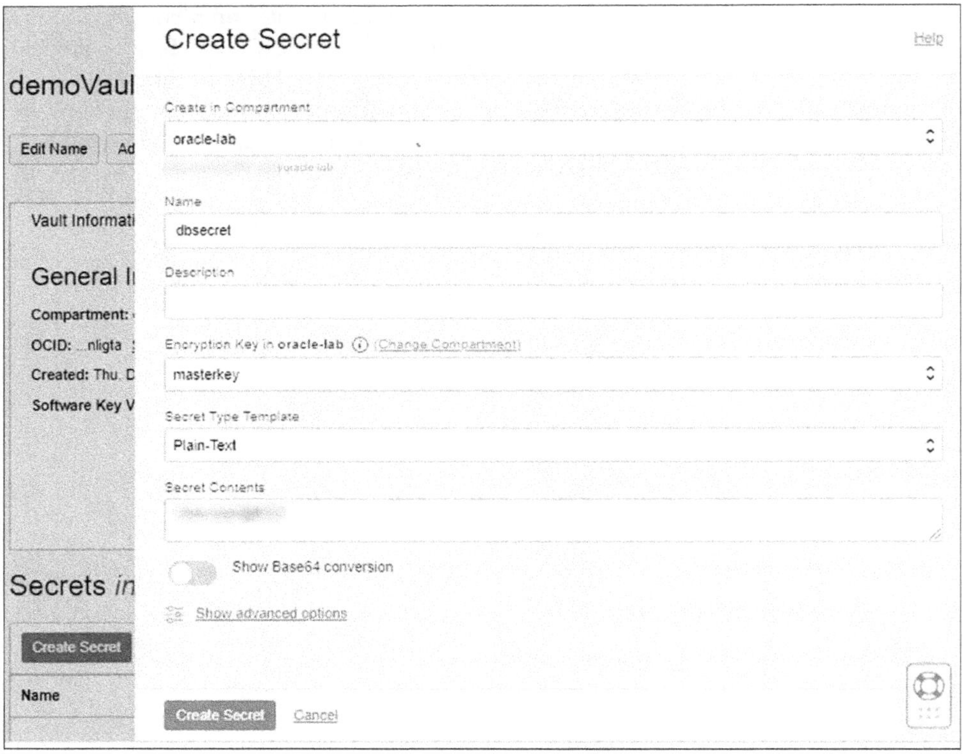

Figure 3-63   Create a Secret

When you are interacting with OCI resources using APIs, storing database passwords and other resource credentials in the vault is useful. This way, passwords are secured throughout the process while accessing the database. Disaster Recovery as a Service (DRaaS) is one of the use cases where you will need to use the vault to store database passwords.

Audit

The *Audit* service provides governance and visibility for OCI tenancy. It automatically logs all activities performed within your tenancy using all supported application programming interface (API) endpoints including the OCI console, command-line interface (CLI), software development kits (SDKs), and any others, including custom clients. All these activities are logged as log events. These log events include very granular information about the event, including user, event name, execution time, resource information, etc. These details allow the administrator to answer important questions, such as which activity occurred, who performed the activity, when was it performed, and from where.

The Audit service helps administrators with monitoring user activity, including overall usage within tenancy, troubleshooting issues, security, and compliance monitoring. Audit events get logged in about 15 minutes from the occurrence of the event. These log events are stored in JSON format. JSON format also makes ingesting these events into other tools easier. You can also copy the entire event or a portion of it.

The Audit service is enabled by default for all tenancies. It cannot be disabled. The tenancy administrator has full access to the Audit service. Similar or restricted access can be granted using IAM policies to other users of the tenancy.

Audit event logs can be searched by date, any keyword within the event, and request action types such as GET, POST, PUT, PATCH, and DELETE. Let's review the Audit service to see how to search for a log event.

Log in to your tenancy by going to https://cloud.oracle.com. Go to the menu and click **Identity & Security > Audit**, as shown in Figure 3-64.

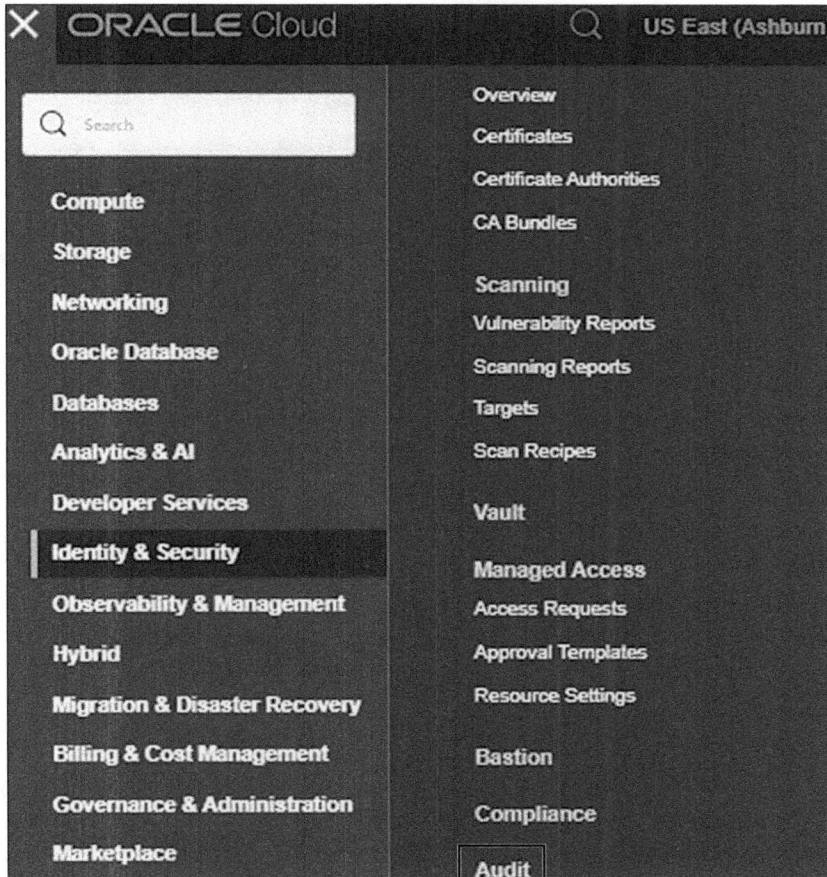

Figure 3-64   Identity & Security Menu

Next, enter the start date, end date, request action type, and keyword to search for within the event and click **Search**, as shown in Figure 3-65.

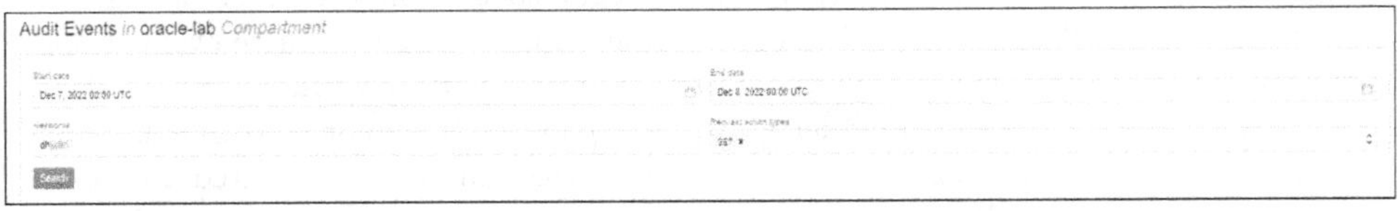

Figure 3-65   Audit Event Search

In this window, you can see all event logs recorded in the timeframe, as shown in Figure 3-66.

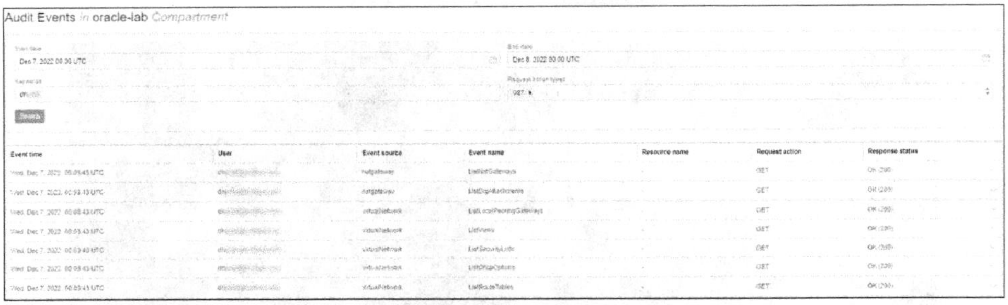

Figure 3-66   Audit Event Search Result

You can check details of the log event by expanding the event, as shown in Figure 3-67. You can even copy the entire event or a portion of it by clicking the copy symbol next to the curly bracket.

Figure 3-67   Audit Event Detail

Audit logs are retained for 365 days by default and cannot be changed. If you need to export audit logs for any reason, you will need to reach out to Oracle support. Oracle support will copy all the logs to object storage in your tenancy.

Summary

In this chapter, you learned that Oracle offers a broad range of Identity & Security services; we went over some of them here. Oracle provides integration between these services to give you necessary tools to secure your tenancy and protect against internal and external modern threats. We will continue exploring more of these services in later chapters. For now, we will change our focus to the Oracle Infrastructure as a Service (IaaS) cloud-native technologies.

4

Oracle IaaS—Cloud-Native Technologies

Cloud-native refers to the design and development of applications that are built specifically to take advantage of the cloud computing model. Cloud-native applications are designed to be scalable, resilient, and highly available, and they are built using microservices architecture and containerization technologies such as Docker and serverless computing.

The term *cloud-native* is also often used to describe applications that are designed to be deployed in a cloud environment, but it can also refer to the infrastructure and tools that support the development and deployment of these applications. This includes cloud-based platforms, tools for continuous integration and continuous delivery (CI/CD), and orchestration tools like Kubernetes. In this chapter, we will focus on several important cloud-native technologies that are commonly used by the DevSecOps team.

In general, the goal of cloud-native design is to enable organizations to build and deploy applications more quickly and efficiently, and to take advantage of the scalability, reliability, and cost benefits of the cloud.

There are several reasons why cloud-native design can be advantageous for organizations:

- **Scalability:** Cloud-native applications are designed to be scalable, meaning they can handle a large volume of traffic or workload without experiencing performance degradation. This capability can be especially important for applications that experience sudden spikes in traffic.
- **Resilience:** Cloud-native applications are also designed to be resilient, meaning they are able to recover quickly from failures or disruptions. This capability can help ensure that applications are available and functioning properly, even in the face of unexpected events.
- **Cost-Effectiveness:** By leveraging the cloud, organizations can take advantage of the pay-as-you-go model to pay only for the resources they use, rather than having to invest in and maintain their own infrastructure. This model can help organizations reduce their costs and increase their efficiency by focusing on the core application logic, and not the supporting infrastructure and services.

- **Speed and Agility:** Cloud-native design can also enable organizations to build and deploy applications more quickly and efficiently, thanks to tools like CI/CD and orchestration tools like Kubernetes. This capability can help organizations respond more quickly to changing business needs and stay competitive in the market. Part of this speed is also leveraging PaaS services like building blocks. This way, the developers can rapidly add application functionality by leveraging services managed by OCI.

Overall, the benefits of cloud-native design can help organizations build and deploy applications more effectively, take advantage of the scalability and reliability of the cloud, and reduce costs.

In this chapter, we will cover the most popular cloud-native options available on OCI, from serverless technologies like Functions, Streams, and Events, to containerized technology like Docker containers managed by Kubernetes.

Functions

Oracle Cloud Functions is a serverless computing platform offered by Oracle Cloud. It enables developers to build, deploy, and run applications and functions without having to worry about the underlying infrastructure.

With Oracle Cloud Functions, developers can write and deploy code in a variety of languages, including JavaScript, Python, Go, and Java. The platform automatically scales the code to meet demand and only charges for the actual execution time used.

Oracle Cloud Functions can be triggered by events such as a change in a database, a message being published to a message queue, or a request to an HTTP endpoint. Developers can use Oracle Cloud Functions to build and deploy a wide range of applications, including microservices, data processing pipelines, and event-driven applications.

Note: Open Source for the Win!

OCI Functions are not proprietary technology! They are based on the FNP project (an open-source, container-driven, serverless platform), which allows the DevSecOps team to deploy their function servers on any cloud or even in existing on-premises environments! This helps avoid the technology lock-in problem experienced when using similar technologies from other cloud service providers. For more information, check out FNProject.io.

Overall, Oracle Cloud Functions is designed to make it easier for developers to build and deploy applications quickly and efficiently, taking advantage of the scalability and cost-effectiveness of the cloud.

You can manage functions in one of three ways:

- **Oracle Cloud Shell:** This tool enables you to use the Oracle Cloud Shell from the OCI console to create, deploy, and invoke functions. It requires minimal setup and is the easiest way to start working with functions and the OCI Command Line Interface (CLI). The shell includes OCI-specific tools and utilities that help the admin be more productive.
- **Local Host:** This host enables you to deploy a Docker instance that enables a command-line interface to create, deploy, and invoke functions. This is a great way for macOS and Linux users to set up the CLI on their daily driver.
- **Oracle Compute Instance:** This tool is similar to a local host but leverages some of the automation to set up Docker on a normal compute instance.

Functions can be deployed in several ways. You can use the Cloud Shell, a server, or an OCI Compute Instance. For this example, we will show how to deploy using a Linux server.

Four basic steps need to be performed:

Step 1: Setting Up the Tenancy: This step includes creating a compartment for the function to run in and the network that it will use. You also will set up the security.

Step 2: Creating the Application: Here, you will set up the application that the function will run in.

Step 3: Setting Up the Linux Host: In this step, you will get the API key and set up a Linux host to manage functions.

Step 4: Creating and Running the Function: In this last step, you will create a Python function and learn how to run it. This will also cover an example of having a function use the Python OCI API.

When using functions, you need to be familiar with a few terms:

- **Application:** A logical grouping of functions
- **Function:** Blocks of code stored as a Docker image
- **Invocation:** The process of running a function
- **Trigger:** An action that can automatically invoke a function
- **Context:** A local installation of a development copy of a function
- **Provider:** A service that holds the Docker image and manages the infrastructure that runs the functions

Setting Up the Tenancy

When setting up the Tenancy to run functions, you should have a security strategy that plans for what users will have access to, in order to author or run the functions. You also need to decide whether the ability to run functions is limited to a specific compartment for the application or for the entire tenancy. For this example, we will create a user group called FunctionDevelopers and include all users who can create and run functions in that group.

Note: Multiple Levels of Security

OCI Function policies do not need to be in the main tenancy. Most policies can be created at the compartment level. This setup allows for more granular security.

Next, a policy needs to be created. This policy will allow the group access to the abilities that functions require. For this example, the policy is called Functions. While the sample sets the policy for the tenancy, you can also set the **allow** statement for a compartment for better security. The following statements are added to the policy:

```
Allow group FunctionDevelopers to use cloud-shell in tenancy
Allow group FunctionDevelopers to manage repos in tenancy
Allow group FunctionDevelopers to read objectstorage-namespaces in tenancy
Allow group FunctionDevelopers to manage logging-family in tenancy
Allow group FunctionDevelopers to read metrics in tenancy
Allow group FunctionDevelopers to manage functions-family in tenancy
Allow group FunctionDevelopers to use virtual-network-family in tenancy
Allow group FunctionDevelopers to use apm-domains in tenancy
Allow group FunctionDevelopers to read vaults in tenancy
Allow group FunctionDevelopers to use keys in tenancy
Allow service faas to use apm-domains in tenancy
Allow service faas to read repos in tenancy where request.operation='ListContainer
    ImageSignatures'
Allow service faas to {KEY_READ} in tenancy where request.
    operation='GetKeyVersion'
Allow service faas to {KEY_VERIFY} in tenancy where request.operation='Verify'
```

When completed, the policy should look similar to that shown in Figure 4-1.

Creating the Application

Functions are contained within a structure known as an application. An application serves as a logical grouping of functions, providing developers with the capability to assign and set up resources for all functions within the application. Additionally, applications allow for the establishment of a shared context for storing configuration variables that can be accessed by all functions in the application while also facilitating function runtime isolation.

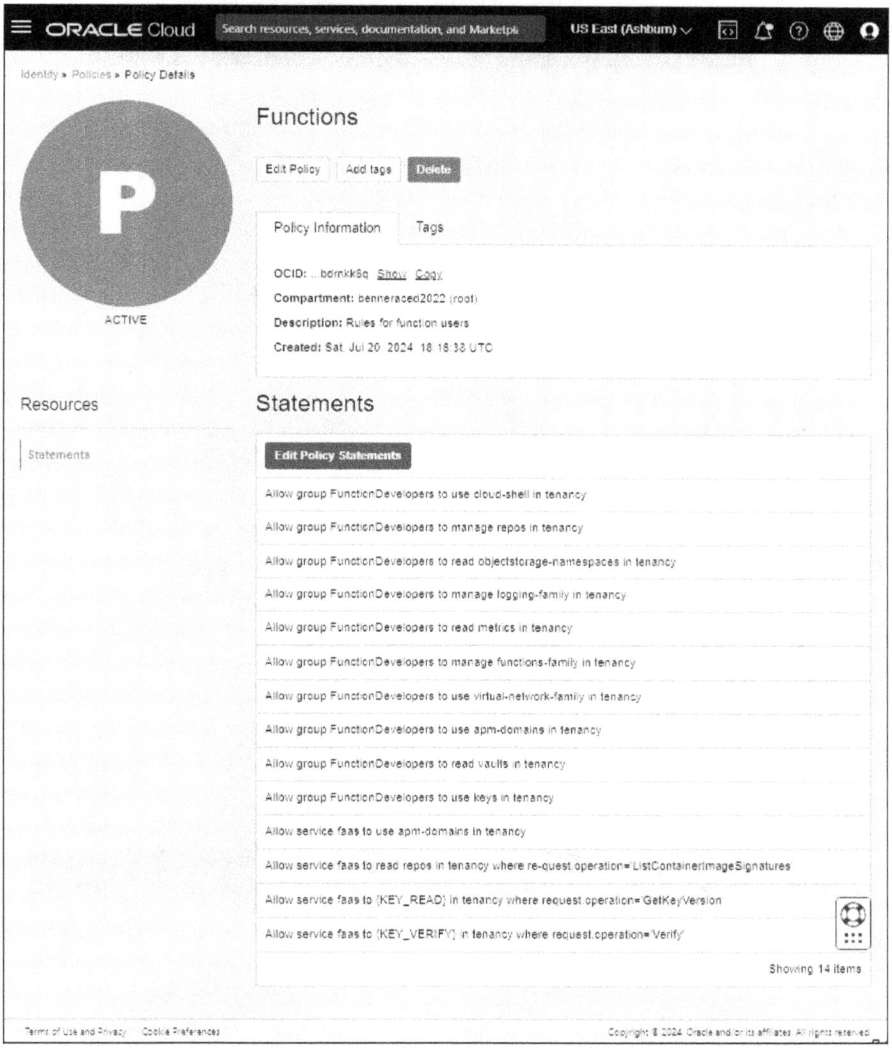

Figure 4-1 Policy for Functions

Applications are easy to create from the Console. Simply navigate to the main menu and select **Developer Services > Functions > Applications**. This is seen in Figure 4-2.

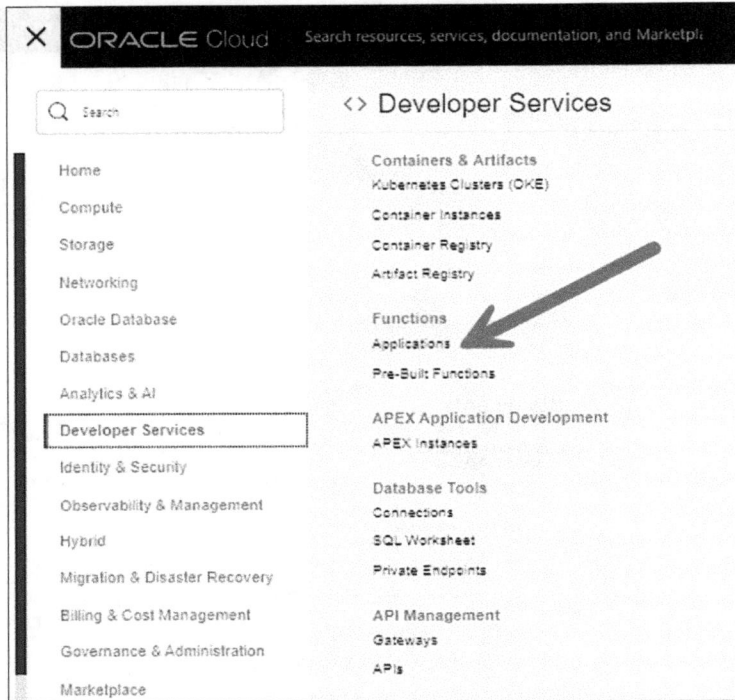

Figure 4-2   Navigating to Applications

From here, click **Create Application**, as shown in Figure 4–3.

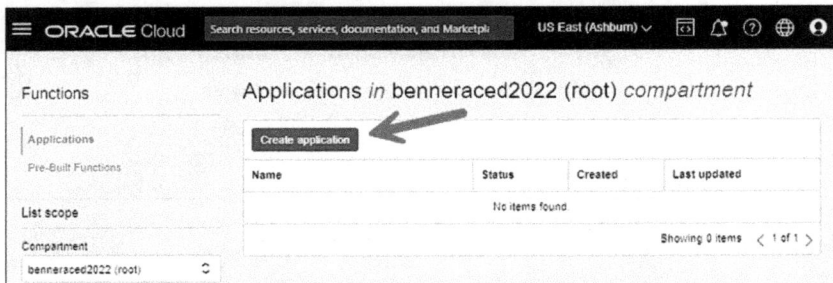

Figure 4-3   Create Application

Next, you need to set up a few details for the function. The first is the name of the application, in this case **Test Application**. Next, select the VCN and subnets that the function can run in. Finally, you can select the shape. The shape is the architecture that the function will run on. You can pick Arm, X86, or both. This allows you to limit a function to a specific architecture if it requires features only available to that architecture.

This step is important because the Docker image user for the function should match the architecture. For the sample, since the development is being done on Arm, Arm is selected. You can see the configuration in Figure 4-4.

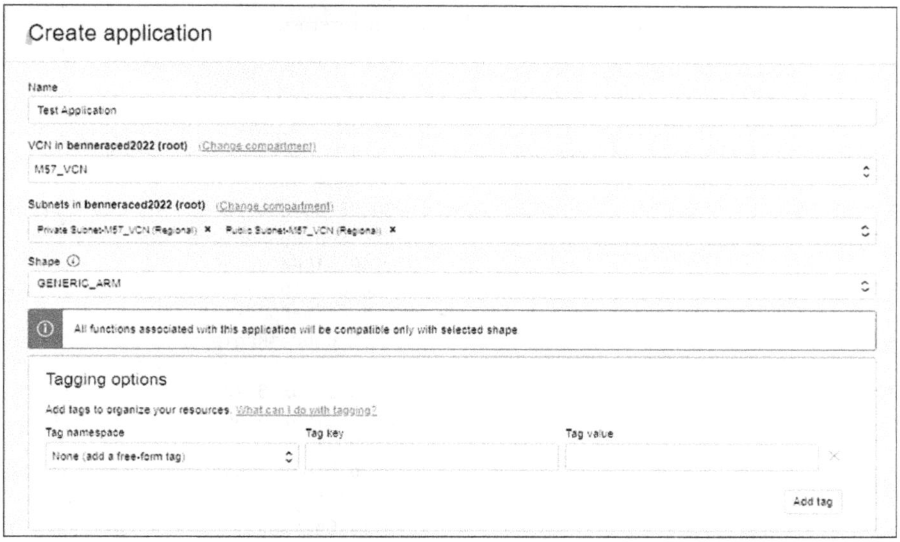

Figure 4-4   Arm-Based Application

When done, click **Create**. You will then be redirected to the Application page.

Setting Up the Linux Host

To set up the function, you first need a host. The host can be nearly any modern operating system, but for this example we will use an AMD system, running Oracle Linux 8. The system will have two cores and 8 GB of RAM, with a 50 GB boot drive. The user erik was also configured to have access to root using **sudo**. Don't worry about only two cores; this is more than enough for editing and testing functions.

The host setup is done in a few steps:

Step 1. Install Docker.
Step 2. Install the Fn CLI.
Step 3. Set up Fn.
Step 4. Log in to a Registry.

To install Docker, you should make sure that the **addons** repo is configured. This is done by running the command **sudo dnf repolist**, the results of which are shown in Example 4-1.

Note: What's a Repo?

In Linux, a repo (short for repository) is a location on the network that hosts .rpm files that are used to install and patch the operating system. Different software can be organized into different repos based on the area of interest.

Example 4-1   Installing Docker

```
[erik@functions ~]$ sudo dnf repolist
repo id                                  repo name
ol8_MySQL80                              MySQL 8.0 for Oracle Linux 8 (aarch64)
ol8_MySQL80_connectors_community         MySQL 8.0 Connectors Community for
                                         Oracle Linux 8 (aarch64)
ol8_MySQL80_tools_community              MySQL 8.0 Tools Community for Oracle
                                         Linux 8 (aarch64)
ol8_UEKR7                                Latest Unbreakable Enterprise Kernel
                                         Release 7 for Oracle Linux 8 (aarch64)
ol8_addons                               Oracle Linux 8 Addons (aarch64)
ol8_appstream                            Oracle Linux 8 Application Stream
                                         (aarch64)
ol8_baseos_latest                        Oracle Linux 8 BaseOS Latest (aarch64)
ol8_ksplice                              Ksplice for Oracle Linux 8 (aarch64)
ol8_oci_included                         Oracle Software for OCI users on
                                         Oracle Linux 8 (aarch64)
 [erik@functions ~]$
```

If ol8_addons is not installed, you can enable it by using the command **sudo dnf config-manager --enable ol8_addons**.

Next, you need to install Docker. If Docker is already installed, you can skip this step. To check whether Docker is installed, run the command **sudo Docker version**. (On most new installs, Docker is not installed.)

```
[erik@functions ~]$ sudo Docker version
sudo: Docker: command not found
[erik@functions ~]$
```

Next, to install Docker, you first need to add in the Extra Packages for Enterprise Linux (EPEL) library.

```
sudo dnf install -y epel-release
```

Next, point dnf to the Docker repo, using the following command:

```
sudo dnf config-manager -y --add-repo=https://download.Docker.com/linux/centos/
  Docker-ce.repo
```

Next, install the community edition of Docker:

```
sudo dnf install Docker-ce -y
```

The next commands will start the server and enable it to restart on reboot:

```
sudo systemctl enable Docker
sudo systemctl start Docker
```

Now, let's make sure Docker is running by using the following command:

```
sudo systemctl status Docker
```

Check the status results to make sure Docker is running. You should see **active (running)** in the Active: section. Figure 4-5 shows a good example with Docker running.

```
[erik@functions ~]$ sudo sudo systemctl status docker
 docker.service - Docker Application Container Engine
   Loaded: loaded (/usr/lib/systemd/system/docker.service; enabled; vendor preset: disabled)
   Active:              since Sat 2024-07-20 23:11:45 GMT; 3min 20s ago
     Docs: https://docs.docker.com
 Main PID: 12475 (dockerd)
    Tasks: 10
   Memory: 33.3M
   CGroup: /system.slice/docker.service
           └─12475 /usr/bin/dockerd -H fd:// --containerd=/run/containerd/containerd.sock

Jul 20 23:11:44 functions systemd[1]: Starting Docker Application Container Engine...
Jul 20 23:11:44 functions dockerd[12475]: time="2024-07-20T23:11:44.4836148252" level=info msg="Starting up"
Jul 20 23:11:45 functions dockerd[12475]: time="2024-07-20T23:11:44.5507531472" level=info msg="Loading containers: start."
Jul 20 23:11:45 functions dockerd[12475]: time="2024-07-20T23:11:45.4218080882" level=info msg="Firewalld: interface docker0 alre
Jul 20 23:11:45 functions dockerd[12475]: time="2024-07-20T23:11:45.5613252472" level=info msg="Loading containers: done."
Jul 20 23:11:45 functions dockerd[12475]: time="2024-07-20T23:11:45.5818628232" level=warning msg="Not using native diff for over
Jul 20 23:11:45 functions dockerd[12475]: time="2024-07-20T23:11:45.5920217042" level=info msg="Docker daemon" commit=8e96db1 com
Jul 20 23:11:45 functions dockerd[12475]: time="2024-07-20T23:11:45.5822706652" level=info msg="Daemon has completed initializati
Jul 20 23:11:45 functions dockerd[12475]: time="2024-07-20T23:11:45.6611284652" level=info msg="API listen on /run/docker.sock"
Jul 20 23:11:45 functions systemd[1]: Started Docker Application Container Engine.
[erik@functions ~]$
```

Figure 4-5 Docker Running

You can also test that Docker is running by using it to run the hello-world container, as shown in Example 4-2.

Example 4-2 Testing That Docker Is Running by Using It to Run the hello-world Container

```
[erik@functions ~]$ sudo Docker run hello-world
Unable to find image 'hello-world:latest' locally
latest: Pulling from library/hello-world
478afc919002: Pull complete
Digest: sha256:1408fec50309afee38f3535383f5b09419e6dc0925bc69891e79d84cc4cdcec6
Status: Downloaded newer image for hello-world:latest

Hello from Docker!
This message shows that your installation appears to be working correctly.

To generate this message, Docker took the following steps:
 1. The Docker client contacted the Docker daemon.
 2. The Docker daemon pulled the "hello-world" image from the Docker Hub.
    (arm64v8)
 3. The Docker daemon created a new container from that image which runs the
    executable that produces the output you are currently reading.
```

4. The Docker daemon streamed that output to the Docker client, which sent it
   to your terminal.

To try something more ambitious, you can run an Ubuntu container with:
$ Docker run -it ubuntu bash

Share images, automate workflows, and more with a free Docker ID:
  https://hub.Docker.com/

For more examples and ideas, visit:
  https://docs.Docker.com/get-started/

Now, add the user working on the function to the Docker group

usermod -aG Docker erik

You can test by using the command **Docker version**. The output should look
similar to that shown in Figure 4-6.

```
[erik@functions hello]$ docker version
Client: Docker Engine - Community
 Version:           26.1.3
 API version:       1.45
 Go version:        go1.21.10
 Git commit:        b72abbb
 Built:             Thu May 16 08:34:39 2024
 OS/Arch:           linux/amd64
 Context:           default

Server: Docker Engine - Community
 Engine:
  Version:          26.1.3
  API version:      1.45 (minimum version 1.24)
  Go version:       go1.21.10
  Git commit:       8e96db1
  Built:            Thu May 16 08:33:34 2024
  OS/Arch:          linux/amd64
  Experimental:     false
 containerd:
  Version:          1.6.32
  GitCommit:        8b3b7ca2e5ce38e8f31a34f35b2b68ceb8470d89
 runc:
  Version:          1.1.12
  GitCommit:        v1.1.12-0-g51d5e94
 docker-init:
  Version:          0.19.0
  GitCommit:        de40ad0
[erik@functions hello]$ ▓
```

Figure 4-6   Docker Version Output

On some systems, you may need to reboot for this to work for non-root users.

Next up is getting an API key, which is needed for the Fn commands to access OCI. To get an API key, from the OCI console, navigate to **Profile > User Settings > Resources – API Keys**. This will bring you to the API Key page shown in Figure 4-7.

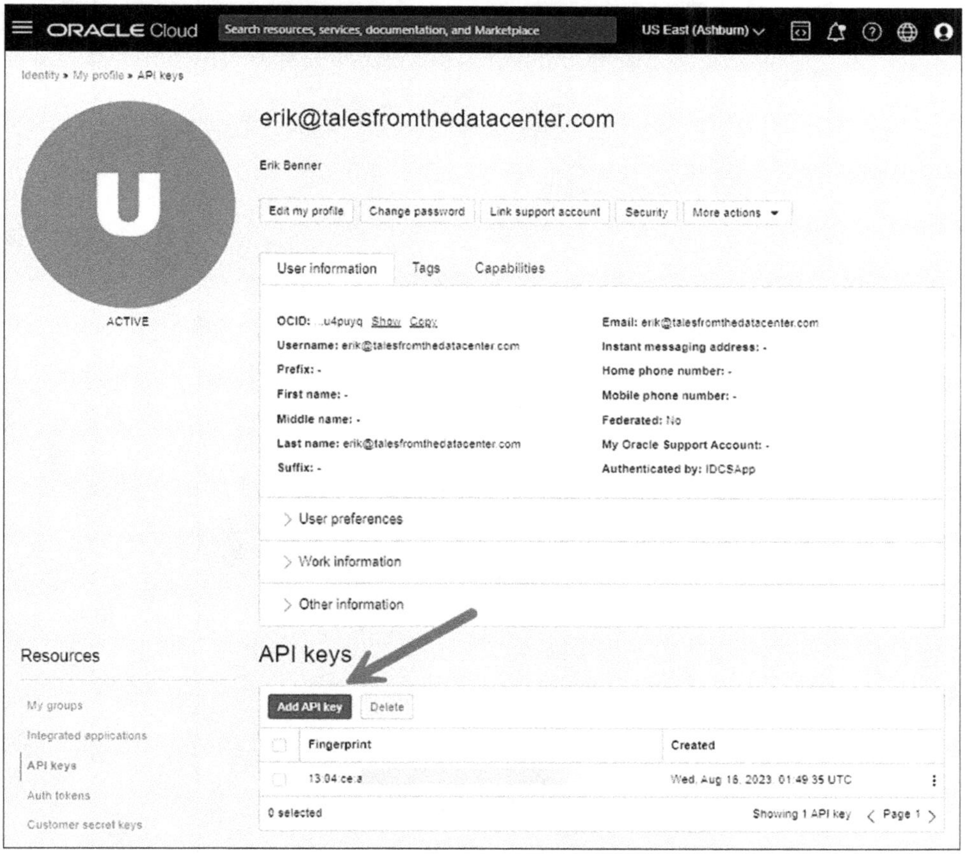

Figure 4-7   Create a New API Key

Note: You Get One Chance, So Make It Count

API keys can be tricky. Once you create a key, you get one chance to download the private key. Be thoughtful and make a backup of the download; otherwise, you will need to rekey.

Next, click **Add API Key**. This takes you to the Add API Key dialog box, where you can download the new private key, as shown in Figure 4-8.

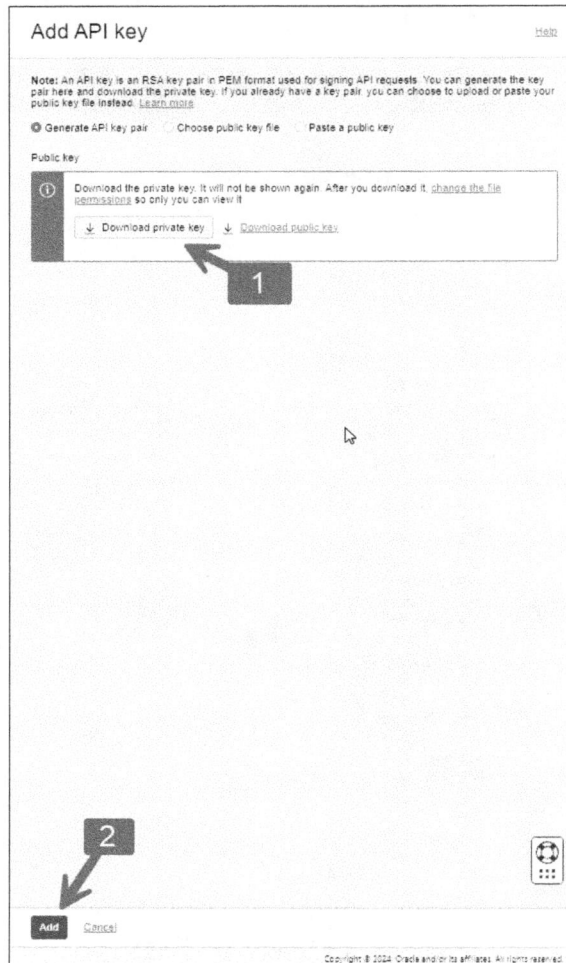

Figure 4-8   API Key Dialog Box

Once the key is added, you will see the configuration file preview. Go ahead and copy the config file preview as well. Next, take the /pem file you download and the sample config and put them into the ~/.oci directory. Name the config file **config**.

Now edit the config file and add in the location of the .pem file. Once completed, it should look like the following.

```
[DEFAULT]
user=ocid1.user.oc1..aaaaaaaac7z4b2mycsdmglfyflz4qomu6cmmltwq3g64vroh622cuqu4puyq
fingerprint=f9:a2:62:59:df:ac:61:08:5a:87:93:98:bf:5f:61:38
```

```
tenancy=ocid1.tenancy.oc1..
  aaaaaaaa257pjnvghqbiutozu4nsos4xt667ml34i4vvpyhxe2tcugfyr23e
region=us-ashburn-1
key_file=/home/erik/.oci/oci.pem
```

Finally, secure the .pem file with the **chmod** command. Change the name of the file as needed.

```
chmod go-rwx oci.pem
```

Next, you need to install the Fn Project CLI by using the following command:

```
sudo curl -LSs https://raw.githubusercontent.com/fnproject/cli/master/install |
  sh
```

When completed, you should see a text version of the Fn logo and the version installed, as in Figure 4-9.

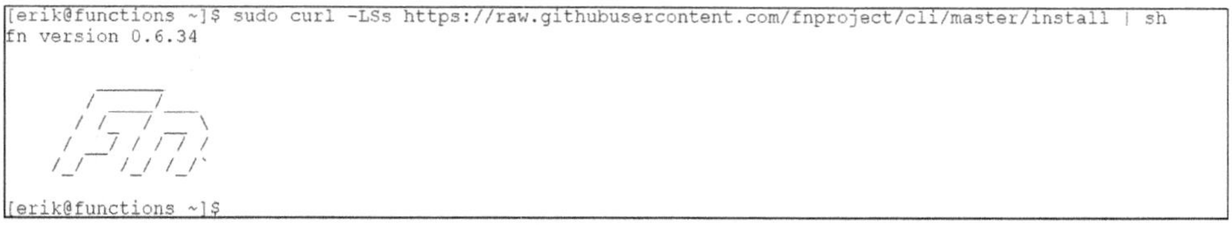

```
[erik@functions ~]$ sudo curl -LSs https://raw.githubusercontent.com/fnproject/cli/master/install | sh
fn version 0.6.34


     /‾‾‾‾/
   / /‾‾/ ‾‾\
  / ‾/ / /7 /
 /_/‾ /_/ /_/`

[erik@functions ~]$
```

Figure 4-9 Fn Installed

Now you need to create a new context for the function, using OCI as the provider:

```
fn create context myappcontext --provider oracle
```

Next, you can use this context:

```
fn use context myappcontext
```

Now you can update the context to use the OCI credentials. In this case, use the DEFAULT profile in the Oracle config file.

```
fn update context oracle.profile DEFAULT
```

Now, set the compartment that you will use:

```
fn update context oracle.compartment-id \ ocid1.compartment.oc1..
  aaaaaaaacqt1rn4xkj4xuyozvaljeweem7gfzxmnxe6y3j3p2hrcqjbondnq
```

Next, you need to point to the API URL. Each OCI region will have a unique URL. This is in the format of **functions.$REGION.oci.oraclecloud.com**:

```
fn update context api-url https://functions.us-ashburn-1.oci.oraclecloud.com
```

The last setup of the context is to set the object storage to be used to hold the images. The format for the Registry is **$REGION.ocir.io/$NAMESPACE/$bucket**:

```
fn update context registry iad.ocir.io/idizdwpbvdsb/function_bucket
```

Next up, you need an authentication token. The token is a short string of text characters; it is used to allow Docker to log in to OCI to access images. Navigate to **Console > Identity > My Profile > Auth Tokens** and then select the **Generate Token** button. You should see the dialog box shown in Figure 4-10.

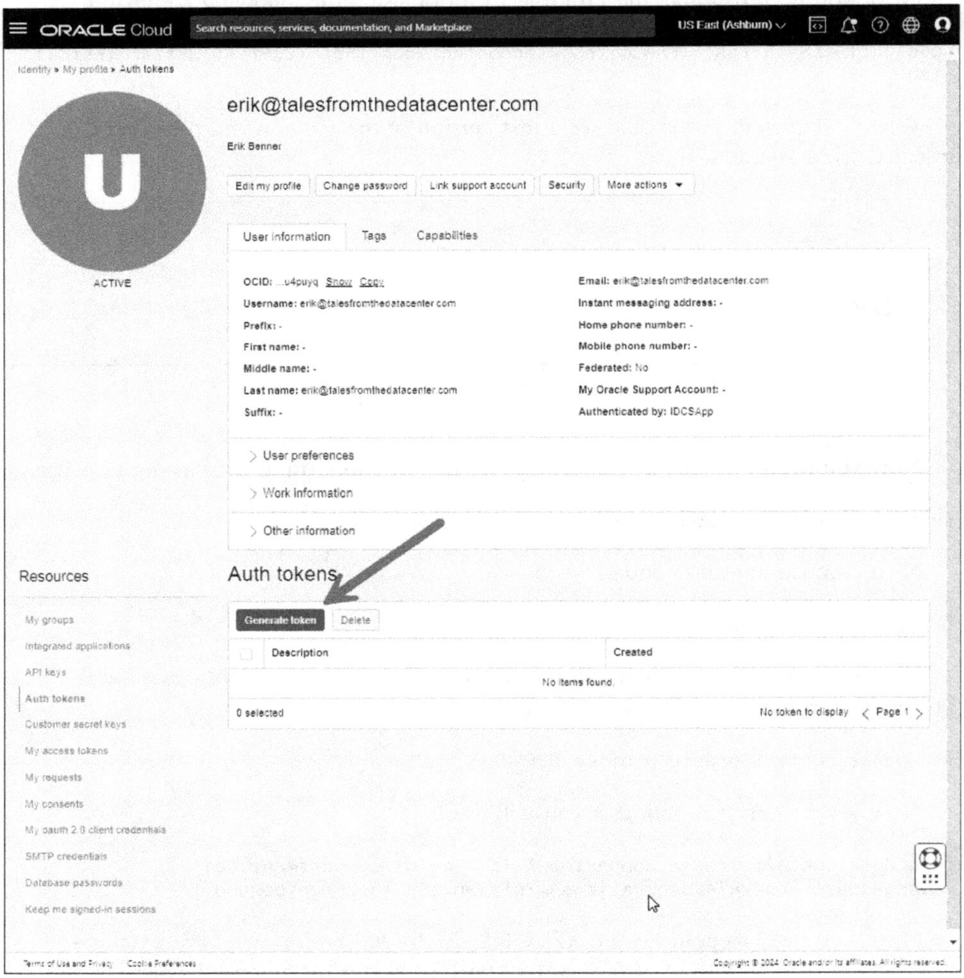

Figure 4-10   Token Management

The next dialog box will allow you to name the token. First, pick a descriptive name and then click **Generate Token**, as shown in Figure 4-11.

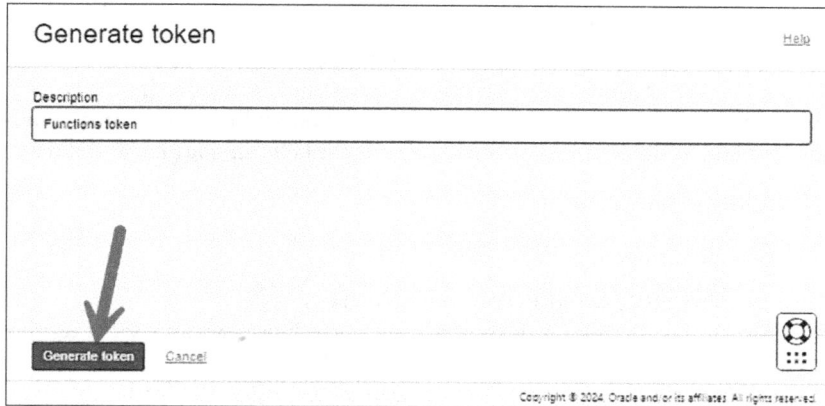

Figure 4-11   Generate Token

OCI will generate a token for your use. If you lose the token, you will need to generate a new one. You are limited to only two tokens.

Note: Make a Secure Backup of the Token

It is *very* important to copy and save the token for future use. You will not have an opportunity to retrieve the token after this step.

You can easily copy the token by clicking the **Copy** option in the Generated Token dialog box, shown in Figure 4-12.

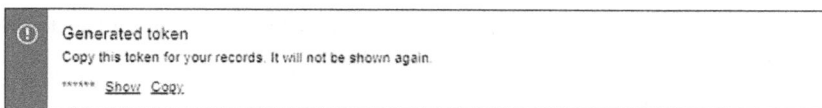

Figure 4-12   Generated Token

Once you have the token, you can log Docker in to OCI by using the **Docker login** command. You will pass it the **$REGION.ocir.io** and the **$NAMESPACE/$USER** variables. The **$USER** should include the domain when using a user in an identity domain:

```
Docker login iad.ocir.io -u yournamespace/youruser
```

The same approach is shown in the following:

```
Docker login  -u 'idizdwpbvdsb/Default/erik@talesfromthedatacenter.com'
   iad.ocir.io
```

When prompted for a password, use your auth token.

Now that Docker is connected, you can create a sample function. In this example, you will use the default Python HelloWorld sample. You will use the **fn init** command, specifying **python**. This will create a directory named hello in your current directory:

```
fn init --runtime python hello
```

The directory has three files:

- **func.py:** The HelloWorld Python source code
- **func.yaml:** The definition of the function, including the name, what runtime language to use, and also what versions are used
- **Requirements.txt:** The libraries that need to be made available to the function when it runs

Note: 404 Errors

When you're deploying a function, 404 errors are commonly caused by a missing library in the requirements.txt file.

Creating and Running a Function

Next, you can deploy the application to OCI, using the **fn deploy** command, passing the application where the function will be located:

```
fn -v deploy --app "Test Application"
```

Now that the function is deployed, you can invoke it for testing, using **the fn invoke** command, passing the application and function name:

```
fn invoke "Test Application" hello
```

Now, let's make a more complex function that will call the hello world function. You can call this function **test**. Use the **fn init** command so that you have a good start with the requirements.txt and YAML:

```
fn init --runtime python test
```

When you do this, you need to make sure that you add that to the requirements.txt file. Just add the line **oci** to the existing file, as shown in the following:

```
[erik@functions test]$ more requirements.txt
fdk>=0.1.75
oci
```

Now, we will need some information from the existing function—mainly its OCID and invoke endpoint. You can get that from the function info page. To locate it, from the main console, navigate to the main menu and select **Developer Services > Applications**, then select **Test Application** then your application, as shown in Figure 4-13.

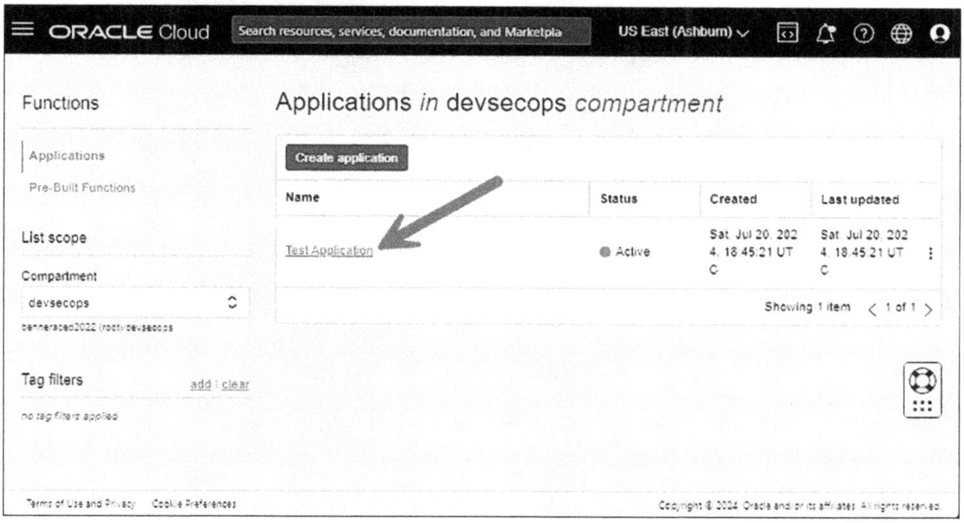

Figure 4-13   Selecting the Application

Now you should see a list of all functions for the application. Click the three dots on the right side to copy the OCID and invoke endpoint, as indicated in Figure 4-14.

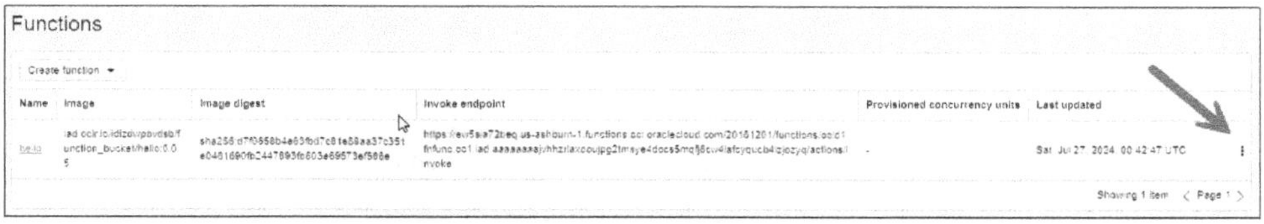

Figure 4-14   Accessing Function Options

From here, not only can you copy information about the function, but you can also delete the function, open a support request for the function, and edit the functions. These options are available in the following pop-up function options shown in Figure 4-15.

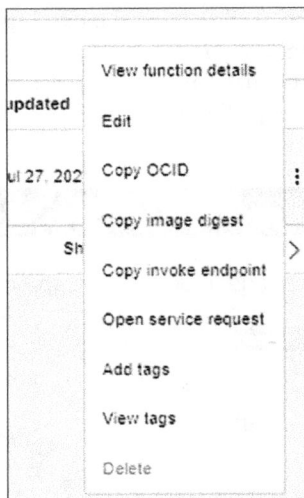

Figure 4-15   Function Options

Save the copied endpoint and OCID. You will need it for the sample to set the correct values for the **function_endpoint** and **function_ocid** variables. This is shown in Example 4-3.

Example 4-3   Sample Function

```
import logging
import oci

from fdk import response


def handler(ctx, data: io.BytesIO=None):
    try:
        function_endpoint =  "https://ew5sia72beq.us-ashburn-1.
functions.oci.oraclecloud.com/20181201/functions/ocid1.fnfunc.oc1.iad.
aaaaaaaajvhhzrlaxooujpg2tmsye4docs5mqfj6cw4lafcyqucb4izjozyq/actions/invoke"
        function_ocid = "ocid1.fnfunc.oc1.iad.
aaaaaaaajvhhzrlaxooujpg2tmsye4docs5mqfj6cw4lafcyqucb4izjozyq"
        function_body = ""
    except (Exception) as ex:
        print('ERROR: Missing key in payload', ex, flush=True)
        raise

    signer = oci.auth.signers.get_resource_principals_signer()
    client = oci.functions.FunctionsInvokeClient(config={}, signer=signer,
service_endpoint=function_endpoint)
    resp = client.invoke_function(function_id=function_ocid, invoke_function_
body=function_body)
    print(resp.data.text, flush=True)
```

```
return response.Response(
    ctx,
    response_data=resp.data.text,
    headers={"Content-Type": "application/json"}
)
```

You can now deploy the function:

```
fn -v deploy —app "Test Application"
```

Finally, you can invoke it as follows:

```
fn invoke "Test Application" test
```

Streams

Oracle Cloud Streams is a fully managed, cloud-based messaging service offered by Oracle Cloud. It enables organizations to build real-time, event-driven applications by providing a secure and scalable messaging platform. The service allows developers to publish and subscribe to messages, enabling them to build applications that can process and react to events in real time. The platform supports a wide range of messaging patterns and protocols, including publish-subscribe, point-to-point, and request-response.

A producer publishes messages to a stream, which is an append-only log. These messages are distributed among Oracle-managed partitions for scalability. Partitions allow you to distribute a stream by splitting messages across multiple nodes (or brokers). Each partition can be placed on a separate machine, allowing multiple consumers to read a stream in parallel. A consumer reads messages from one or more partitions. Consumers can read from any partition regardless of where the partition is hosted. Each message within a stream is marked with an offset value, so a consumer can pick up where it left off if it is interrupted. Messages from a partition are guaranteed to be delivered in the same order they were produced. Consumers can read messages explicitly by providing the partition and offset, or as a member of a consumer group, which coordinates the consumption of an entire stream by the members of the group.

Some examples of how Oracle Cloud Streams can be used include building microservices architectures, real-time data processing pipelines, and event-driven applications. The platform can be integrated with other Oracle Cloud services, such as Oracle Functions and Oracle Autonomous Transaction Processing, to build and deploy cloud-native applications.

When setting up Streams, you should be aware of the following concepts.

- **Consumer:** An entity that reads messages from one or more streams.
- **Consumer Group:** A group of instances that work together to consume messages from all partitions in a stream. At any given time, messages from a specific partition can be consumed by only a single consumer in the group.
- **Cursor:** A reference to a specific position in a stream, such as an offset or time in a partition, or a group's current location.

- **Instance:** A consumer group member is defined when a group cursor is created and group membership is maintained through interaction. Lack of interaction leads to a timeout and removes the instance from the consumer group.
- **Key:** An identifier used to group related messages.
- **Message:** A message encoded in Base64 is published to a schema-agnostic stream. The stream accepts various message formats, such as XML, JSON, CSV, and gzip. Producers and consumers must agree on the format.
- **Offset:** The offset is the position of a message within a partition. Each message is identified by its offset, and consumers can choose to read messages starting from any offset. If the reading process is interrupted, the offset can be used to restart reading from where it left off in the stream.
- **Partition:** A section of a stream. Partitions make it possible to distribute a stream by splitting messages across multiple nodes. This also enables multiple consumers to read from a stream simultaneously.
- **Producer:** An entity that publishes messages to a stream.
- **Stream:** A partitioned, append-only log of messages.
- **Stream Pool:** A grouping that you can use to organize and manage streams, including any shared Apache Kafka or security settings.

Overall, Oracle Cloud Streams is designed to make it easier for organizations to build real-time, event-driven applications by providing a scalable and secure messaging platform in the cloud.

Events

Oracle Cloud Events is a fully managed, cloud-based event management service offered by Oracle Cloud. It enables organizations to build and run event-driven applications by providing a platform for publishing, subscribing, and reacting to events. With Oracle Cloud Events, developers can create and publish events using various sources, including HTTP requests, database changes, and message queues. They can then subscribe to these events and create actions or functions triggered in response to the events. Oracle Cloud Events supports a wide range of event types and sources, and it can be integrated with other Oracle Cloud services, such as Oracle Functions and Oracle Autonomous Transaction Processing, to build and deploy cloud-native applications.

Before you use events, you need to add in a security policy. You also need to make a user group for the Event admins. In Example 4-4, the group is EventAdmins, and the policy is Events, with the policy being applied to the tenancy. Optionally, you can apply the policy at the compartment level.

Example 4-4   Adding a Security Policy

```
allow group EventAdmins to inspect compartments in tenancy
allow group EventAdmins to use tag-namespaces in tenancy
allow group EventAdmins to inspect streams in tenancy
```

```
allow group EventAdmins to use stream-push in tenancy
allow group EventAdmins to use stream-pull in tenancy
allow group EventAdmins to use virtual-network-family in tenancy
allow group EventAdmins to manage function-family in tenancy
allow group EventAdmins to use ons-topic in tenancy
allow group EventAdmins to manage cloudevents-rules in tenancy
```

The policy should look similar to that shown in Figure 4-16.

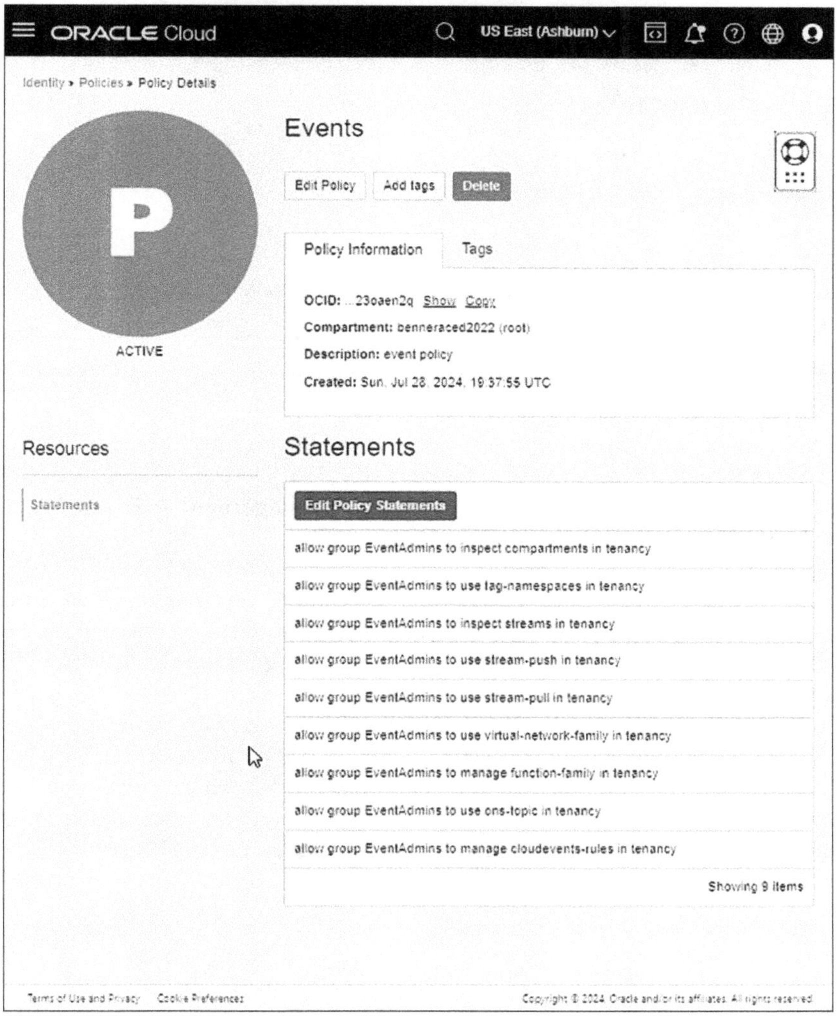

Figure 4-16   Events Policy

One of the most common event use cases is to run a function when an object is uploaded to object storage. To set this up, you need to navigate to **Storage > Object Storage**.

From here, you can see all of your buckets (as in Figure 4-17). You can either modify an existing bucket or create a new bucket. In this case, create a new bucket by clicking **Create Bucket**.

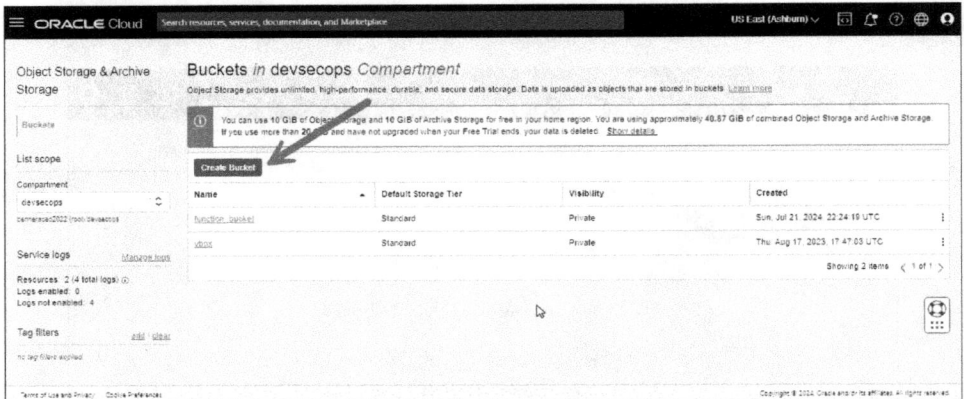

Figure 4-17   Bucket List

As with any bucket, you have several options. The one of interest here is Emit Object Events. Click **Create** as highlighted in Figure 4-18.

Next, you need to navigate to **Observability & Management > Event Service > Rules**. You should see the page shown in Figure 4-19.

Next, click **Create Rule**, which will bring up the Create Rule dialog box. In this dialog, you will be able to set up the rule. In this case, the condition is an Event Type. The service is Object Storage when an object is created. The rule will then run a function in the DevSecOps compartment from the test application called test. The completed sample is shown in Figure 4-20.

Although you are using the event to run a function, it has many more use cases. You can also generate a notification based on an event or push data to a stream. This is a capability that has many uses to both improve security and automate tasks.

Overall, Oracle Cloud Events is designed to make it easier for organizations to build and run event-driven applications by providing a scalable and reliable event management platform in the cloud.

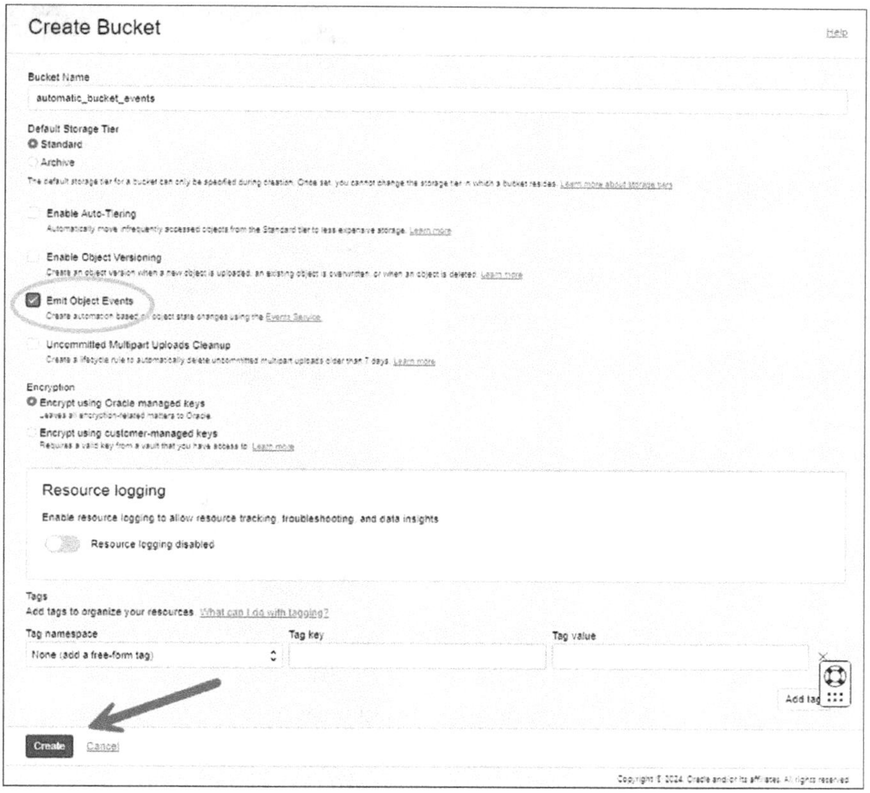

Figure 4-18   Creating a Bucket

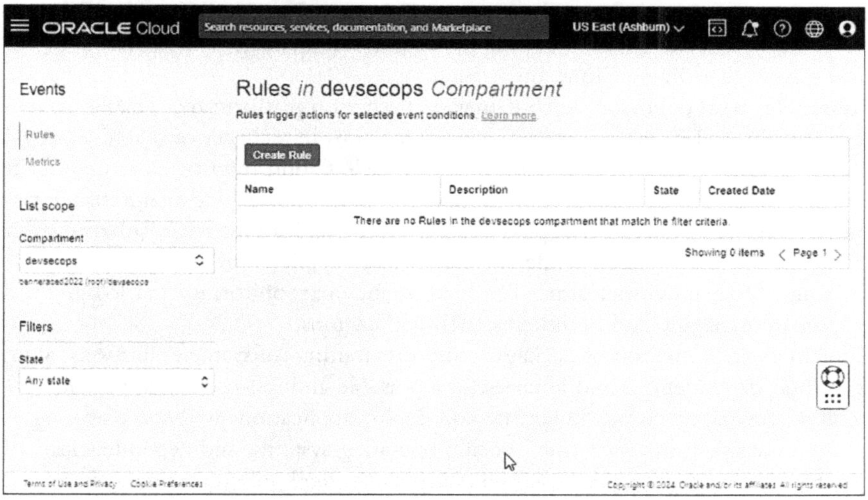

Figure 4-19   Event Rules

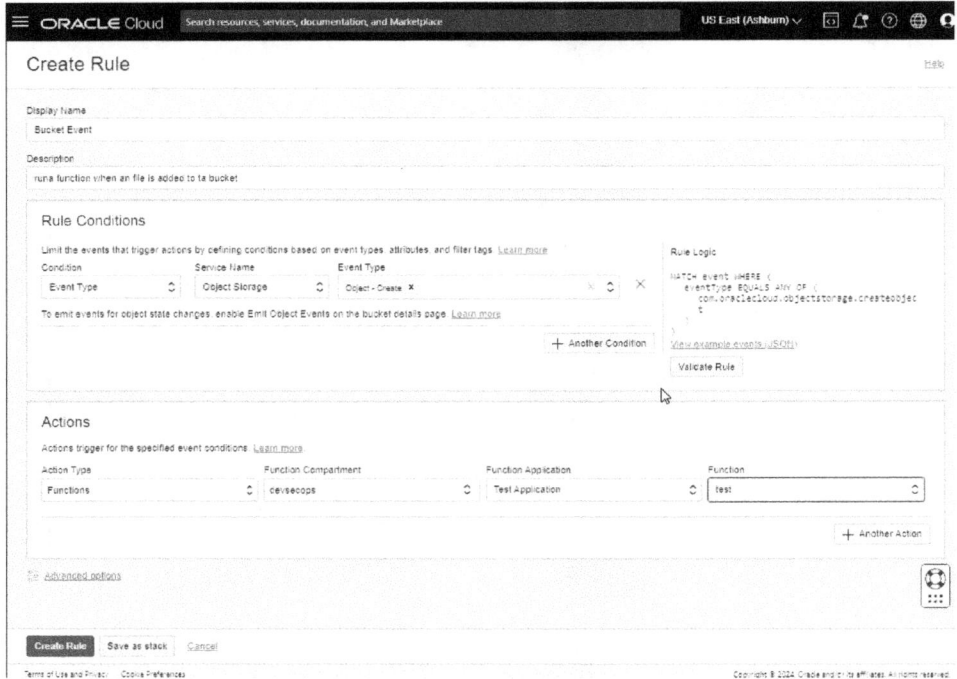

Figure 4-20   Object Event

Oracle Kubernetes Engine (OKE)

Oracle Kubernetes Engine is a fully managed Kubernetes service offered by Oracle Cloud. OKE enables organizations to deploy, scale, and manage containerized applications on the Oracle Cloud Infrastructure.

Kubernetes is an open-source container orchestration platform that enables developers to deploy, scale, and manage containerized applications in a cluster of machines. OKE simplifies the utilization of Kubernetes on the Oracle Cloud Infrastructure by offering a fully managed service that handles the underlying infrastructure and maintenance tasks. By using OKE, developers can deploy containerized applications with Kubernetes, and the platform will automatically scale and manage the applications based on demand. Additionally, OKE provides features like load balancing, monitoring, and logging to assist developers in managing and optimizing their applications.

Containers are a method of packaging and distributing software applications, along with all their dependencies and libraries, in a portable and self-contained manner. They allow developers to quickly create and deploy applications without worrying about the underlying infrastructure, specific operating systems, and dependencies needed to run the application. Using containerization technology, containers create a lightweight, standalone, executable package that includes everything an application needs to run, such as the application code, system tools, libraries, and runtime. This makes it easy to deploy applications in any environment, whether it's on a local machine, in a cloud environment, or on-premises. Containers are often used alongside container orchestration platforms like Kubernetes, which enable developers to manage and deploy large numbers of containers at scale. The most widely used container today is Docker.

Docker

Docker is a containerization platform that enables developers to package and distribute software applications in a portable and self-contained way. Docker uses containers to create lightweight, standalone, executable packages that include everything an application needs to run, including the application code, system tools, libraries, and runtime. Docker allows developers to build and deploy applications quickly and easily, without having to worry about the underlying infrastructure or the specific operating system and dependencies required to run the application. This makes it easy to deploy applications in any environment, whether it's on a local machine, in a cloud environment, or on-premises.

Key Terms

There are several key technologies that you need to first understand:

- **Serverless Kubernetes with Virtual Nodes:** Virtual nodes offer a serverless Kubernetes experience for running containerized applications at scale, without the need to spend extra resources on managing, scaling, upgrading, and troubleshooting cluster infrastructure.

  With virtual nodes, Kubernetes sees these nodes as regular ones, allowing for precise pod scaling with per-pod pricing. This means you can scale your deployments without having to consider the cluster's capacity, making it easier to handle scalable workloads like high-traffic web applications and data processing jobs.
- **Managed Nodes:** Managed nodes are worker nodes that are created within a customer's tenancy and operated with shared responsibility between OKE and the customer. Customers can define the desired specifications for their worker node pools, and OKE streamlines the provisioning of these nodes. OKE offers features to automate and simplify key ongoing operations for these worker nodes, including on-demand cycling to automate updating worker nodes, self-healing of worker nodes upon detection of failure, autoscaling, and more. Managed nodes are suitable for customers who require worker nodes with configurations or compute shapes that are not supported by virtual nodes.
- **Self-Managed Nodes:** Self-managed nodes in OKE provide additional customization and control for running containerized workloads that need unique compute configurations or advanced setup across the stack not supported by managed nodes. This allows customers to utilize specialized infrastructure options such as RDMA-enabled bare metal HPC/GPU, confidential computing, or other specialized use cases. While customers still benefit from a managed control plane, they are responsible for managing the worker nodes, including Kubernetes upgrades and OS patching.

- **Control Plane Nodes:** These nodes were previously referred to as master nodes. This is where the scheduler, manager, and the API server run. For redundancy, three nodes are often used.
- **Worker Nodes:** This is where the containers run. They communicate to the control nodes for management.
- **K8s:** This is a common abbreviation for Kubernetes. The 8 represents the numbers of characters between the *k* and the *s*!
- **Managed Cluster:** This system utilizes specialized systems to oversee the K8s cluster. While it provides greater control, it comes with a significant cost. Managed nodes are OCI Compute instances that run in your tenancy and can be controlled and configured with shared operational responsibility.
- **Virtual Cluster:** This cluster utilizes VMS for the nodes, which helps reduce costs. Virtual nodes offer precise, pod-level elasticity and pay-per-use pricing. This allows you to scale deployments without worrying about the cluster's capacity, making it easier to handle scalable workloads like high-traffic web applications and data processing jobs. Resources are allocated at the Pod level.

Note: One Less Thing to Manage and Patch

One advantage of OKE is that it is a managed Kubernetes service; it's not a proprietary frontend to Kubernetes. It does, however, include some advantages versus building and managing your own Kubernetes software and cluster.

- **Authentication and Authorization:** You can control access and permissions using native OCI identity and access management (IAM), Oracle Identity Cloud Service, and Kubernetes role-based access control. You can also configure OCI IAM multifactor authentication. Workload Identity allows you to establish secure authentication at the pod level for OCI APIs and services. By following a zero-trust approach, you can ensure that users have access only to necessary resources. This helps enhance your security by reducing the potential for security breaches or unauthorized access.
- **Compliance:** Compliance starts with clusters that already have industry-standard regulatory frameworks approved, such as FedRAMP High, HIPAA, PCI, and SOC 2.
- **Container Image Scanning:** OKE supports container image scanning. This capability allows you to ensure that your application images are free of serious security vulnerabilities and that the integrity of the container images is preserved when deployed by enforcing image signing. You can easily scan for known common vulnerabilities and exposures (CVE).
- **Encryption:** Oracle encrypts block volumes, boot volumes, and volume backups at rest using the Advanced Encryption Standard (AES) algorithm with 256-bit encryption.
- **Strong Isolation at the Pod Level:** Virtual nodes provide strong isolation for each Kubernetes pod. Pods do not share any underlying kernel, memory, or CPU resources. This pod-level isolation enables you or your organization to run untrusted workloads, multitenant applications, and sensitive data.

A Kubernetes cluster is a collection of nodes, which are machines running applications. Nodes can be either physical machines or virtual machines, and their capacity in terms of the number of CPUs and amount of memory is defined at the time of their creation. Typically, a cluster consists of three control nodes and enough worker nodes to handle the workload. There are two types of clusters:

- **Enhanced Clusters:** Enhanced clusters support all available features, including features not supported by basic clusters (such as virtual nodes, cluster add-on management, workload identity, and additional worker nodes per cluster). Enhanced clusters come with a service-level agreement (SLA).
- **Basic Clusters:** Basic clusters offer all the essential functionality provided by Kubernetes and Container Engine for Kubernetes, but they do not include the advanced features of Container Engine for Kubernetes. Basic clusters have a service-level objective (SLO) but do not come with a service-level agreement.

Creating a cluster is quick and easy to do. Navigate to **Developer Services > Kubernetes Clusters (OKE)** (see Figure 4-21). From here, you can see any existing clusters in the compartment and create a new cluster.

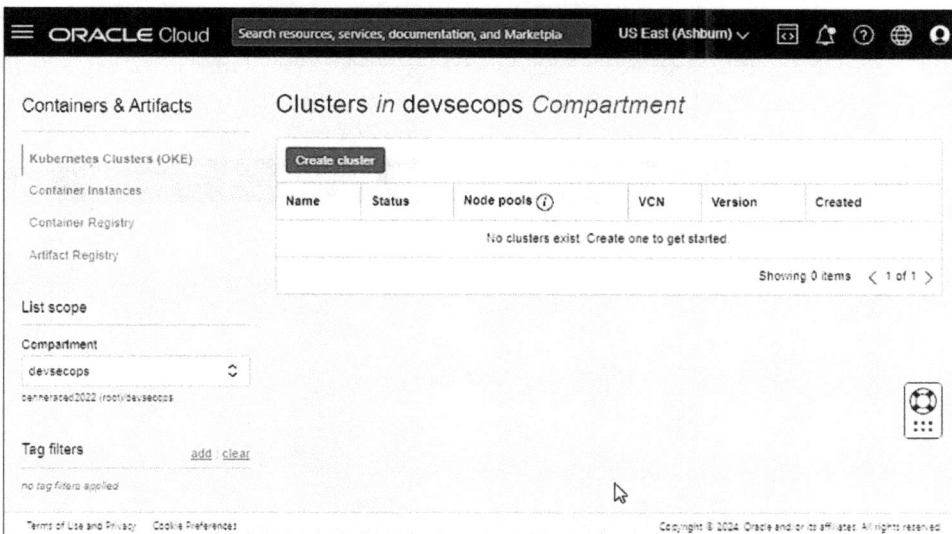

Figure 4-21   K8s Clusters

Next, select **Create Cluster** to start the dialog process shown in Figure 4-22.

For most new clusters, you should use the Quick Create approach. This option will correctly create all new resources for the cluster to isolate it from existing workloads. For this sample, let's create a managed cluster.

The cluster will have a public endpoint, allowing access to manage the cluster from the Internet, but the workers will be on a private subnet. This is seen in the first part of the creation dialog shown in Figure 4-23.

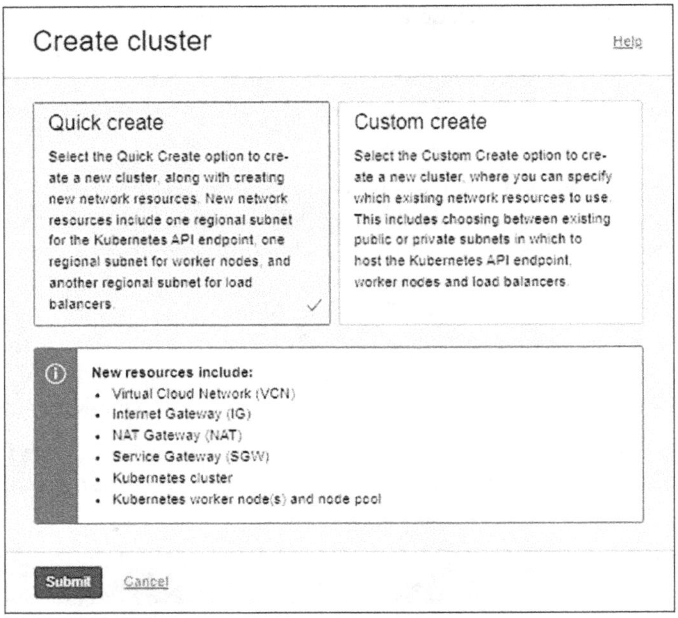

Figure 4-22   K8s Creation Dialog Box

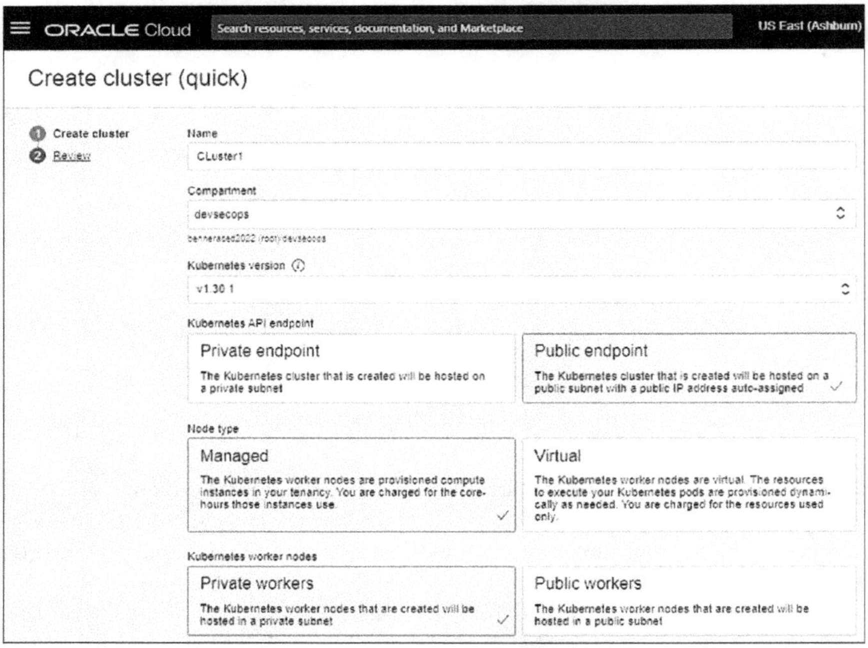

Figure 4-23   K8s Creation Part 1

Next, set the initial node configuration. For the sample, three nodes, each with one OCPU and 9 GB of RAM, will be used. Each uses Oracle Linux 8 with K8s 1.30.1 You can see how the shape is set in Figure 4-24.

Figure 4-24   K8s Creation Part 2

Note

Building a shape with odd amounts of RAM or CPU is an efficiency advantage that OCI has when compared to other cloud service providers. You can assign exactly the resources required and are not limited to preselected combinations for CPU/RAM.

Click **Next** to continue to the review page. From here, you can review the settings, shown in Figure 4-25.

Figure 4-25   K8s Review

Click **Create Cluster** to continue. The system will then create all of the dependency resources and the K8s cluster. When you return to the list of clusters in the compartment, you should see the cluster now, as shown in Figure 4-26.

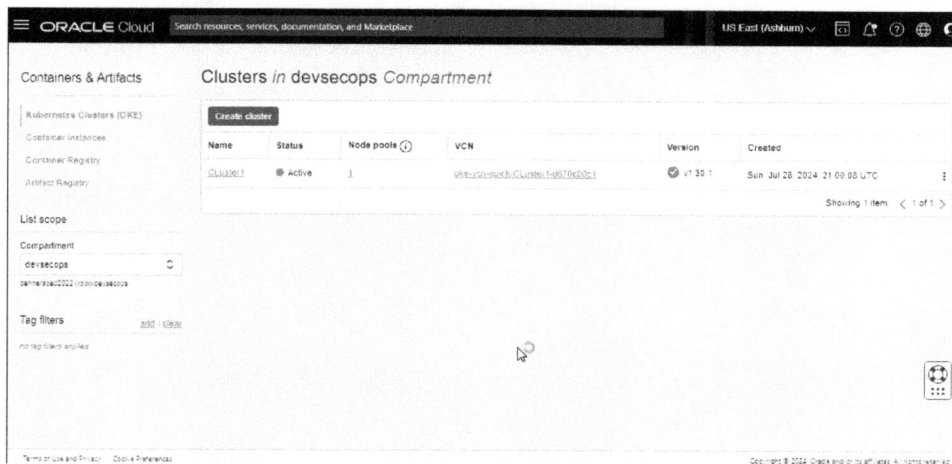

Figure 4-26 K8s Cluster Created

From here, you can manage the cluster by using the **kubectl** command, just like you would for any other K8s cluster!

Summary

In this chapter, you learned about OCI cloud-native technologies, how to create serverless computing functions, how events can be used, what streams are, and also how to set up a K8s cluster. In the next chapter, you will learn more details about OCI networking options.

Oracle IaaS—Network

Cloud networking is the foundation of your cloud infrastructure architecture. Here, you define how your resources access other internal and external resources and systems, and how access to these resources is controlled at the network level. In an on-premises data center, this responsibility traditionally fell on the network engineering team (who now should be the *cloud network engineering team*). However, for DevSecOps cloud practitioners, an understanding of the fundamentals of cloud networking is not only beneficial but also imperative.

The benefit of OCI is that it offers on-demand, self-service network management, allowing you to create and secure your cloud network in a matter of minutes without the need to procure expensive network hardware and appliances. How you design your network to support your applications, databases, and other systems is up to your cloud network engineer. No two networks are alike, and often carving out the network into subnets, restricting and allowing access through firewall and security policies, and using DNS and DHCP are some of the typical setups required.

In this chapter, we will focus on the fundamentals of cloud networking within OCI. We will walk through concepts and the creation of basic networks. We will also provide a glimpse into some advanced cloud networking concepts and security at the end.

Getting Started with OCI Networking

Like most other cloud services, cloud networks are virtual. Thus, setting up a virtual cloud network is a matter of clickthrough navigation. Though a lot of the complexities of configuration are simplified in OCI, for those new to virtual cloud networking, we will first address a few concepts.

Understanding Concepts and Terminology

Table 5-1 lists the basic OCI networking terminology needed to get started on your first network setup.

Table 5-1   Basic OCI Networking Terminology

Term	Explanation
VCN	Stands for *virtual cloud network*, a private network in the Oracle cloud data center. Each VCN has an IPv4 CIDR block assigned to it.
CIDR	Stands for *Classless Inter-Domain Routing*. It is also referred to as *supernetting*. For example, an IP address of 10.0.0.15 in the network associated with the netmask of 255.255.255.0 is identified using the CIDR notation of 10.0.0.15/24.
Subnet	A subdivision of a VCN. Each VCN can have multiple subnets. A subnet contains VNICs that you attach to compute instances. Each subnet will have an IP range that should not overlap with other subnets. For example, you may consider a subnet for your applications and a separate one for your databases. A subnet can exist in a single availability domain (AD) or can be spaced across an entire region, which is a common layout (and referred to as a *regional subnet*).
VNIC	Stands for *virtual network interface card*. This is similar to a traditional network card attached to physical devices. Every compute instance will have a primary VNIC that cannot be deleted, but secondary ones can be added and can be in a different subnet.
Private IP	An IPv4 private IP address. Each VNIC will have a primary IP, but additional IPs can be added.
Internet Gateway	One of many gateway types, but this is a virtual router that serves to connect to the Internet from your VCN.
Route Table	Includes route rules that define how to route the network traffic, specifically a destination CIDR block and the next hop that matches that CIDR.
Security Rules	Consists of ingress and egress firewall rules to allow access to ports/protocols in your VCN. Each VCN comes with a default security list with default security rules.
Security List	Consists of a number of security rules and applies to the entire VCN. Optionally, a network security group can be used for more fine-tuned firewall management by applying a set of security rules against specific resources in that group.

Walking Through a Basic Network Architecture Diagram

Figure 5-1 shows a standard topology for a basic OCI network architecture. Here, a single VCN is configured across two availability domains in a single region. When created, this VCN has been configured with an IPv4 CIDR block of 192.0.0.0/16 (which is a Class B block). This means that this entire VCN, which includes all of its subnets, can have IP addresses between the 192.0.1.x to 192.0.252.x range, of exactly 65,000 IPs.

Now Subnet A within this VCN has been created with a CIDR block of 192.0.1.0/24, which includes all IP addresses between 192.0.1.1 and 192.0.1.252, and similarly Subnet B may have a CIDR block of 192.0.2.0/24 but on a different subnet. Thus, each subnet has its own nonoverlapping ranges.

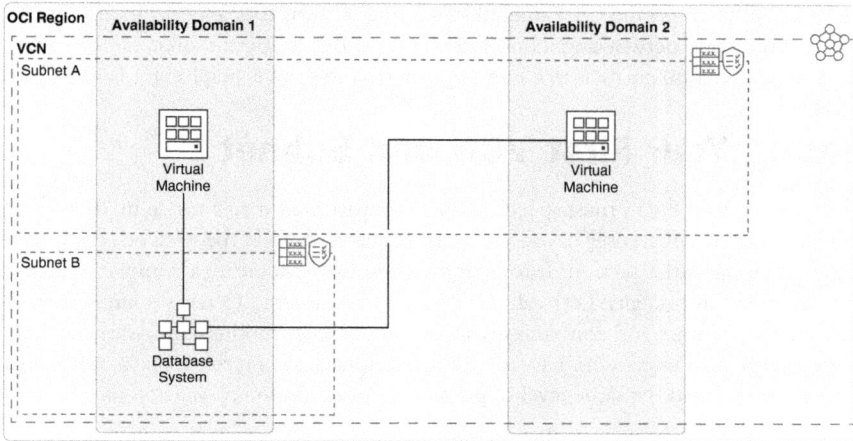

Figure 5-1 Understanding the OCI Network Architecture Diagram

Each subnet has its own *route table* and *security list*, designated by the smaller icons (see Figure 5-2 for a description of these icons). Each VCN automatically comes with a default route table, and each subnet created uses this default route table. As your network expands and connectivity requirements change, route rules (or routing tables) can be added or removed at any time. Security lists control the ingress and egress rules, referring to inbound and outbound virtual firewall rules, respectively.

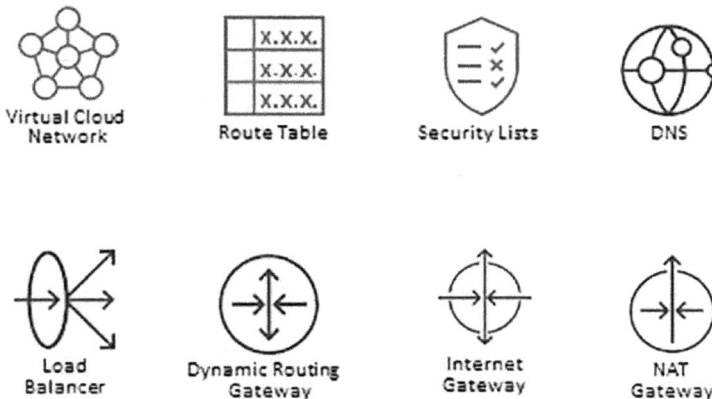

Figure 5-2 Sample of Networking Icons

Both a VCN and a subnet can exist only in a single region but can span multiple availability domains (ADs).

Each of the services within a subnet, whether it is a compute instance or Database as a Service (DBaaS), may have one or more IP addresses assigned to it, but these IPs must be within the range of that subnet.

Figure 5-1 is based on the OCI unified visual language for topology diagrams. Figure 5-2 lists a few of the main networking icons. Full details of this diagram toolkit can be found at https://docs.oracle.com/en-us/iaas/Content/General/Reference/graphicsfordiagrams.htm.

Creating Your First VCN and Subnet

When creating a VCN, you must specify which compartment it will reside in. The *compartment* controls which user has access to its resources, such as the network components we will be creating in this section. It is recommended that you create a compartment specific to your network components. Let's call this *NetworkCompartment*. Other resources such as block storage volumes and compute instances can reside in another compartment, say *ComputeCompartment*. Users who have administrative privileges on the *ComputeCompartment* do not necessarily need the same level of privileges on the *NetworkCompartment*.

Creating a VCN

A VCN automatically comes with a default route table (with no route rules), security list (with default security rules), and DHCP (with default values). Creating a VCN is relatively straightforward (see Figure 5-3):

Step 1. Navigate to the OCI console menu and click **Networking > Virtual Cloud Networks**.

Figure 5-3   Creating a VCN

Step 2. Click **Create VCN** to enter the creation wizard.

Step 3. Give a name to the VCN (such as appvcn).

Step 4. Provide an IPv4 CIDR block range (such as 192.0.0.0/16).

Step 5. Click **Create VCN**.

Keep in mind that the policies on the IAM compartment apply immediately to the VCN just created.

After the VCN is created, under the Resources tab on the left, you will notice one of each of the following resources created: CIDR Blocks/Prefixes, Route Tables, Security Lists, and DHCP Options.

Creating a Subnet

Creating a subnet in this VCN is equally easy. When designing your cloud network, you should put some thought into the following:

- **How many VCNs will you have?** Consider the various tiers of services, business units, and other factors in your architecture and segregate appropriately.
- **Which compartment will these VCNs reside in?** Having a VCN reside in its own compartment outside of your other cloud resources helps control access, if separation of duty among your cloud administrators is required.
- **What is the IPv4 CIDR block of your VCN?** This determines the range of IP addresses across the subnets in this VCN.
- **What are the IPv4 CIDR blocks of each of your subnets?** This determines the range of IP addresses within your subnets.
- **What firewall access will you allow on each subnet?** This is controlled through security lists.

Creating a subnet is relatively straightforward:

Step 1. Within the VCN, click **Subnets** on the left; then click **Create Subnet**.

Step 2. Give a name to the subnet (such as appsubnet).

Step 3. Select whether the subnet will be Regional or Availability Domain-specific. Regional was introduced recently and is recommended so that the subnet can span multiple ADs.

Step 4. Provide an IPv4 CIDR block range that is contained in the VCN CIDR blocks (such as 192.0.1.0/24; this CIDR block is a subset of 192.0.0.0/16).

Step 5. Select a route table. This would have already been automatically created in your VCN earlier.

Step 6. Select the subnet access: Private Subnet or Public Subnet. A public subnet allows public IP addresses in it.

Step 7. Select a route table. This would have already been automatically created in your VCN earlier.

Step 8. Click **Create Subnet**.

Now that your VCN and a subnet have been created, when you create a resource such as a compute instance, during the provisioning process you can select for these resources to reside in this VCN and subnet. Figure 5-4 shows a snippet of the networking options under the compute instance creation page.

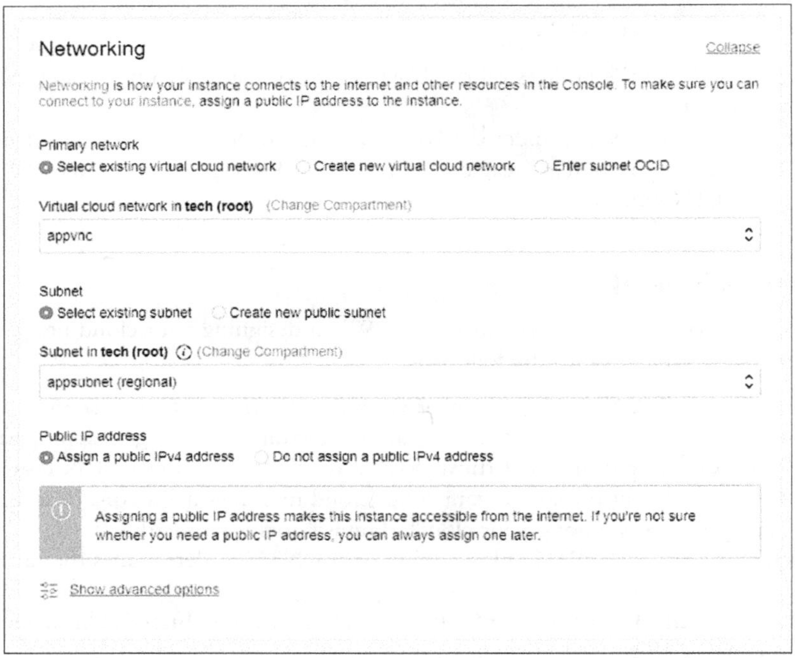

Figure 5-4   Selecting the Network During the Creation of a Compute Instance

You cannot move a compute instance from one subnet to another. Some creative approaches exist though. It is possible for some instance shapes that support multiple VNICs to add a VNIC in the new subnet and detach the old one, but the private and/ or public IP addresses will change. Alternatively, you can create a custom image and launch a new instance from that image in the new subnet.

Updating the Security List

A *security list* is a set of virtual firewall rules for your VCN. You specify the source CIDR, which determines the range of the inbound source IP address. You specify a protocol: TCP or UDP. Finally, a destination port range, though optional, is recommended. The rule would essentially allow traffic to the designated port in your subnet from the source IP range.

A security rule can be *stateful* or *stateless*. Stateful is the common option, and it is intended for high-volume externally facing websites. Stateless rules do not inspect traffic, otherwise referred to as *connection tracking*.

For example, Figure 5-5 shows the ingress rules after adding an inbound rule for port 443 from the public Internet.

Ingress Rules

Add Ingress Rules   Edit   Remove

	Stateless ▾	Source	IP Protocol	Source Port Range	Destination Port Range	Type and Code	Allows	Description	
☐	No	0.0.0.0/0	TCP	All	22		TCP traffic for ports: 22 SSH Remote Login Pr otocol		⋮
☐	No	0.0.0.0/0	ICMP			3, 4	ICMP traffic for: 3, 4 D estination Unreachabl e: Fragmentation Need ed and Don't Fragment was Set		⋮
☐	No	192.0.0.0/16	ICMP			3	ICMP traffic for: 3 Desti nation Unreachable		⋮
☐	No	0.0.0.0/0	TCP	All	443		TCP traffic for ports: 44 3 HTTPS	Allow public access to p ort 443	⋮
☐	No	0.0.0.0/0	ICMP			8	ICMP traffic for: 8 Echo	Allow ping from the publ ic Internet	⋮

0 Selected   Showing 5 Items   < 1 of 1 >

Figure 5-5   Adding an Ingress Rule for Port 443 and ping

The same figure shows another ICMP rule with type 8 added. By default, ping is disabled. This ICMP rule allows ping from the public Internet.

Connecting VCNs Through Local Peering

Consider the network architecture example in Figure 5-6. Here, we have two separate VCNs; each VCN has a single subnet and hosts the compute instances shown. For one VCN to communicate with another, we set up a *local peering gateway (LPG)*. An LPG is a virtual router that is added to each VCN to establish "peering" between the networks.

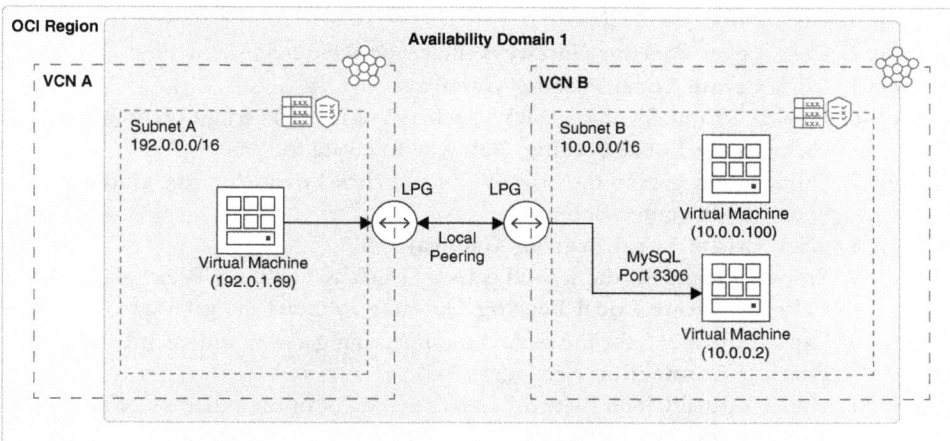

Figure 5-6   Target Network Architecture for Our Example

After you set up the LPG, it is possible to open the entire Subnet B to Subnet A. This is done by adding the appropriate rule under Subnet B's security list. However, as depicted in Figure 5-6, we specifically want only Subnet A to access the MySQL port 3306 on host (10.0.0.2) on Subnet B. Both security lists and *network security groups (NSGs)* allow you to define security rules to control inbound and outbound network traffic. Security lists apply to an entire subnet, but an NSG applies only to attached VNICs. Instead of opening up port 3306 to all compute instances in the entire subnet, you can restrict it to the VNICs attached to the NSG. The steps involve doing the following:

Step 1. Create an LPG on both VCNs. This is a virtual gateway.

Step 2. Establish peering between both LPGs so that both networks are now connected.

Step 3. Add a route rule to both VCNs, which allows routing between the two networks.

Step 4. Create an NSG on Subnet B and create a rule to allow ingress to port 3306.

Step 5. Attach the VNIC of the host (10.0.0.2) to the NSG.

After this setup, the virtual firewall now only allows hosts on Subnet A to access the target host on Subnet B.

Creating Local Peering Gateways and Establishing Peering

To achieve the target network architecture depicted in Figure 5-6, an LPG must be created on both VCNs. When creating the second VCN, you will establish "peering" with the other VCN. The order of creation of the LPGs makes no difference. The steps are as follows:

Step 1. Navigate to **Networking > Virtual Cloud Networks**.

Step 2. Identify the two VCNs from the VCNs listed in the table.

Step 3. Click one of the VCNs.

Step 4. Click **Local Peering Gateways** under the Resources submenu on the left.

Step 5. Click **Create Local Peering Gateway**.

Step 6. Provide a name for this gateway (such as Vcn1LocalPeeringGateway) and click **Create Local Peering Gateway** to create the gateway.

Step 7. Similarly, navigate to the other VCN and click **Local Peering Gateways** under the Resources submenu.

Step 8. Click **Create Local Peering Gateway**.

Step 9. Provide a name for the second gateway (such as Vcn2LocalPeeringGateway) and click **Create Local Peering Gateway** to create the gateway.

Step 10. Expand the menu for the second local peering gateway and click **Establish Peering Connection** (see Figure 5-7).

Step 11. Under Virtual Cloud Network, select the VCN of the other VCN in the drop-down menu.

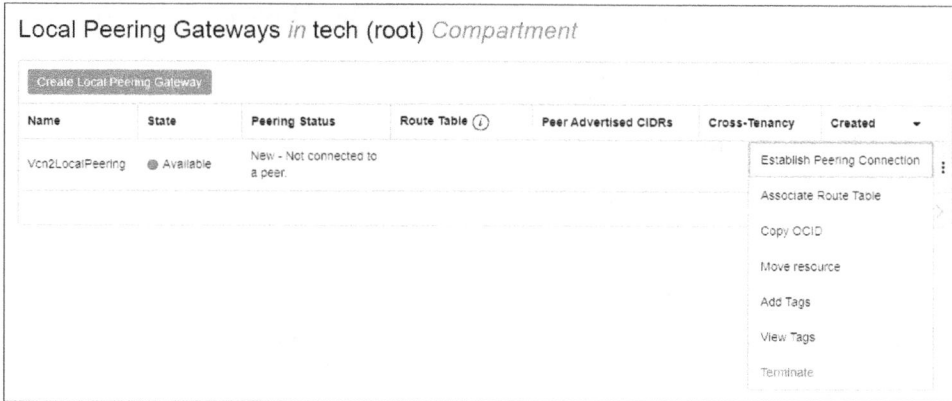

Figure 5-7   Establishing a Peering Connection Between Two VCNs

Step 12. Under Unpeered Peer Gateway, select the unpeered local gateway of the other gateway in the drop-down menu.

Step 13. After being redirected back to the main page, confirm that the Peering Status has changed from New – Not Connected to a Peer to Pending – Establishing a Connection to a Peer and finally Peered – Connected to a Peer.

You have now successfully connected two local VCNs in the same region. This does not mean that they can access each other yet, because new route rules need to be added and the firewall has not been open yet. We will walk through this process shortly.

If you want to connect your VCN to an on-premises network, a *dynamic routing gateway (DRG)* would be used instead. Connecting to a VCN in a different region requires a *remote peering connection (RPC)* added to a DRG instead of an LPG. OCI offers various gateways to support your network connectivity needs, and the setup is generally similar in concept. These gateways are listed in Table 5-2.

Adding a New Route Rule to the Route Table

After you create the local peering gateway, a new route rule is added to each VCN's route table. The steps are as follows:

Step 1. Navigate to **Networking > Virtual Cloud Networks**.

Step 2. Identify the two VCNs from the VCNs listed in the table.

Step 3. Click the target VCN.

Step 4. Click **Route Tables** under the Resources submenu on the left.

Step 5. Click the route table, which should already exist.

Step 6. Click **Add Route Rules**.

Step 7. On the Target Type drop-down, select **Local Peering Gateway**.

Step 8. In Destination CIDR Block, enter **192.0.0.0/16**, which is the CIDR of the other network.

Step 9. Under Target Local Peering Gateway, select **Vcn2LocalPeeringGateway**, which is the LPG on the other VCN.

Step 10. Click **Add Route Rules**.

Step 11. Similarly, click the source VCN.

Step 12. Click **Route Tables** under the Resources submenu on the left.

Step 13. Click the route table, which should already exist.

Step 14. Click **Add Route Rules**.

Step 15. On the Target Type drop-down, select **Local Peering Gateway**.

Step 16. In Destination CIDR Block, enter **10.0.0.0/16**, which is the CIDR of the target network.

Step 17. Under Target Local Peering Gateway, select **Vcn1LocalPeeringGateway**, which is the LPG on the other VCN.

Step 18. Click **Add Route Rules**.

The route tables on each of the VCNs have now been configured to route two-way traffic to the respective target networks.

Creating Network Security Groups (NSGs)

An NSG is not required when setting up local peering. An NSG can be used for any type of communication but is demonstrated here to set up the access defined in Figure 5-6. Here, we will create an NSG on the target VCN to restrict access to MySQL port 3306 to connections initiating from the source network (it would not even allow access from other hosts from its same subnet). The steps are as follows:

Step 1. Navigate to **Networking > Virtual Cloud Networks**.

Step 2. Click the VCN that is running the host with a MySQL database (see virtual machine 10.0.0.2 in Figure 5-6).

Step 3. Click **Network Security Groups** under the Resources submenu on the left.

Step 4. Click **Create Network Security Group**.

Step 5. Provide a name (such as DbNetworkSecurityGroup) and click **Next**.

Step 6. Set up an ingress rule to TCP destination port 3306 from the other VCN's CIDR (192.0.0.0/16); then click **Create** (see Figure 5-8).

At this point, the two networks are connected, with the source network allowed inbound access to port 3306 on the target network. However, we have not yet defined which hosts (specifically VNICs) are attached to this newly set up NSG on the target network. The next subsection covers this process.

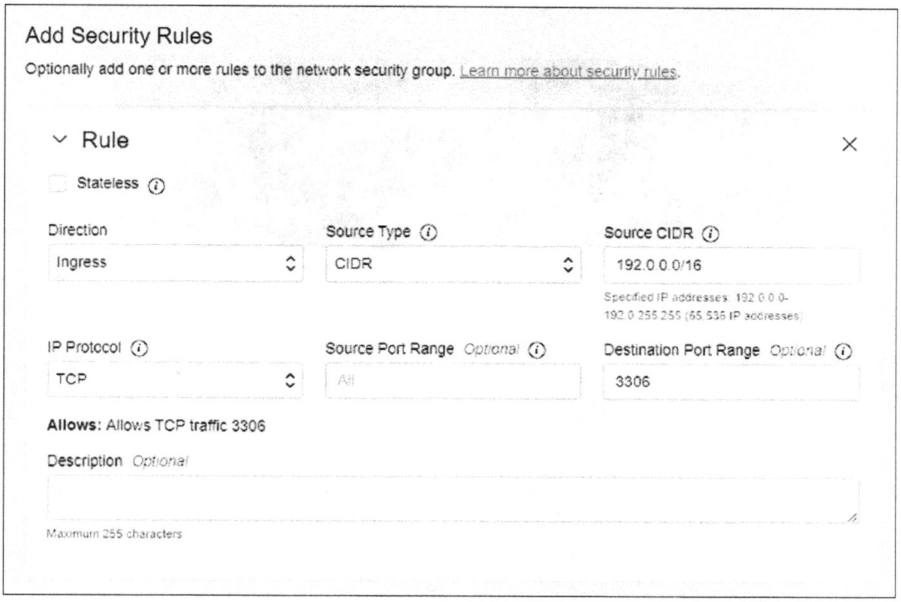

Figure 5-8   Adding an Ingress Security Rule for MySQL Port 3306 to an NSG

Attaching VNIC to the Network Security Group

On the target subnet, you will attach the VNIC of the target host to the newly created NSG, effectively allowing inbound access from the source subnet to port 3306. The steps are as follows:

Step 1. Navigate to **Compute > Instances**.

Step 2. Click the instance running the MySQL database (with IP address 10.0.0.2 as per Figure 5-6).

Step 3. Under the heading Primary VNIC and under Network Security Groups, click **Edit**.

Step 4. From the drop-down, select the NSG (that is, DbNetworkSecurityGroup) and click **Save Changes**.

Step 5. Confirm that the NSG is configured correctly.

The target host is now attached to its respective network security group in its respective VCN. A simple **netcat (-v Verbose - information on incoming network connections)** command from the source host to the target host confirms successful connectivity, as demonstrated in Figure 5-9.

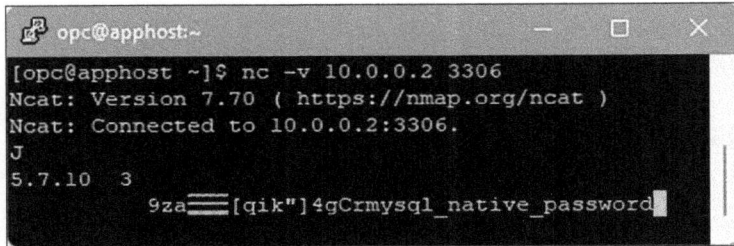

Figure 5-9   Testing the Connection from Different VCNs

Creating Flow Logs

If you create a resource and connectivity to this resource is not working as expected, this is where *flow logs* can be helpful. Flow logs provide a mechanism to troubleshoot security lists or view the traffic to and from your VNICs.

Creating a flow log for your network requires taking advantage of the logging features under Observability and Management as follows:

Step 1. Navigate to **Observability & Management > Logs**.
Step 2. Click **Enable Service Log**.
Step 3. Under Service, select **Virtual Cloud Network – Subnets**.
Step 4. Under Resource, select your subnet.
Step 5. Under Log Category, select **Flow Logs – All Records**.
Step 6. Under Log Name, give a name to the log (such as appsubnet_flowlog).
Step 7. Under Log Group, select a log group (create one if one does not exist).
Step 8. Click **Enable Log**.

Under the logging service, you will find a new log name, as shown in Figure 5-10.

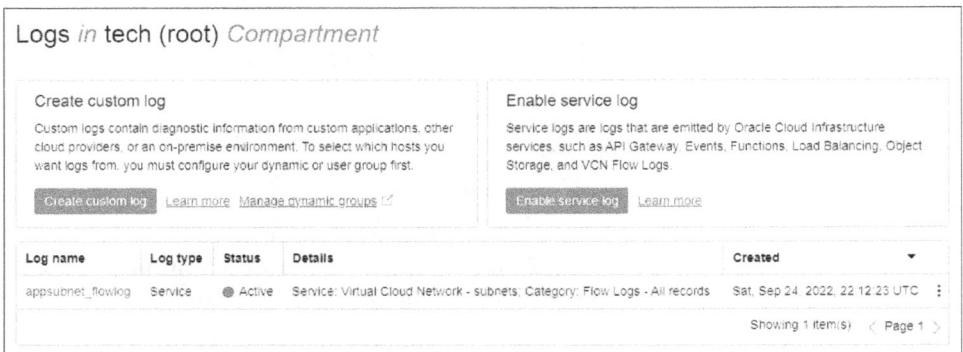

Figure 5-10   Viewing a List of Logs

Click this newly created log name; then click **Explore with Log Search**. Customize the search criteria and click **Search**. Under the Actions button, you can customize the fields to display or even visualize them. Figure 5-11 shows an example of the output of this flow log search operation.

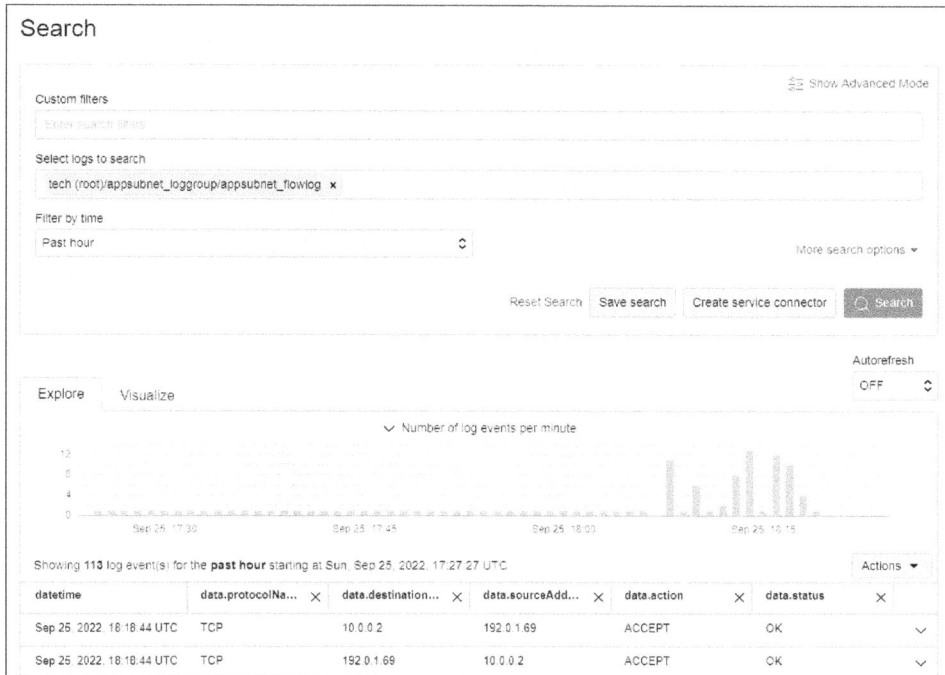

Figure 5-11   Searching Through the Flow Logs

Here, you can see typical firewall logging information, such as source and destination IPs, status, port, protocol, and bytes.

Using Network Path Analyzer

A common challenge most cloud practitioners run into when setting up or expanding their cloud infrastructure is connectivity issues. When a source system cannot connect to a target system, is the problem a rule missing in a security list or a service issue? Is it the local firewall at the OS level or a missing gateway configuration? This is where the *Network Path Analyzer (NPA)*, a component under the *Network Command Center*, comes in handy.

On the console, navigate to **Networking > Network Path Analyzer**. Here, you can create an analysis of your network path. Figure 5-12 shows the configuration page for creating the path analysis. It is as simple as entering the source and target IP addresses, protocol, and target port.

Figure 5-12   Running a Path Analysis on the Network Using NPA

Clicking Run Analysis returns the results of this analysis, as shown in Figure 5-13. This figure depicts an unsuccessful path, but more importantly, it highlights where the blockage is. As you can see in the figure, the traffic was successful up until it was denied by the security list and the network security group listed (because neither had a security rule allowing for ingress TCP port 1521). The NPA is an extremely handy tool and is often used in conjunction with flow logs to troubleshoot and audit network connectivity.

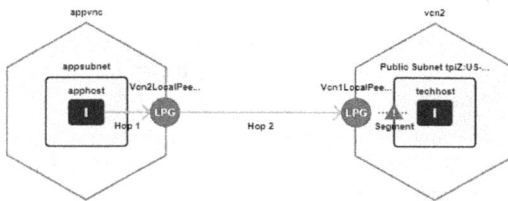

Figure 5-13   Reviewing the Results of the NPA Path Analysis

Understanding Gateways

Earlier in this chapter, we demonstrated the use of the local peering gateway to connect two separate VCNs. OCI offers a number of other gateways and gateway services, each serving a different purpose. Table 5-2 lists these network gateways and their function.

Table 5-2   OCI Network Gateways

Gateway Type	Purpose
Local Peering Gateway (LPG)	A virtual router added to a VCN to let one VCN communicate with another without traversing the Internet. Each VCN requires its own LPG.
Dynamic Routing Gateway (DRG)	A virtual router added to a VCN to connect it to an on-premises network via VPN or OCI FastConnect. It can also be used to establish a high-throughput, low-latency, private interconnection with Microsoft Azure.
Remote Peering Connection (RPC)	A connection added to a DRG to allow peering of VCNs in different regions.
Network Address Translation (NAT) Gateway	A virtual router that allows private IP addresses in your VCN access to the Internet.
Service Gateway	A virtual router added to a VCN to allow access from a VCN to other OCI services such as Object Storage.

Securing Your Network

Network security is a vast topic and requires continuous review and revision as your cloud network expands. As you progress on your cloud networking journey, consider the following areas to improve your network security posture:

- Subnet configuration, whether public or private
- Security rules (defined in security lists or network security groups)
- Firewall rules at the compute instance level
- Gateways to manage connectivity to external networks
- Route tables to control and appropriately route traffic to other networks
- IAM policies to restrict access to OCI network management
- Security zones, a function of Oracle Cloud Guard, that include policies (called *security zone recipes*) at the compartment level to ensure compliance with the Oracle maximum security architecture and best practices

Summary

OCI networking is a vast topic, and this chapter introduced the steps involved in setting up and connecting to your first cloud networks. VCNs and subnets are the foundation of your network. Security lists and network security groups provide firewall-like capabilities. The various virtual gateways provided by OCI allow you to connect to other external networks, inside OCI or outside of it.

OCI provides an extensive list of network features and capabilities that cover all aspects of cloud network management and include support for IPv6, DHCP, DNS, VPN, BYOIP (Bring Your Own IP), redundancy, monitoring, performance, and much more.

In the next chapter, you will learn more about compute instances.

6

Oracle IaaS—Compute

Compute is often the heart of any Infrastructure as a Service (IaaS) offering because it is the engine that processes the data. This concept initially sounds simple, but DevSecOps teams need to consider several nuances, other than the basics of building virtual machines (VMs) using compute. These considerations include what CPU architecture to use, what billing model to use, and even where to get the operating system.

In this chapter, we will cover the different compute options available on OCI, from bare metal to virtualized systems, as well as the many CPU manufacturers and families available. Additionally, we will cover different options for consuming compute, along with how to manage virtual images for customer OS images that are available in the OCI Marketplace or managed by the DevSecOps team.

Building a VM

Before we drill down into more details of using a virtual machine, let's start with the basic task of creating a machine in OCI. From the OCI console, navigate to the main menu and select **Compute > Instances**. From this page (shown in Figure 6-1), you can see what systems have been created and whether they are running. You can also see any VMs that were recently terminated (deleted).

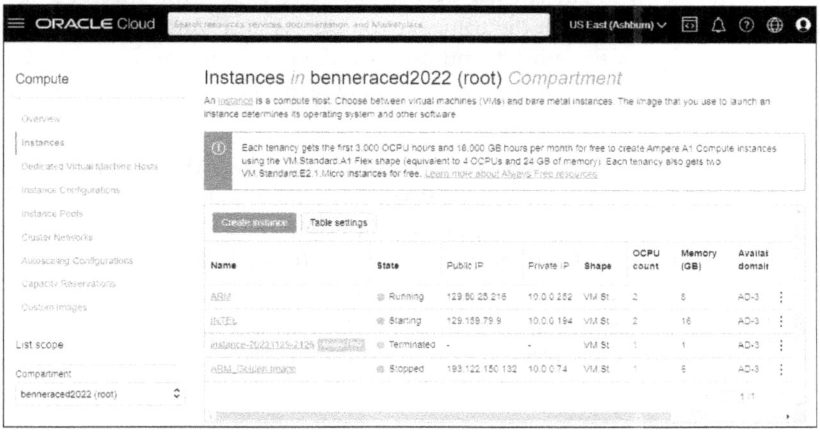

Figure 6-1 Compute Instances

There are also several other options in the Compute menu:

- **Overview:** This page links to the main Compute page, showing the overall CPU and memory utilization, as well as a summary of instances and their states.
- **Instances:** This page shows a list of instances, if they're active, shut down, or terminated.
- **Dedicated Virtual Machine Hosts:** There are bare metal systems that can run virtual machines. This page allows you to guarantee that your VMs are not hosted on shared physical servers with other customers. This way, the team can control what other VMs might compete for resources on the same physical host. It also helps improve security, by guaranteeing that no hostile VMs are running on the same hypervisor, just in case there is a security issue with the isolation within the hypervisor.
- **Instance Configurations:** Using these configurations, you can manage templates that define settings used when creating an instance. This includes the shape, operating system network settings, SSH keys, storage, and the like. This page is useful for the DevSecOps team to standardize on common settings.
- **Instance Pools:** This is where a pool is managed. A pool is a group of instances running behind a shared load balancer. This page helps to scale horizontally.
- **Cluster Networks:** Cluster networks are used for HPC workloads and shapes. These are very low latency high-bandwidth networks.
- **Autoscaling Configurations:** Autoscaling configuration drives the number of running instances in an instance pool. You can configure scale-out and scale-in rules to have the appropriate number of application servers for your current workload. This option helps align costs with workload.
- **Capacity Reservations:** This page is where capacity reservations are managed. It enables you to reserve computer capacity without running the instances. This option offers a small cost savings versus running the reserved compute all the time.
- **Custom Images:** This page is where custom images can be managed.

Next, to build a new instance, click **Create Instance** to start the wizard. This wizard process is lengthy and starts with the name, as you can see in Figure 6-2.

From this first page of the wizard, you can pick the compartment for the VM and its name. Additionally, there are five sections that allow you to modify the instance to meet your needs:

- **Placement:** Here, you can pick the availability domain (AD) and the fault domain (FD). Normally, it is recommended that you let OCI pick the FD. Think of the AD as an isolated group of racks in the region and the FD as a subset of servers that are isolated. AD allows for high availability (HA), and FD allows you to keep both nodes in a cluster or load balancer group from being on the same server or a related single point of failure. Not all regions have multiple ADs, but all ADs have multiple FDs. A sample placement is shown in Figure 6-3.

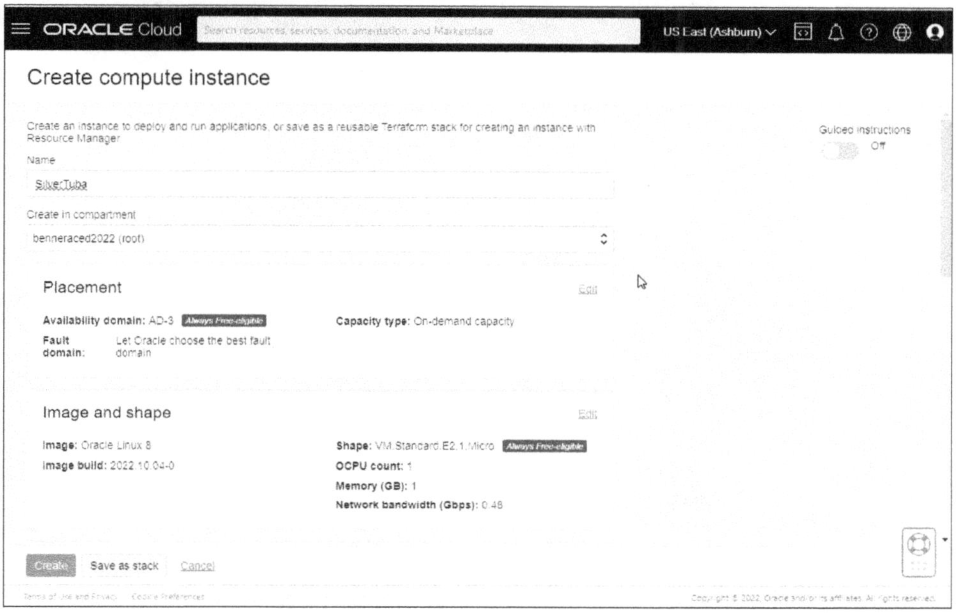

Figure 6-2   Instance Configuration

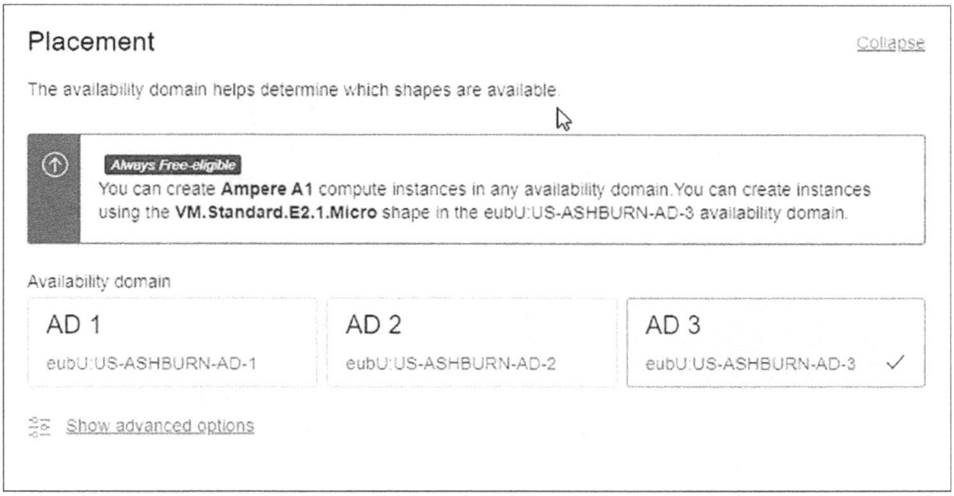

Figure 6-3   Image Placement

- **Image and Shape:** Here, you can pick the CPU, instance size, and OS. An image shape can also be a bare metal server, where you have an entire server dedicated to you. Figure 6-4 shows a basic configuration.

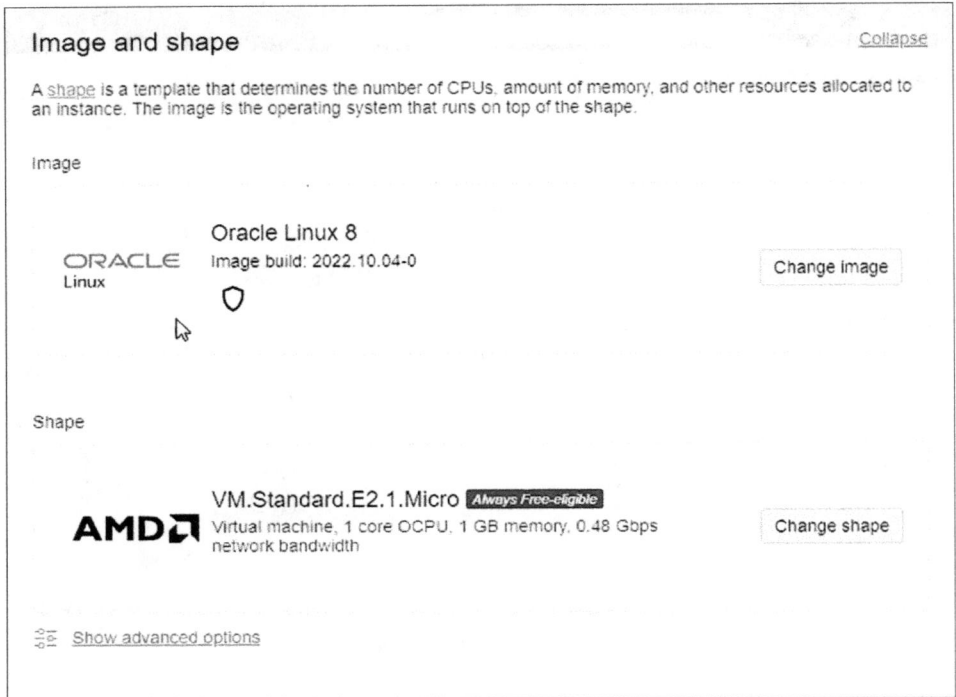

Figure 6-4   Image and Shape

- **Networking:** Here, you can assign the correct network to the instance. This includes both public and private networks, as well as a public IPv4 address. This is an Internet-facing IP address that is NATed to the instance on a one-to-one IP address, so the Internet IP also NATs to the IP on the compute VM. While this approach adds security functionality, the VM will not show the publicly visible IP address on the server. Figure 6-5 shows a sample configuration.
- **Add SSH Keys:** Here, you can either upload or create an SSH key for the instance. Figure 6-6 shows that a public SSH key was uploaded to be used by the system. New systems using Oracle Linux images use SSH and the user named opc to access the operating system.
- **Boot Volume:** Here, you can edit the size and security of the boot volume. The default boot volume is 50 GB, using balanced storage performance. The default is shown in Figure 6-7.

After you have set your options, click the **Create** button. This will start a job that will create the instance. After the instance is created, you can see its IP address. Both the Internet and private IP address are highlighted in Figure 6-8.

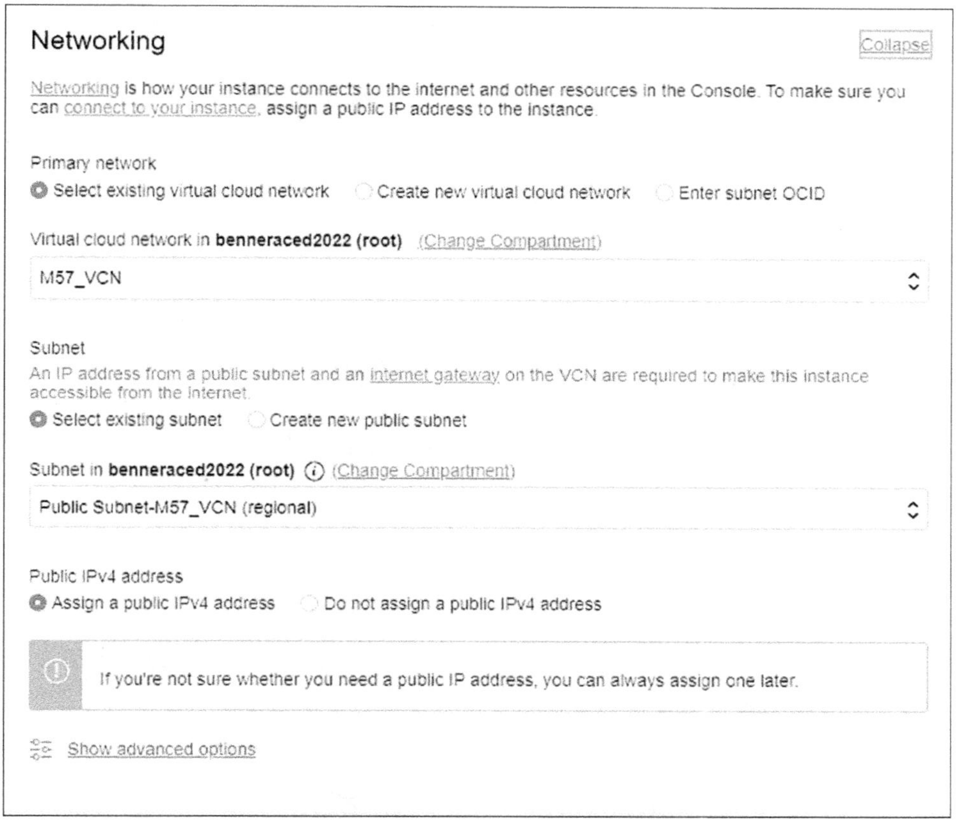

Networking

Collapse

Networking is how your instance connects to the internet and other resources in the Console. To make sure you can connect to your instance, assign a public IP address to the instance.

Primary network
- ⦿ Select existing virtual cloud network   ◯ Create new virtual cloud network   ◯ Enter subnet OCID

Virtual cloud network in **benneraced2022 (root)**   (Change Compartment)

| M57_VCN | ⌄ |

Subnet
An IP address from a public subnet and an internet gateway on the VCN are required to make this instance accessible from the internet.
- ⦿ Select existing subnet   ◯ Create new public subnet

Subnet in **benneraced2022 (root)** � (Change Compartment)

| Public Subnet-M57_VCN (regional) | ⌄ |

Public IPv4 address
- ⦿ Assign a public IPv4 address   ◯ Do not assign a public IPv4 address

> ⓘ   If you're not sure whether you need a public IP address, you can always assign one later.

Show advanced options

Figure 6-5   Image Networking

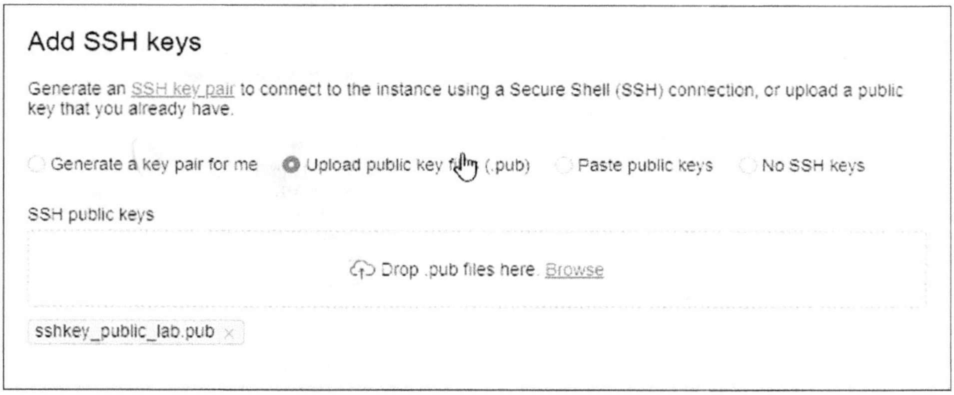

Add SSH keys

Generate an SSH key pair to connect to the instance using a Secure Shell (SSH) connection, or upload a public key that you already have.

◯ Generate a key pair for me   ⦿ Upload public key file (.pub)   ◯ Paste public keys   ◯ No SSH keys

SSH public keys

> ⌂ Drop .pub files here. Browse

sshkey_public_lab.pub ×

Figure 6-6   Image SSH Keys

Boot volume

A boot volume is a detachable device that contains the image used to boot the compute instance.

☐ Specify a custom boot volume size

Volume performance varies with volume size. Default boot volume size: 46.6 GB. When you specify a custom boot volume size, service limits apply.

☐ Use in-transit encryption

Encrypts data in transit between the instance, the boot volume, and the block volumes

☐ Encrypt this volume with a key that you manage

By default, Oracle manages the keys that encrypt this volume, but you can choose a key from a vault that you have access to if you want greater control over the key's lifecycle and how it's used. How do I manage my own encryption keys?

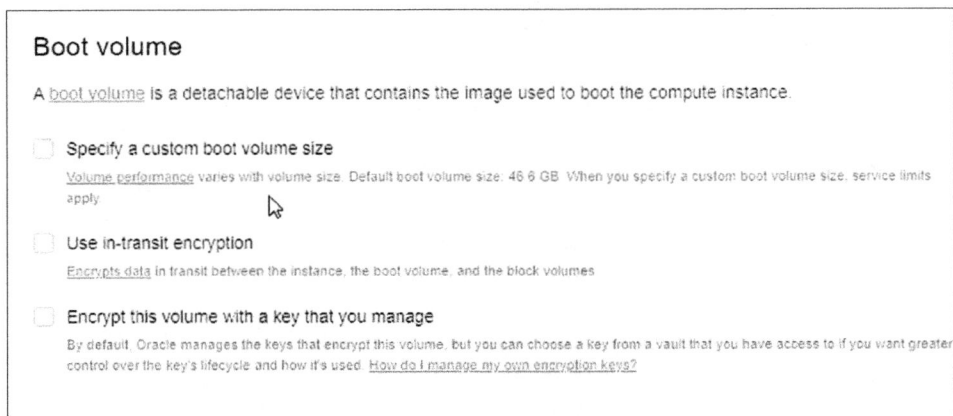

Figure 6-7 Boot Options

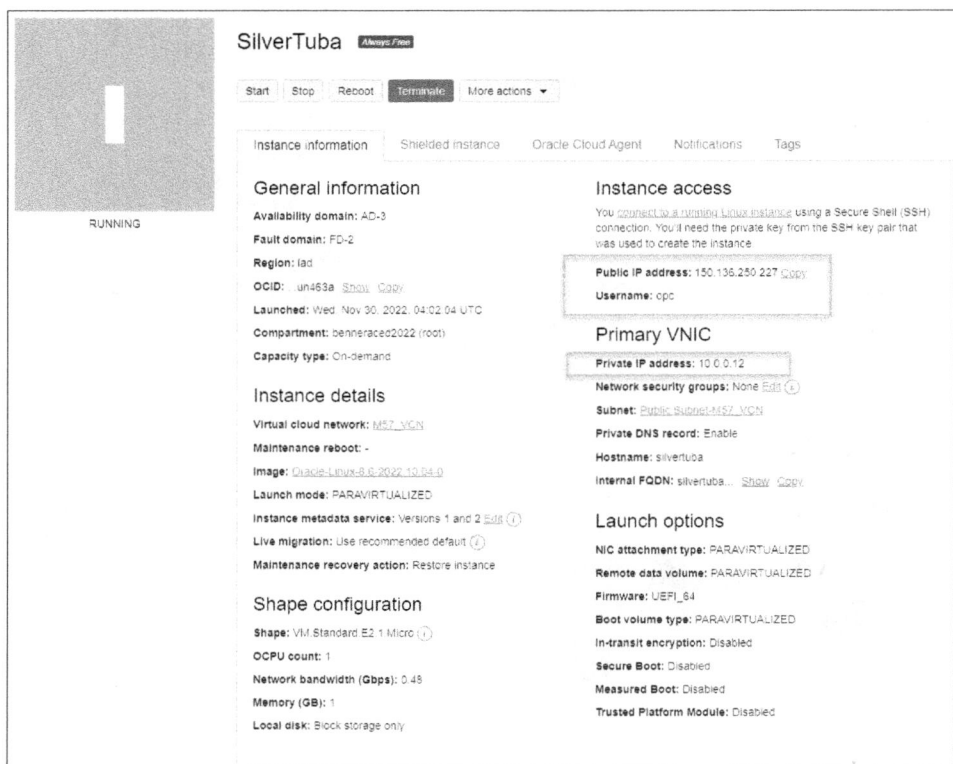

SilverTuba Always Free

Start Stop Reboot Terminate More actions ▼

Instance information Shielded instance Oracle Cloud Agent Notifications Tags

RUNNING

General information

Availability domain: AD-3
Fault domain: FD-2
Region: iad
OCID: ...un463a Show Copy
Launched: Wed, Nov 30, 2022, 04:02:04 UTC
Compartment: benneraced2022 (root)
Capacity type: On-demand

Instance details

Virtual cloud network: M57_VCN
Maintenance reboot: -
Image: Oracle-Linux-8.6-2022.10.04-0
Launch mode: PARAVIRTUALIZED
Instance metadata service: Versions 1 and 2 Edit ⓘ
Live migration: Use recommended default ⓘ
Maintenance recovery action: Restore instance

Shape configuration

Shape: VM.Standard.E2.1.Micro ⓘ
OCPU count: 1
Network bandwidth (Gbps): 0.48
Memory (GB): 1
Local disk: Block storage only

Instance access

You connect to a running Linux instance using a Secure Shell (SSH) connection. You'll need the private key from the SSH key pair that was used to create the instance.

Public IP address: 150.136.250.227 Copy
Username: opc

Primary VNIC

Private IP address: 10.0.0.12
Network security groups: None Edit ⓘ
Subnet: Public Subnet-M57_VCN
Private DNS record: Enable
Hostname: silvertuba
Internal FQDN: silvertuba... Show Copy

Launch options

NIC attachment type: PARAVIRTUALIZED
Remote data volume: PARAVIRTUALIZED
Firmware: UEFI_64
Boot volume type: PARAVIRTUALIZED
In-transit encryption: Disabled
Secure Boot: Disabled
Measured Boot: Disabled
Trusted Platform Module: Disabled

Figure 6-8 Instance Created

Next, let's drill down into the options in more detail.

X86 and ARM, AMD vs. Intel... What's the Scoop?

In DevSecOps, it is important for both the developers and operators to understand the difference in compute architectures. Not only does this improve the performance of the application, but it also can reduce costs and in some cases also reduce the possible security threat surface.

When cloud first became mainstream, there was generally only a single choice for the CPU, and that was Intel. Yes, there are different CPU families within Intel, but the market was dominated by that CPU technology and the x64 architecture. The x64 architecture included all of the 64-bit Intel processors, as well as the Advanced Micro Devices (AMD) processors, where the 64-bit processing mode was developed way back in 2000. The x64 mode allowed for 32-bit software to run on the same 64-bit CPU, enabling the industry to have a mostly smooth transition to a 64-bit CPU. When AMD launched x86 (also known as AMD64), it was mainly seen as a desktop technology company, with a focus on lower-cost, lower-performing CPUs.

The Intel Xeon family of processors was more powerful and dominated the server marketspace. This situation changed in 2017 when ADM announced its Epyc (pronounced *epic*) CPU, focused on the server market. This newer Epyc CPU was based on a new chiplet design that made design and manufacturing more reliable and less complicated. A chiplet is a small subset of integrated circuits that can easily be combined on the CPU. Think building blocks to build an entire CPU, allowing one block to be I/O control, one block for the processing core, one block for memory management, and so on. This new design allowed AMD to offer a lower-cost but high-performing CPU that competed with the Intel Xeon family of chips.

Intel countered, with some cost adjustments, and a CPU battle started, for dominance in the cloud. This battle benefits cloud customers, due to the competitive nature, with Intel and AMD leapfrogging each other generation after generation of tech. At the current time, the fourth-generation Epyc CPU is commonly seen as faster and lower cost for CPU-intensive workloads. Intel is still a great option, especially because workloads can take advantage of Intel-specific acceleration logic for machine learning and artificial intelligence workloads. Both Intel and AMD systems provide good performance for both integer and floating-point operations.

Then a little company called Ampere entered the market, with a new CPU specifically designed for cloud workloads based on the ARM architecture. ARM used to be an acronym for Advanced RISC Machines, but has since become its own term for a family of Reduced Instruction Set Computer (RISC)–based CPUs. Initially, ARM CPUs were seen in embedded devices like cellphones and Internet of Things (IoT) devices like thermometers. This changed radically with Ampere, which produced a data center scaled-up ARM processor, called the Ampere Altra, known as the *A1 compute* in OCI. These CPUs offer cloud service provider (CSP) systems with low power consumption and high-density compute. At cloud scale, imagine a single rack of x64 servers, consuming 12.5 kW of power supporting 2240 x64 cores running at 2.2 GHz. With the Ampere Altra, that same rack can support 3200 cores running at

2.6 GHz, a 44 percent improvement. This improvement directly translates to lower cost for the ARM-based servers in the cloud. Ampere then released the AmpereOne CPU, significantly increasing the memory throughput, core density, and real-world performance. Benchmarks with AmpereOne can be deceiving, though, but in real-world applications like AI, Java, and web services, it is faster than the previous generation.

This capability sounds too good to be true, so many ask, Is there a downside to ARM? The answer is *kinda*. First, the ARM processor is single threaded; there is no hyperthreading as there is in the x86 platform. This single threading can be both good and bad. Single-threaded processes run very well with ARM and can outperform an x86 system, but a process that uses many threads will need more cores. ARM historically also has slower floating-point and memory operations, though recent improvements from companies like Ampere are slowly changing that. The good news is that with OCI the rate of A1 is currently $.01 per core per hour, whereas Intel starts at $.04 per core per hour.

We also need to mention what an OCPU is. OCPU, also known as Oracle Compute Processing Unit, is a single core on the processor allocated to the VM. It is the full core, including any threads that may be native to the architecture. So the x64 CPUs each have two threads, whereas an OCPU is one core with two threads. Other CSPs use the virtual CPU (vCPU) metric, where the VCPU is *kinda* a thread. The description *kinda* is very accurate here because a VCPU is not always a thread but is a metric of compute native to the CSP that sold the VM. Understanding this distinction is important, because it shows the importance of reading the fine print with your CSP. Keep in mind that eight VCPUs does not always mean eight threads and four full cores. It can mean something much smaller.

An additional challenge to understand with ARM is the availability of an operating system and additional software. If you leverage a modern operating system like Oracle Linux, then you have the same experience across ARM and the x64 processors. This includes technologies like Java, Nginx, Docker, PHP, Python, and Apache that are all native to the Linux distribution. That being said, not all Linux distributions have an ARM build, and Microsoft has yet to release its upcoming ARM versions of Windows and its related software. Since there are several Linux options, the real challenge becomes with third-party software that is not compiled for the ARM platform.

All of these factors considered, ARM is rapidly increasing in popularity, so many independent software vendors (ISVs) are starting to make their applications available on ARM. One example is Oracle Java, which is available for x64 and ARM. With Java applications, it really doesn't matter if Java is running on x64 or ARM. Applications written for Java should run fine on either platform. The same is true for applications running on Python, PHP, Perl, and so on.

Let's compare these platforms using sysbench, a performance benchmarking tool built into Oracle Linux. Each platform will be compared for two and eight threads, or two ARM cores and one x86 core versus eight ARM cores or four x64 cores.

Each OCPU grants the VM 1 Gbps of network bandwidth per interface, with a maximum of 40 Gbps throughput per interface for A1 and AMD CPUs. Intel standard VMs max out at 32 Gbps per interface. Intel also offers optimized instances that offer 4 Gbps per OCPU for bandwidth with a maximum of 40 Gbps per interface.

Baseline CPU and memory throughput will be compared. ARM has only a single thread, compared using the total thread count, instead of the core counts. In Table 6-1, the sysbench tool was used to calculate the maximum number of events that could be run in 10 seconds for CPU performance. For memory, the total amounts of MiB transferred through RAM in 10 seconds were compared. All results are an average of five runs on the same day.

Table 6-1 CPU Performance

Compute	Arch	OS Procs	Events	Memory MiB/s	RAM (GB)	Hourly Rate
A1	arm	2	68691	5484	16	$0.04
A2	arm	2	15733	4667	16	$0.06
AMD E4	x64	2	40809	7096	16	$0.07
AMD E5	x64	2	46775	9356	16	$0.09
Intel	x64	2	29578	6366	16	$0.10
A1	arm	8	278082	7438	64	$0.18
A2	arm	8	63024	12691	64	$0.24
AMD E4	x64	8	164078	7266	64	$0.30
AMD E5	x64	8	186979	7951	64	$0.37
Intel	x64	8	117837	9738	64	$0.42

As you can see, there is a fair amount of difference between each CPU architecture and how they scale. This can also be seen with the difference between A1 and A2, as the A2 is not optimized for floating-point operations but can excel at workloads that are not floating-point heavy, like NGINX servers or most Java applications. There is no single right choice, and OCI gives the DevSecOps team the option to pick the right CPU with the right amount of RAM to meet the unique needs of the application.

Note: No Proprietary CPUs

One really great advantage of Oracle's computing choices is that all of the CPU options are available not only in the cloud but also in other clouds and on-premises servers. You are not locked into a specific CPU that is only available on OCI. This way, you can develop in the cloud and deploy on the same CPU on-premises if you need to.

A VM Is More Than a VM; There Are Options...

The DevSecOps team needs to be aware of differences with OCI's compute offering. How you provision CPU and memory to VMs is also very different when compared to other CSPs. With most other CSPs, different amounts of CPU and RAM are bundled together and sold. This is often called a *shape*, and this bundling of fixed amounts brings challenges to the DevSecOps team. One challenge is in efficiency, because most applications do note the ratio of CPU to memory that the CSP offers. You could have an application that is memory intensive but CPU light, like a Java-based content management system or an in-memory accelerated database. The opposite could also be true, with an application that is CPU heavy and memory light. With the other major CSPs, you have to buy your VM shape based on the combined CPU/memory requirements. Let's say your CSP offers two choices: SHAPE-A with four threads and 8 GB of RAM and SHAPE-B with eight threads and 16 GB of RAM. Now look at your application that is currently using two threads and 10 GB of RAM. As an architect, you likely would pick SHAPE-B because it has the required RAM and more CPU than is required. The problem now is that your application would be paying for six threads more than is required and 6 GB of RAM that is not required. This is very inefficient…leading to higher cloud costs.

OCI changes this arrangement by allowing you to use what are called Flex shapes, which enable you to pick the OCPU count and the RAM separately. With this Flex model, you can provision the six threads and 10 GB of RAM, exactly what your application needs. This way, not only are your costs in alignment with the application's needs, but you also have a smaller footprint, reducing the expense and environmental impact of using the inefficient SHAPE-B option. Additionally, CPU and RAM can be individually adjusted as the needs of the application change, allowing for a more agile deployment while keeping costs manageable.

To see this in the console, navigate to the main menu and select **Compute > Instances > Instance Details** for a VM, and then go to **More Actions** and click **Edit**, as shown in Figure 6-9.

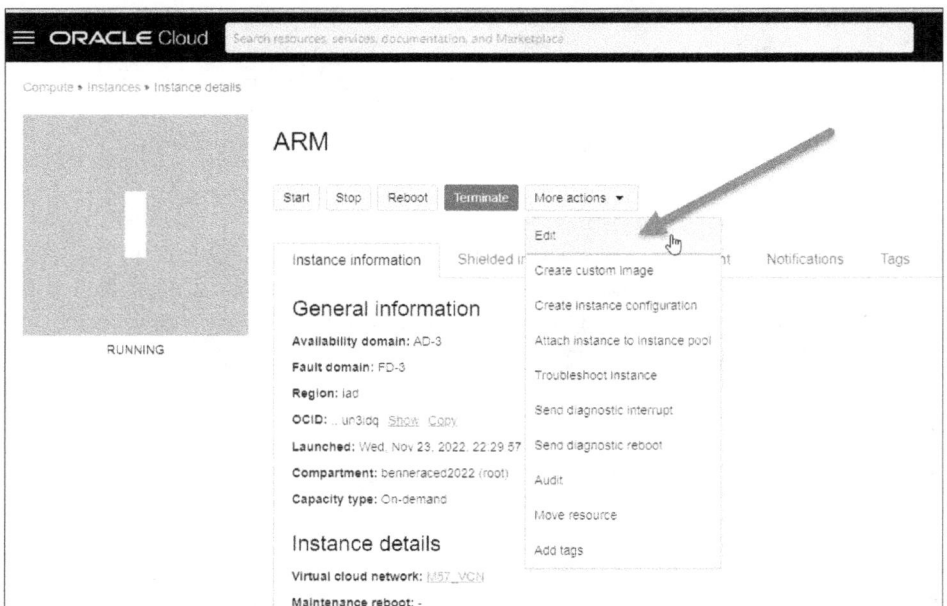

Figure 6-9   Edit VM

From here, click **Edit Shape** in the Shape Summary section, shown in Figure 6-10.

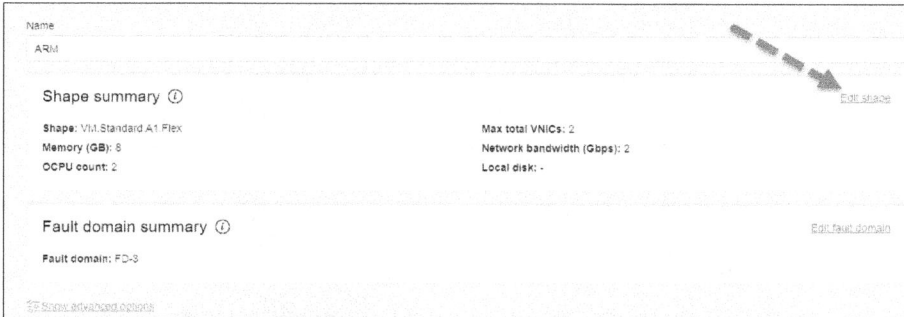

Figure 6-10   Edit Shape

From here, you will see the shape and its details. You can also expand the small arrow on the right side, as shown in Figure 6-11, to expand the CPU/Memory allocation option.

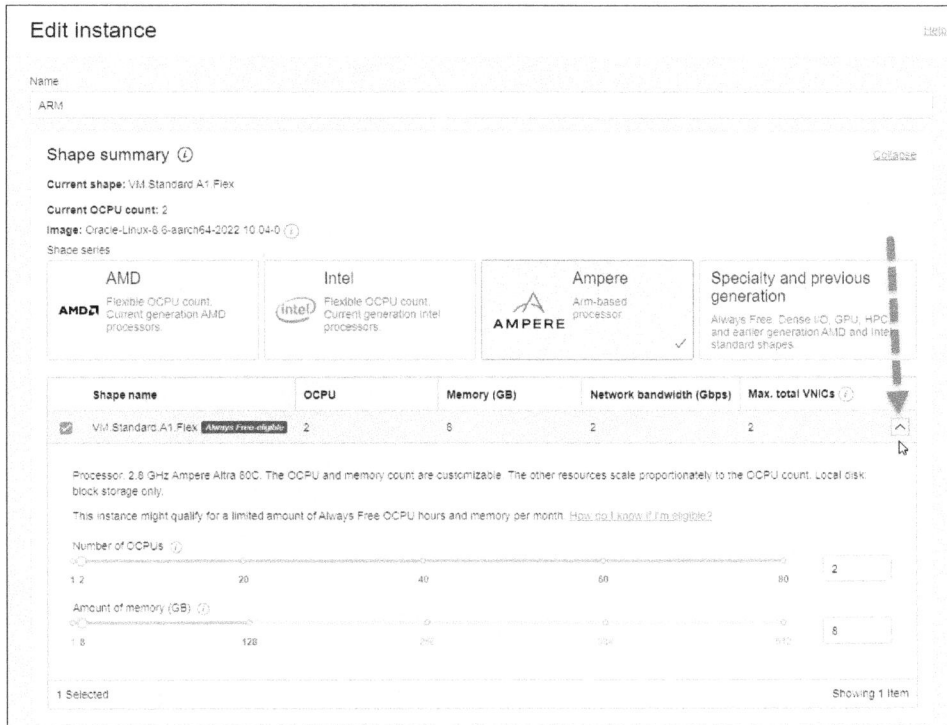

Figure 6-11   Edit Instance

Once you have expanded the OCPU and RAM sliders, you can easily change the CPU and memory separately. You can also click the number in the box on the right and change the allocated number manually. Not only can you change the OCPU/memory, but on many VMs, you can also move to other products. An example is moving a VM from Intel FLEX to AMD FLEX, or selecting a specialty shape under the Specialty and Previous Generation box. If the shapes are not compatible, you will get an error message, and no changes will happen. An example of an incompatible change is moving an AMD VM to an ARM shape.

When provisioning a VM, the DevSecOps team needs to be aware of some additional capacity options. When creating a VM, in the Placement section, click **Show Advanced Options** to see the options shown in Figure 6-12.

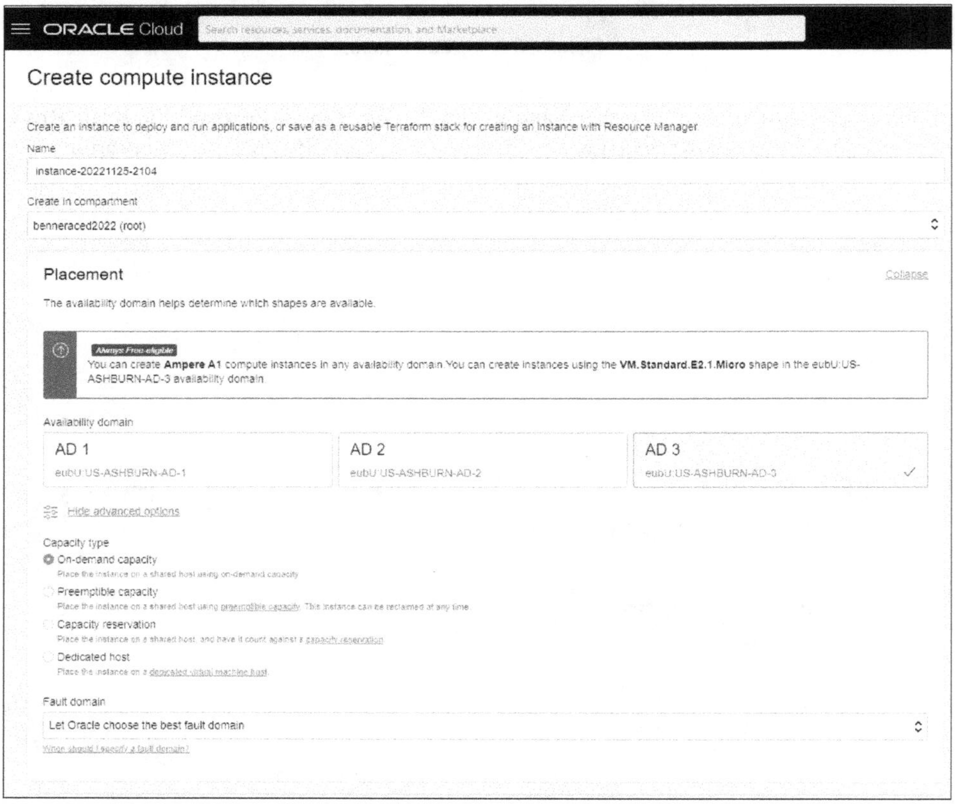

Figure 6-12   Advanced Options

Four capacity-type options are available to the team:

- **On-Demand Capacity:** This is the default behavior.
- **Preemptible Capacity:** These instances can be deleted by OCI at any time. This does come with a significant price savings to the customer, currently 50 percent of

the normal price. This option is useful for workloads that are short term in nature or that can scale easily, like HPC.

- **Capacity Reservation:** This option holds the capacity in OCI without actually starting the VM. It is useful for guaranteed availability of resources for disaster recovery, or unplanned growth where the capacity needs to be available instantly. This reservation is currently billed at 85 percent of the normal rate.
- **Dedicated Host:** This option enables you to run the VM on a host dedicated to your tenancy. To use this option, you first must provision a dedicated virtual host. Billing is based on the size and number of dedicated virtual host machines, plus any additional costs for marketplace images or Windows OS.

From a security side, there are also several options for the DevSecOps team. They are found under the advanced options under the Image and Shape section and can been seen at the bottom of Figure 6-13.

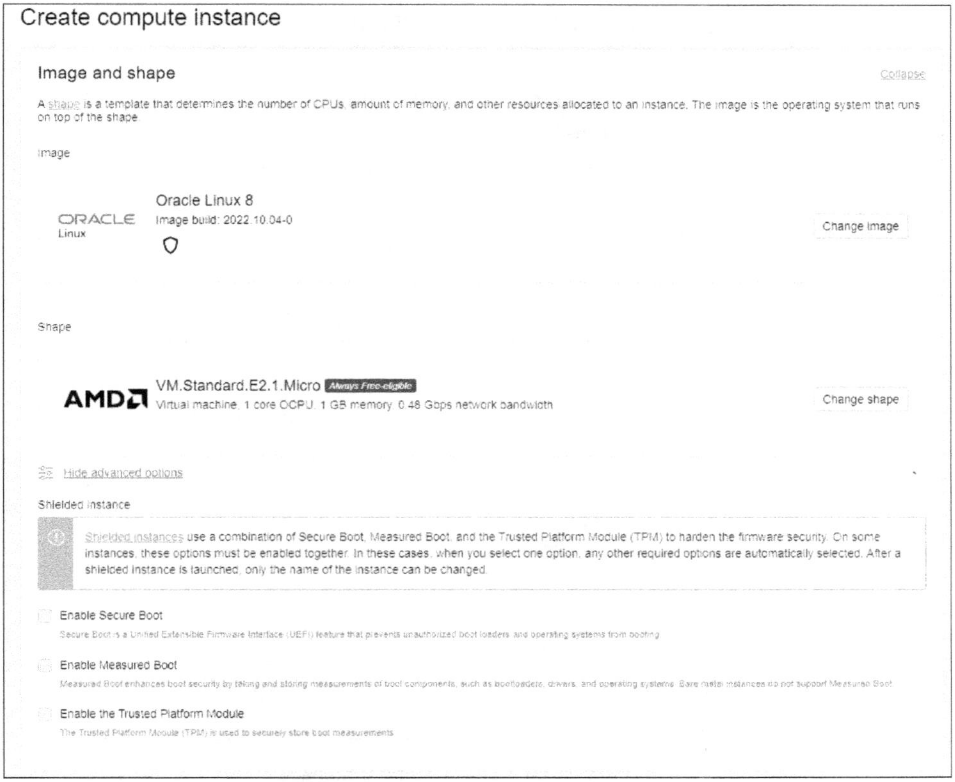

Figure 6-13 Shielded Instance

When all these options are used, the instance is referred to as a *shielded instance*, and offers additional security to the booting of the OS:

- **Enable Secure Boot:** This option enables the Unified Extensible Firmware Interface (UEFI) firmware option that prevents unauthorized boot loaders or operating systems from booting. Using this option requires additional administrative effort.
- **Enable Measured Boot:** This option enhances boot security to maintain a list of measurements (a digital signature) of boot components like drivers, bootloaders, and operating systems. This helps prevent unauthorized changes to these components but does require additional effort to maintain the systems.
- **Enable the Trusted Platform Module:** The Trusted Platform Module (TPM) is a security chip on the server that is used by measured boot to securely store the boot measurements. Measured boot will check each startup component, including the firmware, all the way to the boot drivers, and it will store this information in the TPM. When used on a VM, a virtual TPM is used to store this data. This ensures that there are no external changes to the operating system.

Additionally, under the Boot Volume section, the administrator has the following three options, as shown in Figure 6-14:

Figure 6-14   Boot Volume Options

- **Specify a Custom Boot Volume Size:** This option enables the admin to create a boot block device from 50 to 32,768 GB (32 TB) in size. You can also assign custom volume performance units (VPUs) to the boot volume if needed.

- **Use In-Transit Encryption:** This option automatically encrypts the boot and data volumes because data is accessed from the VM as the data is used. This helps prevent anyone sniffing the storage traffic to read data.
- **Encrypt This Volume with a Key You Manage:** This option allows an admin to encrypt the volume at rest with a key that is managed by the admin. This allows the security side of the DevSecOps team to control the encryption algorithm used, as well as who has access to the keys leveraging the OCI Vault service.

OS Images and the Marketplace

One of the features of OCI that is often overlooked is the Marketplace. The OCI Marketplace is where you can get customer images for your environment, as well as virtual appliances and even services. The Marketplace is an online store, with a mix of free and paid offerings. The Marketplace is broken into two major sections: Applications and Services. From here, the focus will be Applications.

Don't let the name *Applications* fool you. Although applications (such as Oracle Enterprise Manager 13c) are available to install in your tenancy, a large number of virtual appliances and even operating systems also are available in the Marketplace. Several free operating systems like Rocky Linux and AlmaLinux are available free in the Marketplace. While many of the images are free, there are also OS images from companies like the Center for Internet Security (CIS) that are paid images, and charge an hourly rate for their use. To get to the Marketplace, go to **Marketplace > All Applications** in the OCI console. This will take you to the list of all the available free and paid applications, as shown in Figure 6-15.

From here, you can search for keywords to find a specific image, or you can use the filters to narrow down from a broader list. The following filters are available:

- **Type**
  - **Image:** This is a single image, usually an OS or a simple appliance.
  - **Stack:** This is a full-tech stack, which can include VMs, databases, and other Platform as a Service (PaaS) technologies that can be deployed on multiple systems.
- **Architecture**
  - **X86:** For Intel and AMD systems
  - **Arm:** For ARM compute like the A1
- **Roving Edge Exportability**
  - **Roving Edge Exportable:** These images can be deployed on Oracle's Roving Edge Device.
- **Publisher**
  - This is a long list of companies that have published images available for use on OCI.

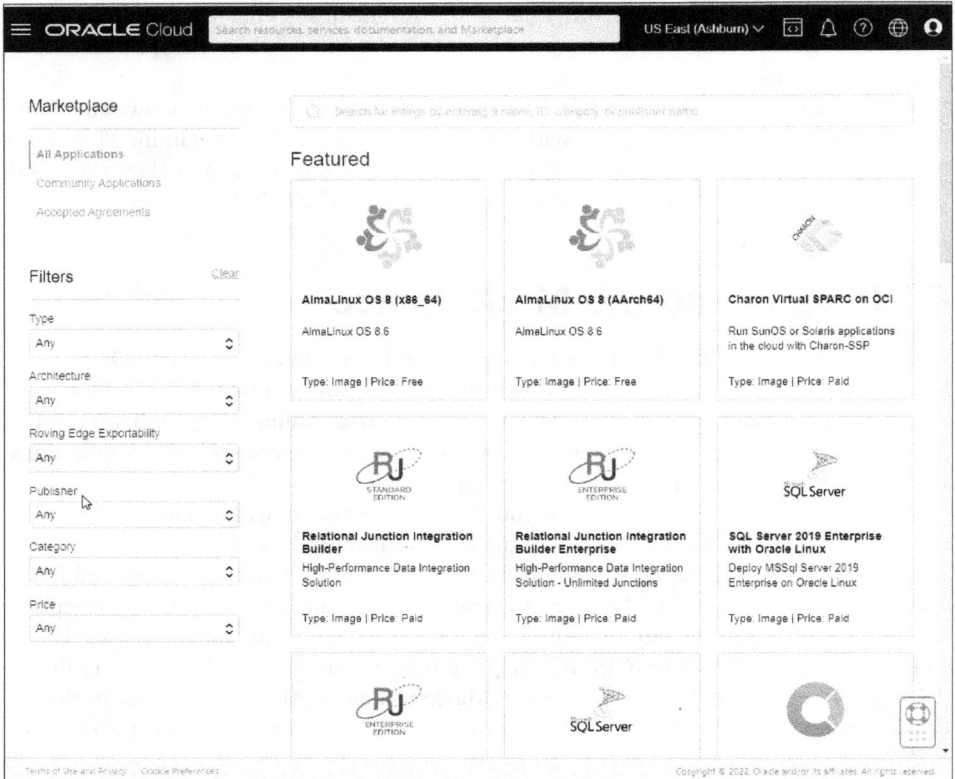

Figure 6-15   The Marketplace

- **Category**
  - This is a list of categories, like Operating System, Application Development, Big Data, and more.
- **Price**
  - **BYOL:** Bring Your Own License, where a license is required but paid for outside of the OCI Marketplace.
  - **Free:** These are free images.
  - **Paid:** These images have an hourly rate that is charged against your OCI tenancy.

So, let's say you want to deploy Microsoft SQL Server in a compute node. You can search the Marketplace by simply entering **Microsoft SQL** in the search box, as shown in Figure 6-16.

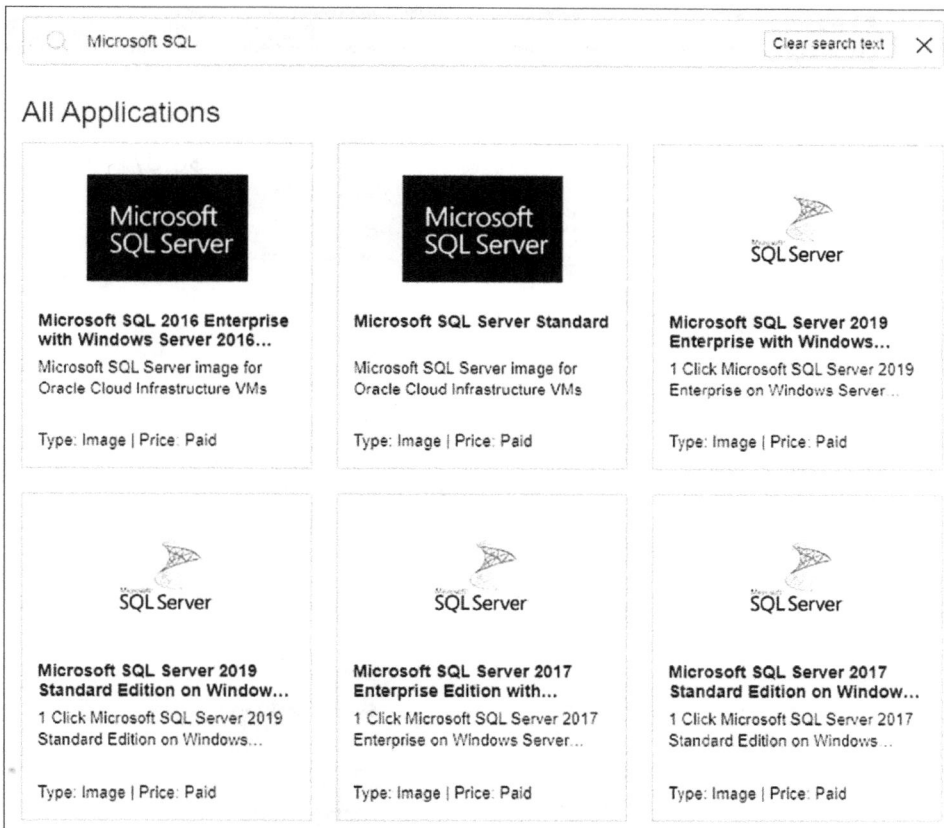

Figure 6-16   Marketplace Search

Here, you can see multiple results, with each result telling you the type and price. When the image has a price, you can click the image to see the details. The details will also give you other important information, such as what compute shapes can be used. A sample is shown in Figure 6-17.

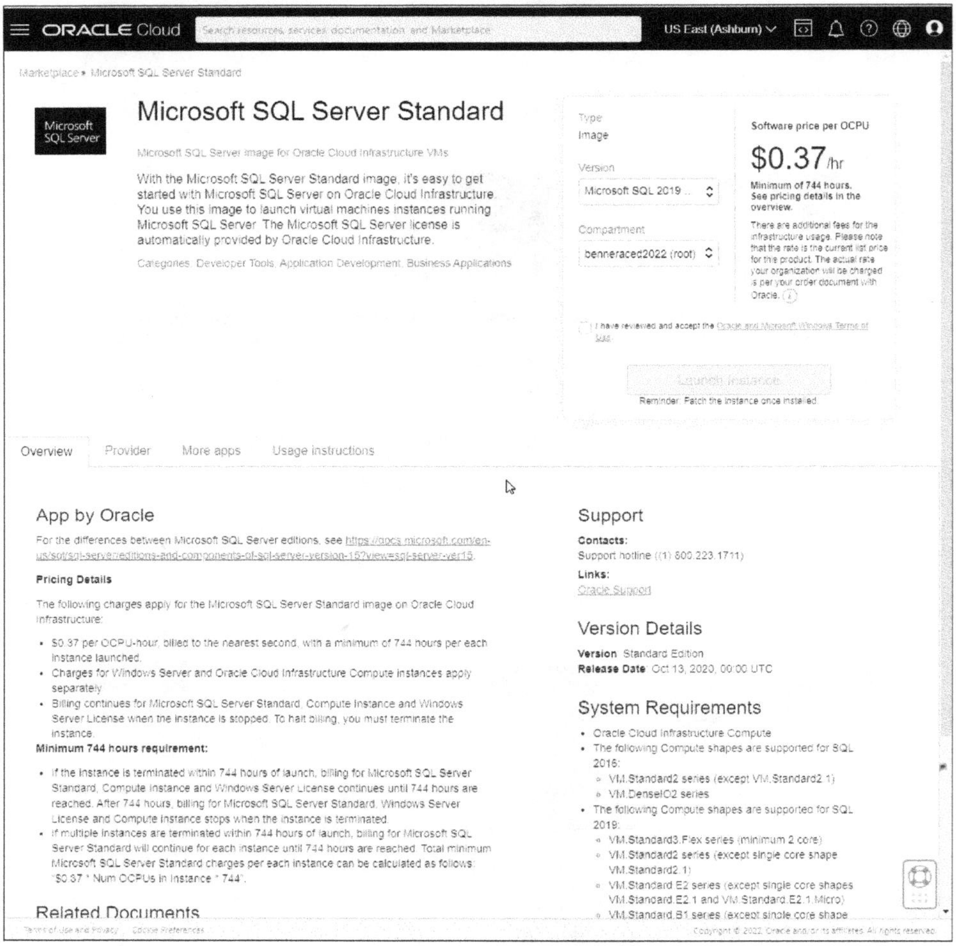

Figure 6-17   Marketplace Details

Here, you can see this image costs $0.37 an hour per OCPU. It also can be deployed on a wide variety of compute shapes, including the legacy VM standard shapes as well as the more modern and agile FLEX shapes. Plus, you can see who provided the image (Oracle in this case) as well as contact information for tech support.

For a sample deployment, let's use a free stack. In this example, we'll use the Oracle ZFS Storage Marketplace stack. It will provision both the compute and storage required for the stack, with several options. The ZFS stack has all the features of Oracle's on-premises ZFS appliance and offers a large number of features.

To launch the stack, review and accept the Oracle terms of use, and then click **Launch Stack**, as shown in Figure 6-18.

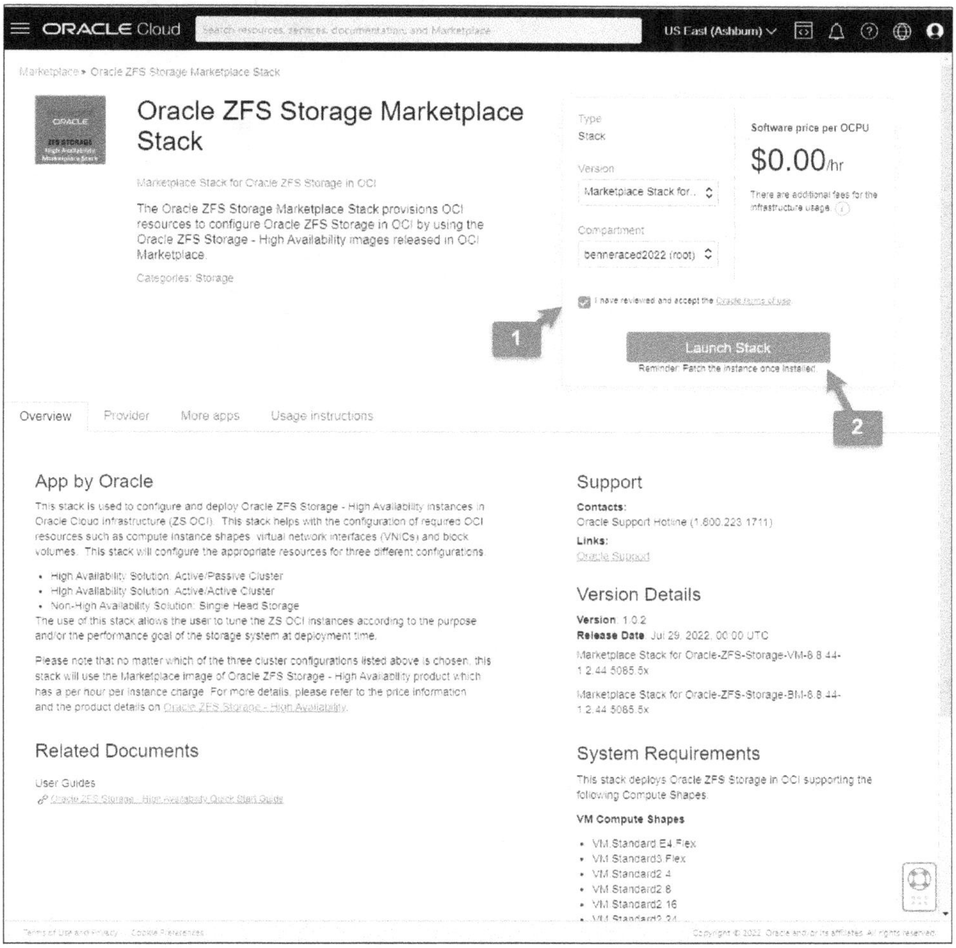

Figure 6-18   Launching a Stack

From here, you will be taken to a wizard that is specific to the stack but has many common components. On the first screen (shown in Figure 6-19), you set the name, description, and any optional tags or Terraform providers.

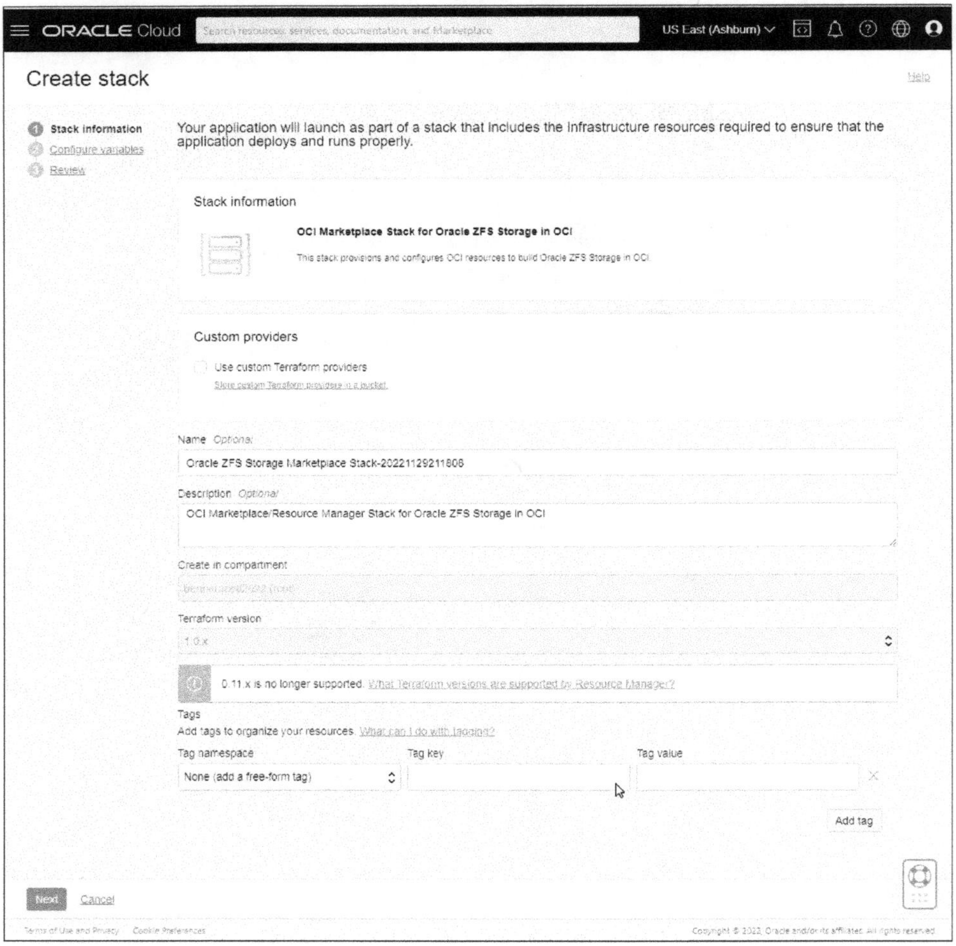

Figure 6-19   Step 1 Marketplace Stack

The second step has more options for the stack. These options will vary because they are stack specific. In this example, let's deploy a single node using the E4 Flex compute. There are many options with this stack; you can see a sampling in Figure 6-20.

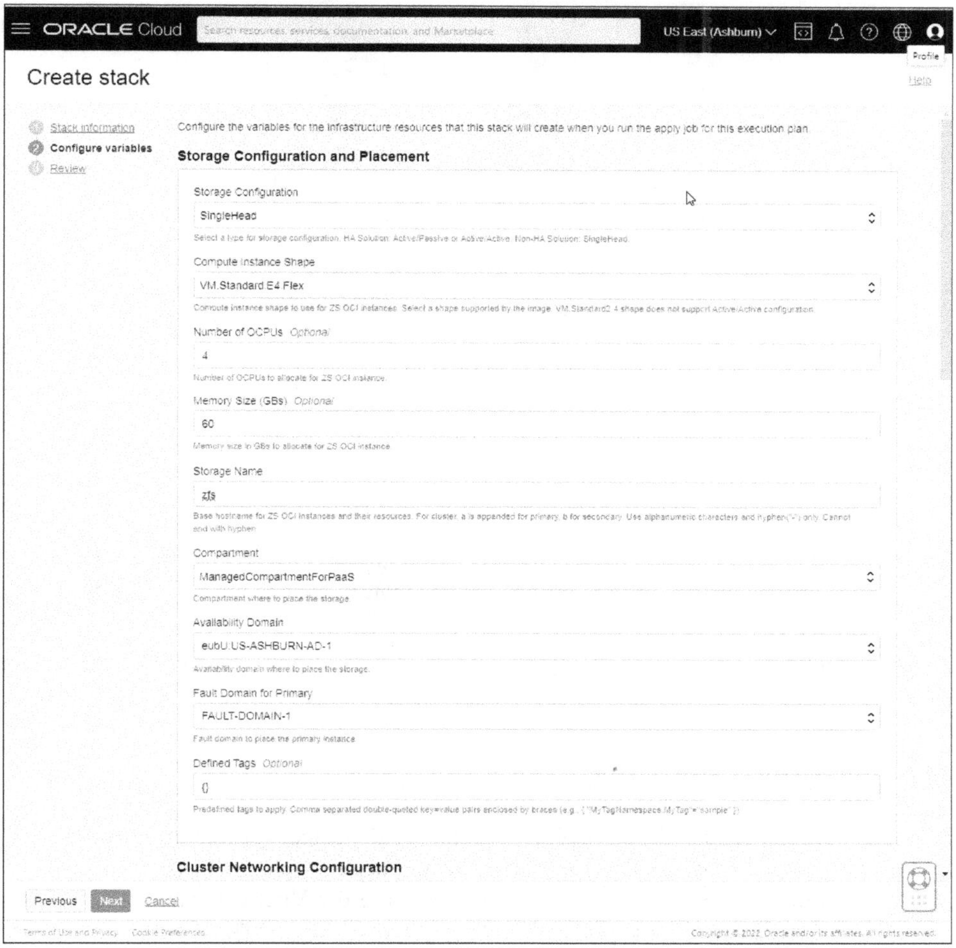

Figure 6-20   Step 2 Stack Deployment

The third step is a review of all the options. From there, click **Create** to start the build. A job will launch and can be monitored from the screen, including the logs and progression, as shown in Figure 6–21.

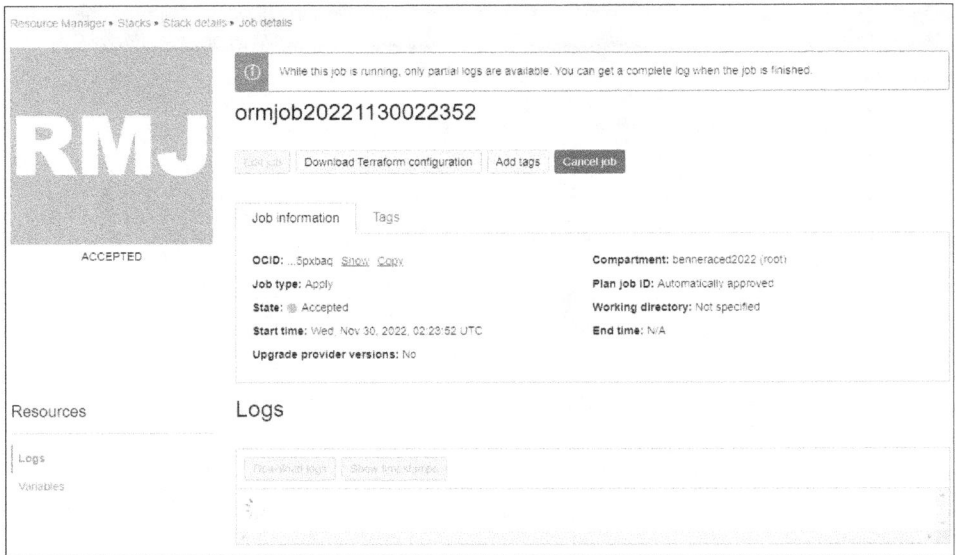

Figure 6-21   Job Status

Once complete, the stack is deployed, and any additional steps are specific to the stack or image deployed.

Custom OS Images

Not only can complex stacks be deployed via the Marketplace; you can also deploy custom OS images. Additionally, you can create and deploy your own custom images. While this process can be complex, the easiest way is to use VirtualBox and then upload your image from VirtualBox to OCI.

An easier way to build a custom image is to simply take an existing OS image and modify it to meet your needs; then you can save it as a custom image. To do this, first create a VM and make the changes needed to the VM. This could be a custom filesystem layout, custom security settings, additional software installed, or even default users added to the image. Don't forget to enable the firstboot options and do a system unconfig.

Next, after all of this is done, you can clone the image to object storage and then use that as an image. To do this, navigate in the OCI console to **Compute > Instances** and then click the system that you want to make a custom image.

From the Instance Details page, click **More Actions** and then **Create Custom Image** from the drop-down, as shown in Figure 6-22.

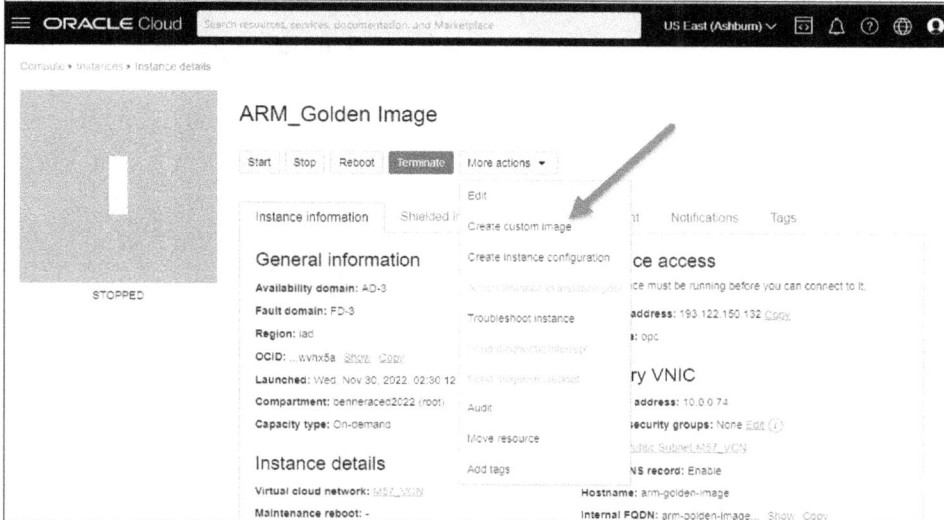

Figure 6-22   Create Custom Image

From here, you will need to select a compartment and pick a name for the image, as shown in Figure 6-23.

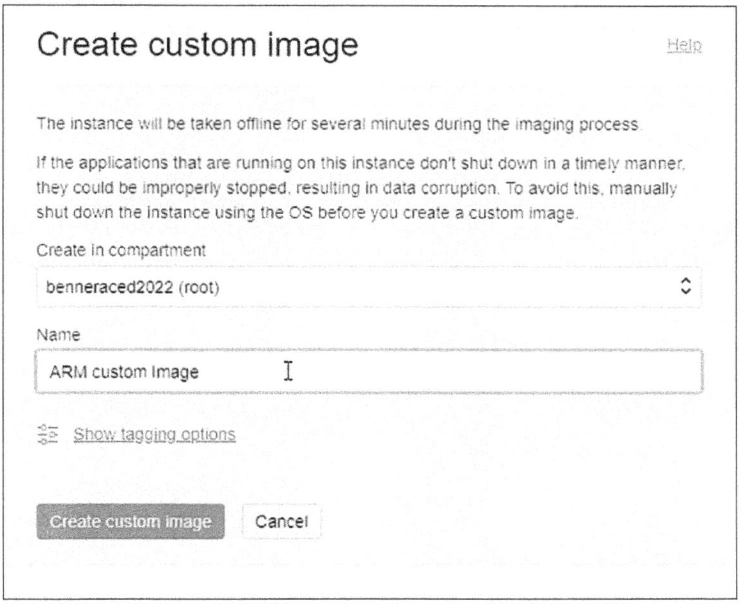

Figure 6-23   Image Location and Name

Under the hood, OCI is creating an image. You can track this progress by clicking **Resources > Work Requests** from the Image Details page that is the source for the custom image. This output is shown in Figure 6-24.

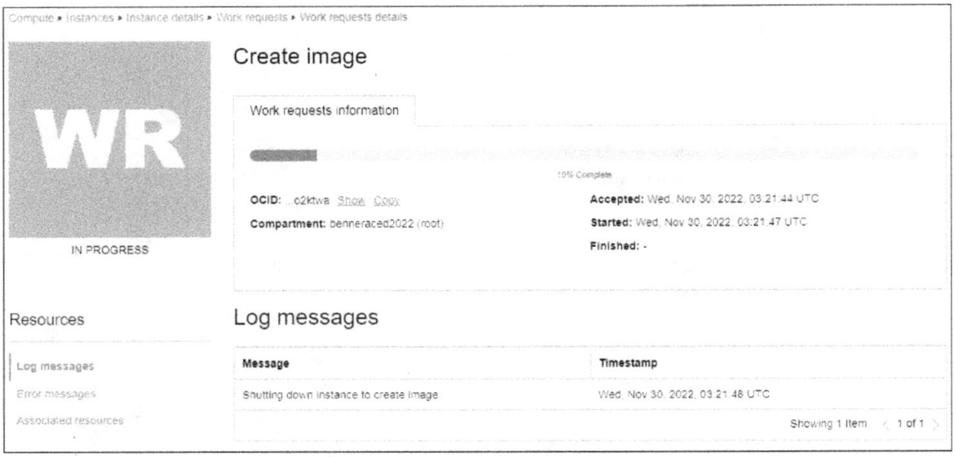

Figure 6-24   Image Creation Status

After the image is created, you can use it when creating a new VM. To select the image, when creating the VM, under Image and Shape, click **Edit** and then click **Change Image**, and under Image Source, select **Custom Images** from the drop-down. You will then see the custom images available, as shown in Figure 6-25.

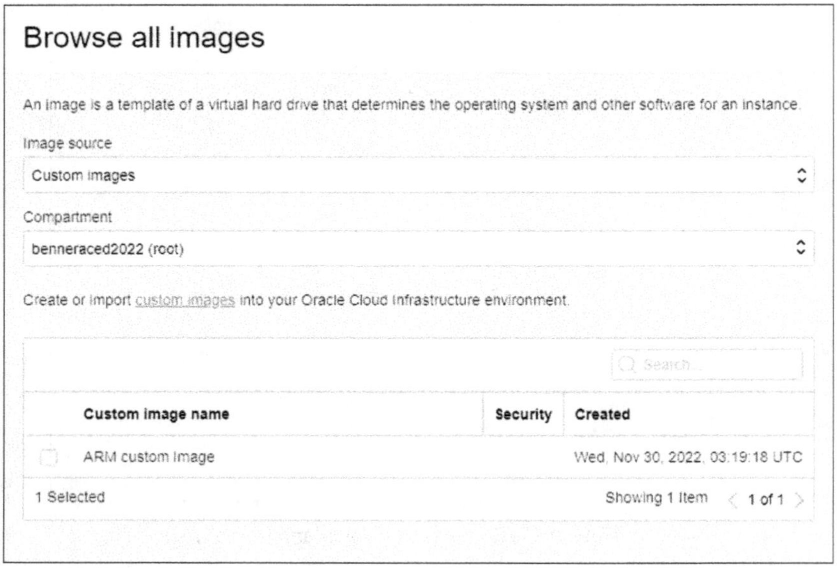

Figure 6-25   Custom Image Selection

Summary

In this chapter, you learned about OCI compute, how to create a VM, the processor options along with the pros and cons, as well as many of the advanced options to better secure and standardize OS deployments in your tenancy. In the next chapter, you will learn more details about OCI storage options.

7

Oracle IaaS—Storage

OCI offers highly reliable storage options that deliver consistently high performance and scalability and are backed by an availability service-level agreement (SLA). Numerous cloud storage options are available. These options are low cost, on demand, and address different workload requirements depending on the purpose. Table 7-1 summarizes the main cloud storage options that OCI offers and the use case they can serve.

Table 7-1   Cloud Storage Products

Storage Type	Purpose
Block Volumes	Provides storage to compute instances
Object Storage	Stores unstructured data of any content type
File Storage	Provides an enterprise-grade network file system (NFS)
Archive Storage	Provides storage service for infrequently accessed data
Data Transfer Appliance	Enables you to securely move terabytes or petabytes of data offline between on-premises data centers and the cloud
Storage Gateway	Enables you to store and retrieve data on OCI Object Storage from on-premises data centers

In this chapter, we will discuss the setup and configuration of block volumes, object storage, file storage, and archive storage. *Block volumes* are low latency, SSD-based storage that are attached to compute instances. *Object storage* is intended to store unstructured data and can be accessed through the browser, CLI, REST API, or OCI SDK. This storage is ideal for data lakes, for example. Users have the ability to upload any type of raw data such as images, logs, backups, and text. *File storage* can be accessed from any instance in the VCN and supports the Network File System version 3.0 (NFSv3) protocol, allowing its data to be accessed simultaneously by multiple hosts. *Archive storage* is similar to object storage but is designed to store seldomly accessed data for long periods of time, which can drastically reduce storage cost for archived data.

Although inbound data transfer is free in OCI, as opposed to other cloud service providers, the time to migrate large volumes of data to the cloud may be weeks or months, depending on network bandwidth. This is where the *Data Transfer Appliance* is used to securely migrate extremely large volumes of data from on-premises data centers to OCI in only days. Lastly, the *Storage Gateway* extends the local file systems in on-premises data centers to access object storage in OCI at no extra charge, essentially extending your storage options for your on-premises systems.

In this chapter, we will cover the first four storage options. They can be accessed from the Storage link in the OCI console (see Figure 7-1). The chapter concludes with information on OCI's security-first architecture as it pertains to cloud storage.

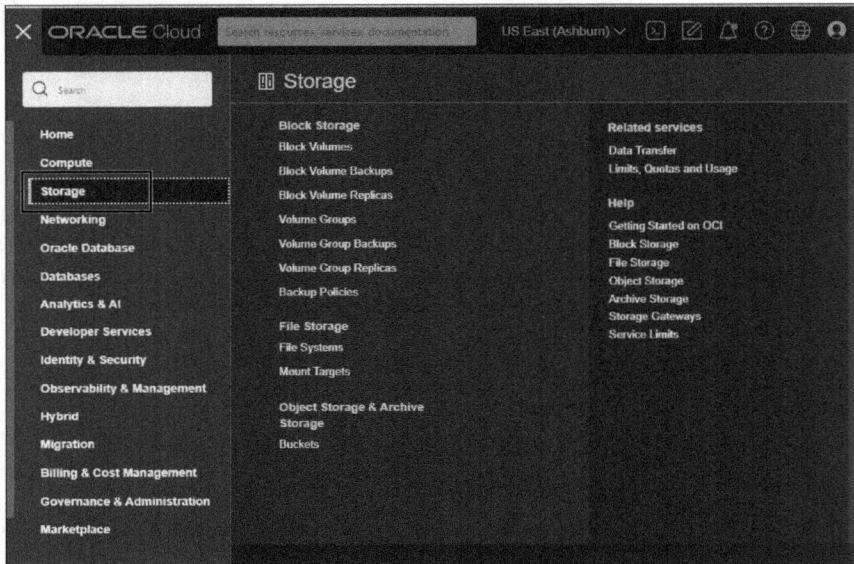

Figure 7-1   Accessing the Storage Options in the Console

Block Volume

OCI provides the ability to create, attach, resize, and move a *block volume*, also referred to as a *block storage volume*. It is essentially SSD-based storage that can be attached to any available compute instance and generally maintains all software, binaries, and data needed for your application.

Block volumes are the most common storage types that you will use in your cloud journey. The two types of block storage options are block volume and boot volume. Boot volumes are created during the creation of a compute instance and hold the OS binaries. These volumes can be viewed, managed, and terminated in the same way as block volumes and are accessible under the Boot Volumes menu in the service.

Creating and Attaching

Once a block volume is created and attached to a compute instance, it can be used similarly to a hard drive. When it is detached, the data residing on it remains intact and can be reattached to the same or another host. When it is detached, charges still accrue on the block volume.

You can attach a volume by navigating to the volume itself and selecting a compute instance, or you can connect to a compute instance and attach the block volume.

Creating a Block Volume

For the quick creation of a 1 terabyte block volume, follow these steps:

Step 1. Navigate to the OCI console menu; then click **Storage > Block Volumes**.

Step 2. Click **Create Block Volume** to enter the creation wizard.

Step 3. Enter the block volume name. All other settings are prefilled with defaults. Customize other settings as needed.

Step 4. Click **Create Block Volume** to create the volume.

Compartment, availability domain, size, performance, backup policies, replication, and encryption can be customized as necessary. Block volumes can have a minimum size of 50 GB and a maximum size of 32 TB. All tenancies receive 200 GB of always-free block volume storage.

Attaching a Block Volume to an Instance

After the block volume is created, its details will immediately appear in the details page, as shown in Figure 7-2.

```
opc@freehost:~                                          —    □    ×

[opc@freehost ~]$ # Before executing iscsiadm commands
[opc@freehost ~]$ lsblk
NAME                  MAJ:MIN RM   SIZE RO TYPE MOUNTPOINT
sda                       8:0    0 46.6G  0 disk
├─sda1                    8:1    0  100M  0 part /boot/efi
├─sda2                    8:2    0    1G  0 part /boot
└─sda3                    8:3    0 45.5G  0 part
  ├─ocivolume-root 252:0    0 35.5G  0 lvm  /
  └─ocivolume-oled 252:1    0   10G  0 lvm  /var/oled
[opc@freehost ~]$
[opc@freehost ~]$ # After executing iscsiadm commands
[opc@freehost ~]$ lsblk
NAME                  MAJ:MIN RM   SIZE RO TYPE MOUNTPOINT
sda                       8:0    0 46.6G  0 disk
├─sda1                    8:1    0  100M  0 part /boot/efi
├─sda2                    8:2    0    1G  0 part /boot
└─sda3                    8:3    0 45.5G  0 part
  ├─ocivolume-root 252:0    0 35.5G  0 lvm  /
  └─ocivolume-oled 252:1    0   10G  0 lvm  /var/oled
sdb                      8:16    0  100G  0 disk
[opc@freehost ~]$ █
```

Figure 7-2   Reviewing the Block Volume Details

The attachment type can either be iSCSI or Paravirtualized. Paravirtualized is simpler to set up because it does not require additional iSCSI configuration commands to be run. iSCSI, however, does not have the virtualization overhead and thus has better input/output operations per second (IOPS) performance than Paravirtualized for larger block volumes, but requires connecting to the host and mounting the volume to make it usable. IOPS is a standard measurement for how many read/write operations a volume can carry out every second. The higher the number, the better the volume performs.

The most common access type is Read/Write, but other options such as Read/Write - Shareable and Read-only - Shareable are available.

From here, it is possible to attach this volume to an instance (the instance must be running) by following these steps:

Step 1. Click **Attached Instances**.

Step 2. Click **Attach to Instance**.

Step 3. Though optional, preferably select a Device Path.

Step 4. Select the running instance from the drop-down.

Step 5. Click **Attach**.

Even though the volume is attached, since the default attachment type is set to iSCSI, a few extra steps are required:

a. On the details page of the block volume, click the menu icon and select **iSCSI Commands & Information**, as demonstrated in Figure 7-3.

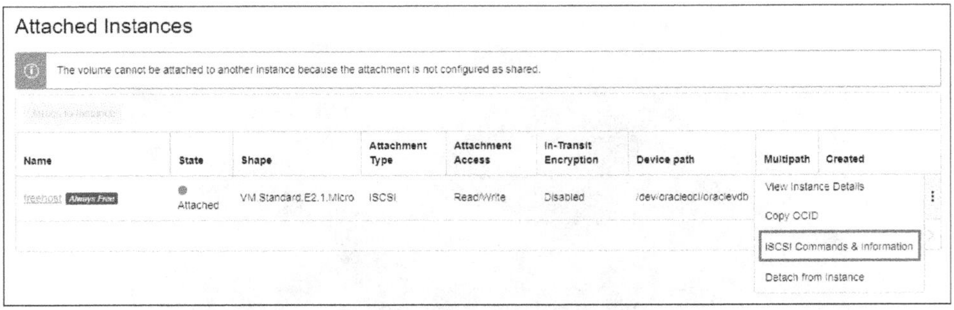

Figure 7-3   Capturing the iSCSI Commands

b. Copy the commands under the Attach Commands section.

c. Log in to your host and execute the three **iscsiadm** commands. There is no need to make changes to these commands because they already take into account your system details. Then format and mount the filesystem volume.

Example 7-1 walks through not only an example of executing the iSCSI commands but also the remaining steps required to view, format, and mount the file system.

Example 7-1   Mounting the iSCSI Volume as root

```
# Run the iscsiadm commands below on the compute instance
# The parameters are specific to the volume and instance
# These commands should be copied and executed from the OCI console as is
sudo iscsiadm -m node -o new -T iqn.2015-12.com.oracleiaas:13c56eb9-639a-4fa1-
   b8ea-5378b9e0c7f0 -p 169.254.2.5:3260
sudo iscsiadm -m node -o update -T iqn.2015-12.com.oracleiaas:13c56eb9-639a-4fa1-
   b8ea-5378b9e0c7f0 -n node.startup -v automatic
sudo iscsiadm -m node -T iqn.2015-12.com.oracleiaas:13c56eb9-639a-4fa1-b8ea-
   5378b9e0c7f0 -p 169.254.2.5:3260 -l

# View available disks
# The volume will appear as a 'disk' with the correct size shown
lsblk

# Confirm that the file system is a 'data' volume
file -s /dev/sdb

# One time creation of the file system as ext4; all data will be lost
mkfs.ext4 /dev/sdb

# Create a local directory in which the file system will be mounted to
mkdir /u01

# Mount the filesystem
mount /dev/sdb /u01

# Confirm that file system is mounted and available
df -h
```

Configuring Performance

The performance levels of a block volume can be changed at any time, but it must be detached and reattached to the instance. Oracle delivers consistent, low-latency performance of up to 200 IOPS/GB to a maximum of 300,000 IOPS and 2,680 MBps of throughput per volume.

By default, block volumes are created with a "balanced" performance level. The balanced level operates at 10 VPUs. *VPU* stands for volume performance unit and indicates how much performance resources are allocated to a volume. At 10 VPUs, the block volume is expected to deliver 6,000 IOPS with a throughput of 48 MBps. At 100 VPUs, it will deliver 19,500 IOPS with a throughput of 156 MBps.

How does changing the VPU fare in the real world? For example, moving from a 10 VPU volume to a 20 VPU volume can yield a 16 percent improvement in I/O performance. The balanced performance level is generally a good level to start at unless you start experiencing or have high performance I/O needs.

Using Ultra High Performance Volumes

The benefits of an ultra high performance volume are considerable. Creating a 30 GB XFS file takes 10 minutes and 53 seconds on a 10 VPU volume, but 3 minutes and 21 seconds on an ultra high performance 100 VPU one, a 325 percent performance improvement.

Any volume that is 30 VPUs or higher is considered ultra high performance, or *UHP*. To take advantage of this performance, the compute instance shape must support multipath attachments. Refer to the documentation at https://docs.oracle.com/en-us/iaas/Content/Block/Concepts/blockvolumeperformance.htm#shapes_vm_iscsi and find a compute shape that has Yes under the Supports Ultra High Performance (UHP) column.

After selecting a VM shape that supports multipath attachments and during the creation of the compute instance, do the following on the Create Compute Instance page:

Step 1. Click **Show Advanced Options**.

Step 2. Click the **Oracle Cloud Agent** tab.

Step 3. Select the **Block Volume Management** check box.

Step 4. Click **Create**.

Keep in mind that UHP volumes do not have iSCSI commands to run and show up differently when running the **lsblk** command when viewing the available block devices (see Figure 7-4).

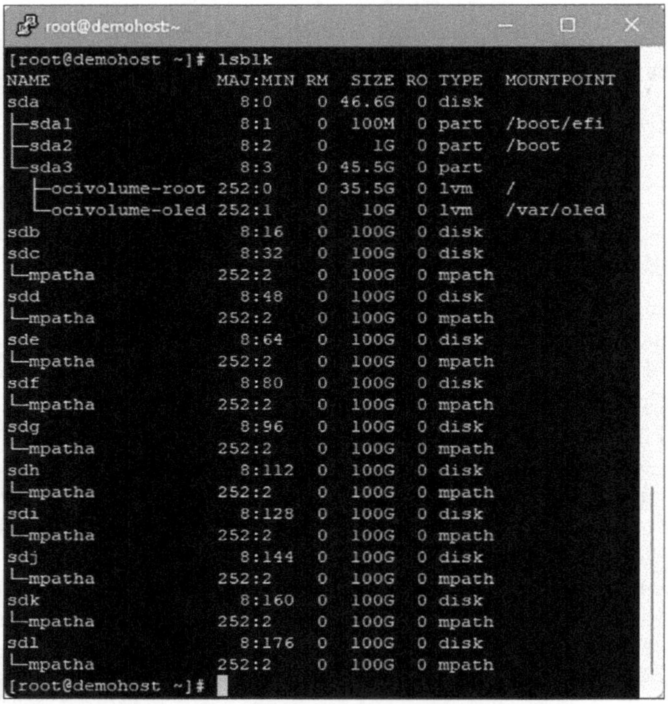

Figure 7-4   Viewing the Attached Volumes in the Linux OS

Mounting the UHP iSCSI volume for the OS requires slightly different steps. These steps are demonstrated in Example 7-2.

Example 7-2   Mounting the UHP iSCSI Volume as root

```
# Retrieve device name from the friendly name (e.g., mpatha)
multipath -ll

# Create the filesystem; all data will be lost
mkfs.ext4 /dev/mapper/mpatha

# Create a local directory in which the filesystem will be mounted to
mkdir /u02

# Mount the filesystem
mount /dev/mapper/mpatha /u02

# Confirm that filesystem is mounted and available
df -h
```

Monitoring Volume Performance

Each volume has a Metrics page, which allows you to view various metrics such as Volume Read Throughput (in bytes per second), Volume Write Throughput (in bytes per second), Volume Read Operations (I/O reads), and Volume Write Operations (I/O writes). This data can be represented in various statistical formats, though the most common ones are *rate*, *sum*, and *mean*. This page is demonstrated in Figure 7-5.

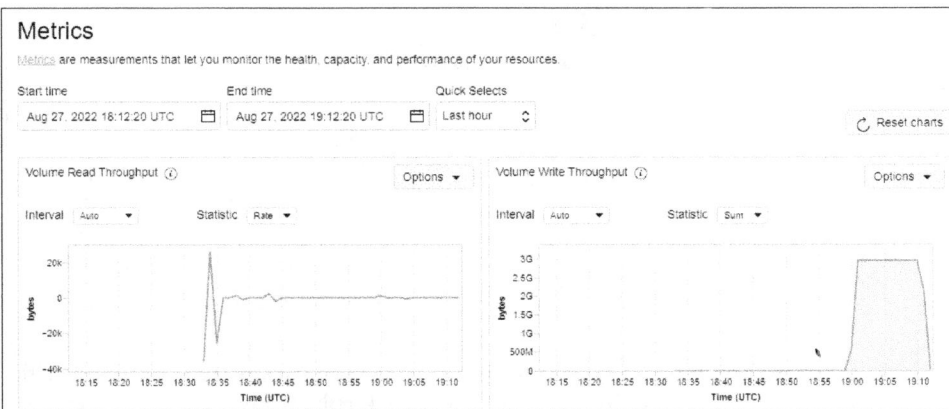

Figure 7-5   Viewing Block Volume Metrics

Performing a Backup

To have a complete understanding of block volume backups, you must understand a few concepts. First, when you navigate to your block volume, click **Block Volume Backups** and create a *block volume backup*. This manual, on-demand operation can create a full or an incremental backup. However, to schedule backups, you must first create a *backup policy* and then add a *schedule* to this policy.

For example, as seen in Figure 7-6, a backup policy named Non_Prod_Backup_Policy has a full weekly backup and incremental daily backups.

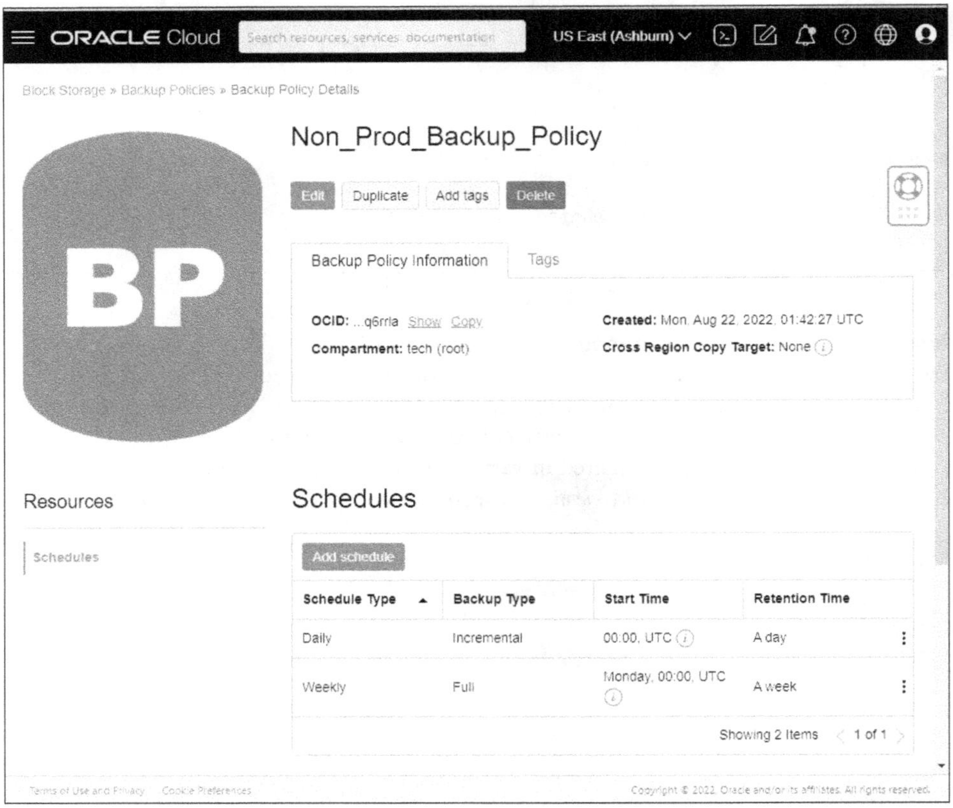

Figure 7-6   Backup Schedules Defined in the Block Volume Backup Policy

Now that this backup policy is defined, you can navigate back to and edit the specific block volume. To do so, click **Edit** to change the block volume, and under Backup Policies, select the user-defined backup policy named **Non_Prod_Backup_Policy**, as shown in Figure 7-7.

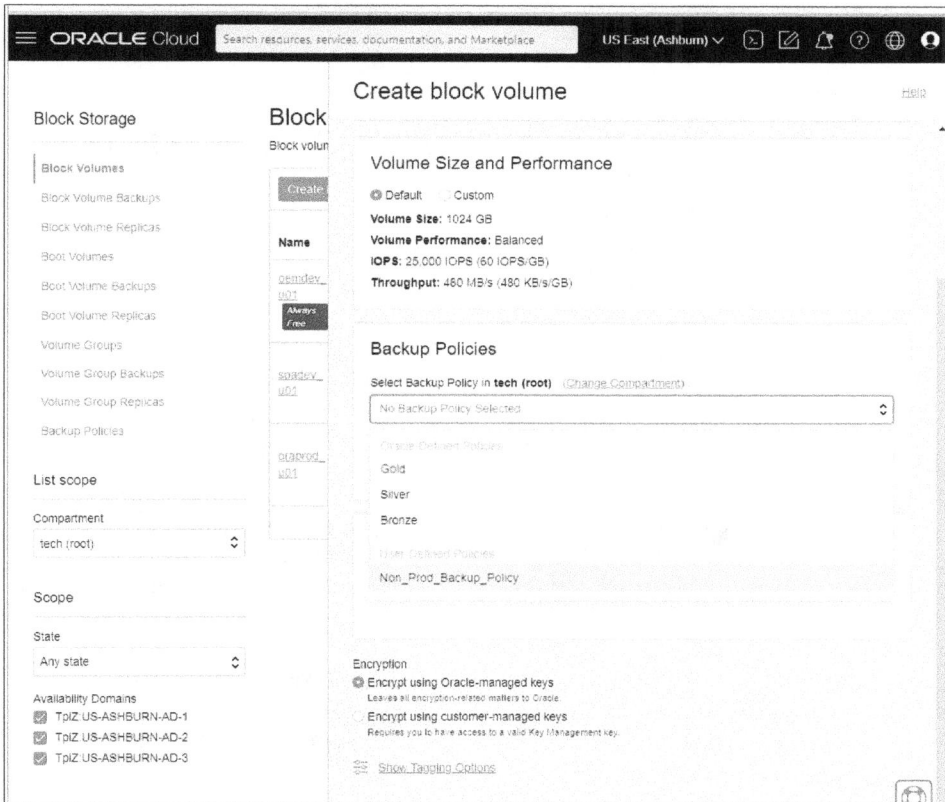

Figure 7-7 Attaching a Backup Policy to a Block Storage Volume

Restoring a Backup Volume

Restoring a block volume is rather straightforward. The backups can be accessed from the block volume details page or by navigating to the Block Volume Backups menu.

When you're restoring a block volume, a new block volume is created from the backup. You could specify the same settings as you would when creating a block volume. At minimum, you must provide a name.

After you restore a block volume, it appears as a new volume in your list (see Figure 7-8). At this point, to revert your compute instance to use this volume, you must unmount and detach the original volume, and then attach and mount the restored volume.

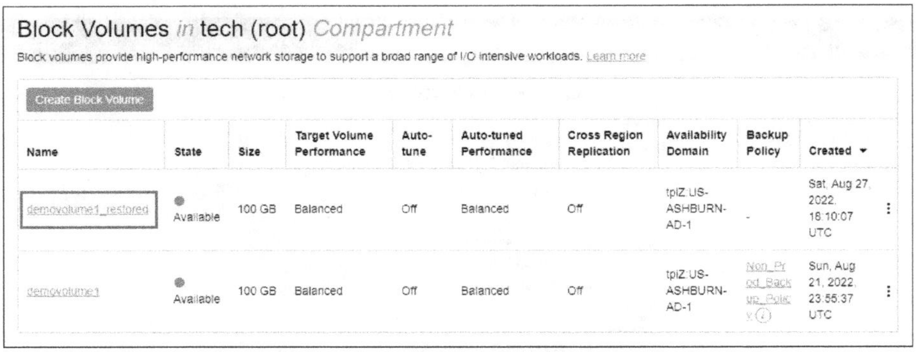

Figure 7-8   Viewing the Restored Block Volume

Using Volume Groups

The Block Volume service allows you to group block and/or boot volumes together in a *volume group*. The primary purpose of volume groups is to group volumes together where they can be backed up or cloned together. Often, one or more compute instances may have multiple volumes attached to them, and it would be desirable to take a point-in-time backup of the boot volume and all block volumes all at once. This is where volume groups come in.

For example, Figure 7-9 shows how the boot volume and the two block volumes are added to a single volume group. Thus, a backup policy can be attached to the volume group (as opposed to each of the block volumes separately) to ensure that a crash-consistent backup is taken every time.

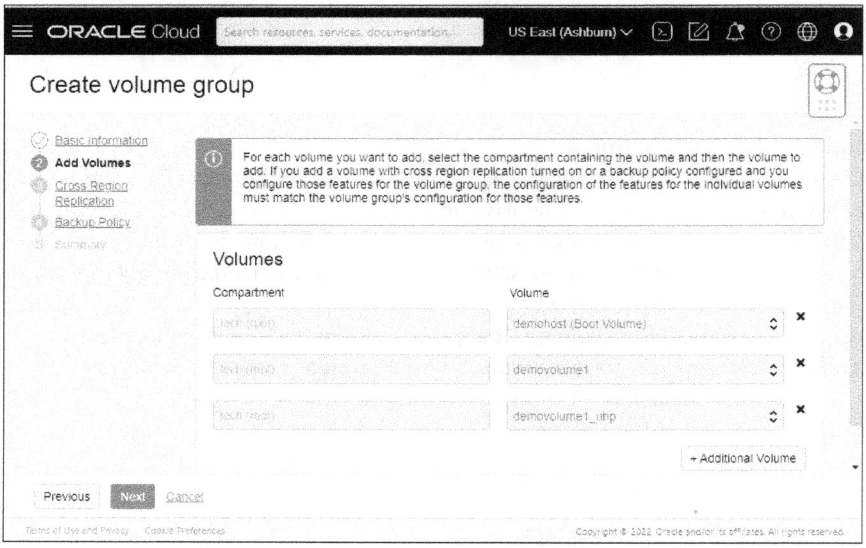

Figure 7-9   Adding Volumes to a Volume Group

The following are some points worth noting about volume groups:

- A maximum of 32 volumes can be added to a volume group.
- A total maximum size of 128 TB is supported in each volume group.
- Each volume may be in only one volume group.
- Deleting a volume group does not delete the volumes.
- It is necessary to remove a volume from a volume group before deleting it.

Cloning a Volume

Cloning a volume takes a point-in-time snapshot and copies it to another volume. The cloned volume is now treated as a new block volume. If you are trying to back up a volume, though much faster, cloning is not the approach to consider. Unlike a typical volume backup that is stored in object storage, clones are created as another block volume, thus incurring a higher cost. They do not have backup retention policies either. But they are effective ways to quickly create a copy of a volume for reuse in another compute instance.

Object Storage

Object storage is designed to store unstructured data of any content type in its native format. For example, object storage is high performance and secure. Any data uploaded as an "object" is stored in a *bucket*.

Uploading objects entails the following steps:

Step 1. Click the menu icon in the console and navigate to Storage.

Step 2. Click **Buckets**.

Step 3. Click **Create Bucket** and give it a name (such as Non_Prod_Unstructure_ Text).

Step 4. Navigate to the newly created bucket by clicking the name.

Step 5. Though optional, preferably select a Device Path.

By default, buckets are set to private visibility but then can be configured as public to let anonymous and unauthenticated users access data stored in the bucket. Select this option at your own risk.

Files can be uploaded through the web console on the browser directly to the bucket, assuming the user has the appropriate permissions. They can be uploaded via the REST API and OCI SDK. Alternatively, they can be uploaded through the OCI, as demonstrated in Figure 7-10. Here, the CLI is used to upload a document and then execute an object list command to view the available objects in the bucket.

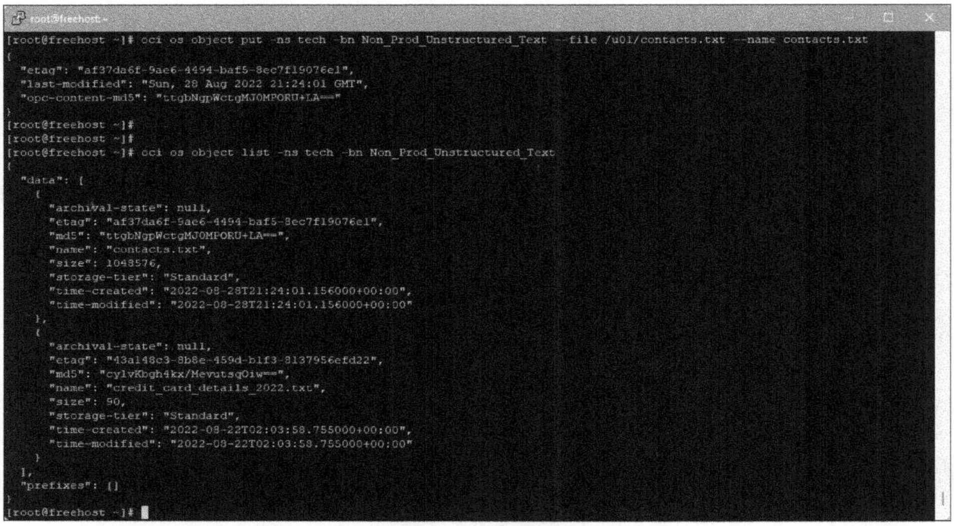

Figure 7-10   Uploading a Document to a Bucket Using the CLI and Then Listing Contents

Similarly, these objects will appear on the console as well, as seen in Figure 7-11.

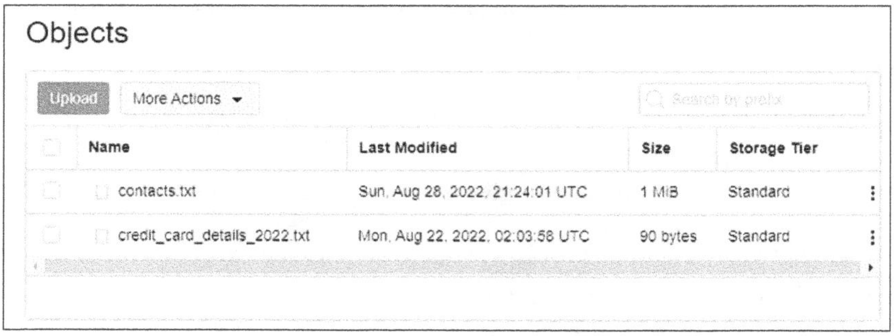

Figure 7-11   Viewing Objects in a Bucket on the Web Console

File Storage

The File Storage service allows you to create a *file system* (aka network file system or NFS) that can be shared across multiple compute instances. Writing to this file system on one instance will make it available to the other instance, since the file system is shared. Each file system resides in a VCN and has its own internal IP address. The maximum allowable size of the file system is 8 EB (exabytes). In fact, it would report as such in the OS (see Figure 7-12). Similar to other types of storage offered by OCI, snapshots can be configured to ensure data availability.

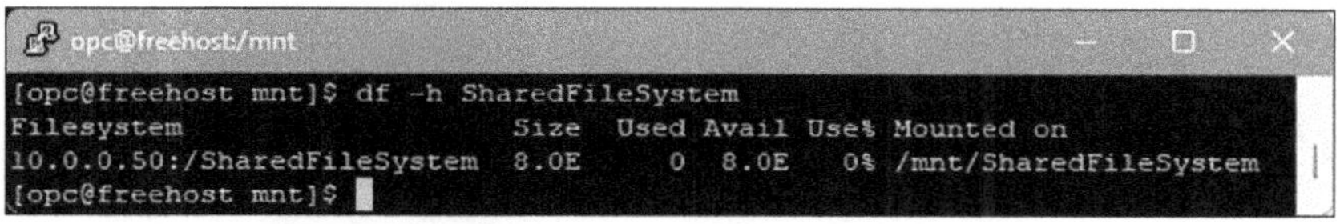

Figure 7-12   Viewing the Available Size of the NFS File System

Every file system will have one or more *mount targets*. Each mount target will have its IP address, which is used by NFS clients to connect to the file system. Each mount target can accept up to 100,000 NFS client connections.

Creating file storage is extremely straightforward; simply navigate to **File Storage > Create File System**. That's it. You can configure the export path and mount target information (as shown in Figure 7-13), wherein you can customize which VCN and subnet this file system resides.

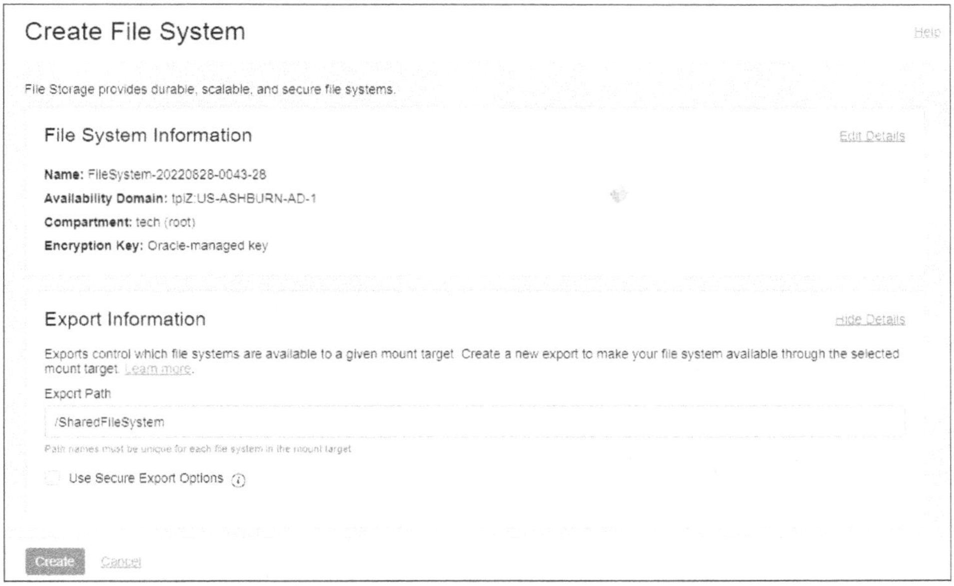

Figure 7-13   Creating a File Storage File System

After you create the file system, the *export path*, which was created during the creation of the file system, is shown here, as depicted in Figure 7-14. The process of clicking the three dots at the right of the window and selecting **Mount Commands** provides you with the exact commands to be executed as is on your compute instances.

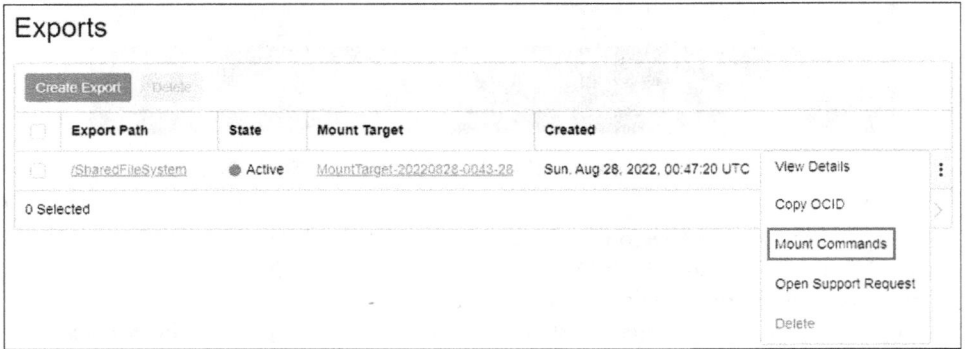

Figure 7-14   Locating the Commands to Mount the File System to a Compute Instance

Example 7-3 shows the commands used.

Example 7-3   Mounting a File Storage Export to a Compute Instance

```
# Install the NFS client
sudo yum install nfs-utils

# Create a local mount point directory
sudo mkdir -p /mnt/SharedFileSystem

# Mount the file system
sudo mount 10.0.0.50:/SharedFileSystem /mnt/SharedFileSystem
```

However, prior to running these commands, you would need to add some rules to your security list to allow access; otherwise, you may experience a mount.nfs: Connection timed out error. Table 7-2 lists the rule type (ingress or egress), protocol (TCP or UDP), and port ranges required.

Table 7-2   Security List Requirements to Be Able to Mount a File System

Rule Type	Source CIDR	IP Protocol	Destination Port Range
Ingress	10.0.0.0/16	TCP	111
Ingress	10.0.0.0/16	TCP	2048–2050
Ingress	10.0.0.0/16	UDP	111
Ingress	10.0.0.0/16	UDP	2048
Egress	10.0.0.0/16	TCP	111
Egress	10.0.0.0/16	TCP	2048–2050
Egress	10.0.0.0/16	UDP	111

Archive Storage

Archive storage is used for specifically that—archiving storage. Any object that is infrequently accessed can be uploaded or moved to archive storage as a more cost-effective solution, almost at one-tenth of the cost. However, data retrieval takes time.

Objects are uploaded to archive storage in exactly the same way as that of object storage. From a usage perspective, the process is completely identical. The difference is during the bucket creation. Navigate to the Object Storage & Archive storage service and create a bucket. As seen in Figure 7-15, simply select the **Archive** default storage tier instead.

Figure 7-15 Creating an Archive Storage Bucket

To retrieve an object from archive storage, you must first restore it. By default, it is 24 hours for an object to be available for download, but can be configured anywhere from 1 to 240 hours. Similar to object storage, archive storage can be accessed via the console, CLI, REST API, or OCI SDK.

How to Secure Your Storage

OCI adopts a security-first design architecture that utilizes built-in tenant isolation, least privilege access, and data encryption at rest. Resources such as block volumes, archive storage, and file systems by default are encrypted at rest using the Advanced Encryption Standard (AES) algorithm with 256-bit encryption. The Block Volume service employs data eradication after volume deletion. To ensure additional security of your storage, there are a number of tasks you should perform. Some of these include the following:

- **Restrict access through IAM policies:** This includes assigning least privilege to OCI users to perform their responsibilities. Consider restricting the ability to delete volumes and backups to those who need it.
- **Encrypt storage using custom keys and frequently rotate keys:** Though all volumes and their backups are encrypted using Oracle-provided encryption keys, it

is recommended that you create and manage your own custom encryption keys in the Oracle Vault service.

- **Schedule frequent backups:** Furthermore, limit the users who have permissions to delete backups.
- **Configure and enable Cloud Guard:** This cloud-native service automatically inspects, reports, and also can perform corrective actions when security weaknesses are identified.

All storage services described in this chapter are integrated into Oracle Identity and Access Management to centrally manage access and permissions. For example, as demonstrated in Figure 7-16, consider creating a policy to disallow the deletion of volumes and their backups.

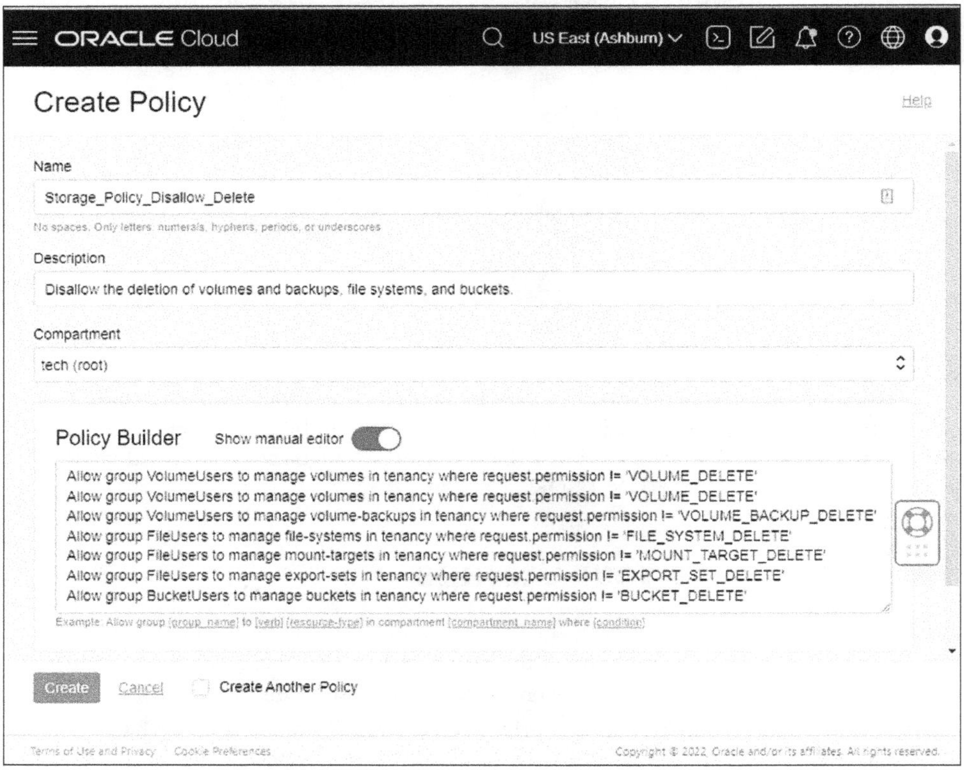

Figure 7-16   Creating a Policy to Allow All Actions on Storage Except Deletion

Once these primary tasks are performed, you can explore more advanced setup.

Summary

In this chapter, you learned that OCI offers a number of storage options, each serving a different function. This can include adding available disks to running compute instances, creating an NFS share among multiple compute instances, or creating an object storage to dump all sorts of files into.

The various OCI storage services have a lot of options to ensure performance, availability, and security of your storage solutions. These can all be dynamically configured and customized as needed.

In the next chapter, you will learn about database as a service.

8

Oracle DBaaS—Databases

Database as a Service (DBaaS) is a managed service where a cloud provider manages the underlying infrastructure and database software. As a result, the customer can rapidly deploy the database and automate the operations. It is a very cost-effective approach because all overhead expenses, such as setup, administration, and maintenance of infrastructure, are not part of the customer's responsibility. DBaaS is also very useful for the DevSecOps team because of the ability to provision the database quickly and efficiently for today's Agile approach. Oracle offers not only its world-class Oracle database but also MySQL, NoSQL, and JSON databases. In this chapter, we will go over all the different DBaaS options available in OCI. This DBaaS product lineup offers machine learning capabilities, clustering, high availability, and a range of security features.

Oracle's DBaaS Offerings

Oracle offers the following Oracle database services:

- Autonomous Database on Shared and Dedicated Infrastructure
- Autonomous Transaction Processing (ATP)
- Autonomous Data Warehouse (ADW)
- Autonomous JSON Database
- Oracle Base Database (VM and Bare Metal)
- Exadata Database Service (Public Cloud)
- Exadata Cloud@Customer
- MySQL Database Service (Standalone, High Availability, HeatWave)

In OCI, Oracle Database editions are categorized by what options and packs are included with it:

- **Standard Edition (SE):** This edition allows you to create the database and develop applications with Oracle Standard Edition 2. Unlike on-premises SE, you get access to limited features such as transparent database encryption, Oracle Machine Learning, Oracle Spatial and Graph, and Oracle APEX. However, this edition lacks many advanced functionalities such as Data Guard, Real Application Cluster (RAC), and Multitenant. SE supports up to eight threads per database.

- **Enterprise Edition (EE):** This edition allows you to create the database and develop applications securely in a highly available manner. It includes all features of SE and also includes Oracle Data Safe, Data Masking Pack, Diagnostic Pack, and Tuning Pack. In addition, it includes the Data Guard option and other features that are not available with on-premises EE licensing.
- **Enterprise Edition—High Performance (HP):** This edition includes all operations and packs of Enterprise Edition. In addition, it allows you to use more options and packs like Partitioning, Advanced Encryption, and Advanced Compression.
- **Enterprise Edition—Extreme Performance (EP):** This edition includes all options and packs of Enterprise Edition—High Performance. In addition, it includes Real Application Cluster, Active Data Guard, Sharding, and In-Memory Database features.
- **Enterprise Edition—Bring Your Own License (BYOL):** Under this edition, you can bring your existing on-premises license and use it in OCI. This option allows access to some of the basic options and packs. Plus, you can purchase other features separately as needed.

Let's look at all these details in Table 8-1 for a better understanding of what is included in each of these editions. The legend for this table is as follows:

- B: Buy the license separately
- I: Included with DBaaS subscription
- N: Not available with that subscription

Table 8-1   Oracle Database Editions Offering

Pack	Description	EE	HP	EP	BYOL
Diagnostic	Helps identify and troubleshoot database performance	I	I	I	I
Tuning	Helps with automatic SQL tuning	I	I	I	I
Data Masking and Subsetting	Allows masking of data for security reasons	I	I	I	I
Real Application Testing (RAT)	Allows performance application testing on production workloads	I	I	I	I
Oracle Machine Learning (formerly known as Advanced Analytics)	Allows you to perform data analytics within the database	I	I	I	B
Spatial and Graph	Allows you to perform geographical analysis and visualization	I	I	I	B
Multitenant	Allows you to create more than three pluggable databases that share the same physical resources	N	I	I	B

Pack	Description	EE	HP	EP	BYOL
Partitioning	Partitions tables to achieve better query performance, storage usage, and so on	N	I	I	B
Advanced Compression	Allows data compression	N	I	I	B
Advanced Security	Allows data encryption at rest and data redaction to mask database queries	N	I	I	B
Label Security	Provides row-level access based on user security levels	N	I	I	B
Database Vault	Helps prevent unauthorized users from accessing privileged data or making unauthorized data changes	N	I	I	B
Oracle On-Line Analytical Processing (OLAP)	Provides an analytics engine for multidimensional cube analytic workload processing	N	I	I	B
Database Lifecycle Management Pack	Covers complete lifecycle of discovery, configuration, compliance management, and data guard for the database	N	I	I	B
Cloud Management Pack	Allows you to build a private cloud using the Oracle database	N	I	I	B
Real Application Cluster (RAC)	Provides multinode scalability and zero-time downtime clustering for the Oracle database	N	N	I	B
In-Memory Database	Allows real-time analytics on production data without requiring a separate reporting database	N	N	I	B
Active Data Guard	Allows you to create a read-only database with continuous recovery running in background	N	N	I	B
Sharding	Allows geographic distributed tables	N	N	I	B

Note: Oracle Support Rewards

With the Oracle Support Rewards Program, BYOL customers get a 25 percent rebate of their total spend for Oracle Support renewal, while ULA customers get a 33 percent rebate. The rebate is based on the monthly OCI spend and can be applied to the support invoice for Oracle core technology like database licenses. If you spend $100,000 on OCI, you would have a $25,000 rebate you can apply to your onprem support invoice.

Database as a Base Database Service

Oracle Base Database Service allows you to create a virtual machine and bare metal with the following options:

- Single-node DB systems with either bare metal or virtual machines
- Two-node RAC DB systems on virtual machines

Each database home can have a maximum of one database. A bare metal DB system allows multiple database homes. A virtual machine DB system allows only a single database home, scalable storage, and scalable CPU. Oracle offers flex shapes for DB systems, making it a more agile infrastructure. Compute is referred to as *Oracle CPU (OCPU)* in OCI. OCPU is equivalent to two vCPUs. You can increase the OCPU from 1 to 64 in increments of 1 at a minimum. For each OCPU, 16 GB RAM gets added to the systems.

These Base Database Service choices allow you to quickly provision complete DB systems with minimal effort based on your specific requirements. Consequently, it is very useful for development and testing purposes.

Note: Be Careful Making Manual Changes

Do not drop the database created as a part of a database system. It is required when you're scaling up and possibly performing other system operations.

Exadata Cloud Service and Exadata Cloud@Customer

Exadata Engineered System is tailor-made to run Oracle Database for all types of workloads. Exadata systems come in different shapes and sizes to meet customers' specific requirements. Exadata hardware includes database servers, storage servers, persistent memory, PCI NVMe flash storage, high-capacity disk drives, and cluster network fabrics to provide high-speed internal connectivity between servers. Exadata has redundant hardware components and provides the highest level of availability. Exadata system software helps achieve the highest level of performance with reliability and consistency. One of the unique features is Smart Scan technology. It offloads data-intensive SQL operation to storage servers. Queries get processed in parallel on disk and flash. Only relevant data is passed back to database servers. Other features like Storage Indexes, Smart Flash Logging, Hybrid Columnar Compression, and more provide unique capabilities to the Exadata system to deliver unparalleled performance. Oracle offers the latest Exadata X11 systems as a part of its cloud infrastructure.

Oracle provides the Exadata Database service on a dedicated infrastructure in the public OCI and on Exadata Cloud@Customer. In a dedicated infrastructure, Oracle manages complete hardware infrastructures, and the customer is responsible for VMs and databases. In other words, all administration, management, and maintenance tasks fall under the customer's responsibilities now, unlike the Autonomous Database Service or the Base Database services.

If a customer cannot move to the cloud for security, compliance, or other reasons, then the Autonomous Database service is available on Exadata Cloud@Customer. This Exadata system will reside in a customer's data center within their network; Oracle still manages the infrastructure. The fully managed Autonomous Database and Exadata Database services run concurrently on Exadata Cloud@Customer.

Exadata Cloud@Customer also opens the door for a hybrid cloud, which is an integration of some resources running on-premises and some on a public cloud. Some of the examples of these resources are databases, applications, or computing infrastructures. Consequently, organizations can follow their security requirements, government guidelines, or any other constraints that otherwise prevent them from using the cloud. Exadata Cloud@Customer plays an important role in this hybrid cloud architecture. It allows organizations to keep the data secured within their on-premises environment and allows applications to move to the cloud or allows organizations to develop native cloud applications. Management of this system also becomes a shared responsibility between organizations and public cloud providers, as we saw in this section.

Autonomous Database Services

Oracle's most unique DBaaS offering is the Oracle Autonomous Database Service, also know as an Autonomous Database. This database service uses the Exadata infrastructure under the hood. Exadata is the best-in-class engineered system offered by Oracle to run Oracle Database.

Autonomous Database is a fully managed database service. It means Oracle takes care of hardware and software installation, administration, and maintenance. You do not need to perform any administration tasks. Autonomous Database will perform all database-related administration tasks such as handling database growth, backing up, patching, and upgrading. You just create the Oracle Database and start using it.

Autonomous Database is a fully elastic database service. You can scale the compute and store it independently without any downtime. Compute is allocated in increments of 1 OCPU or ECPU (a new billing metric introduced in early 2023). Two ECPUs are the equivalent of one OCPU though it is not directly tied to a CPU thread, and storage is allocated in multiples of 1 TB. Autonomous Database also offers auto scaling. With auto scaling, compute and storage will scale up to three times from the original allocated resources during the creation. You can also disable auto scaling if you choose to do so. With compute auto scaling enabled, you will be charged based on the average OCPU consumption within an hour.

Autonomous Database is based on the same Oracle Database. Currently, you can create Oracle Database 23ai as Autonomous Database. Oracle Database 23ai is a converged database, and it supports multimodel, multitenant, and multiworkload capabilities. Customers therefore can create a single database and use it for multiple purposes instead of creating a database for individual requirements like OLTP, OLAP, and JSON.

- **Multimodel:** Supports diverse data models, including relational, JSON, and graph, within a single database. This flexibility is ideal for applications with mixed data requirements.

- **Multitenant:** Enables consolidation of multiple pluggable databases (PDBs) under a single container database (CDB), simplifying management and improving resource utilization.
- **Multiworkload:** Seamlessly handles OLTP, OLAP, and JSON workloads without compromising performance, ensuring an all-encompassing solution for varying application needs.

Autonomous Database supports all existing applications and tools in the cloud or on-premises that support Oracle Database. It also supports machine learning integration and incorporates the creation and execution of machine learning notebooks or models directly within the database environment. Advanced Analytics performs graph and spatial analytics for enhanced data concepts. You can connect to Autonomous Database using Oracle Net Services, such as JDBC Thin Driver, JDBC OCI, Oracle Call Interface (OCI), and ODBC Driver, and database tools such as SQL Developer, SQL*Plus, and SQLcl.

You will need to download a credentials wallet from the Autonomous Database page. There are two types of client credentials wallets available:

- **Instance wallet:** Enables you to connect to the specific database
- **Regional wallet:** Enables you to connect to all databases in the region

OCPU/ECPU pools provide granular control over resources and resource allocation in autonomous databases. These features allow customers to dynamically scale compute resources based on workload demands, as mentioned previously, ensuring cost-efficiency and performance optimization within autonomous databases to auto scaling. Let's say you're running the Autonomous Data Warehouse database and reporting runs during early morning hours.

Oracle offers an Always-Free Autonomous Database service. You can create a free Oracle Cloud account and start using the Autonomous Database service for trial purposes without incurring any cost. There are some restrictions that you should be aware of and follow before using this service, however. Some of the most notable restrictions for using the Always-Free Autonomous Database are

- Maximum 1 OCPU
- Maximum 20 GB Exadata storage per database
- Maximum 2 Always-Free Autonomous Databases per OCI tenancy

You can find more details on this free service at https://www.oracle.com/cloud/free/.

Note: Autonomous Databases Still Need DBAs

While Autonomous Database takes care of a majority of tasks, you will still need a Database Administrator (DBA) to steward the day-to-day database tasks like SQL tuning.

The Autonomous Database service is available on shared and dedicated Exadata infrastructure on OCI.

In a *shared Exadata infrastructure*, multiple customers/tenants share physical resources. An autonomous database on a shared infrastructure has the lowest cost; in other words, this could be a starting point to familiarize yourself with a service without incurring a lot of cost. The autonomous database is created as a pluggable database in this scenario.

In a *dedicated Exadata infrastructure*, the customer's environment is isolated from other customers/tenants. The customer gets complete governance controls and access to all physical resources. Exadata infrastructure is managed by fleet administrators responsible for operating environments and database administrators responsible for database environments. This is a good example of a private Database as a Service.

An autonomous database can be created based on the following workload requirements:

- **Autonomous Database for Transaction Processing (ATP):** It is best suited not just for OLTP workloads but also mixed workloads. It supports all applications from standard to mission-critical, requiring scalable query performance.
- **Autonomous Database for Analytics and Warehousing (ADW):** It is best suited for OLAP workloads supporting business intelligent (BI) tools and all types of SQL processing.
- **Autonomous Database for APEX:** APEX is a low-code application development platform. This autonomous database option allows you to rapidly deploy databases and use APEX to deploy the application rapidly.
- **Autonomous JSON Database (AJD):** It is designed for NoSQL JSON documents. It provides the same benefits and features as Oracle Database.

MySQL and MySQL HeatWave

MySQL is one of the most popular open-source databases. Oracle offers a MySQL database service as a fully managed service. Oracle takes care of all administration, management, and maintenance of the service. These database tasks include scaling, backing up, patching, configuring, and handling OS tasks such as installing, patching, and performing all other hardware-related tasks. The customer is responsible only for managing data.

Oracle offers the following options for MySQL DBaaS:

- Standalone MySQL database system
- High-availability MySQL database system with three MySQL instances with failover and zero data loss capabilities
- HeatWave Cluster database system that allows accelerated query processing for OLTP and OLAP workloads

MySQL Enterprise Edition is available only from OCI. It offers advanced security, including audit, authentication, masking and de-identification, transparent data encryption (TDE), encryption, and firewall.

The MySQL database faces the same challenges in that you need an individual database for different types of workloads. Oracle has introduced the MySQL HeatWave service to resolve this issue. It allows users to run OLTP and OLAP workloads from a single MySQL database. MySQL HeatWave is the only MYSQL service to do so. Users do not need to run the extract, transform, load (ETL) process to move data from one MySQL database to another MySQL database to run analytics. Data is moved from the MySQL database to the HeatWave Analytic cluster in real time and integrated into the high-performance memory accelerator. This in-memory acceleration produces reports significantly faster than Amazon Redshift or Snowflake at a fraction of the price.

MySQL HeatWave provides HeatWave ML, which is native, in-database machine learning. It also provides machine learning–based automation to perform a number of administration and management tasks. MySQL HeatWave also uses built-in machine learning algorithms and provides the ability to create custom machine learning models. These machine learning models can be built using familiar SQL commands, so you don't need any special skill to learn them.

When you create the MySQL database system as HeatWave, you can add a HeatWave cluster with a minimum of 1 and a maximum of 64 nodes. MySQL database nodes and HeatWave cluster nodes interact seamlessly without any user intervention. Whenever certain requirements are met for queries, they are offloaded to a HeatWave cluster, and results are returned to the MySQL database node. This way, the user or application has to interact with the MySQL database only. This also allows the existing application to work without requiring any changes.

MySQL Heatwave is available in the cloud and on-premises with Oracle Dedicated Region Cloud@Customer. Oracle has also made MySQL HeatWave available to Amazon Web Services (AWS).

NoSQL

Traditional RDBMS is perfect for most cases, but when it comes to a very large amount of data, which is common for today's Internet-driven companies, it comes with limitations such as supported data types and constraint issues. The NoSQL database becomes one of the common answers for these cases. The NoSQL database allows more flexibilty in different types of structured and unstructured data in high volumes. Oracle provides the NoSQL database service in the form of JSON documents, plus column and key-value data models.

The NoSQL database is a fully managed service provided by Oracle. So not only is it serverless, but it also provides autoscaling and is highly available in a dedicated environment for all customers. Like other fully managed database services, NoSQL databases are encrypted at rest and in motion and patched without any interuptions. These services also offer Atomicity, Consistency, Isolation, and Durability (ACID) transactions without performance impact. Oracle delivers single-digit millisecond response times for NoSQL databases. This NoSQL database is similar to what you have on-premises, so no application change is required.

How to Provision Databases

So far we have gone over the different types of database services offered by Oracle. Now let's go over how to provision some of these services. You can follow a similar process to provision all of these database services, with some changes depending on the service type.

Provisioning Base Database Service

Go to https://cloud.oracle.com site and log on to your tenancy. At the top-left corner, click the main menu and select **Oracle Database > Oracle Base Database (VM, BM)**, as shown in Figure 8-1.

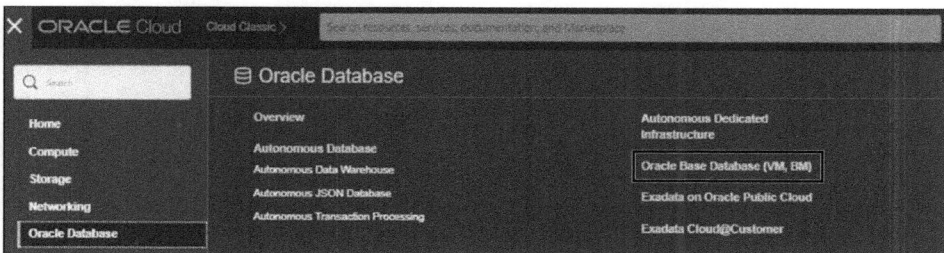

Figure 8-1   Oracle Database Menu

Select the desired compartment on the left-side menu. Click **Create DB System**, as shown in Figure 8-2.

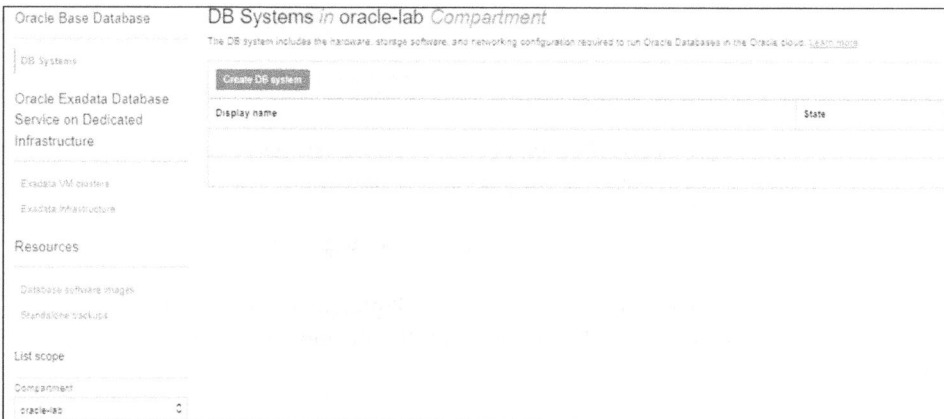

Figure 8-2   Base DB System Home Page

You will be presented with a page to specify a basic configuration for the DB system, as shown in these next steps. Fill in the compartment, DB system name, availability domain, shape type, shape, storage, and server-related information, as shown in Figure 8-3.

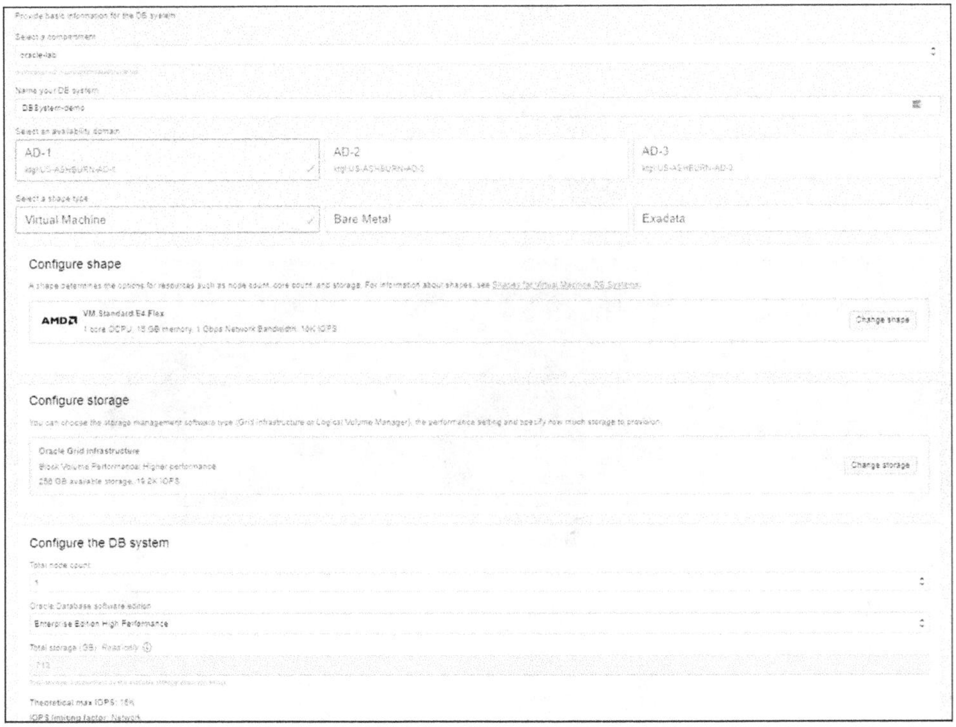

Figure 8-3   Create DB System Page Part 1

You can download the private key or upload or paste your personal public key to access the server. Next, choose the license type and network information, as shown in Figure 8-4.

Then select the appropriate diagnostic collection settings and click **Next**, as shown in Figure 8-5.

A page requesting database information will be displayed, as shown in the following steps. Fill in the database name, administrator credentials, and workload type, as shown in Figure 8-6.

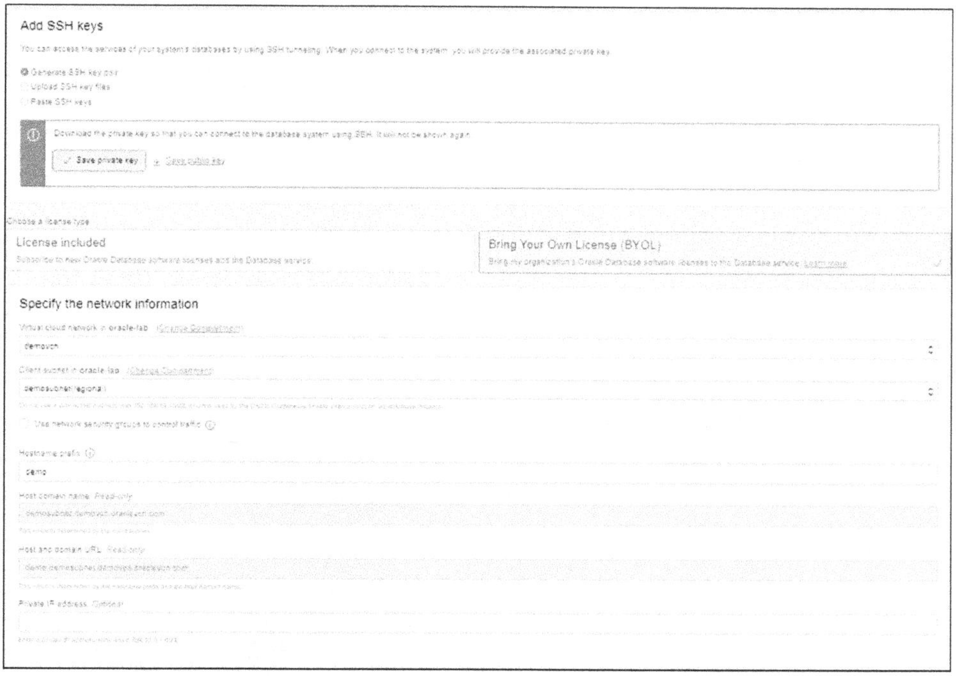

Figure 8-4   Create DB System Page Part 2

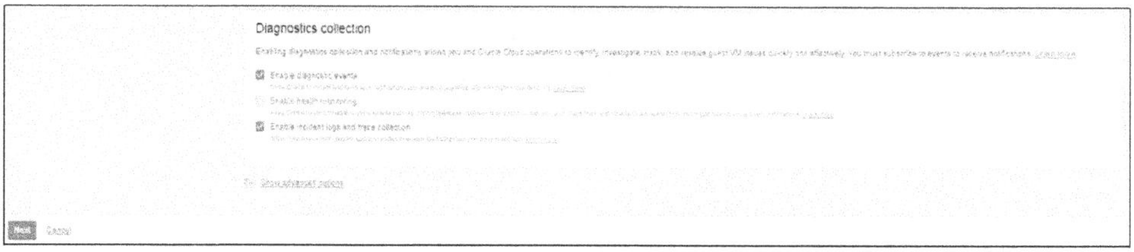

Figure 8-5   Create DB System Page Part 3

Warning

Do not forget your password. Oracle cannot recover it for you. This is an important security feature that helps protect your data from the cloud service provider.

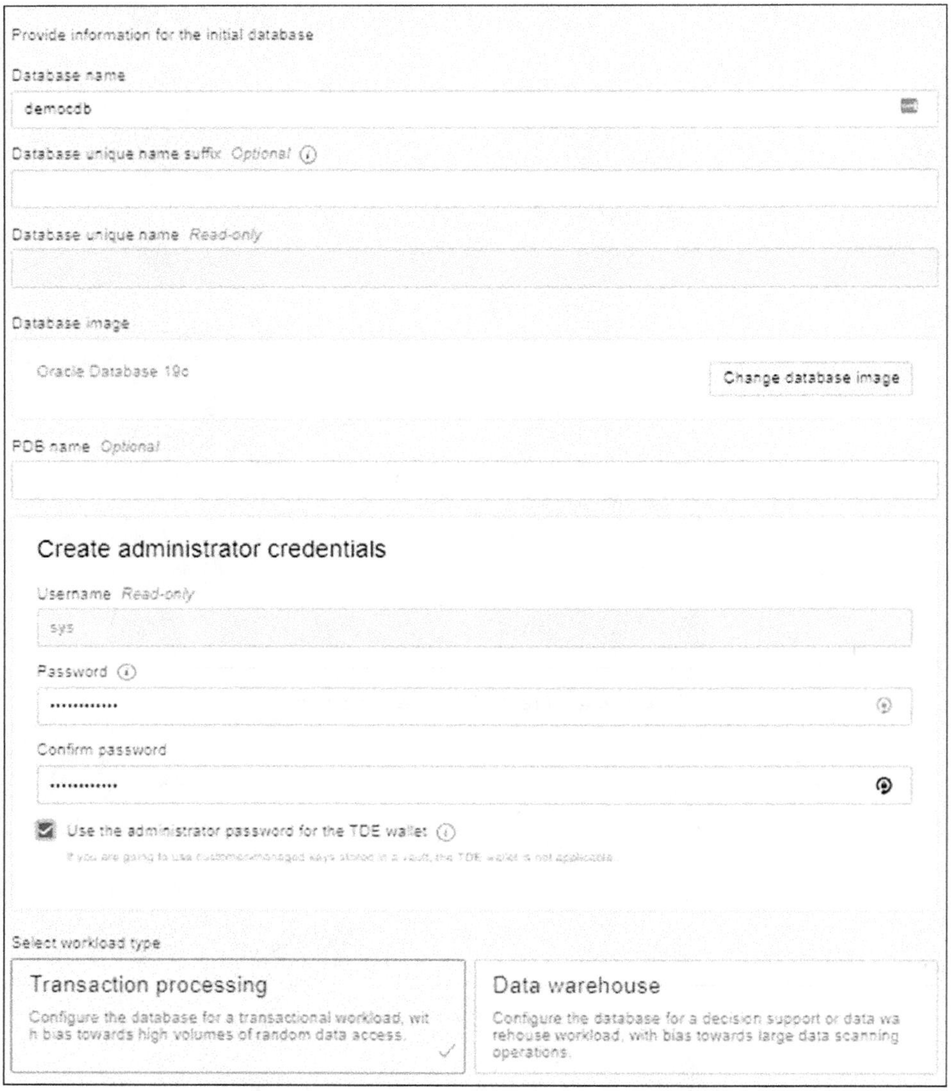

Provide information for the initial database

Database name

demodb

Database unique name suffix *Optional* (i)

Database unique name *Read-only*

Database image

Oracle Database 19c   [Change database image]

PDB name *Optional*

Create administrator credentials

Username *Read-only*

sys

Password (i)

············

Confirm password

············

☑ Use the administrator password for the TDE wallet (i)
 If you are going to use customer-managed keys stored in a vault, the TDE wallet is not applicable.

Select workload type

Transaction processing	Data warehouse
Configure the database for a transactional workload, with bias towards high volumes of random data access.	Configure the database for a decision support or data warehouse workload, with bias towards large data scanning operations.

Figure 8-6   Create DB System Page Part 4

Configure your database backup information and click **Create DB System**, as shown in Figure 8-7.

OCI will take you to the DB System creation page. There, you will find all basic information for the DB system, network, and so on, as shown in Figure 8-8.

Configure database backups

☑ Enable automatic backups ⓘ

ⓘ **Important:** All prerequisites for backing up to Oracle Cloud Infrastructure Object Storage must be met for automatic backups to work.

Backup retention period

30 days

You can change the backup retention period after provisioning.

Backup scheduling (UTC) ⓘ

Anytime

☷ Show advanced options

Previous   **Create DB system**   Cancel

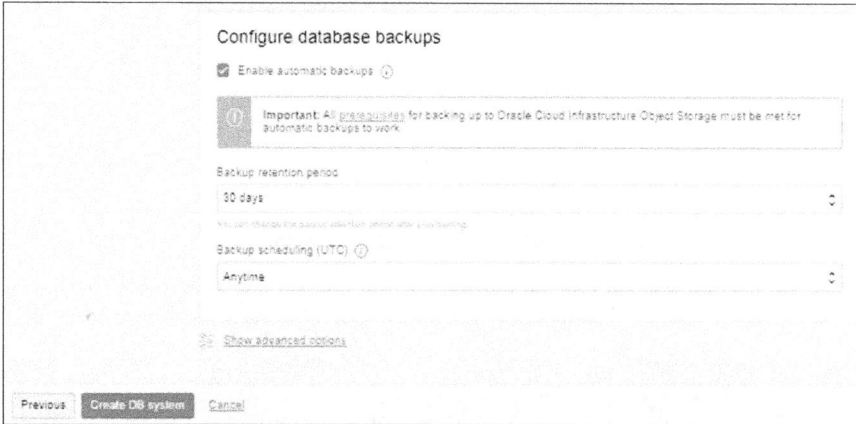

Figure 8-7   Create DB System Page Part 5

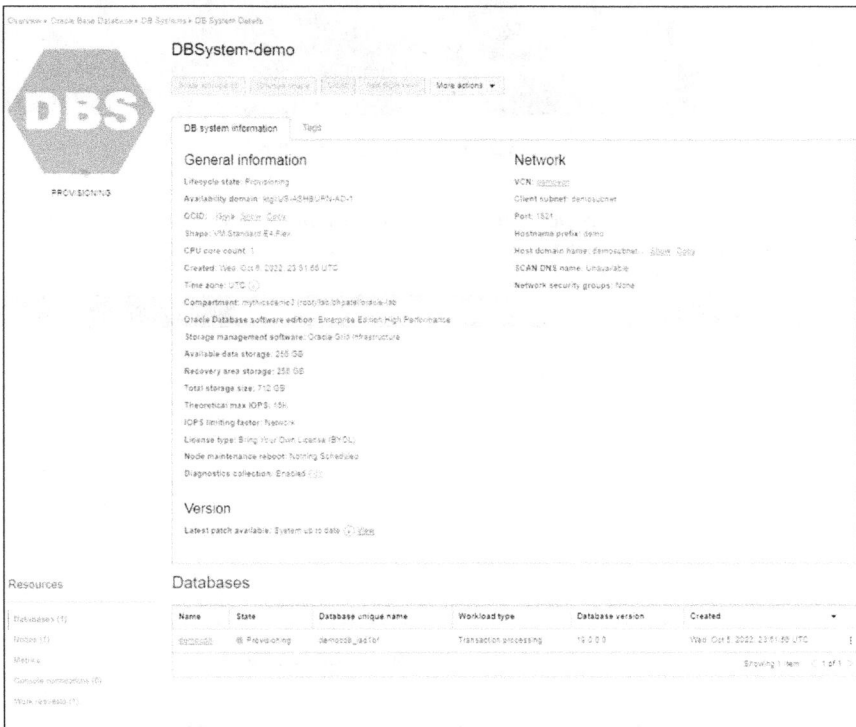

DBSystem-demo

DB system information   Tags

General information

Lifecycle state: Provisioning
Availability domain: kkg/us-ASHBURN-AD-1
OCID: ...rkyra Show Copy
Shape: VM.Standard.E4.Flex
CPU core count: 1
Created: Wed, Oct 5 2022, 23:51:56 UTC
Time zone: UTC ⓘ
Compartment: mythicsdemo2 (root)/lab/bhpatel/oracle-lab
Oracle Database software edition: Enterprise Edition High Performance
Storage management software: Oracle Grid Infrastructure
Available data storage: 256 GB
Recovery area storage: 256 GB
Total storage size: 712 GB
Theoretical max IOPS: 15K
IOPS limiting factor: Network
License type: Bring Your Own License (BYOL)
Node maintenance reboot: Nothing Scheduled
Diagnostics collection: Enabled Edit

Network

VCN: demovcn
Client subnet: demosubnet
Port: 1521
Hostname prefix: demo
Host domain name: demosubnet... Show Copy
SCAN DNS name: Unavailable
Network security groups: None

Version

Latest patch available. System up to date ⓘ View

Databases

Name	State	Database unique name	Workload type	Database version	Created	
demodb	⬤ Provisioning	demodb_iad1of	Transaction processing	19.0.0.0	Wed, Oct 5 2022, 23:51:56 UTC	⋮

Showing 1 item ‹ 1 of 1 ›

Figure 8-8   Base DB System Creation Progress

After the DB system is created, you can go to the Base DB System home page to review the system summary, as shown in Figure 8-9.

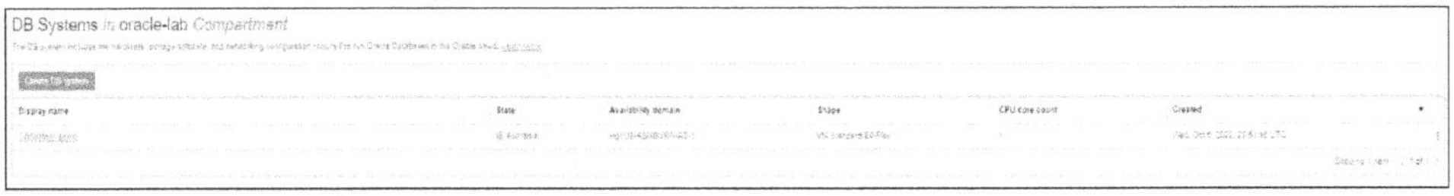

Figure 8-9   Base DB System Status

Provisioning the Autonomous Database Service

Go to https://cloud.oracle.com site and log on to your tenancy. At the top-left corner, click the menu and select **Oracle Database > Autonomous Database**, as shown in Figure 8-10.

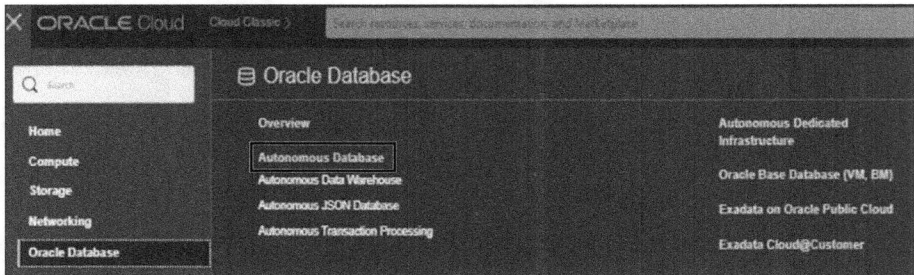

Figure 8-10   Oracle Database Menu

Select your desired compartment on the left-side menu. Click **Create Autonomous System**, as shown in Figure 8-11.

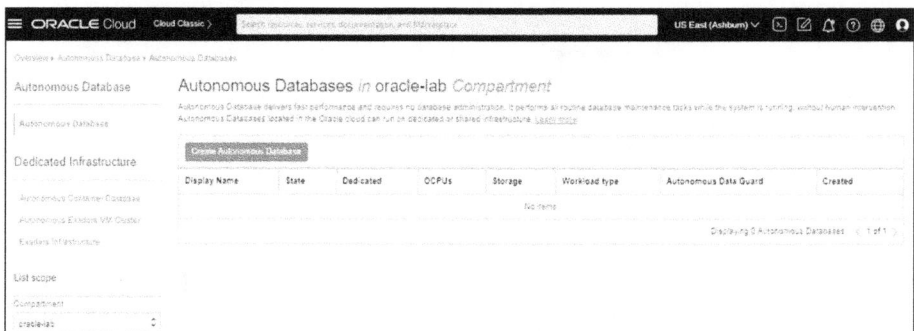

Figure 8-11   Autonomous Database Page

Click **Oracle Autonomous Database**. Next, provide some mandatory information about the database, including workload type, deployment type, physical resources, network access, license type, and database edition, as shown in Figure 8-12.

Set the password for the ADMIN user. You will be logging in to the database as this user. You can specify multiple email addresses as contact for operational notifications and announcements, as shown in Figure 8-13.

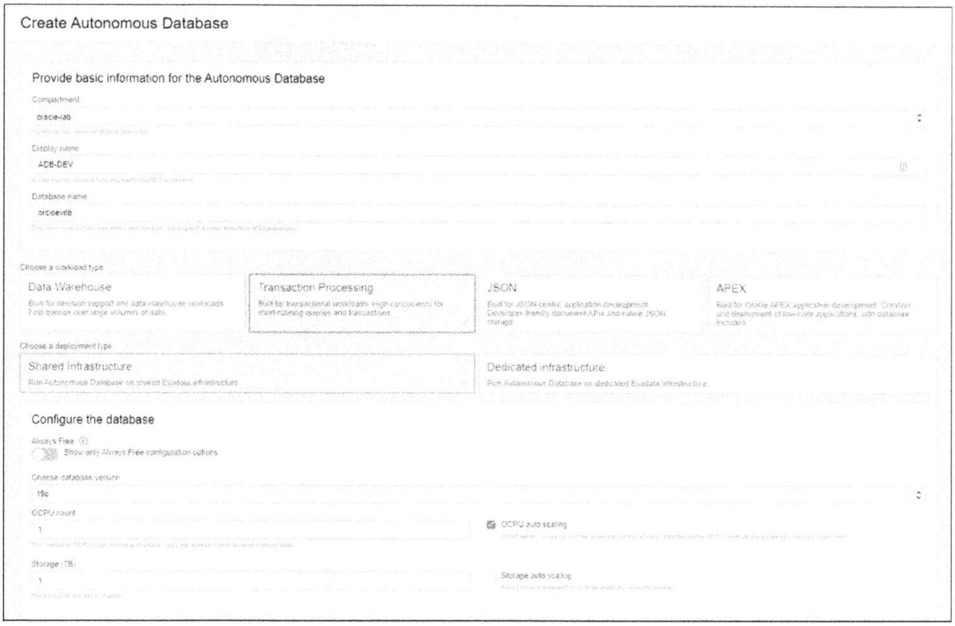

Figure 8-12   Configure Autonomous Database Part 1

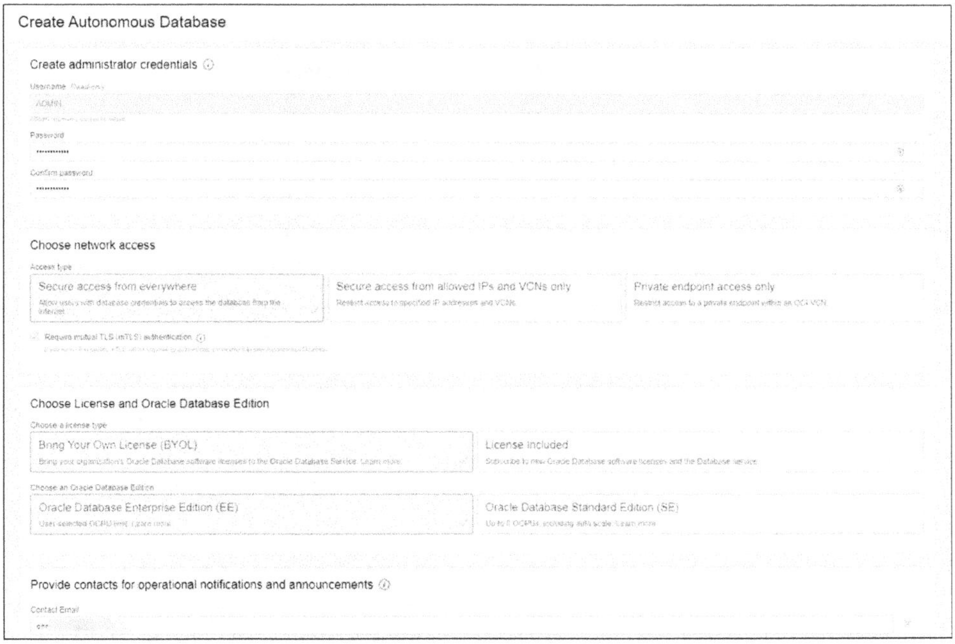

Figure 8-13   Configure Autonomous Database Part 2

Review the advanced options to choose the encryption key, patching maintenance, character and national character sets, and add tags. Now click **Create Autonomous Database** at the bottom-left corner. You will be taken to the Autonomous Database page shown in Figure 8-14.

> **Note**
> Memory will be allocated based on the OCPU selected per the following calculation: 1 OCPU = 16 GB RAM.

Figure 8-14   Autonomous Database Review

Once the database creation is complete, you can see the database in the available state on the main page, as shown in Figure 8-15.

You can connect to the autonomous database using SQL Developer by downloading the database credentials wallet as shown here. First, click **Display Name** for the autonomous database name. Next, click **DB Connection**, as shown in Figure 8-16.

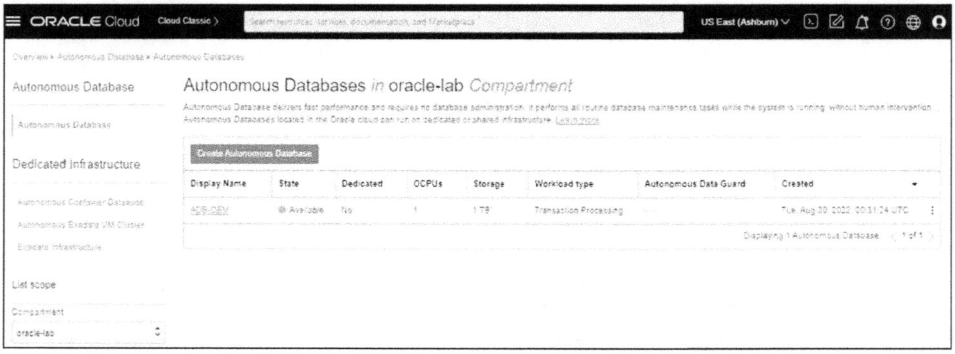

Figure 8-15   Autonomous Database Main Page

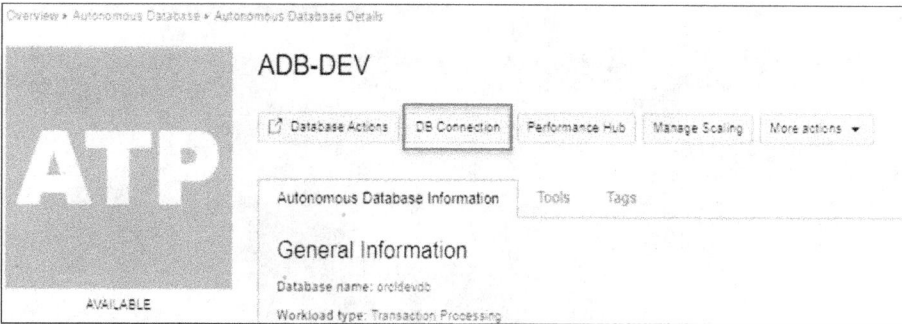

Figure 8-16 Accessing DB Connection

Then select the appropriate wallet type and click **Download Wallet**, as shown in Figure 8-17.

You can provide this wallet zip file to the SQL Developer utility and log in as the ADMIN user.

Provisioning MySQL Database

Let's go over how to create the MySQL HeatWave database service step-by-step. You can create a single or high-availability MySQL database the same way by choosing the appropriate configuration.

Click the menu and select **Databases > MySQL**, as shown in Figure 8-18.

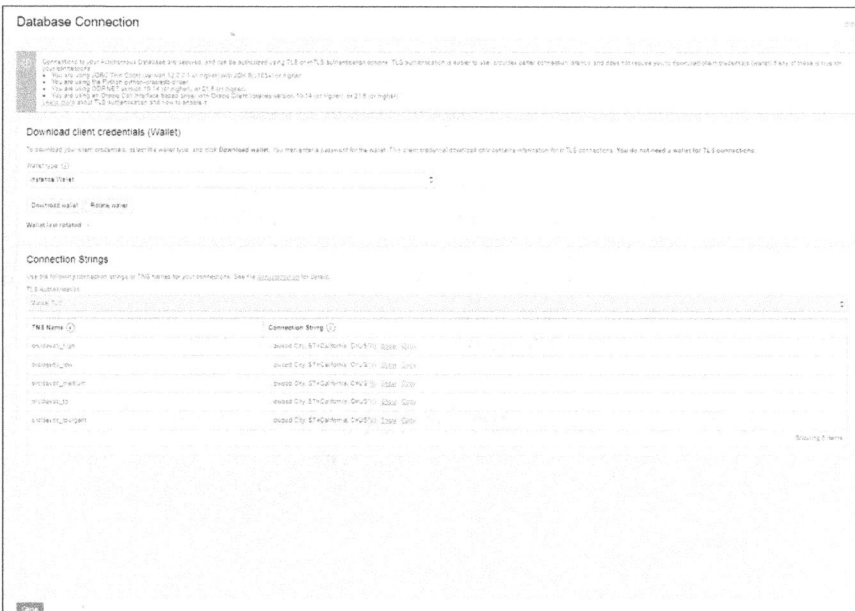

Figure 8-17 Database Connection

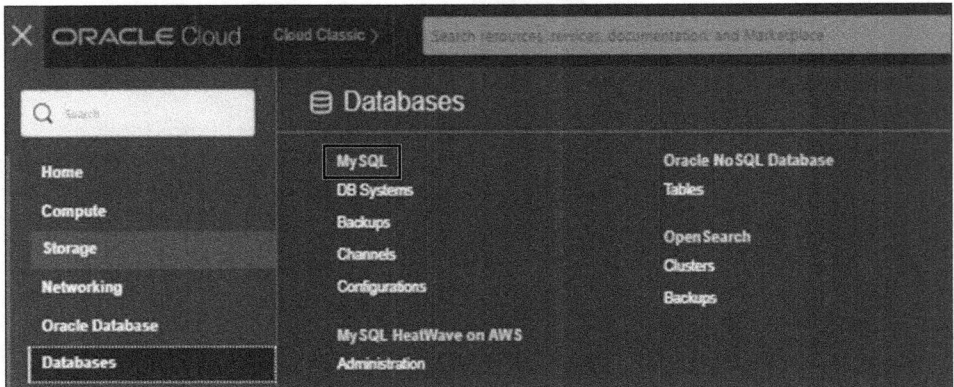

Figure 8-18   Database Menu

Click **Create DB System**, as shown in Figure 8-19.

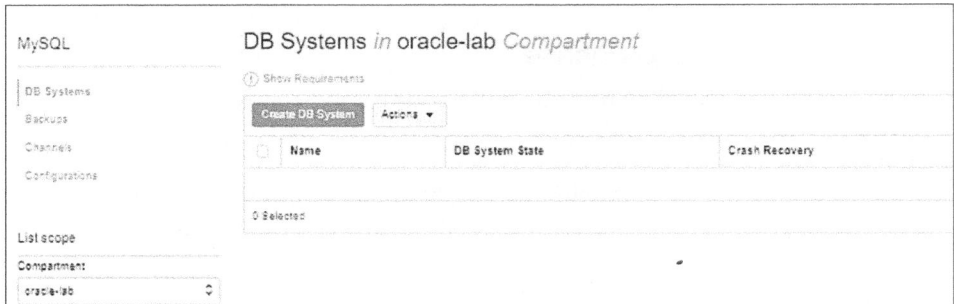

Figure 8-19   MySQL Database Page

Next, provide some required database information, including the configuring network, placement, hardware, and backup plan. Select **HeatWave** as the configuration and create administrator user credentials for the database. Then review the advanced options to configure a backup deletion plan, MySQL system shape and version, crash recovery, maintenance window time, network, data import options, and tags. Click **Create** to create the MySQL DB Systems, as shown in Figure 8-20.

Warning: Keep a Backup of Your Password

Do not forget your password. Oracle cannot recover it for you. This is an important security feature that helps protect your data from the cloud service provider.

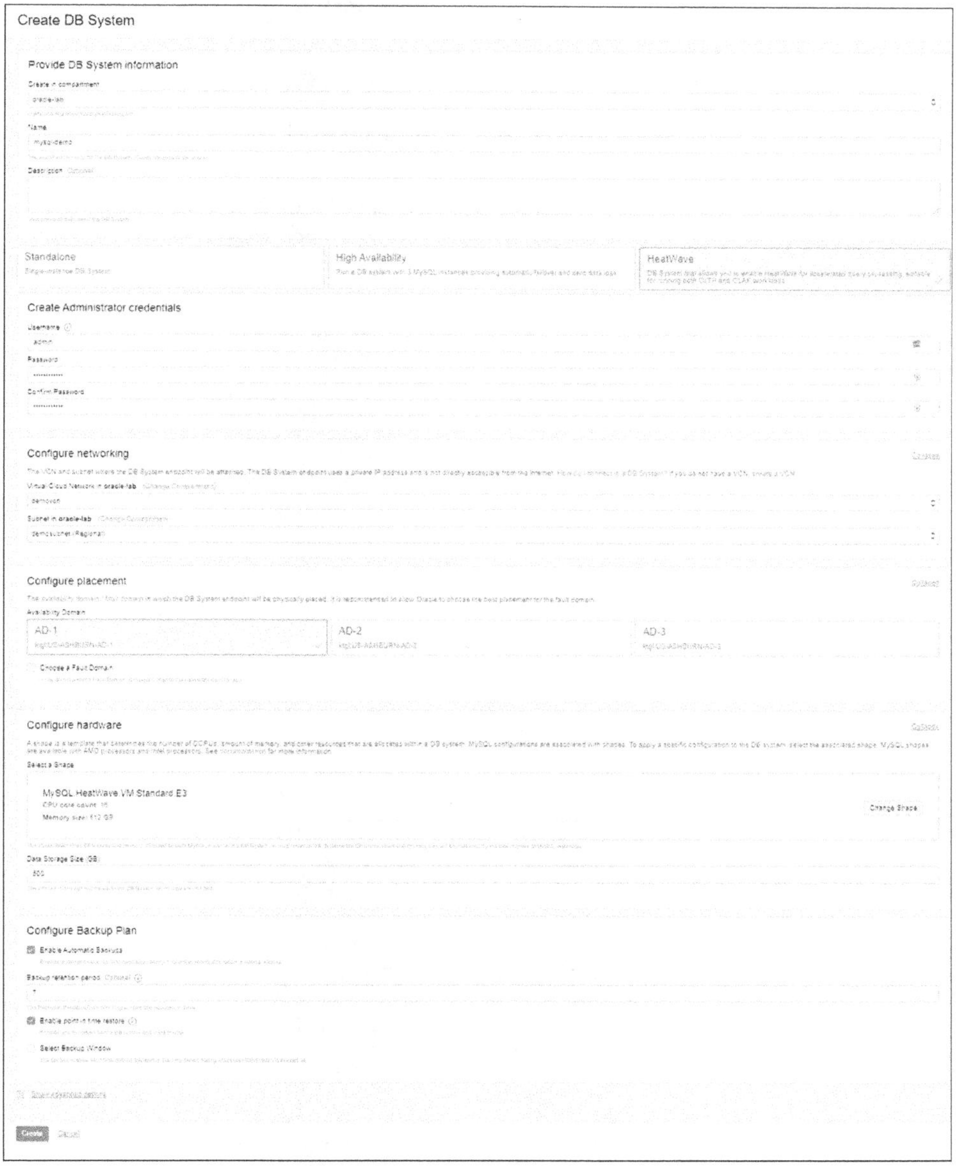

Figure 8-20 MySQL Database Configuration

Once the DB system is created, you should see it on the DB Systems page, as shown in Figure 8-21. You will see all options and their status.

Figure 8-21   MySQL DB System Page

Let's create the HeatWave cluster now. First, click the three dots on the right-hand side, as shown in Figure 8-21, to see all available options. Then click **Add HeatWave Cluster**, as shown in Figure 8-22.

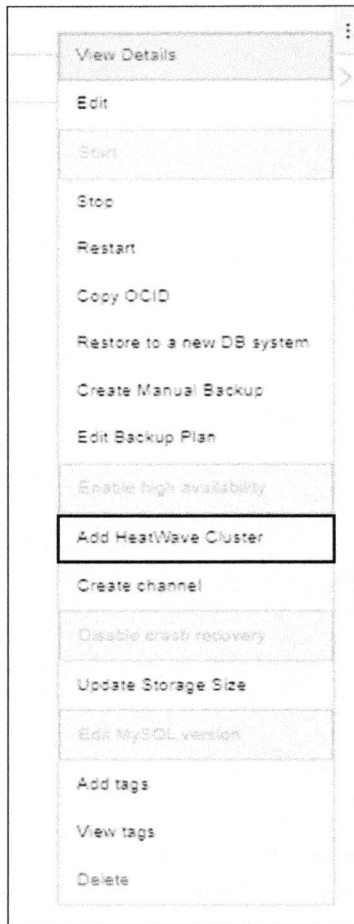

Figure 8-22   MySQL Database Options

Select the appropriate shape and provide a node count (from 1 to a maximum of 64). You can also click **Estimate Node** to get a suggestion based on the shape and size of the data. Then click **Add HeatWave Cluster**, as shown in Figure 8-23.

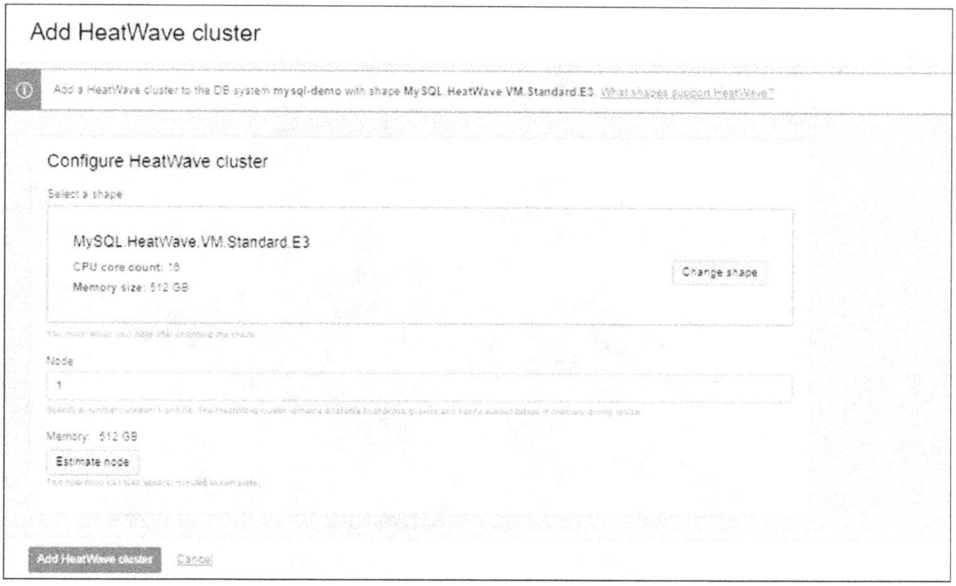

Figure 8-23   HeatWave Configuration

After the HeatWave cluster is added, you will notice the HeatWave Cluster setting is Enabled and the HeatWave State is Active on the main page of MySQL Database Systems, as shown in Figure 8-24.

Figure 8-24   MySQL HeatWave Status

Provisioning the NoSQL Database

To provision the NoSQL database, go to the https://cloud.oracle.com site and log on to your tenancy. At the top-left corner, click the menu and select **Databases > Oracle NoSQL Database**, as shown in Figure 8-25.

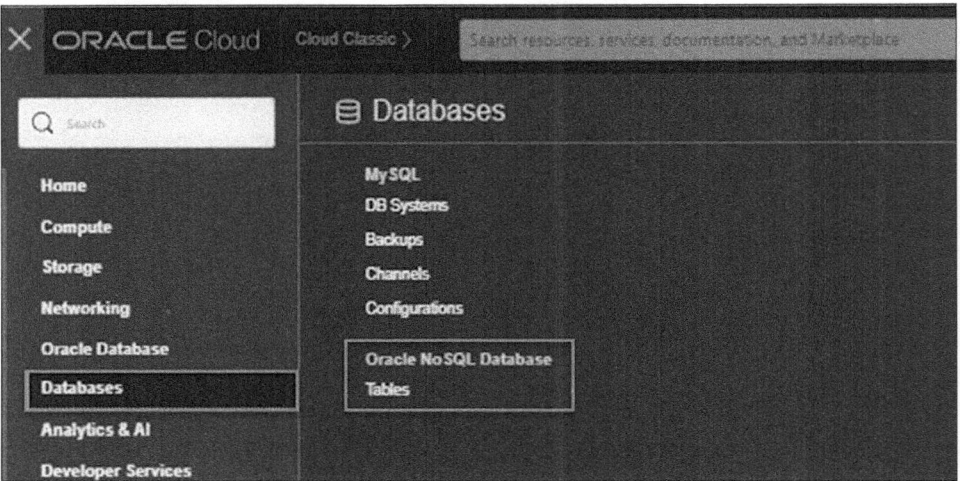

Figure 8-25   NoSQL Database Menu

Next, click **Create Table**, as shown in Figure 8-26.

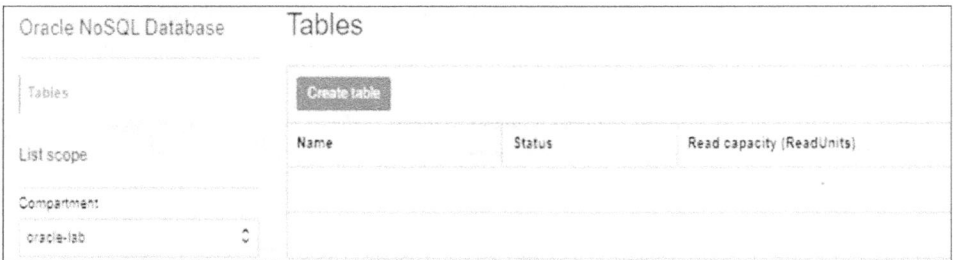

Figure 8-26   NoSQL Database Main Page

Next, provide the table creation mode, capacity mode, table name, and column details, as shown in Figure 8-27.

When the NoSQL table creation is complete, you will see its summary on the Oracle NoSQL Database main page, as shown in Figure 8-28.

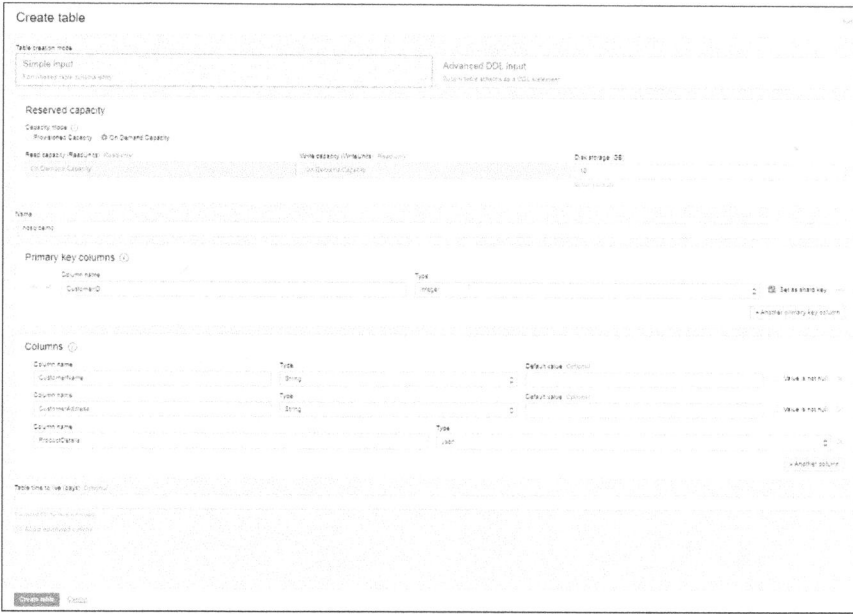

Figure 8-27 NoSQL Database Configuration

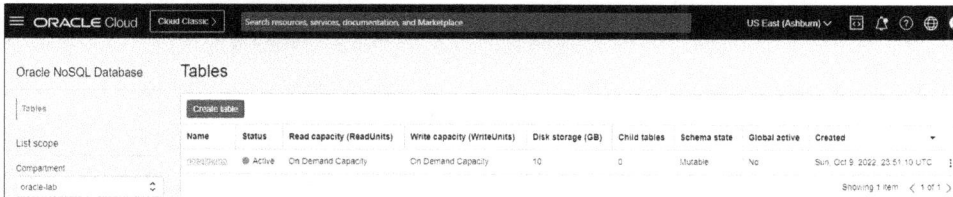

Figure 8-28 NoSQL Database Main Page

Summary

In this chapter, you learned that *Oracle* is a synonym for the world's best database, so it's no surprise that each DBaaS offered in OCI has unique characteristics and perspectives to it. The Autonomous Database service is one kind of DBaaS offered by Oracle. It provides customers with a means to test cloud database features and a path to ease migration to the cloud. In this chapter, we described all the different types of database services offered by OCI, such as Oracle, MySQL, and NoSQL. Some of the most common reasons why a customer chooses a specific DBaaS are the level of control over the environment and how all management tasks are handled. In the next chapter, we will explore DevOps services offered by OCI.

OCI DevOps Service

When we mention *continuous integration and continuous delivery*, also known as *CI/CD*, the image shown in Figure 9-1 is often at the forefront of these discussions. This image is intended to display an infinite loop of build, deployment, and release stages that never end. It is a continuous release process. Benefits of CI/CD include everything from faster software release cycles to bridging the gap between developers and operators. In practicality though, CI/CD is summed up as an approach to infuse extreme automation in the stages of application development. CI/CD fits well into the Agile culture of software development where small, incremental releases are pushed out instead of a single big bang deployment. While there is no shortage of methods to introducing automation into your build and deploy processes (which can include custom approaches), modern tools such as Jenkins and GitLab exist and have standardized our way of delivering continuous integration and continuous delivery. *Oracle Cloud Infrastructure DevOps*, or *OCI DevOps* for short, is one such platform that simplifies the automation of your software development lifecycle releases.

Note: CI/CD Development or Delivery?

CI/CD empowers teams to quickly and consistently deliver high-quality software by automating the processes of building, testing, and deploying applications. The one bit of confusion often arises from its name: continuous integration/continuous *delivery* or continuous *deployment*. Both "delivery" and "deployment" are commonly used interchangeably, and both terms are correct.

CI/CD is the foundation of DevOps. While CI/CD is the practical implementation of software delivery, DevOps is more of a methodology. A combination of the words *development* and *operations*, DevOps embodies a collaborative culture among these two teams to encourage rapid, continuous deployments and it reduces processes that hamper software releases.

In this chapter, we will focus on core concepts and terminology of CI/CD and how it relates to OCI DevOps.

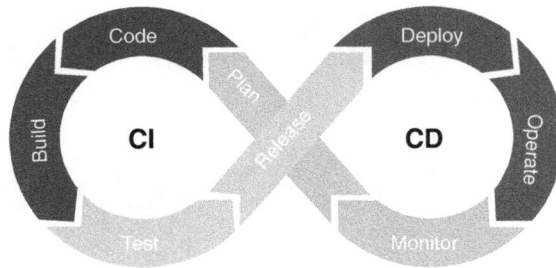

Figure 9-1   The Stages of CI/CD

Overview of OCI DevOps

OCI DevOps is a platform that enables you to deliver end-to-end CI/CD. From here, you can collaborate and integrate changes through the building, testing, and deployment of your software and applications to Oracle Cloud.

OCI DevOps is a service under the Developer Services group within OCI (see Figure 9-2).

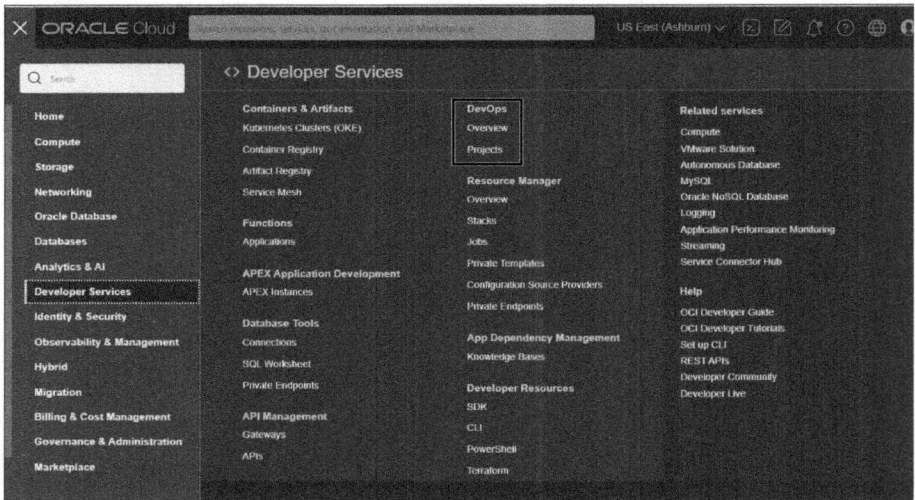

Figure 9-2   OCI DevOps

As seen in the overview page of OCI DevOps in Figure 9-3, this becomes your starting point. A *DevOps Project* is the foundation of your automation because it includes all resources needed to implement your CI/CD workflow. This workflow can include artifacts, build pipelines, deployment pipelines, code repositories or external connections to other repositories, triggers, and target deployment environments. The next section delves deeper into many of these components.

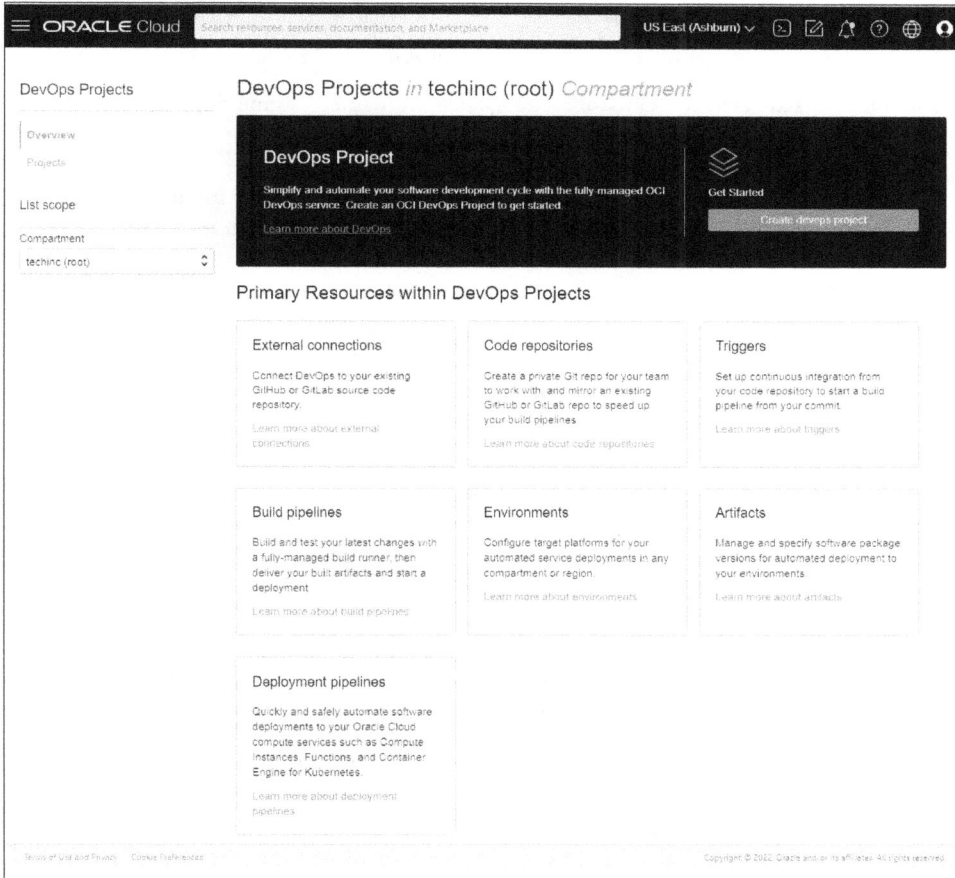

Figure 9-3 OCI DevOps Overview Page

OCI DevOps can be leveraged in a number of ways that include

- Connecting to external repositories such as GitLab, GitLab Server, GitHub, Bitbucket Cloud, Bitbucket Server, and Visual Builder Studio
- Triggering a build automatically when source code is committed or a pull request is initiated
- Testing changes during a build pipeline
- Supporting blue-green and canary deployment strategies
- Automating provisioning of OCI services (such as compute or database)
- Integrating with CI/CD tools such as Jenkins, GitHub, and GitLab

There is no charge to take advantage of OCI DevOps, though any OCI resources created to support your pipeline may incur their respective cost.

Deployment Environments

OCI DevOps can deploy to one of three types of *deployment environments*:

- **Oracle Kubernetes Cluster:** The Oracle Container Engine for Kubernetes (OKE) is a fully managed service that supports the deployment and management of containers in the cloud.
- **Compute Instances:** The OCI Compute service can launch instances of varying hardware specifications to run compute hosts in the cloud. These are also referred to as *instance groups* in OCI DevOps.
- **Functions:** Oracle Functions is a managed Function-as-a-Service (FaaS) platform in the cloud.

Deployment Strategies

OCI DevOps supports two types of deployment strategies to OKE or instance groups: *blue-green deployment strategy* and *canary deployment strategy*. Both of these strategies reduce downtime and support the ability to roll back as well.

Figure 9-4 demonstrates a blue-green deployment strategy. In the top diagram in this figure, two parallel production environments are running, but only one of them (green) is live and accepting requests. The new version 2 of the application is deployed to the blue (just-deployed) environment. Then the environments are switched. On the bottom diagram, the new version 2 of the application is now live and considered the green environment, while the previous version 1 becomes the blue standby environment.

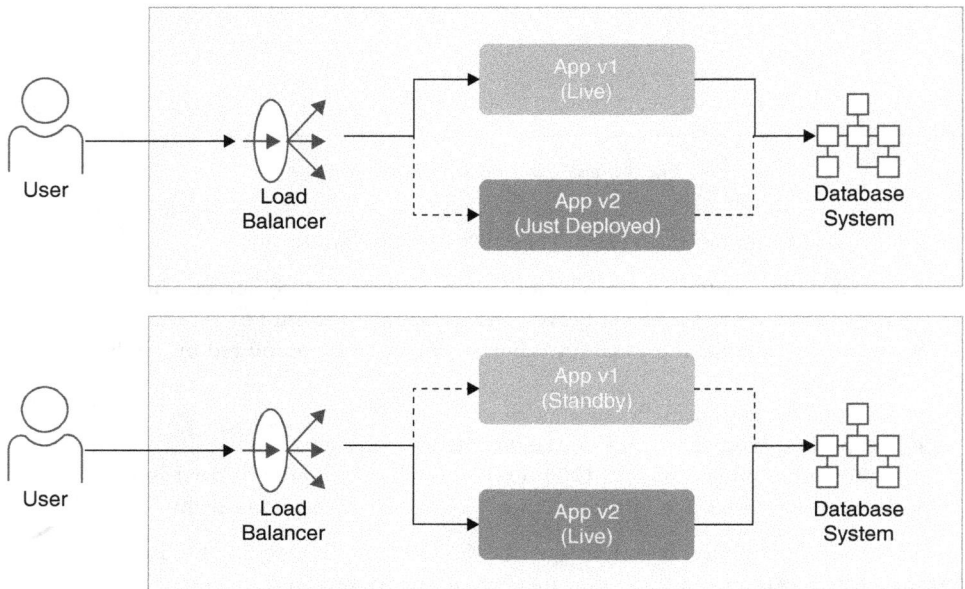

Figure 9-4   Blue-Green Deployment Strategy

Rollback is simple, because traffic can be immediately reverted back to the previous version of the application.

Figure 9-5 demonstrates a canary deployment strategy. The new version 2 of the application is deployed incrementally, with initially no traffic being routed to it. The new canary version can be tested (preferably automatically through a release pipeline) before opening it up to user traffic, usually to a small number of users in the beginning. If problems are experienced, the new canary deployment can be taken offline or out of load. When successful, the process is repeated for all other nodes.

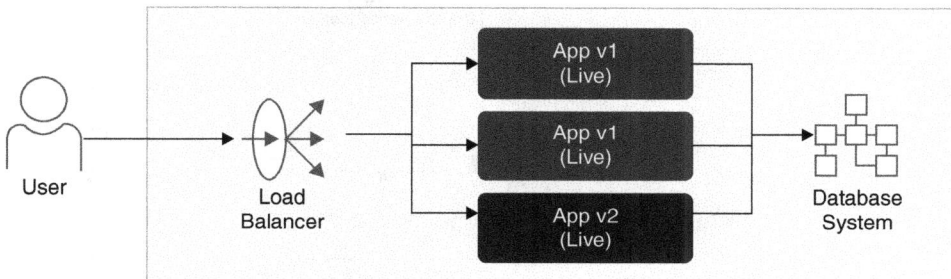

Figure 9-5   Canary Deployment Strategy

DevOps Components and Resources

Let's observe Figure 9-6. This figure demonstrates a high-level flow of a typical pipeline. The target deployment environment here is *Oracle Functions*, which is a serverless Function-as-a-Service platform, similar to AWS Lambda or Azure Functions. The code artifacts are maintained in a *repository*. The pipelines define the stages needed to deliver the artifacts to the target deployment environment—in this case, Oracle Functions. When the code is committed to the code repository, it triggers a build pipeline wherein the output is stored in the container register as Docker images. The deployment pipeline then deploys it to the OCI Functions environment.

The end-to-end checkout, build, and deployment can be fully automated with a click of a button, or for example, triggered upon code commit. Once you create a DevOps project, multiple resources are available at your disposal to create your project (see the menu options in Figure 9-7). A DevOps project is merely a logical grouping of these resources.

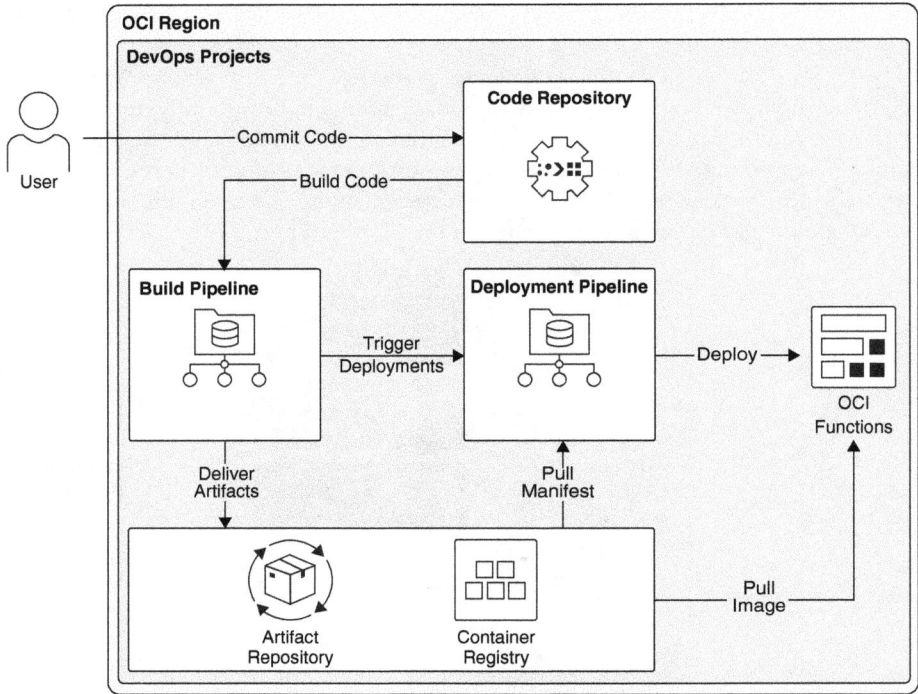

Figure 9-6   DevOps Deployment Pipeline

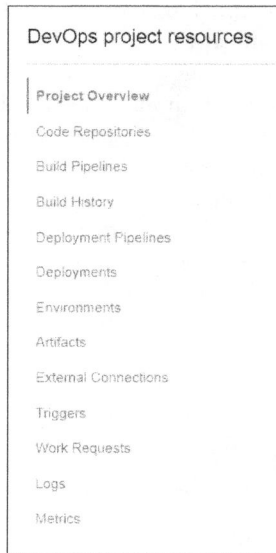

Figure 9-7   DevOps Project Resources

Artifacts are maintained in one of several locations:

- **Code Repository:** This is a private repository to the DevOps project where code can be viewed, accessed, and committed. Standard branching and Git tags are supported. This console is accessible under the DevOps project.
- **Container Registry:** This is a private Docker registry for OKE deployments, accessible via the Containers & Artifacts service under Developer Services.
- **Artifacts Registry:** This registry maintains software development packages for deployment to services such as Oracle Functions or YAML deployment configurations, accessible via the Containers & Artifacts service under Developer Services.
- **External Connections:** This feature establishes a connection to an external repository such as GitHub, GitLab, Bitbucket Cloud, Visual Builder Studio, Bitbucket Studio, and GitLab Server.

Figure 9-7 shows the menu options as they appear in the console, and Table 9-1 describes the purpose of some of the main ones.

Table 9-1   DevOps Project Resources

Term	Explanation
Code Repository	This is a private code repository.
Build Pipeline	This is a pipeline that contains stages of the build process, which includes compiling and testing the application. The build pipeline can trigger a deployment pipeline.
Deployment Pipeline	This pipeline contains stages that define the flow needed to deploy your artifacts to an environment. The deployment stage includes individual actions within a pipeline. The different stage types supported are *rolling deployment, wait, manual approval,* and *invoke function.*
Deployment	Running a deployment pipeline will appear as an execution here. From here, you can view details of the execution, including the parameters passed and log details.
Environment	The target deployment environment can be OKE, instance groups (for compute), or functions.
Artifact	This is a pointer to the source location of the actual artifact which will be deployed to the target deployment environment. Each artifact has a name and a version. For example, artifacts such as a container image or a Kubernetes manifest are hosted on OCI repositories such as Container Registry and Artifact Registry.
Trigger	A trigger can be created against a code repository with an action defined (an action specifies which build pipeline to trigger).
Work Request	This request enables you to view and monitor the progress of operations.

Oracle provides automated scripts to set up a sample DevOps deployment for each of the three environments: OKE, compute instance groups, or functions. The sample DevOps walkthroughs leverage a combination of Terraform code and stacks in the

OCI Resource Manager service to provision this environment. Even if you don't have an understanding of either Terraform or Resource Manager, this is a point-and-click approach to setting up a sample DevOps environment in OCI with all the dependencies taken care of to get you inspecting the various components under OCI DevOps. You can access this sample at https://docs.oracle.com/en/solutions/build-pipeline-using-devops/index.html. Figure 9-8 shows a snippet of this web page.

Figure 9-8   Deploying Oracle's Sample DevOps Service to Play Around With

How to Create a Working Sample Project

In this section, we will create and execute the sample pipeline depicted in Figure 9-9. This is a slight variation of the instance group pipeline in the Oracle sample linked to previously.

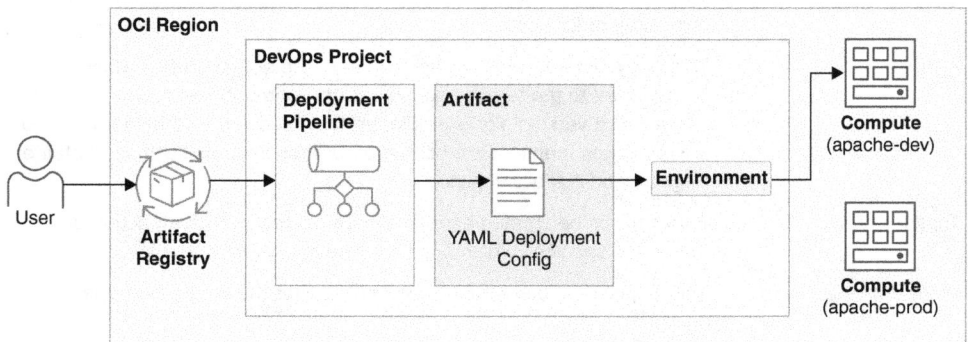

Figure 9-9   Logical Architecture of Our Sample Pipeline

This example demonstrates the use of DevOps to implement *Infrastructure as Code (IaC)*, which is meant to deploy infrastructure, such as the Apache HTTP Server in this case, through an automated means instead of manually. Thus, this pipeline can be run against any number of target environments, ensuring consistency. The deployment pipeline will download the shell script deploy_apache.sh from the OCI Artifact Registry, and execute a YAML configuration that deploys it to the apache-dev compute instance environment. The same pipeline can be used to execute against the next target environment, apache-prod, should we choose to. Thus, the project will consist of the following resources:

- Two compute instances (one development and one production instance)
- One Artifact Registry, which includes
  - One artifact (deployment script deploy_apache.sh)
- One DevOps project, which includes the following components:
  - One deployment pipeline
  - One environment (references the compute apache-dev instance)
  - One general artifact (reference to the file in the Artifact Registry)
  - One inline artifact (instance group deployment configuration)

Creating Compute Instances to Deploy To

The first step is to create a compute instance named apache-dev. For the purpose of this example, it can be created as Always Free tier instance shapes. Figure 9-10 shows the list of these compute instances.

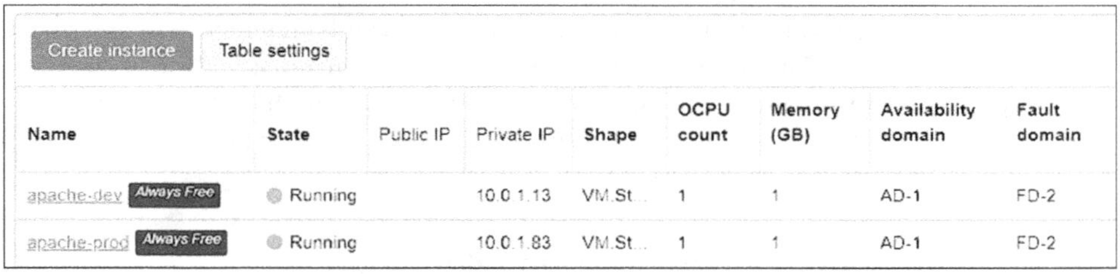

Name	State	Public IP	Private IP	Shape	OCPU count	Memory (GB)	Availability domain	Fault domain
apache-dev *Always Free*	● Running		10.0.1.13	VM.St...	1	1	AD-1	FD-2
apache-prod *Always Free*	● Running		10.0.1.83	VM.St...	1	1	AD-1	FD-2

Create instance   Table settings

Figure 9-10   Post-Creation of the Compute Instances

Granting Permissions to Compute Instance Run Command Plug

Because the script used to install the Apache HTTP Server will require sudo permissions, log in to the apache-dev compute instance via SSH and grant sudo permissions to the Compute Instance Run Command plug-in to be able to run the command. This is a one-time activity specific to this sample.

Step 1. Log in to the apache-dev compute instance.

Step 2. Run the commands listed in Example 9-1 to create a sudoers configuration file.

Step 3. Confirm that response output of the final command is "parsed OK."

Example 9-1   Creating a sudoers Configuration File

```
# Login as root
sudo su - root
# Navigate to the sudoers directory
cd /etc/sudoers.d
# Create file (an existing 100-oracle-cloud-agent-run-command may exist)
echo "ocarun ALL=(ALL) NOPASSWD:ALL" > 101-oracle-cloud-agent-run-command
# Validate the syntax in the configuration file
visudo -cf ./101-oracle-cloud-agent-run-command
```

Creating an Artifact Registry to Host Artifacts

In these steps, we will create an Artifact Registry. The process to create a registry that will host our files is rather straightforward:

Step 1. Navigate to the OCI console menu and click **Developer Services > Containers & Artifacts**.

Step 2. Click **Artifact Registry**.

Step 3. Click **Create Repository**.

Step 4. Enter the name **apache-artifact-repository** and click **Create**.

Uploading a Script to the Artifact Registry

Now that the registry is created, upload a prewritten shell script to it. The shell script deploy_apache.sh is provided in Example 9-2. This script will be referenced as an artifact in the DevOps project. The script is straightforward, self-explanatory, and all-inclusive in its steps; it downloads and installs Apache from the Yum repository, opens the local Linux firewall ports 80 and 443 to allow access to the Apache web server, creates a sample index.html file, and starts Apache.

Example 9-2   Contents of the deploy_apache.sh Script

```
# Download and install Apache from Yum repository
sudo yum -y update
sudo yum -y install httpd

# Open local firewall to ports 80 and 443
sudo firewall-cmd --permanent --add-port=80/tcp
sudo firewall-cmd --permanent --add-port=443/tcp
sudo firewall-cmd --reload

# Create sample HTML file
sudo systemctl start httpd
```

```
sudo echo "Successfully deployed ${version}" > /tmp/index.html;
sudo cp /tmp/index.html /var/www/html/index.html;

# Start Apache
sudo systemctl start httpd;
```

Step 1. Create a file called deploy_apache.sh on your local workstation with the contents shown in Example 9-2.

Step 2. Since the registry apache-artifact-repository is created, click **Upload Artifact** to upload the script deploy_apache.sh.

Step 3. For Artifact Path, enter a path structure such as **apacheproject/deploy_ apache.sh**.

Step 4. For Version, provide a version such as **1.0**.

Step 5. Upload the file from your local workstation. See Figure 9-11 for reference.

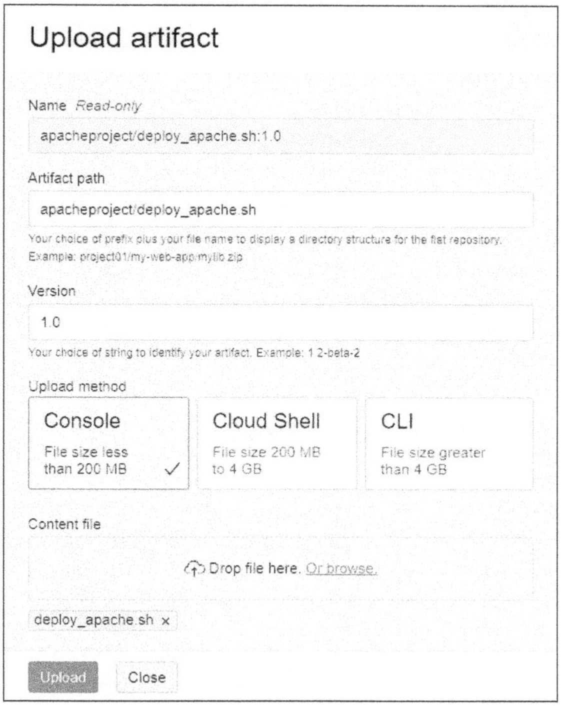

Figure 9-11   Uploading a Shell Script to the Artifact Registry

Step 6. Click **Upload**.

Creating a Notification Topic

Prior to creating a DevOps project, you must create a *topic* that is used for the DevOps project notifications. A topic is required during the creation of the DevOps project.

Step 1. Navigate to the OCI console menu and click **Developer Services > Notifications** (it will be under the Application Integration submenu).

Step 2. Click **Create Topic**.

Step 3. Enter the name **apacheprojecttopic** and click **Create**.

Creating a DevOps Project

A DevOps project is a logical grouping of the resources required for your DevOps implementation. On its own, it does nothing. After it is created, you would subsequently create any number of pipelines, reference artifacts, set up target environments, and view the work requests of your deployments.

Step 1. Navigate to the OCI console menu and click **Developer Services > DevOps**.

Step 2. Click **Projects**.

Step 3. Click **Create Devops Project**.

Step 4. Enter the project name **apacheproject**.

Step 5. Click **Select Topic** and select **apacheprojecttopic**, which was the topic created in the previous section. Then click **Select Topic**.

Step 6. Click **Create Devops Project**.

Step 7. On the confirmation page, you will see an orange warning stating "Logging is required to run build and deployment pipeline." Click **Enable Log**.

Step 8. Toggle the **Enable Log** button; then click **Enable Log**.

Creating an Environment in the DevOps Project

An environment could be an instance group, as is the case in our sample here. We will have one instance group for the development server. Note that each instance group can potentially have multiple compute instances in them; for instance, production may have four compute instances that we would like to deploy to all at once. In this section, we will create a single instance group that will host the single apache-dev compute instance.

Step 1. Navigate to the OCI console menu, then click **Developer Services > DevOps**.

Step 2. Click **Projects**.

Step 3. Click your project name **apacheproject**.

Step 4. Click **Environments** on the leftmost menu.

Step 5. Select **Instance Group**, since we are deploying to compute instances.

Step 6. Enter the name **apache-dev-servers** and then click **Next**.

Step 7. Click **Add Instance** and select the **apache-dev** compute instance.

Step 8. Click **Create Environment**.

Observing the breadcrumb menu at the top of Figure 9-12, we are in the apacheproject under the Environments menu. In the Environments page, we have selected apache-dev-servers to show the details of this environment. At the moment, only one compute instance, apache-dev, is in this instance group.

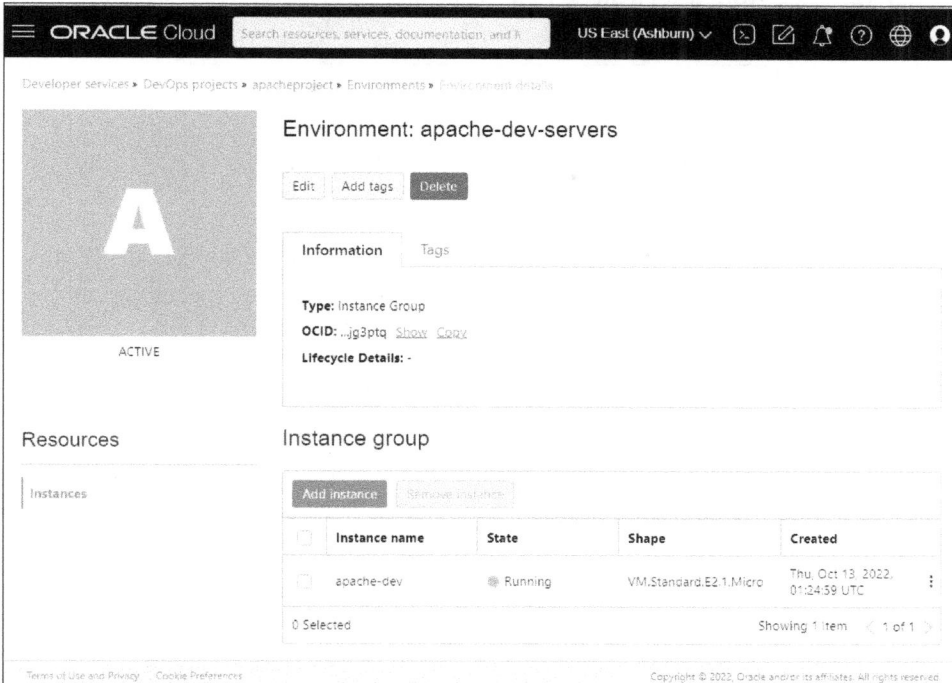

Figure 9-12   Post-Creation of a DevOps Project Environment

Adding an Artifact from the Artifact Registry to the DevOps Project

In an earlier step, we uploaded the shell script deploy_apache.sh to the Artifact Registry. The steps here add a reference of this artifact to this DevOps project.

Step 1. Navigate to the OCI console menu and click **Developer Services > DevOps**.

Step 2. Click **Projects**.

Step 3. Click your project name **apacheproject**.

Step 4. Click **Artifacts** on the leftmost menu.

Step 5. Click **Add Artifact**.

Step 6. Enter the name **deploy_apache.sh**.

Step 7. Select the type **General Artifact**.

Step 8. Select the artifact source **Artifact Registry Repository**.

Step 9. Select the artifact registry repository **apache-artifact-repository**.

Step 10. Select the artifact location **Select Existing Location**.

Step 11. Select the artifact **apacheproject/deploy_apache.sh/1.0**.

Step 12. Click **Add**. See Figure 9-13 for reference.

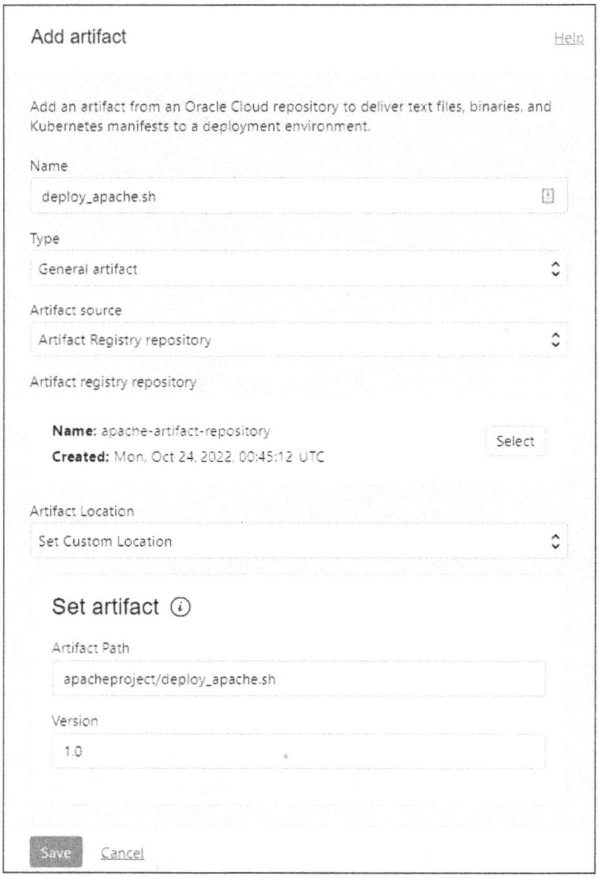

Figure 9-13   Adding an Artifact from the Artifact Registry to the DevOps Project

Adding an Instance Group Deployment Configuration Artifact

Prior to executing the deploy_apache.sh script on our target environment, an *instance group deployment configuration* is required. The deployment configuration to be used is documented in Example 9-3. It specifies the user used to execute the artifact deploy_apache.sh, which would be hosted under the /tmp folder.

Example 9-3 Contents of the Instance Group Deployment Configuration

```
# Configuration used only for instance group deployments
version: 1.0
component: deployment
runAs: root
env:
  variables:
    version: "v1.0"
files:
  # Define where the files will be put on the compute instance
- source: /
  destination: /tmp
steps:
  # Define the scripts to execute on the instance after it is copied over
  - stepType: Command
    name: Install Apache Web Server
    command: /tmp/apacheproject/deploy_apache.sh
    runAs: root
    timeoutInSeconds: 600
```

Step 1. While still in the DevOps project apacheproject, click **Artifacts** on the leftmost menu.

Step 2. Click **Add Artifact**.

Step 3. Enter the name **instance_group_deployment_configuration**.

Step 4. Select the type **Instance Group Deployment Configuration**.

Step 5. Select the artifact source **Inline**.

Step 6. Paste the contents of Example 9-3 into the Value text box.

Step 7. Uncheck **Allow Parameterization**.

Step 8. Click **Add**.

Observe Figure 9-14. Here, you can see two artifacts in the DevOps project. One references a shell script in the Artifact Registry, and the other is an inline configuration file local to the DevOps project.

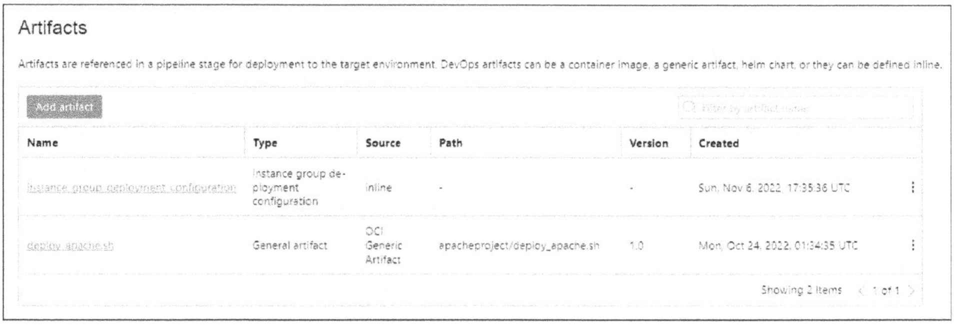

Figure 9-14 Listing All Artifacts in the DevOps Project

Creating a Deployment Pipeline

A pipeline is a series of steps, each performing a particular series of operations running either sequentially or in parallel. A pipeline is intended to be automated and repeatable. A deployment pipeline specifically defines the stages needed to deliver the artifacts to the target deployment environment. The following series of steps will create our deployment pipeline.

Step 1. While still in the DevOps project apacheproject, click **Deployment Pipelines** on the leftmost menu.

Step 2. Click **Create Pipeline**.

Step 3. Enter the pipeline name **apachedeploypipeline**.

Step 4. Click **Create Pipeline**.

Step 5. Click **Add Stage**.

Step 6. A number of Deploy, Control, and Integrations stages are listed. These enable you to perform different sets of tasks as required. Select **Deploy Incrementally Through Compute Instance Groups**.

Step 7. Enter the stage name **Deploy Apache (dev)**.

Step 8. Enter the environment **apache-dev-servers**.

Step 9. Under Deployment Configuration, click **Select Artifact**.

Step 10. Check the box beside the artifact name **instance_group_deployment_configuration**.

Step 11. Click **Save Changes**.

Step 12. Under Select One or More Artifacts, click **Select Artifact**.

Step 13. Check the box beside the artifact name **deploy_apache.sh**.

Step 14. Click **Save Changes**.

Step 15. Enter the Instance rollout by percentage value **100**.

Step 16. Click **Add**.

The view of the deployment pipeline can be seen as shown in Figure 9-15. Here, the deployment pipeline is simple and consists of only one stage. The Deployments tab shows a history of executions of this pipeline. The Parameters tab provides the ability to pass parameters to the pipeline if the deployment configuration allows it (ours does not).

Running the Deployment Pipeline

Now that the deployment pipeline is created, it can be executed. These steps will perform a manual instantiation of the pipeline (meaning we will invoke it, as opposed to an automated trigger kicking it off).

Step 1. While still in the deployment pipeline apachedeploypipeline, click **Run Pipeline**.

Step 2. Click **Start Manual Run**.

Once the pipeline is run, the deployment details are shown as depicted in Figure 9-16. The middle panel shows the stages, while the rightmost panel lists the log information. Task statuses, errors, and commands are logged.

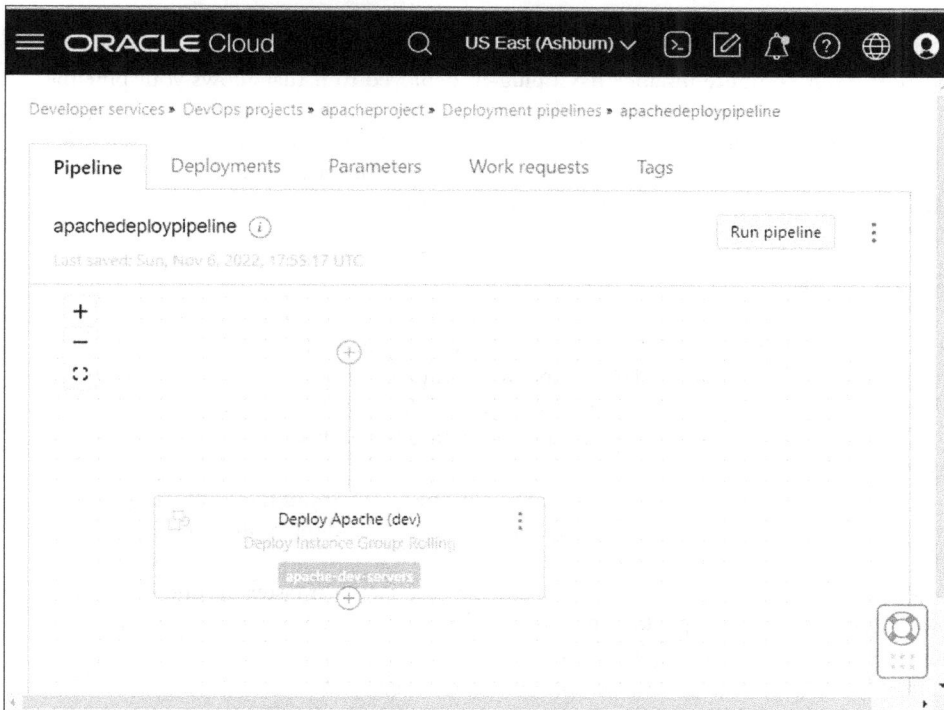

Figure 9-15   Viewing the Deployment Pipeline After Its Creation

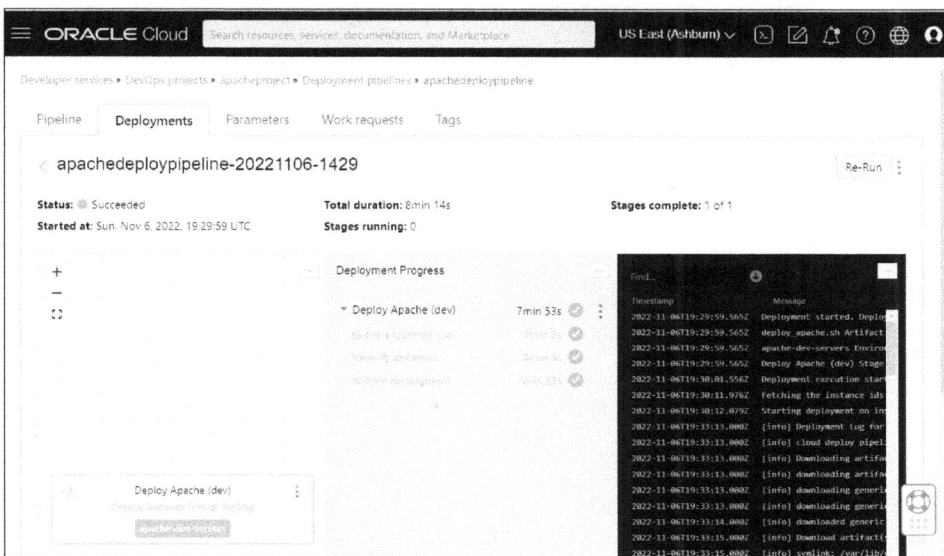

Figure 9-16   Reviewing the Output of the Pipeline Deployment

Compute instance group deployments leverage the Compute Instance Run Command plug-in that is necessary for OCI DevOps to remotely execute commands. In short, your compute instance has a plug-in deployed to it that allows your pipeline to make remote calls. A few plug-in logs worth noting include /var/log/oracle-cloud-agent/plugins/runcommand/runcommand.log and /var/lib/ocarun/commands/wd/latestDeployment/stdout. They contain the same content displayed on the console and are handy for troubleshooting and auditing purposes.

Summary

This chapter provided a glimpse into OCI DevOps. Through it, fully automated, continuous, and repeatable CI/CD pipelines can be created to build, test, and deploy your code to various OCI services that include OKE, functions, and compute. Smaller releases can be pushed out incrementally, providing the ability to keep up with the faster pace of change needed today.

Pipelines can be manual or automated, and can be deployed in sequence or in parallel using various strategies such as blue-green or canary. Handling failures and rolling back can also be designed into the pipeline.

When implemented correctly, OCI DevOps can result in faster product delivery, reduced risk of defects, quicker and easier rollback of changes if necessary, and an accurate reporting on all deployments.

In the next chapter, you will learn more about Data Safe.

Data Safe

Oracle Data Safe is a database security cloud service offered by Oracle. It provides a unified GUI to view all security and compliance monitoring in one place for the entire Oracle database footprint either on-premises or in the cloud. Security is one of the main pillars of DevSecOps, and Oracle Data Safe is a useful tool in achieving that. Oracle Data Safe features include security assessment, user assessment, data discovery, data masking, and activity auditing. In this chapter, we will go over Oracle Data Safe service options available in OCI.

Oracle Data Safe is a fully integrated cloud service to address security and compliance requirements. It provides a single pane of glass for all Oracle database security tasks and monitoring. You can register on-premises or in the cloud, including third-party cloud provider Oracle databases, with Data Safe.

To enable and manage the Oracle Data Safe service, you will need to be a member of a tenancy's Administrator group or have manage permission to either data-safe resources or the Oracle Data Safe family resource. Oracle Data Safe is a regional service, meaning you will have to enable it in each region of your tenancy. Oracle Data Safe stores all assessment, masking, audit, and other security-related data in its own Oracle database in OCI.

Oracle Data Safe provides the following features:

- Security Assessment
- Data Discovery
- Data Masking
- Activity Auditing
- Alerts
- User Assessment

Databases can be configured to use some or all of these features. Let's go over each of these features in detail.

Security Assessment

The Security Assessment feature performs a comprehensive analysis of your database configuration. It analyzes the database configuration, user access, and other security controls. These findings are categorized by risk summary and target summary, as shown in Figure 10-1. Risk levels are categorized as High, Medium, Low, Advisory, and Evaluate. You can also view these risk levels by target.

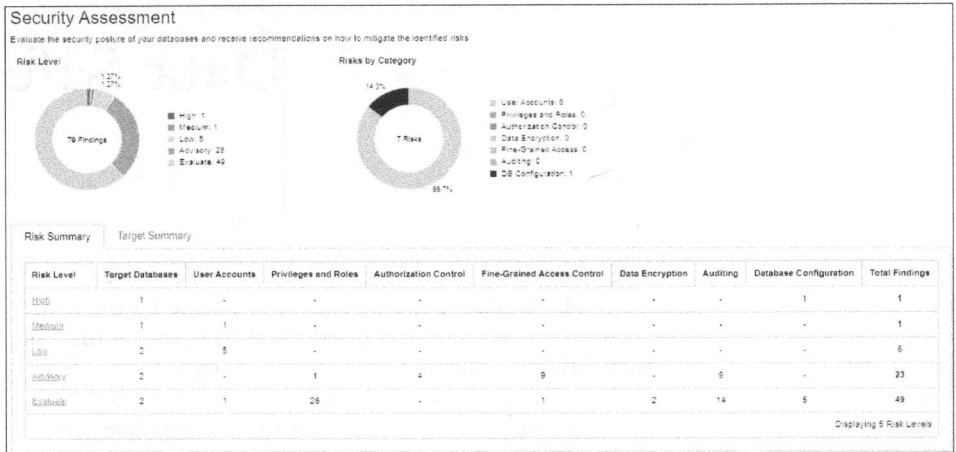

Figure 10-1 Security Assessment

All findings are reported with the appropriate recommendations to remediate or mitigate risks. These recommendations are also derived from benchmarks, such as the Center for Internet Security (CIS), Defense Information Systems Agency (DISA), Security Technical Implementation Guides (STIGs), and European Union General Data Protection Regulation (EU GDPR).

You can also define the baseline for an assessment and then perform drift assessment to find out any changes to the configuration. To do so, click the main menu and select **Oracle Database > Data Safe – Data Security > Assessment History** under Related Resources, as shown in Figure 10-2. It will list all security assessment that has been run for all databases.

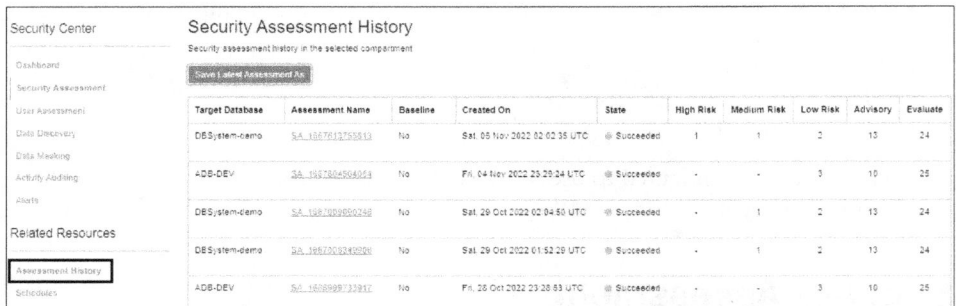

Figure 10-2 Security Assessment History

Click the assessment to review details, set the assessment as a baseline, and generate and download reports. You will be redirected to a similar page, as shown in Figure 10-3.

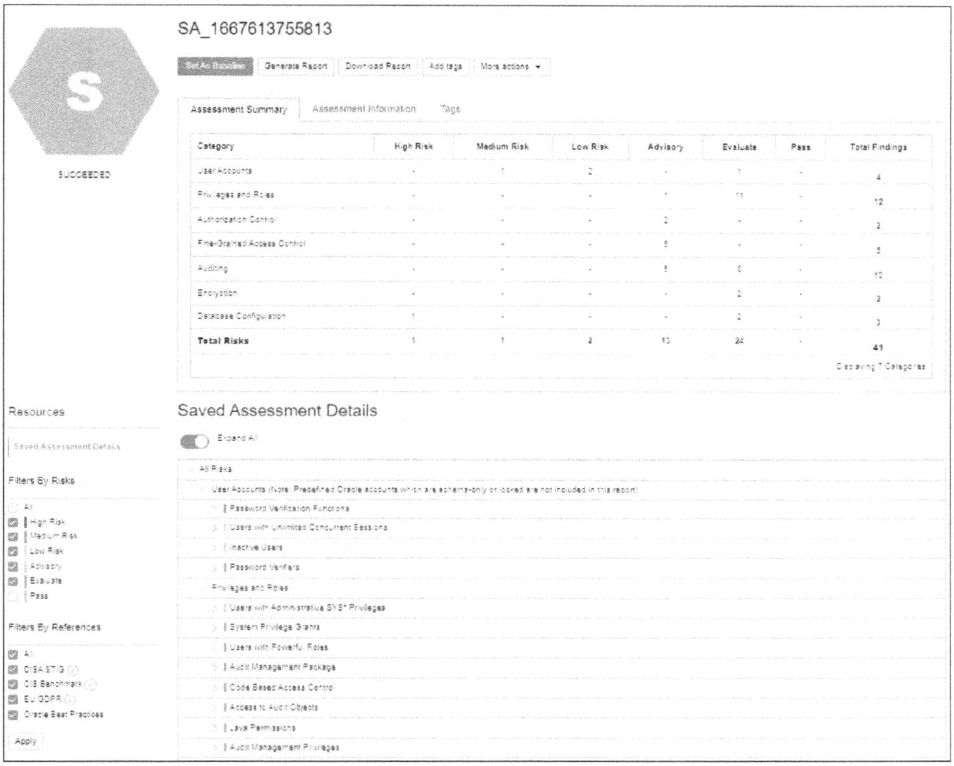

Figure 10-3 Security Assessment Details

Assessment details can be filtered by risks and security references for review. You also can generate assessment reports in PDF or XLS format, as shown in Figure 10-4.

Figure 10-4 Generate a Security Assessment Report

Once a report is generated, it can be downloaded to your desktop, as shown in Figure 10-5. It is also available for downloading later.

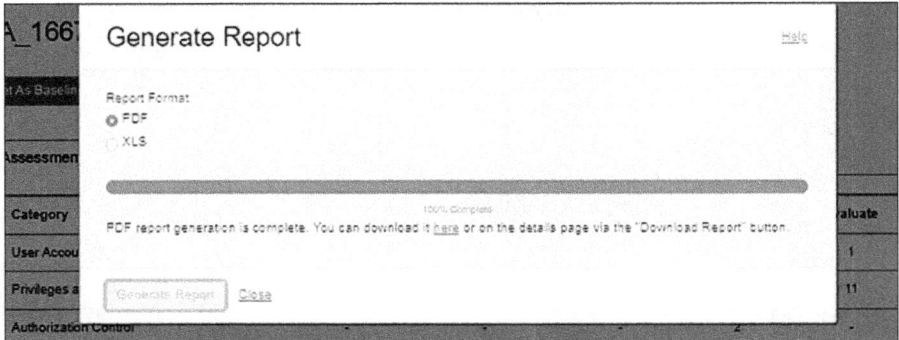

Figure 10-5   Download the Security Assessment Report

User Assessment

The User Assessment feature helps you identify overprivileged users within the database. This feature uses the privileges assigned to the user and the user's activities within the database. It also uses vulnerabilities associated with password settings like password policies, last login, and password age. All this information is used to calculate potential risk associated with a user account. These findings are represented by risk summary and target summary, as shown in Figure 10-6. Risk levels are categorized as Critical, High, Medium, and Low. This feature also provides details on the user's activity recorded by auditing.

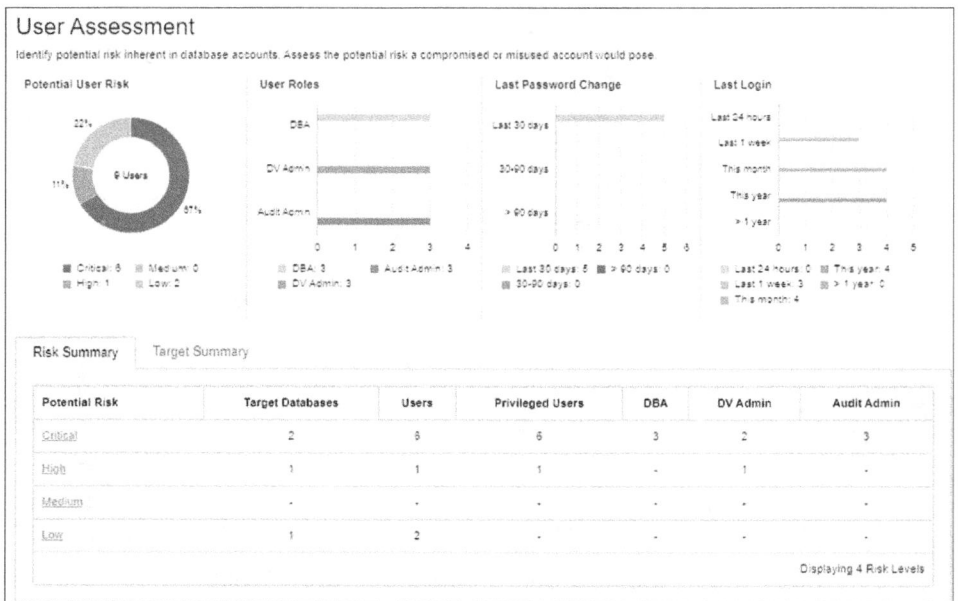

Figure 10-6   User Assessment

All user assessments done to date can be viewed by clicking **Assessment History**, as shown in Figure 10-7.

Figure 10-7   User Assessment History

You can also perform user assessment drift by creating the baseline and comparing future findings against it. Click one of the latest assessments, and it will redirect you to the assessment detail page, as shown in Figure 10-8.

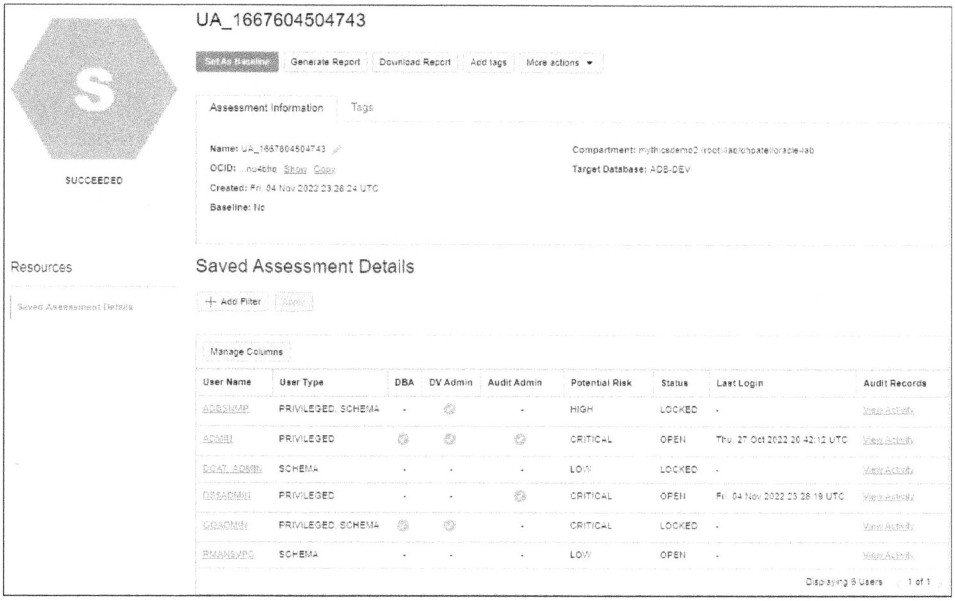

Figure 10-8   User Assessment Details

You can review the assessment details, set it as a baseline, and generate and download a report. With the User Assessment feature, just like Security Assessment, you can generate a report in PDF or XLS format. Once the report is generated, you can download it at the same time or later.

Data Discovery

The Data Discovery feature helps identify sensitive data such as personally identifiable information (PII) in the database. Data Discovery will search through sensitive types, dictionary-based referential relationships and nondictionary referential relationships. Sensitive types are like regular expressions that search through sensitive columns such as Social Security number and birth date. Oracle Data Safe has over 170 predefined sensitive types that you can use. You can also create custom sensitive types per your requirements by going to the main menu and selecting **Oracle Database > Data Safe – Data Security > Data Discovery > Sensitive Types Resource** within the Data Discovery section on the Data Safe main page. Data Discovery searches the data dictionary tables to find primary and foreign key relationships between tables. So it will flag tables with sensitive columns. Oracle Data Safe gives you a choice to discover nondictionary referential relationships in other word application–level relations between columns. These relationships are defined within application only. They are discovered based on column name and column data patterns.

Let's run Data Discovery now on the Oracle Database residing on the Base Database Service in OCI. First, we will create a custom sensitive type and then create a sensitive data model based on predefined and custom sensitive type data. Here, we have used **swingbench** to create a schema SOE and load some data about sales type data. By default, swingbench uses a schema named SOE, but a Sensitive Types scan can be used against any schema.

Go to https://cloud.oracle.com and log on to your tenancy. Click the main menu and select **Oracle Database > Data Safe – Data Security > Data Discovery > Sensitive Type > Create Sensitive Type/Category**, as shown in Figure 10-9.

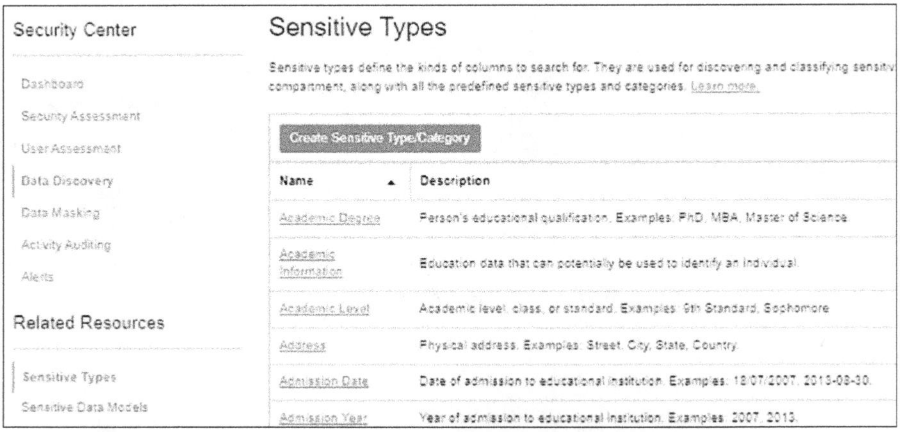

Figure 10-9   Sensitive Types Main Page

Click on **Create a Sensitive Category**, as shown in Figure 10-10. This allows you to keep all your sensitive column types in one place.

Figure 10-10   Create a Sensitive Category

Now let's look at the other option by going back to the Sensitive Types page and clicking **Create Sensitive Type/Category**, as shown in Figure 10-9. This time we are going to create a sensitive column type, as shown in Figure 10-11, in the category created in the previous step. Here, we've specified the exact column name, since this is the only place this data exists. You can provide a regular expression for the column name, column comment, and/or column data to discover sensitive columns per your requirements.

Go to Data Safe and click **Data Discovery > Discover Sensitive Data**, as shown in Figure 10-12.

Select an appropriate sensitive database model name, a compartment to store the model, and a target database to run discovery, as shown in Figure 10-13. Then click **Next**.

In the next window, you will see a message to refresh database schemas. It is a good idea to refresh now in case some changes occurred to any schema. For this specific example, select the **SOE** schema, as shown in Figure 10-14. Then click **Next**.

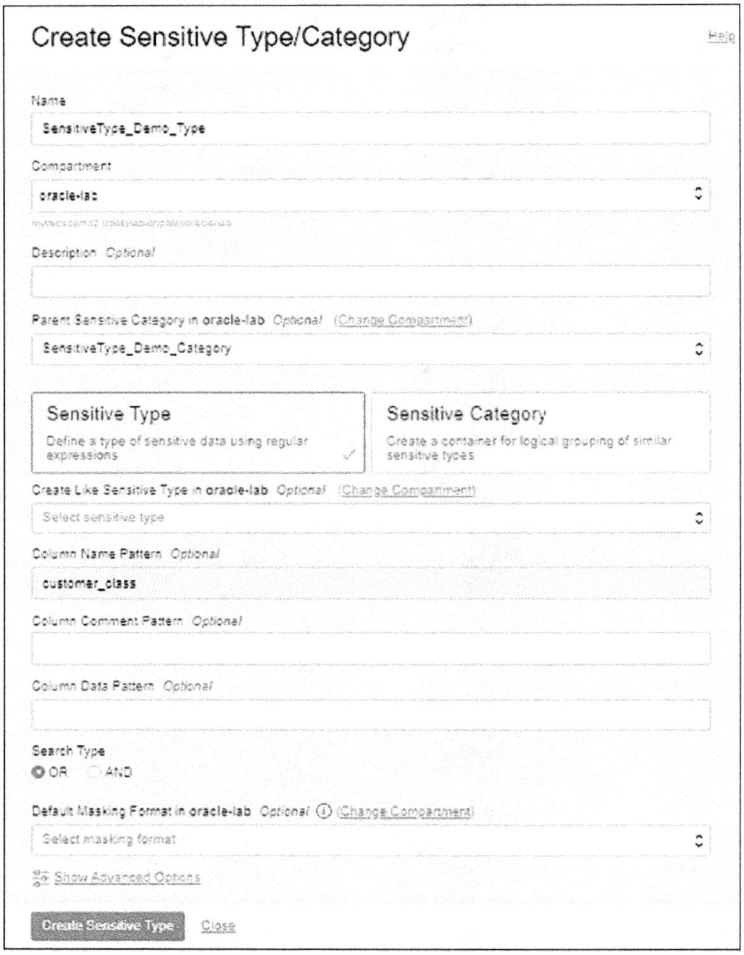

Figure 10-11   Create a Sensitive Type

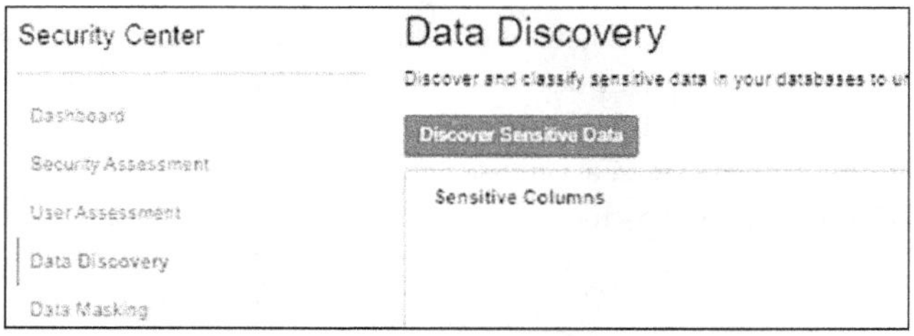

Figure 10-12   Discover Sensitive Data

Figure 10-13   Provide Basic Information

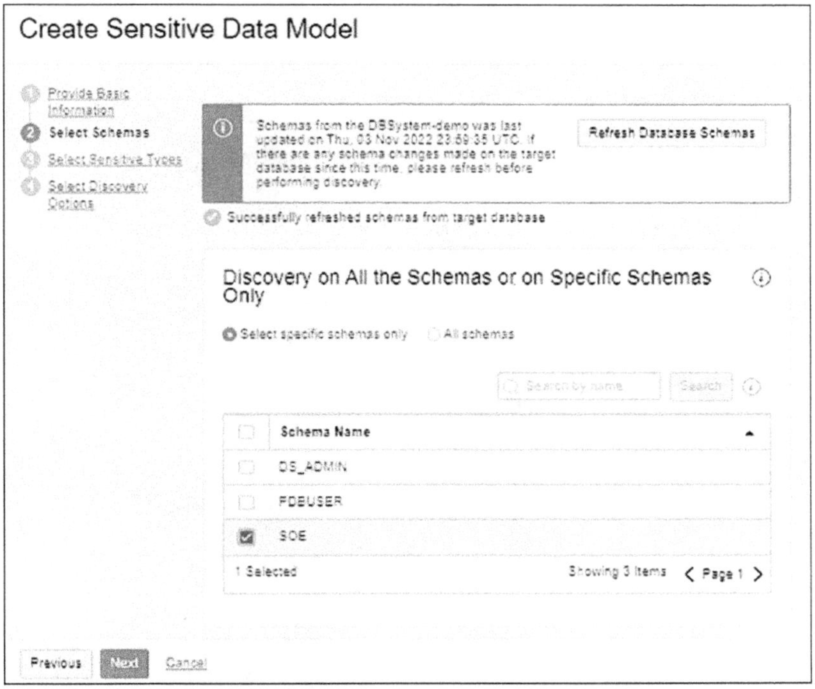

Figure 10-14   Select Schemas

Select sensitive types for Data Discovery, as shown in Figure 10-15. Click **Next**.

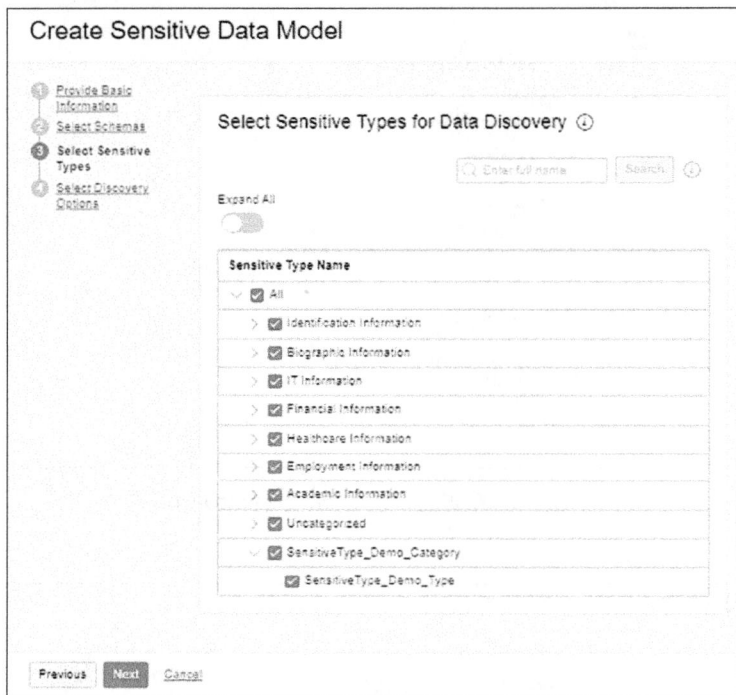

Figure 10-15   Select Sensitive Types

Now select discovery options, as shown in Figure 10-16. Then click **Create Sensitive Data Model**.

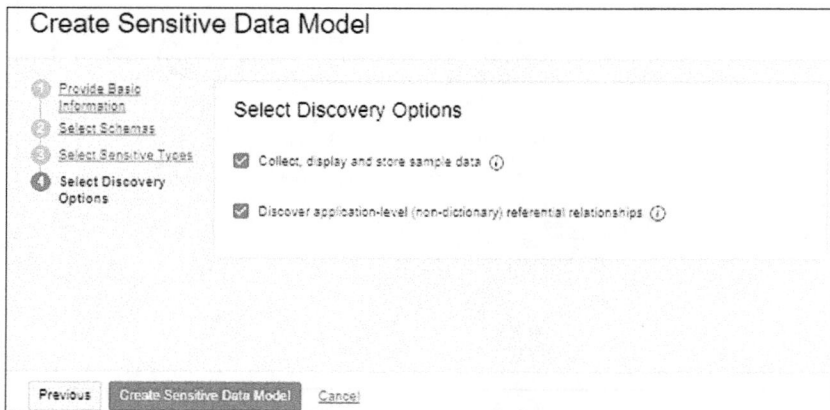

Figure 10-16   Select Discovery Options

As a result of this process, a sensitive data model gets created, as shown in Figure 10-17, with some information. Based on your choice, this model will include sample data within it. This model can also perform incremental updates to capture any changes that occurred to the database over time.

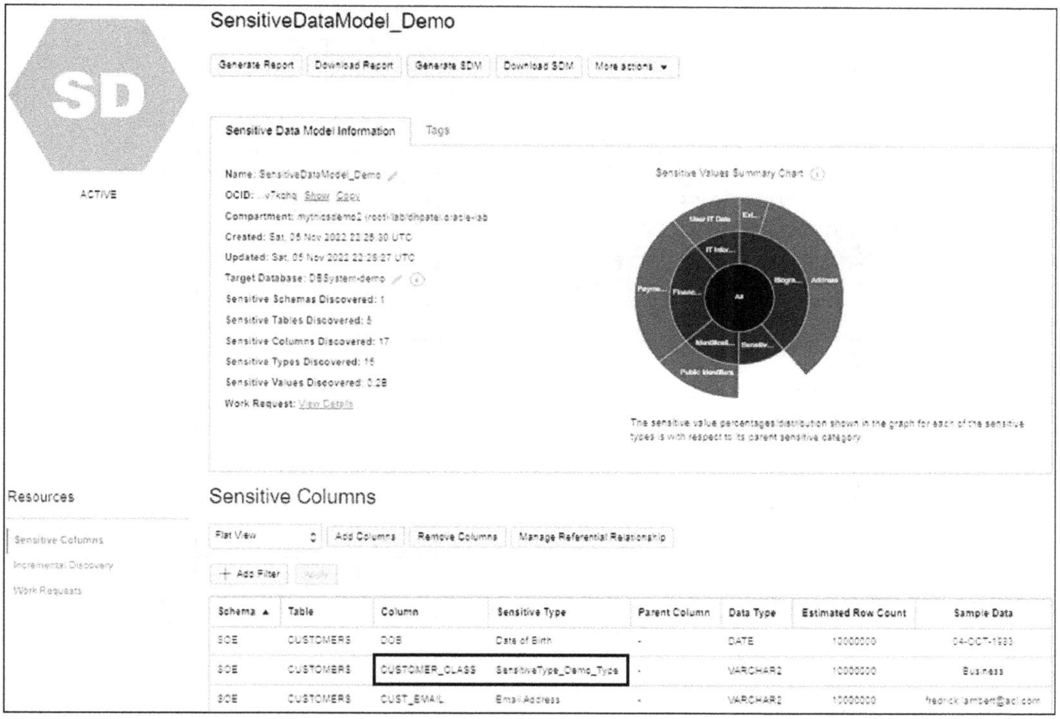

Figure 10-17   Sensitive Model Information

You can generate and download reports of this model in XLS or PDF format. A sample of the report is shown in Figure 10-18. You can also download the sensitive data model in XML format. This model can also be used to implement the data masking process.

Data Discovery				ORACLE Data Safe	

Sensitive Data Model : SensitiveDataModel_Demo
Target   : DBSystem-demo
Report Time   : 2022-11-05T22:33:31   All times are in UTC

Summary					
Total Columns Scanned	Total Values Scanned	Total Sensitive Types	Total Sensitive Tables	Total Sensitive Columns	Total Sensitive Values
80	1236144635	15	5	17	217978892

Sensitive Columns							
Sensitive Type	Schema Name	Table Name	Column Name	Sensitive Value Count	Column Data Matched	Column Name Matched	Column Comment Matched
Date of Birth	SOE	CUSTOME RS	DOB	10000000	Y	Y	N
SensitiveT ype_Dem o_Type	SOE	CUSTOME RS	CUSTOMER_ CLASS	10000000	N	Y	N
Email Address	SOE	CUSTOME RS	CUST_EMAIL	10000000	Y	Y	N
Card Spending Limit	SOE	CUSTOME RS	CREDIT_LIMI T	10000000	N	Y	N
Last Name	SOE	CUSTOME RS	CUST_LAST_ NAME	10000000	N	Y	N
First Name	SOE	CUSTOME RS	CUST_FIRST _NAME	10000000	N	Y	N
Card Security Code	SOE	CARD_DET AILS	SECURITY_C ODE	15000000	Y	Y	N
Card Expiration Date	SOE	CARD_DET AILS	EXPIRY_DAT E	15000000	Y	Y	N
Card Type	SOE	CARD_DET AILS	CARD_TYPE	15000000	Y	Y	N
SensitiveT ype_Dem	SOE	ORDERS	CUSTOMER_ CLASS	14297900	N	Y	N

Figure 10-18   Sensitive Data Model Report

Data Masking

The Data Masking feature allows you to mask sensitive data such as Social Security numbers, credit card information, and blood type. It replaces actual data with some random realistic-looking data. This feature prevents security breaches for sensitive or confidential data in nonproduction database environments and stays compliant with data privacy standards like EU GDPR. It also maintains complex data relationships, which allows application development and testing to continue without any data-related issues.

Oracle provides more than 60 data masking formats, and you can also create a custom masking policy to mask data with specific formats. Oracle Data Safe provides easy steps to follow and overall simplifies the data masking process. Data Safe allows you to create a data masking policy based on the data discovery model, which includes sensitive data and referential relationships in a target database. These policies can be applied against a target database to perform masking.

We will go through the process of data masking for the same database we used for the Data Discovery feature. We will also use the same data discovery model created with predefined and custom sensitive columns. To begin, go to the Data Safe main page and click **Data Masking > Masking Policies**, as shown in Figure 10-19.

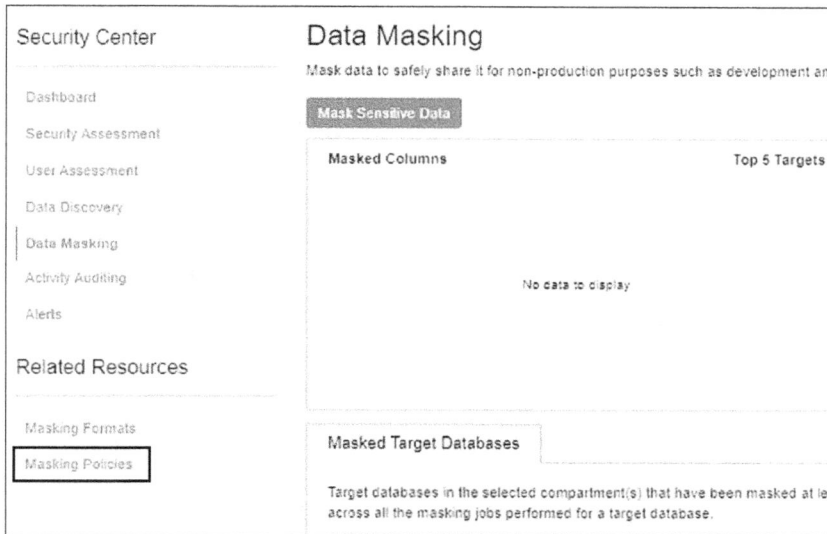

Figure 10-19   Data Masking Main Page

Here, you can either choose to create a new masking policy or upload one in XML format. In our scenario, we are going to create a new masking policy. So click **Create Masking Policy**, as shown in Figure 10-20.

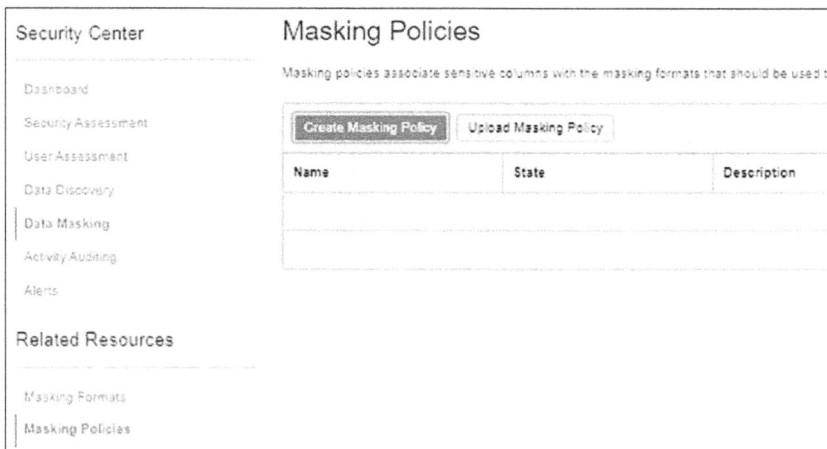

Figure 10-20   Masking Policy

In the window that appears, provide a masking policy name, compartment, and the sensitive data model name created earlier, as shown in Figure 10-21. Then click **Create Masking Policy**.

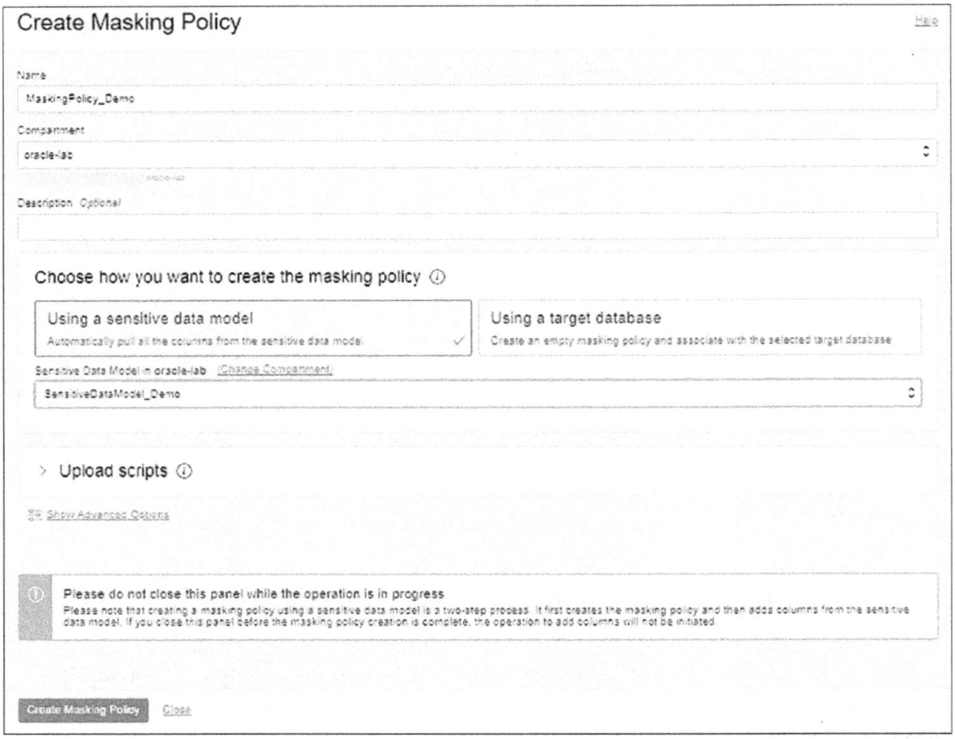

Figure 10-21   Create Masking Policy

Once the data masking policy is created, you will find some basic information and columns requiring that masking be listed, as shown in Figure 10-22. Notice that the appropriate masking format is selected for each column. You can change it to a different format if needed. The masking policy document can be generated in XML format and downloaded as well.

From the Data Masking main page, click **Mask Sensitive Data**, as shown in Figure 10-23.

Next, provide the target nonproduction database and masking policy created earlier and click **Mask Data**, as shown in Figure 10-24. This selection will kick off the masking job, and the process will take some time depending on the data getting masked.

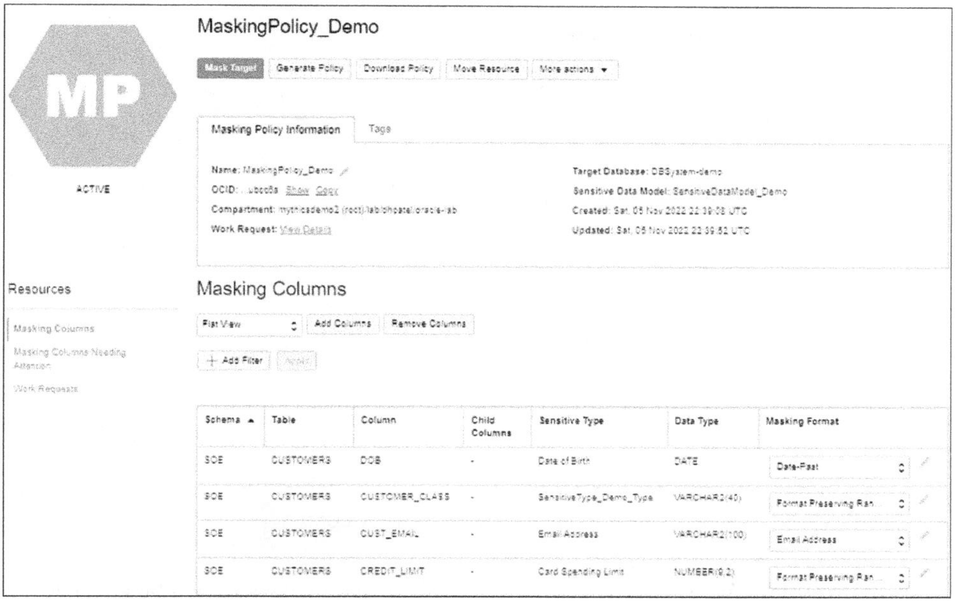

Figure 10-22   Masking Policy Information

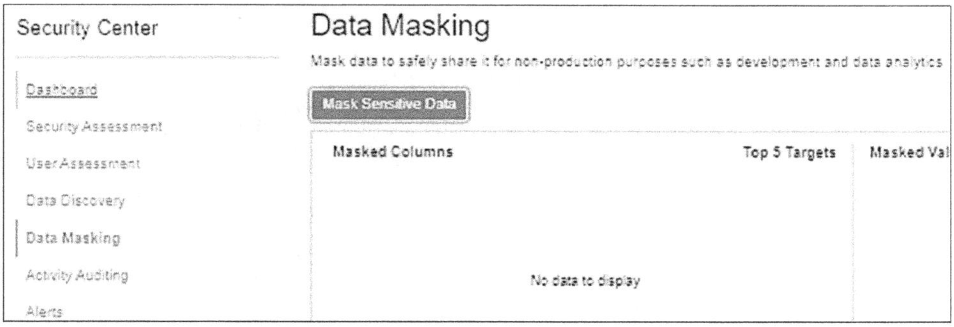

Figure 10-23   Data Masking Main Page

Warning

Do not select a production database. Be very careful while selecting the target database for the masking operation.

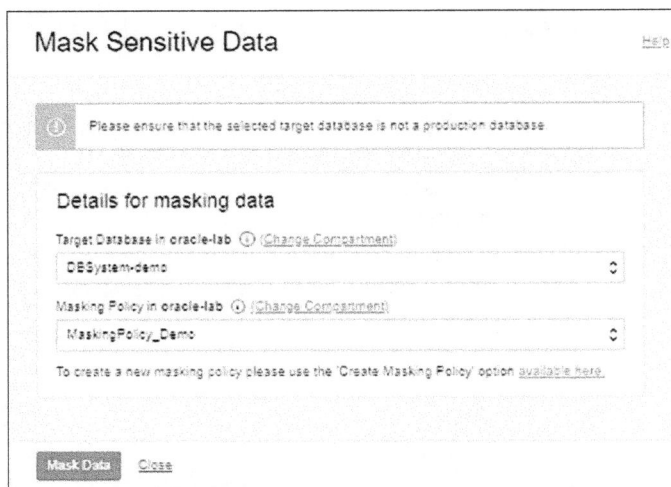

Figure 10-24   Mask Sensitive Data

A data masking operations summary of all masked target databases will be available on the Data Masking main page, as shown in Figure 10-25. Click **Masked Target Database** to generate a masking report, download a masking report, and download masking logs. Reports are available in PDF or XLS format.

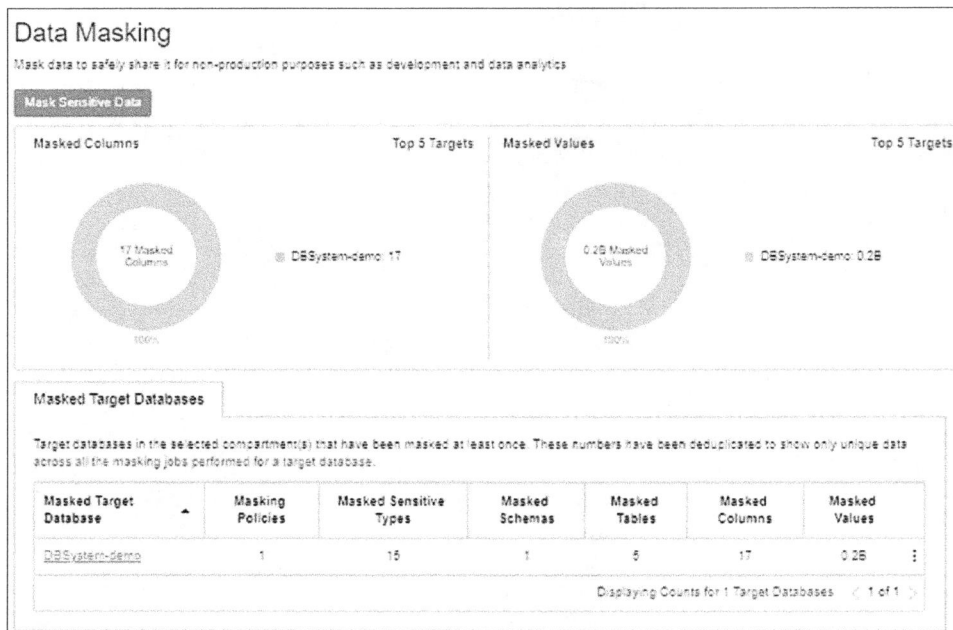

Figure 10-25   Data Masking Summary

Activity Auditing

The Activity Auditing feature utilizes audit data collected from the database using audit policies enabled for it. Audit resources like audit profiles, audit policies, and audit trails are auto-created on registered database targets. You can modify them as required.

Data Safe creates an audit profile when you register a target database. On the Activity Auditing page, go to the Audit Profile section under Resources and click a target database. It will take you to the Audit Profile page, as shown in Figure 10-26. The audit profile name and description can be updated here. This page enables you to update the online data retention period for up to 12 months and the offline data retention period for up to 72 months. You can also discover any new audit trails available for the database and collect audit records beyond free usage. Audit records can be computed for each audit trail type by Data Safe. This capability allows you configure audit records collection settings appropriately.

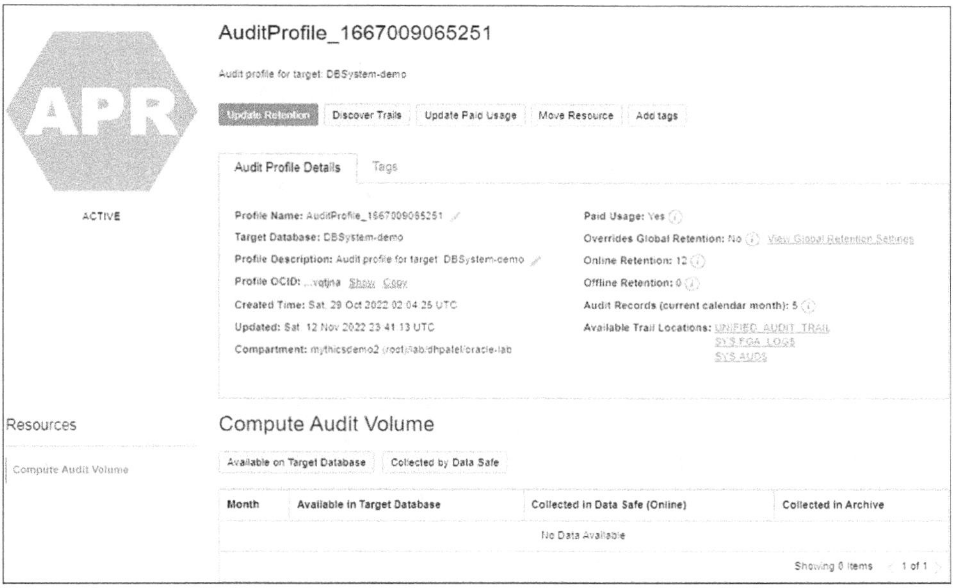

Figure 10-26 Audit Profile

Audit policies include basic auditing, admin user activity auditing, user activity auditing, Oracle predefined policies, custom policies, and audit compliance standards like the Center for Internet Security (CIS). On the Activity Auditing page, go to Audit Policies under the Resources section and click a target database to get to the Audit Policy page, as shown in Figure 10-27. The audit policy name and description can be updated here. You can enable and disable each of these options by clicking **Update and Provision**. You also can retrieve the latest audit policies from the target database.

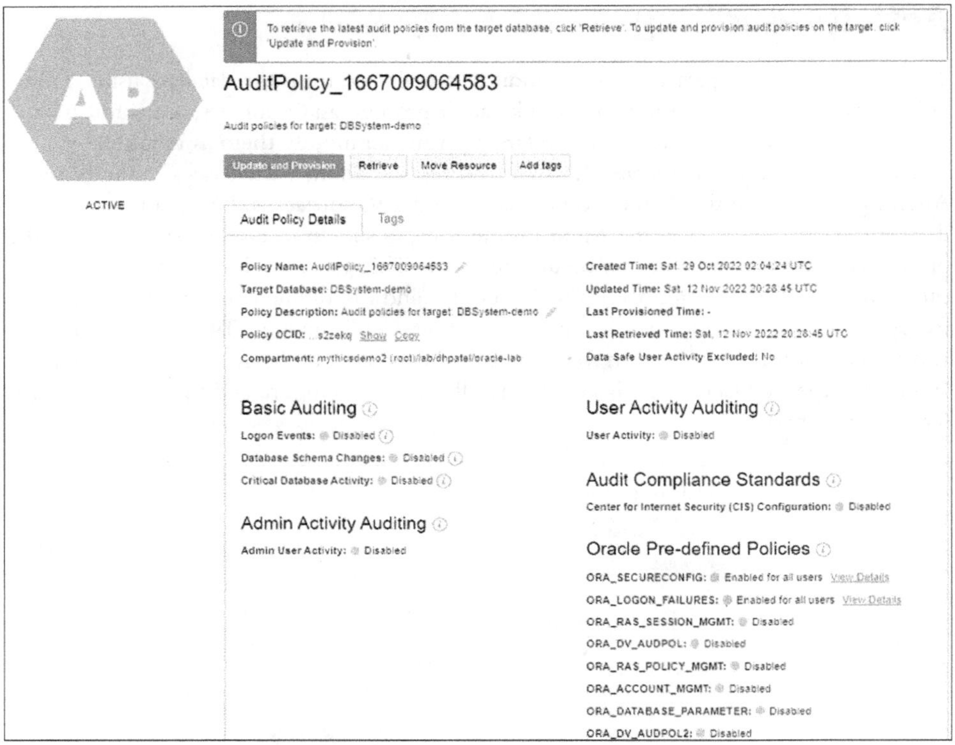

Figure 10-27 Audit Policy

Data Safe discovers audit trails at the time of database registration. It supports different audit trails such as SYS.AUD$, SYS.FGA_LOG$, UNIFIED_AUDIT_TRAIL, and DVSYS.AUDIT_TRAILS$ (for Database Vault), depending on the database version and edition. On the Activity Auditing page, go to Audit Trails under the Resources section and click a target database with a specific trail location to get to the Audit Trail page, as shown in Figure 10-28. The audit trail name and description can be updated here. You can start or stop the audit trail collection. Also, make sure to define a purge policy to control the audit data growth over time.

Oracle provides predefined auditing reports that can be downloaded in PDF or XLS formats. You can also create custom reports based on your specific requirements, as shown in Figure 10-29.

Figure 10-28   Audit Trail

Figure 10-29   Audit Reports

Alerts

Oracle Data Safe provides a set of alert policies that can be applied to one or more targets. These alert policies are based on audit policies that generate audit events. This feature will notify you if any unusual activities are captured. These violations can be database parameter changes, failed logins by users, and other predefined sets of alert rules.

To use this feature, go to https://cloud.oracle.com and log on to your tenancy. On the Data Safe home page, click **Alerts** and then **Alert Policies** under Resources, as shown in Figure 10-30. Data Safe will list all alert policies. You can click each of them and apply it to one or more target databases. You can also click **Target-Policy Associations** to find out all alert policies enabled for each target database.

Figure 10-30   Alert Policies

In addition, you can download alert reports in PDF or XLS format. Oracle also allows you to create customer alert reports per your specific requirements. Click **Reports** under Related Resources and then **All Alerts**, as shown in Figure 10-31, for reporting.

Figure 10-31   Alert Reports

How to Add a Database

Oracle Data Safe can register the following target databases:

- Autonomous Databases
  - Autonomous Data Warehouse Database

- Autonomous Transaction Processing Database
- Autonomous JSON Database
- Oracle Cloud Database
  - Oracle Base Database (VM, BM)
  - Exadata on Oracle Public Cloud
- Oracle Databases on Compute
  - Databases in Oracle Cloud Infrastructure
  - Databases in other cloud environments
- Oracle Cloud@Customer Databases
  - Exadata Cloud@Customer
- Oracle On-Premises Databases

We will go over a few of these scenarios on how to register autonomous databases, the Oracle Base Database System, and on-premises databases. You can follow similar processes to register other databases as targets for Oracle Data Safe.

One important consideration here is to create a service account for Oracle Data Safe. The autonomous database is an exception from this task because a service account named DS$ADMIN is already created and locked. When you register the autonomous database with Oracle Data Safe, this account will get unlocked, and the password will be reset.

Registering an Autonomous Database

Go to https://cloud.oracle.com and log on to your tenancy. Click the main menu and select **Oracle Database > Data Safe – Data Security**, as shown in Figure 10-32.

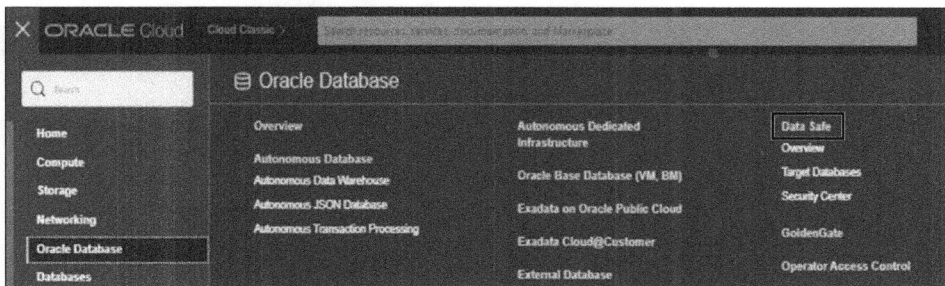

Figure 10-32   Oracle Database Menu

Now we're going to register the autonomous database with Data Safe. Click **Start Wizard** for registering Autonomous Databases, as shown in Figure 10-33.

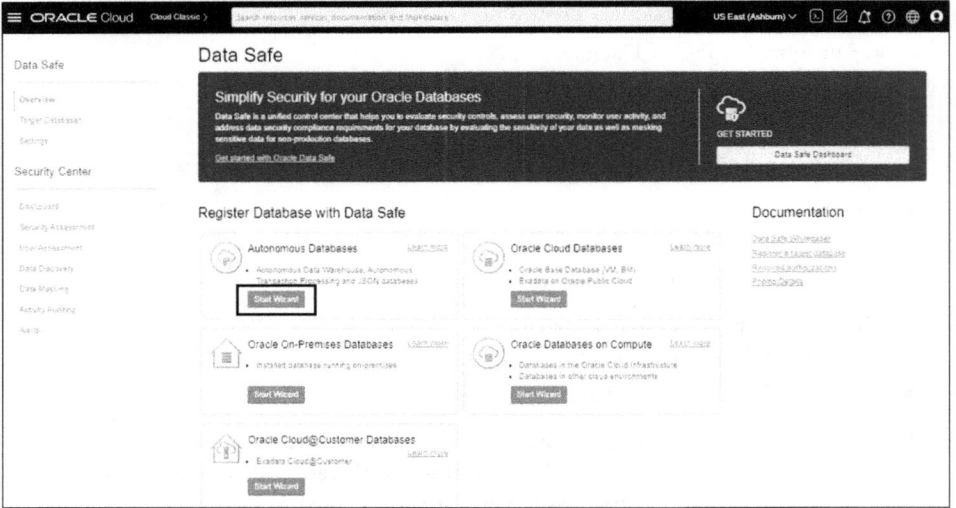

Figure 10-33   Data Safe Database Wizard

Select the appropriate compartment and the database within it and click **Next**, as shown in Figure 10-34.

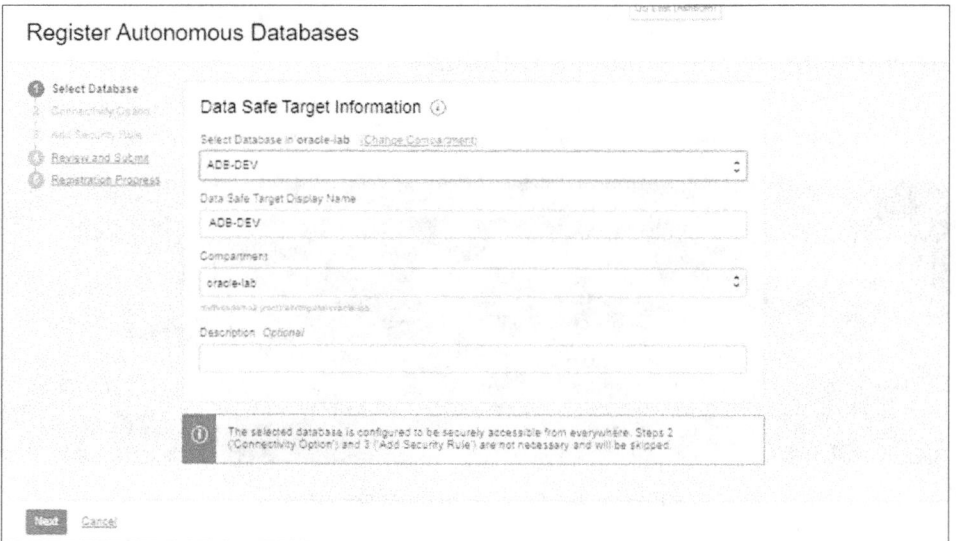

Figure 10-34   Data Safe Database Selection

Now review the target database information and click **Register**, as shown in Figure 10-35.

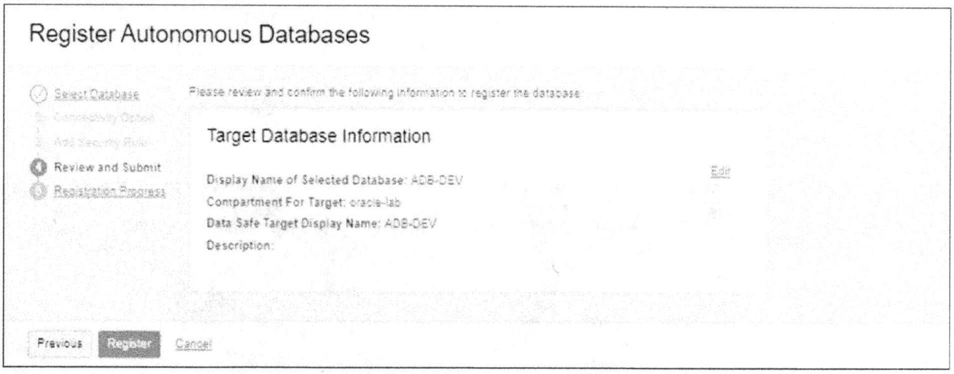

Figure 10-35   Review Registration Information

Once the registration is complete, you will see the target database ADB-DEV as active, as shown in Figure 10-36.

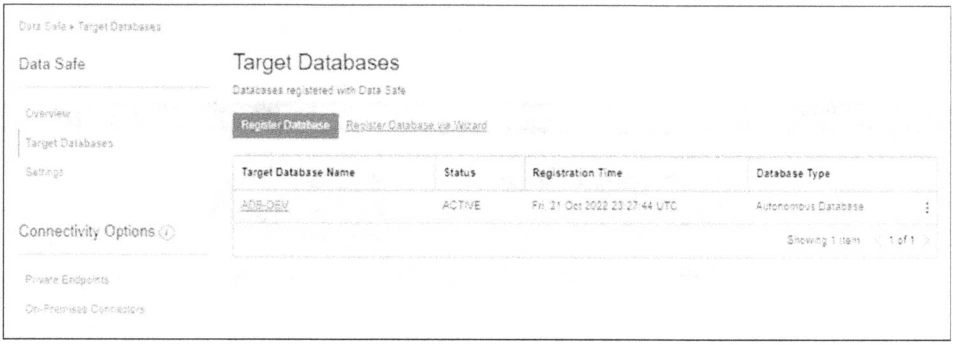

Figure 10-36   Target Database Status

Registering an Oracle Base Database System

There are a few prerequisite tasks that you will need to complete before registering Oracle database. First, let's create an Oracle Data Safe service account. Log on to the pluggable database and create a service account named ds_admin, as shown in Example 10-1.

Example 10-1   Creating a Data Safe Administrator User

```
SQL> alter session set container=DEMOCDB_PDB1;
SQL> create user ds_admin identified by ds_admin default tablespace ds_data
  temporary tablespace temp;
SQL> grant connect, resource to ds_admin;
```

Next, grant required roles to the service account named ds_admin. You will need to download the datasafe_privileges.sql script from OCI, as shown in the following steps.

Go to https://cloud.oracle.com and log on to your tenancy. Go to the menu and select **Oracle Database > Data Safe**, as shown in Figure 10-37.

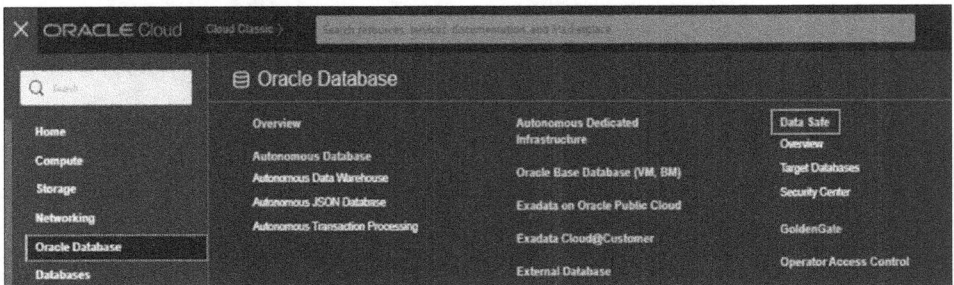

Figure 10-37   Oracle Database Menu

Click **Start Wizard** under the Oracle Cloud Databases section, as shown in Figure 10-38.

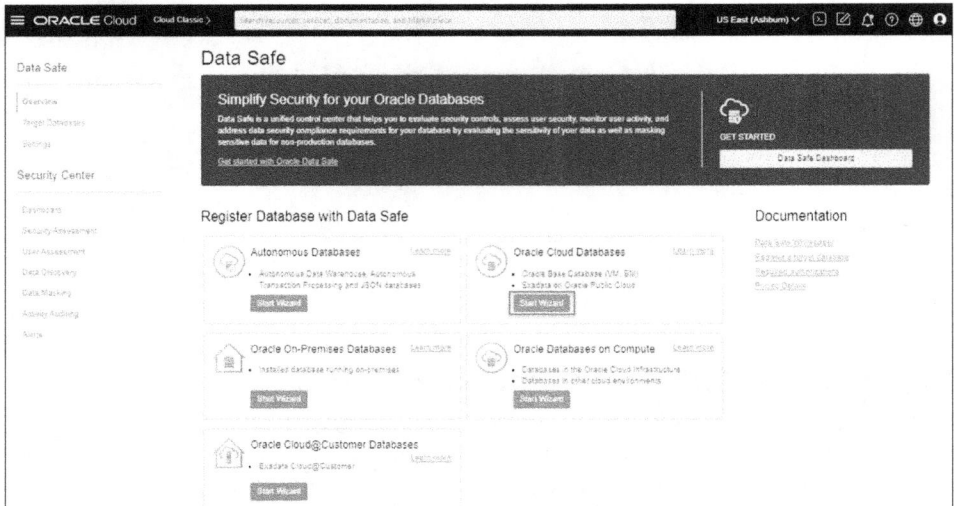

Figure 10-38   Data Safe Database Wizard

Click **Download Privilege Script**, as shown in Figure 10-39.

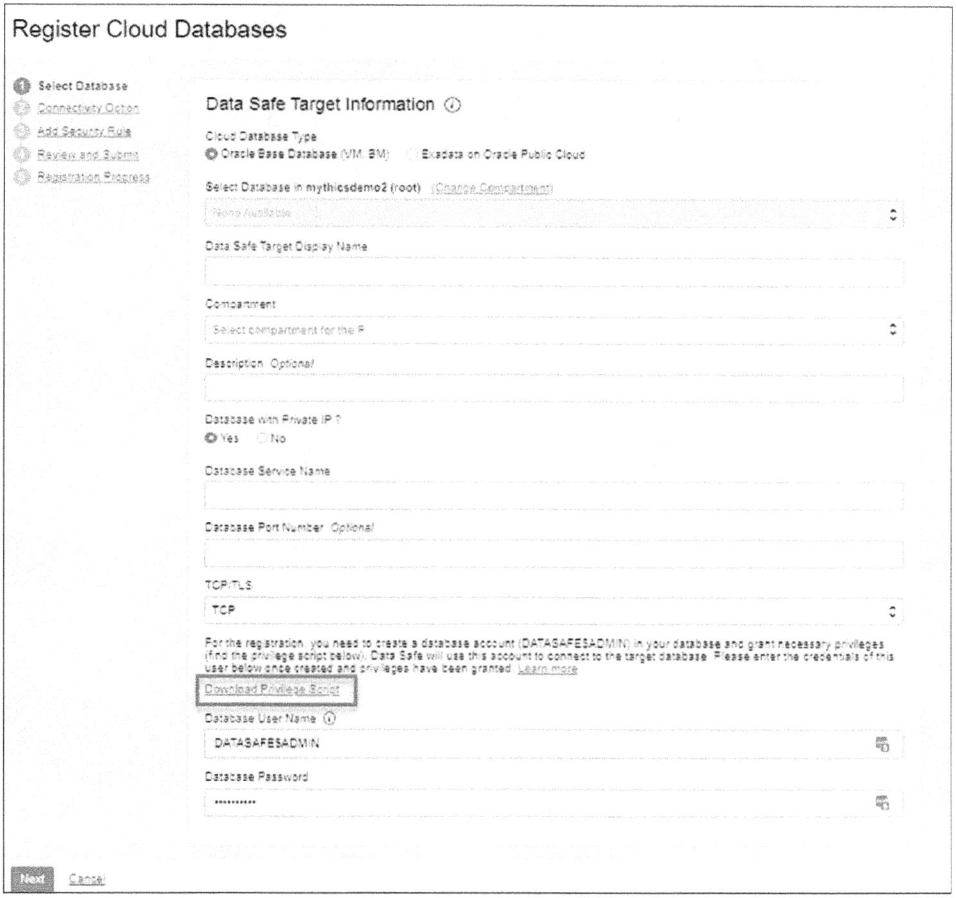

Figure 10-39 Select Database

Next, copy this script to the database server and run it, as shown in Example 10-2.

Example 10-2 Data Safe Administrator Privileges Assignment

```
SQL> @/home/oracle/datasafe_privileges.sql DS_ADMIN GRANT ALL
Enter value for USERNAME (case sensitive matching the username from dba_users)
Setting USERNAME to DS_ADMIN
Enter value for TYPE (grant/revoke)
Setting TYPE to GRANT
Enter value for MODE (audit_collection/audit_setting/data_discovery/masking/
  assessment/all)
Setting MODE to ALL
Granting AUDIT_COLLECTION privileges to "DS_ADMIN" ...
Granting AUDIT_SETTING privileges to "DS_ADMIN" ...
Granting DATA_DISCOVERY role to "DS_ADMIN" ...
```

```
Granting MASKING role to "DS_ADMIN" ...
Granting ASSESSMENT role to "DS_ADMIN" ...
Done.
```

Now you can register this database with Oracle Data Safe. To do so, start the target registration wizard, as shown in Figure 10-38. Fill in the database information, including database system name, service name, and service account credentials, and click **Next**, as shown in Figure 10-40.

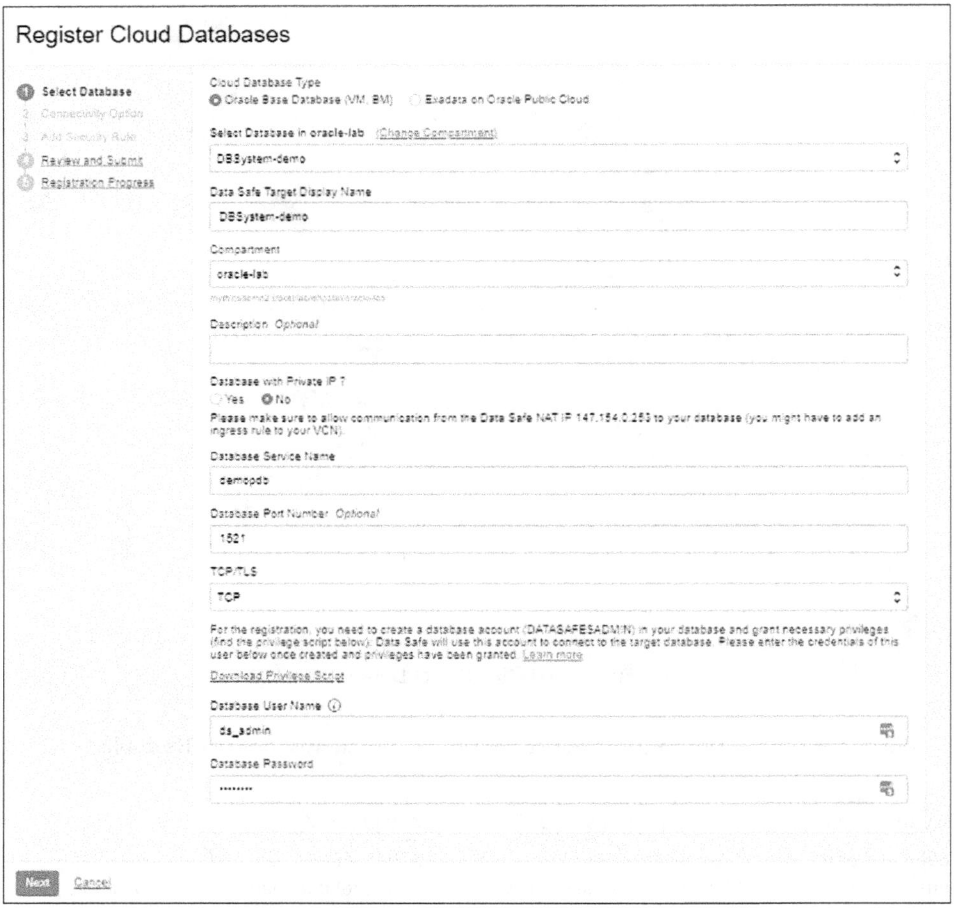

Figure 10-40   Register a Cloud Database

Both bare metal and virtual database systems are created with one private IP address. Private endpoints will be created to allow Data Safe to access the target database. Provide VCN details to create this private endpoint and click **Next**, as shown in Figure 10-41.

Now provide a security list where ingress and egress rules will be created and click **Next**, as shown in Figure 10-42.

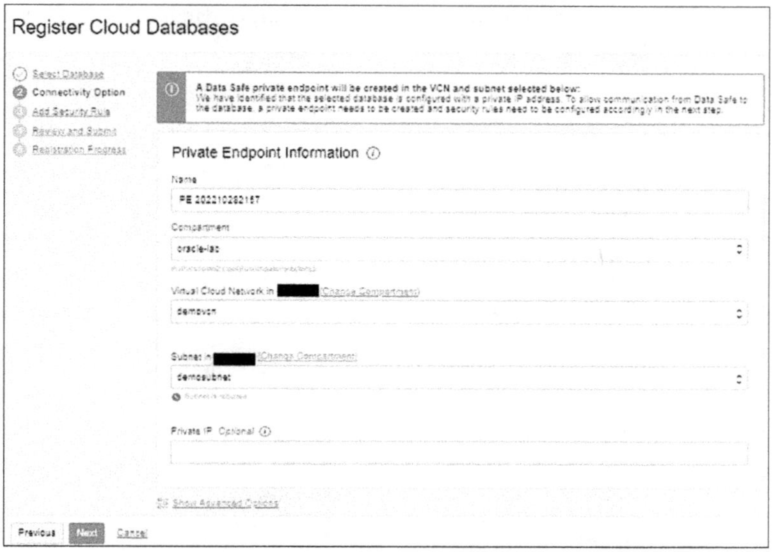

Figure 10-41   Connectivity Options

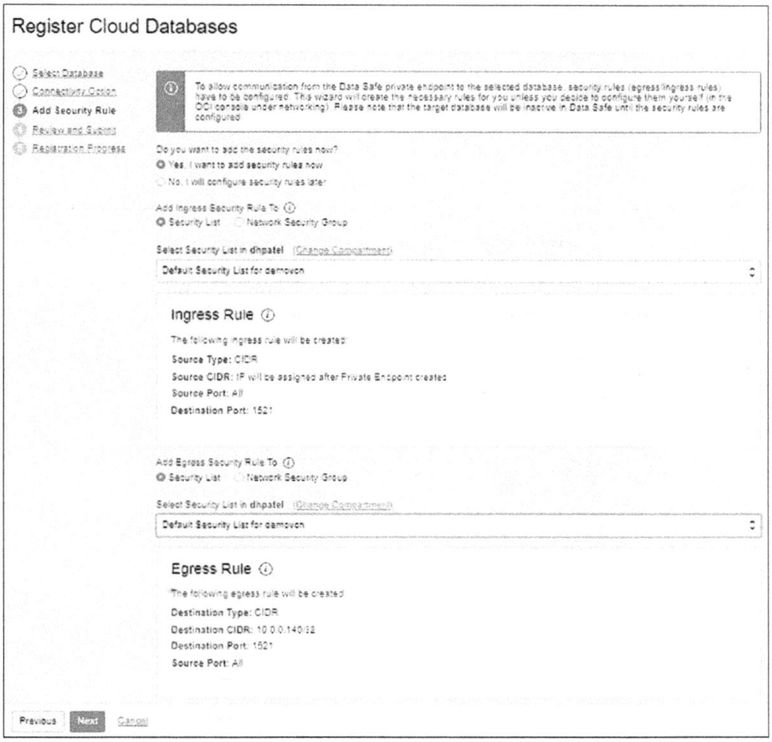

Figure 10-42   Add Security Rules

Review all the information provided so far for the target database registration and click **Register**, as shown in Figure 10-43.

Figure 10-43   Review the Information

The registration progress with be displayed, as shown in Figure 10-44.

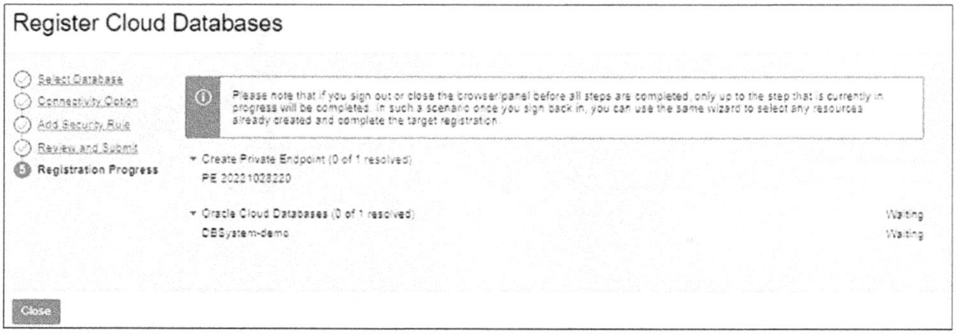

Figure 10-44   Registration Progress

It will take a minute or two to finish the registration process. Once it is complete, you will notice a database with active status on the main Target Databases page, as shown in Figure 10-45.

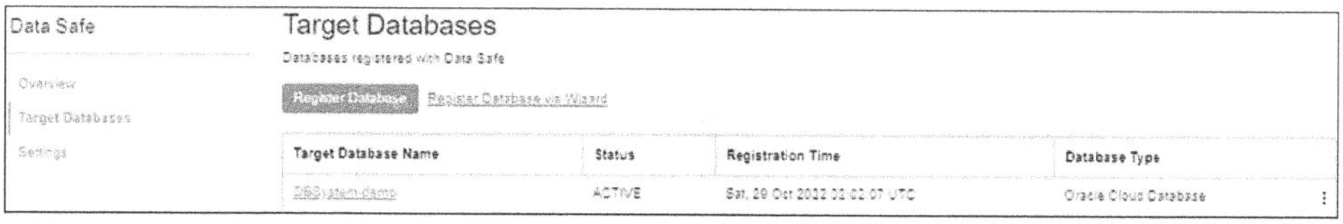

Figure 10-45   Target Database Status

Registering an On-Premises Database

Data Safe can also provide security controls for on-premises databases. The process to register is almost identical to the one shown for registering the OCI Database System in the previous section. One of the major differences is how on-premises databases communicate with Data Safe. This communication can be achieved by using either private endpoints or on-premises connectors. Earlier, we showed how to use private endpoints to register the OCI Database System, so now we will go over the on-premises connector option. On-premises connectors allow Data Safe to connect to on-premises databases, and you can create up to five on-premises connectors.

Oracle recommends that you create a separate server (other than the database server) to install the on-premises connector. The on-premises connector can also be installed on two servers to achieve high availability. You can install the on-premises connector on the database server as well though. In the following scenario, we will install the on-premises connector on the database server.

Go to https://cloud.oracle.com and log on to your tenancy. Then go to **Data Safe > Target Databases > On-Premises Connectors**. You will get to the page shown in Figure 10-46. Click **Create On-Premises Connector**.

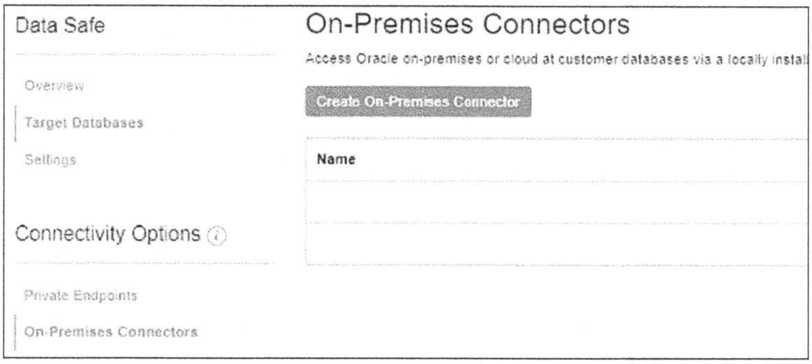

Figure 10-46   On-Premises Connectors Main Page

Next, provide a compartment name, on-premises connector name, and optional description, as shown in Figure 10-47.

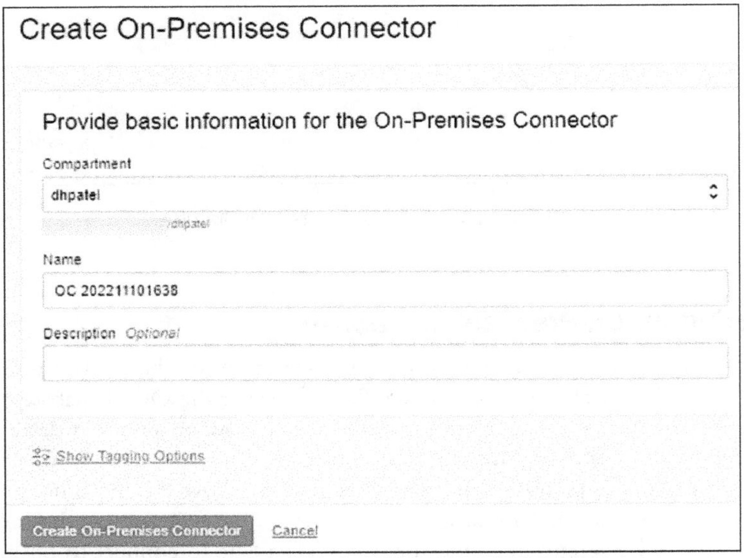

Figure 10-47   Create an On-Premises Connector

The on-premises connector is created as INACTIVE. Click **Download Install Bundle**, as shown in Figure 10-48. It will download the zip file with all required files to install the on-premises connector. Copy this file to the database server.

Figure 10-48   On-Premises Connector Status

Now you need to install the on-premises connector as an Oracle user. You can install it as any user other than root user. Installation steps are shown in Example 10-3.

Example 10-3 Installing an On-Premises Connector

```
$ export JAVA_HOME=/tmp/jdk-18.0.2.1/
$ export PATH=$JAVA_HOME/bin:$PATH
$ scl enable rh-python38 bash
$ python setup.py install --connector-port=1560
Enter install bundle password:
Data Safe on-premises connector installation in progress...
Data Safe on-premises connector successfully installed
```

Now you will notice that the on-premises connector status has changed to ACTIVE, as shown in Figure 10-49.

Figure 10-49 On-Premises Connector Status

At this point, you are ready to register the on-premises database with Data Safe by following the process shown earlier.

Summary

In this chapter, you learned that Oracle Data Safe is a fully integrated data security service for Oracle databases in the cloud and on-premises offered in OCI. It helps protect sensitive data, manage database configuration, control user access, and audit all database activities. Data Safe helps track database security configuration changes using drift management, allowing organizations to avoid tons of security challenges caused by rigorous application development cycles. Auditing helps you troubleshoot any security issues created from any exploited, overprivileged accounts. In the next chapter, we will look into one of the important pillars of security: Identity and Access Management.

Identity and Access Management

Identity and Access Management (IAM) is a modern access management service offered by Oracle in OCI. It provides fine-grained access control with authentication and authorization. IAM plays a critical role for workloads running across multiple clouds and on-premises. IAM helps to provide secure user access to only required resources. In other words, the right people have the right access, which is one of the most challenging tasks. IAM provides an organization with the tools to achieve its zero trust strategy.

We briefly touched on IAM in Chapter 3, "Oracle IaaS—Security." Here, we will focus on some of its important components. We will also cover one of the most used and important concepts: federations with Active Directory.

Compartments

A *compartment* is one of the most common and fundamental components of OCI. It is a logical unit containing all related resources. Compartments are global, meaning you can create resources across multiple regions within the same compartment.

During tenancy creation, the root compartment gets created. All resources are created under this root compartment. Best practice is to create user compartments within this root compartment to isolate resources based on the needs of the organization. For example, you can create production, test, and development compartments to organize a database environment appropriately. You can create one or more compartments within each compartment like a hierarchical structure. OCI allows up to six levels of nesting for compartments. We will look at a compartment nesting scenario while dealing with the policies example later in this chapter.

As you've noticed, each resource created within a tenancy belongs to a compartment. Resources can be moved from one compartment to another compartment. With appropriate groups and policies defined, you can control the access between resources residing in different compartments.

Users

As the name suggests, a *user* represents an individual person or a system. These users require access to different resources within your environment. Customers can create *local users* or *federated users*. Local users and their access are controlled in OCI. We will cover how to set up a federation later in this chapter.

Oracle offers Oracle Identity Cloud Service (IDCS) and Identity and Access Management (IAM) user choices. IDCS is an Identity as a Service (IDaaS). It integrates seamlessly with all other services like Platform as a Service (PaaS) and Software as a Service (SaaS) to manage user access controls. IDCS supports HTTP protocols for authentication, coarse-grained authorization, identity federation like Security Assertion Markup Language (SAML) 2.0, and user/role profile (SCIM). IDCS is recommended to create day-to-day users.

Identity and Access Management is a native authentication service used to manage user access for OCI resources such as compute, networking, storage, and analytics. Recently, Oracle released a new update to merge IDCS capabilities into native IAM services. As a result, IAM now includes all core functions of IDaaS, allowing unified administration and user experience.

Users can manage their accounts with different types of authentication requirements. You can access these settings by going to the user details page.

- **API Keys:** This setting allows the application to use API and CLI to authenticate the user.
- **Auth Tokens:** These are Oracle-generated token strings. They allow third-party APIs to authenticate with OCI. For example, the Docker containers registry tries to upload images to object storage, or a Swift services client uses Oracle Recovery Manager (RMAN) to back up the database to object storage.
- **Customer Secret Keys:** This setting allows the Amazon S3 compatibility API to work with object storage.
- **Database Passwords:** This setting allows you to access the Oracle database and manage database passwords in one place instead of local to each database.
- **OAuth 2.0 Client Credentials:** This setting allows you to interact with services using the OAuth 2.0 authentication protocol (Oracle Analytics Cloud and Oracle Integration Generation 2).
- **SMTP Credentials:** This setting allows you to send email through the Email Delivery service.

We will go over two of the most common authentication settings used by customers: Database Passwords and API Keys.

Database Passwords

Database passwords allow users themselves to create and manage their own passwords. Users do not need to reach out to database administrators to change passwords anymore. Passwords are only visible to users.

For our sample scenario, we will use an existing autonomous database named GDAGJTLHW0V4D0HT. Some prerequisite steps need to be performed in the database for IAM credentials to work, however. Log on to the autonomous database as the ADMIN user using SQL Developer version 22.2.1 or higher. (We covered how to log on to an autonomous database using SQL Developer in Chapter 8, "Oracle DBaaS—Databases.")

Enable IAM authentication on the database and verify it afterward, as shown in Example 11-1. If another external authentication is already enabled, then include the **force => TRUE** argument. In this case, there is no external authentication, so you can skip this argument.

Example 11-1   IAM Authentication Configuration

```
BEGIN    DBMS_CLOUD_ADMIN.ENABLE_EXTERNAL_AUTHENTICATION(
        type => 'OCI_IAM' );
END;
/
SELECT NAME, VALUE FROM V$PARAMETER WHERE NAME='identity_provider_type';
```

Add the IAM user and roles on the database, as shown in Example 11-2.

Example 11-2   IAM User and Roles

```
CREATE USER dhpatel IDENTIFIED GLOBALLY AS 'IAM_GROUP_NAME=LabUsers';
CREATE ROLE iam_role;
GRANT connect, resource TO iam_role;
ALTER ROLE iam_role IDENTIFIED GLOBALLY AS 'IAM_GROUP_NAME=LabUsers';
```

Now go to https://cloud.oracle.com and log on to your tenancy to create a database password for IAM user dhpatel. Click your profile in the top-right corner of the page, then click the main menu and select **Identity & Security > Domain > User Settings**, as shown in Figure 11-1.

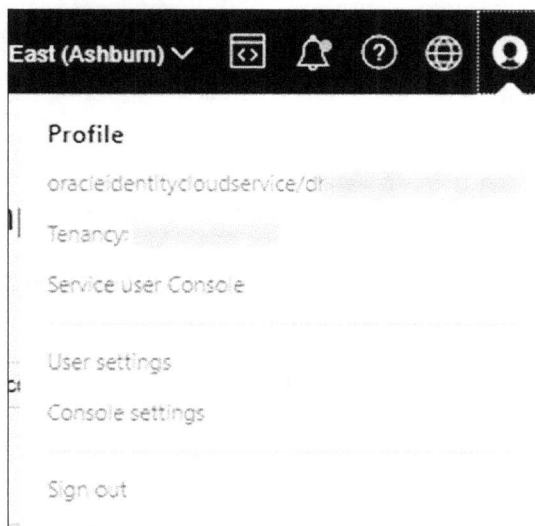

Figure 11-1   Profile Menu

Click **Resources > Database Passwords,** as shown in Figure 11-2.

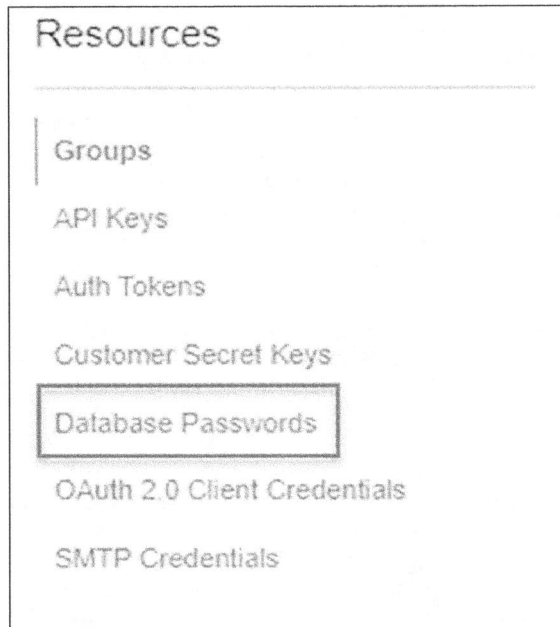

Figure 11-2   User Resources

Click **Create Database Password,** as shown in Figure 11-3.

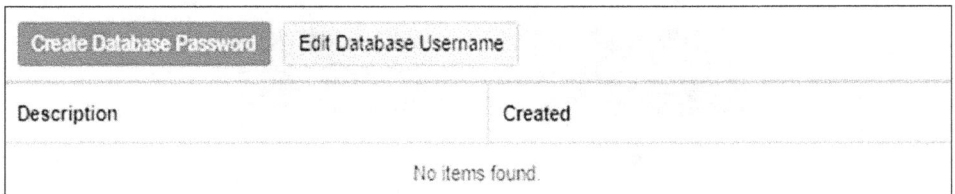

Figure 11-3   Database Password List

Next, enter a description and password; then click **Create Database Password,** as shown in Figure 11-4.

Now edit the database username to remove all extra characters in it. To do so, click **Edit Database Username,** as shown in Figure 11-5.

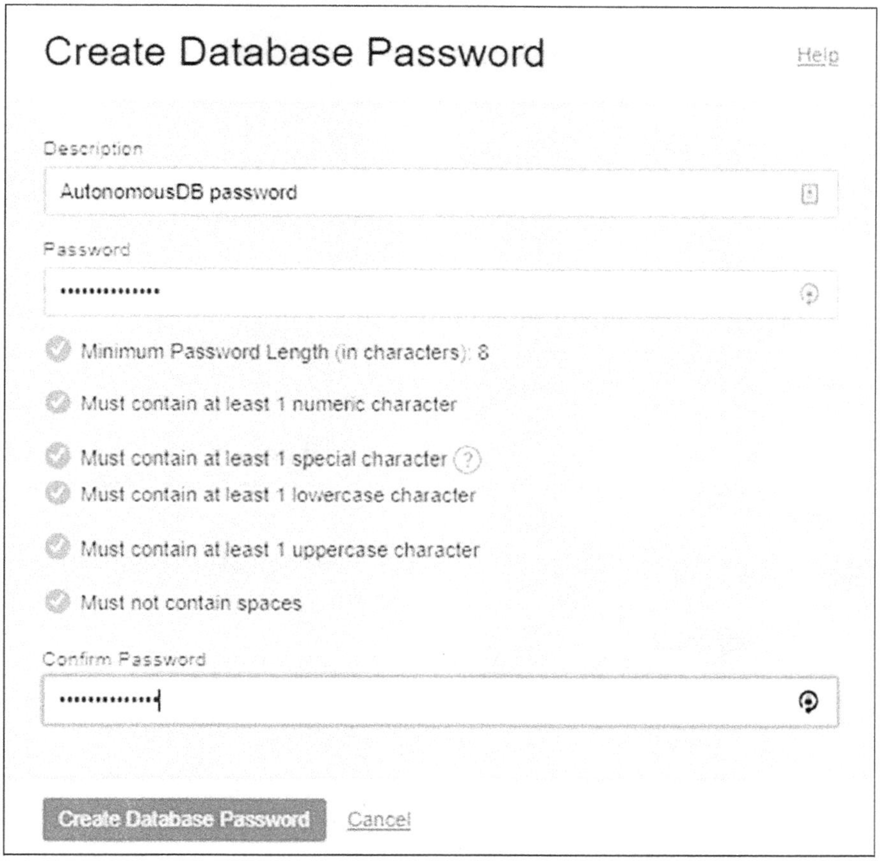

Figure 11-4   Create Database Password

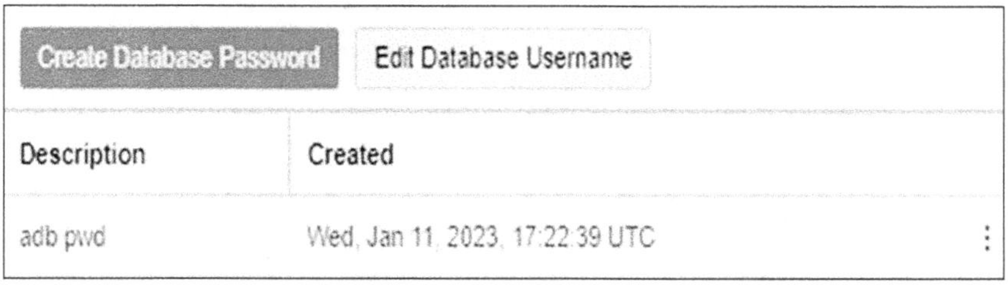

Figure 11-5   Database Password List

Replace your long username with a short username and click **Save Changes**, as shown in Figure 11-6.

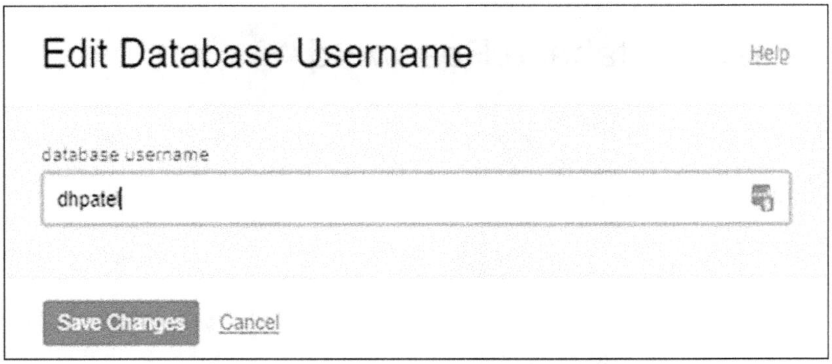

Figure 11-6   Edit Database Username

Now you are ready to log on to the autonomous database using IAM user dhpatel. Go to SQL Developer and create a connection for this database with the appropriate credentials and cloud wallet zip file, and then click **Test**, as shown in Figure 11-7.

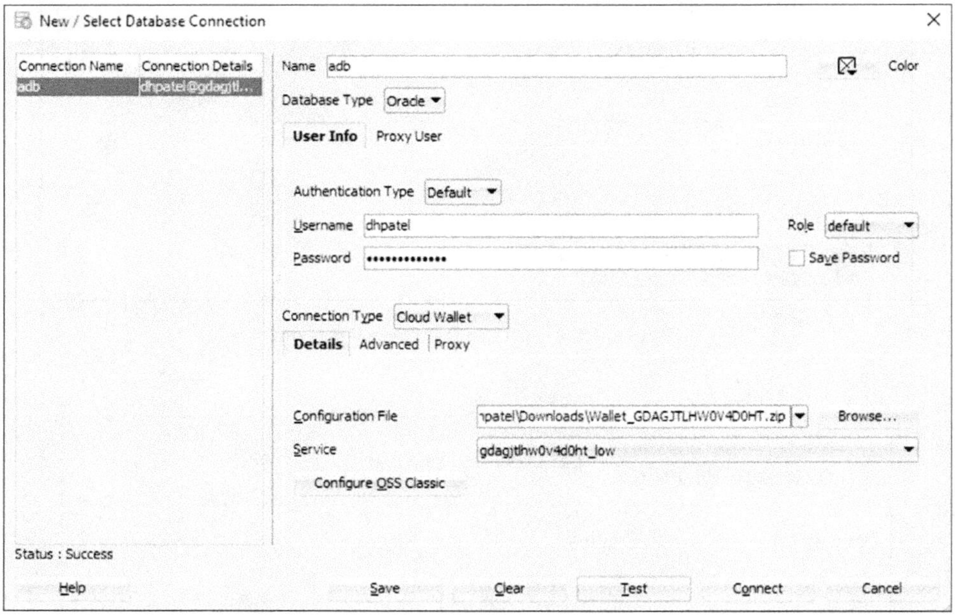

Figure 11-7   SQL Developer Connection

After you log on, verify the session by running the **show user** command, as shown in Figure 11-8.

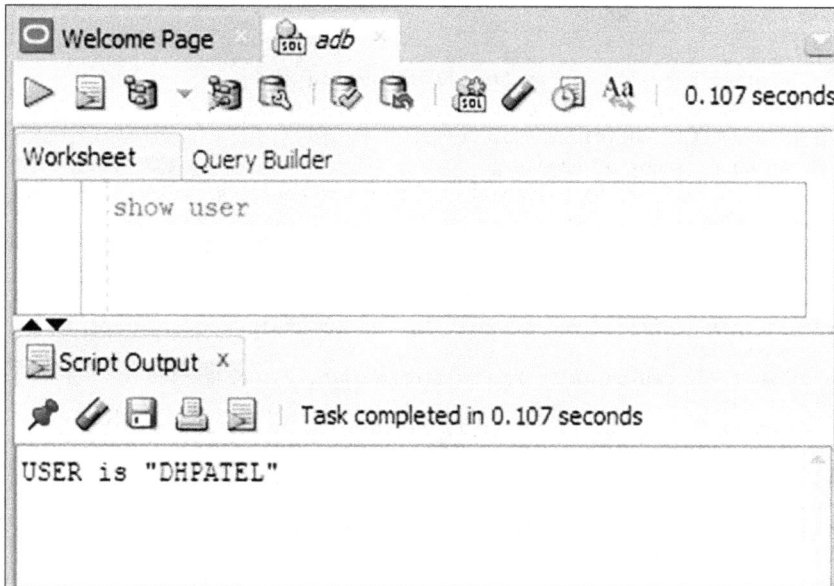

Figure 11-8   SQL Developer Script Output

As you can see, the user dhpatel is logged on to the autonomous database using IAM database credentials.

API Keys

Using API keys is another common authentication method that customers use. When using API keys, an IAM user can get authenticated without storing a password in any place on the instance.

API keys can be used with the OCI command-line interface (CLI), software development kit (SDK), and any custom-developed application. For our example, let's go over how to use API keys with the OCI CLI. All the following commands are run on an OCI compute instance running Oracle Linux 8.

First, install the OCI CLI by installing the packages shown in Example 11-3.

Example 11-3   Package Installation

```
# dnf install oraclelinux-developer-release-el8 -y
# dnf install python36-oci-cli -y
```

You can use your custom private key and public key, but for simplicity, we will be generating keys during the configuration. Let's begin with configuring the OCI CLI, as shown in Example 11-4.

Example 11-4   OCI CLI Setup

```
# oci setup config
Enter a location for your config [/root/.oci/config]:
Enter a user OCID: ocid1.user.oc1..
Enter a tenancy OCID: ocid1.tenancy.oc1...
Enter a region by index or name(e.g.
1: af-johannesburg-1, 2: ap-chiyoda-1, 3: ap-chuncheon-1, 4: ap-dcc-canberra-1,
    5: ap-hyderabad-1,
6: ap-ibaraki-1, 7: ap-melbourne-1, 8: ap-mumbai-1, 9: ap-osaka-1, 10: ap-seoul-1,
11: ap-singapore-1, 12: ap-sydney-1, 13: ap-tokyo-1, 14: ca-montreal-1,
    15: ca-toronto-1,
16: eu-amsterdam-1, 17: eu-dcc-milan-1, 18: eu-frankfurt-1, 19: eu-madrid-1,
    20: eu-marseille-1,
21: eu-milan-1, 22: eu-paris-1, 23: eu-stockholm-1, 24: eu-zurich-1,
    25: il-jerusalem-1,
26: me-abudhabi-1, 27: me-dcc-muscat-1, 28: me-dubai-1, 29: me-jeddah-1,
    30: mx-queretaro-1,
31: sa-santiago-1, 32: sa-saopaulo-1, 33: sa-vinhedo-1, 34: uk-cardiff-1,
    35: uk-gov-cardiff-1,
36: uk-gov-london-1, 37: uk-london-1, 38: us-ashburn-1, 39: us-gov-ashburn-1,
    40: us-gov-chicago-1,
41: us-gov-phoenix-1, 42: us-langley-1, 43: us-luke-1, 44: us-phoenix-1,
    45: us-sanjose-1): 38
Do you want to generate a new API Signing RSA key pair? (If you decline you will
    be asked to supply the path to an existing key.) [Y/n]: Y
Enter a directory for your keys to be created [/root/.oci]:
Enter a name for your key [oci_api_key]:
Public key written to: /root/.oci/oci_api_key_public.pem
Enter a passphrase for your private key (empty for no passphrase):
Private key written to: /root/.oci/oci_api_key.pem
Fingerprint: ca:89:e8:7b:a0:76:03:1c:b2:1e:09:86:11:83:27:44
Config written to /root/.oci/config
```

As a result of the configuration process shown in Example 11-4, the OCI CLI configuration file, private key, and public key get created, as shown in Example 11-5.

Example 11-5   OCI CLI Configuration and Key Files

```
# ll .oci/
total 12
-rw-------. 1 root root  296 Jan 11 20:07 config
-rw-------. 1 root root 1704 Jan 11 20:07 oci_api_key.pem
-rw-------. 1 root root  451 Jan 11 20:06 oci_api_key_public.pem
```

Review the configuration file for all parameters set for the OCI CLI, as shown in Example 11-6, to use while making API calls.

Example 11-6   OCI CLI Configuration File Content

```
# cat .oci/config
[DEFAULT]
user=ocid1.user.oc1..
fingerprint=ca:89:e8:7b:a0:76:03:1c:b2:1e:09:86:11:83:27:44
key_file=/root/.oci/oci_api_key.pem
tenancy=ocid1.tenancy.oc1..
region=us-ashburn-1
```

Now let's create an API key in OCI by uploading a public key. To do this, go to the user settings page and click **API Keys** under Resources, as shown in Figure 11-9.

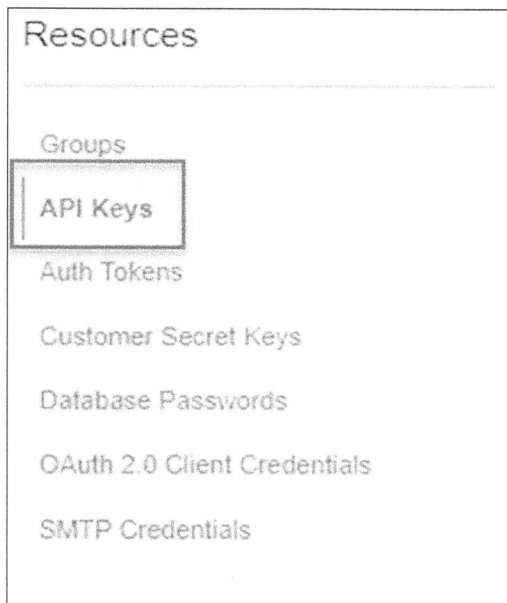

Figure 11-9   User Resources

Click **Add API Key**, as shown in Figure 11-10.

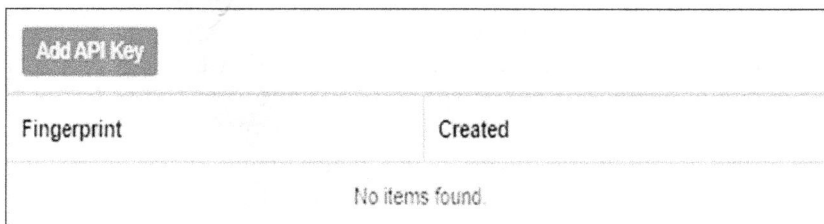

Figure 11-10   API Key List

Select the **Paste Public Key** option, paste the key created during the OCI CLI configuration (/root/.oci/oci_api_key_public.pem), and click **Add**, as shown in Figure 11-11.

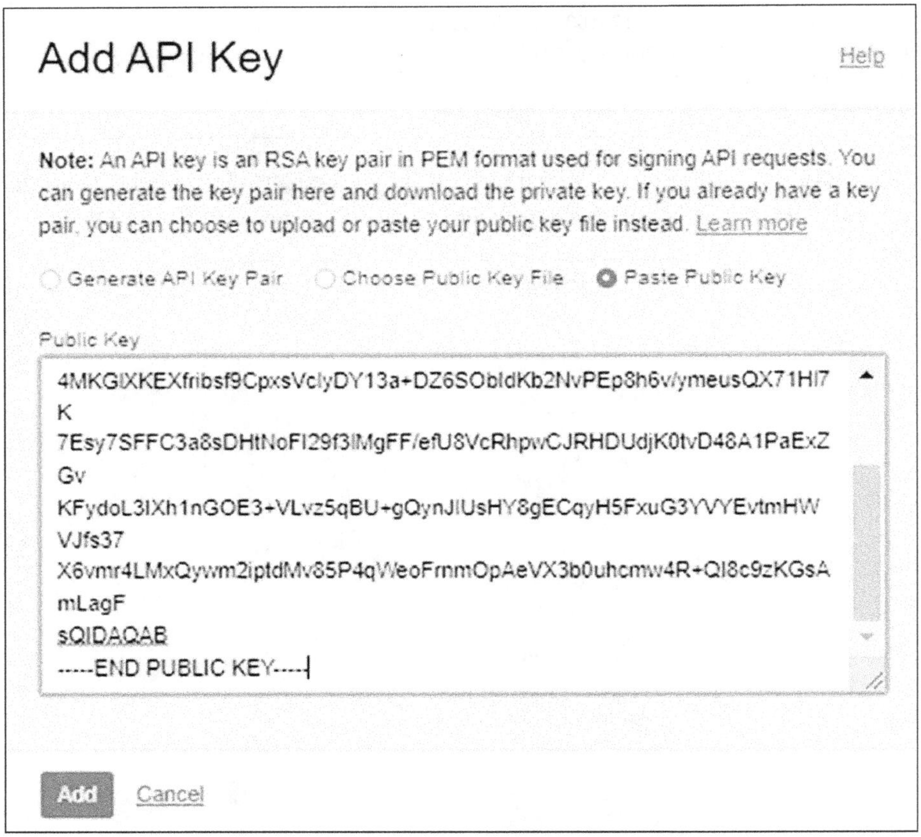

Add API Key   Help

Note: An API key is an RSA key pair in PEM format used for signing API requests. You can generate the key pair here and download the private key. If you already have a key pair, you can choose to upload or paste your public key file instead. Learn more

○ Generate API Key Pair   ○ Choose Public Key File   ● Paste Public Key

Public Key

```
4MKGlXKEXfribsf9CpxsVclyDY13a+DZ6SObldKb2NvPEp8h6v/ymeusQX71HI7
K
7Esy7SFFC3a8sDHtNoFI29f3lMgFF/efU8VcRhpwCJRHDUdjK0tvD48A1PaExZ
Gv
KFydoL3lXh1nGOE3+VLvz5qBU+gQynJlUsHY8gECqyH5FxuG3YVYEvtmHW
VJfs37
X6vmr4LMxQywm2iptdMv85P4qWeoFrnmOpAeVX3b0uhcmw4R+Ql8c9zKGsA
mLagF
sQIDAQAB
-----END PUBLIC KEY-----
```

Add   Cancel

Figure 11-11   Add API Key

The configuration file uses this API key from the OCI CLI/SDK, as shown in Figure 11-12. This is similar to the configuration file created when the OCI CLI **config** command was executed earlier. If you are going to use your own private and public keys, you need to create API keys for the IAM user in OCI first. It will give you the configuration file to copy the content and create the OCI CLI configuration file manually.

You're ready to run the OCI CLI commands now. You can find all instances running in the oracle-demo compartment, as shown in Example 11-7.

Configuration File Preview   Help

Note: This configuration file snippet includes the basic authentication information you'll
need to use the SDK, CLI, or other OCI developer tool. Paste the contents of the text
box into your ~/.oci/config file and update the key_file parameter with the file path to
your private key. If you already have a Default profile in your config profile, you'll need
to perform some additional steps. Learn more

Select API Key Fingerprint

```
ca:89:e8:7b:a0:76:03:1c:b2:1e:09:86:11:83:27:44
```

Configuration File Preview Read-only

```
[DEFAULT]
user=ocid1.user.oc1.

fingerprint=ca:89:e8:7b:a0:76:03:1c:b2:1e:09:86:11:83:27:44
tenancy=ocid1.tenancy.oc1.
```

Paste the contents of the text box into your ~/.oci/config file.   Copy

Close

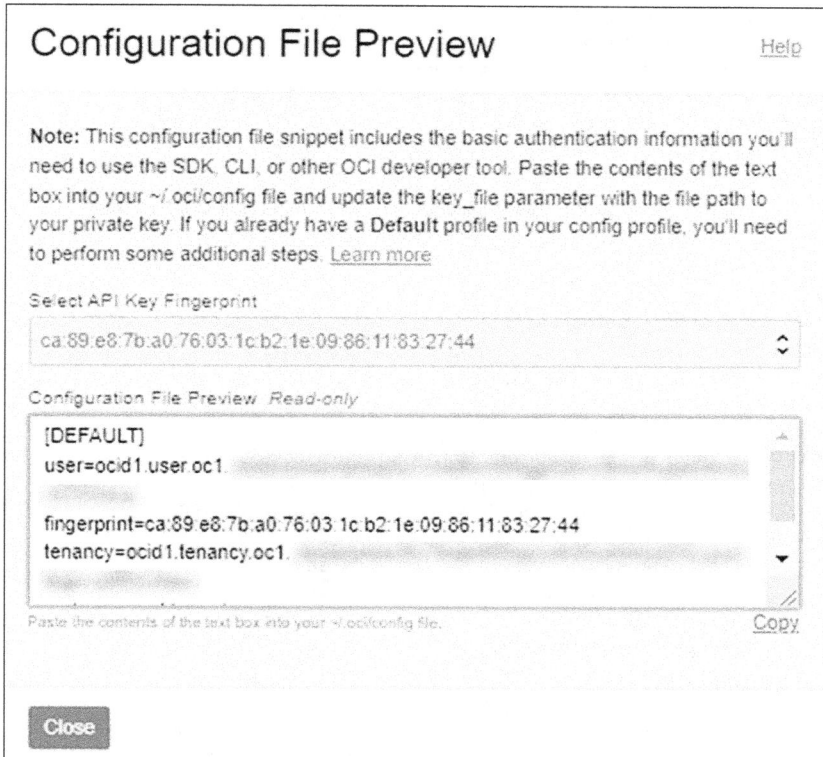

Figure 11-12   OCI CLI/SDK Configuration File Preview

Example 11-7   OCI CLI Example

```
# oci compute instance list --compartment-id ocid1.compartment.oc1..
  aaaaaaaasv3xucogay6qhyddgomsrz7vqctguxqhof3ipo3cbhtbuqx5fxoa --lifecycle-state
  RUNNING
{
  "data": [
    {
      "agent-config": {
        "are-all-plugins-disabled": false,
        "is-management-disabled": false,
        "is-monitoring-disabled": false,
        "plugins-config": null
      },
      "availability-config": {
        "is-live-migration-preferred": null,
        "recovery-action": "RESTORE_INSTANCE"
      },
```

```
    "availability-domain": "ktgl:US-ASHBURN-AD-1",
    "capacity-reservation-id": null,
    "compartment-id": "ocid1.compartment.oc1..
aaaaaaaasv3xucogay6qhyddgomsrz7vqctguxqhof3ipo3cbhtbuqx5fxoa",
    "dedicated-vm-host-id": null,
    "defined-tags": {
      "Oracle-Tags": {
        "CreatedBy": "oracleidentitycloudservice/dhpatel@mythics.com",
        "CreatedOn": "2022-12-12T17:38:51.673Z"
      }
    },
    "display-name": "wordpress",
    "extended-metadata": {},
    "fault-domain": "FAULT-DOMAIN-3",
    "freeform-tags": {},
    "id": "ocid1.instance.oc1.iad.
anuwcljsnlpusgychyxsjj6sxntnbdvbact6synyzvrtce7wjecme323uzoa",
    "image-id": "ocid1.image.oc1.iad.
aaaaaaaaxnniiwolr6k5smo4gybuys37zraeodjip6rxjghtzg76ajryeioq",
    "instance-options": {
      "are-legacy-imds-endpoints-disabled": false
    },
    "ipxe-script": null,
    "launch-mode": "PARAVIRTUALIZED",
    "launch-options": {
      "boot-volume-type": "PARAVIRTUALIZED",
      "firmware": "UEFI_64",
      "is-consistent-volume-naming-enabled": true,
      "is-pv-encryption-in-transit-enabled": false,
      "network-type": "PARAVIRTUALIZED",
      "remote-data-volume-type": "PARAVIRTUALIZED"
    },
    "lifecycle-state": "RUNNING",
    "metadata": {
      "ssh_authorized_keys": "ssh-rsa AAAAB3NzaC1yc2EA…XCKTgkXf7JH6C7pNZGiBu/
AfUJ\n",
      "user_data": "I2Nsb3VkLWNvbm…
G91Y2gsIC90bXAvY2xvdWQtaW5pdC1jb21wbGV0ZSBdCg=="
    },
    "platform-config": null,
    "preemptible-instance-config": null,
    "region": "iad",
    "shape": "VM.Standard.E2.1",
    "shape-config": {
      "baseline-ocpu-utilization": null,
      "gpu-description": null,
      "gpus": 0,
      "local-disk-description": null,
      "local-disks": 0,
```

```
      "local-disks-total-size-in-gbs": null,
      "max-vnic-attachments": 2,
      "memory-in-gbs": 8.0,
      "networking-bandwidth-in-gbps": 0.7,
      "ocpus": 1.0,
      "processor-description": "2.0 GHz AMD EPYC\u2122 7551 (Naples)"
    },
    "source-details": {
      "boot-volume-size-in-gbs": null,
      "boot-volume-vpus-per-gb": null,
      "image-id": "ocid1.image.oc1.iad.
aaaaaaaaxnniiwolr6k5smo4gybuys37zraeodjip6rxjghtzg76ajryeioq",
      "kms-key-id": null,
      "source-type": "image"
    },
    "system-tags": {},
    "time-created": "2022-12-12T17:38:52.457000+00:00",
    "time-maintenance-reboot-due": null
  }
 ]
}
```

Groups

A *group* is a collection of users with a common factor such as organization or access requirement. In OCI, privileges are assigned at the group level. So, you will need to create at least one group for administrators. This also means all users will need to be part of at least one group. You can create a local group to manage local users, or you can create and manage groups using federation.

Dynamic Groups

A dynamic group member is referred to as a *principal*. A principal is a service or resource trying to access another resource. A principal can be an infrastructure, stacked, or ephemeral principal. An example of an *infrastructure principal* is an instance. IAM allows instances and applications running on it to interact and perform actions on another resource. An example of a *stacked principal* is an Oracle database. A stacked principal is the principal created on top of another principal. An example is an Oracle database created on an infrastructure principal like an instance. An *ephemeral principal* is a principal requiring temporary access to another resource. An example of such a principal is an Oracle function. These principals are grouped together within dynamic groups, and their access is controlled using policies.

For dynamic groups, principal members are not added explicitly. Instead, *matching rules* are created to define which members will be part of this dynamic group. So, based on the matching rules for infrastructure principals, a new instance gets added if it qualifies and terminated instances get removed from the dynamic group. Depending on the access granted to the group, a compute instance can make API calls to other resources like object storage.

Let's go over a few examples showing how to create dynamic groups with different types of matching rules. To start, go to https://cloud.oracle.com and log on to your tenancy. Click on the main menu and select **Identity & Security > Dynamic Groups**, as shown in Figure 11-13.

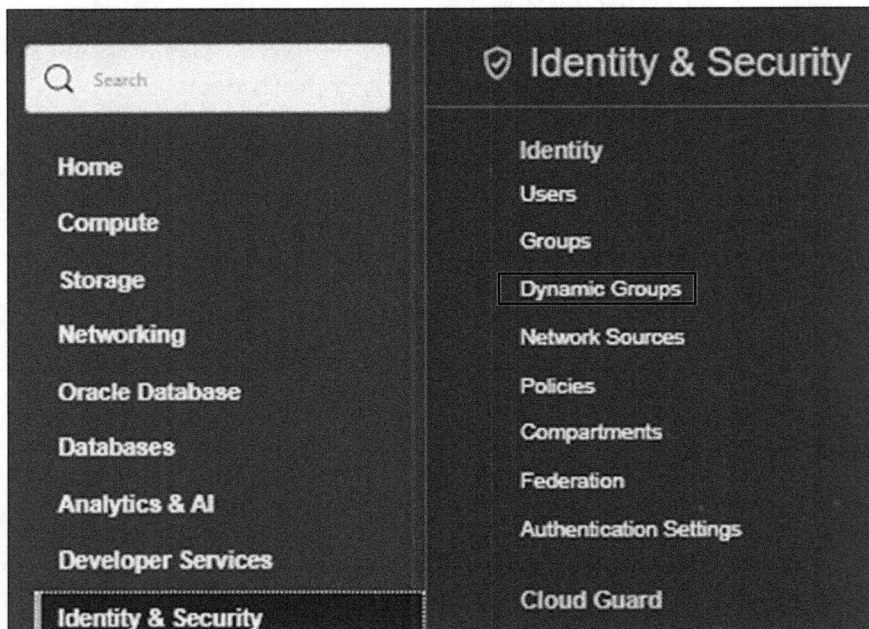

Figure 11-13   Identity & Security Menu

Click **Create Dynamic Group**, as shown in Figure 11-14.

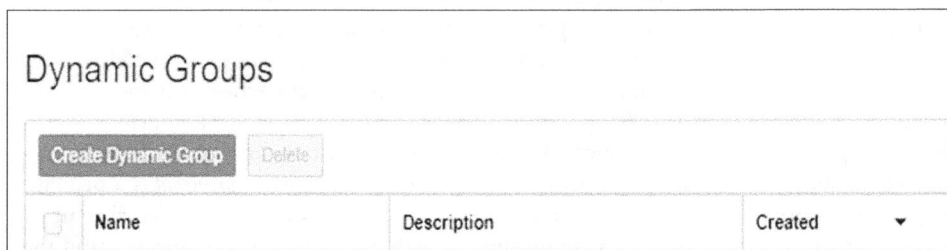

Figure 11-14   Dynamic Group List

Next, provide a group name and description. You can define the rule based on the example rule shown here and to match any or all rules. For this example, click **Rule Builder**, as shown in Figure 11-15.

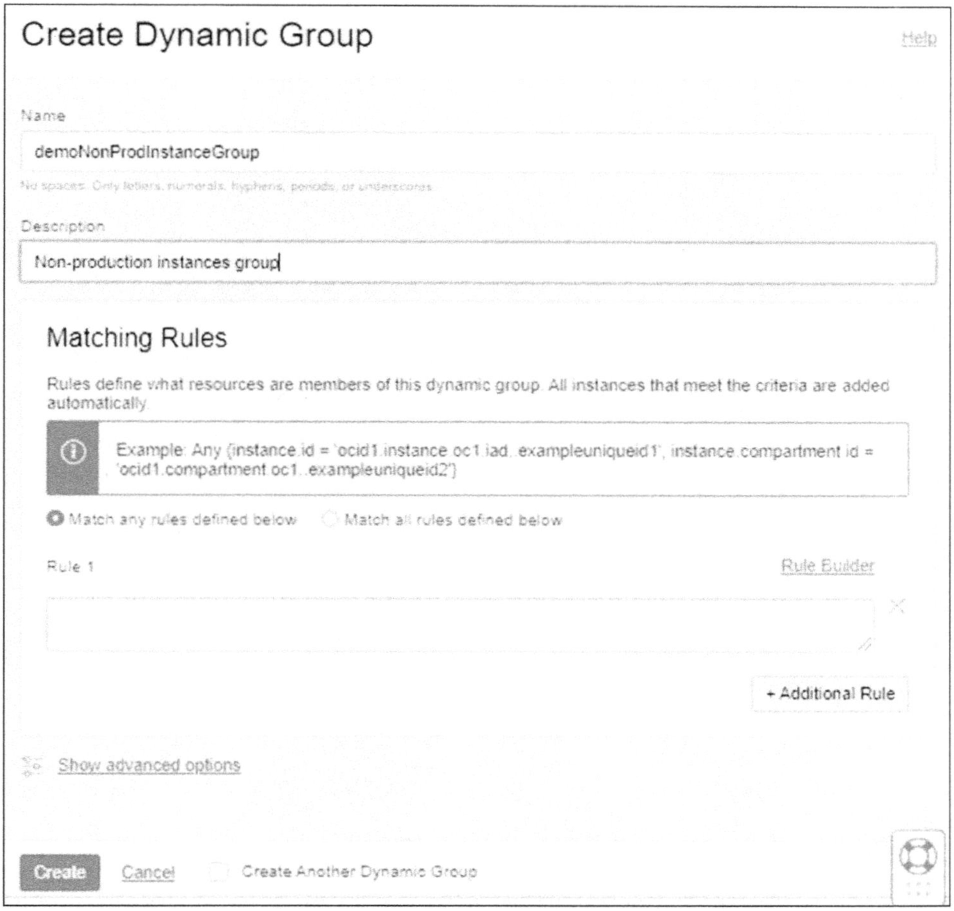

Create Dynamic Group

Help

Name

demoNonProdInstanceGroup

No spaces. Only letters, numerals, hyphens, periods, or underscores.

Description

Non-production instances group

Matching Rules

Rules define what resources are members of this dynamic group. All instances that meet the criteria are added automatically.

ⓘ Example: Any {instance.id = 'ocid1.instance.oc1.iad..exampleuniqueid1', instance.compartment.id = 'ocid1.compartment.oc1..exampleuniqueid2'}

⦿ Match any rules defined below   ○ Match all rules defined below

Rule 1   Rule Builder

                                                                              ⤬

                                                                    + Additional Rule

Show advanced options

Create   Cancel   ☐ Create Another Dynamic Group

Figure 11-15   Create Dynamic Group

Select all of the following to include an instance that matches the rule. For rule, select a compartment ID and provide an OCID for it. Here, we have provided the compartment OCID of oracle-demo compartment. Now click **Add Rule**, as shown in Figure 11-16.

Review all the information entered and click **Create**, as shown in Figure 11-17.

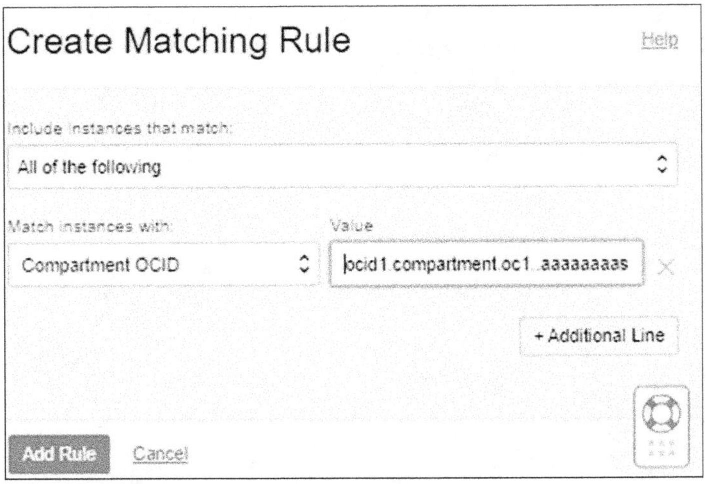

Figure 11-16   Dynamic Group Matching Rule

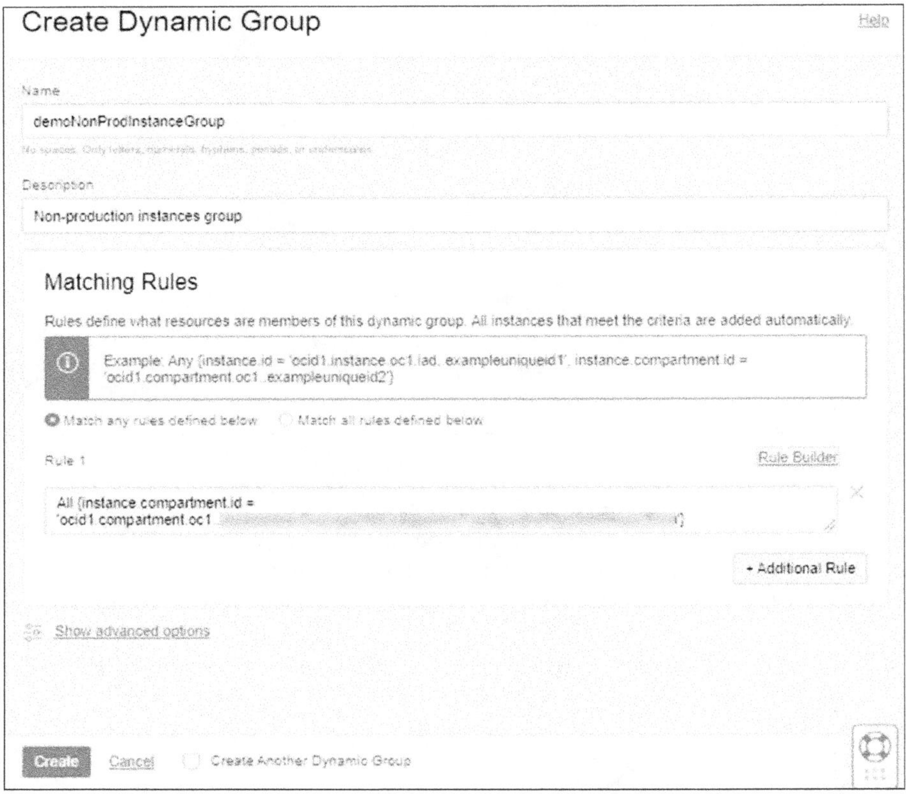

Figure 11-17   Review Dynamic Group Configuration

Now all instances created in the oracle-demo compartment will be added as members to the demoNonProdInstanceGroup dynamic group.

Rule builders have some limitations, so to utilize more rule options, you should write matching rules manually. Let's look at some examples:

1. Create a dynamic group to include all Oracle databases from a specific compartment:

```
ALL {resource.type = 'dbaas',resource.compartment.id='cid1.compartment.oc1..
aaaaaaaasv3xucogay6qhyddgomsrz7vqctguxqhof3ipo3cbhtbuqx5fxoa'}
```

2. Create a dynamic group to include a specific function:

```
ALL {resource.type = 'fnfunc', resource.id = 'ocid1.fnfunc.oc1.iad.
aaaaaaaa7jeinsl4tteswjae7rvttwzlp5ipuvqabfm3xx5mubldq2ychdaa'}
```

3. Create a dynamic group to include all instances having a specific tag namespace, key, and value. Oracle tagging allows you to organize resources per your specific requirements.

```
tag.production.app.value='#'
```

Policies

A *policy* is one of the critical components of IAM. It defines who has what access and how. A policy only allows access to resources, meaning by default all access is denied. In other words, your tenancy will have at least one policy to control access to your resources.

You define a policy by using the following types of statements:

```
Allow group <group_name> to <verb> <resource_type> in tenancy
Allow group <group_name> to <verb> <resource_type> in compartment <compartment_
  name>
```

In these statements, **verb** refers to the type of access. Table 11-1 shows possible values for it.

Table 11-1   Verbs and the Types of Access They Grant

Verb	Type of Access
Inspect	Ability to observe, list, and monitor resources with more or less information, depending on the resource type but without any confidential information.
Read	Ability to access the resource with metadata. Includes inspect-level access.
Use	Ability to modify the resources to a different degree, depending on the resource type. Includes user-level access.
Manage	Full access to resources such as creating or deleting resources.

The following family resource types are some of the most common and include other individual resource types:

- Cluster-family
- Compute-management-family
- Database-family
- Instance-family
- Object-family
- Virtual-network-family
- Volume-family

A policy can contain multiple policy statements.

Now go to https://cloud.oracle.com and log on to your tenancy. Click on the main menu and select **Identity & Security > Policies**, as shown in Figure 11-18.

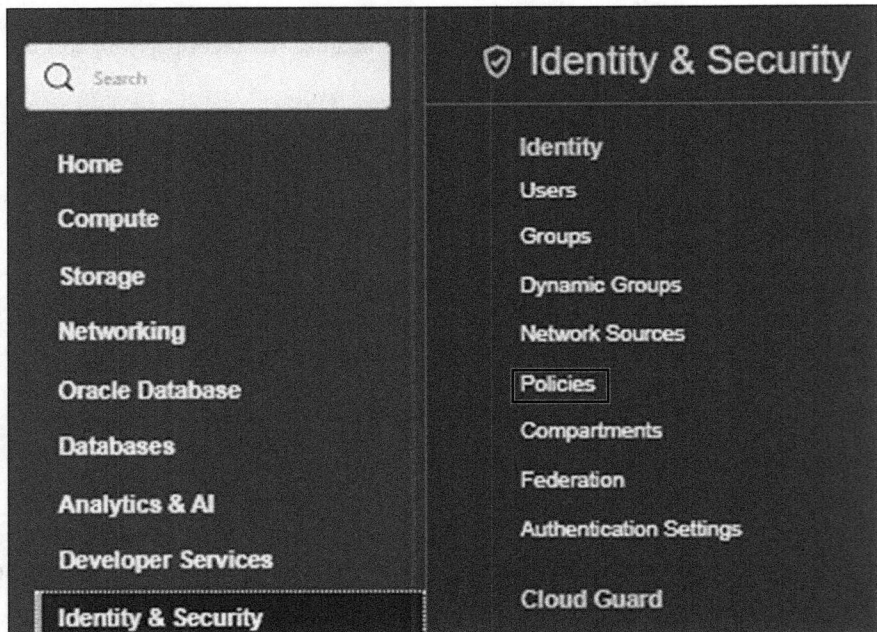

Figure 11-18   Identity & Security Menu

Click **Create Policy**, as shown in Figure 11-19.

Next, you will see a policy builder where you can create policies based on common policy templates. For this example, enable **Show Manual Editor** to enter the policies manually, as shown in Figure 11-20. Here, we are giving the LabUsers group privileges to manage instances in conjunction with using volume and virtual network resources. This policy also allows the users to launch instances from image listings.

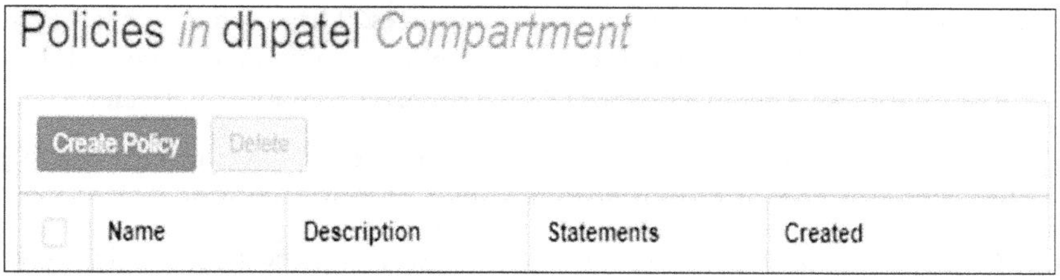

Figure 11-19   Policy List

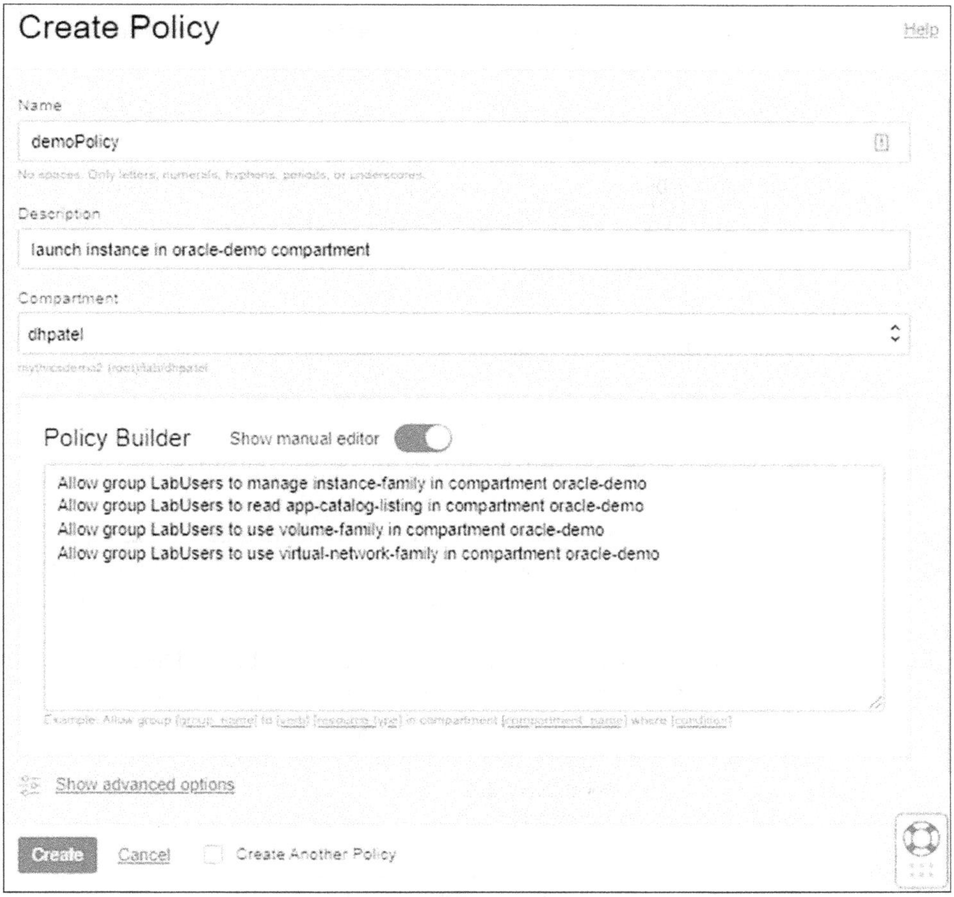

Figure 11-20   Create Policy

Policies can provide further fine-grained access using one or more conditions. Each condition can have multiple variables with values to compare. These variables can be related to source resources or relevant to target resources. These conditions get evaluated to true, false, or not applicable, and accordingly, user access will be determined. Let's review some examples to better understand how to write conditional policies.

1. Modify the demoPolicy created earlier to restrict the LabUsers group, allowing it to launch instances only in the Ashburn region:

```
Allow group LabUsers to manage instance-family in compartment oracle-demo
where request.region='ash'
Allow group LabUsers to read app-catalog-listing in compartment oracle-demo
where request.region='ash'
Allow group LabUsers to use volume-family in compartment oracle-demo where
request.region='ash'
Allow group LabUsers to use virtual-network-family in compartment oracle-demo
where request.region='ash'
```

2. Modify the Junior DBA group so that it is not be able to delete the database backup of the Base Database service:

```
Allow group  JuniorDBA to manage db-backups in compartment oracle-demo where
request.operation!='DeleteBackup'
```

Warning

Policy condition matching *is not* case sensitive. So be cautious while specifying resource names that *are* case sensitive.

You should also understand how policies impact the parent and child compartments. As you saw earlier, a policy gets attached to a compartment during the creation. So, in the case of hierarchical compartment structure, any policy granting manage access to the resource and policies applied to a compartment get inherited by all child compartments. Policies need to refer to the compartment appropriately while dealing with hierarchical compartment structure.

Let's review this hierarchy with the example shown in Figure 11-21. DevelopmentDB is a parent compartment with BaseDB and AutonomousDB as child compartments. AutonomousDB has two more child compartments: ATP and ADW.

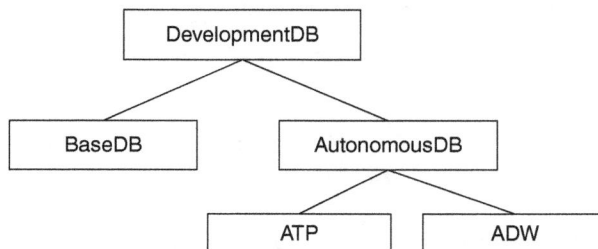

Figure 11-21 Compartment Hierarchy

Following the policy examples in accordance with the compartments shown in Figure 11-21, the layout can be created as follows at the DevelopmentDB compartment:

- **Policy 1:** The dba-admin should be able to manage databases in the DevelopmentDB, BaseDB, and AutonomousDB compartments.

  ```
  Allow group dba-admin to manage database-family in the DevelopmentDB
  compartment.
  ```

- **Policy 2:** The junior-dba-admins should be able to manage databases only in the BaseDB compartment.

  ```
  Allow group junior-dba-admins to manage database-family in the BaseDB
  compartment.
  ```

- **Policy 3:** The dw-dba-admins should be able to manage databases only in the ADW compartment.

  ```
  Allow group dw-dba-admins to manage database-family in the AutonomousDB:ADW
  compartment.
  ```

Pay close attention to the Policy 3 example here. Because the policy is written at the DevelopmentDB compartment, the ADW compartment is referenced as AutonomousDB:ADW. If the policy was written at the AutonomousDB compartment, then you could reference the compartment as ADW in the policy. In other words, a parent compartment is only aware of an immediate child compartment and not aware of the further hierarchy of these child compartments. Therefore, when you reference a compartment in a policy, make sure to be aware of the hierarchy level to reference it correctly.

Federation

All organizations use an identity provider (IdP) for Identity and Access Management. Among the most common IdPs used are Microsoft Active Directory and Okta. To access OCI, customers need to create a login ID for all users. And now administrators have to manage at least two separate systems for IAM. This will add more complexity to their existing IAM processes. OCI provides identity federation to solve this issue. OCI offers federation support with Microsoft Active Directory, Okta, Microsoft Azure Active Directory, and other identity providers supporting the Security Assertion Markup Language (SAML) 2.0 protocol.

Here, we will go over how to set up a federation between Oracle Identity Cloud Service and Microsoft Active Directory. For our example, Active Directory and related software required for federation are installed and configured on the thetechiewizard.com ADS server. The domain name being federated is thetechiewizard.com. For this specific AD server, we can download the SAML metadata document for the AD federation server by going to https://ads.thetechiewizard.com/FederationMetadata/2007-06/FederationMetadata.xml. This is just a reference as an example URL; depending on the system you are federating to, the URL will be different.

The file will be downloaded as FederationMetadata.xml. We've also created the user dhpatel and the group OCI_Administrators in AD for this scenario. User dhpatel is a member of the OCI_Administrators group.

Go to https://cloud.oracle.com and log on to your tenancy. Click on the main menu and select **Identity & Security > Federation**, as shown in Figure 11-22.

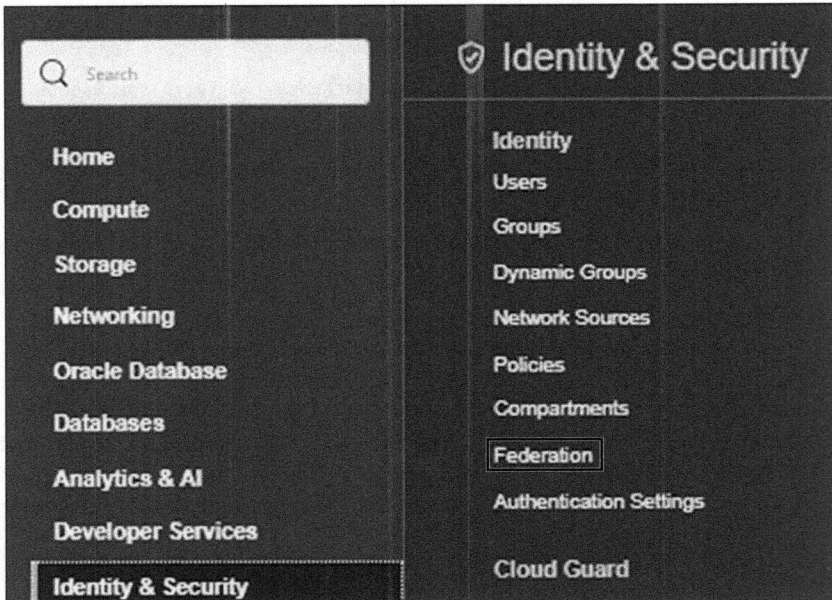

Figure 11-22   Identity & Security Menu

Click **Add Identity Provider**, as shown in Figure 11-23.

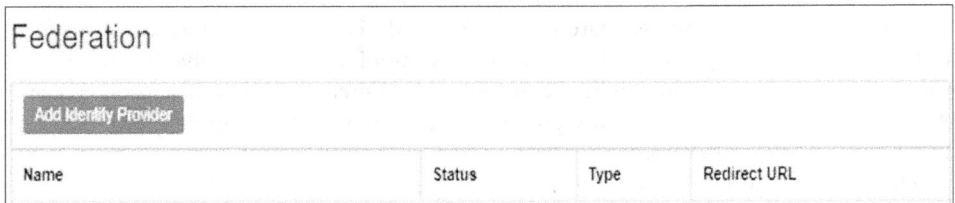

Figure 11-23   Federation List

Next, provide a name and description. Then select **Microsoft Active Directory Federation Service (ADFS)** and upload the FederationMetadata.xml file downloaded earlier. Select **Encrypt Assertion**, select **Force Authentication**, leave Authentication Context Class References, and click **Continue**, as shown in Figure 11-24.

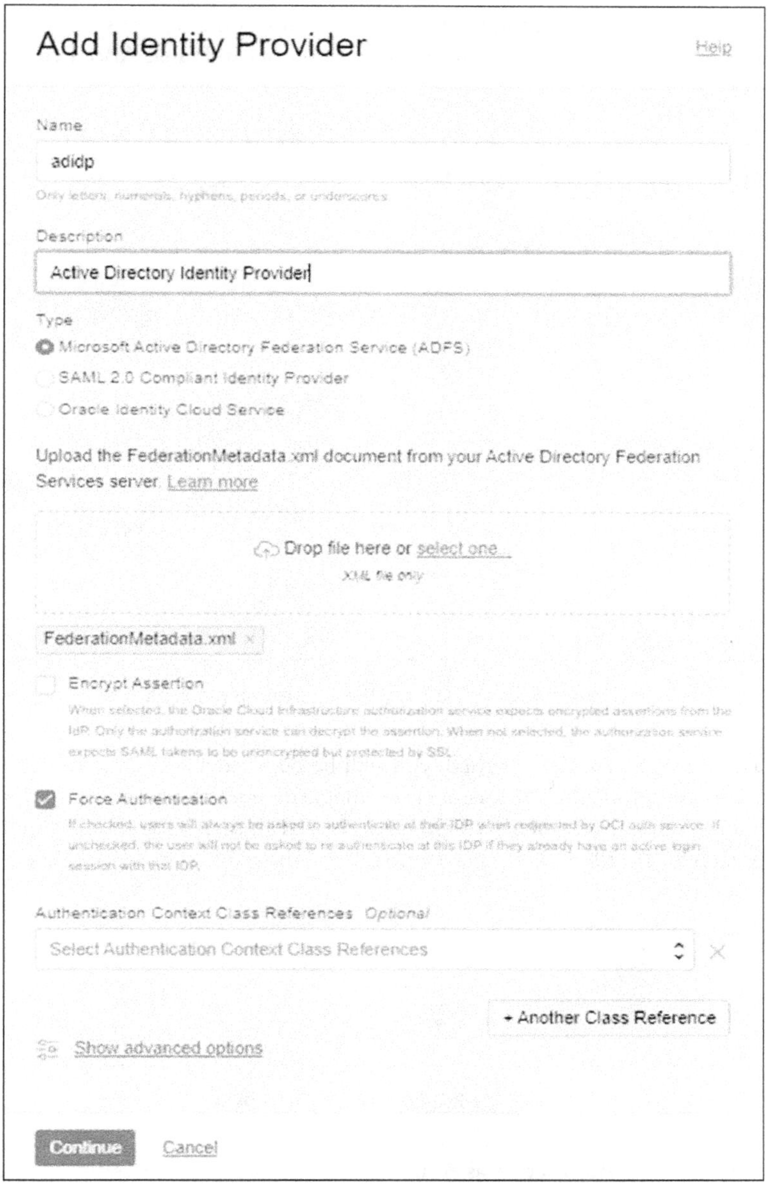

Figure 11-24   Add Identity Provider

Next, you can provide group mapping between OCI and AD. You can also skip this mapping and do it later after the provider is added. You can create different groups for network admins, system admins, and so on and map them to the appropriate OCI groups with required policies assigned to them. For this example, just map the AD group OCI_Administrators with the OCI group Administrators and click **Add Provider**, as shown in Figure 11-25.

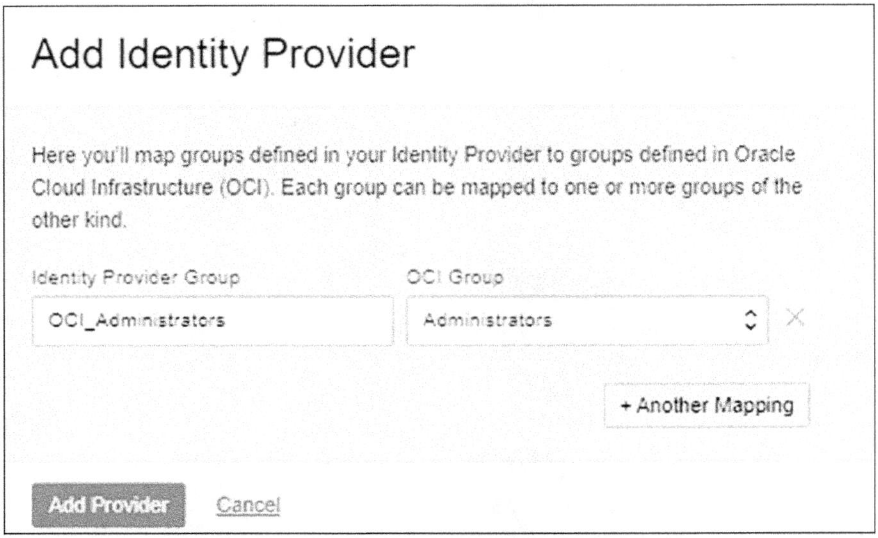

Add Identity Provider

Here you'll map groups defined in your Identity Provider to groups defined in Oracle Cloud Infrastructure (OCI). Each group can be mapped to one or more groups of the other kind.

Identity Provider Group   OCI Group

OCI_Administrators   Administrators   ⌄ ✕

+ Another Mapping

Add Provider   Cancel

Figure 11-25   Identity Provider Group Mapping

Once the identity provider is added, you will be taken to the Federation home page. Here, you can download the OCI Federation metadata document like you did for AD in earlier steps. Click the **Download this document** link, as shown in Figure 11-26. We have renamed this file to OCImetadata.xml and moved it to the ADS server hosting Active Directory.

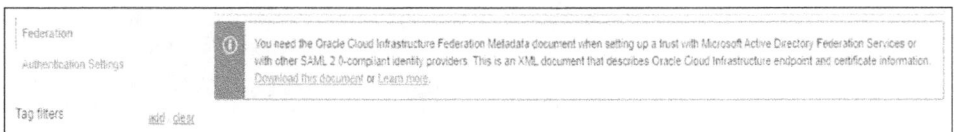

Federation

Authentication Settings

Tag filters   add clear

You need the Oracle Cloud Infrastructure Federation Metadata document when setting up a trust with Microsoft Active Directory Federation Services or with other SAML 2.0-compliant identity providers. This is an XML document that describes Oracle Cloud Infrastructure endpoint and certificate information. Download this document or Learn more.

Figure 11-26   Federation Page

Now log on to the ADS server as Administrator to make the necessary configurations on the Active Directory end. Click the startup menu and select **AD FS Management**, as shown in Figure 11-27.

Figure 11-27   Windows Startup Menu

On the AD FS Management Console, right-click **AD FS** and click **Add Relying Party Trust**, as shown in Figure 11-28.

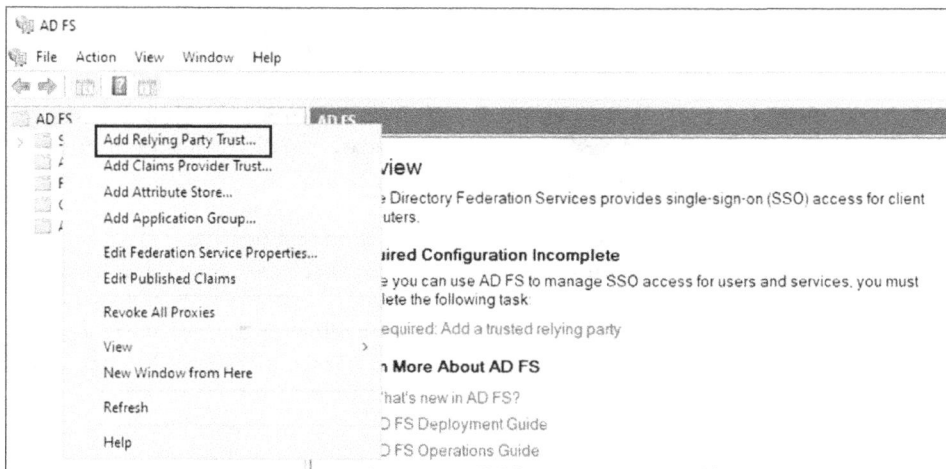

Figure 11-28   AD FS Management Console

The Add Relying Party Trust Wizard will open. Leave the default selection of the Claims Aware option and click **Start**, as shown in Figure 11-29.

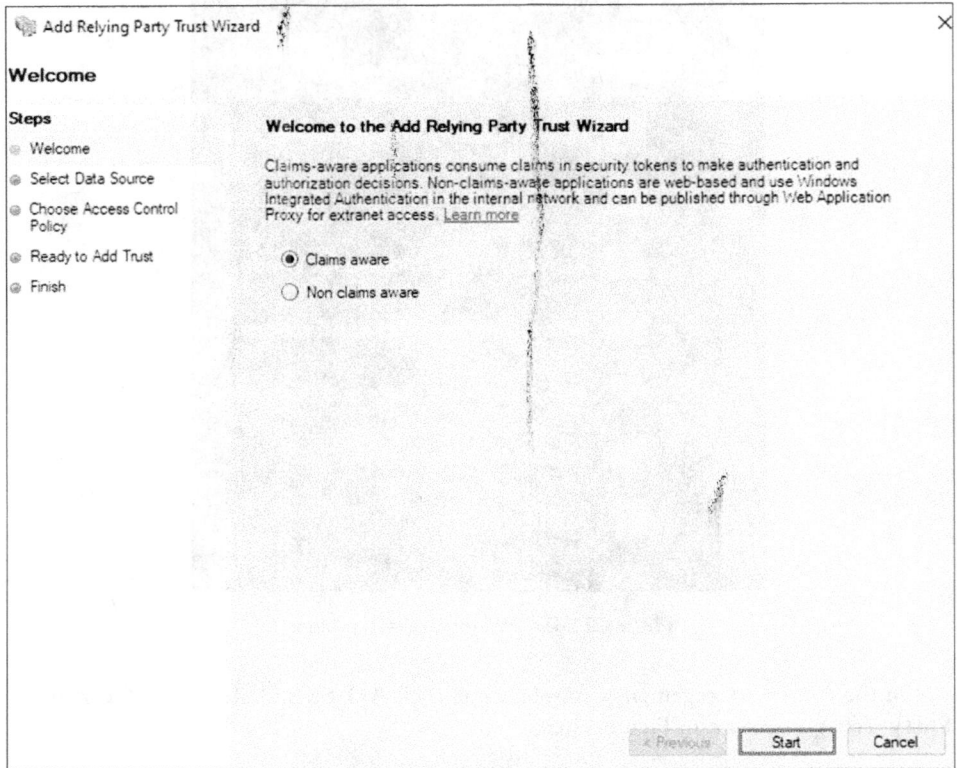

Figure 11-29   Add Relying Party Trust Wizard

Select the **Import Data About the Relying Party from a File** option, upload the file we downloaded from the AD server OCIMetadata.xml file, and click **Next**, as shown in Figure 11-30. This filename can change, depending on what system you are federating to.

Next, provide a trust display name and click **Next**, as shown in Figure 11-31.

By default, the Permit Everyone access control policy is selected. Keep this default and click **Next**, as shown in Figure 11-32. You can choose multiple access control policies to restrict access, depnding on how you want to allow or disallow user logging from specific groups or the intranet, with multifactor authentication (MFA) or any other requirements.

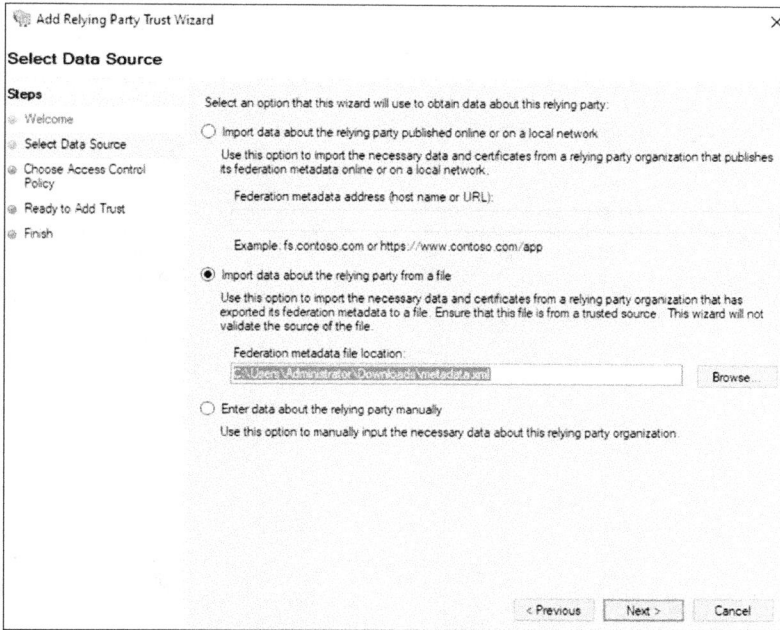

Figure 11-30   Select Data Source

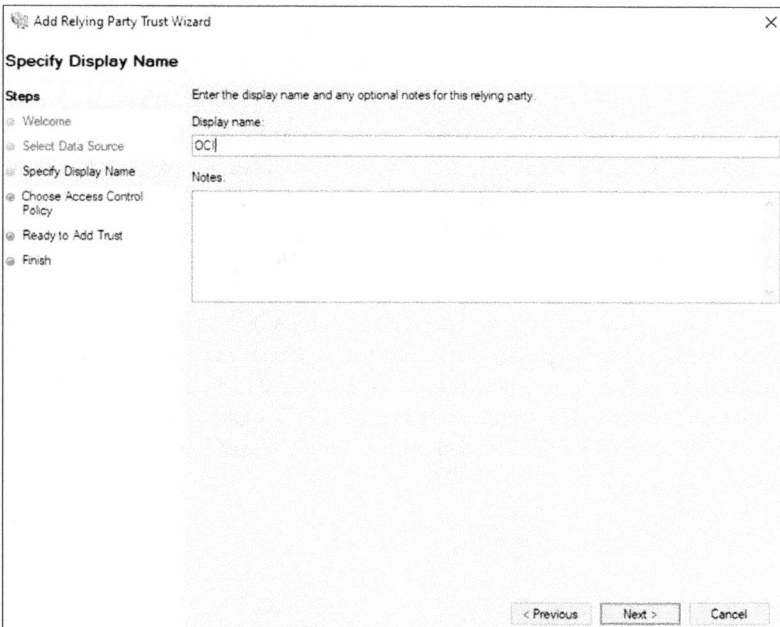

Figure 11-31   Select Display Name

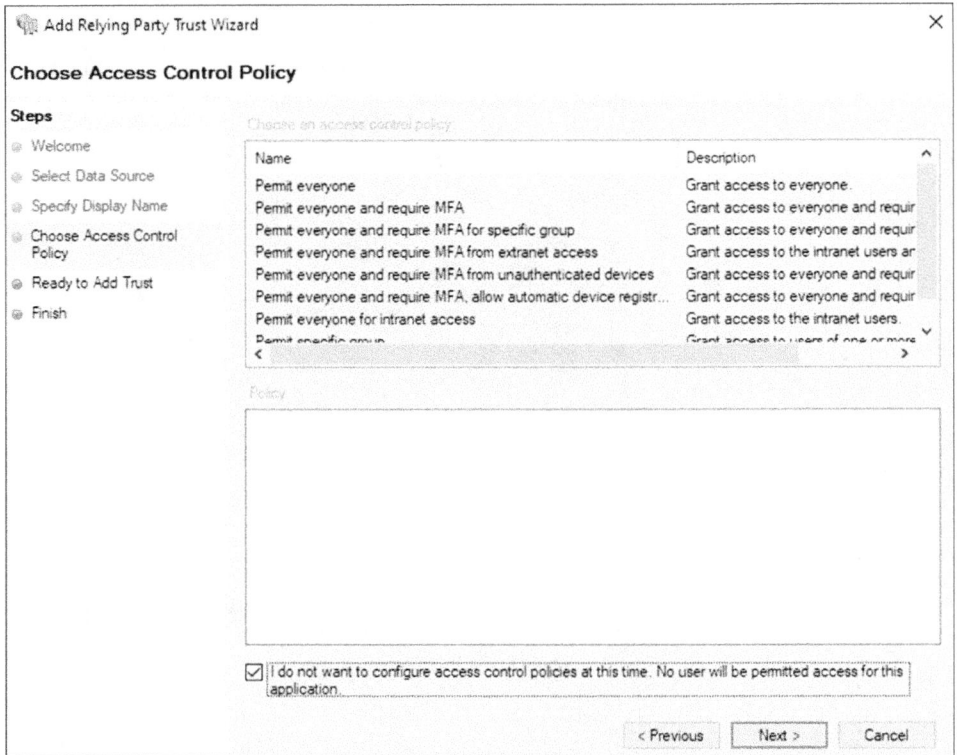

Figure 11-32   Choose Access Control Policy

Review all trust settings and click **Next**, as shown in Figure 11-33.

Next, leave the default selection of Configure Claims Issuance Policy for This Application and click **Close**, as shown in Figure 11-34. If you decide to configure claims issuance policies later, you can reopen this window by right-clicking the **Relying Party Trusts OCI** and clicking the **Edit Claim Issuance Policy** option. The claim issuance policy contains a set of rules. These rules will determine which claim to add with a security token for application access. These claims are AD attributes such as name and email address. Let's put these pieces into perspective. Once the application has received a user authentication request, the application will contact AD Federal Services. AD Federal Services will then contact AD. Once authenticated, AD will return the claim to AD Federal Services. Now AD Federal Services will send the necessary token with this claim to the application.

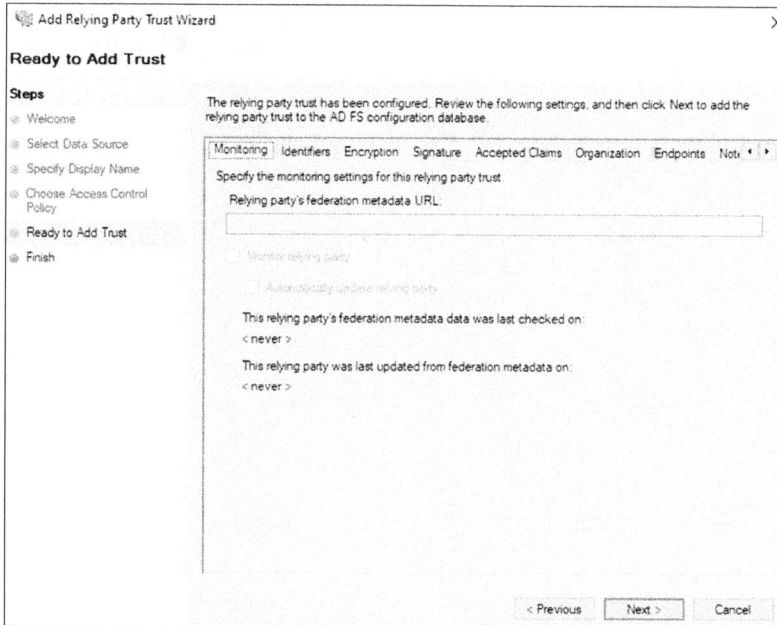

Figure 11-33   Review Trust Information

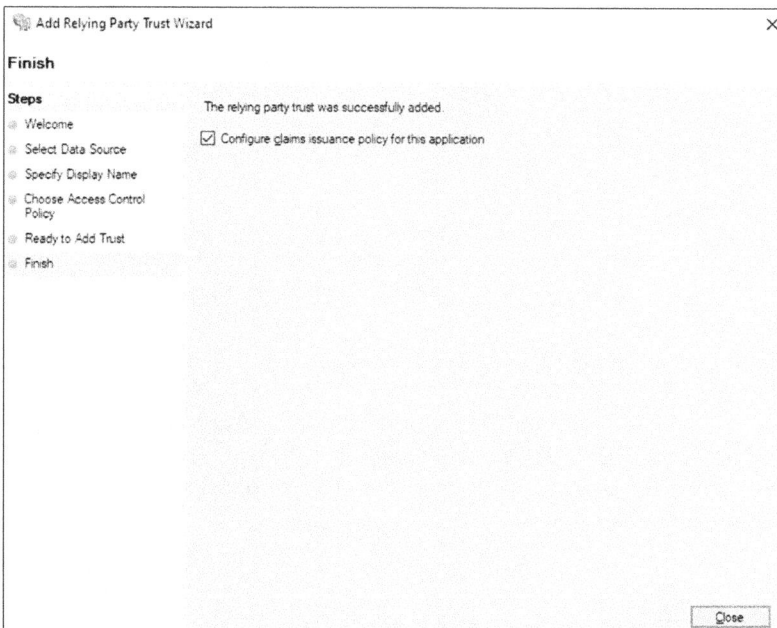

Figure 11-34   Add Trust

These claims rule configurations added to the SAML authentication response are required by OCI. This configuration is for name ID and group. Click **Add Rule**, as shown in Figure 11-35.

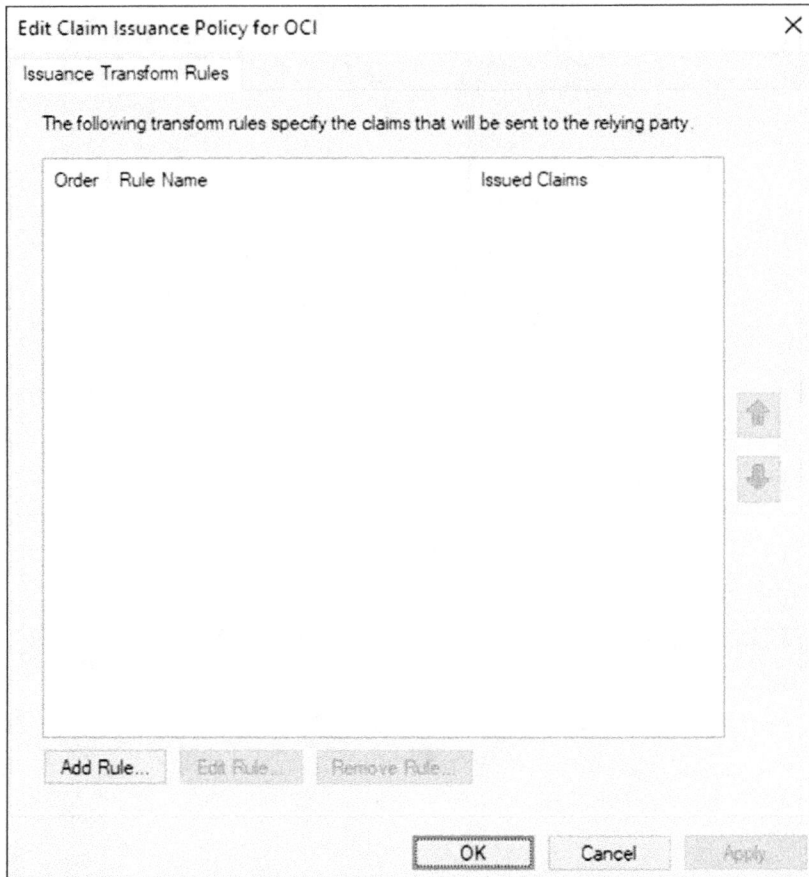

Figure 11-35   Edit Claim Issuance Policy

For the rule template, select **Transform an Incoming Claim** and click **Next**, as shown in Figure 11-36.

Next, enter a claim rule name. Then select **Windows Account Name** for the incoming claim type, **Name ID** for the outgoing claim type, and **Persistent Identifier** for outgoing name ID format. Then select **Pass Through All Claim Values** and click **Finish**, as shown in Figure 11-37.

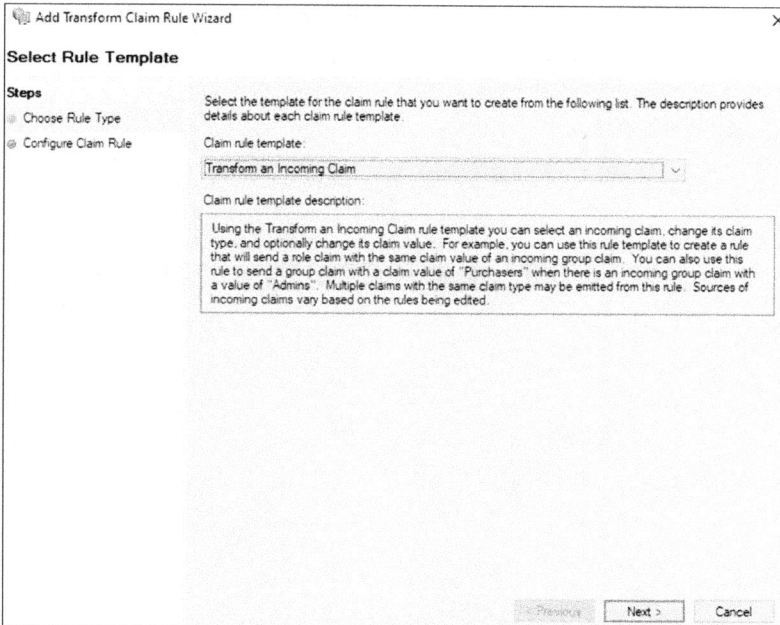

Figure 11-36   Choose Rule Type

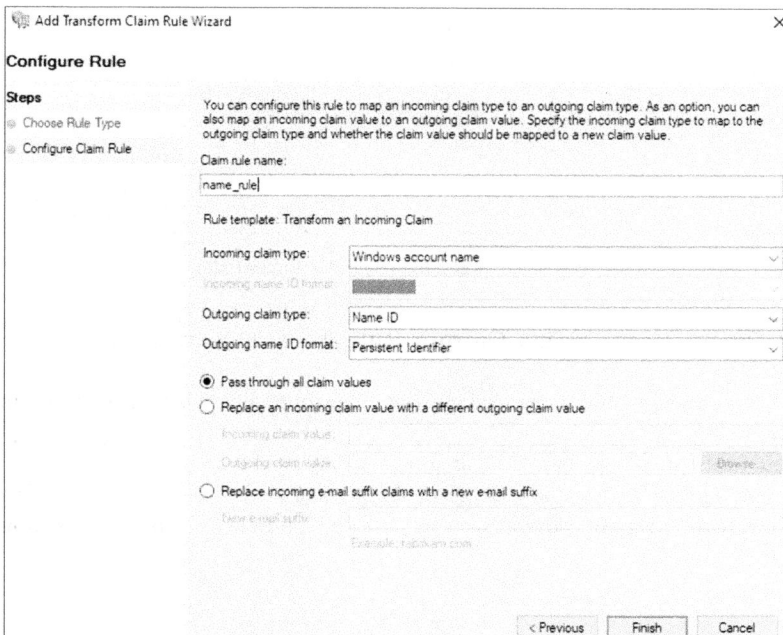

Figure 11-37   Configure Claim Rule

To add another rule for group, click **Add Rule**, as shown in Figure 11-38.

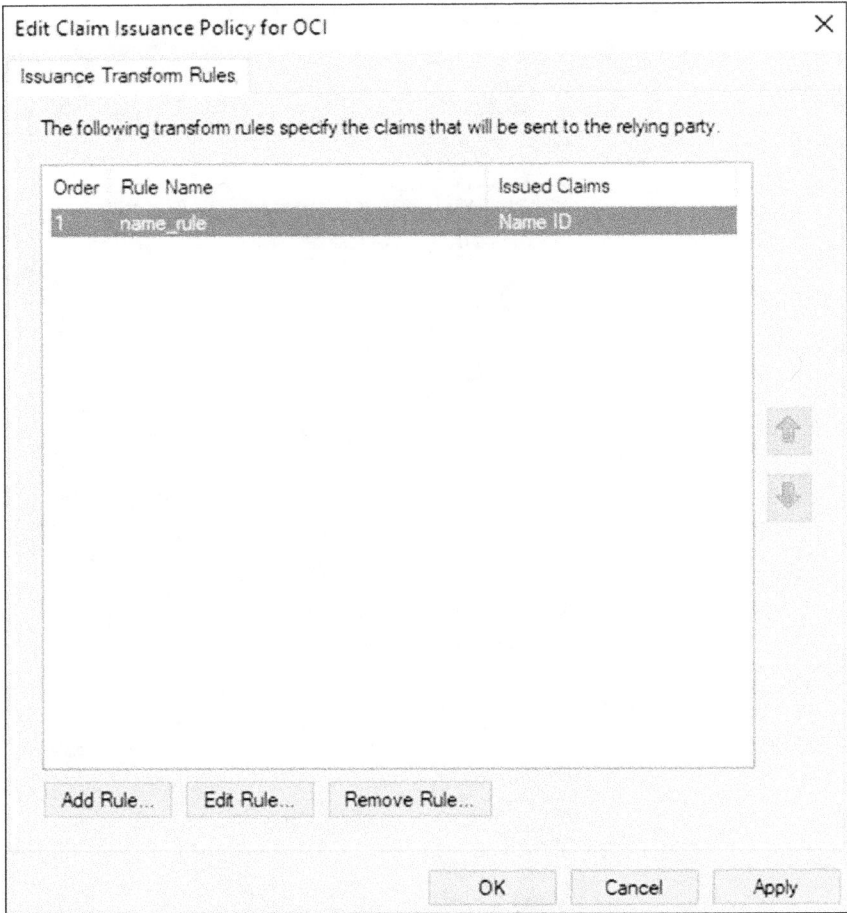

Figure 11-38   Edit Claim Issuance Policy

Select **Send Claims Using a Custom Rule** and click **Next**, as shown in Figure 11-39.

Next, enter a claim rule name and custom rule; then click **Finish**, as shown in Figure 11-40.

Review both rules and click **OK**, as shown in Figure 11-41.

Now you're ready to test the federation setup. Go to the OCI login page of your tenancy, select the identity provider you just created, and click **Continue**, as shown in Figure 11-42.

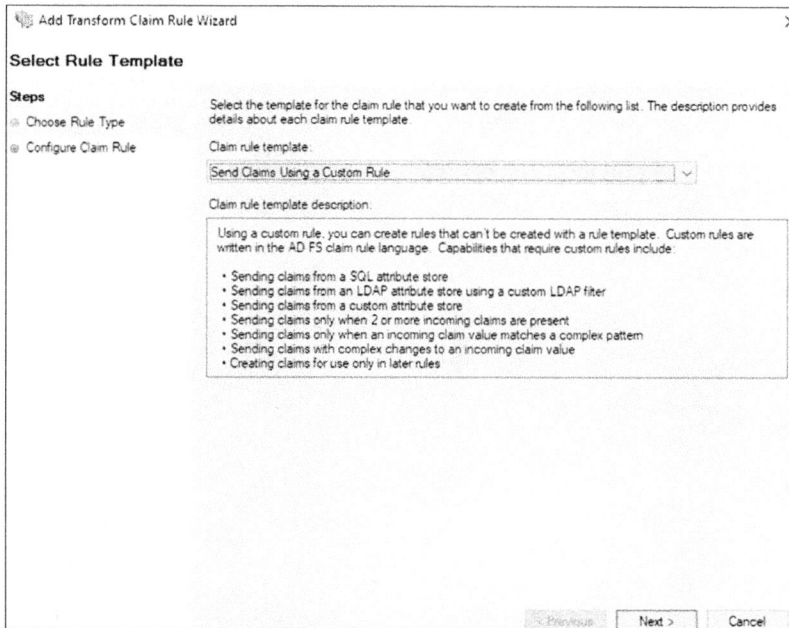

Figure 11-39   Select Rule Template

Figure 11-40   Configure Rule

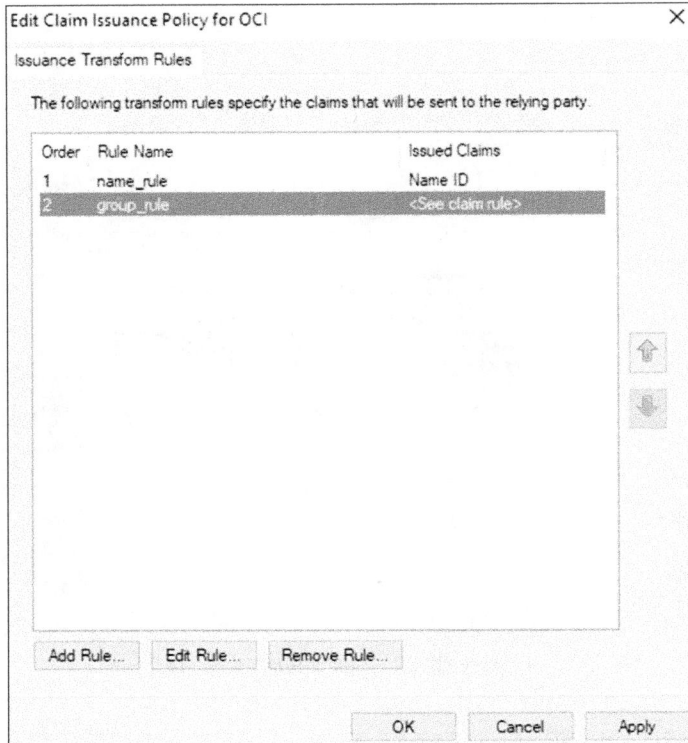

Figure 11-41   Review Claim Issuance Policy

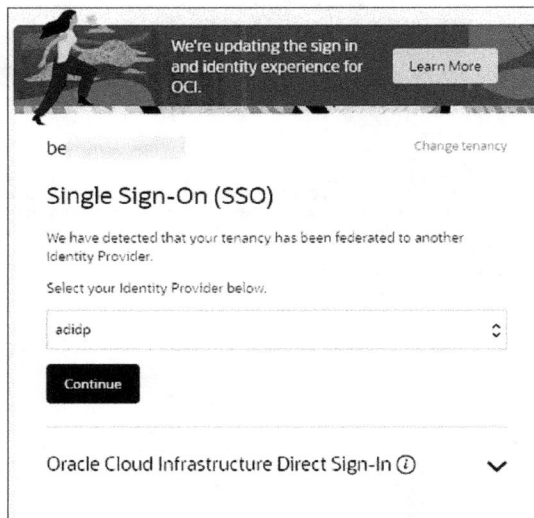

Figure 11-42   OCI Login Page

Next, enter the username and password of your AD account user and click **Sign In**, as shown in Figure 11-43.

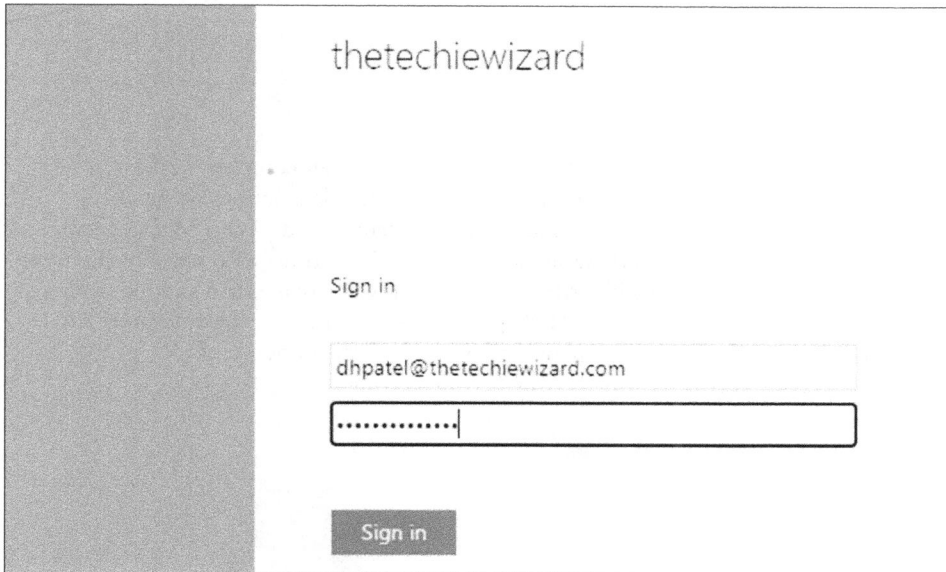

Figure 11-43   OCI Federation Login Page

You will be taken to the OCI home page, as shown in Figure 11-44.

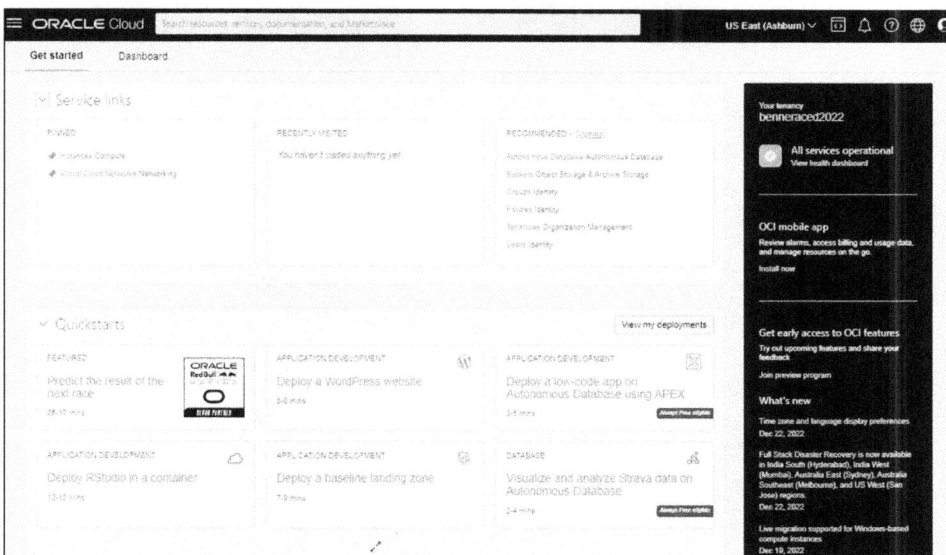

Figure 11-44   OCI Home Page

At this point, you've concluded the federation sample scenario. Federation is the feature most commonly used by organizations. It gives them greater control and lessens complexities for identity and security management when OCI is added to their existing environmental footprints.

Summary

In this chapter, you learned that today's organization requires complex workforce structures to operate efficiently. It requires stable and reliable solutions to support on-premises and hybrid cloud environments. OCI Identity and Access Management (IAM) fits the bill perfectly in these situations. Using federations with some of the most widely used identity providers like Microsoft AD and Okta makes IAM adoption more appealing and convenient. In the next chapter, we will continue exploring more OCI service offerings by looking into operating system security services.

Operating System Security

The Linux operating system accounts for 90 percent of all servers provisioned in the cloud. Its dominance and popularity can be attributed to its cost, reliability, open-source nature, and large community support. With the majority of global websites running Linux, its security becomes of the utmost importance. Proactively securing Linux becomes especially critical in order to protect against expanding cybersecurity threats. However, most Linux patching is traditionally disruptive and requires planning and downtime. This poses problems when zero-day vulnerabilities are identified.

In this chapter, we will present a number of OCI services and features to address some of these challenges and to augment the security of your Linux operating systems. These are

- **Oracle Ksplice:** A feature in Oracle Linux that supports the immediate and nondisruptive patching of the Oracle Linux operating system with zero downtime and no reboots
- **Oracle Autonomous Linux:** An OCI managed service that monitors for critical events and performs automatic daily updates of Linux operating systems, taking advantage of Oracle Ksplice to offload operating system management duties from your administrators
- **Vulnerability Scanning Service (VSS):** A free OCI service that checks hosts and containers for vulnerabilities

Each of these services is powerful on its own, and this chapter will offer an insight into each of them, walking through steps to get you started.

Oracle Ksplice

Most Linux kernel upgrades and security patches require a system reboot. This operation often requires coordination and planning. For instance, if a kernel upgrade is required on a database server, that server would need to be rebooted. The database may need to be rebooted gracefully in a rolling fashion, application connection pools rerouted to active nodes, and validations and restarts performed afterwards. These upgrades and patching are disruptive in nature.

Enter Ksplice. Ksplice is an open-source extension to the Linux kernel that allows for kernel upgrades and security patches to be applied without the need of a reboot. Ksplice was created in 2009, and the company that supported it, Ksplice, Inc., was later acquired by Oracle in 2011. Additional background and information can be found at https://ksplice.oracle.com.

Certain prerequisites on your Oracle Linux system are necessary to using Oracle Ksplice though:

- The host must be set up as an Oracle Ksplice client.
- The host must be connected to the Internet.
- The host must be registered with the Unbreakable Linux Network if Ksplice is configured in online mode.

Online mode allows Ksplice to apply updates automatically. For this, it must have access to and register with the Unbreakable Linux Network through the Internet. Oracle Ksplice can run on any Oracle Linux system, including on-premises hosts. Fortunately, it is automatically installed on all compute instances created in OCI and does not need to be registered with the Unbreakable Linux Network. Ksplice is incredibly easy to use for instances created in OCI.

Example 12-1 provides some key commands to manage Ksplice. They are all run as the root user.

Example 12-1   Key Commands to Manage Ksplice

```
# View the help page
man ksplice

# View the summarized help page
ksplice -help

# List patches that have been applied
ksplice all show

# List all available updates
ksplice all show --available
ksplice -n all upgrade

# Apply all available updates
ksplice -y all upgrade

# List available kernel updates only
ksplice kernel show --available
ksplice -n kernel upgrade

# Apply available kernel updates only
ksplice -y kernel upgrade
```

```
# Remove all applied patches
ksplice user remove --all

# Disable automatic updates
touch /etc/uptrack/disable

# Enable automatic updates
rm /etc/uptrack/disable
```

Ksplice enables you to apply all security updates or just kernel-specific ones. Figure 12-1 displays the output of the command to list all available kernel updates. As you review Example 12-1, two of the commands shown can list the available kernel updates. One is shown in Figure 12-1, and the other is simply the **apply** command with the **-n** option. This option just lists available updates without installing. Both yield the same result.

```
root@dev:/root> ksplice kernel show --available
Available updates:
[jiss0g31] Known exploit detection.
[5993roz1] Known exploit detection for CVE-2019-9213.
[asr6mujr] Known exploit detection for CVE-2017-1000253.
[lqk35m32] Known exploit detection for CVE-2016-5195.
[i5qf2uj7] Known exploit detection for CVE-2021-27363.
[19t3hu97] Known exploit detection for CVE-2021-27364.
[5ql8vxnt] Known exploit detection for CVE-2021-27365.
[3gs7m6hr] Known exploit detection for CVE-2021-22543.
[jn7beiz1] Known exploit detection for CVE-2020-8835.
[h0m4pvoo] Known exploit detection for CVE-2021-4034.
[76gyo37t] Known exploit detection for CVE-2017-11176.
[e0d0a40p] CVE-2022-39188: Denial-of-service in MMU-based Paged Memory Management Support.
[r0nwi7jc] Denial-of-service in 802.1Q VLAN Support.
[oxettdpq] NULL pointer dereference when logging a filesystem event.
[aylqwdqr] Known exploit detection for CVE-2022-0847.
```

Figure 12-1 Viewing Available Ksplice Kernel Updates

Figure 12-2 displays the tail end of the output of the command that applies the kernel updates. In this example, there were a significant number of updates. But in a matter of minutes, the effective kernel version was upgraded from 5.4.17-2136.312.3.4.el8uek to 5.4.17-2136.318.7.2.el8uek. No reboot or downtime was necessary.

```
Installing [27jjkx15] Parallelize mapping and unmapping operations of large a
Installing [lmjgn7pg] CVE-2022-27672: Information disclosure due to Cross-Thr
Installing [gw2zwhqy] CVE-2023-2162: Use-after-free during iSCSI login.
Installing [rn3xcc35] CVE-2023-0459: Information leak during userspace access
Installing [4do10s8f] CVE-2022-3108: NULL pointer dereference in AMD GPU driv
Your kernel is fully up to date.
Effective kernel version is 5.4.17-2136.318.7.2.el8uek
root@dev:/root>
```

Figure 12-2 After Successfully Applying Kernel Updates with Ksplice

There is little explanation needed to justify keeping your Linux systems updated. The footprint of Linux is massive, and keeping up-to-date with security and kernel patching is essential. Using Ksplice is still an operation that must be managed by your system administrator though. In the following section, we will discuss Oracle Autonomous Linux, which takes advantage of Ksplice, among other things, to relieve your administrators of those manual responsibilities.

Oracle Autonomous Linux

Unlike other autonomous services in OCI, Oracle Autonomous Linux (or Autonomous Linux for short) is a service that manages a Linux compute instance, but it does not create one. Compute instances managed by the Autonomous Linux service require you to first create the compute instances as you normally would, but must be created using the Oracle Autonomous image.

Autonomous Linux provides some key capabilities that include

- **Automatic Updates:** Automatic daily updates to Linux compute instances, including zero-downtime Ksplice updates
- **Event Monitoring:** Instance monitoring by capturing events that can be viewed in the console, CLI, or API
- **Notifications:** Notifications on updates and events

A number of prerequisites are needed for Autonomous Linux to work. These include setting up appropriate IAM policies, the required agent (specifically the Oracle Cloud Agent), and required plug-ins (specifically the OS Management Service Agent and Oracle Autonomous Linux plug-in). One of the notable prerequisites is the necessary use of the August 2021 Oracle Autonomous Linux image or later. Neither free tier nor custom images are supported.

When creating a compute instance, select one of the Oracle Autonomous Linux images available. See Figure 12-3 for an example. You can select from a number of image build versions. These are often released every month, and the latest will be the most current one.

As mentioned earlier in this chapter, all newly created compute instances in OCI now will automatically include the Oracle Cloud Agent and the OS Management Service Agent plug-in. But since this is an Autonomous Linux image, it will also include an Oracle Autonomous Linux plug-in.

Log in to the Autonomous Linux compute instance and run the command shown in Example 12-2 to confirm that the Oracle Autonomous Linux plug-in is running.

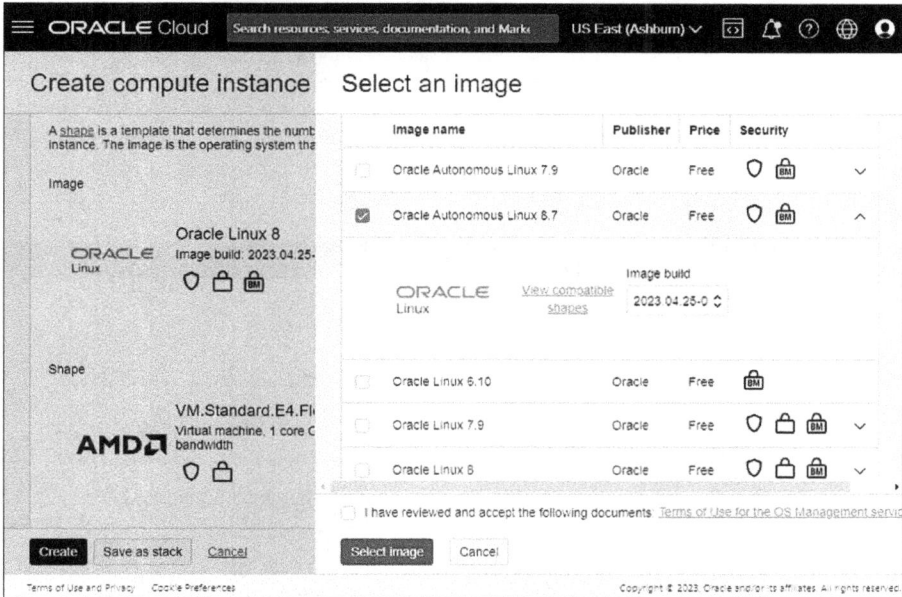

Figure 12-3 Selecting an Oracle Autonomous Linux Image

Example 12-2 Confirm That the Oracle Autonomous Linux Plug-in Is Running

```
# This should return 1 process
ps -elf | grep oci-alx | grep -v grep
```

If you navigate to the compute instance of this Autonomous Linux instance and navigate to the Oracle Cloud Agent tab, you will find that the Oracle Autonomous Linux plug-in is enabled, as depicted in Figure 12-4.

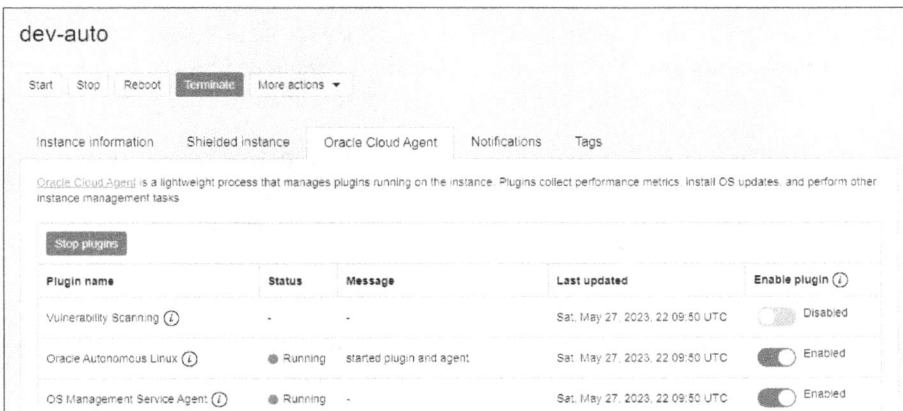

Figure 12-4 Confirming the Oracle Autonomous Linux Plug-in Is Enabled

When you navigate back to the OS Management Service dashboard on the console, a new scheduled job is now created, as shown in Figure 12-5. This is a controlled scheduled job managed by the Oracle Autonomous Linux service. Clicking this will take you to its page, which includes two work requests: Ksplice Update and Package Install/ Upgrade. Each of these work requests includes log messages and error messages available for viewing. This scheduled job can be executed on demand, the next run can be skipped, or the job deleted altogether.

Figure 12-5   Viewing the Newly Created Autonomous Linux Scheduled Job

There is no cost to using the Oracle Autonomous Linux image, and the monitoring, management, and maintenance of Linux packages and kernel updates are completely offloaded to the Oracle Autonomous Linux service. Environments with strict release management processes that include testing and approval tasks may struggle with this service because package maintenance is effectively surrendered. The nature of the cloud infrastructure promotes the use of managed services to bear responsibility for most tedious and manual management tasks, but at the expense of control. Oracle Autonomous Linux is not a fully managed service though. Root access is still available, and all administrative privileges also remain available to the system administrator.

Vulnerability Scanning Service (VSS)

Vulnerability Scanning Service is a free host-scanning service exclusive to OCI. It periodically scans compute instances and, in its search for CVEs in the file system, reports on the security risk, and identifies if patching is required. VSS can scan for vulnerabilities in compute instances and container registry images. This section provides an overview of host scanning.

CVE stands for Common Vulnerabilities and Exposures. Publicly disclosed cybersecurity vulnerabilities in the form of documented CVEs are available at https://cve.mitre.org. CVEs are not restricted to operating systems and can be issued against web servers, database servers, libraries, and more. When a CVE is identified on a particular set of software, this is evidence that a publicly disclosed vulnerability exists.

Navigate to a compute instance, click **OS Management** on the submenu on the left, and then click the **Oracle Cloud Agent** tab on the top of the page. This tab shows a few of the plug-ins on the Oracle Cloud Agent. The Vulnerability Scanning plug-in will be disabled by default on all OCI hosts.

To start, first perform a one-time setup of the group, policy, and user of VSS by following these steps:

Step 1. Navigate to the OCI console menu and click **Identity & Security > Identity**.

Step 2. Click **Groups > Create Group**.

Step 3. Enter a name (such as VSSAdmins) and a description (such as VSS Security Group).

Step 4. Click **Policies > Create Policy**.

Step 5. Enter a name (such as vss-security-policy) and a description (such as VSS Security Policy).

Step 6. Click **Show Manual Editor** and enter the policy in Example 12-3. Then click **Create**.

Step 7. Click **Users** and select the user to add the newly created VSSAdmins group to by clicking **Add User to Group**.

Example 12-3   IAM Policies Granting Permissions to All Compute Instances in the Tenancy

```
allow group VSSAdmins to manage vss-family in tenancy
allow service vulnerability-scanning-service to read compartments in tenancy
allow service vulnerability-scanning-service to manage instances in tenancy
allow service vulnerability-scanning-service to read vnics in tenancy
allow service vulnerability-scanning-service to read vnic-attachments in tenancy
```

Now that the user has the appropriate permissions, it's time to create a *scan recipe*. Scan recipes are assigned to *targets*. Scan recipes dictate the folder(s) to scan and the frequency of the scan. A target is a grouping of instances to scan.

Scan recipes can be set up without a host agent or with an agent that is installed on the compute instances. This agent can be an OCI-based agent (free) or a Qualys agent, which is a premier offering requiring a license. The following example uses the OCI agent.

Both scan recipes and targets are created in the Scanning service using the following instructions:

Step 1. Navigate to the OCI console menu; click **Identity & Security > Scanning**.

Step 2. If taken to a dashboard page with no menu option on the left, click **Skip** on this page.

Step 3. Click **Scan Recipes > Create**.

Step 4. For type, select **Compute**.

Step 5. Enter a name (such as VSS-Host-Scan-Recipe).

Step 6. Note that the check box for Agent Based Scanning is already selected.

Step 7. Note that the check box for Enable File Scans is already selected.

Step 8. Enter the Linux folders to scan and separate them by using commas (for example, /home, /tmp).

Step 9. Select a file scan schedule (for example, Bi Weekly - Sunday).

Step 10. Select a schedule (such as Daily).

Step 11. Click **Create Scan Recipe**.

At this point, although the scan recipe is created, it is not yet associated with a target. To do so, follow these steps:

Step 1. On the confirmation page after creating the scan recipe, click **Create Target**.

Step 2. Enter a name (such as Dev-Targets).

Step 3. Under Scan Recipe, select the newly created **VSS-Host-Scan-Recipe**.

Step 4. In the Targets section, select **Selected Compute Instances in the Selected Target Compartment** and add to it all compute instances to include in this target.

Step 5. Click **Create Target**.

Referencing Figure 12-6, which is the page to create a target, it is possible to select particular compute instances to add to the target. Only actively running instances are available for selection. Alternatively, as depicted in the figure, all compute instances in the selected target compartment and its subcompartments can be added.

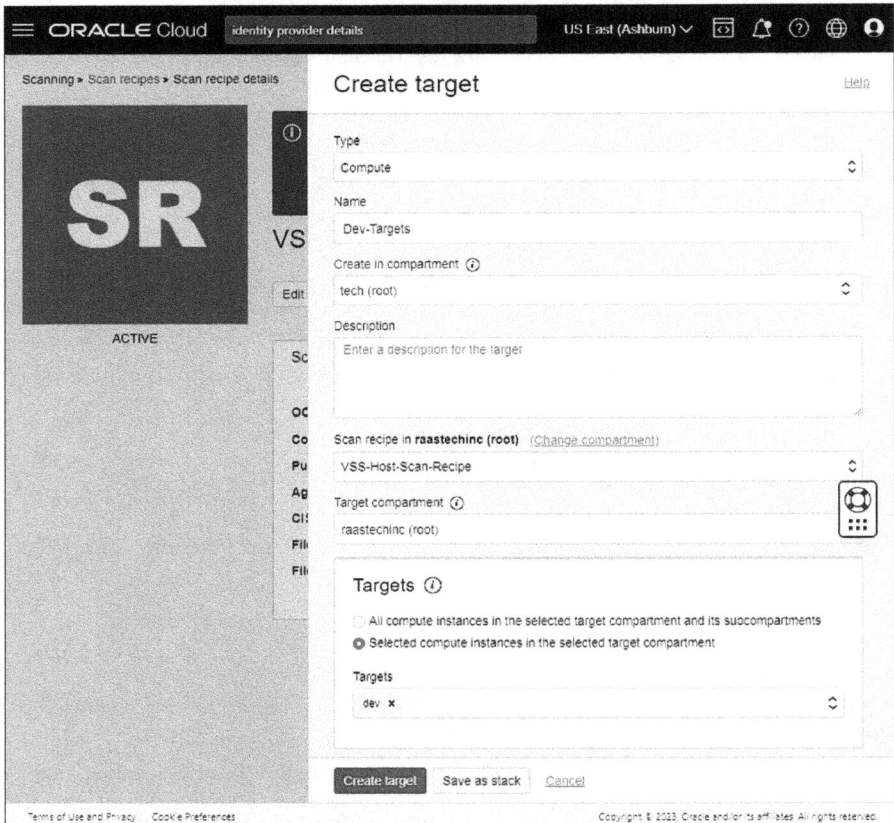

Figure 12-6   Creating a Target for a Scan Recipe

On the confirmation page after creating the target, click **View Scan Result**. Alternatively, you can view the results via the Scanning Report link on the left of the page.

Summary

In this chapter, you learned the benefits to leveraging services such as Ksplice, Autonomous Linux, and VSS, which are all intended to ensure the security posture of your operating system. But the benefits are more than just that, and include

- **Maintaining a high security and compliance posture:** One way to outpace cybersecurity threats is by frequently applying patch and kernel updates, as well as continuing to scan for vulnerabilities.
- **Improving availability:** This is through the use of zero-downtime services such as Ksplice.
- **Reducing operational costs:** Scheduling and applying updates across an entire group of instances and leveraging managed services for kernel or patch updates all provide the ability to optimize operations while scaling your infrastructure. Services such as Autonomous Linux assist in this.

This chapter provided a glimpse of several OCI-related security services as they pertain to operating system security. Understanding these services and what they have to offer is important in your overall DevSecOps journey. In the next chapter, you will learn more about observability and management.

Observability and Management

Any IT infrastructure or software system these days maintains its own logs to capture a variety of information including performance, access information, events, and other diagnostic information. This is no different with the OCI cloud service. When enabled on the cloud, each of the resources captures a significant amount of logging information across potentially and incredibly a large number of services. Identifying what to search, and more importantly, where to search for it, can become a daunting task. OCI offers services to ease the process of log management.

In Chapter 5, "Oracle IaaS—Network," we briefly discussed flow logs—how to configure them and view them. This chapter will go deeper into the two areas of logging: the *OCI Logging Service* and *Oracle Cloud Logging Analytics*. While both serve different yet complementary functions, regardless of how you use OCI, it is important to understand the fundamentals of logging in Oracle Cloud.

OCI Logging Service

The OCI Logging Service is a fully managed service that is highly scalable. In it, you can ingest, search, and analyze OCI resource logs in a consolidated pane. From the OCI Logging Service dashboard, shown in Figure 13-1, you can create, manage, and view all aspects of the Logging Service.

On the OCI console, navigate to **Observability & Management > Logging** to get to this service.

Log Format

When you're viewing the logs on the browser, by default, only the *datetime*, *type*, and *data.message* columns are displayed. An example of this can be observed later in Figure 13-5. These fields can be customized, but expanding this data via the down arrow to the right reveals the entire JSON object showing all the log data captured. An example of a full entry of a log is shown in Example 13-1.

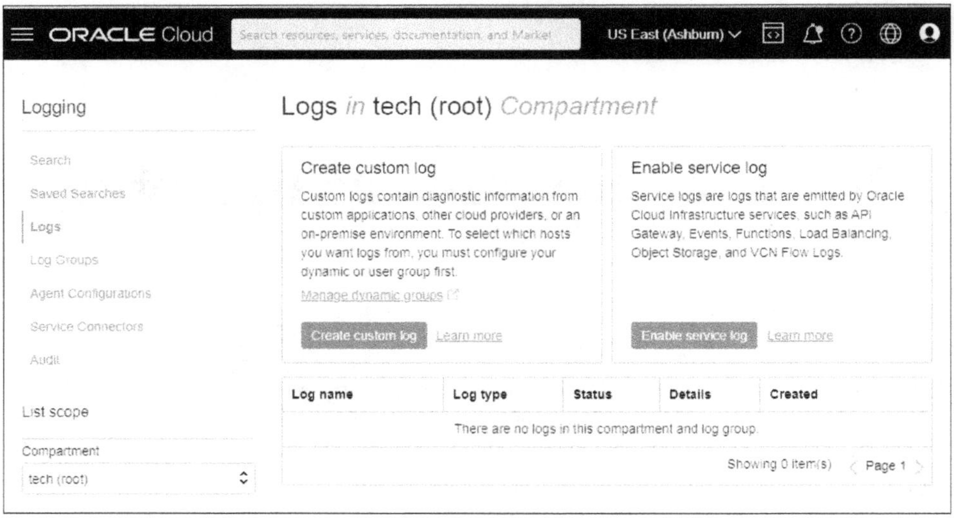

Figure 13-1 The OCI Logging Service Dashboard

Example 13-1 Log Entry in JSON Format

```
{
  "datetime": 1676227024000,
  "logContent": {
    "data": {
      "action": "ACCEPT",
      "bytesOut": 484,
      "destinationAddress": "10.0.0.2",
      "destinationPort": 443,
      "endTime": 1676227024,
      "flowid": "6b3474ab",
      "packets": 3,
      "protocol": 6,
      "protocolName": "TCP",
      "sourceAddress": "49.7.21.134",
      "sourcePort": 62975,
      "startTime": 1676227024,
      "status": "OK",
      "version": "2"
    },
    "id": "2e24aca8",
    "oracle": {
      "compartmentid": "ocid1.tenancy.oc1..aaaaa75c6q…",
      "ingestedtime": "2023-02-12T18:37:31.728Z",
```

```
      "loggroupid": "ocid1.loggroup.oc1.iad.amaaywe6do…",
      "logid": "ocid1.log.oc1.iad.amaagpyiad…",
      "tenantid": "ocid1.tenancy.oc1..aaaa75c6q7…",
      "vniccompartmentocid": "ocid1.tenancy.oc1..aa6q7svhjk…",
      "vnicocid": "ocid1.vnic.oc1.iad.abuwcljgfp…",
      "vnicsubnetocid": "ocid1.subnet.oc1.iad.aaaaabyclj…"
    },
    "source": "-",
    "specversion": "1.0",
    "time": "2023-02-12T18:37:04.000Z",
    "type": "com.oraclecloud.vcn.flowlogs.DataEvent"
  }
}
```

The log data can always be exported in its entirety to JSON.

Log Types

There are three types of logs in the Logging Service: service logs, audit logs, and custom logs.

Several, but not all, OCI services already include built-in logging capabilities. Each of these services captures diagnostic information specific to the type of service. These are referred to as *service logs*. The supported services that have built-in logging are

- Analytics Cloud
- API Gateway
- Data Flow Batch Service
- Email Delivery
- Events Service
- Functions
- Integration
- Load Balancers
- Media Flow
- Network Firewall
- Object Storage
- Operator Access Control Service
- Site-To-Site VPN
- Virtual Cloud Network—subnets
- WAA Service
- WAF Service

Each of these services has predefined log categories. For example, the API Gateway service captures *access logs* and *execution logs*. The DevOps service captures DevOps logs. And the Object Storage service captures *read access events* and *write capture events*.

As you use various OCI services, you can enable logging from the service itself. Figure 13-2 shows the deployment logs on the API Gateway service. For this particular service, the Logs section on this page shows two types of log categories—access logs and execution logs—each of which can be enabled or disabled. When clicking either of the log names, you are redirected to the Logging Service where you can view or search on these logs.

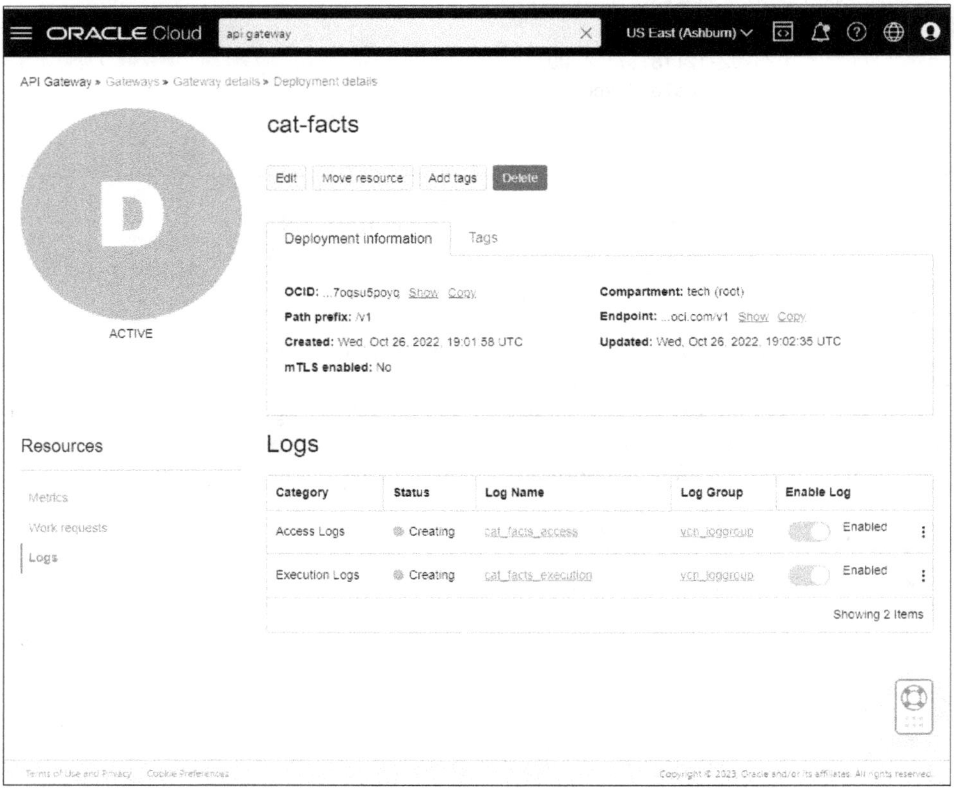

Figure 13-2   Enabling a Log on the API Gateway Service

Audit logs are captured by the Audit Service. They capture information about API calls made internal to OCI. These API calls can be instantiated from the console, CLI, SDK, or other means. These logs are not specific to any of the provisioned services or the resources created under these services. Figure 13-3 shows a number of events captured, such as GET and POST operations made to a number of APIs, some of them to search the logs (through the browser), others internal to the service itself such as a DHCP lookup, and so on.

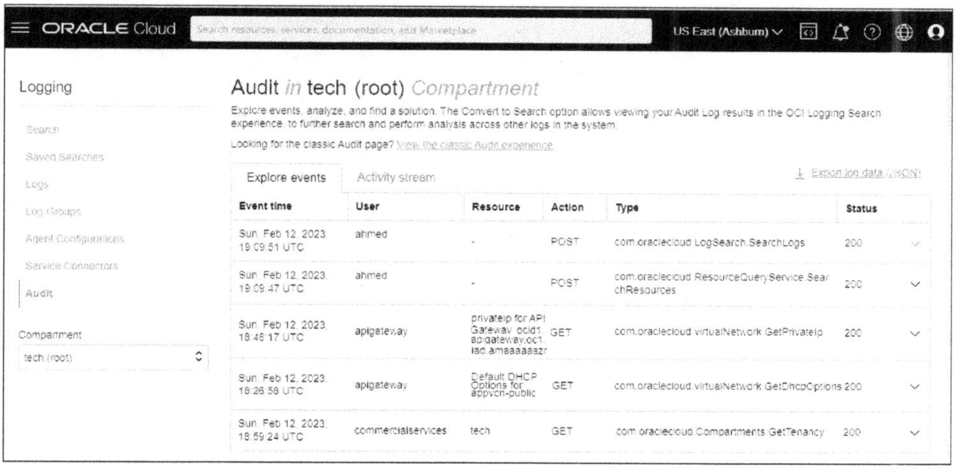

Figure 13-3 Viewing Audit Logs

Custom logs are used to ingest logs from custom applications, OS hosts, or even on-premises systems. In many cases, a *Unified Monitoring Agent* would need to be configured. Later in this chapter, we walk through how to ingest syslogs from a host Linux OS. A number of prebuilt parsers are available for Linux logs, such as SYSLOG, AUDITD, JSON, CSV, APACHE2, REGEXP, and MULTILINE. Windows event logs (specifically system, application, and security logs) are also supported.

Log Groups

Log groups are exactly what they sound like; they are logical groupings of logs. Each log has its own Oracle Cloud Identifier (OCID) and is stored in a log group. Benefits of log groups include the ability to

- Organize your logs and control access to them
- Move them from one compartment to another
- Perform searches and analysis, and view metrics at the log group level

Exercise 1: Enabling a Service Log

In this sample walkthrough, we will enable, search, and view the service log for VCN subnets. Following Figure 13-4 as a guide, the steps involved are straightforward and begin with creating a log group as follows:

Step 1. Navigate to **Observability & Management > Log Groups**.

Step 2. Click **Create Log Group** and give it a name (such as vcn_loggroup); then click **Create**.

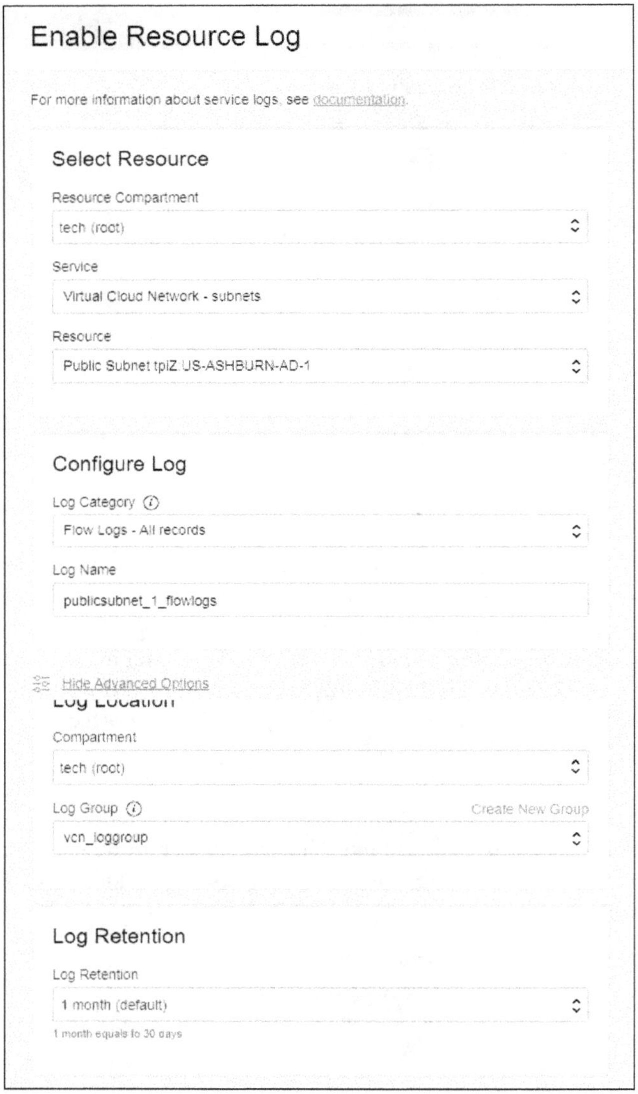

Enable Resource Log

For more information about service logs, see documentation.

Select Resource

Resource Compartment

| tech (root) | ⬍ |

Service

| Virtual Cloud Network - subnets | ⬍ |

Resource

| Public Subnet tpiZ:US-ASHBURN-AD-1 | ⬍ |

Configure Log

Log Category ⓘ

| Flow Logs - All records | ⬍ |

Log Name

| publicsubnet_1_flowlogs |

Hide Advanced Options

Log Location

Compartment

| tech (root) | ⬍ |

Log Group ⓘ   Create New Group

| vcn_loggroup | ⬍ |

Log Retention

Log Retention

| 1 month (default) | ⬍ |

1 month equals to 30 days

Figure 13-4   Enabling a VCN Subnet Service Log

Now you can enable (not create) the logging for the VCN subnet service and group the logs under the log group created earlier. The steps are as follows:

Step 1. Navigate to **Observability & Management > Logs**.
Step 2. Click **Enable Service Log**.

Step 3. Under Service, select **Virtual Cloud Network – Subnets**.

Step 4. Under Resource, select your subnet. In this example, we are selecting a public subnet (i.e., Public Subnet tpiZ:US-ASHBURN-AD-1).

Step 5. Under Log Category, select **Flow Logs – All records**.

Step 6. Under Log Name, give a name to the log (such as publicsubnet_1_flowlogs).

Step 7. Click **Show Advanced Options**.

Step 8. Select the log group named **vcn_loggroup** created earlier.

Step 9. Under Log Retention, select a value (such as 1 month [default]).

Step 10. Click **Enable Log**.

Click this newly created log name; then click **Explore with Log Search**. Customize the search criteria (or keep it as the default) and click **Search**. Under the Actions button above the output, you can customize the fields to display or even visualize them. Figure 13-5 shows an example of the output of this flow log search operation.

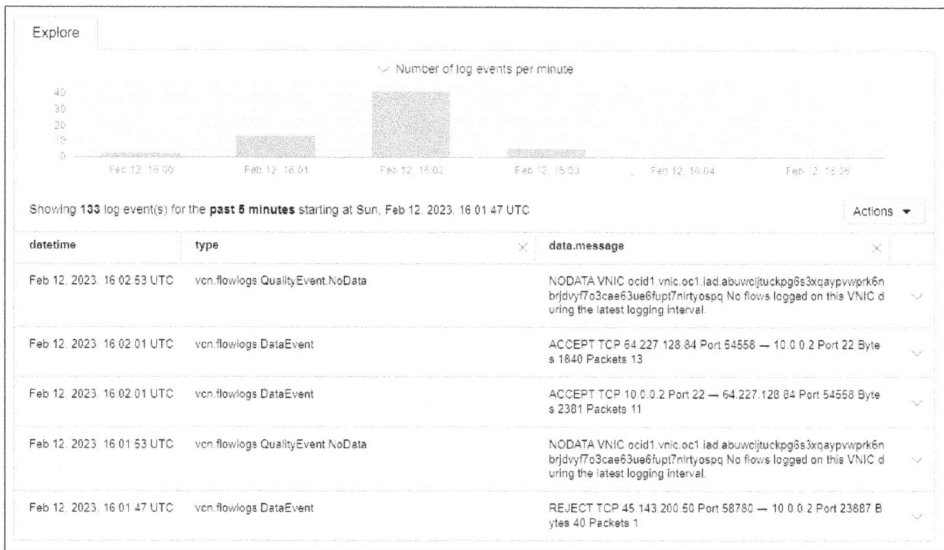

Figure 13-5 Exploring the Service Log

A few moments after enabling the service log, when you click the publicsubnet_1_ flowlogs log that you created, you immediately start seeing network-related traffic. Look at Figure 13-5 as an example.

What if you want to search for traffic hitting a specific port on your compute instances? As observed in Figure 13-6, the custom filter provides an auto-complete function, making it unnecessary to recall specific rules or keywords, and provides all searchable values.

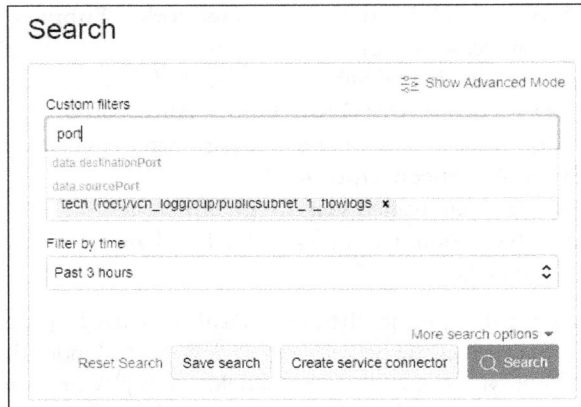

Figure 13-6   Searching the Service Log for Traffic to a Specific Destination Port

Adding a custom filter of **data.destinationPort=443** displays all network traffic to that host on port 443. The Logging Search feature allows you to slice and dice and visualize the output in a number of ways, from different chart types to controlling the intervals. Figure 13-7 visualizes the logs in a stacked graph format for the last 3 hours, with an interval capture of 5 minutes.

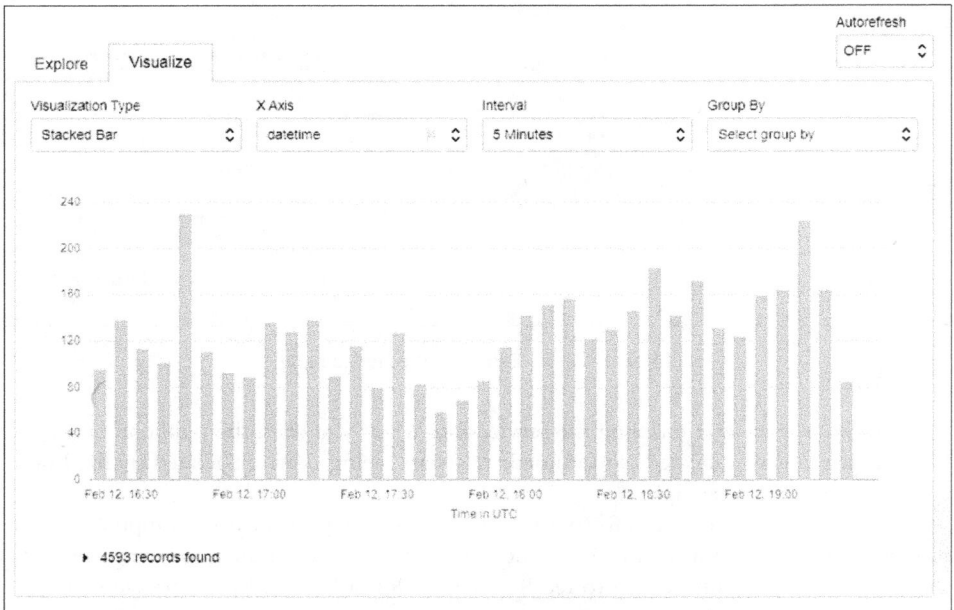

Figure 13-7   Providing a Visualized View of the Log Data

Note that the log information in this example is the number of events accessing port 443. They are not web access logs, but rather network events.

Exercise 2: Creating a Custom Log

In this walkthrough, we will create a *custom log*. We will also create an *agent configuration* that defines which hosts to ingest logs from and the location of the log. Custom logs require selecting which hosts to log from by configuring dynamic or user groups. Furthermore, the Logging and Monitoring agent must be enabled on the hosts.

Before creating the custom log, navigate to your compute instances and ensure that the logging and monitoring plug-in is enabled for each host you wish to ingest logs from. To do so, follow these steps:

Step 1. Navigate to **Compute > Instances**.

Step 2. Click an instance name.

Step 3. Click **Custom Logs** on the submenu on the left.

Step 4. If they are not enabled, under the Custom Logs heading, click **Enable Logging and Monitoring** (see Figure 13-8). This option will appear only if it is not enabled.

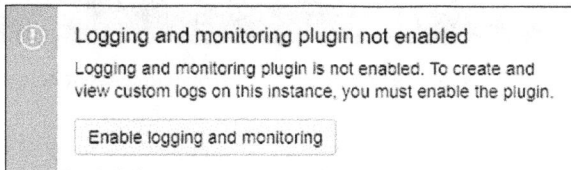

Logging and monitoring plugin not enabled

Logging and monitoring plugin is not enabled. To create and view custom logs on this instance, you must enable the plugin.

Enable logging and monitoring

Figure 13-8   Enabling Logging and Monitoring for a Compute Instance

You can enable the Unified Monitoring Agent during the creation of the compute instance. Otherwise, you will have to install the agent manually. The Oracle documentation at https://docs.oracle.com/en-us/iaas/Content/Logging/Concepts/agent_management.htm describes how to do so. The following steps provide instructions on installing and verifying the agent on Oracle Linux 7, which was not initially created with an agent:

Step 1. Log in as root to your compute instance.

Step 2. Run the commands in Example 13-2.

Example 13-2   Installing and Verifying the Unified Monitoring Agent on OEL 7

```
# Download the RPM for Oracle Linux 7
# See Oracle documentation for download links to other operating systems
wget https://objectstorage.us-phoenix-1.oraclecloud.com/n/axmjwnk4dzjv/b/unified-
  monitoring-agent-ol-bucket/o/unified-monitoring-agent-ol-7-0.1.1.rpm
```

```
# Install Unified Monitoring Agent RPM
yum install -y unified-monitoring-agent-ol-7-0.1.1.rpm

# Verify agent installation
systemctl status unified-monitoring-agent
```

Figure 13-9 shows the successful output of the verification command and confirmation that the service is running. If not, a message stating "Unit unified-monitoring-agent.service could not be found" would appear.

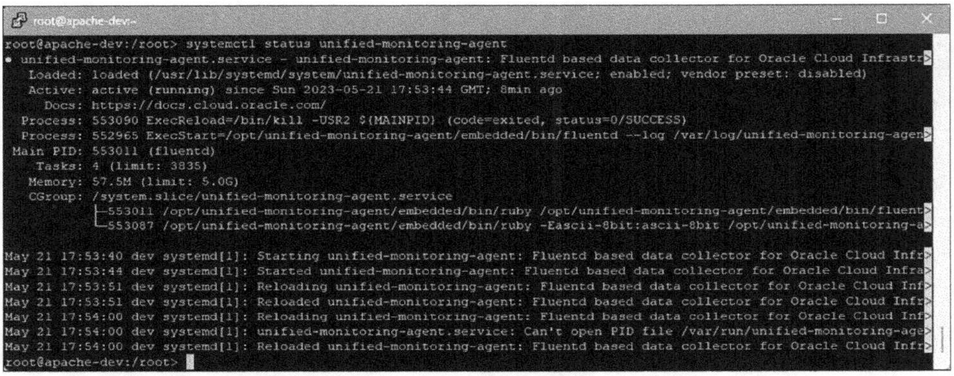

Figure 13-9   Verifying That the Unified Monitoring Agent Is Running

Now that the prerequisites at the host level are completed, the next task is to create a custom log as follows:

Step 1. Navigate to **Observability & Management > Logs**.

Step 2. Click **Create Custom Log**.

Step 3. Under Custom Log Name, give a name to the log (such as custom_syslog).

Step 4. Select the log group named **vcn_loggroup** created earlier.

Step 5. Click **Create Custom Log**.

After creating the custom log, you are taken to the Create Agent Config screen to create a new configuration:

Step 1. Under Configuration Name, give a name for the agent configuration (such as custom_syslog_configuration).

Step 2. Enter a description (this is a mandatory field).

Step 3. Under Host Groups, select a group type of **User Group** and group as **Administrators**. These settings can be changed depending on the existing groups defined in your compartment.

Step 4. In the Agent Configuration section, select an input type of **Log Path**, input name of **syslog**, and file path of **/var/log/messages** (see Figure 13-10).

Figure 13-10   Entering the Log Information for the Agent Configuration

Step 5. Click **Advanced Parser Options**.

Step 6. Select a parser of **SYSLOG** and click **Save Changes**.

Step 7. Under Select Log Destination, select a log group of **vcn_loggroup**.

Step 8. Under Log Name, select **custom_syslog**.

Step 9. Click **Create Agent Config**.

Logs can be viewed from the Logging Service similar to service logs or under the custom logs submenu of the compute instance.

Oracle Cloud Logging Analytics

Oracle Cloud Logging Analytics is a powerful service that performs a number of log analysis functions across all applications and resources. It provides advanced analysis and visualizations as well as anomaly detection. Logging Analytics was created out of the need to make some sense out of the massive volumes of log data and provide meaningful insight into your environment. It leverages built-in machine learning algorithms to correlate logs from any and all sources and identify problems and root causes. The documentation for Oracle Cloud Logging Analytics can be found at https://docs.oracle.com/en-us/iaas/logging-analytics/index.html.

Setting Up Logging Analytics for the First Time

OCI has simplified and streamlined the process of getting started with Logging Analytics. A wizard is available on the Logging Analytics dashboard for first-time users to quickly set up the service without having to go through lengthy manual setup steps. This approach is ideal for nonproduction environments to get started and familiarized with Logging Analytics. To add it, follow these instructions:

Step 1. Navigate to **Observability & Management > Logging Analytics**.

Step 2. Click **Start Using Logging Analytics** (see Figure 13-11).

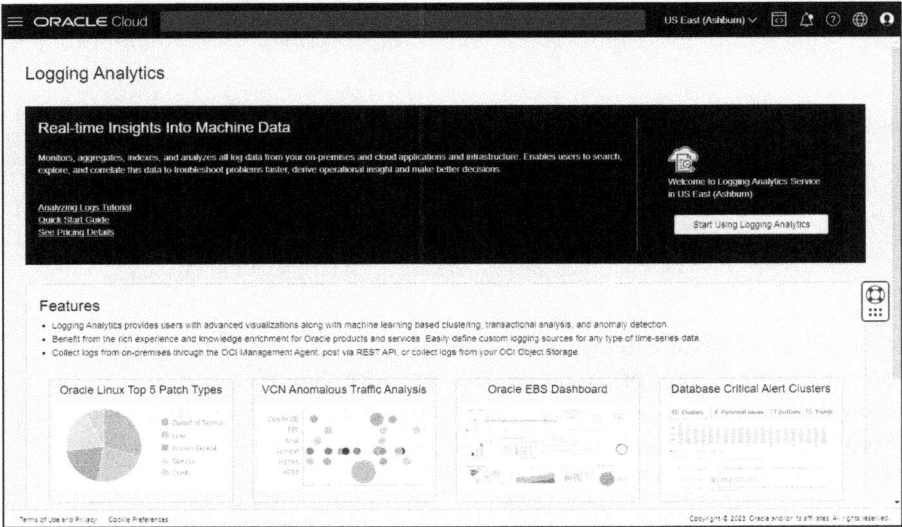

Figure 13-11   Starting to Use Logging Analytics for the First Time

Step 3. Click **Set Up Ingestion** (see Figure 13-12).

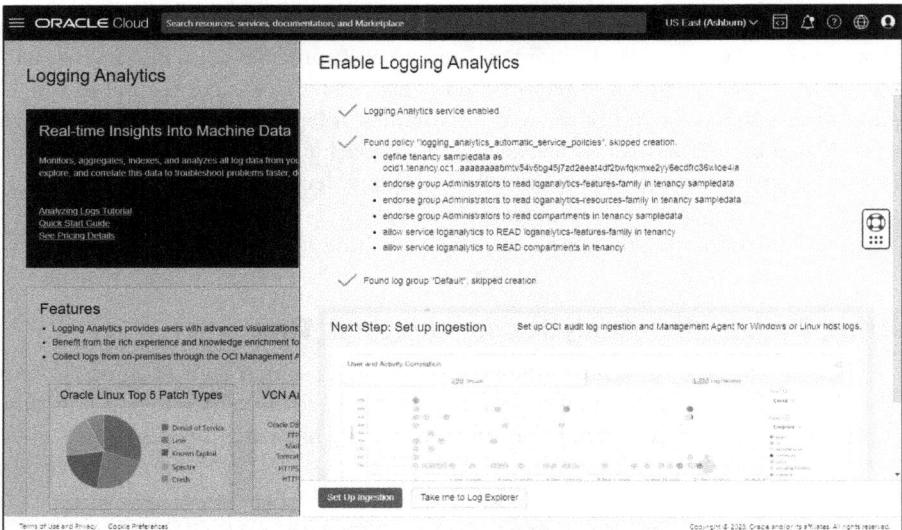

Figure 13-12   After Enabling Logging Analytics and Creating Required Policies

Step 4. Click **Next** (see Figure 13-13).

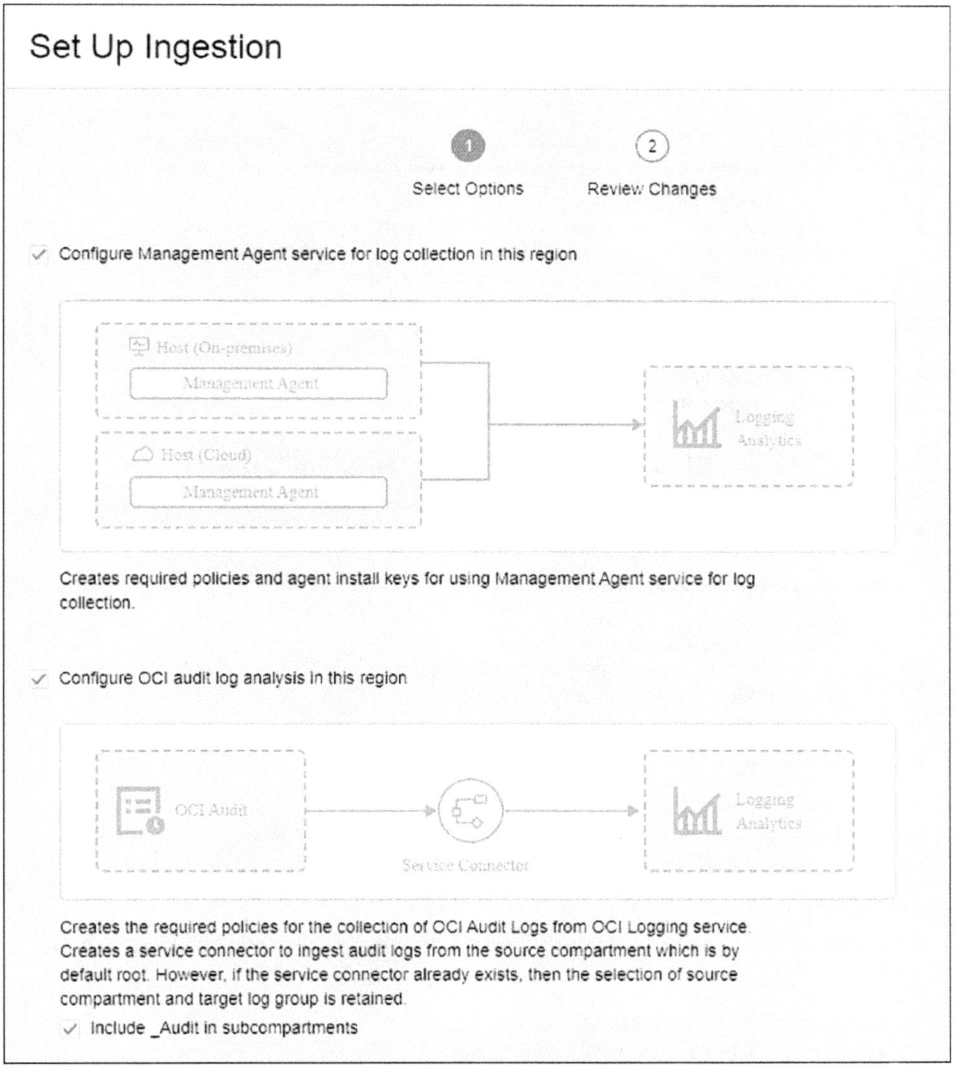

Set Up Ingestion

Figure 13-13 Setting Up Ingestion for the First Time

Step 5. On the final confirmation page, click **Set Up Ingestion** (see Figure 13-14).

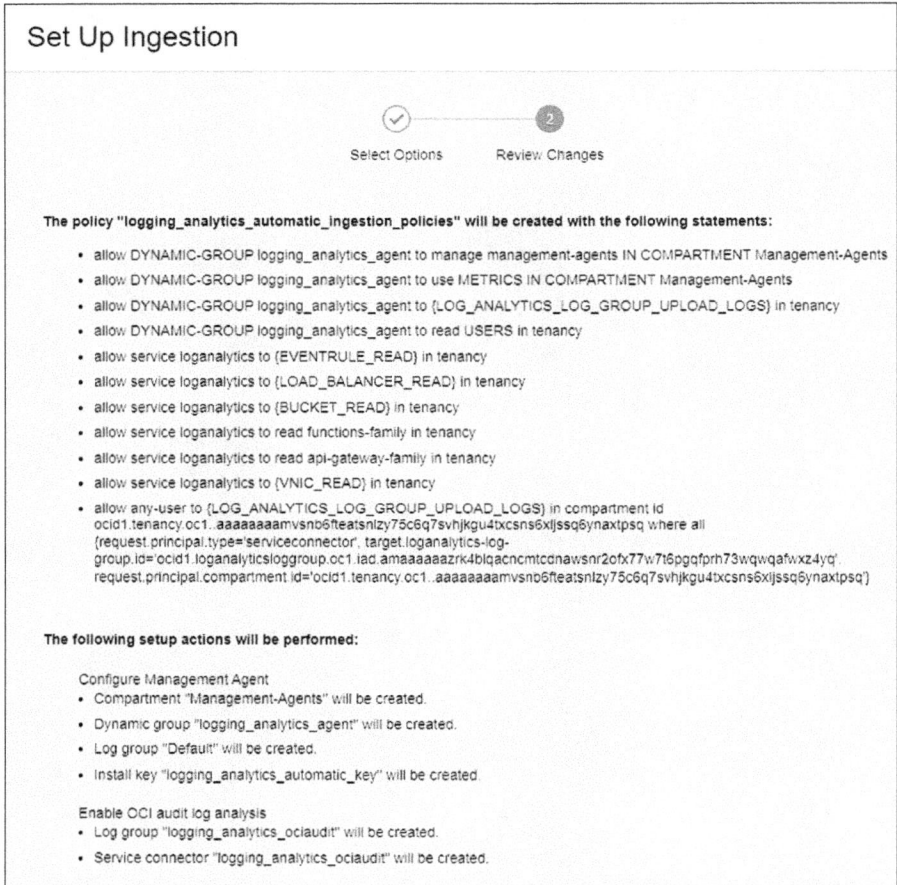

Figure 13-14   Reviewing the Confirmation Page Before Setting Up Ingestion

Completing this activity through the wizard performs two major functions behind the scenes:

- Configures the Management Agent:
  - Creates a compartment named Management-Agents
  - Creates a dynamic group named logging_analytics_agent
  - Creates a log group named Default
  - Creates a policy named logging_analytics_automatic_ingestion_policies
  - Creates an Agent install key named logging_analytics_automatic_key
- Enables OCI audit log analysis:
  - Creates a log group named logging_analytics_ociaudit

- Creates a policy named logging_analytics_automatic_ingestion_policies
- Creates a service connector named logging_analytics_ociaudit

If any of these resources already exists, its creation is skipped. However, another operation is still needed, and that is installing the Management Agent.

Downloading and Installing the Management Agent

The Management Agent software must be downloaded and installed to each host to tie into the Logging Service. The Management Agent only supports Java 8 with a minimum version of JDK 8u281 (and not Java 11). To add it, follow these steps:

Step 1. Navigate to **Observability & Management > Management Agent**.
Step 2. Click **Download and Keys**.
Step 3. For Linux, for example, download the agent for LINUX (X86_64) RPM (named oracle.mgmt_agent.230427.2233.Linux-x86_64.rpm) and transfer it to your Linux hosts.
Step 4. If Java 8 is not installed, download the RPM from https://www.oracle.com/in/java/technologies/javase/javase8u211-later-archive-downloads.html.
Step 5. As the root user, run the command **rpm –i jdk-8u361-linux-x64.rpm**.
Step 6. As the root user, run the command **yum install –y oracle.mgmt_agent.230427.2233.Linux-x86_64.rpm**.

The Agent install log files are located at /opt/oracle/mgmt._agent/installer-logs/installer.log.0.

An Agent install key was already created in the previous section. Now obtain the Management Agent response file, which includes the Agent install key:

Step 1. On the same page on the browser, scroll down to the Install Keys section.
Step 2. Beside the key named logging_analytics_automatic_key, click the three dots and select **Download Key to File** (see Figure 13-15).

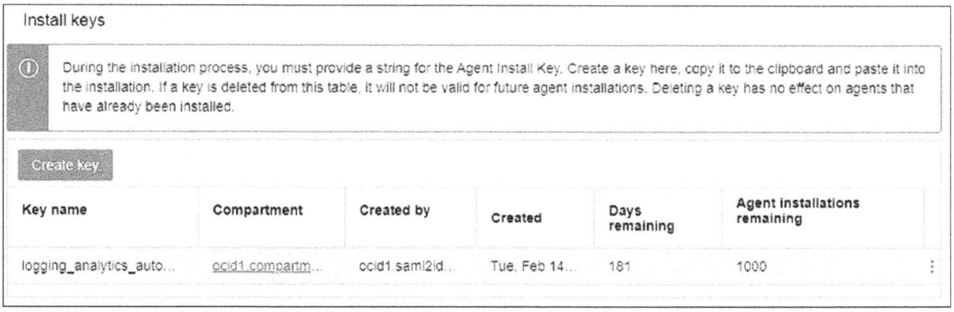

Install keys

During the installation process, you must provide a string for the Agent Install Key. Create a key here, copy it to the clipboard and paste it into the installation. If a key is deleted from this table, it will not be valid for future agent installations. Deleting a key has no effect on agents that have already been installed.

Create key

Key name	Compartment	Created by	Created	Days remaining	Agent installations remaining	
logging_analytics_auto...	ocid1.compartm...	ocid1.saml2id...	Tue, Feb 14...	181	1000	⋮

Figure 13-15 Downloading the Agent Install Key to a File

Step 3. Transfer this file (named logging_analytics_automatic_key.txt) to your Linux hosts to the /tmp folder.

Step 4. On each host, modify this file and add a value to AgentDisplayName and CredentialWalletPassword. Enter a complex password with at least 16 characters (see Figure 13-16).

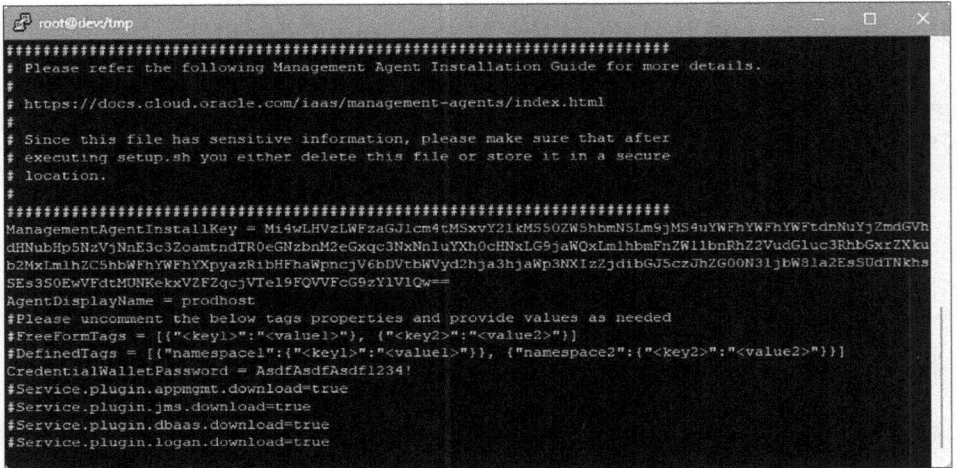

Figure 13-16   Updating the Agent Install Key File

Step 5. Run the command **chown mgmt_agent /tmp/logging_analytics_ automatic_key.txt**.

The next series of steps involves configuring the Management Agent with the recently installed setup.sh script (which is available through the RPM):

Step 1. As the root user, run the command **/opt/oracle/mgmt_agent/agent_ inst/bin/setup.sh opts=/tmp/logging_analytics_automatic_key.txt**. The output should be similar to Example 13-3.

Step 2. Delete the Agent install key file named logging_analytics_automatic_key.txt.

Example 13-3   Installing and Verifying the Unified Monitoring Agent on OEL 7

```
root@prodhost:/root/agent> /opt/oracle/mgmt_agent/agent_inst/bin/setup.sh opts=/
tmp/logging_analytics_automatic_key.txt

Executing configure

        Parsing input response file
        Validating install key
        Generating communication wallet
```

```
        Generating security artifacts
        Registering Management Agent

Starting agent...
Agent started successfully

Agent setup completed and the agent is running.
In the future agent can be started by directly running: sudo systemctl start
  mgmt_agent

Please make sure that you delete /tmp/logging_analytics_automatic_key.txt or store
  it in secure location.
```

The final task is to deploy the Logging Analytics plug-in to the agent and verify that it is active. To do so, follow these steps:

Step 1. Navigate to **Observability & Management > Management Agent**.

Step 2. Click **Agents**.

Step 3. Select the compartment name (such as Management-Agents).

Step 4. Click the name of the Management Agent.

Step 5. Click **Deploy Plug-ins**.

Step 6. Select the **Logging Analytics** plug-in and click **Update**.

Figure 13-17 shows the status of the agent as Active and lists the Logging Analytics plug-in as deployed to this agent.

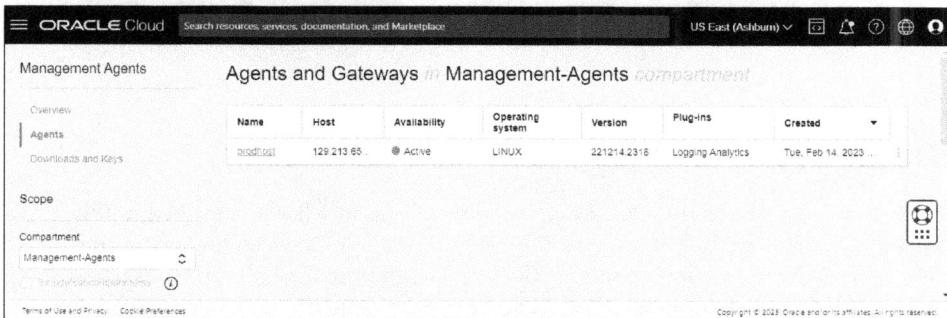

Figure 13-17   Confirming Installation of Management Agent

Logging Analytics is not a free service and is not supported in the free tier. The price is based off a Logging Analytics Storage Unit Per Month, ranging from $223 to $372 per unit per month depending on how many units are used. A *unit* is defined as 300 GB of logs stored. Though the cost appears to be manageable for an enterprise, it is difficult to estimate in advance and can quickly balloon. It is recommended to start small and monitor cost for the first few months.

Clearing and Resetting Logging Analytics

The Start Using Logging Analytics button is removed after Logging Analytics is set up. But if there is a need to clear and clean up the existing Log Analytics resources to start from scratch, follow these steps:

Step 1. Navigate to **Observability & Management > Logging Analytics**.

Step 2. From the drop-down menu, select **Administration**.

Step 3. Click **Service Details**.

Step 4. Click **Terminate**.

This action will offboard your tenancy from Logging Analytics. Any changes that were previously performed on sources, parsers, or other configurations, as well as any log data that has been ingested, will be permanently lost.

If you navigate back to the home page of the Logging Analytics service, an update will appear stating that logging analytics is being disabled (see Figure 13-18).

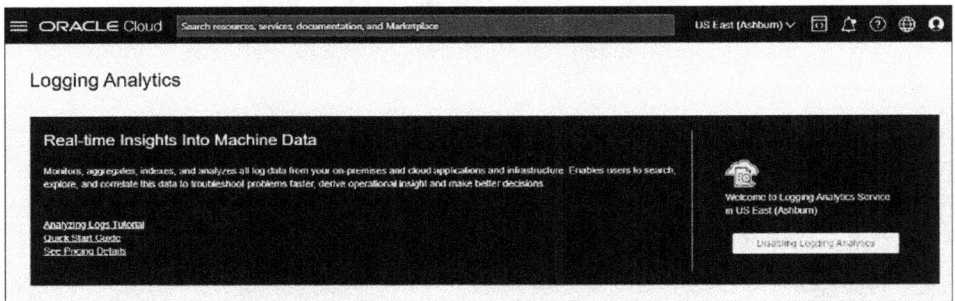

Figure 13-18   Disabling Logging Analytics

Summary

There is much more to the OCI Logging Service beyond what is described in this chapter. Log data can be exported to Object Storage. The Service Connector Hub can transfer data from a source service (such as Logging) to a target service (such as Notifications). Searches can be saved. But the biggest benefit to the Logging Service is a single pane view to all logging across your OCI services and resources. In the next chapter, you will learn more about Cloud Guard.

Cloud Guard

Oracle Cloud Guard is a strong security management and monitoring service in Oracle Cloud Infrastructure. It aims to improve the security of cloud environments by identifying, assessing, and mitigating security threats and misconfigurations. It provides a comprehensive, automated approach to cloud security, helping organizations maintain a secure, compliant, and resilient cloud infrastructure.

Oracle Cloud Guard is designed to continuously monitor and protect cloud resources by automatically identifying security vulnerabilities, misconfigurations, and anomalous activities that could pose a risk. It aggregates security information across OCI to provide actionable insights and automate responses to security incidents. This proactive approach allows organizations to manage their security landscape effectively, ultimately reducing the potential for breaches and data loss. The key advantages of Oracle Cloud Guard include improved visibility, automatic threat detection, and swift response to security incidents. By centralizing security monitoring and automating responses, Cloud Guard minimizes the manual effort required to uphold cloud security, empowering IT teams to concentrate on strategic initiatives rather than reactive security management. This, in turn, leads to heightened operational efficiency, decreased risk of human error, and expedited mitigation of threats.

Furthermore, Oracle Cloud Guard is integrated with other OCI services to ensure that security is ingrained in the cloud environment right from the start. This fosters a culture of continuous security and compliance, benefiting organizations with a proactive security approach that protects against current threats and adapts to address emerging risks in the ever-changing cloud landscape.

Integrating Cloud Guard with other OCI services makes it an ideal centralized security hub. It aggregates data from various OCI services and resources to provide a comprehensive view of the security status. This includes monitoring compute instances, storage services, databases, and networking components to ensure that all cloud infrastructure elements are protected.

There are several key features that you will need to understand:

- **Detector and Responder Recipes:** Detector recipes are preconfigured or customizable sets of rules that define what constitutes a security issue within OCI.

Detectors monitor various aspects, such as configuration compliance, activity anomalies, and threats. Examples include detecting overly permissive IAM policies, unencrypted storage, or unusual login patterns.

Responder recipes define automated actions or responses that Cloud Guard can take when a security issue is detected. Responses can be passive, such as generating alerts, or active, like automatically revoking access, correcting misconfigurations, or quarantining affected resources. This automation helps to quickly remediate security issues, reducing the time to respond to threats.

- **Security Zones:** This is one of the most essential tools to secure an environment and keep it secure. Security zones are specialized compartments that enforce stringent security policies. Resources deployed in these zones must comply with best practice security configurations, and Cloud Guard monitors compliance continuously. If deviations from the policies are detected, Cloud Guard can automatically enforce corrections, ensuring ongoing compliance and security.

- **Customizable Policies and Rules:** Organizations can customize Cloud Guard's detection and response capabilities to meet their specific security requirements. By creating custom detector and responder recipes, they can define what constitutes a security risk and how it should be dealt with, allowing for a personalized security approach that adheres to organizational policies and regulatory standards.

- **Comprehensive Dashboard and Reporting:** The Cloud Guard dashboard provides a comprehensive overview of security findings. It displays current and historical data on detected issues, their severity, and the actions taken. This enables security teams to promptly evaluate the overall security status of their cloud environment and prioritize remediation efforts. The reporting capabilities also assist in compliance management by offering the required documentation and insights for audits and security reviews.

In summary, Oracle Cloud Guard is a critical tool for organizations using OCI, providing a comprehensive, automated, and customizable security management solution that helps safeguard cloud resources, streamline compliance, and maintain a strong security posture in an increasingly complex digital environment.

Initial Configuration

To use Cloud Guard, you need to add some initial IAM policies to the tenancy. You can do this by adding in a policy that allows members of a group to access and manage Cloud Guard. The easiest way to do this is to use the wizard.

Let's navigate to the admin pages for Cloud Guard. From the main console, navigate to the main menu and select **Identity & Security > Cloud Guard > Overview**. This is seen in Figure 14-1.

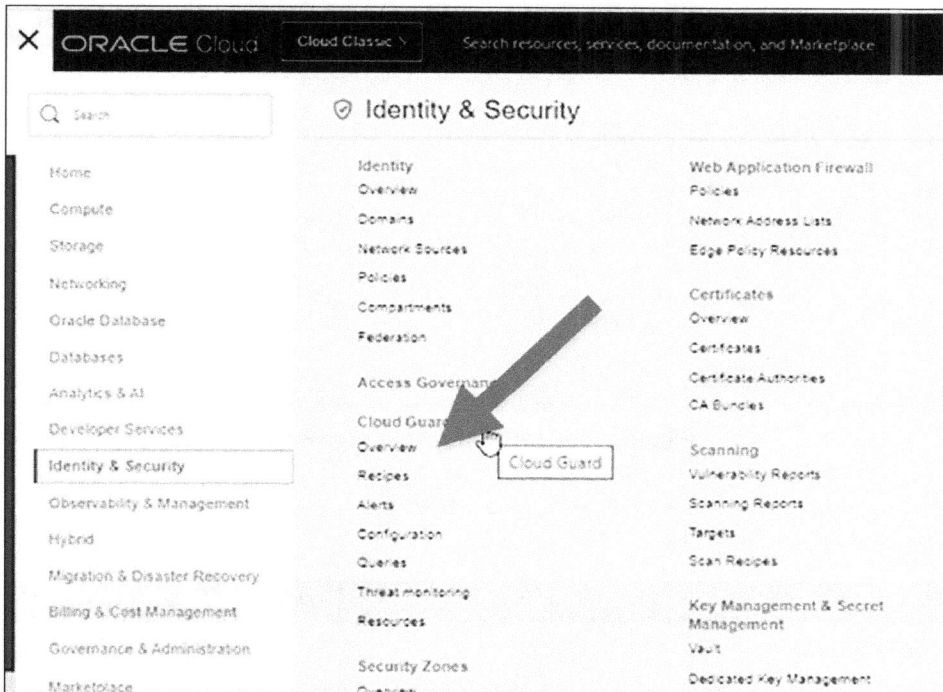

Figure 14-1   Navigating to the Cloud Guard Admin Pages

The first time you use this page, you will get a notification that Cloud Guard needs to be enabled. To enable Cloud Guard, click the **Enable Cloud Guard** button, as shown in Figure 14-2.

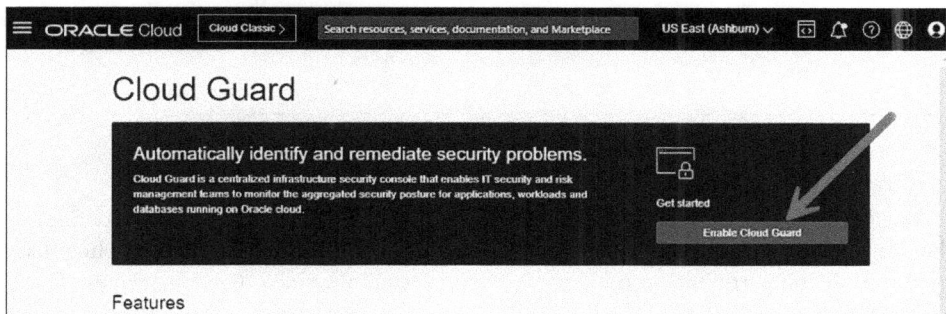

Figure 14-2   Enabling Cloud Guard

Next, if needed, the wizard will add the required policies to the tenancy. If the policies already exist, you will see they are not added. This is shown in Figure 14-3.

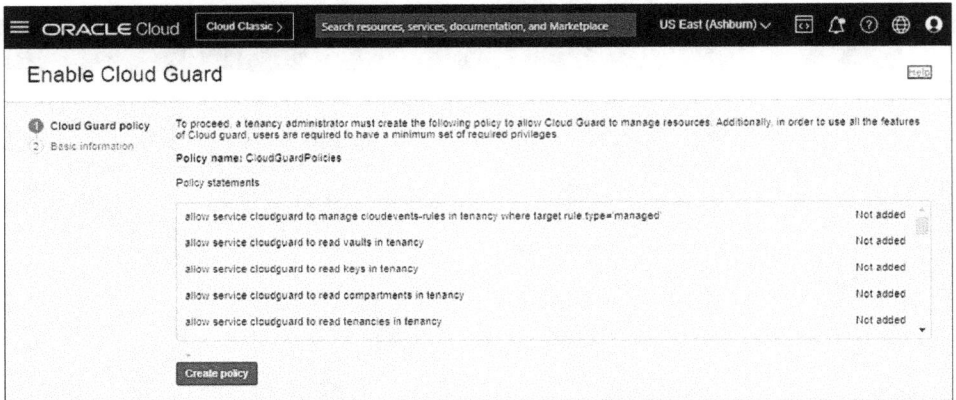

Figure 14-3   Cloud Guard Automatic Policy

If the wizard adds the policies, you will see that they have been successfully added. This is shown in Figure 14-4.

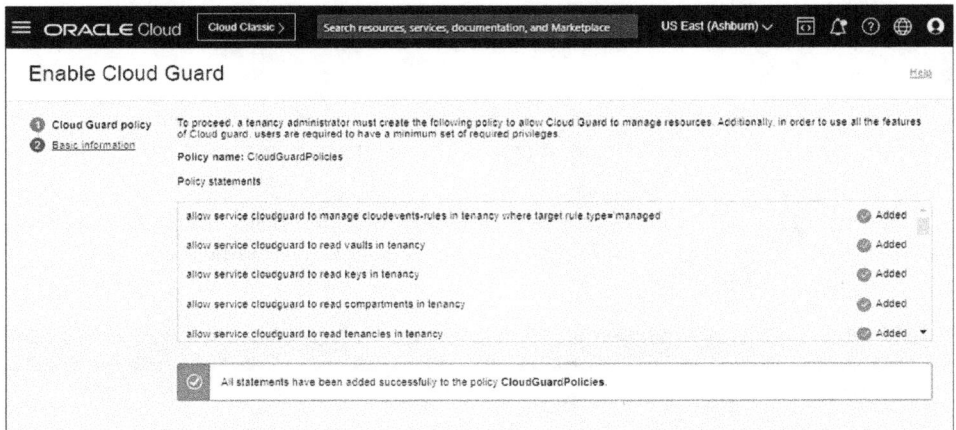

Figure 14-4   Automatic Policies Created

Next, you will be prompted to add your first Cloud Guard policy. A policy defines the scope of the initial detector. In the following example, we have created a policy that monitors all compartments in the tenancy, using Oracle-provided detector recipes. This is shown in Figure 14-5.

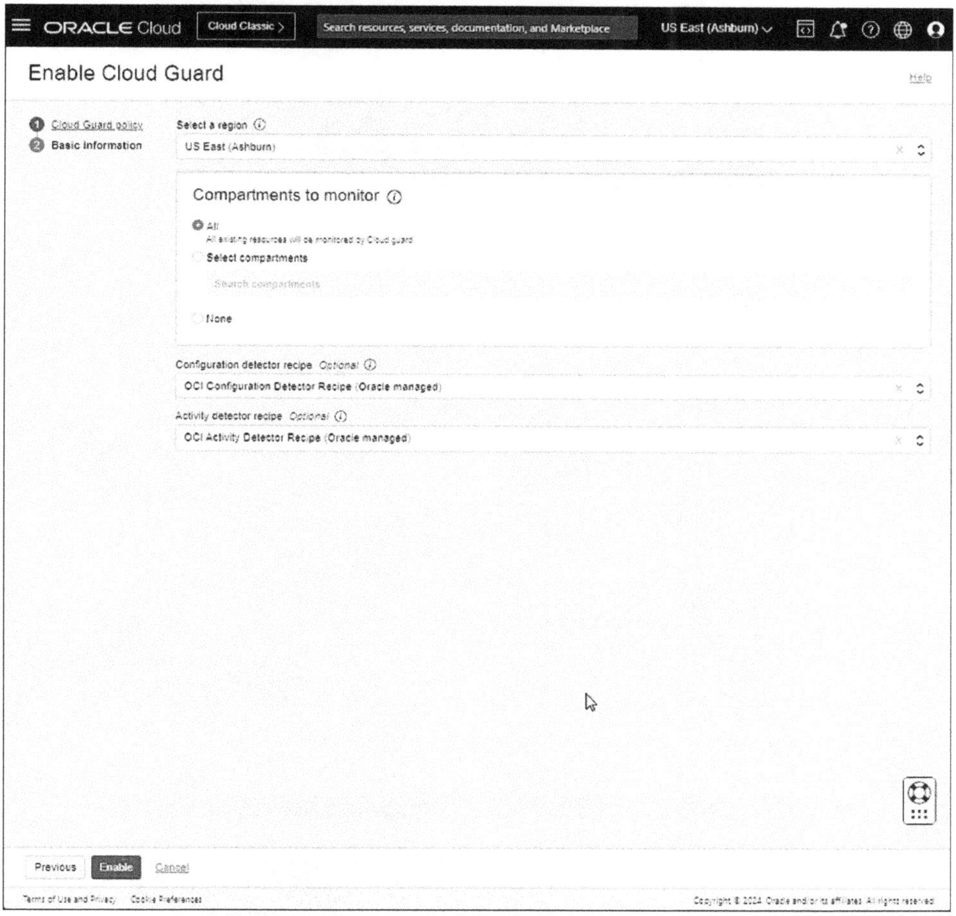

Figure 14-5   Cloud Guard Initial Options

After you click Enable, you will go back to the main Cloud Guard page, as shown in Figure 14-6. You can select **Go to Cloud Guard** to go to the main report.

Initially, you will see no problems, as in Figure 14-7. No, this doesn't mean that you are secure; rather, Cloud Guard has not processed any detector yet.

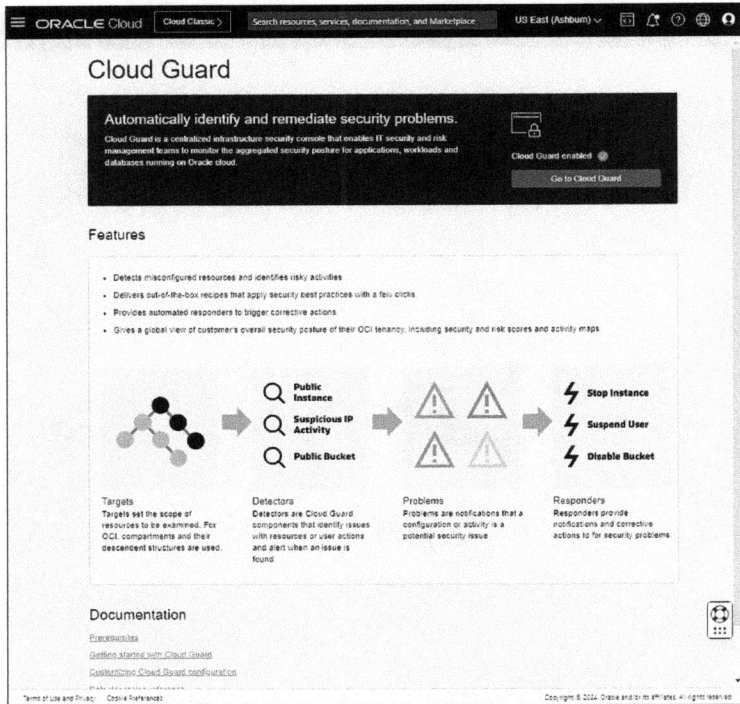

Figure 14-6   Cloud Guard Enabled

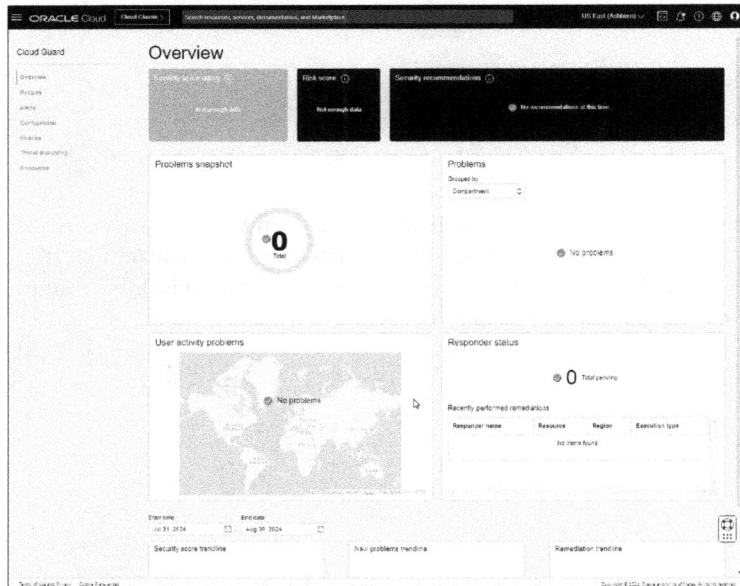

Figure 14-7   Initial Dashboard

You must wait for the last 4 hours to start seeing the data. Each detector will run over the next 24 hours, fully populating the report, as shown in Figure 14-8.

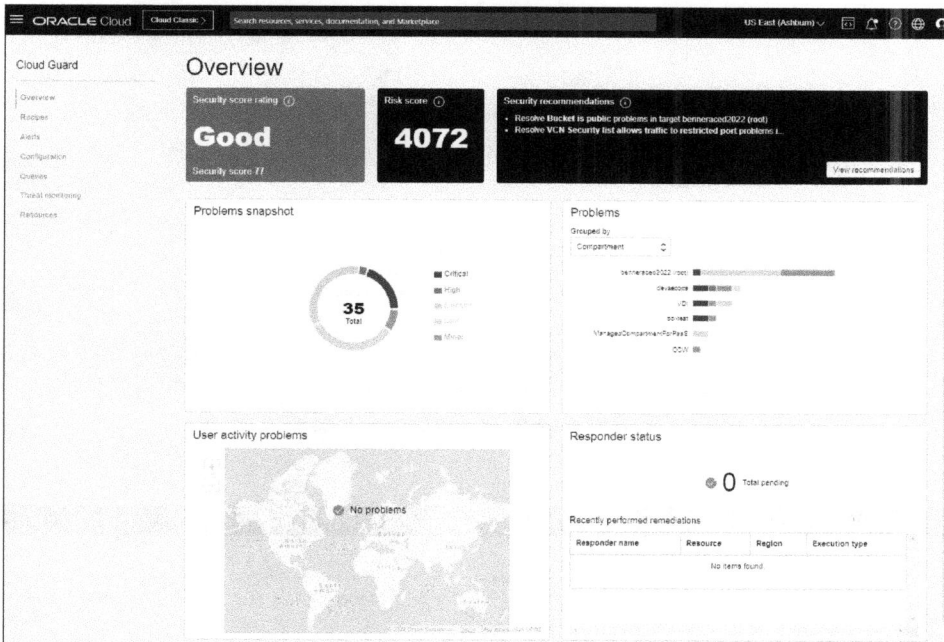

Figure 14-8   Populated Dashboard

Note: There Are Occasionally Dependencies

Some detectors require that additional services be enabled, like VSS. Before configuring Cloud Guard, you might want to initially configure services like the Operating System Management Hub (OSMH) and the Vulnerability Scanning Service (VSS).

From this menu, you can also select **Alerts**. This selection will allow you to see and sort all alerts generated by detectors. A subset of the screen is shown in Figure 14-9.

From here, you can see all of the alerts and sort by multiple fields. Simply click the header to sort by that column. Additionally, you can limit the alerts to specific times, compartments, resource types, and status. More importantly, you can click the **Problem Name** to see the details for that event. A sample is shown in Figure 14-10.

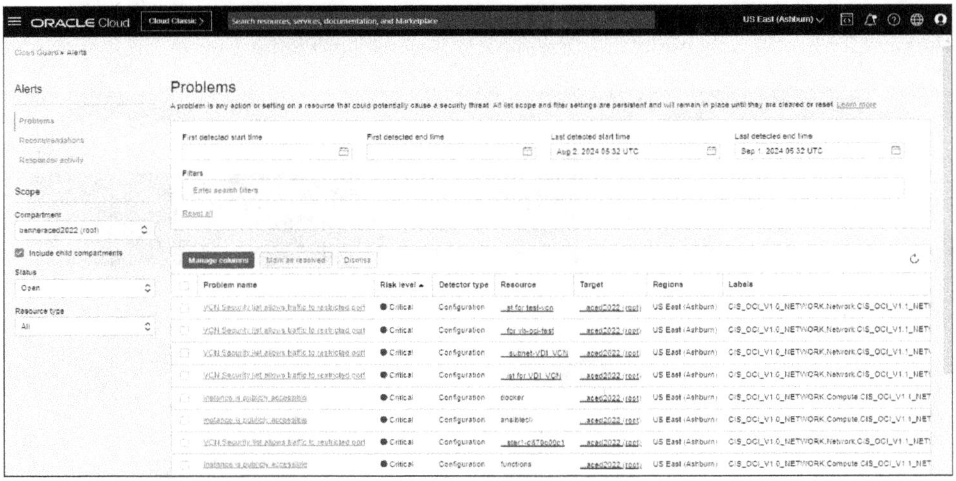

Figure 14-9   Cloud Guard Alerts

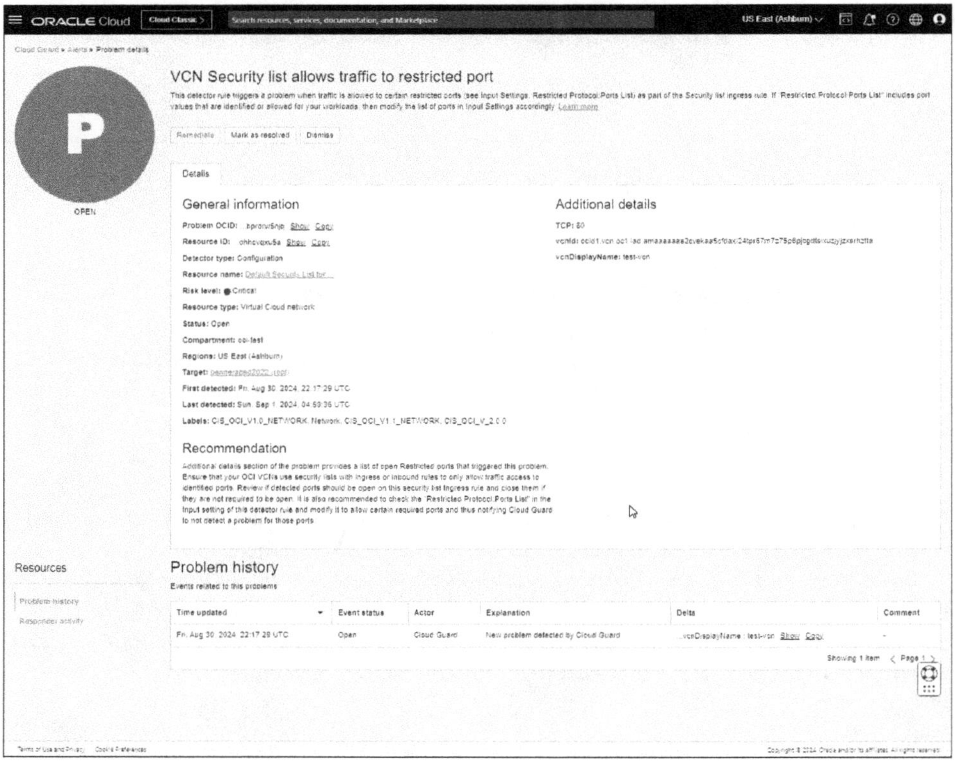

Figure 14-10   Alert Sample

Here, you can see the Details, as well as the Problem History and any responder activity. Cloud Guard will also provide recommendations for the issue and suggestions on how to resolve the potential vulnerability. You also can choose **Remediate, Mark as Resolved**, or **Dismiss**.

The Remediate option is available only for select responders. Remediation involves taking corrective actions to resolve the security problems identified by Cloud Guard detectors. These actions can range from simple configuration changes to more complex responses, such as adjusting permissions or disabling compromised resources. The goal of remediation is to remove vulnerabilities or misconfigurations that could potentially be exploited by malicious actors, thereby improving the security of your cloud resources. There are two types of remediation:

- **Automated Remediation:** Cloud Guard can automatically apply remediation actions using responder recipes configured to respond when specific security issues are detected. For instance, if a detector identifies an open security group rule that exposes sensitive ports, an automated responder could close the port or tighten the security group rules.
- **Manual Remediation:** In some cases, security teams may choose to manually review alerts and take corrective actions. This approach allows for more granular control and is useful for complex issues that require a detailed analysis before making changes.

When you are remediating detected alerts, you have three basic types of actions to take:

- **Configuration Corrections:** Adjusting settings to comply with security best practices, such as enabling encryption on storage services or adjusting network configurations to close unnecessary open ports
- **Access Controls:** Modifying access permissions to restrict overly permissive roles or users, thereby reducing the attack surface
- **Resource Management:** Stopping or terminating resources that are deemed to be a security risk, such as unused instances that could be exploited if left running

Automating the remediation of your alerts has several advantages. By taking proactive measures to identify and resolve security issues, organizations can markedly enhance their resistance to cyber attacks. Utilizing automated remediation processes alleviates the manual burden on security teams, empowering them to direct their efforts toward strategic initiatives instead of routine corrective tasks. Automated responders are capable of promptly addressing security concerns as they arise, thereby reducing the timeframe during which vulnerabilities are exposed and mitigating the potential impact of security incidents.

When automating the remediation, there are three things you should always consider:

- **Set Appropriate Responders:** Carefully configure responder recipes to ensure that remediation actions align with your security policies and do not disrupt business operations.

- **Test Automated Actions:** Before you implement automated remediation, it is crucial to thoroughly test the actions in a controlled environment to verify that they function as intended and do not lead to any unforeseen adverse effects.
- **Monitor and Review:** It is crucial to consistently monitor remediation efforts and thoroughly evaluate the results to identify any recurring patterns or issues. This will help you determine whether additional security measures are needed or if adjustments should be made to detection methods. One effective way to monitor and review is by using a feedback loop process. A feedback loop is vital in securing cloud environments because it allows for continual improvement and adjustment of security measures in response to new threats, vulnerabilities, and changes in the cloud landscape. In the context of cloud security, a feedback loop involves the process of identifying security issues, analyzing and addressing them, learning from the results, and then using this information to improve and strengthen security strategies and settings.

Outside of using a responder to automate the resolution, you also have two options to mark the alert as resolved or dismiss it:

- **Mark as Resolved:** Once a security issue has been dealt with, you indicate that by marking the alert as resolved. This action signifies that the underlying security problem has been successfully remedied. For instance, if a detector identifies an open port and that port is subsequently closed, the alert can then be marked as resolved. These resolved alerts are logged in the system as instances where issues were effectively addressed. This documentation is valuable for monitoring the progress of remediation efforts and for audit purposes, because it serves as evidence that the security team has taken proactive steps in response to the alert. The alert then transitions to a "Resolved" state, which indicates that the risk has been mitigated, and unless the problem recurs, no further action is necessary.
- **Dismiss:** When an alert is dismissed, it indicates that the alert has been reviewed and determined to be unnecessary to act upon or to be a false positive. Dismissing an alert does not require immediate resolution of the underlying issue; instead, it simply removes the alert from the active list. This action acknowledges the alert but deems it not actionable. Situations that may lead to an alert being dismissed include intentional configurations that trigger alerts but still comply with internal security policies or acceptable risk levels. Once dismissed, the alert moves to a "Dismissed" state, signifying that no action will be taken for that specific alert. It's important to note that dismissed alerts are typically not considered in the evaluation of the overall security posture.

A question that often comes up for new administrators is when to use Mark as Resolved and when to use Dismiss. Use Mark as Resolved when the issue identified by the alert has been fixed. This ensures an accurate record of resolved security problems and reflects the cloud environment's security posture. Use Dismiss when the alert is not relevant, is a known false positive, or represents an acceptable risk that does not need fixing. This action helps to clean up the dashboard by removing irrelevant alerts without necessarily improving security.

It's important to keep in mind that, regardless of the tools you use, it is crucial to consistently review and assess alerts to determine the appropriate course of action, whether it's resolving or dismissing them, in line with your organization's security policies and risk tolerance. It's essential to maintain detailed records of why alerts were resolved or dismissed, because this context can prove invaluable for future audits or reviews. Such records can also provide insight into recurring issues and aid in enhancing detector configurations.

Additionally, if specific alerts are frequently dismissed, it may be beneficial to consider customizing detector recipes to better align with your organization's security posture. This approach can lead to a reduction in unnecessary alerts, allowing for a more focused approach on actionable items.

By understanding the nuances between these actions, you can establish and maintain an organized and responsive method for managing security alerts within OCI Cloud Guard.

Recipe Management

Recipes are a vital component of Cloud Guard, serving as a mechanism for the detection and response to configuration changes and security settings. Detector recipes play a crucial role in identifying security issues, while responder recipes enable automated responses to the identified security threats. These recipes are highly customizable and allow organizations to tailor Cloud Guard's monitoring and response actions to meet their specific security needs and policies. By defining the methods for detecting and responding to security issues, recipes facilitate automated security management, reducing the need for manual intervention and enabling faster risk mitigation.

Moreover, recipes provide a unified approach to security across the entire OCI tenancy, streamlining security management, especially in large or complex cloud deployments. Notably, they can be updated and refined as security needs evolve, empowering organizations to continuously enhance their security posture in response to emerging threats and changing compliance requirements. This adaptability ensures that Cloud Guard can effectively adapt to the unique needs of each organization's cloud environment.

Using Detector Recipes

Detector recipes serve as the blueprint for Cloud Guard to pinpoint potential security vulnerabilities. These recipes encompass detectors, which act as guidelines that dictate which configurations, activities, or behaviors should be flagged as possible security risks. Detectors span a wide range of security domains, covering aspects such as configuration compliance, anomaly detection, and threat identification. Oracle offers a collection of predefined detectors to address common security concerns, such as identifying open ports, unencrypted data, excessive permissions, or inactive resources that could pose a security risk. Additionally, organizations have the flexibility to create custom detectors tailored to their specific environment and unique requirements.

In a detector recipe, every individual detector can be fine-tuned with specific parameters to adjust sensitivity levels and set thresholds for identifying potential security threats. This level of customization minimizes false alarms and directs attention toward the most critical security issues. Detector recipes can be either applied across all compartments in an OCI tenancy or targeted to specific compartments, offering a focused approach to security monitoring.

Using Responder Recipes

Responder recipes define the actions that Cloud Guard will take when a security issue is detected by a detector. Responders can be configured to either alert security teams or take automatic corrective actions, thus streamlining the incident response process.

Responders can be classified into two main types:

- **Remediative Responders:** These responders take automated actions to remediate the identified security issues, such as closing open ports, revoking excessive permissions, or disabling noncompliant resources.
- **Notification Responders:** These responders send alerts or notifications to the relevant security personnel, allowing for manual intervention when necessary.

As with detectors, Oracle provides predefined responders for common scenarios, but organizations can also create custom responders to fit their unique security policies and workflows. Actions within a responder recipe can be configured based on the severity of the security issue or the type of resource involved, providing flexibility in how security incidents are handled.

Managing OCI Cloud Guard recipes involves configuring, customizing, and updating the detector and responder recipes to align with your organization's security policies and requirements. Proper management of these recipes ensures that Cloud Guard effectively monitors for security issues and responds appropriately to mitigate risks. The following sections provide a detailed guide on how to manage Cloud Guard recipes.

Accessing Cloud Guard Recipes

When you want to navigate to Cloud Guard, log in to the Oracle Cloud console; then go to the Cloud Guard service under the Identity & Security section. From there, click **Recipes**. This option is shown in Figure 14-11.

From the Cloud Guard dashboard, you can access both detector and responder recipes. There, you'll find a list of predefined (default) recipes and any custom recipes you've created. Figure 14-12 shows the initial detector recipes provided by Oracle.

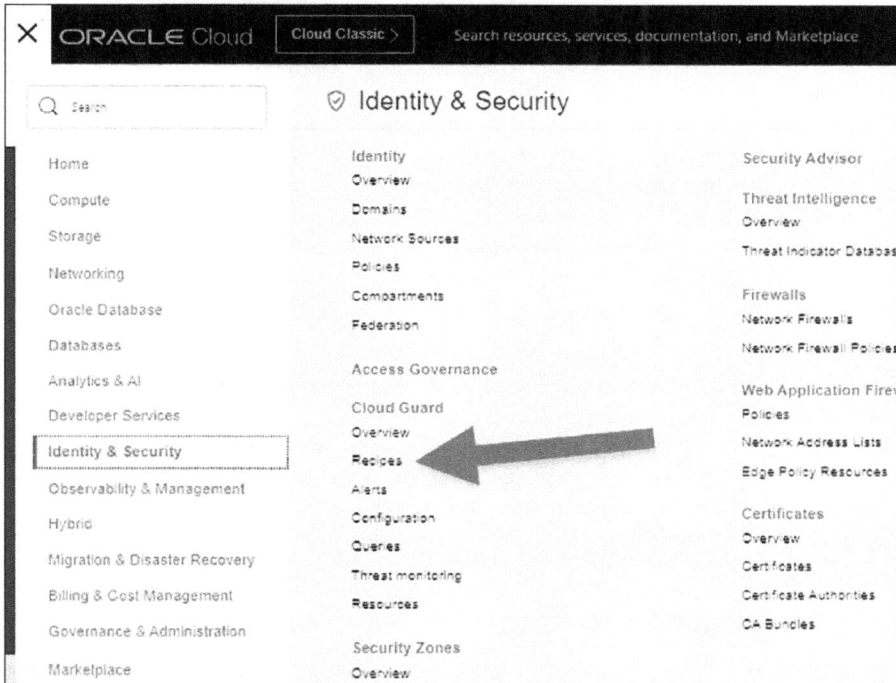

Figure 14-11   Accessing Recipes

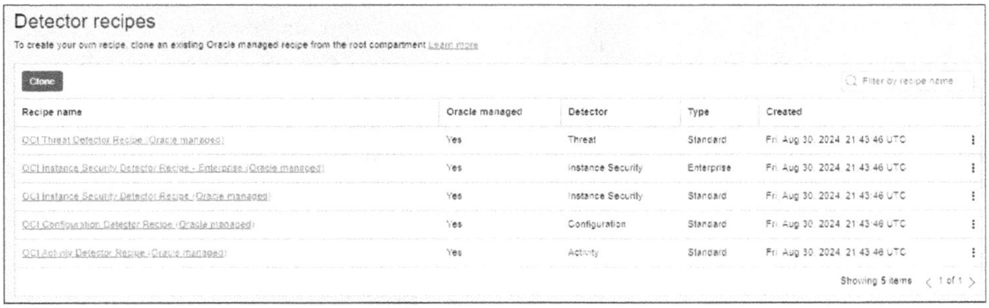

Figure 14-12   Standard Recipes

Managing Detector Recipes

Detector recipes define the rules for identifying security issues. You can use predefined recipes provided by Oracle or create custom recipes to meet specific needs. These recipes come with default rules for common security concerns, such as open ports, misconfigured security settings, or unauthorized access attempts.

The easiest way to enhance them for your environment is to clone and then modify a recipe. The following actions can be performed against recipes to customize them:

- **Clone a Recipe:** Start by cloning an existing predefined recipe if you want to customize it to modify rules without affecting the default configurations.
- **Modify Rules:** In the cloned recipe, you have the option to enable or disable specific detectors, adjust detection thresholds, or modify rule parameters to align with your specific security posture.
- **Add Custom Detectors:** You can develop personalized detectors to address specific security needs by establishing new rules that focus on particular security concerns that are important to your organization.

Regardless of what change you make, you should always test custom or modified detector recipes in a controlled environment to ensure that they work as expected and do not produce excessive false positives.

After you make any changes, it's important to deploy the recipe. You'll need to apply detector recipes to specific compartments or across the entire tenancy depending on where you want the rules to be enforced. It's also crucial to regularly review the alerts generated by your detectors to assess their effectiveness and adjust rules as necessary.

Managing Responder Recipes

Responder recipes define the actions Cloud Guard should take when a security issue is detected. They can be configured for automated responses or to simply notify security teams. You can use the existing predefined responders. This is a great way to get started with predefined responders, such as those that automatically block access, correct configurations, or alert administrators.

As with detector recipes, you can clone a predefined responder recipe to customize it. You can also adjust the parameters of responder actions based on the severity of the security issues or organizational policies. You can also create new responders to handle specific types of incidents that are unique to your cloud environment. Regardless of whether you clone or create a new responder, you should always configure responders to prioritize actions based on the criticality of the alert. For example, high-severity alerts might trigger immediate automated remediation, while lower-severity alerts may simply generate notifications.

Before deploying, test the responder actions to ensure they do not disrupt business operations. Validate that actions are appropriate for the types of alerts they are meant to handle. Once you have tested the new responder, apply it to the relevant compartments or tenancies, ensuring that the appropriate automated actions are taken across the right resources.

Let's clone and modify a recipe.

The task of cloning and customizing recipes is quick and is the same for any recipe type! Navigate to the recipes, and select either a responder or detector category. From there, click the three dots on the left, and then select **Clone**. This action is shown in Figure 14-13.

Next, fill in the name, descriptions, and any needed tags. You can see this step in Figure 14-14, using Test of Cloning as the name. Click **Clone** to finish the process.

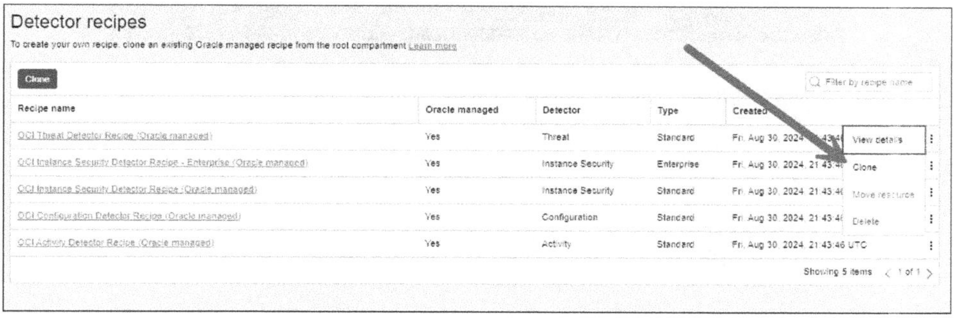

Figure 14-13 Cloning a Recipe

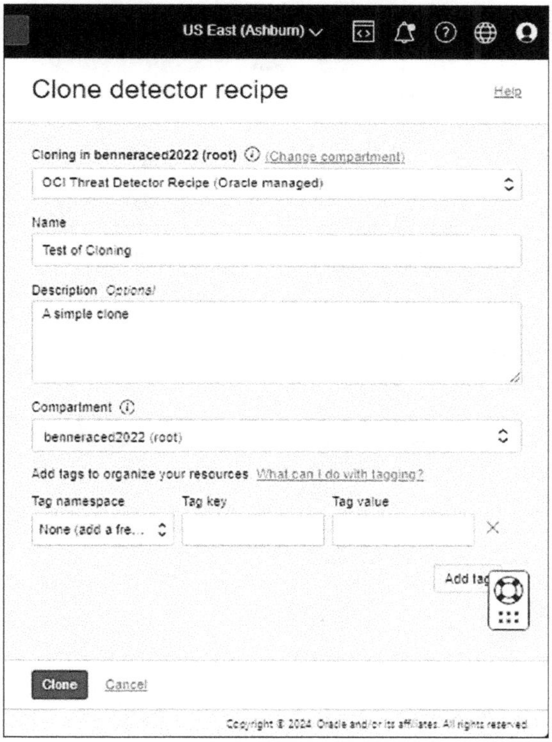

Figure 14-14 Cloning Details

Now that you have cloned the recipe, you can edit it. Click the recipe name from the list to enter the recipe. Each recipe will have different components; in this sample (shown in Figure 14-15), you are simply looking for rogue users.

By clicking the expand icon (the three dots), you can expand the rule to see the list of rules, as shown in Figure 14-16.

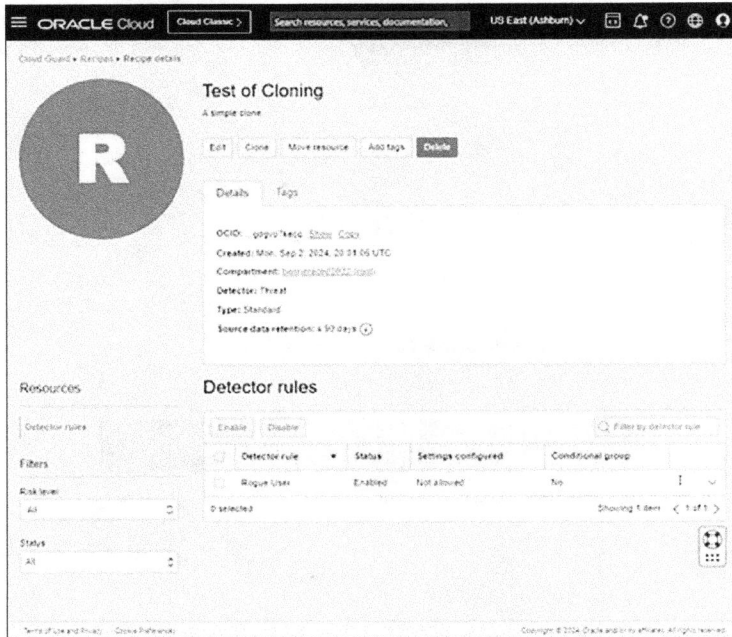

Figure 14-15   Recipe Details

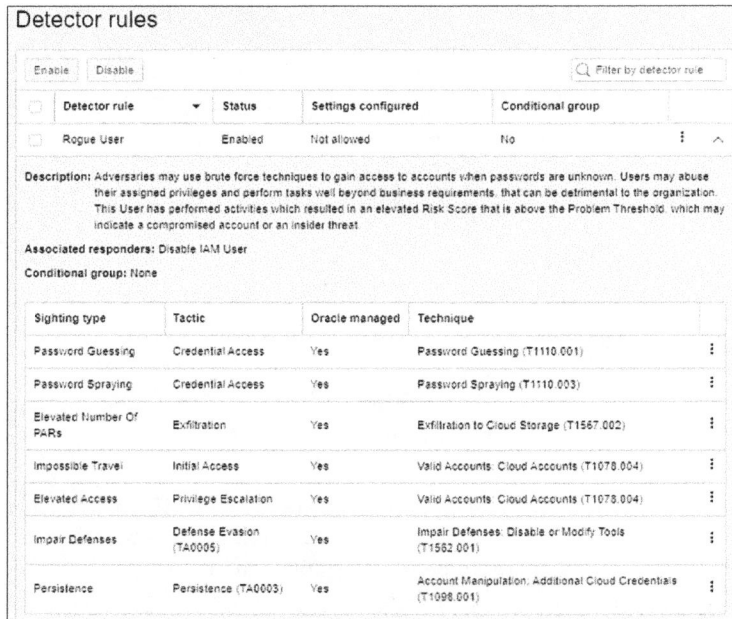

Figure 14-16   Rules List

Each rule will be different, with attributes specific to the use case. You can also add a conditional group to the detector. This will allow you to exclude the rules from specific targets. An example would be to add in a rule that ignores this for a specific user, likely due to a large number of false positives. A sample is shown in Figure 14-17.

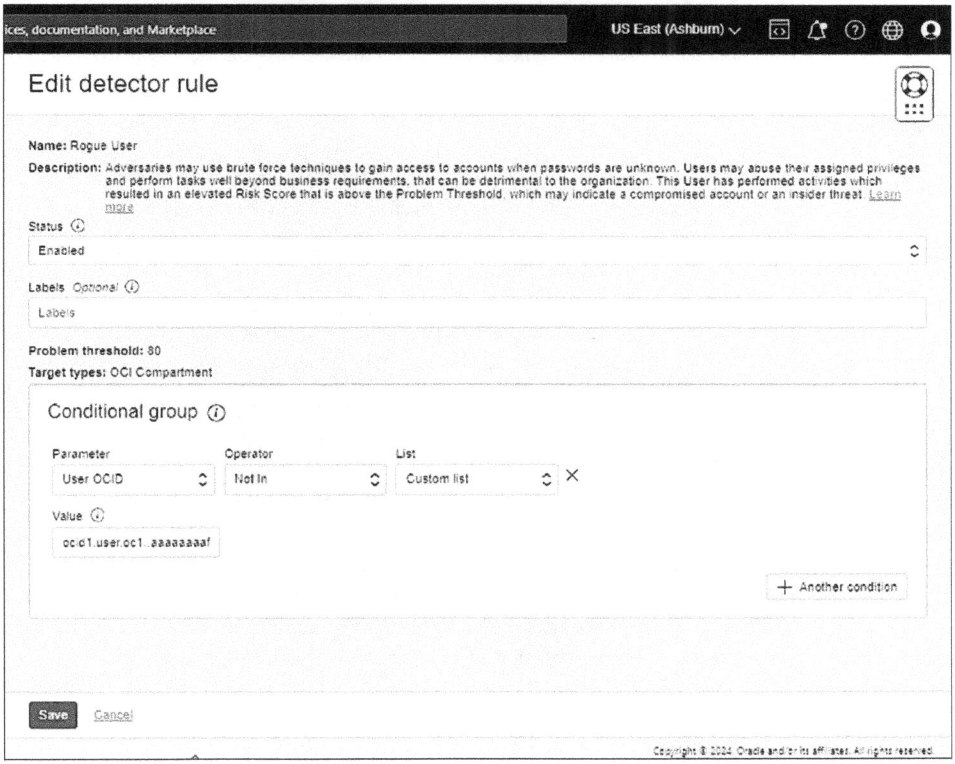

Figure 14-17 Sample Conditional Rule

Here, the rule applies to users who are not in the custom list that contains the OCID of users. While it would be rare to exclude a user from the rules, a more common example of excluding rules would be rules that are being applied to a compute instance with Internet accessibility. Imagine getting alerts for every attempt to log in as the root user on a Linux system!

Best practices for updating and maintaining recipes include the following:

- **Regular Reviews:** Make sure to regularly review and revise both detector and responder recipes to ensure they are in line with the latest security needs, emerging threat landscapes, and advancing cloud infrastructures.
- **Version Control:** It's important to keep track of different versions of your recipes, particularly the custom ones. By monitoring changes and making sure that updates

don't unintentionally compromise the efficacy of your security monitoring and response, you can maintain a robust system.

- **Audits and Compliance:** Utilize the information gathered from audits and compliance checks to make necessary modifications to recipes, guaranteeing that they comply with regulatory standards and internal security protocols. This should be part of your feedback loop process.
- **Alert Analysis:** Make sure to consistently keep an eye on the alerts produced by Cloud Guard and track the responses made by the team. Take the time to analyze the patterns to pinpoint any deficiencies in your security configurations or areas that may require modifications.
- **Sensitivity Adjustments:** Adjust the sensitivity of the detectors to minimize the occurrence of inaccurate security alerts, allowing your security team to concentrate on responding to critical and actionable alerts.
- **Stakeholder Feedback:** Gather feedback from security teams and other stakeholders who interact with Cloud Guard. Use their insights to improve recipe configurations and overall security workflows. Your feedback with these critical team members is an important part of the security process.

Effective management of OCI Cloud Guard recipes involves ongoing configuration, customization, testing, and monitoring to ensure they are optimally aligned with your security goals. By regularly updating and fine-tuning these recipes, organizations can maintain a proactive and adaptive security posture, effectively protecting their cloud environments from evolving threats.

In summary, Cloud Guard recipes are a powerful tool within Oracle Cloud Guard, enabling automated, scalable, and customizable security management for OCI environments. By defining both the detection of security issues and the appropriate response actions, these recipes help organizations maintain a strong and adaptive security posture.

Security Zones

Oracle Cloud Infrastructure offers a powerful feature called security zones to provide robust security enforcement for resources within specified compartments. Security zones play a critical role in ensuring that all cloud resources adhere to stringent security policies and compliance standards. By automatically preventing any operations that would violate these security policies, security zones reduce the risk of security misconfigurations and bolster the overall security posture of the cloud environment. These zones apply a comprehensive set of predefined or custom security policies to resources within designated compartments, covering areas such as data encryption, network access, and resource configuration. Any action that would breach these policies is swiftly thwarted, ensuring strict compliance with the organization's security requirements. Moreover, security zones play a vital role in maintaining adherence to industry standards and regulatory requirements by rigorously enforcing security configurations aligned with these frameworks. By actively enforcing security policies, security zones significantly reduce the administrative burden on security teams, providing a built-in governance model that prioritizes security within the Oracle Cloud Infrastructure.

Through the automatic implementation of security policies, security zones play a critical role in mitigating misconfigurations and reducing the risk of human error, a common contributor to security breaches. By upholding industry standards, security zones ensure that resources consistently adhere to specified security protocols, thereby lessening the reliance on manual verifications and interventions. By proactively enforcing security best practices, security zones fortify the overall security posture of cloud environments, bolstering their resilience against potential threats and vulnerabilities. Furthermore, security zones enable security teams to direct their focus toward high-level strategic initiatives, rather than continuously monitoring and rectifying configurations. The automated prevention of noncompliant actions decreases the necessity for manual oversight.

Security zones are defined by security zone recipes, which consist of policies that determine what is allowed and what is not allowed within the zone. OCI offers predefined recipes like the Maximum Security Zone, which includes a complete set of strict security rules. You also have the option to create custom recipes to suit specific security requirements. Four common security policies are enforced in security zones:

- **Data Encryption:** Ensure that all data at rest and in transit is encrypted using appropriate encryption standards.
- **Network Configuration:** Ensure that access to the public is restricted and that security group configurations are properly enforced to minimize the organization's exposure to the internet.
- **Identity and Access Management:** Ensure the implementation of stringent access controls, which involves carefully managing user and service access permissions to make sure that they have the least privilege necessary to perform their tasks.
- **Resource Configuration:** Remember to implement best practices to enhance security, like preventing the use of outdated services, making sure that backups are activated, and mandating the use of multifactor authentication (MFA) for sensitive tasks.

Security zones also integrate with OCI services. Security zones integrate seamlessly with OCI Cloud Guard, enhancing monitoring and remediation capabilities. Cloud Guard can alert on or automatically remediate violations detected within security zones. Additionally, it is integrated with OCI's logging services, where actions within security zones are logged and auditable, providing transparency and traceability for security operations and compliance checks.

The most common use cases involve enforcing security policies in development and testing environments to ensure that configurations align with production standards. This helps reduce security risks when promoting code and configurations to production. When combined with Cloud Guard, it is also ideal for workloads that need to comply with regulatory requirements, such as those in finance, healthcare, or government sectors where strict security controls are mandatory. This is an important solution for securing applications that handle sensitive data within security zones, ensuring that all resources adhere to high security standards, such as mandatory encryption and restricted network access.

OCI security zones provide a robust framework for ensuring that cloud resources are deployed and managed in a secure manner. By automatically enforcing security policies, they help organizations maintain compliance, reduce risks associated with misconfigurations, and improve their overall security posture. Whether used for protecting sensitive workloads, ensuring compliance, or securing development environments, security zones are a key component of a comprehensive cloud security strategy in OCI.

Adding a New Security Zone

Adding a security zone in Oracle Cloud Infrastructure involves creating a compartment designated as a security zone, where only resources that comply with strict security policies can be deployed. Security zones enforce best practices for cloud security, ensuring that resources adhere to rules such as mandatory encryption, restricted network access, and proper configuration of security controls.

In the OCI console, navigate to **Identity & Security > Security Zones**, as shown in Figure 14-18.

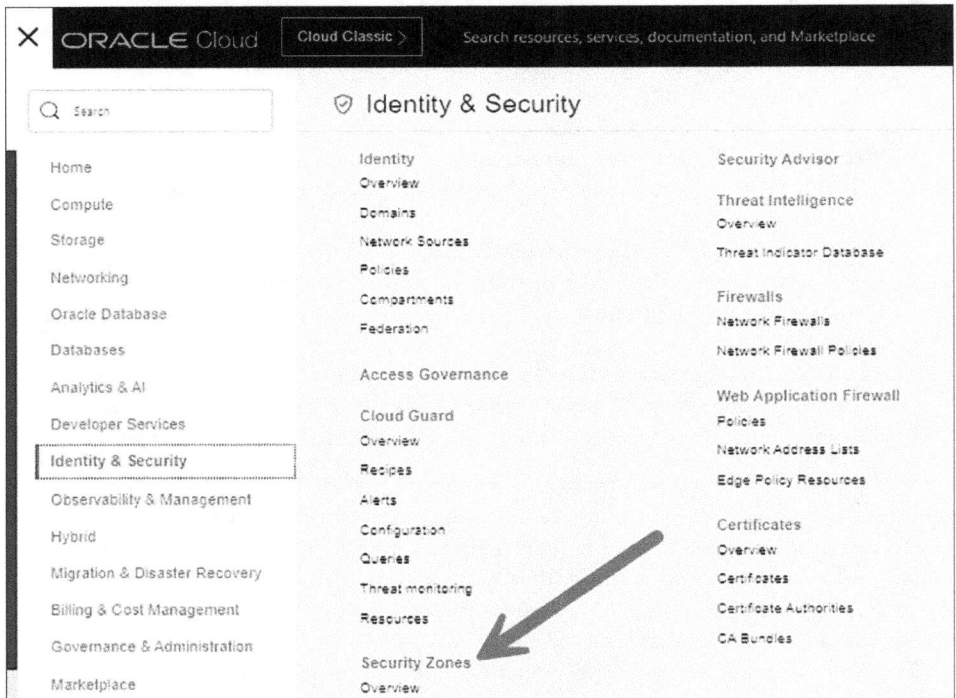

Figure 14-18   Accessing Security Zones

Next, click **Create Security Zone**. This selection will open the security zone creation wizard, as shown in Figure 14-19.

When setting up your security zone, you need to provide essential details such as the name of the security zone and a description to provide more context on its intended use. You should also choose a compartment for the zone. It's important to note that only empty compartments or compartments without conflicting resources according to security policies can be selected. Once complete, the form should resemble that shown in Figure 14-20.

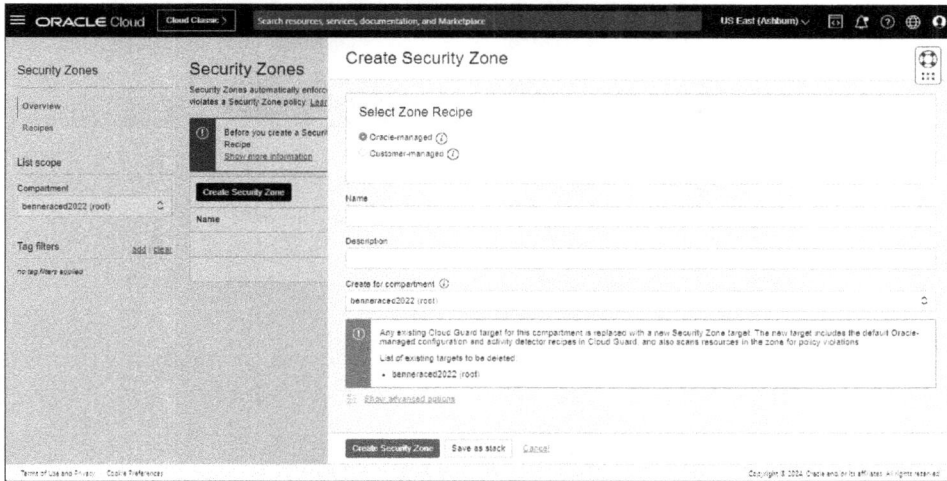

Figure 14-19   Security Zone Creation

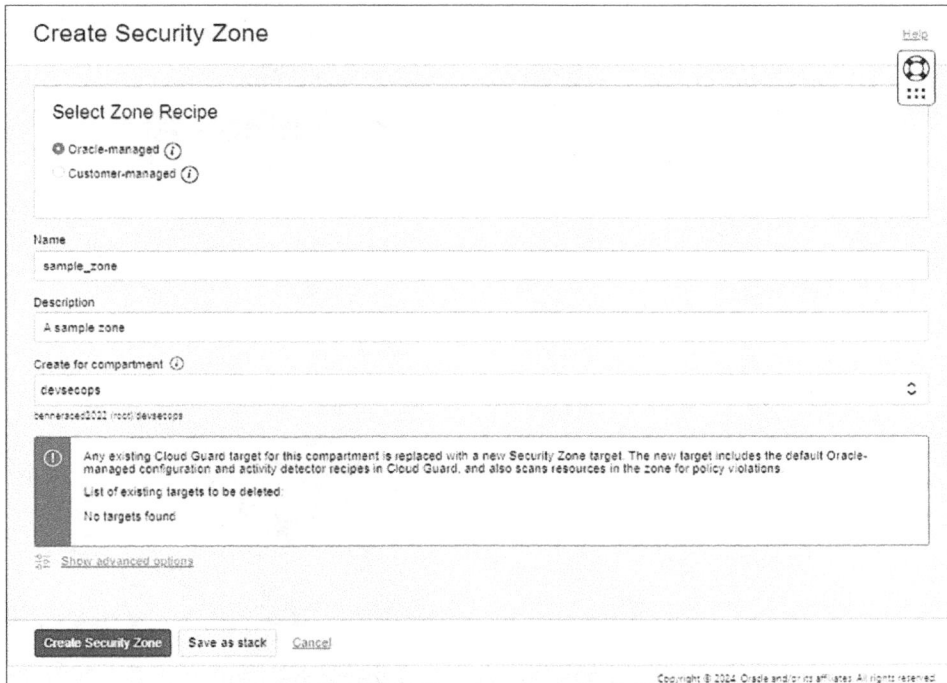

Figure 14-20   Sample Zone Creation

Click **Create Security Zone** to finish the creation. By default, the zone will use the Maximum Security Recipe. Before doing this, go ahead and clone the recipe and make any modifications needed. This follows the same basic process that all recipes use!

Next, navigate to the list of security zones, and select the zone you want to update, as shown in Figure 14-21.

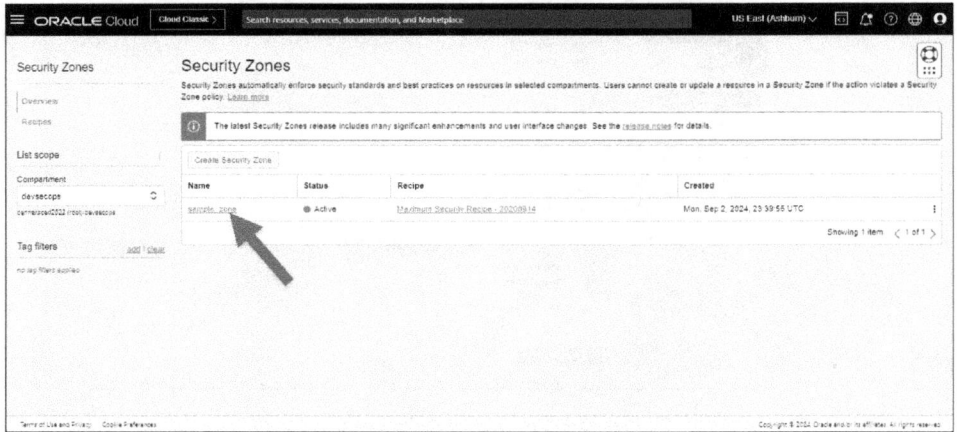

Figure 14-21   Selecting a Security Zone

From here, select the current recipe and use the edit button. In Figure 14-22, you can see where you can use a drop-down to select an alternative recipe.

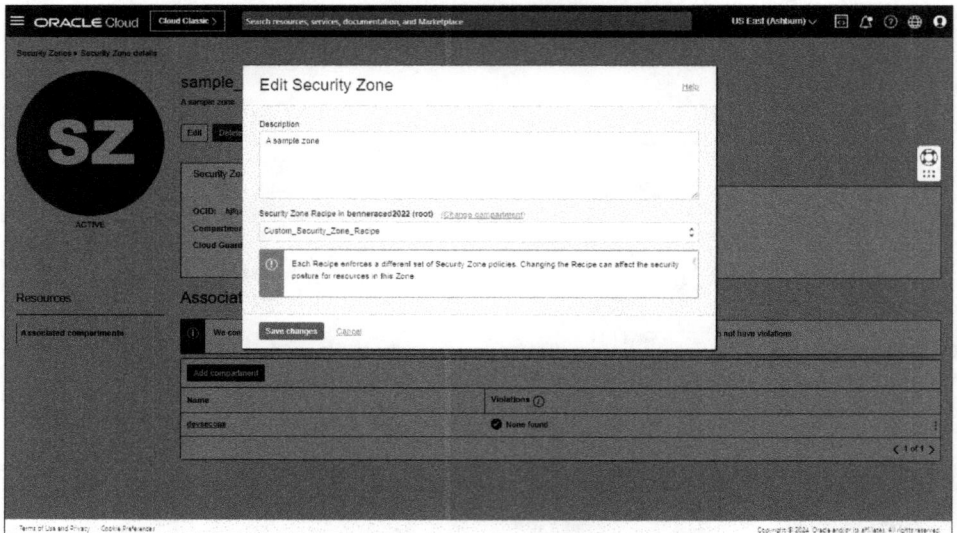

Figure 14-22   Selecting a New Recipe

Save the change, and you will now start using the new recipe to enforce its rules on the compartment.

A straightforward but powerful way to enforce robust security policies across your cloud resources is to create and manage security zones in OCI. By carefully selecting the appropriate security zone recipes and continuously monitoring compliance, you can ensure that your cloud infrastructure adheres to best security practices, reducing the risk of misconfigurations and potential security breaches.

Summary

In this chapter, you learned about Oracle's Cloud Guard service, how to deploy it, manage it, and leverage it to add significant security automation to your tenancy. You also learned how security zones can be used with Cloud Guard to enforce security recipes. In the next chapter, we will cover Ansible, an open-source software tool.

An Introduction to Ansible

What Is Ansible?

Ansible is an incredibly powerful and efficient open-source software tool that enables the automation of various IT operations such as system configuration and software deployment. The tool employs a simple yet readable language called *YAML*, which allows users to create scripts known as *playbooks* that can be easily replicated. These playbooks can be executed either via a command-line interface or a centralized web interface to manage and configure systems. Additionally, Ansible offers a vast collection of predefined functions known as *modules*, which boast a straightforward interface and take input parameters to define the actions to be performed on the target hosts. These modules typically return output data that can be further utilized by other modules or tasks in a playbook. Furthermore, Ansible has a unique feature called a *collection*, which facilitates the packaging and distribution of reusable content, such as playbooks, modules, roles, plug-ins, and inventory scripts, in a format that can be shared among users.

When it comes to managing systems, Ansible is a tool that stands out for its agentless approach. This means that you don't have to install any extra software on the systems you want to manage, making it a hassle-free option. Ansible uses SSH to communicate with most Linux systems, as well as other systems like network switches and firewalls. This makes it not only convenient but also flexible for different needs. When you execute an Ansible command or playbook, it connects to the managed systems via SSH and performs the tasks or commands specified in the playbook. To use SSH with Ansible, you need to set up SSH access on the managed systems. This process usually involves creating an SSH key pair on the Ansible control machine and transferring the public key to the managed systems. Once the public key is placed, the control machine can connect to the managed systems using the corresponding private key. Overall, Ansible's use of SSH makes it an efficient and secure tool for managing diverse systems.

Were you aware that Ansible is not only capable of managing Linux systems but also Windows systems? It achieves this by utilizing the Windows Remote Management (WinRM) protocol to communicate with Windows systems, which is an innate feature in modern versions of Windows. Ansible has a collection of modules that are specifically designed to administer Windows systems, enabling the DevSecOps team to run commands and scripts and to manage services on Windows systems just as they would on Linux systems. Additionally, Ansible allows the use of PowerShell for Windows automation and provides a set of modules for executing PowerShell commands and scripts too. While Ansible is very helpful, it lacks a centralized tool to manage the execution of playbooks. Without a centralized tool, there is no centralized logging and management of playbooks. This limits the ability to scale Ansible usage across the enterprise. An example of what is lacking is the ability to have end users run playbooks on systems that they do not have shell access to. This is where Oracle Linux Automation Manager (OLAM) comes into the picture.

What Is OLAM?

Oracle Linux Automation Manager is Oracle's supported distribution of the open-source AWX project. OLAM is designed to help organizations manage and scale their Ansible deployments. It is similar if not identical to other commercially available AWX-based products, with the major distinction of OLAM being just like Oracle Linux, because it is free to use, free to download, and free to distribute. Support for OLAM is included with an Oracle Linux Premier subscription, which is included with Oracle Cloud Infrastructure at no additional cost. This makes OLAM free to use with 24×7×365 support for OCI-based systems.

Following are some of the things that OLAM provides that Ansible does not include:

- **A Web-Based User Interface:** OLAM provides a user-friendly, web-based interface for managing and monitoring Ansible deployments.
- **Role-Based Access Control (RBAC):** OLAM allows administrators to control access to Ansible resources and functionality based on user roles.
- **Scheduling and Notifications:** OLAM allows users to schedule Ansible jobs to run at specific times and to receive notifications when jobs complete or fail.
- **Reporting and Analytics:** OLAM provides detailed reporting and analytics on Ansible job runs and resource usage.
- **Advanced Authentication:** OLAM provides advanced authentication methods, including LDAP, Active Directory, and others.
- **OLAM API:** OLAM includes a REST API that allows users to programmatically access OLAM functionality.

Organizations that need OLAM include those that need to manage and scale Ansible deployments; that need a web-based user interface; that require advanced authentication, reporting and analytics, and role-based access control; and that need the ability to schedule and receive notifications. Best of all, OLAM is free! Support is included with your OCI services, or an Oracle Linux subscription. Best of all, even without either of these, it's free to download and use.

To date, there have been two major releases of OLAM: 1.0 and 2.0. OLAM 2.0 introduced the concept of a service mesh, external databases, more advanced workflows, and more. A *service mesh* is a distributed system, with nodes performing a specific task. The service mesh allows the OLAM system to have active/active high availability and disaster recovery. Multiple nodes can be deployed in a single location for high availability, with additional nodes deployed in a different location for disaster recovery. The service mesh provides several benefits for DevOps teams, including

- **Scalability:** The service mesh provides a scalable infrastructure that can handle the increasing demands of even global deployments.
- **Security:** The service mesh provides security features like RBAC, authentication, and authorization that help to secure multiple DevSecOps teams in a single service mesh.
- **High Availability and Disaster Recovery:** The service mesh provides both high availability and disaster recovery by allowing multiple nodes of the same role. Since all nodes talk, this enables a true active architecture.

Currently, there are three supported node types:

- **Control Plane:** This node is a critical component of a DevSecOps pipeline that uses the Ansible automation tool. The OLAM control node serves as the central point of management for Ansible playbooks, inventories, job scheduling, and REST API endpoint. It allows DevOps teams to centrally manage their infrastructure, automate repetitive tasks, and quickly respond to changes. The OLAM control node also provides features like version control, role-based access control, and reporting to help DevSecOps teams track changes and manage their automation workflows more efficiently.
- **Execution Plane:** An execution plane is a worker node that executes Ansible playbooks and tasks as part of an automation workflow managed by an OLAM control node. The execution node serves as the endpoint for running Ansible tasks and helps to distribute the workload across multiple nodes in a cluster. This can improve the performance and scalability of automation tasks, especially for large and complex environments. The execution node can also be configured with custom settings, such as the number of concurrent jobs it can run, the maximum memory it can use, or the type of network connection it supports.
- **Hybrid Node:** The hybrid node is a combination of both the control node and execution nodes. It allows for a simple installation, when the DevSecOps team does not need to scale either globally or to size, that supports thousands of playbooks being run on thousands of systems daily.

There is a fourth type of node that is currently not supported but offered as a developer preview. Called a Hop node, it allows communication between mesh members that cannot communicate with each other.

Larger enterprise workloads should consider setting up a service mesh, with a clustered Postgres database system. This will provide additional redundancy and scalability for Enterprise workloads. An Enterprise service mesh will normally use an external PostgreSQL cluster, with multiple control nodes for redundancy and multiple execution planes for scalability. An OLAM execution node can be installed on a dedicated server or a virtual machine, and it requires connectivity to the OLAM control node to receive job instructions and report back the execution results. One limitation to be aware of is that you cannot have more than 20 nodes in a service mesh. A sample architecture is shown in Figure 15-1.

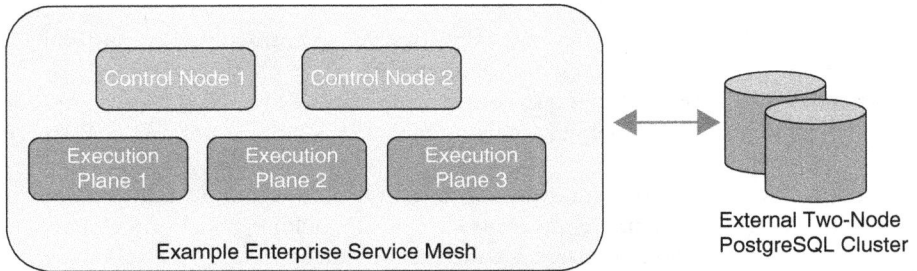

Figure 15-1   Ansible Service Mesh

In the sample service mesh, there are two control nodes, allowing for redundancy for mesh management. This is scaled out with three execution planes, allowing for running larger playbooks against large numbers of systems. This is all backed by a PostgreSQL database cluster where all the persistent data is stored.

Sizing the Deployment

Sizing an OLAM installation can be tricky. The easy way is to use the generic sizing described in Table 15-1 and then grow as needed.

Table 15-1   OLAM Generic Sizing

Node Type	Minimum OCPU	Minimum RAM	Recommended Disk	Notes
Control Node	2	8 GB	100 GB	
Execution Plane	2	8 GB	70 GB	
PostgreSQL Node	2	16 GB	150 GB	Database space may need to be large, based on workload and retention requirements.

If you really want to zero in on specific RAM and CPU requirements, the following sections show how you do it for the execution nodes.

Memory

Memory is sized by the number of forks a job runs. On average, a job uses about 100 MB per fork. This is set in the system parameter SYSTEM_TASK_FORKS_MEM. Assuming this setting is not changed, simply reserve 2 GB of RAM for the overhead and divide by 100, rounding down to the nearest whole number. A system with 8 GB of

RAM would have 2 GB reserved for overhead, leaving 6 GB for forks. This leaves room for 61 forks running at any one time. This is calculated as follows:

$$(8192 - 2048)/100 = 61.44$$

CPU

CPU can be a bit more difficult, because depending on the complexity of the playbook, more CPU may be needed. This being said, by default, the SYSTEM_TASK_FORKS_CPU parameter defaults to 4, allowing for 4 tasks per CPU. A system with 8 cores should be able to run 32 forks at any one time. Also, when you're calculating the CPU, keep in mind that OLAM will reserve a fork for managing the job. So a playbook that is forking 8 times will need 9 forks. Also, some jobs have a fixed value for the number of forks, with inventory and project updates always using a 1, and system jobs always using a 5.

One advantage of OCI's compute for the DevSecOps team is the Agile allocation of compute resources. You can allocate CPU and RAM separately, enabling very efficient deployments of execution nodes in the mesh. A 16-core node can run 54 forks, requiring only 9 GB of RAM. With OCI, this compute node can easily be provisioned. When running on other cloud service providers (CSPs), you might be forced into a node that has significantly more RAM than is required.

Database Disk Space

The PostgreSQL database also needs some special attention in larger deployments. As every job runs, its history and output are logged in to the database. It is recommended to have at least 1000 IOPS at a minimum for the database node and at least 150 GB of space. Depending on the actual workloads and the number of systems, the space can grow faster than anticipated. Let's look at this scenario, where a security check playbook with 100 tasks is run every hour against all Linux systems. In an environment with 100 Linux systems, those would be 2400 executions a day logging 240,000 events in the database daily, or 7,440,000 event monthly. If each task stores only 1200 bytes per task, that would equate to 8.6 GB a month. This may not sound like much, but multiply this amount across more systems, or more playbooks, and it's possible for a database to easily grow 1 GB a day.

Other Requirements

OLAM runs on Oracle Linux 8. To install OLAM, you will need to build an OL8 system. At a minimum, the system should have 4 GB of RAM, 40 GB of disk space (170 GB is recommended), and 2 OCPUs.

Sizing the different nodes in an Enterprise deployment is similar to the stand-alone deployment, with some changes based on the node usage. Actual RAM and CPU may need to be adjusted based on the actual workload.

OCI Authentication

Using OLAM to manage resources in OCI is fairly straightforward. This is done by installing an OCI application key on the OLAM system as a new credential under resources. To do this, you will first need some information from the OCI console and the user that will be used to run the playbooks: OCI OCID, fingerprint, tenant OCID, region, and a private user key.

> ## Note
> If you already have an OCI API key, you can skip to "Adding the OLAM Credential," though reviewing how to generate a key is recommended.

Getting the OCI Information

To get the OCI OCID, log in to the OCI console and navigate to the main menu, then select **Governance & Administration > Tenancy Details**. The details page is shown in Figure 15-2.

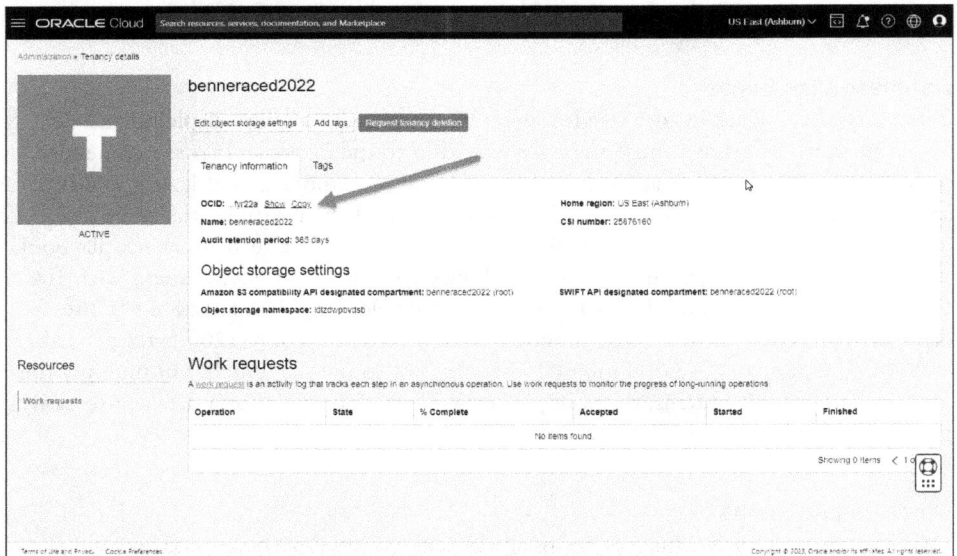

Figure 15-2   Tenancy OCID

From here, you can copy the OCID for the tenancy.

Next, you will need to navigate to the user that you will create an API key for. To do this, from the OCI console, navigate to **Identity & Security > Users** and then select the user you will be creating an API key for. From this user screen (shown in Figure 15-3), you can copy the user's OCID.

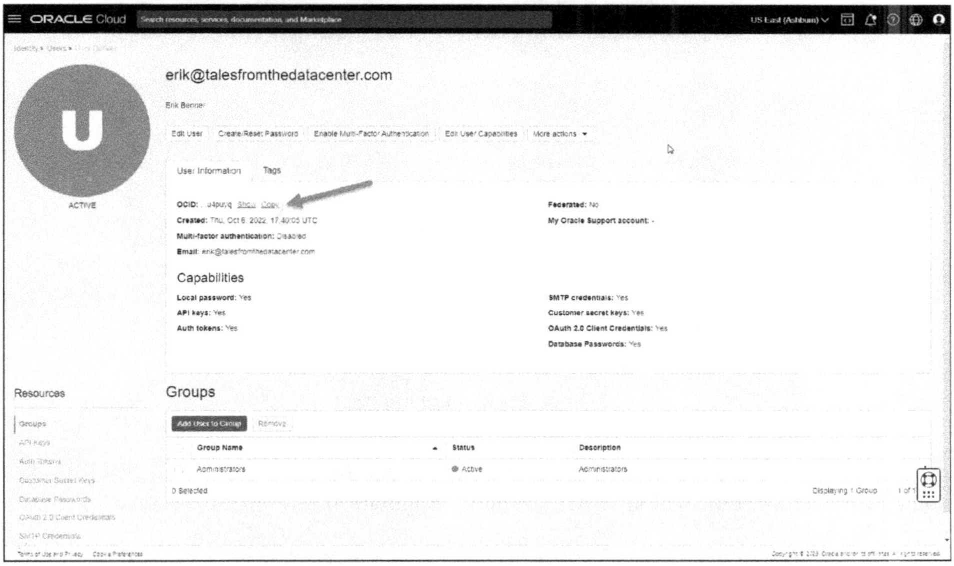

Figure 15-3   User OCID

Next, you will need to create an API key for this user. Select **API Keys** under the Resources section for the user. From the resulting screen (shown in Figure 15-4), you can select **Add API Key** to create a new API key pair.

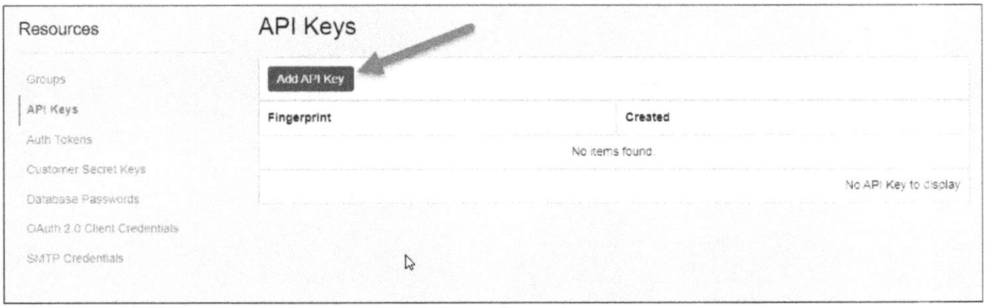

Figure 15-4   API Keys

Next, you have the option of uploading your own API public key file or downloading a new API key pair. For this example (shown in Figure 15-5), you can download both the private and public keys.

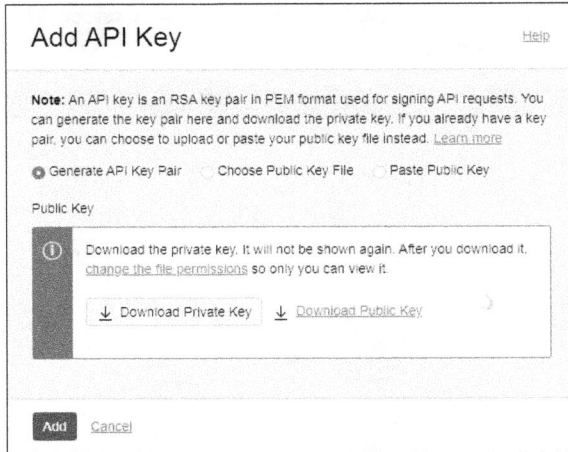

Figure 15-5   Add API Key

Save both of the files because the same API keys can be used later for the OCI CLI. Click **Add**. This action will take you to the Configuration File Preview screen shown in Figure 15-6.

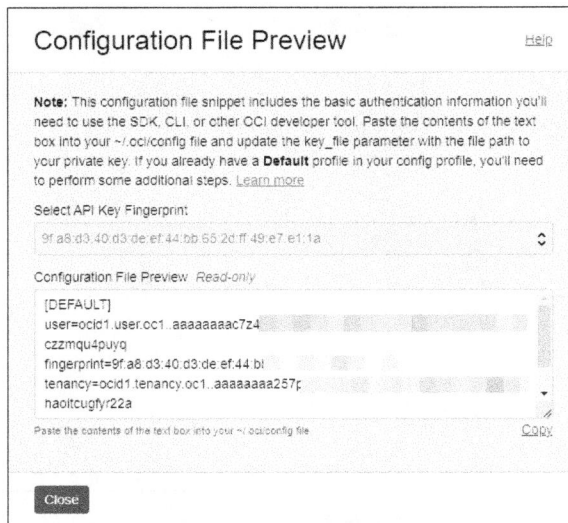

Figure 15-6   Configuration File Preview

Make sure you save the fingerprint and configuration file preview to use later. The configuration file preview will be helpful when you're using the OCI CLI. You can also get your region code from the configuration file. This is the **region=** setting.

A sample config file looks like this:

```
[DEFAULT]
user=ocid1.user.oc1..aaaaaaaac7z4bemycsdmdfgdfgdfgcmkskwiqseedczzmqu4puyq
fingerprint=11:22:33:44:aa:bb:cc:dd:ee:ff:1a:1b:1c:1d:1e:1f
tenancy=ocid1.tenancy.oc1..
  aaaaaaaa257pjnvghqjdk75hswajs8321mchs931dh14dpyhaoitcugfyr22a
region=us-ashburn-1
key_file=<path to your private keyfile> # TODO
```

In this sample, the region code is **us-ashburn-1**.

You now have all the information required to add the credential to OLAM.

Adding the OLAM Credential

To add the credential to OLAM, log in to OLAM and navigate to **Resources > Credentials**. From there, select **Add**. This action will bring up the Create New Credential page.

From the Credential Type drop-down, select **Oracle Cloud Infrastructure** and fill out the form with the information gathered, as shown in Figure 15-7.

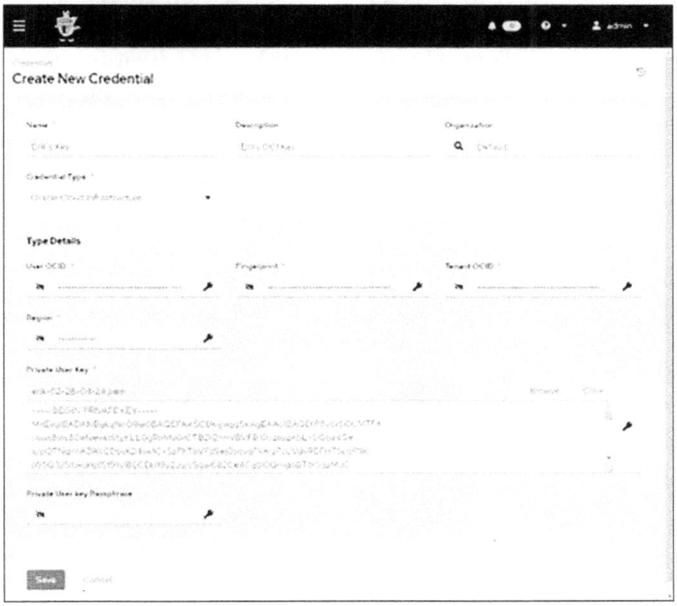

Figure 15-7   Creating a New Credential

After you have verified the information, click **Save**. OLAM will then take you to the details page for the key.

With the credential saved, you can use it to execute Ansible playbooks against OCI.

Collections and Modules

Ansible collections are a game-changer when it comes to sharing and reusing playbooks, modules, roles, plug-ins, and inventory scripts. These collections are structured in a way that makes them easily shareable across different teams and projects. They are essentially self-contained bundles of Ansible content that can be installed and managed separately from the core distribution. To keep things in order, collections are organized into namespaces and packaged as tar.gz archives or Ansible Galaxy roles. With versioning support, users can effortlessly keep track of changes and manage dependencies between different versions. The **ansible-galaxy** command makes installing Ansible collections a breeze because it fetches them from various sources like Ansible Galaxy, Git repositories, or local directories. Overall, Ansible collections streamline the process of sharing and reusing Ansible content, making it easier for teams to collaborate and manage their projects effectively.

It's worth noting that Ansible modules are an incredibly valuable tool for automating specific tasks. These reusable blocks of code can be utilized to manage a wide array of systems and applications. They're written in a variety of programming languages, including Python, PowerShell, Bash, Ruby, and Perl, and are capable of being executed on remote hosts to perform specific actions. Notably, Ansible offers an extensive library of built-in modules that cover many common use cases. Additionally, users can develop their custom modules to enhance Ansible's functionality. One of the most significant advantages of modules is their straightforward interface, which enables them to return output data that can be further utilized by other modules or tasks in a playbook.

Installing the OCI Collection on Your OCI Development System

The OCI Ansible Collection offers a straightforward method for creating and provisioning resources in OCI using Ansible. These modules enable you to write Ansible playbooks that automate the provisioning and configuration of various OCI services and resources, including compute, load balancing, database, and more. When using the collection via the command line, you will need to install and configure it before using it. (The collection is located at https://github.com/oracle/oci-ansible-collection.)

Installation

The following steps show how to install the OCI collection on a system running in OCI for local command-line use. You can easily install the collection on Oracle Linux 8 systems. You simply need to enable the developer and developer_EPEL repositories and then install the collection. This is done with the following commands:

```
sudo yum-config-manager --enable ol8_developer
sudo yum-config-manager --enable ol8_developer_EPEL
sudo yum install oci-ansible-collection -y
```

You also will need to install the OCI CLI because it is helpful to use to test authentication:

```
sudo yum install python36-oci-cli
```

Note

If you do not have Oracle Linux, don't worry. It's free to use, free to download, and free to distribute. It also is practically identical to Red Hat, so there is little learning curve. Also, when you're running Oracle Linux on OCI, support is included with your OCI subscription. You can get Oracle Linux from linux.oracle.com.

If you are on a Mac or other *NIX systems, you can also install the Ansible collection by using the following **curl** command:

```
curl -L https://raw.githubusercontent.com/oracle/oci-ansible-collection/
    master/scripts/install.sh | bash -s -- --verbose
```

Configuration

Once it is installed, you will need to set up a CLI configuration file. This file will contain all of the information required to connect to your OCI tenancy. By default, this data can be in the OCI configuration file located in ~/.oci/config for your user.

Table 15-2 lists the information you will need at a minimum.

Table 15-2 CLI Config Options

Entry	Description and Sample	Required
Region	The OCI region; for example, us-ashburn-1	Yes
Tenancy	The OCID of the tenancy	Yes
User	The OCID of the user	Yes
Fingerprint	The fingerprint of the public key for the user	Yes
Key_file	The full patch to the .pem file for the key	Yes
Pass_phrase	If the key is encrypted, then this is the passphrase	Only if key file is encrypted
Security_token_file	The path to the session token file	Only if session token authentication is being used

A sample configuration file should look similar to this:

```
[DEFAULT]
region=us-ashburn-1
tenancy=ocid1.tenancy.oc1..aaaaaaaa25t4xt667mlfui4vvpyhaoitcugfyr22a
```

```
user=ocid1.user.oc1..aaaaaaaac7z4bemyltwq3g64vroh6czzmqu4puyq
fingerprint=13:04:ce:a3:9b:cf:7d:aa:bb:cc:dd:ee:ff:db:e8:bd
key_file=/home/opc/.oci/user.pem
```

Once this file is installed, you can easily test the configuration using the **oci** command:

```
oci os ns get
```

This command will return the namespace for the tenancy object storage:

```
[opc@ansiblecli .oci]$ oci  os ns get
{
  "data": "iddddweevaab"
}
```

Next, install the Galaxy collection for OCI with the following command:

```
ansible-galaxy collection install -f oracle.oci
```

Next, you can test using Ansible. You can do the same test in Ansible, getting the namespace for the tenancy:

```
[opc@ansiblecli ~]$ ansible localhost -m oracle.oci.oci_object_storage_
  namespace_facts
localhost | SUCCESS => {
    "changed": false,
    "namespace": " iddddweevaab "
}
```

Now that you know things are working, with both the CLI and Ansible, it's time to write a playbook.

Playbooks

An Ansible playbook is a textual configuration file used in Ansible. Ansible is designed to simplify the management and orchestration of IT infrastructure by allowing you to define and automate tasks, configurations, and deployments across multiple systems.

As noted previously, a playbook in Ansible is essentially a file written in YAML (Yet Another Markup Language) format that outlines a series of tasks to be performed on remote systems. These tasks can include a wide range of activities such as

- Installing or updating software packages
- Configuring system settings and files
- Managing users and groups
- Starting or stopping services
- Copying files to remote systems
- Executing commands or scripts on remote systems
- Running complex workflows involving multiple tasks

Playbooks are organized around the concept of *plays*, where a play is a set of tasks targeting a specific group of hosts (servers or devices). Each task in a play specifies a module to use and the required parameters for that module.

Example 15-1 shows a sample playbook. As a note, some of the OCIDs have been shortened for formatting.

Example 15-1   Sample Playbook

```
---
- name : List summary of existing buckets in OCI object storage
  collections:
    - oracle.oci
  connection: local
  hosts: localhost
  tasks:
    - name: List bucket facts
      oci_object_storage_bucket_facts:
        namespace_name: iddddweevaab
        compartment_id: 'ocid1.tenancy.oc1..aaaaaanvaansoscc4vvpyhaoitcugfyr22a'
      register: result
    - name: Dump result
      debug:
        msg: '{{result}}'
```

In Example 15-2, the playbook consists of a single play that targets object storage in OCI. It contains two tasks: one to list all the facts about buckets in the compartment and another to dump the results so you can view the output.

Example 15-2   Output from Sample Playbook Execution

```
[opc@ansiblecli ~]$ ansible-playbook buckets.yml

PLAY [List summary of existing buckets in OCI object storage] ********************
********************************************************************

TASK [Gathering Facts]
********************************************************************
ok: [localhost]

TASK [List bucket facts]
********************************************************************
ok: [localhost]

TASK [Dump result]
********************************************************************
**
ok: [localhost] => {
    "msg": {
        "buckets": [
            {
```

```
                    "compartment_id": "ocid1.tenancy.oc1..
    aaaaaaaa257pjnpyhaoitcugfyr22a",
                    "created_by": "ocid1.saml2idp.oc1..aaaaaf/erik@
    talesfromthedatacenter.com",
                    "defined_tags": null,
                    "etag": "237cd28b-f454b-bdaff1c7c9f5",
                    "freeform_tags": null,
                    "name": "bucket1",
                    "namespace": " iddddweevaab ",
                    "time_created": "2023-08-16T02:37:14.354000+00:00"
                },
                {
                    "compartment_id": "ocid1.tenancy.oc1..aavpyhaoitcugfyr22a",
                    "created_by": "ocid1.saml2idp.oc1..a76ima/erik@
    talesfromthedatacenter.com",
                    "defined_tags": null,
                    "etag": "05020c45-beed-8e46-69da6714c3e3",
                    "freeform_tags": null,
                    "name": "bucket2",
                    "namespace": " iddddweevaab ",
                    "time_created": "2023-08-16T02:37:20.939000+00:00"
                }
            ],
            "changed": false,
            "failed": false
        }
    }

PLAY RECAP
***************************************************************************
localhost                  : ok=3    changed=0    unreachable=0    failed=0
    skipped=0    rescued=0    ignored=0

[opc@ansiblecli ~]$
```

Playbooks can be executed using the **ansible-playbook** command, which reads the playbook file and then connects to the specified hosts to carry out the defined tasks. Playbooks can also use variables, conditionals, loops, and other control structures to make them flexible and dynamic. This can cause some issues though, so always be on the lookout for the following errors:

- **Indentation Errors:** When you're creating playbooks, it's important to use indentation to establish the structure of plays, tasks, and other components. It's essential to avoid mixing spaces and tabs or using irregular indentation because this can result in syntax errors.
- **Misplaced Colons and Dashes:** When you're creating playbooks, it is important to use colons (:) for key-value pairs and dashes (-) for list items. Incorrect use or placement of these characters can result in parsing errors.

- **Incorrect Module Names or Parameters:** To avoid task failures, you must verify the module names and their required parameters in the Ansible documentation. Providing incorrect parameters or using the wrong module name may result in errors. It's always better to double-check before executing any tasks.
- **Missing Quotes:** When you're dealing with parameters that involve strings, like file paths, it's important to remember to enclose them in quotation marks to avoid any errors.
- **Using Variables Improperly:** To correctly reference variables in Ansible playbooks, use the Jinja2 templating syntax by enclosing the variable name in double curly braces (for example, **{{ variable_name }}**). Neglecting to apply this syntax or overlooking the use of curly braces can lead to unexpected outcomes.
- **Undefined Variables:** It is important to avoid using undefined variables in the playbook, inventory, or any other sources to prevent errors. Make sure that your variables are accurately defined before using them.
- **Conditionals and Loops:** Improper implementation of conditional statements (**when**) and loops (**with_items**, **with_dict**, and so on) may result in unintentional skipping or repetition of tasks.
- **Inconsistent Host Naming:** Make sure that the names used in your inventory match those specified in your playbook, whether it's for a group of hosts or a single host. This is a common issue when not using the fully qualified domain name (FQDN) for a host. An example is dbserver versus dbserver.24c.lab.m57. local.
- **Security Considerations:** It is advisable to refrain from sharing confidential information such as passwords, API keys, and private data directly in the playbook. It is recommended that you use secure methods like HashiCorp Vault or a similar tool to handle sensitive data.
- **Global Variables:** It is not recommended to modify global variables such as **ansible_user**, **ansible_ssh_pass**, or **ansible_become** directly in the playbook because this can result in unforeseen outcomes. It is preferable to establish these variables in your inventory or as command-line arguments.
- **Lack of Error Handling:** If error handling mechanisms like **failed_when** or **ignore_errors** are not included, the playbook may continue to run even when tasks fail.
- **Not Testing Playbooks:** Do not develop in production. It is important to test your playbooks in a controlled environment before deploying them to production. You can verify the syntax and task list of your playbook by using the **--syntax-check** and **--list-tasks** options.

As an important note, playbooks are written in YAML, and that has its particularities.

Introduction to YAML

YAML is an abbreviation of Yet Another Markup Language, as noted previously, but also YAML Ain't Markup Language. This format permits the serialization of human-readable data. It is frequently employed in scenarios where data exchange is necessary between languages that have different data structures or when data needs to be saved in a more human-friendly format than traditional programming languages' data structures. YAML is intended to be both readable and writable for humans and machine-parseable. It is a popular configuration file format for various software applications and frameworks, including Ansible, Kubernetes, Docker Compose, and more.

Key features of YAML include

- **Human-Readable:** YAML is a data structuring tool that utilizes indentation and simple punctuation such as colons and dashes. This approach makes it easy for humans to grasp the hierarchy and relationships within the data visually.
- **Indentation-Based Structure:** YAML differs from other data formats in that it employs indentation rather than braces or brackets to depict the hierarchical connections between data elements. This approach is visually straightforward, but it necessitates precise indentation to ensure correct parsing.
- **Support for Complex Data Types:** YAML is capable of supporting a variety of data types, including strings, numbers, lists (arrays), dictionaries (maps), and others. These can be combined in a nested manner to create intricate structures.
- **Comments:** In YAML, you can add comments to give more information or context about the data you are defining. These comments should begin with the hash (#) character.
- **No Compilation or Parsing:** YAML is not compiled or parsed in the traditional sense. It's directly interpreted by the software or tool that reads it.

YAML files can be simple or complex. At its core, a simple YAML file may look like the following:

```
---
# Example YAML file
system:
  IP: 192.168.204.216
  port: 5120
database:
  SID: cdb42
  user: sysdba
```

In this example, the YAML data defines a system with an IP and port, as well as a database with a SID and user.

YAML's simplicity and readability make it a popular choice for configuration files in various software projects, and its support for nested structures and data types allows it to handle a wide range of use cases. This being said, it does have some challenges you need to be aware of. When writing YAML, you should be mindful of a few important things to ensure that your data is correctly structured and interpreted by the software that reads it.

Here are some key items to watch for:

- **Indentation and Whitespace:** When you're working with YAML, it is important to use indentation to establish the data hierarchy. It is recommended that you use spaces instead of tabs for consistency and to ensure that elements are aligned correctly. Combining tabs and spaces can result in unforeseen errors.
- **Spaces in Keys:** When you're creating key-value pairs, it's important to ensure that the keys do not have any spaces. If you do need to include space in a key, simply enclose it in quotes.
- **Quoting:** In certain situations, you may have to use either single (' ') or double (" ") quotes to enclose strings. Quotes can also serve as a means to avoid special characters from being interpreted in a unique manner.
- **Boolean Values:** It is important to use lowercase when writing Boolean values, such as true and false instead of True and False.
- **Lists and Dictionaries:** It is important to exercise caution when defining lists and dictionaries. It is recommended that you maintain a consistent format for the items in the list or the keys and values in the dictionary. Proper usage of colons and dashes is also crucial.
- **Comments:** To add comments in a YAML file, use the hash (#) character. Keep in mind that certain software programs may not support or handle comments as anticipated.
- **Special Characters:** When you're working with YAML, it's important to keep in mind that certain characters have special meanings. This includes colons, dashes, and square brackets, which are commonly used for structuring data. To include these characters as part of your data, you may need to use quotes or escape sequences.
- **Literal Scalars:** Be mindful of the leading spaces when working with literal scalars (text blocks) in YAML. These spaces are considered an integral part of the scalar value by YAML.
- **Aliases and Anchors:** With YAML, you can create aliases and anchors to refer to the same data in various locations. This feature can help minimize repetition. However, improper use may result in unexpected outcomes.
- **Valid YAML:** Always ensure that your YAML is valid according to the YAML specification. There are online YAML validators you can use to check the syntax of your YAML files. Oracle Linux includes yamllint, which works well. To install yamllint, run the following command:

```
sudo dnf install -y yamllint
```

Then use yamllint to check the YAML file. In this sample, there are extra blank lines at the end of the file:

```
[opc@ansiblecli ~]$ yamllint sample.yaml
sample.yaml
  10:1      error    too many blank lines (2 > 0)  (empty-lines)
```

Overall, being consistent with your formatting, paying attention to whitespace and indentation, and testing your YAML in the context of the software that will use it can help you avoid common issues when working with YAML files.

Summary

In this chapter, you learned about Ansible and its relationship to OLAM. We also learned more about OLAM, how to size it and what it does, a bit about manually setting up Ansible, and how to connect it to OCI, along with the basics on playbooks and YAML. In the next chapter, we will describe how to use Ansible in OCI.

Using Ansible in OCI

Using Ansible

Chapter 17, "Ansible—Installing and Managing OLAM," will provide a basic understanding of playbooks and how to set up an Ansible environment to authenticate and run the standard Oracle Cloud Infrastructure Ansible collection. In this chapter, we will cover playbooks in more detail and examine several examples of common tasks that can be done using Ansible in OCI.

Writing Playbooks

Mastering the skill of writing Ansible playbooks is crucial for automating tasks such as configuration management and application deployment across multiple systems. Ansible, an open-source tool, enables users to define tasks using YAML files known as playbooks. This chapter covers the fundamentals of writing playbooks, including variables, loops, and **if** statements. These additional tools are also powerful enablers for adding security into the playbooks.

Basics of Ansible Playbooks

An Ansible playbook contains one or more plays, each targeting a group of hosts from the inventory and specifying tasks to execute on those hosts. The playbook has a basic structure like that shown in Example 16-1.

Example 16-1 Basic Playbook

```
---
- name: A Basic Playbook
  hosts: all
  become: yes
  tasks:
    - name: Ensure nmap is installed on the server
```

```
apt:
  name: nmap
  state: present
```

The key components are as follows:

- **Name:** A human-readable name for the playbook or task helps identify its purpose when running.
- **Hosts:** These are the target hosts for the play. They can be a group of hosts defined in the inventory file, a specific host, or all to target every host.
- **Become:** This component indicates whether the tasks should be executed with elevated privileges, like using **sudo** to obtain root access on Linux systems. On Windows systems, this would be the Administrator account.
- **Tasks:** This list of tasks will be executed on the target hosts. Each task should include a name and a module (such as **apt**, **yum**, **copy**) to specify the action to be performed. It is also important to note that most playbooks will contain multiple tasks.

Example 16-2 shows a simple playbook that installs and starts Nginx on all hosts.

Example 16-2   Nginx Sample

```
---
- name: Install and start Nginx on any host
  hosts: all
  become: yes

  tasks:
    - name: Install Nginx
      apt:
        name: nginx
        state: present

    - name: Start Nginx
      service:
        name: nginx
        state: started
        enabled: yes
```

Variables in Ansible

Variables are crucial in Ansible playbooks because they enable the use of dynamic values, increasing the flexibility and reusability of your playbooks. Variables can be defined in multiple places.

- **Playbooks:** Variables can be defined directly within the playbook under the **vars** keyword. This approach is usually not recommended.

- **Inventory:** Variables can be defined in the inventory file, either globally or per host or group.
- **Host Vars and Group Vars Files:** Variables can be defined in separate YAML files within the host_vars or group_vars directories.
- **Command Line:** Variables can be passed directly when running a playbook using the **-e** option.
- **OLAM:** Variables can be passed from OLAM or an AWX system when the playbook is run. Variables are referenced in playbooks using the syntax **{{ variable_name }}**.

In Example 16-3, **nginx_version** is defined as a variable under **vars**. It is used in the **apt** task to install a specific version of Nginx to make sure all the web servers have the same version.

Example 16-3   Defining a Variable in a Playbook

```
---
- name: Playbook with Variables
  hosts: webservers
  vars:
    nginx_version: "1.26.0"
  tasks:
    - name: Install a specific version of Nginx
      apt:
        name: "nginx={{ nginx_version }}"
        state: present
```

Ansible variables can be defined in multiple places, but not all variables have the same precedence. Here's the order of precedence from lowest to highest:

- Role defaults
- Inventory file variables
- Playbook group_vars/all
- Playbook group_vars/*
- Playbook host_vars/*
- Host facts
- Play vars
- Play vars_files
- Registered variables
- Set facts
- Role vars
- Block vars
- Task vars (only for the task)
- Extra vars (from the command line)

Loops in Ansible

Loops in Ansible allow you to execute a task multiple times with different parameters. This capability is particularly useful for repetitive tasks such as installing multiple packages, creating multiple users, or copying multiple files. The simplest way to use loops is with the **loop** keyword. When you use a loop, a special variable **{{ item }}** is used to define the members of the loop.

In Example 16-4, the **loop** keyword iterates over a list of packages (**nginx, httpd24, wget**) and installs each one. Ansible also supports nested loops, which allow you to iterate over multiple lists simultaneously. When you use a nested loop, the special variable **{{ item }}** gets an additional label based on the loop structure.

Example 16-4   Using a Loop to Install Multiple Packages

```
- name: Install multiple packages
  hosts: all
  tasks:
    - name: Install required packages
      apt:
        name: "{{ item }}"
        state: present
      loop:
        - nginx
        - httpd24
        - wget
```

In Example 16-5, the loop iterates over a list of dictionaries, creating users and assigning them to specific groups.

Example 16-5   Configuring Multiple Users with Different Groups for Each User

```
- name: Create users and assign to groups
  hosts: all
  tasks:
    - name: Create users
      user:
        name: "{{ item.name }}"
        groups: "{{ item.groups }}"
      loop:
        - { name: bubba, groups: 'bbq' }
        - { name: bubbajr, groups: 'beef' }
```

You can control loops with additional keywords like **loop_control** to handle more complex scenarios.

In Example 16-6, **loop_control** is used to create a **pkg_index** variable that tracks the current index in the loop. The **debug** task prints out custom messages that include the loop index and the result of each package installation.

Example 16-6   Customizing a Loop Control

```
---
- name: Install packages with custom loop control
  hosts: all
  tasks:
    - name: Install packages with a control loop
      apt:
        name: "{{ item }}"
        state: present
      loop:
        - nginx
        - httpd24
        - wget
      loop_control:
        index_var: pkg_index
      register: package_results

    - name: Debug loop output
      debug:
        msg: "Package #{{ pkg_index + 1 }}: {{ item }} installation result:
{{ package_results.results[pkg_index].msg }}"
      loop: "{{ package_results.results }}"
```

Conditional Statements in Ansible

Conditional statements in Ansible allow tasks to execute based on specific conditions. This capability is beneficial for managing different environments, operating systems, or other factors influencing task execution. When a keyword is used to specify conditions for executing tasks it simplifies the reuse of the code.

In Example 16-7, the task to install Nginx will only run if the target system's OS family is Solaris.

Example 16-7   Task with a Conditional Statement

```
---
- name: Install Nginx on Solaris-based systems
  hosts: all
  tasks:
    - name: Install Nginx
      apt:
        name: nginx
        state: present
      when: ansible_os_family == "Solaris"
```

You can combine multiple conditions using common logical operators like **and**, **or**, and **not**.

In Example 16-8, the task will run only if the target system is RedHat-based *and* has at least 4 GB of memory.

Example 16-8   Task with Multiple Conditions

```
---
- name: Install Apache only on RedHat-based systems with at least 2GB RAM
  hosts: all
  tasks:
    - name: Install Apache
      yum:
        name: httpd
        state: present
      when: ansible_os_family == "RedHat" and ansible_memtotal_mb >= 4196
```

Note

The family groups Ansible OS families and can contain more than just the returned value:

- RedHat includes Oracle Linux, Rocky Linux, and similar distributions based on Fedora.
- SLED is similar and includes SUSE and OpenSUSE.
- Debian includes Ubuntu.

Ansible facts gathered automatically by the setup module provide a wealth of information about the target system and can be used in conditions as well.

In Example 16-9, different web servers are installed based on the OS family of the target system.

Example 16-9   Doing a Different Task Based on the OS

```
---
- name: Install different web servers based on the OS
  hosts: all
  tasks:
    - name: Install Apache on RedHat
      yum:
        name: httpd
        state: present
      when: ansible_os_family == "RedHat"

    - name: Install Nginx on Solaris
      apt:
        name: nginx
        state: present
      when: ansible_os_family == "Solaris"
```

Advanced Playbook Features

As you become more skilled with Ansible playbooks, you can explore advanced features for improved organization and management. Roles provide a method for organizing playbooks into reusable components. Each role is a directory structure that includes tasks, variables, files, templates, and more, enabling you to encapsulate a specific set of functionalities. The directory structure of a role is shown in Figure 16-1.

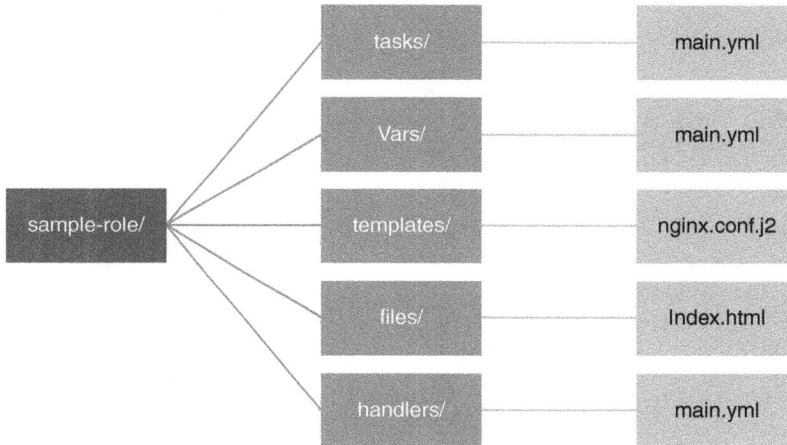

Figure 16-1   Sample Role Directory Structure

Sample Playbooks

In the following sections, we will show several examples of how Ansible can be used with OCI. These are all short examples and ideally would be combined into larger playbooks.

Roles promote reuse and better organization of your playbooks, especially as they grow in complexity (see Example 16-10).

Example 16-10   Using Roles in a Playbook

```
---
- name: Apply The Sample Role
  hosts: all
  roles:
    - sample-role
```

Handlers are another advanced feature; they are special tasks that are triggered by other tasks. They are typically used to restart servers, reload configurations, or perform similar actions that are necessary only after certain changes.

In Example 16-11, the Restart Nginx handler is triggered only if the Nginx configuration file is changed.

Example 16-11   Task Based on a File Change

```
---
- name: Install and configure Nginx
  hosts: all
  become: yes
  tasks:
    - name: Install Nginx
      apt:
        name: nginx
        state: present

    - name: Deploy Nginx configuration
      template:
        src: nginx.conf.j2
        dest: /etc/nginx/nginx.conf
      notify:
        - Restart Nginx

  handlers:
    - name: Restart Nginx
      service:
        name: nginx
        state: restarted
```

Tags enable you to selectively run parts of a playbook (see Example 16-12). This capability is useful when you want to run only specific tasks without executing the entire playbook. Tags are often used with security scripts, where you only need to run specific tasks to resecure a system. You can simply define what individual tasks are to be run within the playbook.

Example 16-12   Using Tags

```
---
- name: Install and configure Nginx
  hosts: all
  become: yes
  tasks:
    - name: Install Nginx
      apt:
        name: nginx
        state: present
      tags: install
```

```
- name: Deploy Nginx configuration
  template:
    src: nginx.conf.j2
    dest: /etc/nginx/nginx.conf
  tags: config

- name: Ensure Nginx is started
  service:
    name: nginx
    state: started
  tags: start
```

You can run only the tasks tagged with **install** using the following command from the command line:

```
ansible-playbook playbook.yml --tags "install"
```

Another useful tool is blocks. Blocks are logical groups of tasks and are a helpful way to deal with errors or decision points. Example 16-13 shows a block being called based on the operating system.

Example 16-13 Using Blocks

```
---
- name: Configure Nginx with blocks
  hosts: all
  become: yes
  tasks:
    - block:
        - name: Install Nginx
          apt:
            name: nginx
            state: present

        - name: Deploy Nginx
          template:
            src: nginx.conf.j2
            dest: /etc/nginx/nginx.conf

      when: ansible_os_family == "RHEL"
      tags: config
```

In Example 16-14, both tasks in the block are executed only if the OS family is RHEL. Ansible provides mechanisms for gracefully handling errors. You can use **ignore_errors** to continue execution even if a task fails, or you can use **rescue** to define a recovery strategy when an error occurs.

Example 16-14   Using `ignore_errors`

```
---
- name: Trying to install a package that may not exist
  hosts: all
  tasks:
    - name: Install custom package
      apt:
        name: packagefromoz
        state: present
      ignore_errors: yes
```

In Example 16-14, when packagefromoz fails to install, the playbook will continue. For most use cases, a better way to deal with the failure is to use the **rescue** option. In Example 16-15, if the installation of Nginx fails, the **rescue** block will execute and attempt to install Apache instead.

Example 16-15   Using `rescue`

```
---
- name: Error handling with rescue
  hosts: all
  tasks:
    - block:
        - name: Install a package
          apt:
            name: nginx
            state: present
      rescue:
        - name: Install an alternative package
          apt:
            name: apache2
            state: present
```

How to Debug and Test Playbooks

Writing playbooks is only part of the job. Debugging and testing are equally important to ensure playbooks work as expected. Ansible provides several tools to help debug playbooks. The **debug** module will print variable values and custom messages during the playbook execution, as shown in Example 16-16.

Example 16-16   Using `debug`

```
---
- name: Debug variables
  hosts: all
```

```
tasks:
  - name: Print OS family
    debug:
      msg: "The OS family is {{ ansible_os_family }}"
```

When you're writing a playbook, it's also a good practice to check the playbook with the **check** option from the command line. This command runs the playbook in a dry-run mode without making any actual changes. For example, the following command will check the playbook named sampleplaybook.yml:

```
ansible-playbook sampleplaybook.yml --check
```

You can also easily compare a playbook with the **diff** option. This command will show the differences in file contents when they are changed:

```
ansible-playbook playbook.yml --diff
```

Testing of playbooks can also be improved by using Lint and Molecule. Lint will check the playbook for best practices and potential issues.

Note

If you have not previously installed pip, you may need to install a few packages first by using the following commands:

```
sudo dnf install bzip2-devel libjpeg-devel python3-devel cargo
sudo pip3 install rust bcrypt neuralpy
```

Lint is installed with pip, using the following command:

```
sudo pip3 install ansible-lint
```

You then can test your playbook with the following command:

```
ansible-lint sampleplaybook.yml
```

Molecule is the tool for testing Ansible roles. It allows you to test your roles in different environments and ensures they work as expected.

As with Lint, installation is done with pip as follows:

```
sudo pip3 install molecule
```

Using Molecule requires that you first initialize the tool and then change into the created directory using **cd** and run a test:

```
molecule init role sample-role
cd sample-role
molecule test
```

Best Practices for Writing Playbooks

To ensure that your playbooks are efficient, maintainable, and scalable, it's important to follow these best practices:

- **Use Roles:** Organize your playbooks into roles to promote reuse and better organization.
- **Avoid manual duplication:** Avoid repetition by using variables, loops, and includes.
- **Use Lint:** Always validate your YAML files to avoid syntax errors.
- **Support partial execution by using tags:** Make your playbooks modular and easier to run partially with tags.
- **Test, test, and test:** Use Ansible Lint and Molecule to test your playbooks and roles before deploying them.
- **Assume failure:** Use error handling mechanisms like **ignore_errors** and **rescue** to make your playbooks robust. Many security issues are caused by ignoring errors.
- **Document:** Your playbook might have made sense at 2 a.m. when you first wrote it, but three years later, it can easily be forgotten and misunderstood. Make sure to include comments and use descriptive task names in your playbooks to enhance clarity and understanding.

Mastering the basics of writing Ansible playbooks, such as defining variables, using loops, and applying conditional logic, is essential for automating IT tasks and managing infrastructure. These skills will enable you to create powerful playbooks capable of handling complex deployments and configurations. As you progress, exploring advanced features like roles, handlers, and error handling will help you create more maintainable and scalable playbooks. When you are able to implement best practices, Ansible playbooks can become a cornerstone of your IT automation strategy, allowing you to manage your infrastructure more efficiently and effectively.

Common OCI Playbooks

In the following sections, we will cover common tasks for your playbooks, broken down by security, networking, storage, and compute tasks. These are just the most common tasks to get you started. Most OCI Platform as a Service (PaaS) and Infrastructure as a Service (IaaS) services are Ansible enabled. You can find the full set of documentation for the OCI Ansible collection at https://github.com/oracle/oci-ansible-collection/tree/master/docs.

Security/Compartments

The following tasks are used to manage basic tenancy security:

- Retrieving a list of availability domains
- Creating a policy
- Creating a group
- Creating a user
- Updating a user's password

For these tasks, we will use these common variables across all samples:

- **compartment_ocid:** The OCID of the compartment we are working in
- **object_read_group:** The name of the read-only group
- **object_read_group_ocid:** The OCID of the read-only group
- **bubba_name:** The user bubba's full name
- **bubba_ocid:** The OCID of the user bubba
- **vcn_name:** A name for the VCN
- **vcn_cidr:** The CIDR block used by the VCN
- **vcn_ig_name:** The name of an Internet gateway
- **vcn_dns_label:** The DNS label for the VCN
- **subnet_ocid:** The OCID of a subnet
- **routing_table_name:** The name for the new routing table
- **routing_table_rules:** The rules for the routing table
- **network_security_group_name:** The security group name
- **object_namespace:** The namespace used for object storage
- **availability_domain:** The AD OCID
- **filesystem_name:** The name for an instance of file storage
- **block_name:** The name of a block volume
- **block_ocid:** The OCID of the block volume
- **compute_instance_ocid:** The OCID of the compute instance
- **compute_instance_name:** The name for the compute instance
- **osimage_ocid:** The OCID of an available OS image

The task shown in Example 16-17 will retrieve the list of ADs that are available for a compartment. The task will return a fact containing all the available ADs.

Example 16-17   Retrieving a List of Availability Domains

```
- name: Get availability domains for vlans
  oci_identity_availability_domain_facts:
    compartment_id: "{{compartment_ocid}}"
  register: oci_ads
- set_fact:
    availability_domain: "{{oci_ads.availability_domains[0].name}}"
```

The task shown in Example 16-18 will create the group that will be assigned to the users and security policies. The task will set the OCID of the group as a fact.

Example 16-18   Creating a Group

```
- name: Create a group for Object readers
      oci_identity_group:
        name: "{{ object_reader_group }}"
        compartment_id: "{{ compartment_ocid }}"
        description: "This group allows read access to an object storage buckets
in a compartment {{ compartment_ocid }}"
```

```
      register: result
    - set_fact:
        object_read_group_ocid: "{{ result.group.id }}"
```

Example 16-19 shows the sample task that will create and assign a policy that allows read-only access to object storage to the group. The task will set the OCID of the policy as a fact.

Example 16-19   Creating a Policy

```
- name: Create a policy statement for a group
      oci_identity_policy:
        name: "Allow_read_access_to_object_storage"
        compartment_id: "{{ compartment_ocid }}"
        description: "Allowed to read buckets and objects in compartment"
        statements: ["Allow group {{ object_read_group }} to inspect buckets in
compartment id {{ compartment_ocid }}",
                        "Allow group {{ object_reads_group }} to inspect objects in
compartment id {{ compartment_ocid }}"]
        register: result
      - set_fact:
          object_read_policy_ocid: "{{ result.policy.id }}"
```

The task shown in Example 16-20 will create the user bubba, returning the OCID of the user. The task will return the text "Created bubba OCID," where **OCID** is the OCID of the created user. Not all tasks need to return facts!

Example 16-20   Creating a User

```
    - name: Create user bubba
      oci_identity_user:
        name: "{{bubba_name}}"
        description: 'Ansible Test User - bubba'
        compartment_id: "{{ compartment_ocid }}"
      register: result
    - set_fact:
        bubba_ocid: "{{ result.user['id'] }}"
    - debug:
        msg: "Created bubba {{ bubba_ocid }}"
```

Example 16-21 will create the group and add the user to the group. It will return the list of group members as a fact.

Example 16-21 Assigning a User to a Group

```
- name: Assign user to group
    oci_identity_user_group_membership:
      user_id: "{{ bubba_ocid }}"
      group_id: "{{ object_reader_ocid }}"
      compartment_id: "{{ compartment_ocid}}"
    register: result
  - set_fact:
      user_group_membership_ocid: "{{ result.user_group_membership['id'] }}"
```

The task in Example 16-22 will assign a password to the user.

Example 16-22 Setting a User's Password

```
- name: Create user password
    oci_identity_ui_password:
      user_id: "{{ bubba_ocid }}"
    register: result
  - set_fact:
      user_password: "{{ result.ui_password['SECUREPASSWORD'] }}"
```

Networking Tasks
The following tasks are used to manage basic networking functionality:

- Creating a VCN
- Creating an Internet gateway
- Creating a routing table
- Creating a security group

The task shown in Example 16-23 will return a fact with the VCN OCID.

Example 16-23 Creating a VCN

```
- name: Creating a VCN
  oci_network_vcn:
    compartment_id: "{{ compartment_ocid }}"
    display_name: "{{ vcn_name }}"
    cidr_block: "{{ vcn_cidr }}"
    dns_label: "{{ vcn_dns_label }}"
  register: result
- set_fact:
    vcn_id: "{{ result.vcn.id }}"
    vcn: "{{ result.vcn }}"
```

The task shown in Example 16-24 will create a new Internet gateway. The task will return the OCID of the new gateway.

Example 16-24   Creating an Internet Gateway

```
- name: Create a new Internet Gateway
  oci_network_internet_gateway:
    compartment_id: "{{ compartment_ocid }}"
    vcn_id: "{{ vcn_id }}"
    name: "{{ vcn_ig_name }}"
    is_enabled: 'yes'
    state: 'present'
  register: result
- set_fact:
    ig_id: "{{ result.internet_gateway.id }}"
```

The task shown in Example 16-25 will create a new routing table with rules. The OCID in the routing table will be returned as a fact.

Example 16-25   Creating a Routing Table

```
- name: Creating a route table
  oci_network_route_table:
    compartment_id: "{{ compartment_ocid }}"
    vcn_id: "{{ vcn_id }}"
    name: "{{ routing_table_name }}"
    route_rules: "{{ routing_table_rules }}"
    state: 'present'
  register: result
- set_fact:
    rt_id: "{{ result.route_table.id }}"
```

The task shown in Example 16-26 will create a network security group. The OCID of the new group will be set as a fact.

Example 16-26   Creating a Security Group

```
- name: creating a network security group
  oci_network_security_group:
    compartment_id: "{{ compartment_ocid }}"
    display_name: "{{ network_security_group_name }}"
    vcn_id: "{{ vcn_ocid }}"
  register: result

- set_fact:
    network_security_group_id: "{{result.network_security_group.id}}"
```

Storage Tasks

The following tasks are used to manage basic storage functionality:

- Getting object storage namespace
- Listing all objects from all the buckets in object storage
- Creating file storage
- Creating a block volume
- Attaching a block volume

The task shown in Example 16-27 will return the object storage namespace. The namespace will be returned as output.

Example 16-27   Getting Object Storage Namespace

```
- name: Get namespace name
  hosts: localhost
  collections:
    - oracle.oci
  tasks:
    - name: Get namespace name
      oci_object_storage_namespace_facts:
      register: output
    - name: Print namespace name
      debug:
        msg: "{{ output }}"
```

The task shown in Example 16-28 will list all objects from all buckets in object storage.

Example 16-28   Listing All Objects from All the Buckets in Object Storage

```
- name: List objects from all the buckets
  hosts: localhost
  collections:
    - oracle.oci
  vars:
    # common vars
    bucket_name: "bucket"
    object_name: "object"

  tasks:
    - name: Get all the buckets in the namespace
      oci_object_storage_bucket_facts:
        namespace_name: "{{ object_namespace }}"
        compartment_id: "{{ compartment_ocid }}"
      register: ocibuckets
```

```
- name: Get all objects from all the buckets
  oci_object_storage_object_facts:
    namespace_name: "{{ namespace_name }}"
    bucket_name: "{{ item.name }}"
  with_items: "{{ ocibuckets.buckets }}"
  register: output
- name: Print the list
  debug:
    msg: 'Bucket: {{item.item.name}}, Objects: {{item.objects}}'
  loop: "{{output.results}}"
  loop_control:
    label: "{{item.item.name}}"
```

You can also manage resources like NFS file systems using Ansible with OCI. The task shown in Example 16-29 will create a file storage share that can then be mounted using NFS. The filesystem OCID will be set as a fact.

Example 16-29   Creating File Storage

```
- name: "Create File Storage"
  oci_file_storage_file_system:
      compartment_id: '{{ compartment_ocid }}'
      availability_domain: '{{ availability_domain }}'
      display_name: '{{ filesystem_name }}'
      state: 'present'
  register: result
- set_fact:
    file_system_id: "{{ result.file_system.id }}"
```

The task shown in Example 16-30 will create a new block volume. This will return the OCID of the new block volume as a fact.

Example 16-30   Creating a Block Volume

```
- name: Create a block volume
  oci_blockstorage_volume:
    availability_domain: "{{ availability_domain }}"
    compartment_id: "{{ compartment_ocid }}"
    name: "{{ block_name }}"
  register: result
- set_fact:
    block_ocid: "{{result.volume.id }}"
```

The task shown in Example 16-31 will attach a block volume to a compute instance. The attachment confirmation will be returned as a fact.

Example 16-31 Attaching a Block Volume

```
- name: attach volume
  oci_compute_volume_attachment:
    instance_id: "{{ compute_instance_ocid }}"
    type: "iscsi"
    volume_id: "{{ block_ocid }}"
    compartment_id: "{{ compartment_ocid }}"
  register: result
- set_fact:
    volume_attachment_details: "{{ result.volume_attachment }}"
```

Compute Tasks

The following tasks are used to manage basic networking functionality:

- Creating an instance
- Stopping an instance
- Resetting an instance
- Deleting an instance

The task shown in Example 16-32 will create a new instance—in this case, an E4 shape with 7 cores and 11 GB of RAM. The ssh will be stored in the file /data/ssh_public_key.

Example 16-32 Creating an Instance

```
- name: Launch/create an instance using an image with custom boot volume size
  oci_instance:
    name: myinstance1
    availability_domain: ""{{ availability_domain }}""
    compartment_id: "{{ compartment_ocid }}"
    shape: "VM.Standard.E4.Flex"
    shape_config:
      ocpus: 7
      memory_in_gbs: 11
    source_details:
      source_type: image
      image_id: "{{ osimage_ocid }}"
      boot_volume_size_in_gbs: 100
    create_vnic_details:
        assign_public_ip: True
        hostname_label: "{{ compute_instance_name }}"
        subnet_id: "{{ subnet_ocid }}"
      metadata:
        ssh_authorized_keys: "{{ lookup('file', /data/ssh_public_key ) }}"
    register: result
```

The task shown in Example 16-33 will stop an instance. Optionally, you can set the state to **startr**, **softreset**, **reset**, and **softstop**.

Example 16-33   Stopping an Instance

```
- name: Stop an instance
  oci_instance:
     id: " {{compute_instance_ocid }}"
state: "stopped"
```

Example 16-34 is almost the same as stopping the instance, but this example shows how to change the state to **reset**.

Example 16-34   Resetting an Instance

```
- name: Reset an instance
  oci_instance:
     id: "{{compute_instance_ocid }}"
     state: "reset"
```

The task shown in Example 16-35 will delete the instance and remove the boot volume.

Example 16-35   Deleting an Instance

```
- name: Terminate/delete an instance and preserve boot volume
  oci_instance:
     id: "{{compute_instance_ocid }}"
     state: "absent"
preserve_boot_volume: yes
```

If you want to delete the boot volume, set **preserve_boot_volume** to **no**.

Summary

In this chapter, you learned about playbooks and how to write them. You also learned a few of the basic tasks that can be done in OCI using Ansible. This is just the start of all the capabilities that are available to the team for building, securing, and running an environment. You can see more examples at https://github.com/oracle/oci-cli.

In the next chapter, we will put all this information together and use OLAM to automate the creation of an application.

Ansible—Installing and Configuring OLAM

Oracle Linux Automation Manager, or OLAM, is a web portal based on the AWX project that provides an enterprise-grade web interface for executing and monitoring Ansible jobs, complete with all the necessary security controls for complex enterprise deployments. This chapter will cover the installation of an OLAM 2.0 single-node system and highlight its major features.

One of the main advantages of OLAM, in addition to being a full-stack technology, is its ability to empower any user in the organization to run a playbook. This capability promotes self-service and enhances repeatability for less experienced members of the DevSecOps team. Imagine a nonsecurity professional being able to apply an organization's security settings to a server or application without needing the assistance of a more senior team member. This task is accomplished by leveraging the power of a playbook, usually written by senior team members, which can then be executed by anyone with the appropriate access.

Installation

Installing OLAM is a fairly straightforward task. In this chapter, we will build a single hybrid node. This approach works well for most small to medium cloud deployments, enabling the DevSecOps team to have their own OLAM server to empower the full stack automation. There are three basic steps to this process: preparing Linux, installing the PostgreSQL database, and then installing OLAM.

Preparing Linux

For the single-node installation used in this chapter, you can use two OCPUs and 16 GB of RAM. You also can use a 500 GB boot disk in a single boot volume group, with the following file system layout. The /var file system might appear to be larger than what you are accustomed to, but this size is needed on any control node because the space is used for OLAM to store containers, logs, and other files. There is also a fair amount of unallocated space, which will be useful later if (and this is not uncommon) /var needs to be grown quickly. On single-node deployments, the database also uses space. A summary of the file systems is shown in Table 17-1.

Table 17-1   Recommended File System Layout

File System	Space
/boot	1 GB
/	70 GB
/var	20 GB
/var/log	5 GB
/home	10 GB
Swap	8 GB
Unallocated	386 GB

Additionally, the system is added in DNS as olam.m57.local.

Next, you will need to open the firewall. This will allow communication to the control node functionality, as well as a port 27199 for mesh communication. This step is accomplished as the root user with the following commands. The **--permanent** option enables the Linux firewall to use these settings after a reboot.

```
firewall-cmd --add-port=27199/tcp --permanent
firewall-cmd --add-service=http --permanent
firewall-cmd --add-service=https --permanent
firewall-cmd --reload
```

Optionally, if you will be using an external database, you will need to open port 5432 on the hosts. You can use the following commands to do this:

```
firewall-cmd --add-port=5432/tcp --permanent
firewall-cmd --reload
```

Next, you will need to add an additional software report to the host. If you're using the Unbreakable Linux Network (ULN) or the OCI base Operating System Management Hub (OSMH) to get patches, make sure the host has the following repos added:

- ol8_x86_64_automation2
- ol8_x86_64_addons
- ol8_x86_64_baseos_latest
- ol8_x86_64_UEKR7
- ol8_x86_64_appstream
- ol8_x86_64_automation2

If this system is using **dnf**, you can add the repos by using the following process. First, add in the OLAM repo:

```
dnf install -y oraclelinux-automation-manager-release-el8
```

Then enable the list of required repos with the following command:

```
dnf config-manager --enable ol8_automation2 ol8_addons ol8_UEKR7 ol8_
  appstream
```

Setting Up PostgreSQL

OLAM uses PostgreSQL as its database. On the sample installation, you will configure the database on the same host that OLAM is running on, but in an enterprise installation, the database would normally be on a clustered pair of hosts. Either PostgreSQL 12 or 13 can be used. For this example, you will use PostgreSQL 13. To do this, reset PostgreSQL and enable the version 13 module by using the following commands:

```
dnf module reset postgresql
dnf module enable postgresql:13
```

Next, install and initialize the database with the following commands:

```
dnf install postgresql-server
postgresql-setup --initdb
```

Next, for security, adjust the password storage mechanism to scram-sha0256:

```
sed -i "s/#password_encryption.*/password_encryption = scram-sha-256/"
  /var/lib/pgsql/data/postgresql.conf
```

Next, start the database with the following command. This will also set PostgreSQL to restart when the system boots.

```
systemctl enable --now postgresql
```

Wait a second, and then verify that the database is running:

```
systemctl status postgresql
```

Look for the Active field to show **active** (running), as in Example 17-1.

Example 17-1   Checking PostgreSQL Status

```
[root@olam ~]# systemctl status postgresql
• postgresql.service - PostgreSQL database server
  Loaded: loaded (/usr/lib/systemd/system/postgresql.service; enabled; vendor
  preset: disabled)
   Active: active (running) since Mon 2023-01-16 14:31:24 EST; 1min 47s ago
  Process: 18635 ExecStartPre=/usr/libexec/postgresql-check-db-dir postgresql
  (code=exited, status=0/SUCCESS)
```

```
Main PID: 18638 (postmaster)
   Tasks: 8 (limit: 99956)
  Memory: 17.0M
  CGroup: /system.slice/postgresql.service
          ├─18638 /usr/bin/postmaster -D /var/lib/pgsql/data
          ├─18639 postgres: logger
          ├─18641 postgres: checkpointer
          ├─18642 postgres: background writer
          ├─18643 postgres: walwriter
          ├─18644 postgres: autovacuum launcher
          ├─18645 postgres: stats collector
          ├─18646 postgres: logical replication launcher
```

Next, add a database user for AWX by using the following command:

```
su - postgres -c "createuser -S -P awx"
```

The command will prompt for a password:

```
[root@olam ~]# su - postgres -c "createuser -S -P awx"
Enter password for new role:
Enter it again:
```

Next, create the database for AWX:

```
su - postgres -c "createdb -O awx awx"
```

At this point, you will need to edit a few configuration files. The /var/lib/pgsql/data/ pg_hba.conf file is a configuration file used by the PostgreSQL database management system. It is used to configure the host-based authentication (HBA) rules for the system, which determine who is allowed to connect to the database and from where. The file typically includes a list of IP addresses, subnets, and/or hostnames that are allowed to connect, along with the authentication method to be used for each.

First, add the following line to the pg_hba.conf file:

```
host  all  all 0.0.0.0/0 scram-sha-256
```

Next, edit the /var/lib/pgsql/data/postgresql.ZZconf file. This configuration file is used by the PostgreSQL database management system. It contains a variety of settings that control the behavior and performance of the PostgreSQL server. In the CONNECTIONS AND AUTHENTICATION section, add the following line. This will have PostgreSQL listen on the public IP of the database host. Don't forget to replace olam.m57.local with your server name.

```
listen_addresses = 'olam.m57.local'
```

The last step is to restart the database:

```
systemctl restart postgresql
```

Once the database is restarted, verify that it is running by using the **systemctl status postgresql** command again. Also, verify that PostgreSQL is listening on the correct IP address. You do this with the following command:

```
netstat -at | grep LISTEN | grep postgres
```

Now, you should see an entry with the hostname postgres as shown:

```
[root@olam ~]# netstat -at | grep LISTEN | grep postgres
tcp        0      0 olam.m57.local:postgres 0.0.0.0:*                LISTEN
```

Installing OLAM

Installing the actual OLAM software is fairly easy because the bulk of the install is in a container. OLAM 2.0 leverages containers to simplify installation of the software, as well as patching and upgrades. There are a few steps to do, which we will cover here:

- Installing the software
- Configuring Redis
- Configuring the database connection
- Installing the container using **podman**
- Creating the initial OLAM configuration
- Configuring Nginx
- Provisioning the OLAM instance
- Cleaning up a few items

The following steps will be done as root, but later we will switch to the awx user.

First, install the software using **dnf**; this step will install all the prerequisite software such as Python, Nginx, and git. Use the following command to do this:

```
dnf -y install ol-automation-manager
```

Next, configure Redis (Remote Dictionary Server), which is an open-source, in-memory key-value data store. It is often used as a database, a cache, a message broker, or for real-time data streaming. Redis supports a wide range of data structures such as strings, hashes, lists, sets, and sorted sets, with atomic operations on them. It also supports advanced data structures such as HyperLogLogs and bitmaps.

Now, append the following lines to the /etc/redis.conf config files:

```
unixsocket /var/run/redis/redis.sock
unixsocketperm 775
```

In cluster installations, you will need to copy the file /etc/tower/SECRET_KEY to the other nodes in the cluster. Make sure the file owner and group are set to **awx**.

Next, in the /etc/tower/settings.py file, edit the entry for CLUSTER_HOST_ID = to point to your host. The default value is **awx**, and this should be changed.

Next, in the same file, you will need to update the database connection information. Set the PASSWORD, HOST, and PORT used when you set up the PostgreSQL database, as shown in Example 17-2.

Example 17-2   Database Configuration

```
DATABASES = {
    'default': {
        'ATOMIC_REQUESTS': True,
        'ENGINE': 'awx.main.db.profiled_pg',
        'NAME': 'awx',
        'USER': 'awx',
        'PASSWORD': 'DATABASE_PASSWORD',
        'HOST': 'DATABASE_HOST_NAME',
        'PORT': '5432',
    }
}
```

Next, you will become the awx user, and run the following commands to install the container:

```
su -l awx -s /bin/bash
podman system migrate
podman pull container-registry.oracle.com/oracle_linux_automation_manager/
  olam-ee:latest
```

The podman container pull is the action of downloading a container image from a registry (such as Docker Hub) to the local machine. Once the image is downloaded, it can be used to create and run new containers.

Once the pull is complete, you can initiate the OLAM instance with the following command:

```
awx-manage migrate
```

Next, create the initial OLAM user with the **amx-manage createsuperuser** command. This command will also specify the username and admin email address. The format is **awx-manage createsuperuser --username admin --email email**. When the command is run, you will also set the admin password. The process should look similar to the following:

```
[awx@olam ~]$ awx-manage createsuperuser --username admin --email erik@m57.local
Password:
Password (again):
Superuser created successfully.
[awx@olam ~]$
```

Now go back to the root user so that Nginx can be configured.

The first step is to create an SSL key for the Nginx server. You can create a test certificate with the following command:

```
openssl req -x509 -nodes -days 365 -newkey rsa:2048 -keyout /etc/tower/
  tower.key -out /etc/tower/tower.crt
```

Answer the information as prompted, making sure that the common name is the system's name in DNS that users will use to access the system.

Next, replace the default nginx.conf file with a new one. Edit the /etc/nginx/nginx.conf file to look like the one shown in Example 17-3.

Example 17-3   Nginx Configuration

```
user nginx;
worker_processes auto;
error_log /var/log/nginx/error.log;
pid /run/nginx.pid;

# Load dynamic modules. See /usr/share/doc/nginx/README.dynamic.
include /usr/share/nginx/modules/*.conf;

events {
    worker_connections 1024;
}

http {
    log_format  main  '$remote_addr - $remote_user [$time_local] "$request" '
                      '$status $body_bytes_sent "$http_referer" '
                      '"$http_user_agent" "$http_x_forwarded_for"';

    access_log  /var/log/nginx/access.log  main;

    sendfile            on;
    tcp_nopush          on;
    tcp_nodelay         on;
    keepalive_timeout   65;
    types_hash_max_size 2048;

    include             /etc/nginx/mime.types;

    default_type        application/octet-stream;

    # Load modular configuration files from the /etc/nginx/conf.d directory.
    # See http://nginx.org/en/docs/ngx_core_module.html#include
    # for more information.
    include /etc/nginx/conf.d/*.conf;
}
```

Now, you can configure a single-node system. This is mainly done as the awx user, so switch to that user for the next few commands:

```
su -l awx -s /bin/bash
```

Next, provision the instance, setting the hostname to the system name. Use the following command to do this, replacing **olam.m57.local** with your hostname:

```
awx-manage provision_instance --hostname=olam.m57.local --node_type=hybrid
```

Then register the control plane using the following command:

```
awx-manage register_default_execution_environments
```

Next, create the initial queue for jobs. It is used to run playbooks:

```
awx-manage register_queue --queuename=default --hostnames=olam.m57.local
```

Then register the control plane:

```
awx-manage register_queue --queuename=controlplane --hostnames=olam.m57.local
```

Now exit the awx user. The last step before starting the system is to clean up the Receptor. The Receptor is responsible for managing nodes, and it enables the execution of playbooks, tasks, and workflows. It also provides real-time feedback to the OLAM server so that the status of the execution can be displayed in the web interface. The Receptor can be installed on a remote node, and it communicates with the OLAM server using a secure connection.

Edit the file /etc/receptor/receptor.conf. Make sure you update the node id to match your host. A sample file is shown in Example 17-4.

Example 17-4   receptor.conf

```
---
- node:
    id: olam.m57.local

- log-level: debug

- tcp-listener:
    port: 27199

- control-service:
    service: control
    filename: /var/run/receptor/receptor.sock

- work-command:
    worktype: local
    command: /var/lib/ol-automation-manager/venv/awx/bin/ansible-runner
    params: worker
    allowruntimeparams: true
#    verifysignature: true
```

Next, start OLAM:

```
systemctl enable --now ol-automation-manager.service
```

Now you can load a set of initial demo data. This will create a demo project and the related data. This is done as the awx user:

```
awx-manage create_preload_data
```

You are now done with a single-node installation. To access the system, point your browser to the host. If you used the demo SSL key, you will need to accept the SSL key error. This error is shown in Figure 17-1.

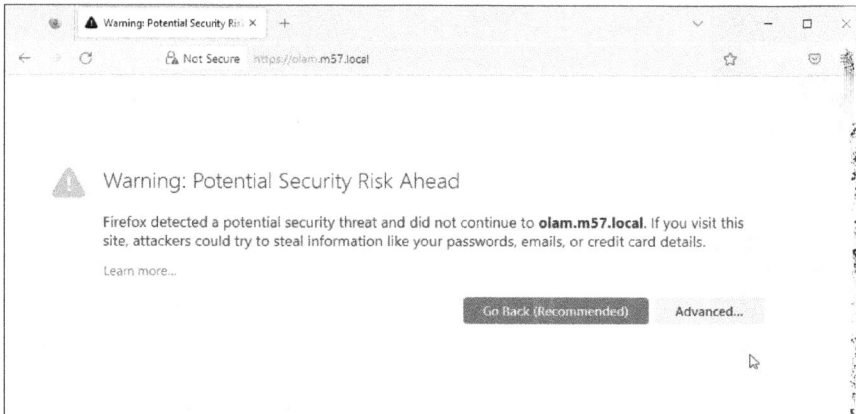

Figure 17-1   SSL Warning

Depending on your browser, the method to accept the test SSL certificate varies. For this example, go ahead and accept the certificate. You will then be prompted with the OLAM login screen, as shown in Figure 17-2.

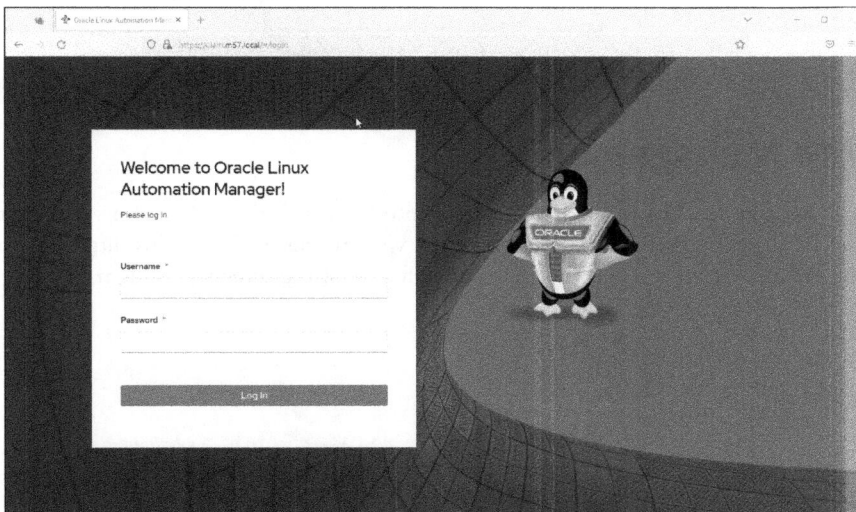

Figure 17-2   OLAM Login

Log in as the Admin user you created. You should then see the default landing page, also know as the main dashboard, shown in Figure 17-3.

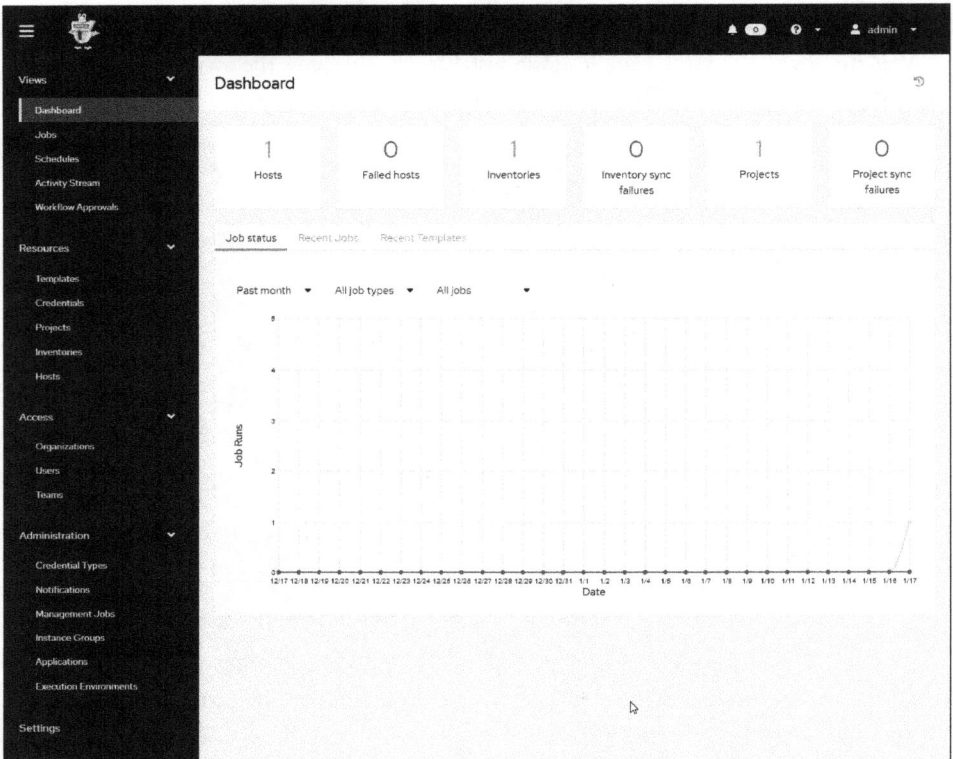

Figure 17-3   OLAM Landing Page

OLAM Management

You can manage OLAM through a web user interface, at the command line, and even with an API. In this section, we will cover the web interface. To use this interface, you use the main navigation menu found on the left side of the screen, as shown in Figure 17-4.

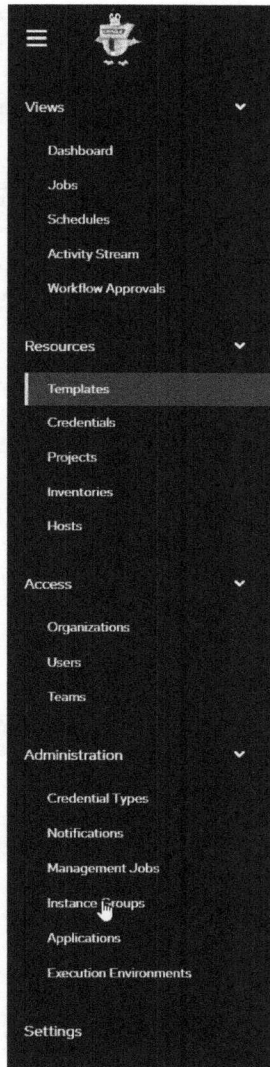

Figure 17-4   OLAM Navigation Menu

This navigation menu gives you access to the following options:

- **Views:** Enables you to manage and access various views of data and resources within the system. This includes views of job templates, workflows, inventory, credentials, and more, which can be customized and filtered to suit specific needs and use cases. Chapter 16, "Using Ansible in OCI," has additional information about this section.

- **Resources:** Provides access to and management of the various resources that are used by the system. This includes resources such as inventories, job templates, workflows, projects, and credentials, as well as other resources that are relevant to managing and automating infrastructure. The Resources menu allows users to create, edit, and delete these resources, as well as to manage access and permissions for different users and teams.
- **Access:** Enables you to manage and control access to various resources within the system. This includes access control for resources such as job templates, workflows, inventory, credentials, and more. The Access menu allows administrators to specify which users and teams have access to specific resources and what level of access they have (for example, read-only, full access). This menu can be useful for enforcing security and compliance policies, and for ensuring that sensitive resources are only accessible by authorized users. By controlling access through the Access menu, administrators can ensure that the right users have the right level of access to the right resources at the right time, improving the overall security and efficiency of the system.
- **Administration:** Enables you to manage and configure the various administrative and system settings for the OLAM installation. This includes settings such as authentication and authorization, user management, system configuration, and more. The Administration menu is intended for use by system administrators and is typically only accessible by users with administrative privileges. The settings and options available through the Administration menu can be used to customize the behavior and operation of OLAM to meet specific needs and use cases and to ensure that the system is secure, reliable, and efficient.
- **Settings:** Enables you to manage and configure various system settings and preferences. This includes settings such as user preferences, system-wide settings, and notifications, among others. The Settings menu allows users to customize their experience within the OLAM user interface, such as setting their preferred language, configuring notification preferences, and specifying default settings for various parts of the system. The options available through the Settings menu can be used to personalize the behavior and operation of OLAM to suit specific user needs and preferences, improving the overall user experience and efficiency.

Resource Management

OLAM resources are the components that make up the OLAM system and are used to manage and automate IT infrastructure. The following OLAM resources are managed via the web interface:

- **Templates:** A predefined set of tasks that can be run against one or more inventory hosts.
- **Credentials:** Securely stored information, such as passwords, keys, and certificates, that can be used in job templates to access remote systems.

- **Projects:** A collection of playbooks, roles, and other files that can be used in job templates.
- **Inventories:** A collection of hosts and groups used to define the systems that OLAM will manage.
- **Hosts:** A collection of targets that OLAM can manage. A host can be an operating system, a switch, a firewall, or any other managed system.

Templates

OLAM *templates* are predefined sets of tasks that can be run against one or more managed systems or servers in the OLAM inventory. In OLAM, templates are created from playbooks, which are written in the Ansible language and specify the actions that should be taken to automate various IT infrastructure tasks.

OLAM templates provide a way to automate IT infrastructure tasks in a consistent and repeatable manner, and can be used for a wide range of tasks, such as software installation, configuration management, and more. Templates can be customized and parameterized, allowing for flexibility and adaptability to different use cases and requirements.

Templates can also be run on demand, on a schedule, or as part of a workflow, making it easier to manage and automate IT infrastructure at scale. When a template is run, OLAM tracks the progress of the tasks, provides real-time updates and notifications, and generates reports, making it easy to understand the status and results of the automation process.

A template has six subsections, broken into tabs: Details, Access, Notifications, Schedules, Jobs, and Survey. To access these sections, click the template. This way, you can see the details for the template, as shown in Figure 17-5.

Figure 17-5   Template Details

The following are some of the key details included in OLAM templates:

- **Playbook:** The playbook is the core component of the template and is written in the Ansible language. It specifies the tasks and actions that should be taken to automate various IT infrastructure tasks.
- **Inventory:** The inventory is a collection of hosts and groups used to define the systems that OLAM will manage. The inventory is associated with the template, and the template will be run against the specified hosts in the inventory.
- **Credentials:** Credentials, such as passwords, keys, and certificates, are securely stored in OLAM and can be used in templates to access remote systems.
- **Variables:** Variables can be used to customize and parameterize the template, allowing for flexibility and adaptability to different use cases and requirements.
- **Job Type:** The job type specifies the type of automation that will be performed, such as check mode, standard job, and cloud inventory update, among others. These job types include
    - **Standard Job:** This is the most common job type and is used to run a playbook against a specified inventory.
    - **Check Job:** This job type runs a playbook in check mode, which means that the playbook will be executed in a simulated environment, without making any actual changes to the systems being managed. It is useful for testing and validating playbooks before running them in a live environment.
    - **Project Update:** This job type is used to update a source control repository, such as Git or Subversion (SVN), used by a project in OLAM.
    - **Sync Job:** This job type is used to synchronize the contents of a source control repository, such as Git or Subversion, with the local copy used by OLAM.
    - **Ad Hoc Command:** This job type allows for the execution of ad hoc commands, either on a single host or across multiple hosts in an inventory.
    - **Workflow Job:** This job type allows for the creation of complex, multistep automation workflows, allowing for the execution of multiple jobs in a specific order, with defined dependencies and conditions.
    - **Cloud Inventory Update:** This job type is used to update the inventory information for cloud-based systems, such as Oracle Cloud Infrastructure (OCI), Amazon Web Services (AWS), or Microsoft Azure, and to keep the inventory data up-to-date.
- **Created:** This shows when the template was last created.
- **Last Modified:** This shows when the template was last modified.
- **Verbosity:** This shows the default verbosity level. There are five levels, starting with 0 and going up to 4. As the level increases, more details are shown about how the job ran and the communication to the target. Normally, only levels 0 and 1 are used.
- **Job Slicing:** Ansible job slicing refers to the ability in OLAM to split a single playbook run into multiple, smaller jobs. This allows for the playbook to be executed in smaller, more manageable chunks, making it easier to manage and

monitor the progress of the automation process. Job slicing can be useful in a variety of scenarios, including when working with large inventories or when dealing with long-running playbooks that may take a significant amount of time to complete. When a job is sliced into smaller pieces, it becomes easier to track progress, identify any potential issues, and adjust the automation process as needed. In OLAM, job slicing can be configured through the use of a slicing specification, which determines the size and structure of the individual jobs. The slicing specification can be based on a variety of factors, including the number of hosts, the size of the playbook, and the available resources of the system.

The next section is Access, as shown in Figure 17-6.

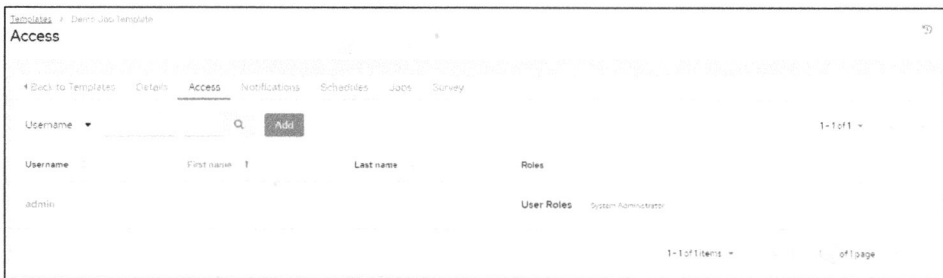

Figure 17-6   Template Access

The Access tab will show which users and groups have access to the template and what their level of access is. These roles include the following:

- **System Administrator:** This role provides full access to all templates, including the ability to create, modify, and delete templates.
- **User:** This role provides read-only access to templates, and users with this role cannot modify or delete templates.
- **Observer:** This role provides read-only access to templates and also includes the ability to view job details and history.

In addition to these predefined roles, custom roles can be created to provide more granular control over template access. For example, a custom role could be created that allows users to modify templates, but only those templates that they have created. To manage access to templates, users are assigned to roles, and the roles are then granted specific permissions to access templates. These permissions can be assigned at the organization or project level, allowing organizations to fine-tune access control to templates as needed.

Next up is the Notifications tab, as shown in Figure 17-7.

This tab will show what notification rules are assigned to the template. This also allows an administrator to select what stats trigger a notification event. The three states are Job Start, Job Success, and Job Failure. It is not uncommon for DevSecOps teams to notify using the notification subsystem only when a job fails. Notifications are covered later.

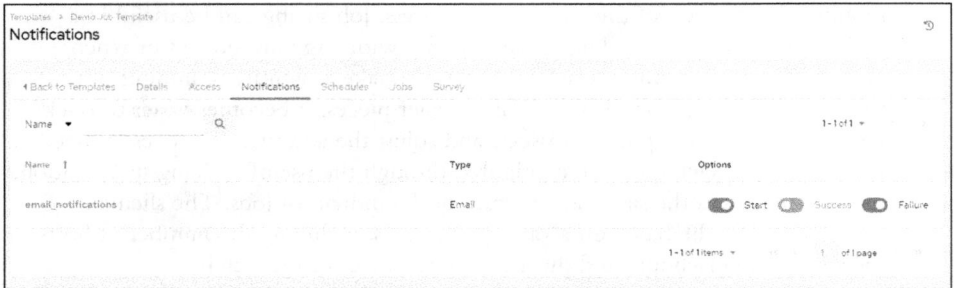

Figure 17-7   Template Notifications

Next up is the Schedules tab, as shown in Figure 17-8.

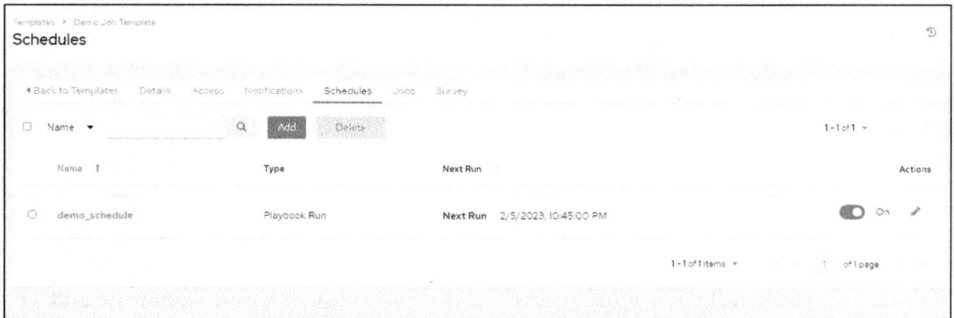

Figure 17-8   Template Schedules

This tab will show what schedules are set for the template. An administrator can select the pencil icon to modify the schedule.

The Jobs tab is up next, as shown in Figure 17-9.

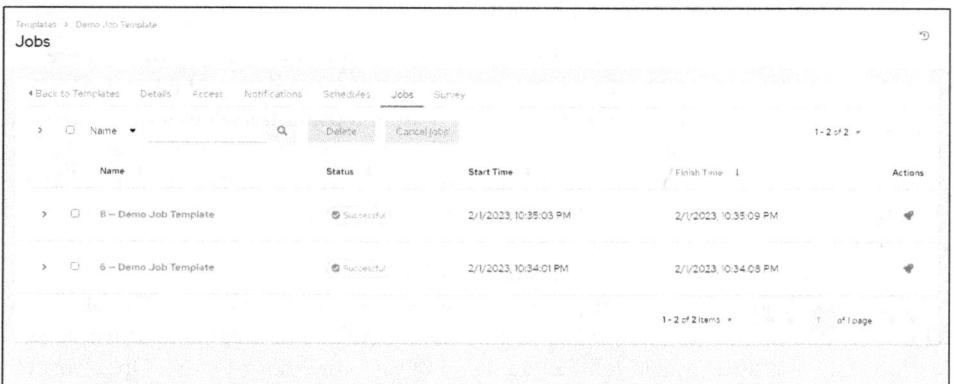

Figure 17-9   Template Jobs

This tab will show the history of when the template was run. You can also click an instance to drill down to see the details of the job. This will redirect you to the Jobs view under the dashboard.

Finally, there is one last tab to explore: the Survey tab, as shown in Figure 17-10.

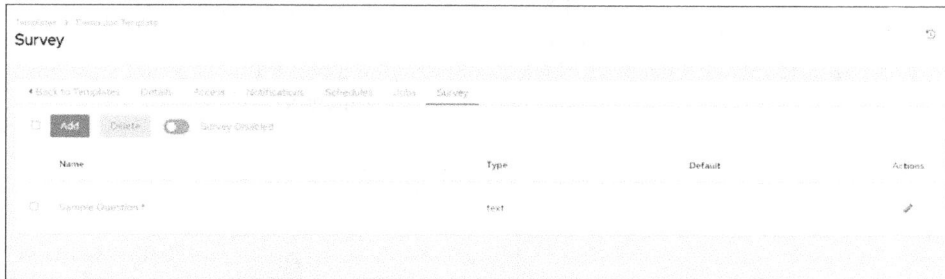

Figure 17-10   Template Survey

Survey is an optional tab and may be blank on a template. An OLAM Template Survey is a feature that allows users to collect input from end users when launching a job template. The survey collects information that can be used to customize the execution of the job, such as providing specific variables or configuration parameters. A survey is created as a part of a job template, and it can contain a variety of questions and response types, such as single-line text, multiline text, password, number, select, and more. The survey can also include optional questions, required questions, and questions with default values. When users launch a job template with a survey, they are presented with the survey questions, and they must answer each question before the job can be launched. The answers to the survey questions are then used as variables in the job execution, allowing users to customize the execution of the job based on their specific needs.

In summary, an OLAM Template Survey is a feature that allows users to collect input from end users when launching a job template. The survey provides a way to customize the execution of the job, and it is created as a part of a job template in OLAM.

Overall, OLAM templates provide a powerful and flexible way to automate and manage IT infrastructure, streamlining workflows and improving overall efficiency.

Credentials

OLAM *credentials* are stored authentication information used to connect to target systems, cloud infrastructure, or other resources that are required to execute an Ansible playbook. This information can include username and password, SSH keys, or API keys, among others.

In OLAM, credentials can be managed centrally and securely, and they can be used across multiple job templates, workflows, and projects. This makes it easy to manage and reuse authentication information, helping to ensure that sensitive information is kept secure and is not duplicated across different playbooks and templates.

OLAM supports several types of credentials that are used to authenticate with different types of systems, infrastructure, or resources. The most common credential types include the following:

- **Machine:** Used to authenticate with remote servers, such as Linux or Windows servers. This type of credential includes information such as username and password, SSH key, or private key file.
- **Source Control:** Used to authenticate with source control management systems, such as Git or Subversion. This type of credential includes information such as username and password, or SSH key.
- **Cloud:** Used to authenticate with cloud infrastructure, such as AWS, Google Cloud, or Azure. This type of credential includes information such as access keys, secrets, and tenant IDs.
- **Network:** Used to authenticate with network devices, such as routers or switches. This type of credential includes information such as username and password or SSH key.
- **Vault:** Used to store encrypted credentials, such as passwords or secrets. This type of credential is encrypted using Ansible Vault.

Credentials can also be assigned to individual users or teams, providing a way to control access to sensitive information. Additionally, OLAM supports the use of encrypted credentials, allowing organizations to securely store sensitive information.

You can view all of the configured credential types by selecting **Credentials** from the menu to open the tab shown in Figure 17-11.

Figure 17-11 Configured Credentials

Next, select a credential to see its details. Different types may show additional details, but the format will be similar to the example shown in Figure 17-12.

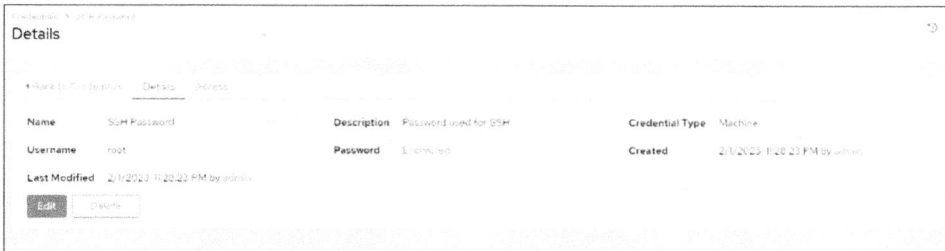

Figure 17-12 Credential Details

In summary, OLAM credentials are stored authentication information used to connect to target systems, cloud infrastructure, or other resources that are required to execute an Ansible playbook. They can be managed centrally, reused across multiple templates, and assigned to users or teams, providing a secure and centralized way to manage authentication information.

Projects

An OLAM *project* is a collection of Ansible playbooks, roles, and related files that are organized together in a single repository. It represents a unit of automation work in OLAM and is used to manage and organize playbooks, inventory, and other related files. A project in OLAM can be linked to a version control system, such as Git or Subversion, allowing users to manage playbooks and related files in a central repository. This makes it easy to manage changes, collaborate with other team members, and ensure that all playbooks are up-to-date. OLAM projects are used as the basis for creating job templates, which are used to run playbooks and manage execution. You can see the list of all the projects from this page. A job template in OLAM includes information such as the playbook to be executed, the inventory to use, and the credentials required to connect to target systems. You can list all of the projects in OLAM by selecting **Resources > Projects** to open the page shown in Figure 17-13.

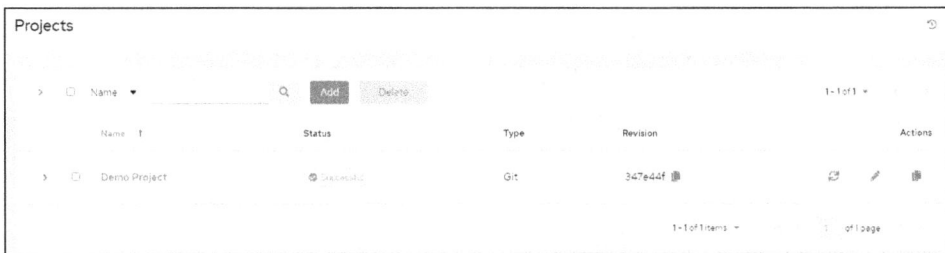

Figure 17-13 Projects List

From here, you can see all projects, and simply click the project name to drill down to the details of the project. A Details page is shown in Figure 17-14.

Figure 17-14 Project Details

The *Project Base Path* is a setting in OLAM that specifies the location within a version control system (VCS) repository where the Ansible playbooks and related files for a project are stored. The base path is used to determine the contents of the project in OLAM, and the playbooks and related files that are available for use in workflows and job templates. The Project Base Path setting is typically set when a project is first created in OLAM. For example, if the base path for a project is set to /ansible/playbooks, OLAM will look for playbooks and related files in the /ansible/playbooks directory within the VCS repository. Any playbooks and related files that are stored outside of the base path will not be available for use in OLAM.

The *Project Cache Timeout* is a setting in OLAM that determines the length of time that the cached version of a project in OLAM will be used before it is updated. The cache timeout is a performance optimization that reduces the number of times that OLAM needs to access a VCS repository, such as Git or Subversion, to retrieve the latest version of the project. The cache timeout is specified in seconds and determines the interval between cache updates. For example, if the cache timeout is set to 600 seconds (10 minutes), the cached version of the project will be used for 10 minutes before OLAM accesses the VCS repository to retrieve an updated version of the project.

The Project Cache Timeout setting is a balance between performance and accuracy. Setting a short cache timeout will ensure that the project in OLAM is always up-to-date but may increase the load on the VCS repository and reduce performance. Setting a longer cache timeout will improve performance but may result in outdated playbooks being used if the cache is not updated frequently enough.

Project Sync is a feature in OLAM that allows you to synchronize the contents of a project with a VCS, such as Git or Subversion. The sync operation pulls the latest changes from the VCS repository into OLAM, updating the project with any new or modified playbooks, roles, or other files. By synchronizing the contents of a project in OLAM with a VCS, you can ensure that all playbooks and related files are up-to-date and consistent across the entire team. This makes it easy to manage changes, collaborate with other team members, and track the history of changes made to playbooks and related files. Project Sync is performed on a regular basis, either manually or automatically, and can be scheduled to run at a specific time or triggered by an event, such as a push to the VCS repository.

In summary, an OLAM project is a collection of Ansible playbooks, roles, and related files that are organized together in a single repository. Projects are used as the basis for creating job templates and provide a central repository for managing playbooks, inventory, and other related files. They are linked to a version control system and make it easy to manage changes, collaborate with other team members, and ensure that playbooks are up-to-date.

Inventory

An *inventory* is a collection of information about the servers, devices, and other resources that are managed by OLAM. The inventory defines the scope of the resources that OLAM can access and manage, and it is used to identify and group the resources that are to be managed by OLAM. An inventory is specified using an inventory file, which is a text file that is written in a specific format and is stored on the Ansible control node. The inventory file is used to specify the hosts, or remote servers, that Ansible is to manage, as well as any variables or connections that are required for those hosts.

An OLAM inventory can be as simple or as complex as needed, and it can be used to manage a small number of hosts, or a large number of hosts spread across multiple environments. The inventory can be organized into groups, and each group can have its own set of variables and connections.

To see the list of inventories available, select **Resources > Inventories**. This selection will show a list, as in Figure 17-15, with the ability to click an inventory to see the details.

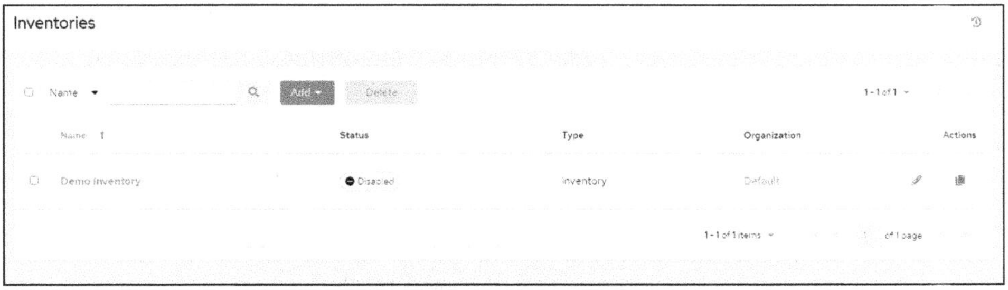

Figure 17-15   Inventory List

Once you click an inventory, you will see the details for that inventory. This initial Details page, as shown in Figure 17-16, will show any variables assigned to the inventory, as well as several navigation tabs.

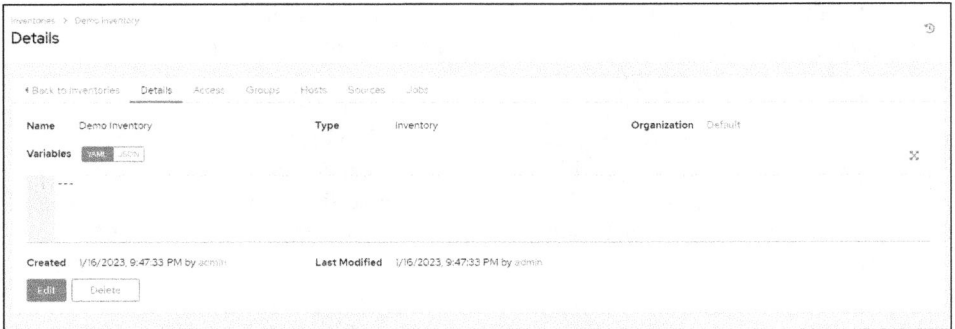

Figure 17-16   Inventory Details

The Access, Teams, and Notifications tabs are similar to the same tabs in Projects. The new tabs are Groups, Hosts, and Sources. The Groups tab shows OLAM inventory groups. These groups are a way to group inventory hosts in OLAM. Inventory groups allow you to categorize your managed servers and apply certain tasks or playbooks to a specific subset of servers, rather than running the same tasks against all servers in your inventory.

The Hosts tab shows what hosts are part of the current inventory, listing each host as in Figure 17-17.

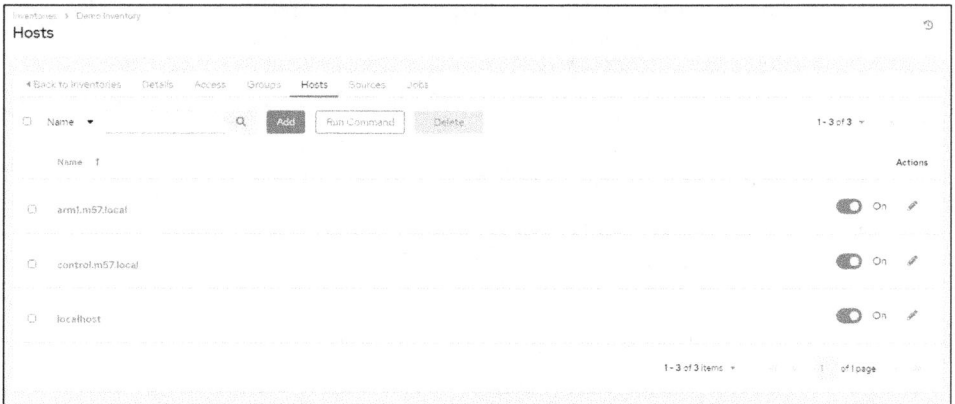

Figure 17-17   Inventory Hosts

From this Hosts tab, you can manually add a host to the group by clicking the **Add** button. Additionally, you can run a command against the hosts by using the **run** command. This capability is useful in DevSecOps because the command can be an Ansible command, a shell command, a **yum** or **apt** command, an SELinux directive, and more. To run a command, select the host(s) you wish to run the command against, and click **Run Command**. From the Run Command page, shown in Figure 17-18, you will be able to pick the module (the type of command, such as shell or SELinux).

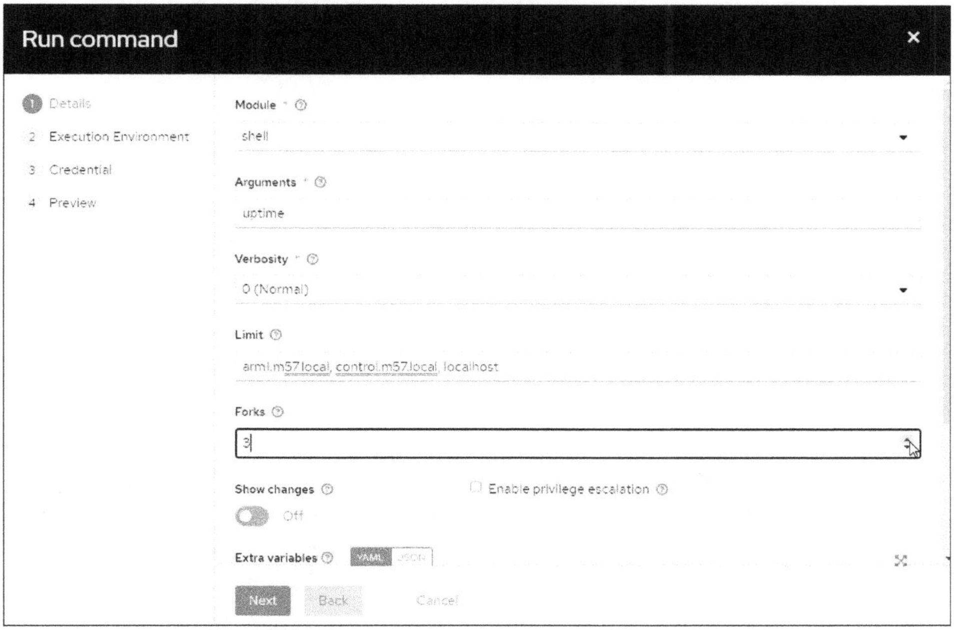

Figure 17-18 Command Details

The module in this case is shell, and the argument is the shell command being run. Limit indicates the hosts that the command is being run against, and forks is the number of simultaneous forks used to run the command. Forking is important to use in larger environments because it effectively distributes the workload across more threads, leading to a faster run time.

Next, you will need to pick the execution environment, as shown in Figure 17-19.

This capability is helpful in a geographically distributed mesh because you can pick the execution environment closest to the hosts. Once you pick the execution environment, you will be prompted to pick the credentials to be used to run the command, as shown in Figure 17-20.

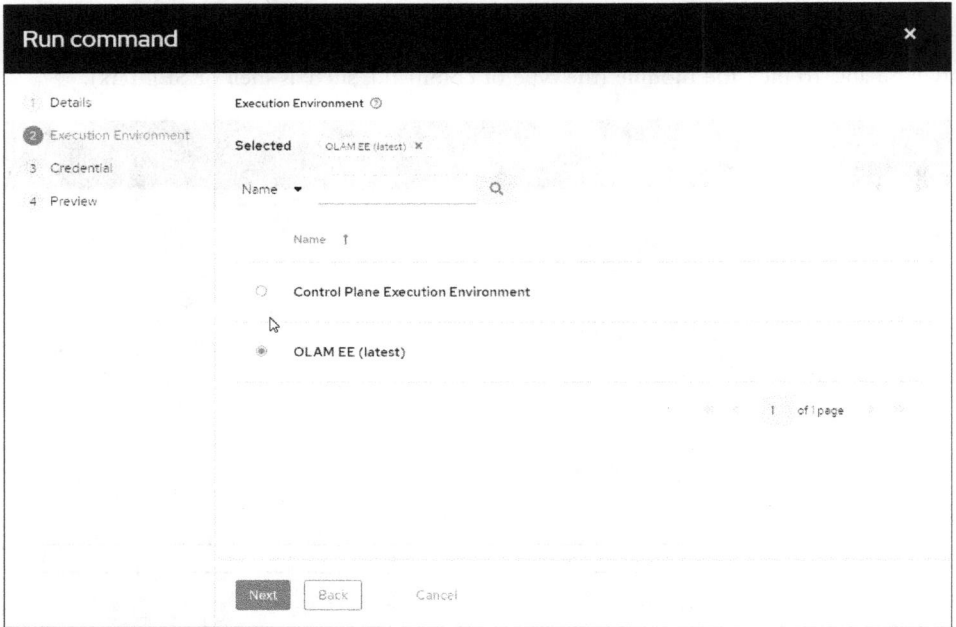

Figure 17-19   Command Execution Environment

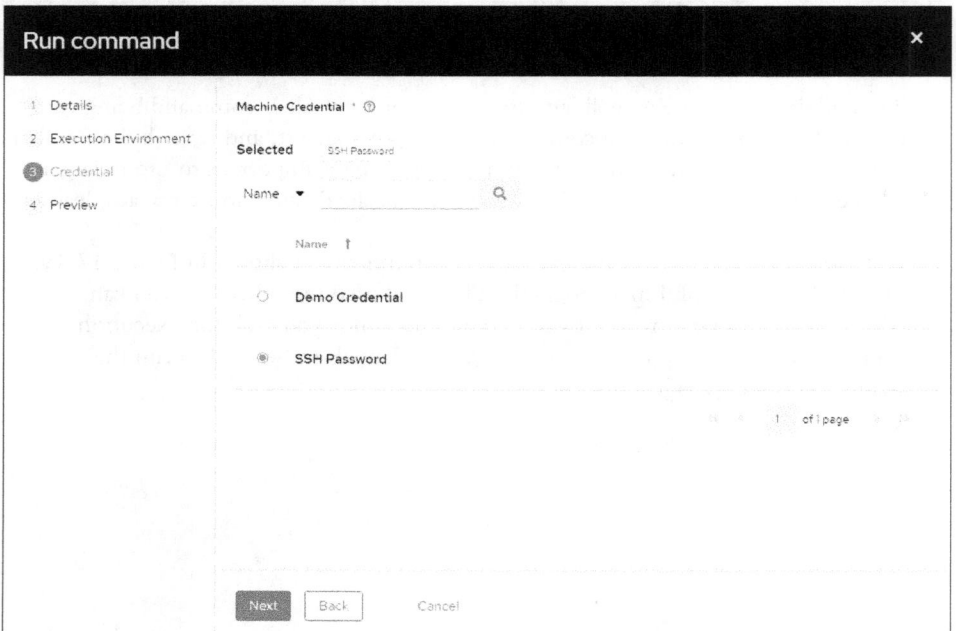

Figure 17-20   Command Credentials

In the sample, the SSH Password will be used. Next, you will have opportunity to verify the job before running it, as shown in Figure 17-21.

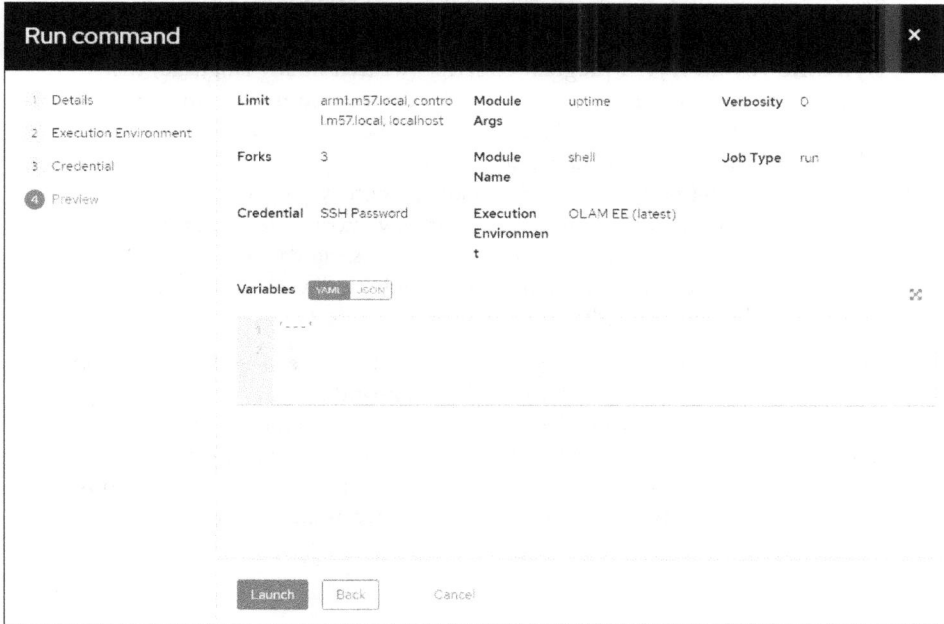

Figure 17-21   Command Preview

Once you are sure this is the command you want to run, click **Launch**. The system will now redirect you to the jobs output, as shown in Figure 17-22.

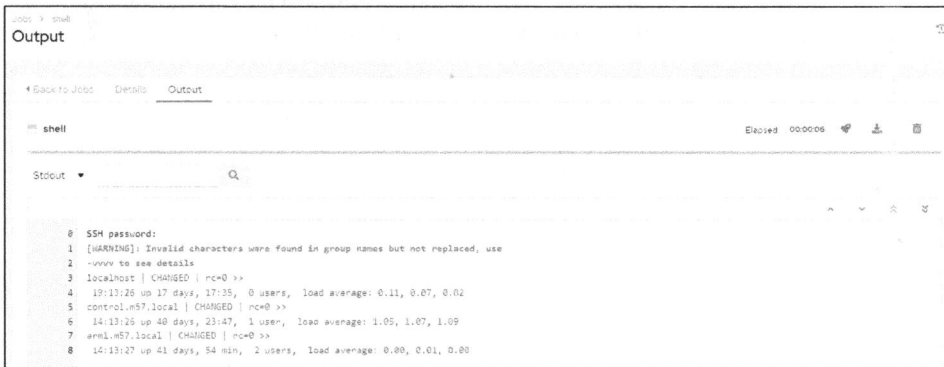

Figure 17-22   Command Output

The last tab is Sources. It might not be populated when the inventory is manually maintained. OLAM can also populate this automatically through four methods:

- **Static Inventory:** A simple text file (INI-style or YAML-style) that lists all managed hosts and groups.
- **Dynamic Inventory:** A program or script (written in any language) that dynamically generates the inventory data based on runtime information such as cloud providers (for example, Amazon AWS, Microsoft Azure, Google Cloud Platform), CMDB systems, LDAP, and so on.
- **Inventory Plug-ins:** OLAM also provides inventory plug-ins, which are scripts written in Python that dynamically generate inventory data, either by querying a source (such as a cloud provider API) or by processing data from a file.
- **Combined Inventory:** A combination of multiple inventory sources, where each source provides additional data for the same set of hosts.

By default, OLAM uses a static inventory file (located at /etc/ansible/hosts), but it can also be specified using the **-I** option on the command line.

In summary, an inventory is a collection of information about the servers, devices, and other resources that are managed by OLAM. The inventory is specified using an inventory file, which is a text file that is stored on the OLAM control node and is used to define the scope of the resources that OLAM can access and manage.

Hosts

A *host* is a remote server, device, or other resource that is managed by OLAM. The host is defined in the OLAM inventory, which is a collection of information about the resources that OLAM is to manage. In the context of OLAM, a host refers to any system that can be connected to and run commands on. A host can be a physical server, a virtual machine, a network device, or any other type of system that is capable of running Ansible modules. To see the list of inventories available, select **Resources > Hosts**. This selection will show a list, as in Figure 17-23, with the ability to click a host to see the details.

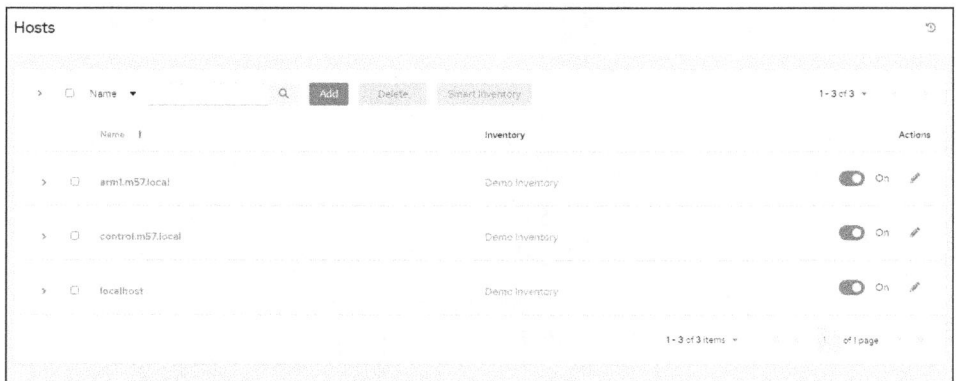

Figure 17-23   Host List

When you select a host, a page will show the details about that host, as shown in Figure 17-24.

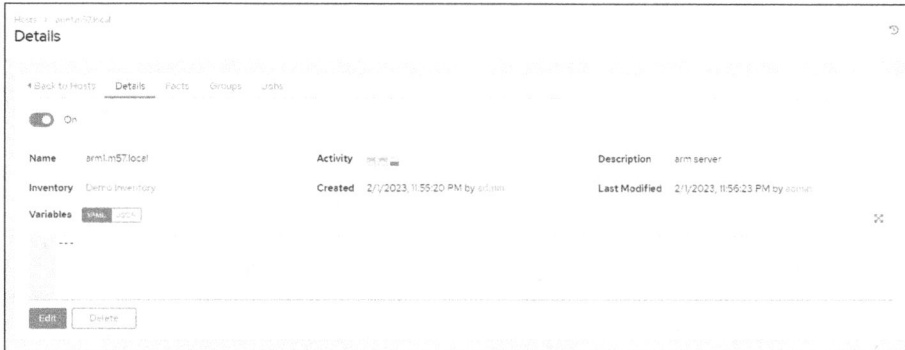

Figure 17-24 Host Details

This screen shows the host name, the inventory it is in, and when it was last created and modified. There are also several tabs. The Facts tab will show the OLAM facts that have been gathered. *Facts* are a collection of data about the system state, including information about the host, network, operating system, and other system information. These facts are gathered at the beginning of each playbook run and made available to playbooks as variables. Facts are commonly used to make decisions in playbooks and to configure managed nodes based on their characteristics. For example, you can use facts to determine the type of operating system a node is running and then execute different tasks based on that information.

You can see host job activity by either selecting the Jobs tab or using the quick reference that shows the status of the last few jobs run against a host. You can mouse over the colored squares in the Activity section, as shown in Figure 17-25. Clicking the event will take you to the Job log.

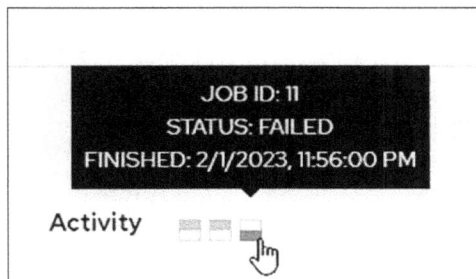

Figure 17-25 Host Job Status

In summary, a host is a remote server, device, or other resource that is managed by OLAM. A host is defined in the inventory, which is a collection of information about the resources that OLAM is to manage.

Access Management

OLAM allows administrators to manage access to resources through organizations, users, and teams.

- **Organizations:** A top-level grouping of resources that can be used to manage access and enforce policies across different teams. Organizations can be used to represent different departments, business units, or customer accounts within an enterprise.
- **Users:** An individual who is granted access to the system. Users can be assigned to one or more organizations and teams, and can have one or more roles that determine what they are allowed to do within the system.
- **Teams:** Groups of users who share common responsibilities or tasks. Teams can be assigned to organizations, and each team can be associated with one or more roles. This allows administrators to control access to resources and manage access policies at a granular level, based on the responsibilities and roles of individual teams.

By combining organizations, users, teams, and roles, OLAM provides a flexible and scalable way to manage access to resources and ensure that sensitive operations are performed by authorized users only.

Organizations

An *organization* is a top-level grouping of resources within OLAM. It allows administrators to manage access and enforce policies across different teams. An organization can represent different departments, business units, or customer accounts within an enterprise. Each organization can have its own set of users, teams, projects, inventories, and job templates, and can be assigned its own role-based access control policies. This allows administrators to manage access to resources at a granular level, based on the specific needs of each organization. By using organizations, OLAM provides a way to control access to resources in a large and complex environment and ensure that sensitive operations are performed by authorized users only.

To see the list of organizations available, select **Resources > Organizations**. This selection will show a list, as in Figure 17-26, with the ability to click an organization to see the details.

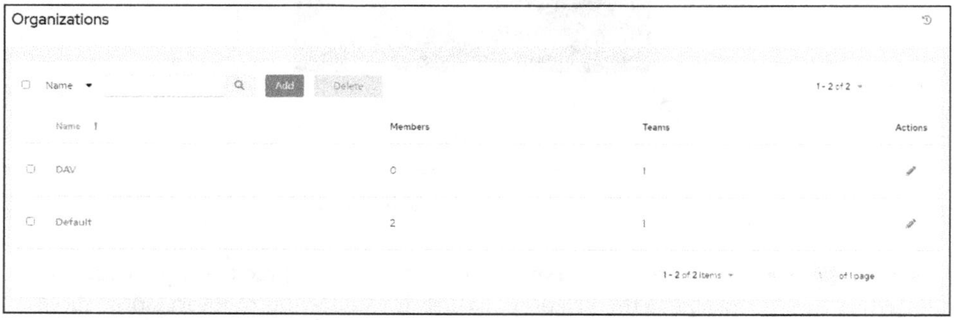

Figure 17-26   Organization List

The Summary will show how many team members are in each organization and how many teams are in each organization. You can drill down into the organization by clicking the organization name. This will bring you to the organization's Details page, as shown in Figure 17-27.

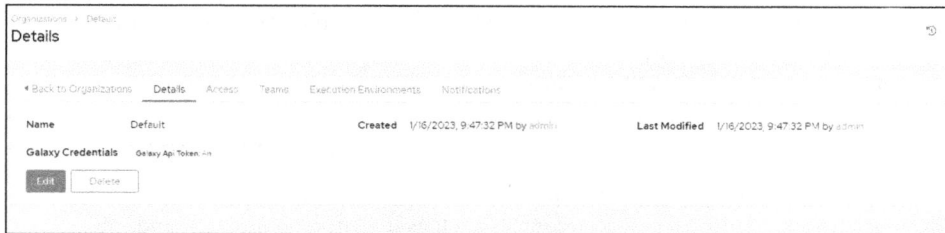

Figure 17-27   Organization Details

This Details page should look familiar because it shows the creation and modification dates, along with the navigational tabs. The Notifications tab serves the same purpose as this tab on other pages. The Access tab, as shown in Figure 17-28, will show what level of access each member of the organization has.

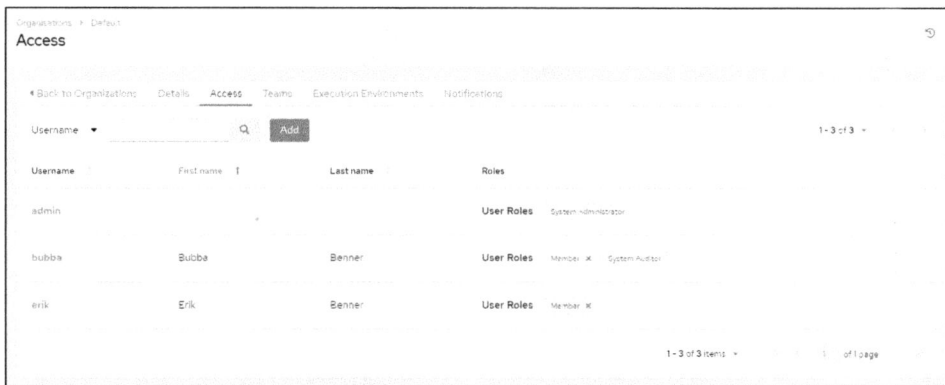

Figure 17-28   Organization Access

For the DevSecOps team, this Access page is important to review to verify that all members of the organization have appropriate access.

The Execution Environment tab shows what execution environment servers can be used by the organization. By default, all organizations can use all execution environments, but in many organizations there is a need to limit this access.

Users

OLAM provides role-based access control for users, which allows administrators to specify what actions each user can perform in the OLAM environment. Some of the tasks that can be controlled include

- **Launching Jobs:** Users can launch jobs to run Ansible playbooks, manage inventory, and perform other tasks.
- **Managing Inventory:** Users can create, edit, and delete inventories, and manage the hosts and groups within them.
- **Monitoring:** Users can view job activity, job results, and system status.

OLAM users can be assigned to one or more organizations, which allows administrators to control access to resources such as inventories, projects, and job templates. This makes it possible to delegate specific tasks to different teams within an organization while still maintaining control over who has access to sensitive data.

Overall, OLAM provides a secure and flexible environment for managing users and their access to resources, making it easier to automate IT operations in a multi-user environment.

To see the list of users in the system, select **Resources > Users**. This selection will show a list, as in Figure 17-29, with the ability to click a user to see the details.

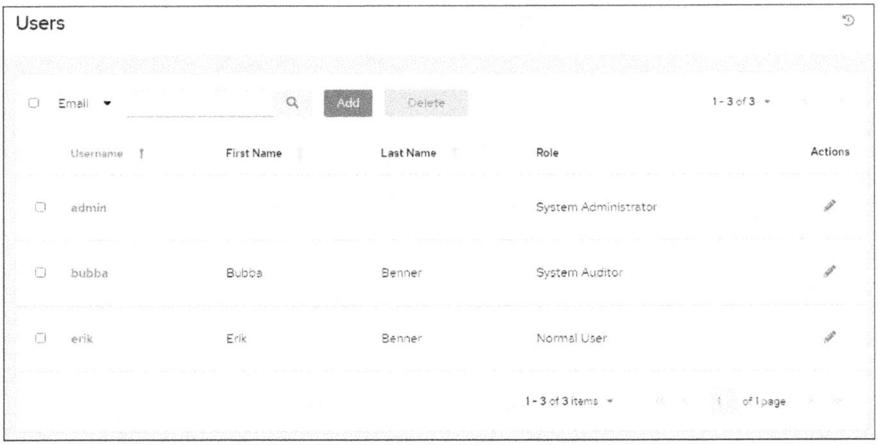

Figure 17-29   User List

This Users page enables you to see all users in the system and what their role is. You can select a user to drill down to see more details, as shown in Figure 17-30.

From this Details page, you will see the expected data like the creation date of the user. There are also other tabs that will show what Teams and Organizations the user is a member of. Additionally, you can select the **Roles** tab, as shown in Figure 17-31, to see all the roles a user has.

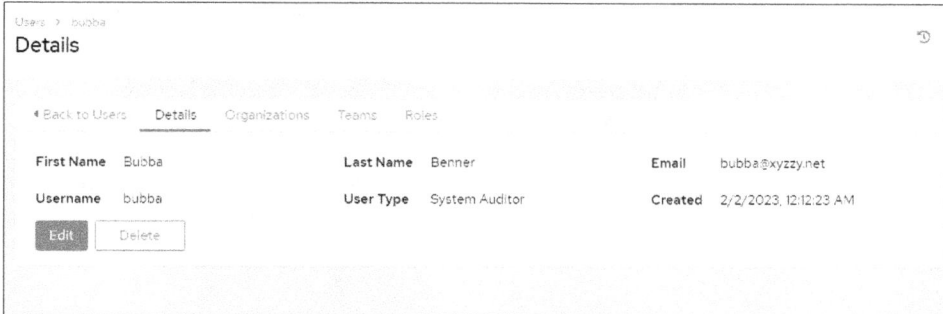

Figure 17-30   User Details

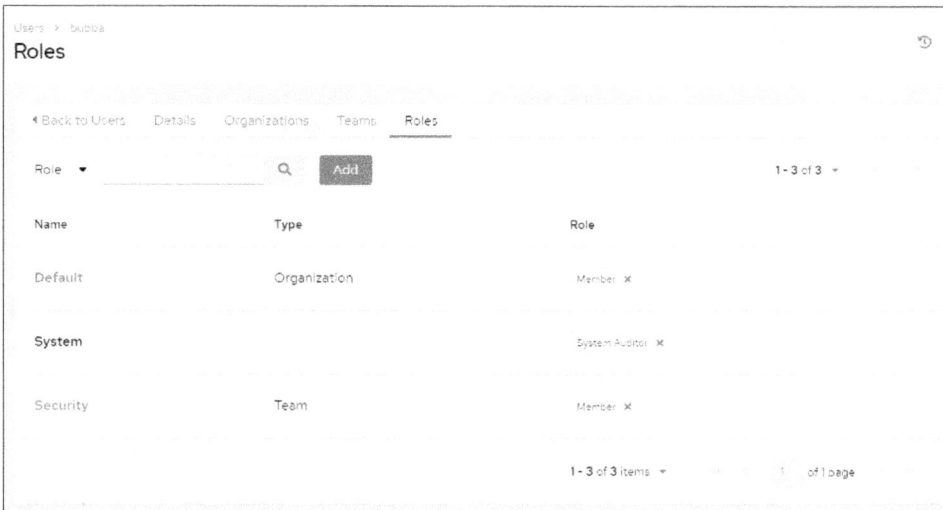

Figure 17-31   User Roles

OLAM provides several built-in user roles that define the actions a user can perform in the environment. The roles are

- **Admin:** A user with the Admin role has complete access to all resources in Ansible Tower, including the ability to manage users, organizations, projects, and job templates.
- **Auditor:** A user with the Auditor role has read-only access to all resources in Tower, including the ability to view job results and system status.
- **User:** A user with the User role has limited access to resources in Tower, including the ability to launch jobs and view job activity.
- **Project Admin:** A user with the Project Admin role has complete access to a specific project, including the ability to manage inventories, job templates, and launch jobs.

- **Read:** A user with the Read role has read-only access to a specific project, including the ability to view job activity and results.

These built-in roles can be customized to meet the specific needs of an organization, making it possible to define custom roles with a specific set of permissions. By using role-based access control, OLAM makes it possible to manage user access to resources in a secure and flexible manner. Overall, OLAM provides a secure and flexible environment for managing users and their access to resources, making it easier to automate IT operations in a multi-user environment.

Teams

OLAM *teams* are groups of users within an organization that have common access requirements to specific resources, such as inventories, projects, and job templates. Teams allow administrators to manage user access to resources in a more flexible and efficient manner, making it possible to delegate tasks to different teams within an organization while still maintaining control over who has access to sensitive data.

Teams are created and managed within an organization, and each team is associated with one or more projects. The members of a team have access to the resources associated with the projects they are a part of. For example, a team of developers could be associated with a project that includes a set of job templates for deploying code to test environments, while an operations team could be associated with a project that includes job templates for monitoring and maintaining production systems.

Teams can be used in conjunction with user roles to provide even more fine-grained control over user access to resources. For example, a user with the Project Admin role for a specific project can manage the resources associated with that project, including adding or removing members from the team.

To see the list of teams in the system, select **Resources > Teams**. This selection will show a list, as in Figure 17-32, with the ability to click a team to see the details.

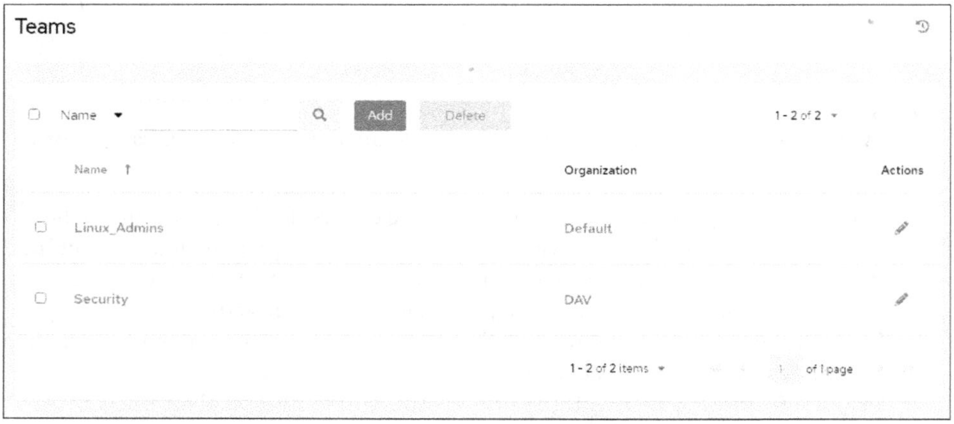

Figure 17-32 Teams List

On the Teams page, you will see a list of all the teams and the organization that each team is in. As with the other resources, you can click the team to drill down to the details, as shown in Figure 17-33.

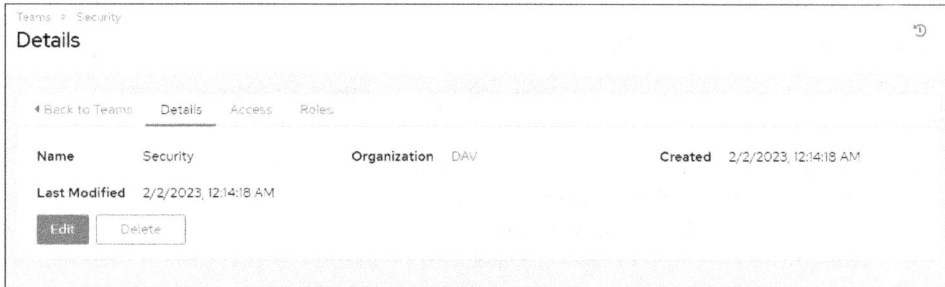

Figure 17-33   Teams Details

From this Details page, you can see the team, when it was created, and the organization the team is in. There are two other tabs: Access and Roles.

Clicking **Access** will show a list of users in the team and their access level, as shown in Figure 17-34.

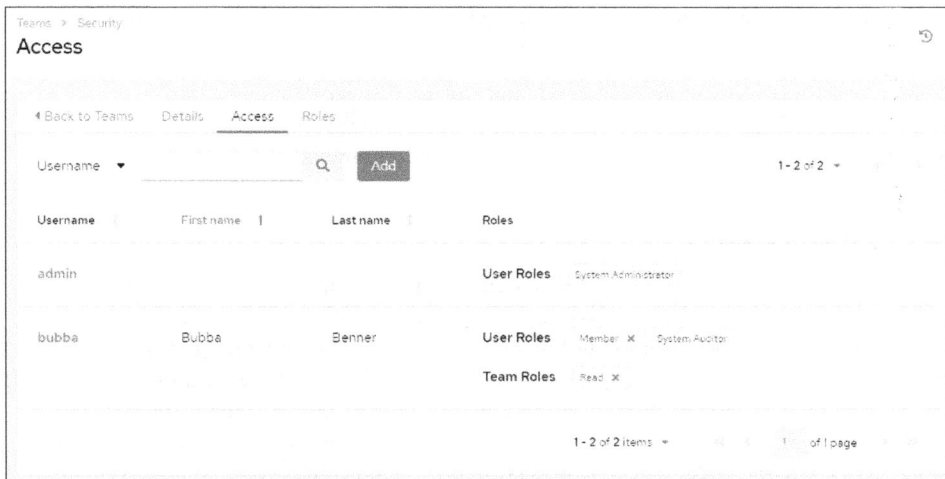

Figure 17-34   Teams Access

Additionally, you can check if there are any roles assigned to the team. Assigning roles to the team is optional; although it is not required, it is a very useful feature for the DevSecOps team because you can use it to customize the security to meet the specific needs of a group of users.

In summary, teams provide a flexible and efficient way to manage user access to resources within an organization, making it easier to automate IT operations in a multi-user environment.

OLAM Administrative Options

OLAM provides several options for managing various aspects of your automation infrastructure, including

- **Credential Types:** Create and manage custom credential types.
- **Notifications:** Configure notifications for job status changes and failures, with options for email, SMS, and webhooks.
- **Management Jobs:** Run jobs that help maintain the OLAM server. Purge old data and sessions.
- **Instance Groups:** Manage dynamic inventories of instances and devices, with options for grouping instances based on criteria such as platform, location, and tag.
- **Applications:** Manage applications and their deployment, with options for defining and managing application workflows, and monitoring the status of deployments.
- **Execution Environments:** Control the environment in which playbooks are executed, with options for defining and managing execution environments, such as containers, virtual machines, and bare metal hosts.

Many of these features are advanced, and not used in smaller single-node environments. This being said, it is important for the DevSecOps team to understand what the possible options are for more advanced configurations.

Credential Types

OLAM enables you to create custom credential types to support specific automation use cases and requirements. Custom credential types can be created using the OLAM API and are stored in the same encrypted manner as the built-in credential types. To create a custom credential type in OLAM, you will need to define the fields and options required for the specific use case, such as username, password, API key, or certificate. You will also need to create a custom script or integration that interacts with the target system or service, using the fields and options defined in the custom credential type. Once you have created a custom credential type, you can use it in the same manner as the built-in credential types, selecting it as the authentication method when running playbooks or ad hoc commands in OLAM.

Custom credential types provide a flexible and powerful way to extend the functionality of OLAM, allowing you to automate a wide range of use cases and systems, and manage sensitive information in a centralized and secure manner.

Notifications

OLAM *notifications* allow you and your users to receive notifications about job status changes and failures, helping you to monitor and respond to automation tasks in real time. Several notification methods are available with OLAM:

- **Email:** Send notifications via email to one or more recipients.
- **Grafana:** Send notifications to Grafana as an easy way to make dashboards.
- **IRC:** Send notifications using the Internet Relay Chat protocol.
- **Mattermost:** Leverage the open-source Mattermost chat service.
- **Pagerduty:** Use the commercial Pagerduty service to alert your teams.
- **Rocket.Chat:** Use the open-source chat technology.
- **Webhook:** Send notifications via an HTTP POST request to a specified URL, allowing you to integrate with third-party services and applications.
- **Slack:** Send notifications to a Slack channel, allowing you to receive updates and alerts directly in your team's collaboration platform.
- **Twilio:** Use this popular commercial messaging system.

To create a notification method, select **Notifications > Add**. This selection will start an interactive form, as shown in Figure 17-35.

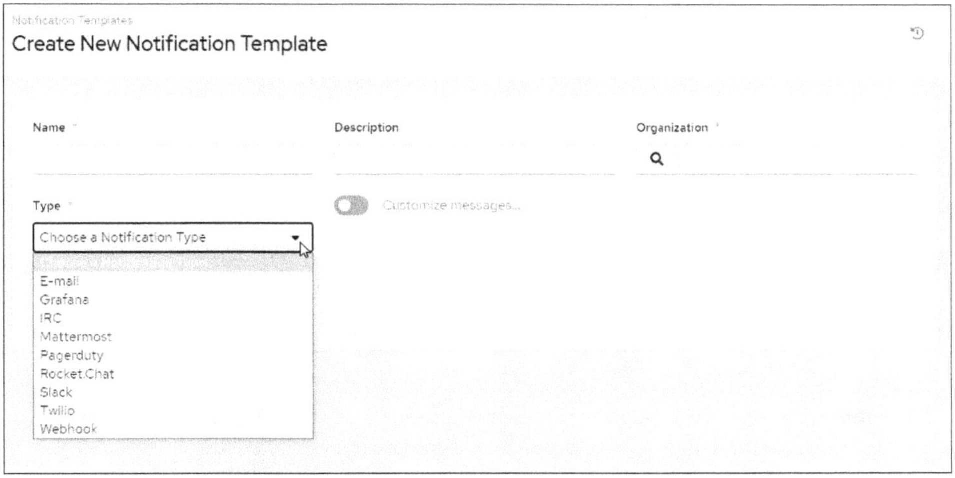

Figure 17-35 Notification Template

From this form, give the method a name, description, organization, and also pick the type. The next screen depends on the type of notification selected. The sample in Figure 17-36 is based on an email notification.

In this email example, you will need to set up the appropriate information for sending emails through your Simple Mail Transfer Protocol (SMTP) relay. Make sure your username and password are correct and that you are using the correct port and encryption methods required by your service. Once you save the new notification server, use the Test button to verify it is working correctly.

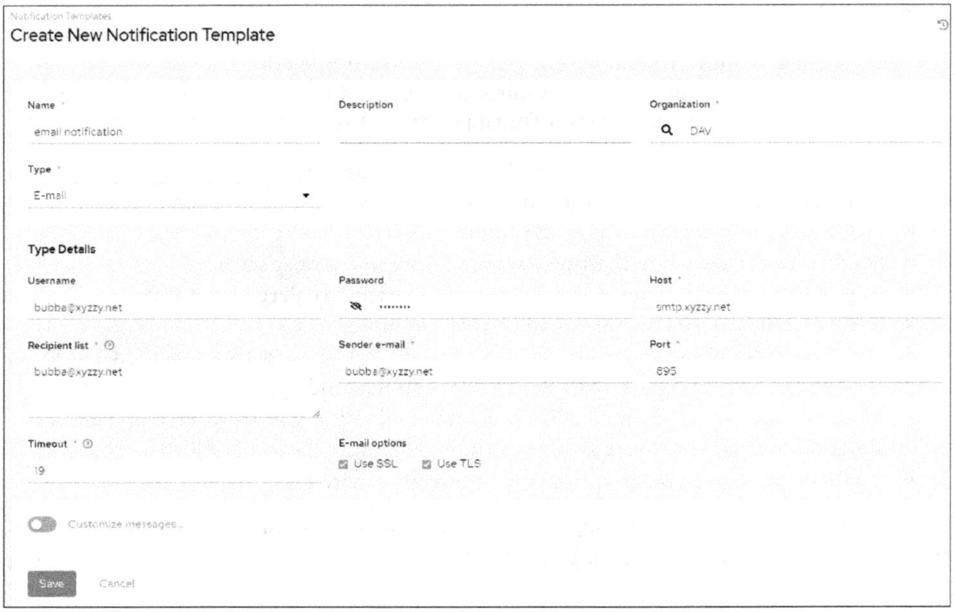

Figure 17-36   Creating an Email Notification

Notifications in Ansible Tower help you to stay informed about the status of your automation tasks and to respond quickly to any issues or failures. You can customize the content and format of notifications to meet your specific needs and requirements.

Management Jobs

As with any system, some periodic maintenance is required. With an OLAM server, four common jobs should be run on some sort of schedule. How often these jobs are run is based on your operation's needs.

- **Clean Up Activity Stream:** This is the process of removing old or unused records from the activity stream. The activity stream in OLAM is a log of all the activities and events that occur in the system, such as job launches, resource changes, and system updates. Over time, the activity stream can become cluttered with outdated or unnecessary records, which can affect the performance of the system and make it difficult to find relevant information. Cleaning up the activity stream helps to keep the system running smoothly and maintain efficient performance. It is important to note that deleting records from the activity stream is permanent and cannot be undone. Before cleaning up the activity stream, administrators should ensure that they have backup copies of any important information that they may need to refer to later.

- **Clean Up Expired OAuth 2 Tokens:** This job starts a playbook that removes or invalidates OAuth 2 access tokens that have passed their expiration date. OAuth 2 is a widely used authorization protocol that enables secure and simplified authorization for applications and services. When an application or service requests authorization, it receives an access token, which is used to make subsequent API calls. Access tokens are issued with an expiration date and can be revoked by the authorization server at any time. When an access token expires, it can no longer be used to make API calls. This can result in errors or denied access if an application continues to use an expired token. To avoid this issue, it is important to regularly clean up expired OAuth 2 tokens and remove them from the system. It is important to note that removing an expired OAuth 2 token will also revoke access to the resources that it was granted access to. Before cleaning up expired tokens, administrators should consider the potential impact on applications and services that may be using them.
- **Clean Up Expired Sessions:** This job starts the process of removing or invalidating user sessions that have passed their expiration date. A user session in OLAM refers to the time period during which a user is logged in to the system and has an active connection to the server. User sessions are typically created when a user logs in to the web interface and are maintained while the user remains active in the system. User sessions are typically assigned an expiration date or timeout value, after which they are automatically terminated or invalidated. This helps to ensure that user sessions do not remain open indefinitely and to protect against security risks, such as unauthorized access.

  It is important to note that removing an expired user session will also terminate the user's active connection to the OLAM server. Before cleaning up expired user sessions, administrators should consider the potential impact on any users who may still be using the system.
- **Clean Up Job Details:** This job removes old job details from the OLAM database. Job details in OLAM are records that store information about jobs that have been executed in the system. This information can include job status, execution logs, resource usage, and other details related to the job execution. Over time, the job details database can become cluttered with outdated or unnecessary information, which can affect the performance of the system and make it difficult to find relevant information. Cleaning up job details helps to keep the system running smoothly and maintain efficient performance.

  It is important to note that deleting job details from the database is permanent and cannot be undone. Before cleaning up job details, administrators should ensure that they have backup copies of any important information that they may need to refer to later. Additionally, administrators should consider the potential impact on any reporting or auditing processes that may be relying on the job details data.

Instance Groups

In OLAM, an *instance group* in a mesh refers to a group of OLAM instances that are connected to each other in a mesh network configuration. This type of configuration can be used to provide redundancy and high availability in an OLAM deployment, allowing for automatic failover in the event of an instance failure. In a mesh configuration, each OLAM instance in the group maintains a connection to multiple other instances in the group. If one instance fails, the other instances in the group can automatically take over its responsibilities, allowing for continuous operation. With instance groups, administrators can manage multiple instances as a single entity, simplifying management tasks such as upgrades, backups, and disaster recovery. Instance groups can be used to manage Ansible Tower instances in different geographic locations, to separate instances based on function (for example, development, test, and production) or to create custom groups based on specific needs.

With a standard installation, the instance group default is created, and this is where all jobs run from.

Applications

OLAM *applications* are external third-party applications that integrate with OLAM to provide additional functionality, such as monitoring, reporting, or other management tasks. Applications can be used to extend the capabilities of OLAM, allowing organizations to manage and automate IT tasks at scale, while also taking advantage of additional tools and features that are not built into OLAM itself.

Examples of Ansible Tower external applications include

- **Grafana:** A popular open-source analytics and monitoring platform that integrates with Ansible Tower to provide real-time visibility into the performance of your IT infrastructure.
- **Jira:** A popular software development tool used for issue tracking and project management. It is widely used by DevSecOps teams to track and manage their work.

To use an application, you will typically need to configure the application to connect to your OLAM instance. This configuration may involve setting up an API connection, configuring webhooks, or using other methods to integrate the two systems.

Once configured, applications can provide additional visibility and insights into your OLAM environment, allowing you to monitor and manage your IT infrastructure more effectively.

Execution Environments

Execution environments are isolated, self-contained environments that provide a controlled and predictable environment for running Ansible playbooks. Environments are used to ensure that playbooks are executed in a consistent and predictable manner, even when there are changes to the underlying infrastructure or the configuration of the playbooks themselves. Each execution environment is defined by a set of parameters, including the version of Ansible that is used, the versions of Python and other dependencies that are required, and any custom plug-ins or modules that are needed. When a playbook is executed within an OLAM execution environment, all dependencies and configurations are automatically managed, ensuring that the playbook is executed as intended. Managed execution groups are groups of hosts that are managed and configured by OLAM. These groups are defined in the inventory file and allow you to target specific sets of hosts with your playbooks or ad hoc commands. By using managed execution groups, you can easily scale your infrastructure and manage multiple hosts with ease.

Execution environments can be used to isolate and control different playbooks and workflows, allowing organizations to manage and execute their Ansible playbooks in a more consistent and predictable manner. This can help to reduce the risk of configuration drift and improve the overall reliability of the IT automation process.

Summary

In this chapter, you learned how to install OLAM and its prerequisites. You also learned about the major features of the tool and how they operate. In the next chapter you will learn how to set up a system with a step-by-step example.

Ansible Full Stack Sample

Ansible in the Real World

Chapter 17, "Ansible—Installing and Configuring OLAM," provided a basic understanding of playbooks and how to set up an Ansible environment to authenticate and run the standard OCI Ansible collection. In this chapter, we will cover how to set up Oracle Linux Automation Manager (OLAM) in a real-world scenario, along with a few new tricks and hints for using OLAM with OCI for full-stack automation. We will start this process by building users and groups to support the DevSecOps teams and then setting up target inventories and projects and running playbooks from GitHub. We will also cover variables and prompting for them when running playbooks and custom execution environments.

Planning a Team

The DevSecOps team is the core of the overall process. From a security aspect, it is best practice to have each team isolated from other teams. This means that users should be members of different teams, with their access limited to their role. In this example, we will create a team called appteam, consisting of the users dba, developer, security, and sysadmin.

Creating Users

Let's start by creating the users. From the main console, select **Access > Users**, as shown in Figure 18-1.

When you first log in to OLAM, only the admin user is created by default. From the Users screen (see Figure 18-2), you can see all users, as well as add or delete users.

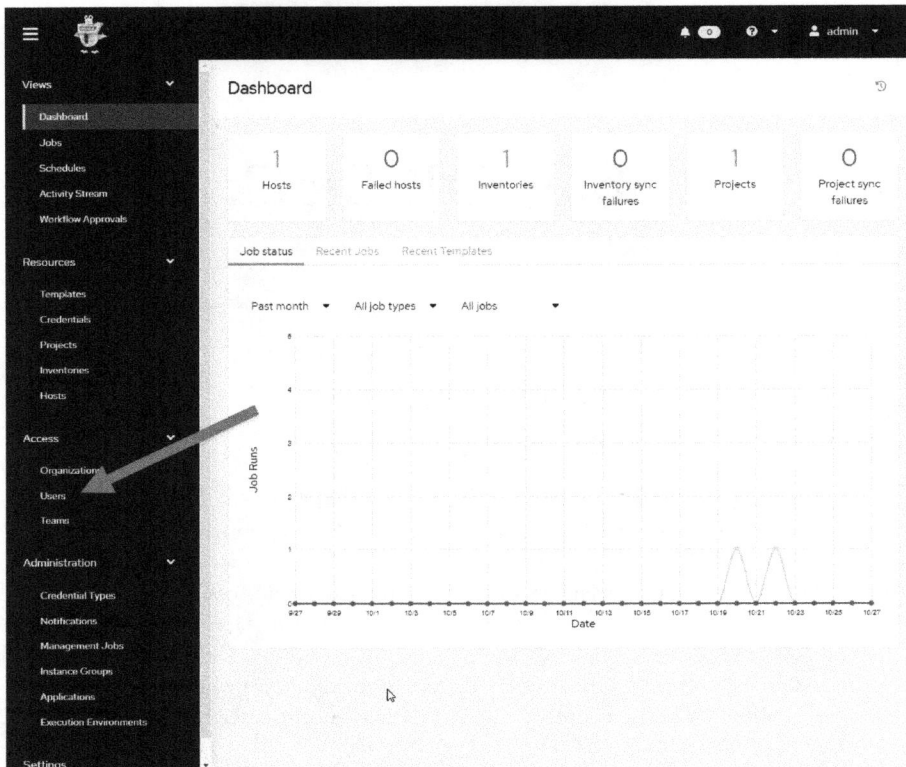

Figure 18-1   Accessing Users

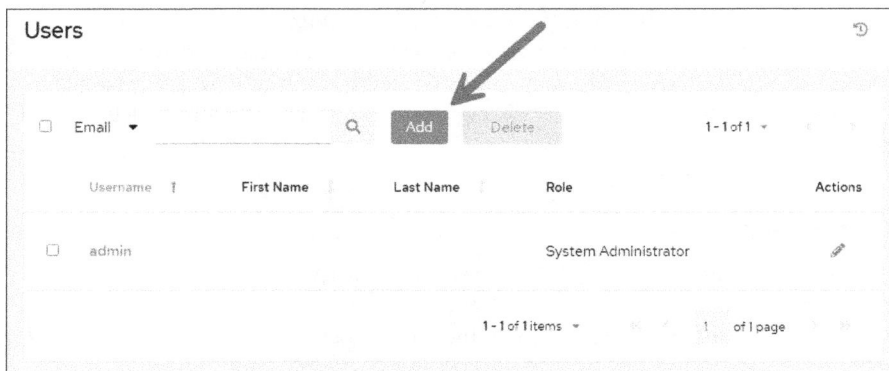

Figure 18-2   Users

Select **Add** to add the users. For this example, we will add the user dba but then repeat the same process for developer, security, and sysadmin. Each user will look similar to the dba user, as seen in Figure 18-3.

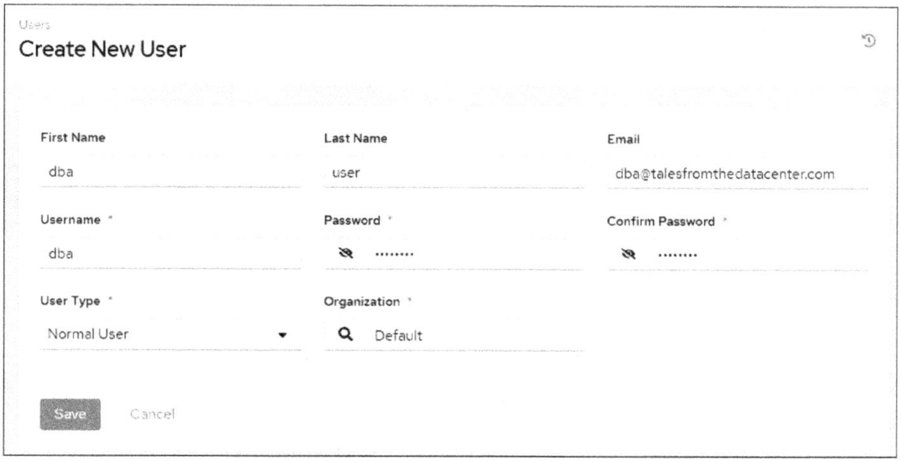

Figure 18-3   Adding a User

This process will be repeated for the other users, with the security user granted the role of System Auditor and the sysadmin user granted the role of System Administrator (see Figure 18-4).

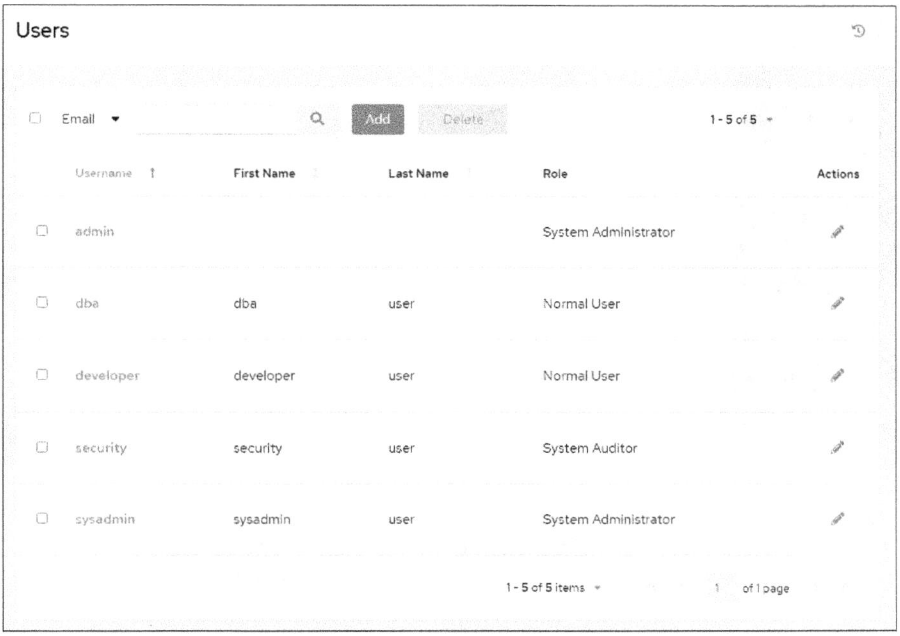

Figure 18-4   Users Created

> **Note**
>
> Of course, your actual users will be different, matching your naming policy. These are just sample names. From a security perspective, the username should not reflect the role.

Now that the users are created, let's create some teams.

Creating Teams

From the main page, select **Access > Teams**. This action will show the teams built into the system. As with users, a fresh installation will have no teams, as you can see in Figure 18-5.

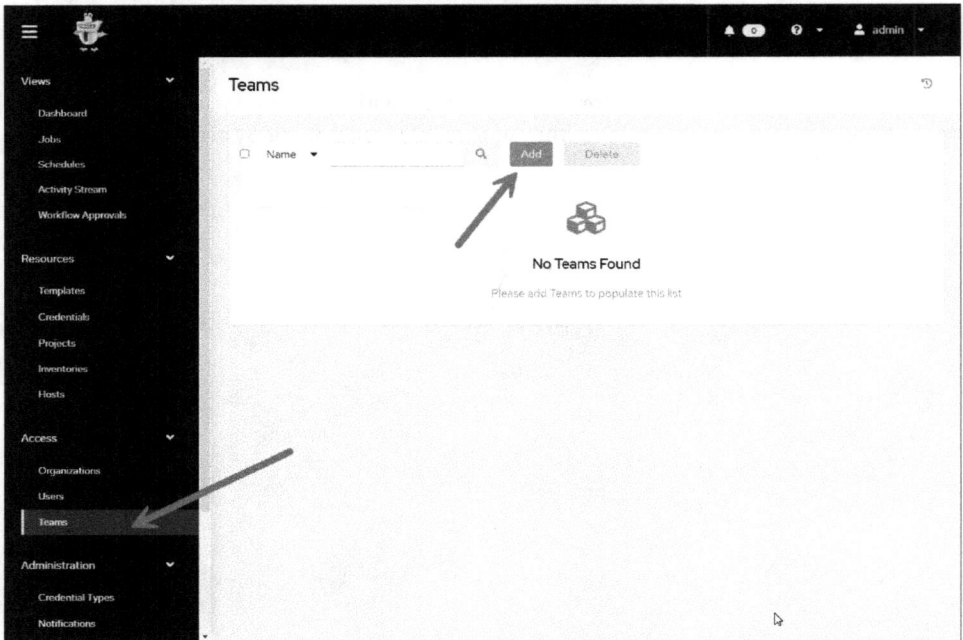

Figure 18-5   Teams

Let's create a few teams now. To start, click **Add** to create a team. The basic information for a team is simple. In this case, make the appteam, as shown in Figure 18-6.

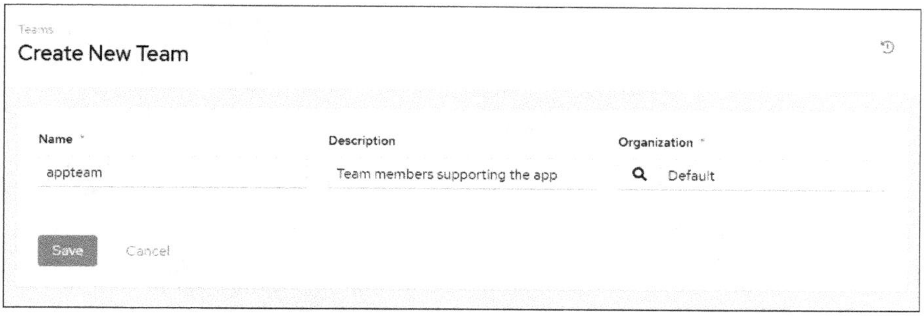

Figure 18-6 Creating a New Team

Once the team has been created, you can see what initial access folks have to the team. Since both security and sysadmin are admins, they will have access to all teams (see Figure 18-7)! Understanding this point is important so you do not accidentally grant more privileges than you want to when using these two built-in roles.

Figure 18-7 Team Access

In a production system, it's not uncommon for folks to be members of different teams—some for their skills (such as DBA or Linux) and others for specific projects or applications.

Next, let's add the developer to the appteam. After selecting **Access > Teams**, select **appteam**, as shown in Figure 18-8.

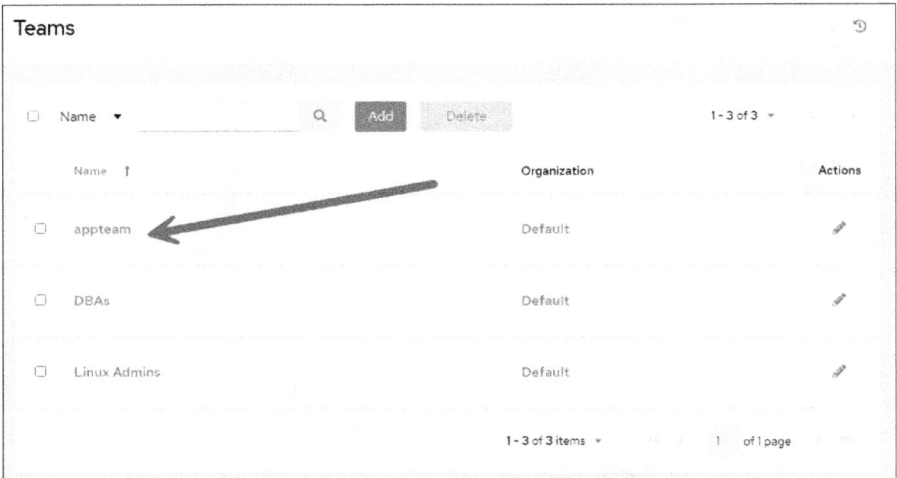

Figure 18-8   Selecting the appteam

From here, you can go to the Access tab and then select the **Add** button, as shown in Figure 18-9.

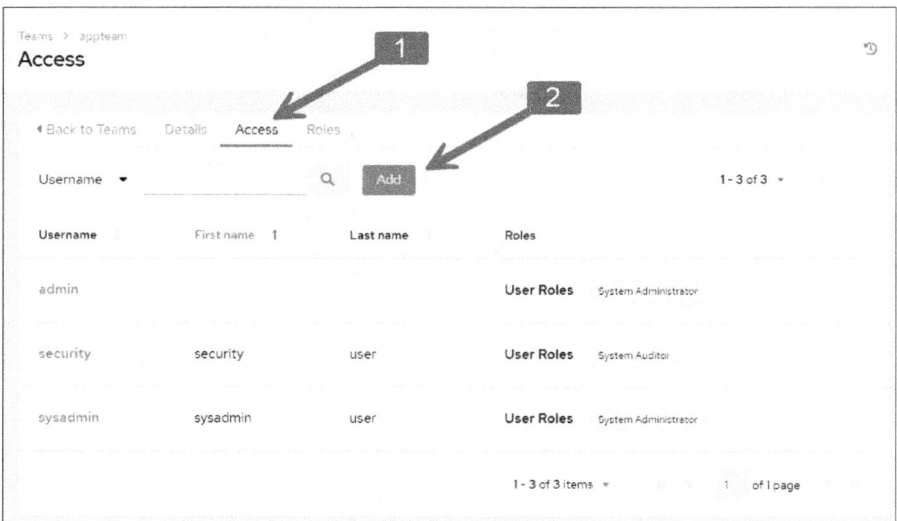

Figure 18-9   Adding a Team Member

From here, you can start with an interactive dialog. First, select **Users** (see Figure 18-10), and then click the **Next** button to proceed to the next step.

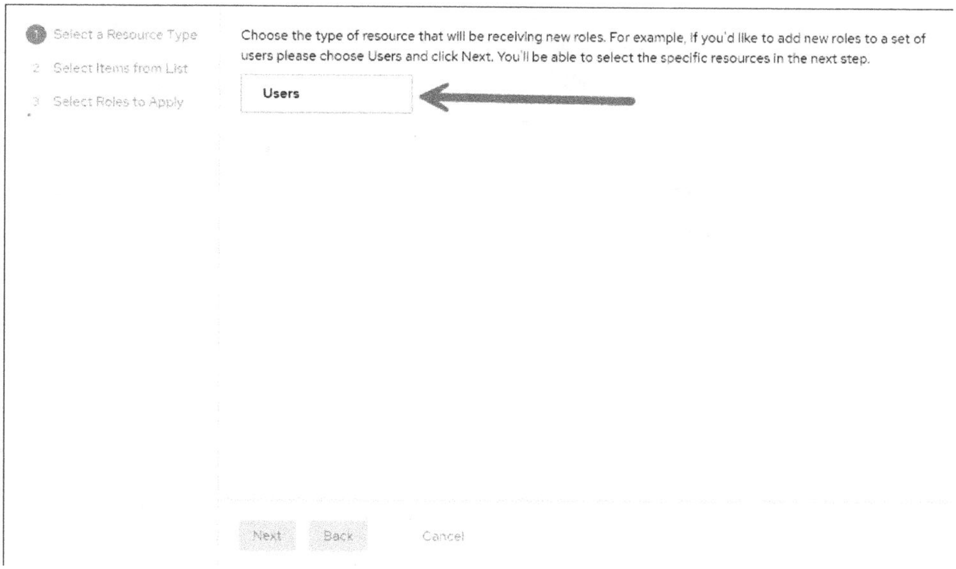

Figure 18-10 Selecting Users

From here, you can search and select what users you want to add to the team. In this case, select the check box next to **Developer** (see Figure 18-11), and then click the **Next** button to continue to the user details where you can apply specific roles.

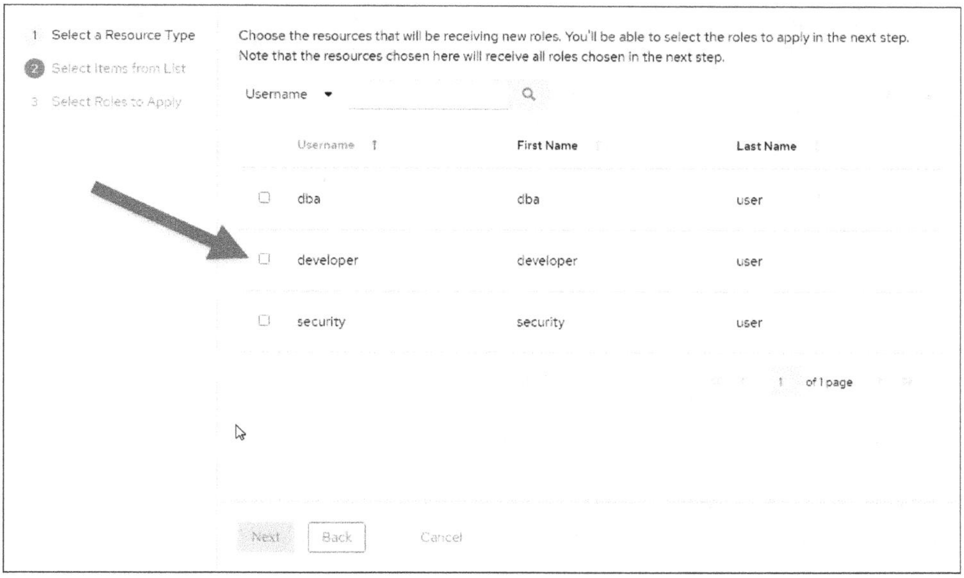

Figure 18-11 Selecting a Developer

You next need to pick what role this user will have. Because you want the developer to have access to run playbooks (maybe this will be used to allow a developer to provision resources, patch servers, and so on), select **Member** (see Figure 18-12).

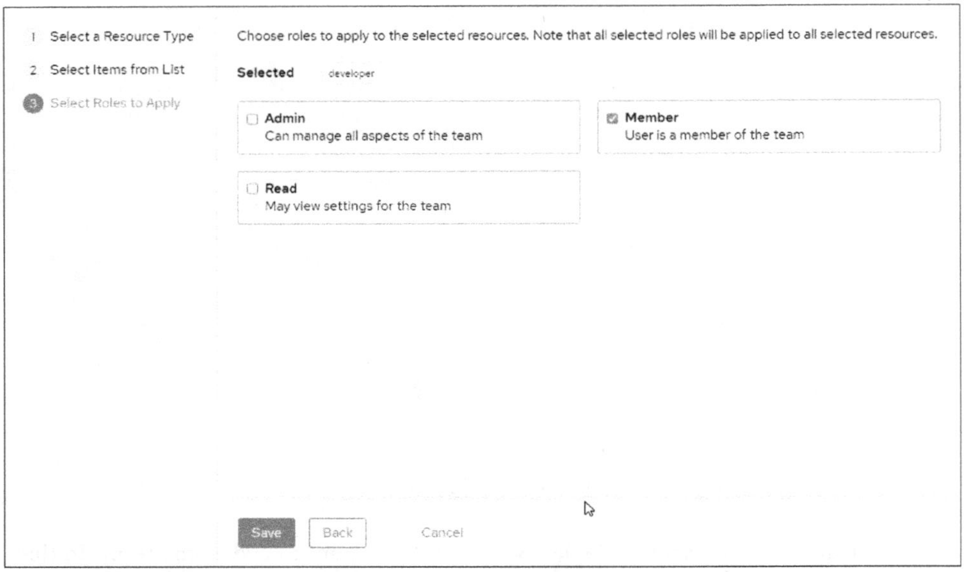

Figure 18-12   Member Access

Team members can have multiple roles, and if a dependency role is required (dependencies are dynamic based on the specifics of your environment and how you set up the roles), it will be automatically added. This is seen in Figure 18-13, where read access was automatically added.

Here, you can see that the developer user was not only added, but this developer was also granted read access to the team because that is a dependency.

Now that we have users and the team created, let's go to the next step—creating a project.

Creating Credentials

Before creating the project, you need some credentials for the team to use. The first credential will be for Git, to access the playbooks. From the main menu, access **Resources > Credentials** and then click **Add**, as shown in Figure 18-14.

Many different credentials can be added: from SSH keys, OCI keys, and even passwords. For this example, add a GitHub credential. From the drop-down, select **GitHub Personal Access Token**. Select the organization and name the token. Then paste the token into the Token field. When completed, the credential should look like Figure 18-15.

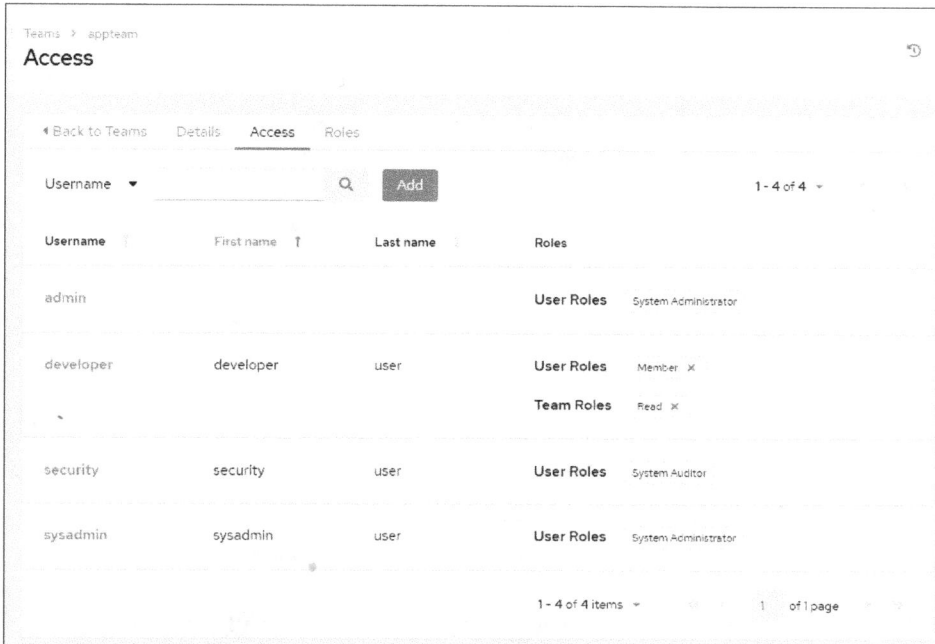

Figure 18-13 New Member Added

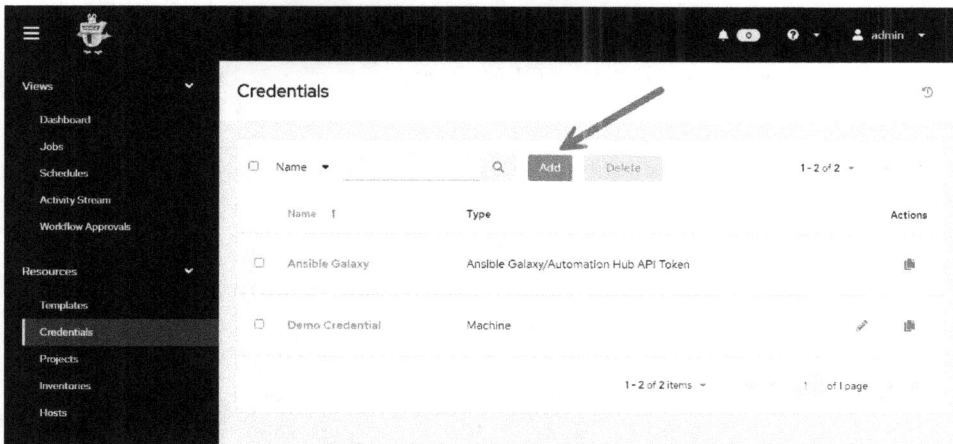

Figure 18-14 Accessing Credentials

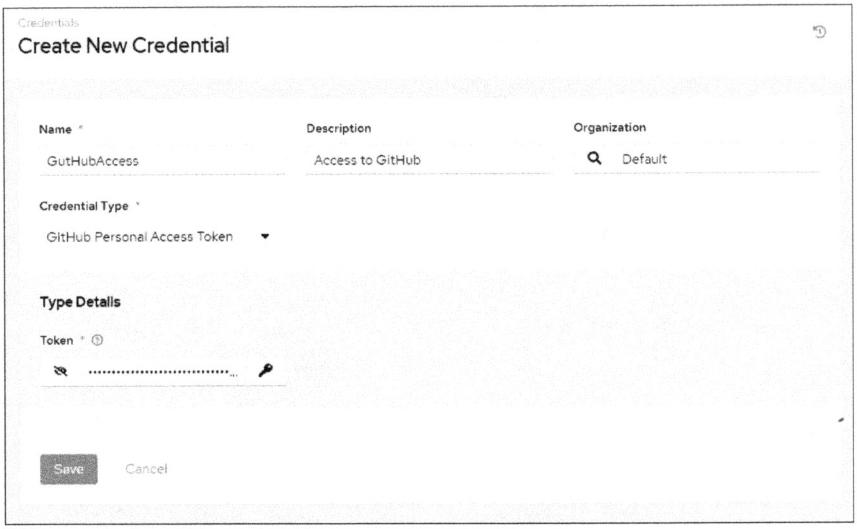

Figure 18-15   GitHub Personal Access Token

Personal access tokens serve as an alternative to using passwords for authentication with GitHub, particularly when utilizing the GitHub API or the command line. These tokens are designed to access GitHub resources on your behalf.

Note
Be careful because these tokens can expire. Expiring tokens are more secure, but don't forget to update them in your OLAM server.

After you have saved the token, you will see the new credential, as shown in Figure 18-16.

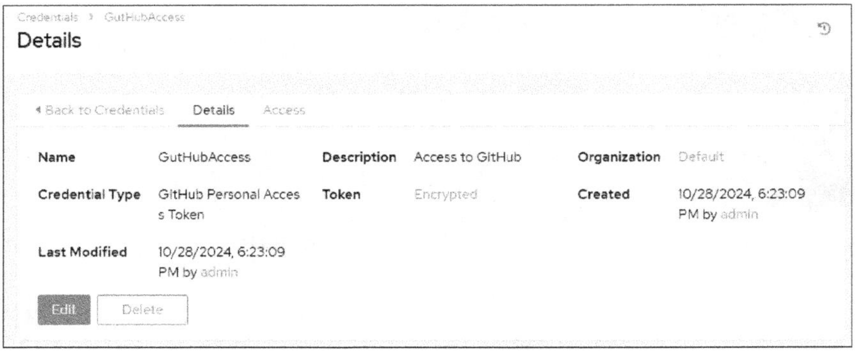

Figure 18-16   GitHub Credential Created

Next, you need to grant access to the team. Click the **Access** tab. This tab will show who has access to use this credential. As you can see in Figure 18-17, not only the admin user can use it but also the security and sysadmin users, due to their roles!

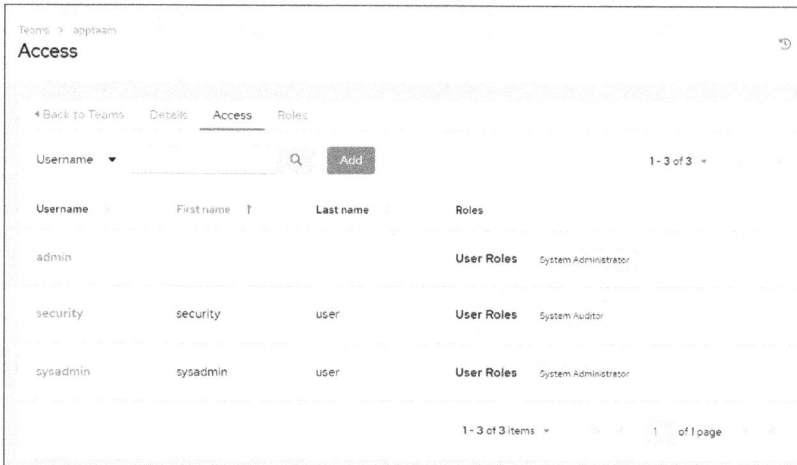

Figure 18-17   Who Can Use the Credential?

Now click **Add**. Clicking this button starts a wizard process, where you first select if access is being granted to a user or a team. Whether you grant access to a specific user or team is up to your security model. In this case, add the team, as shown in Figure 18-18.

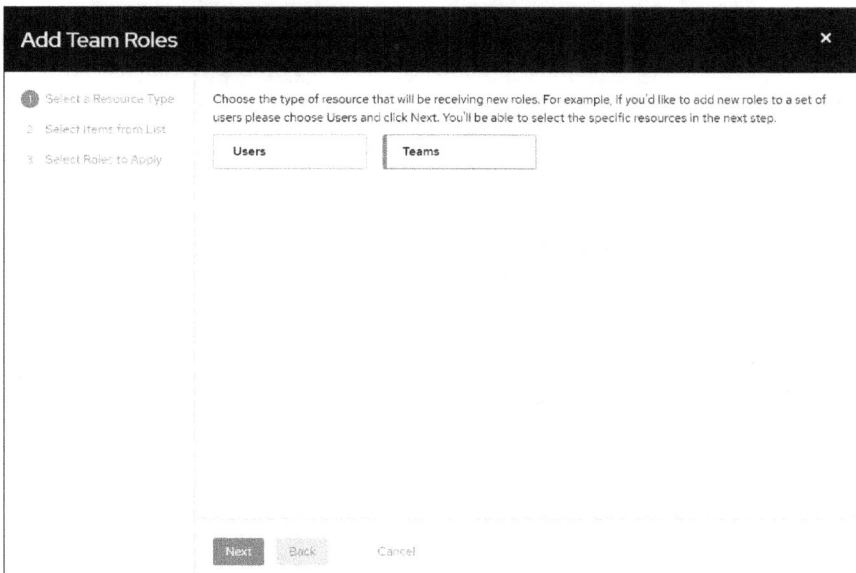

Figure 18-18   Adding Team Access to a Credential

Next, pick the appteam by selecting their check box. Figure 18-19 shows this selection.

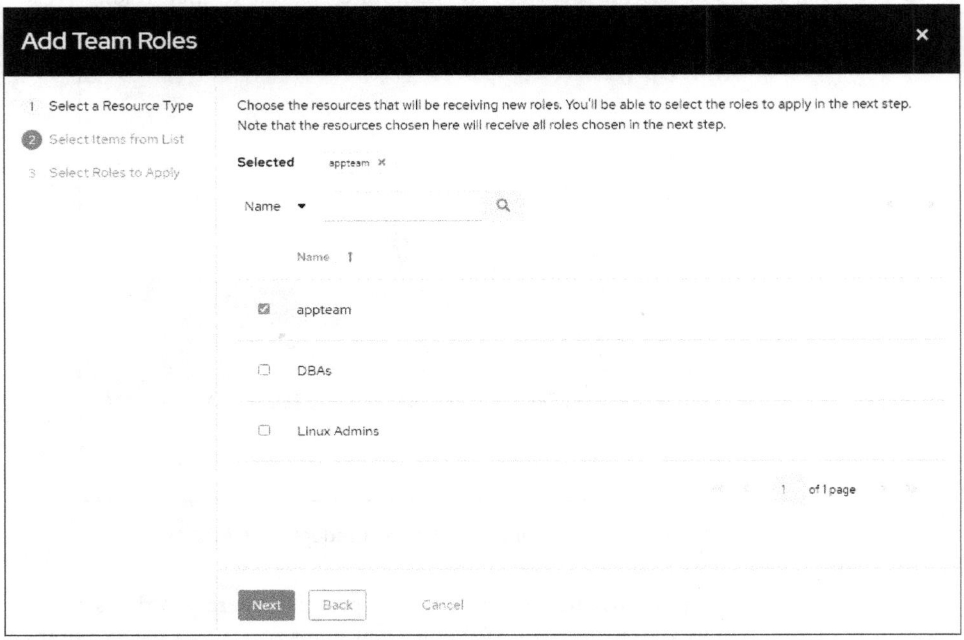

Figure 18-19   Selecting the appteam

Next, you need to set what type of role this is. In this case (see Figure 18-20), only allow the team to use the credential. Optionally, the team or Group can also have full admin access to modify the credential or read-only access where they can see the credential details.

> **Note**
>
> Be careful when using read access because users can easily see the key or password and use that access outside of OLAM.

Now save the access. You will be automatically redirected back to the **Access** tab for the credential, but in this case, you can see that the appteam now has the ability to use this credential, as shown in Figure 18-21.

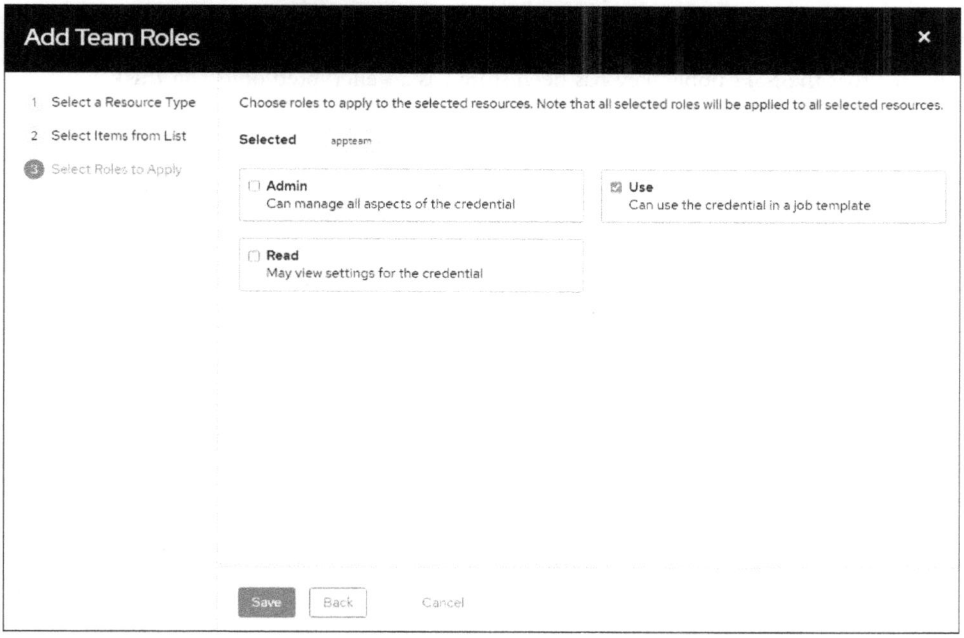

Figure 18-20   Access Role

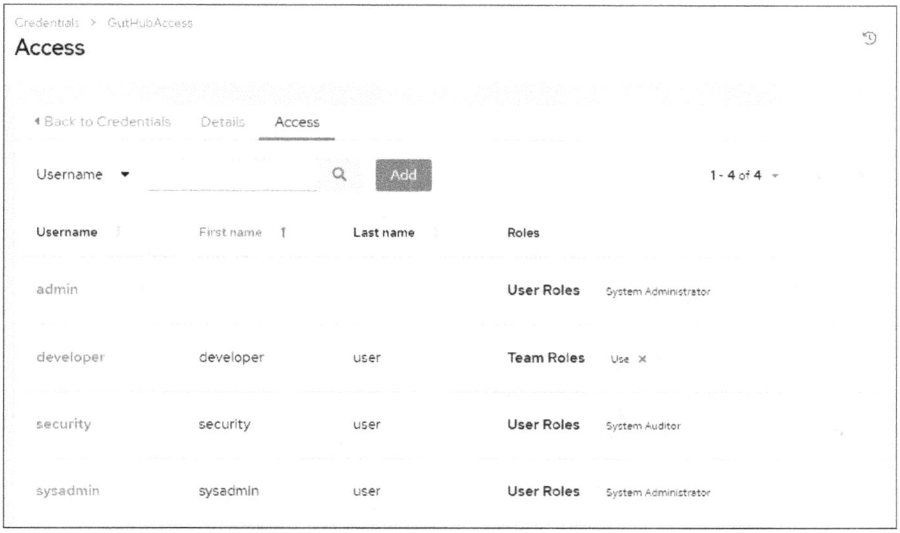

Figure 18-21   appteam Added

The process to add other credentials is similar, using the same overall process. Another popular credential is a machine credential, which is an account password or SSH key. Machine credentials are used when you SSH to a system or device.

In this sample, a credential is set to allow SSH into OCI using the opc user (see Figure 18-22). The credential will also use sudo when needing to access root. You can also see that the SSH public key has been stored as an encrypted object in the key.

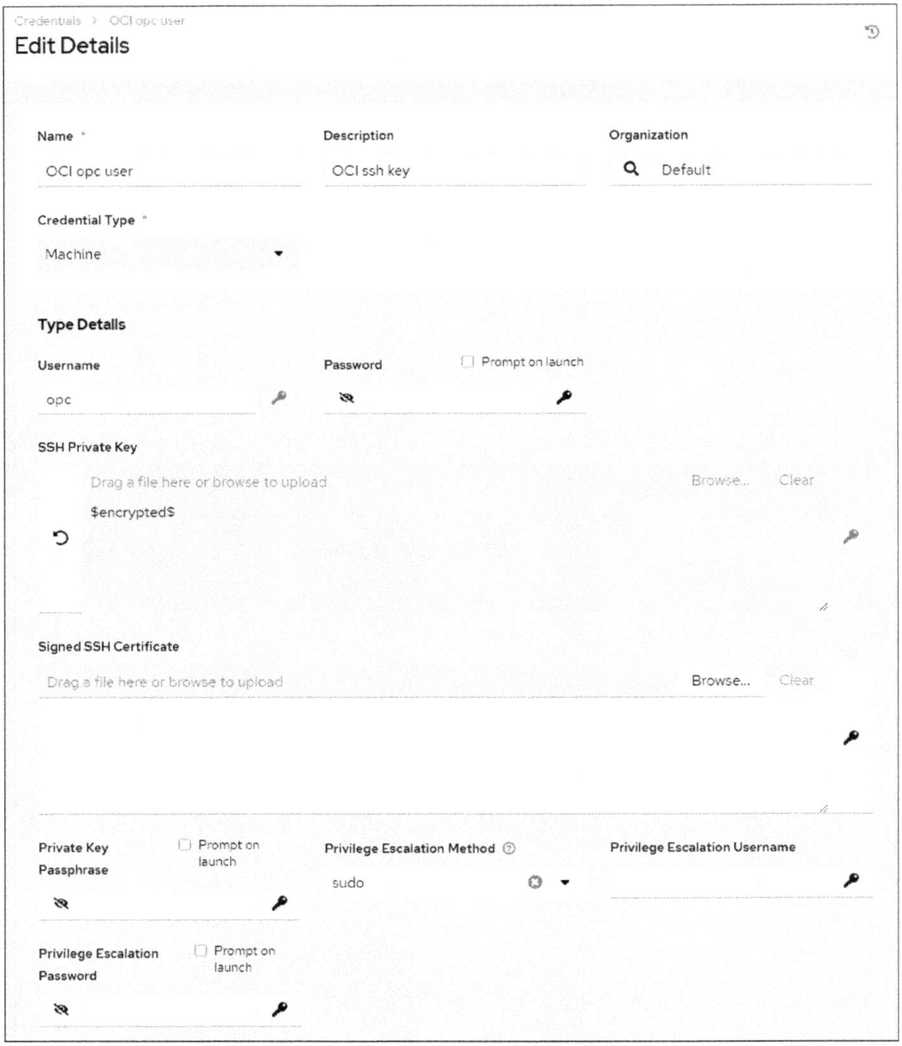

Figure 18-22   Machine Credential

Creating a Project

Projects are a key resource because they allow the security team to align the teams and individuals with the resources they need to manage. To create a project, navigate to **Resources > Projects** and click **Add**, as shown in Figure 18-23.

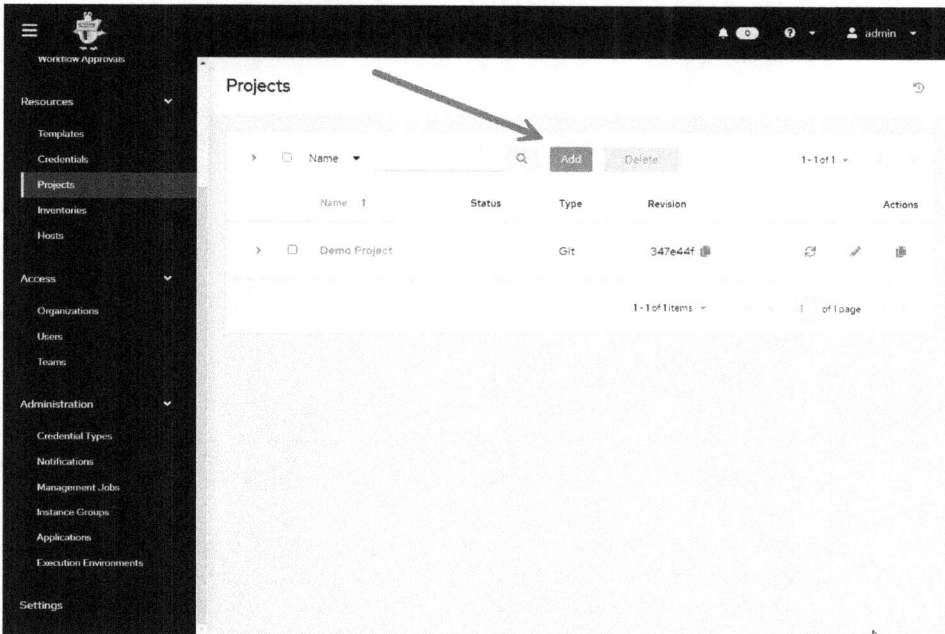

Figure 18-23 Creating a New Project

When creating a project, as you can see in Figure 18-24, you will need an execution environment (EE) and source control credentials predefined. All new OLAM installs come with two EEs, although you can optionally create a custom EE with all the dependencies to run playbooks built into the project.

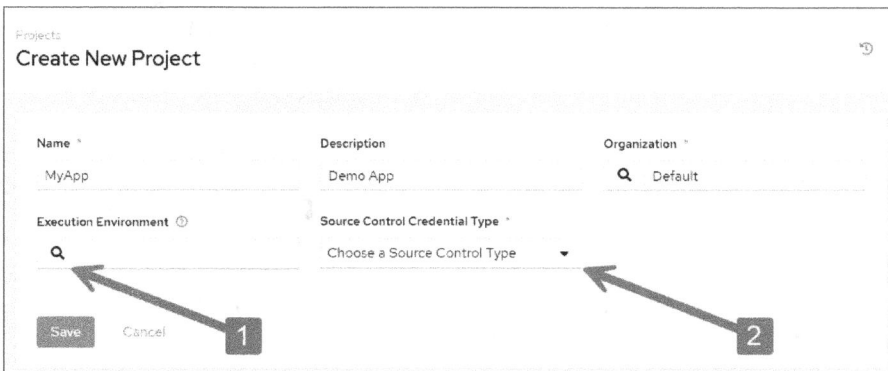

Figure 18-24 New Project

To select an execution environment, click the search icon under Execution Environment. This will start a selection menu, as shown in Figure 18-25. From here, you can pick the execution environment you want to use.

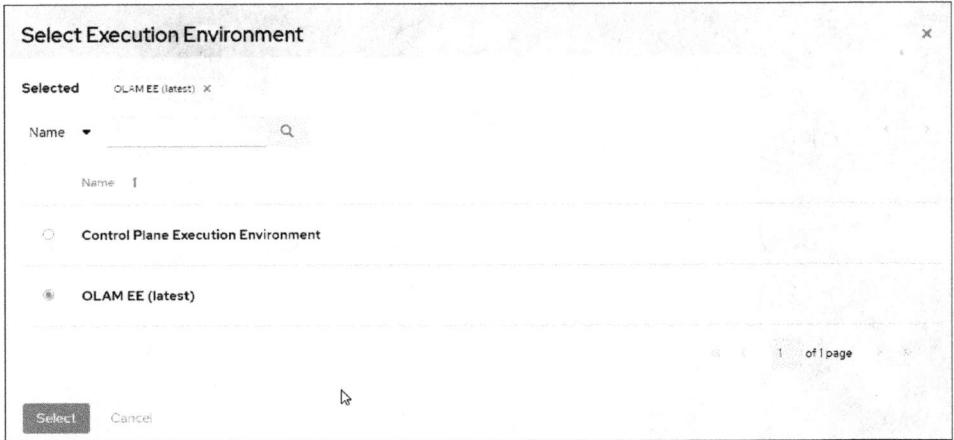

Figure 18-25   Selecting an Execution Environment

Next, select the Source Control Credential Type by selecting **Git** from the drop-down. You can then use the publicly available OCI Ansible collection from https://github.com/oracle/oci-ansible-collection as the URL. Because this is a read-only Git, no authentication is required. Figure 18-26 shows what it should look like.

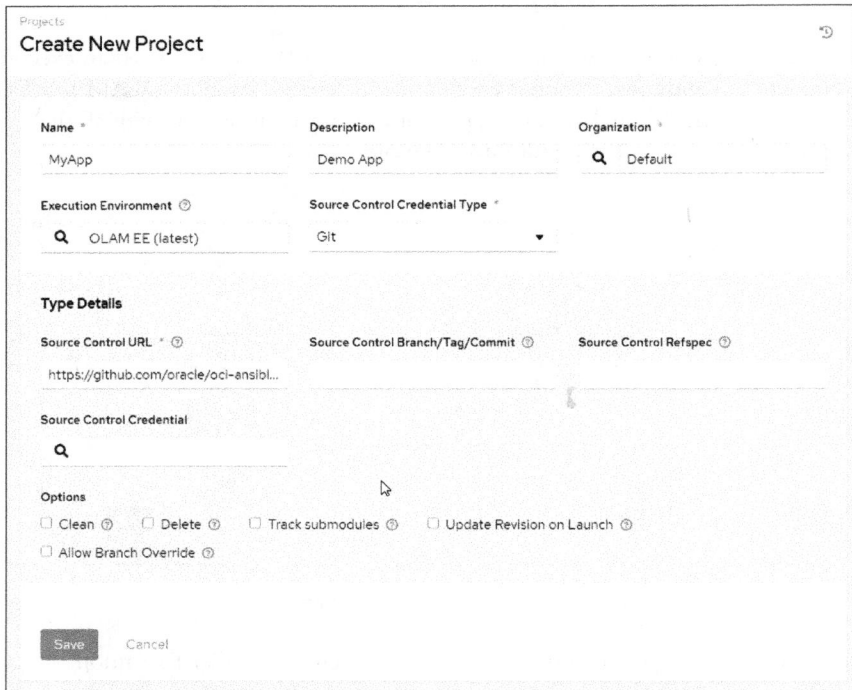

Figure 18-26   Project Using Oracle OCI GitHub

Now that the project is created, you will need to configure the access. This is done by selecting the **Access** tab from the Projects page and then adding the teams as you did with the other credentials.

When done, your Access page should look similar to Figure 18-27.

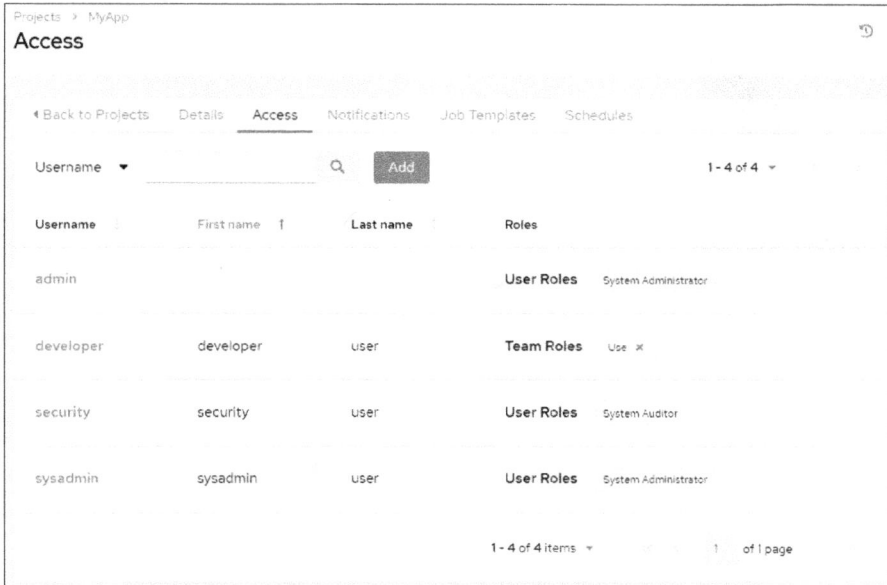

Figure 18-27   Project Access Control

Next, we will set up an Inventory before adding some jobs for users to run.

Setting Up an Inventory

Inventories are key to setting up the security to limit what systems or targets a team can manage with playbooks. Navigate to **Resources > Inventories** to see what inventories have been created and also to add them (see Figure 18-28).

From here, you can see what inventories have been created. You can also create a new inventory by clicking **Add**. When adding new inventories, you have a choice of a regular inventory or a smart inventory, as seen in Figure 18-29.

For this example (shown in Figure 18-30), you can create a regular inventory. That being said, smart inventories are a great tool because they can connect to OCI (or other technologies like Oracle Linux Virtualization Manager or VMWare) to dynamically discover hosts/VMs and update an inventory.

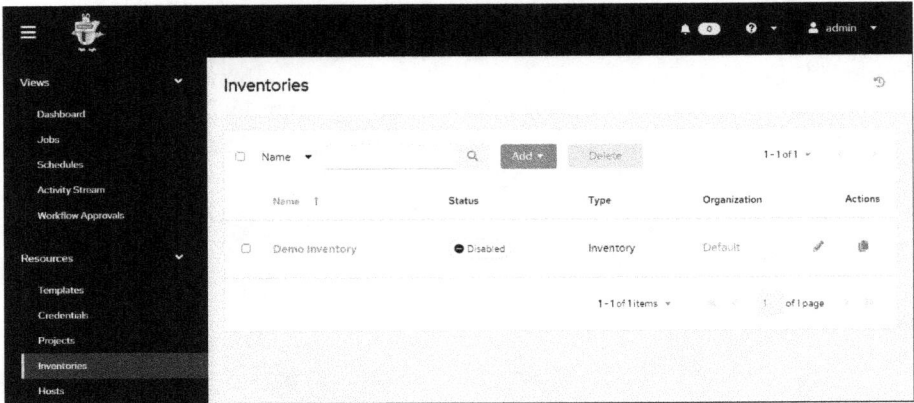

Figure 18-28   Inventory List

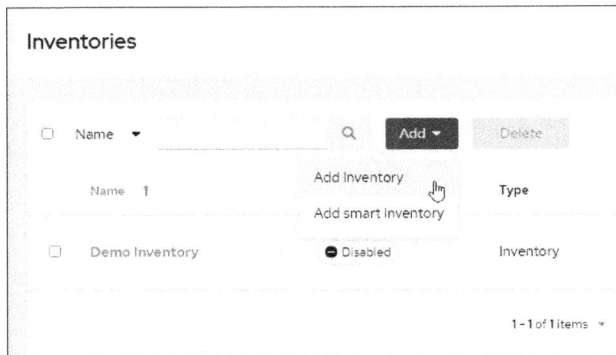

Figure 18-29   Adding an Inventory

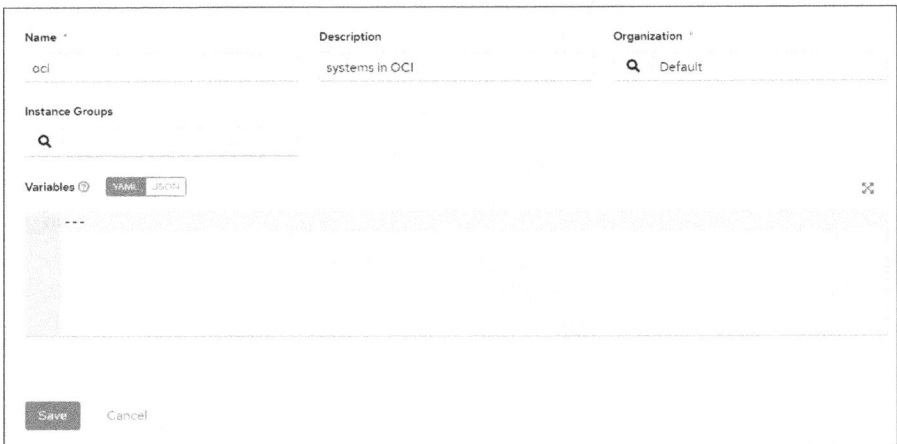

Figure 18-30   Inventory Details

You will then be prompted to provide the name and description of the inventory.

This takes you to the main inventory dialog. From here, you can set up the access and assign roles to teams and users. To do this, click the **Access** tab from the inventory dialog and add the roles in the same way you added roles to other resources. When done, the dialog should look similar to Figure 18-31.

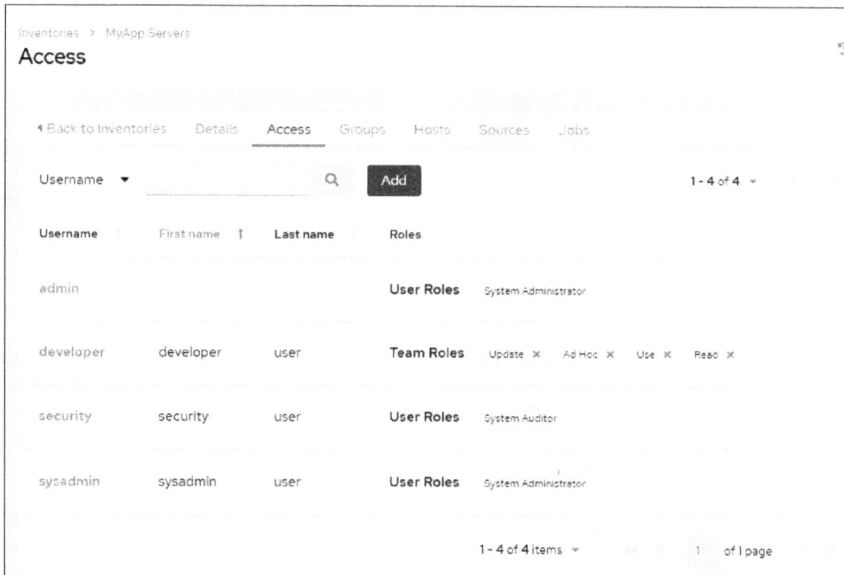

Figure 18-31   Inventory Roles

Next, let's add some hosts. Click the **Hosts** tab to see a list of all hosts in the inventory. In Figure 18-32, you can see there are no hosts yet. Click **Add** to add a host.

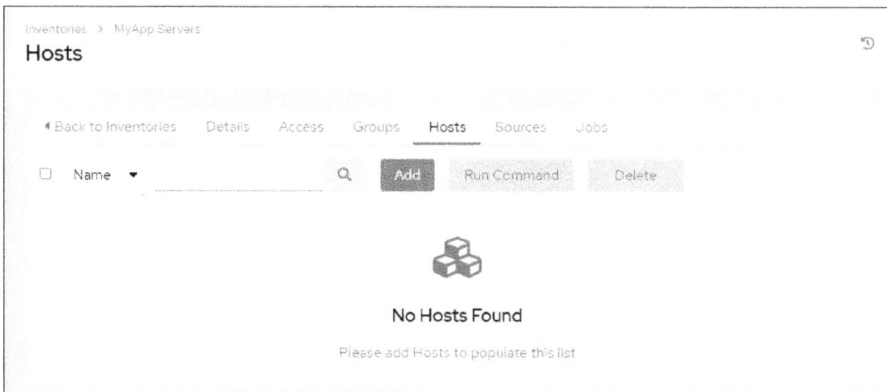

Figure 18-32   Hosts List

When manually adding a host, you should use its name in the Name field. Ideally, use the fully qualified domain name (FQDN), but you can also use an IP address or the short name. In the sample shown in Figure 18-33, you can see the server ociserver2 being added.

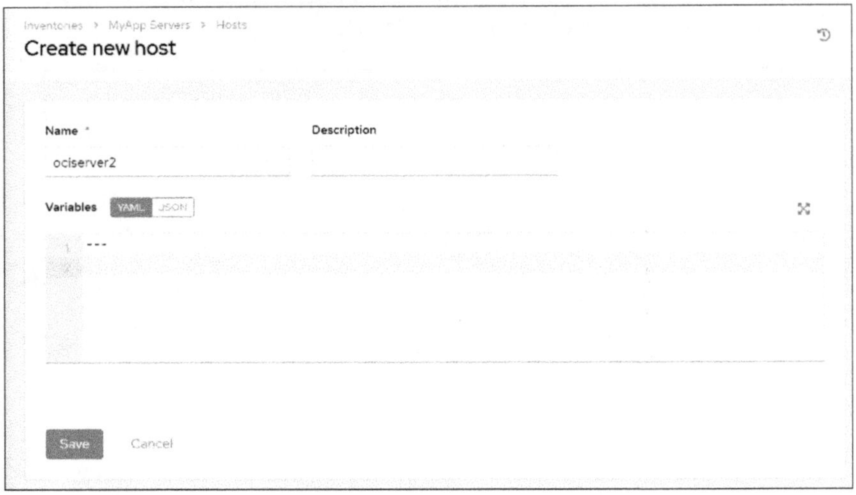

Figure 18-33   Adding a Host

You can continue adding hosts, but you should also test access to all the hosts when you are done adding them. In Figure 18-34, two hosts have been added.

Figure 18-34   Hosts to Test

You can now test access by running a simple command against the host. Select **Run Command**, as shown in Figure 18-35, after selecting the check box for the hosts.

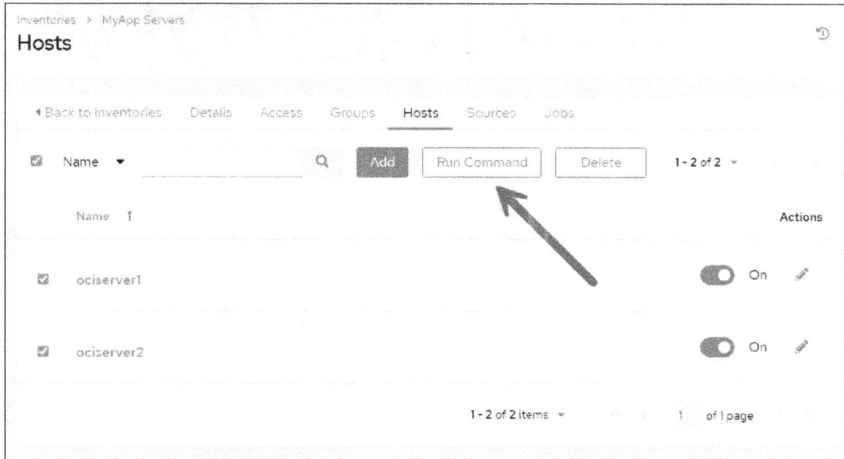

Figure 18-35   Running a Command Against a Host

From here, you have several options. In this sample, just run a shell command on the selected host. From the module, select **shell**, with the arguments being the shell command to run (see Figure 18-36).

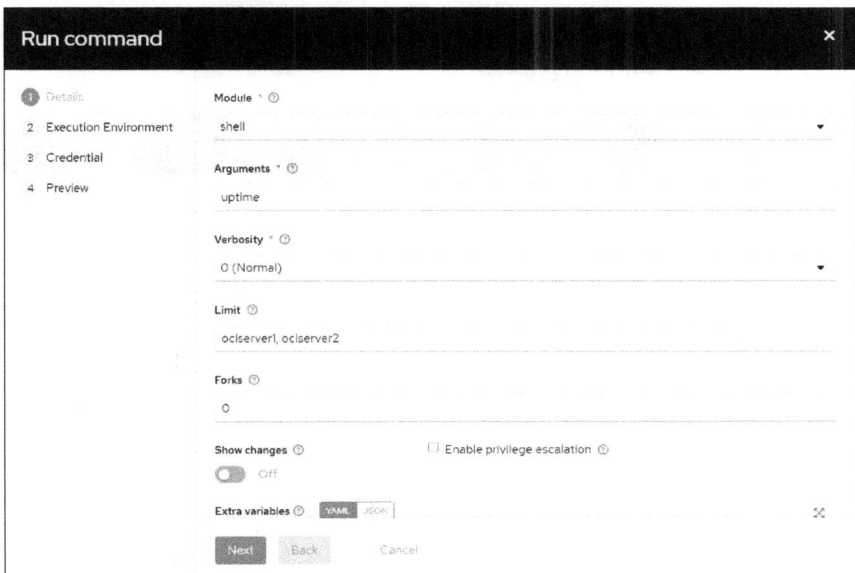

Figure 18-36   Running a Shell Command

Next, you need to select the execution environment to use. For this example, use the stock environment **OLAM EE (latest)**, as shown in Figure 18-37.

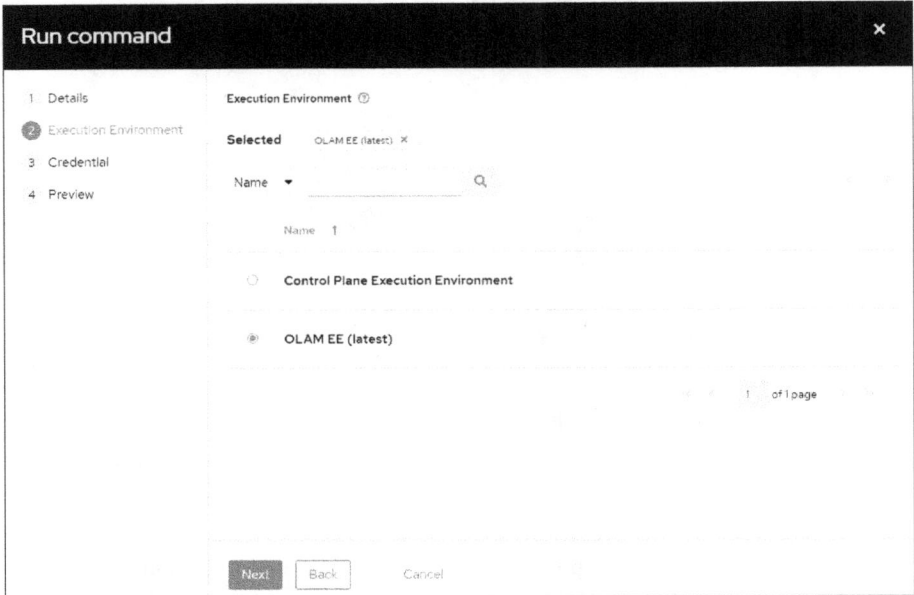

Figure 18-37   Selecting the Execution Environment

You also need to use a credential for this, so you can use the SSH credential previously created, as shown in Figure 18–38.

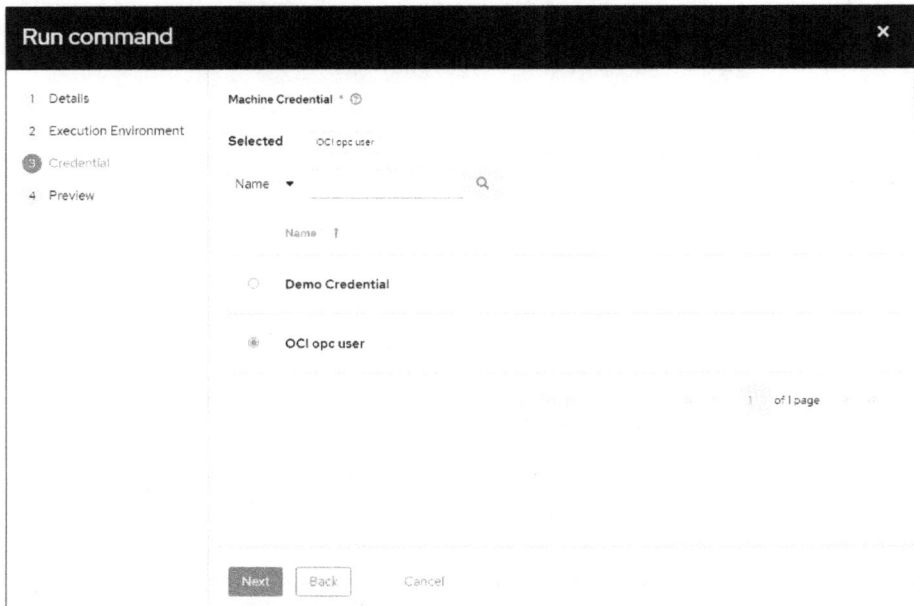

Figure 18-38   Selecting a Credential

Finally, you can run the job by clicking the **Launch** button. This will run the command. Figure 18-39 shows the final screen.

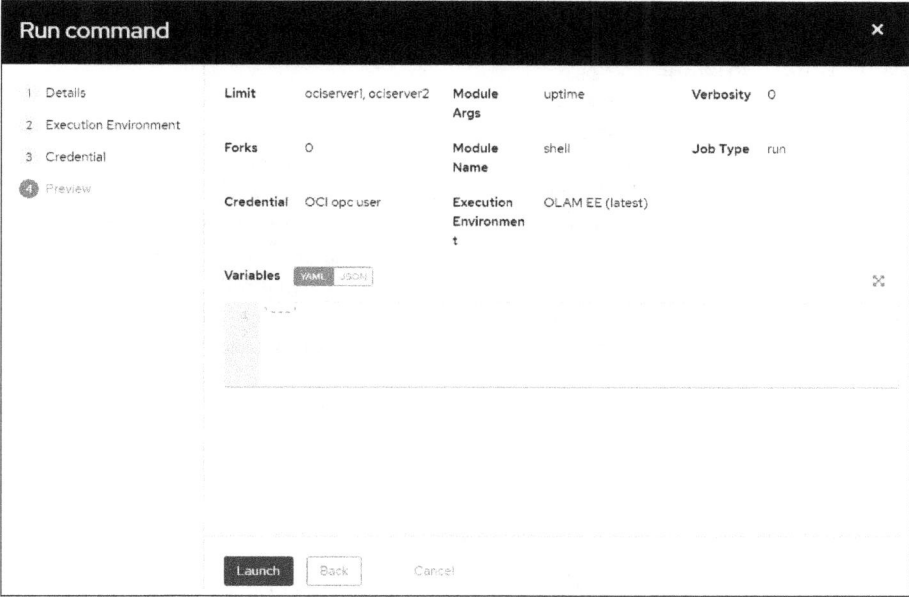

Figure 18-39 Launching the Test

As the job runs, you can see the output, as shown in Figure 18-40.

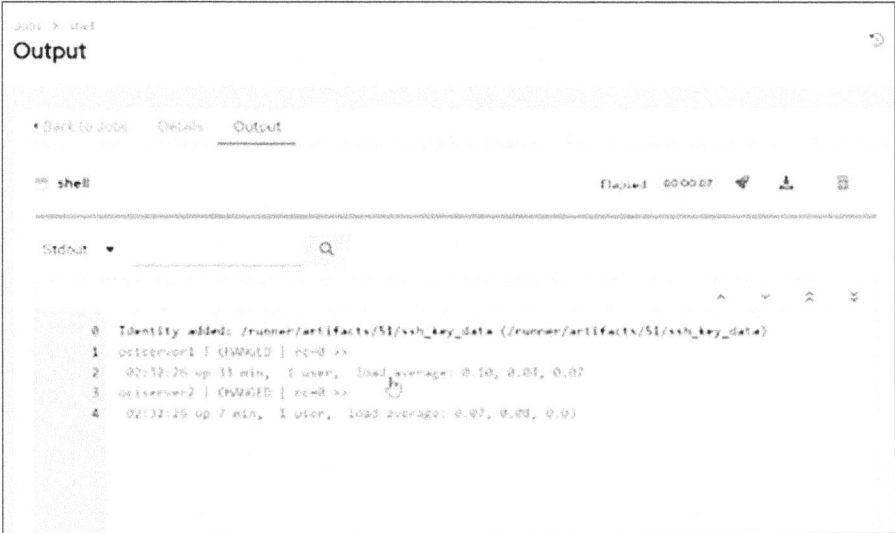

Figure 18-40 Job Output

Here, you can see the results for each host the job runs against. It's always best practice to do a simple test like this when adding inventories because it makes sure communication works as expected.

Making a Job Template

Job templates are one of the final steps before users can utilize the system. A job template contains all the necessary information to define which playbook is executed and what parameters are used. To access the templates, go to the main menu and select **Resources > Templates**. This will lead you to the list of available templates. From there, click **Add** to create a new template. You can choose either a regular template or a workflow template. Workflow templates are more advanced, allowing you to define a sequence of playbook executions that can include decision-making logic and branching. This functionality enables you to orchestrate complex deployments and manage dependencies among multiple tasks. For this example, create a basic template, as shown in Figure 18-41.

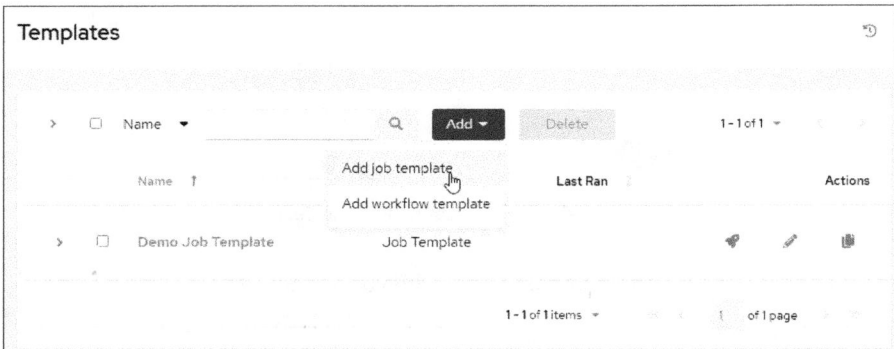

Figure 18-41   Creating a Template

You need to start at the top, with all the basic details. This includes the following options:

- The name and description of the template
- The type of job (You can choose to run or check. Checking jobs only verifies the playbook syntax, tests environment setup, and reports problems without executing the playbook.)
- The inventory that will be used
- The project to use

Note: Projects Have One Important Limitation

A project can only run playbooks that exist in the project. If using multiple playbooks from multiple projects, you should create a new project that contains all the playbooks that are needed.

- The execution environment to use
- A playbook to run (This is gathered from a drop-down list.)
- The credentials to use for the job

Optionally, you can check the prompt on launch to allow users to select that parameter when the job runs. These are all seen in Figure 18-42.

Templates > get time
Edit Details

| Name * | | Description | | Job Type * ⓘ | ☐ Prompt on launch |
| get time | | | | Run | ▾ |

| Inventory * ⓘ | ☐ Prompt on launch | Project * ⓘ | | Execution Environment ⓘ | |
| 🔍 MyApp Servers | | 🔍 MyApp2 | | 🔍 OLAM EE (latest) | |

Playbook * ⓘ
time.yml   ▾

| Credentials ⓘ | | | ☐ Prompt on launch |
| 🔍 SSH: OCI opc user ✕ | | | |

Figure 18-42   Basic Template Options

As you scroll past the basic options, you will find more advanced parameters that can be set (see Figure 18-43).

- **Fork:** This parameter sets the number of simultaneous times the playbook can be run. This allows you to run multiple targets in parallel.
- **Limit:** This parameter sets a pattern for the host to limit where the playbook can be run. This parameter uses the Ansible patterns logic with a colon or comma separating the fields. You can also use an exclamation point (!) as a *not logic expression*. So linux:!phoenix would allow the playbook to run on Linux systems not in Phoenix.
- **Verbosity:** The more verbose, the more information that can be used to troubleshoot. The downside is that high levels like 3 and 4 can bog down the system when run all the time and make it difficult for users to understand the results of the job.
- **Job Slicing:** This setting enables you to distribute the job across multiple hosts. This capability is helpful in larger environments when you need to quickly run

playbooks against large numbers of servers. You will need multiple hosts to run execution engines.

- **Timeout:** This setting overrides the default timeout for jobs, which is normally 0! This is measured in seconds.
- **Show Changes:** This setting will let you see changes to the job made by the task.
- **Instance Groups:** This setting indicates the Instance group to run on.
- **Tags:** This parameter identifies the tags used for controlling the job.
- **Check boxes:**
  - **Privilege Escalation:** Allows the playbook to run as root or administrator.
  - **Provisioning Callbacks:** Enables this job to use a REST call to launch another playbook.
  - **Enable Webhook:** Enables you to interface with GitHub or GitLab SCM systems to launch playbooks. Other SCM systems may be added in the future.
  - **Concurrent Jobs:** Allows jobs to run simultaneously if there is no dependency on each other.
  - **Enable Fact Storage:** Stores the facts from the job in the database.

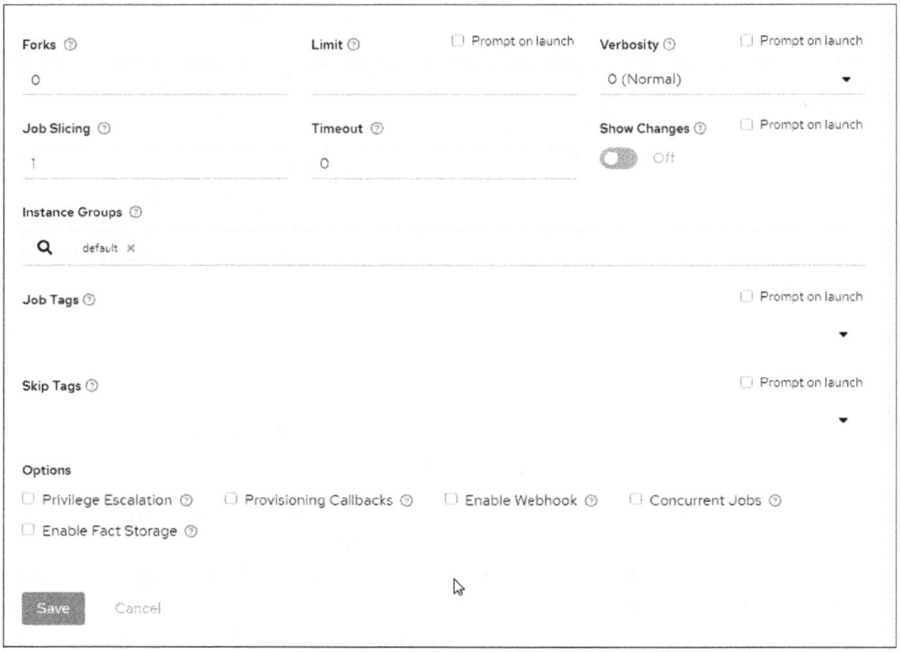

Figure 18-43   Advanced Template Options

Once the template is added, you will go back to the main dialog for the template. This dialog is shown in Figure 18-44.

From here, you can immediately launch the job to test it! As the job runs, you can monitor the status from the job output dialog, as shown in Figure 18-45.

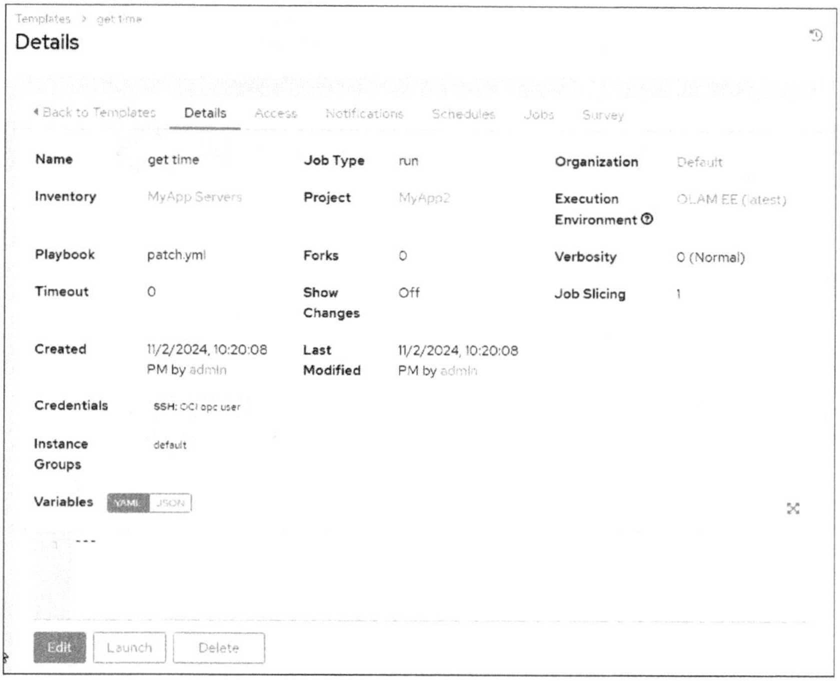

Figure 18-44 Template Main Dialog

Figure 18-45 Job Output

Congratulations, you have a template, and it works! When users want to run the same template, they can log in to OLAM and select **Resources > Templates**. This page will show them the templates that they can run (see Figure 18-46).

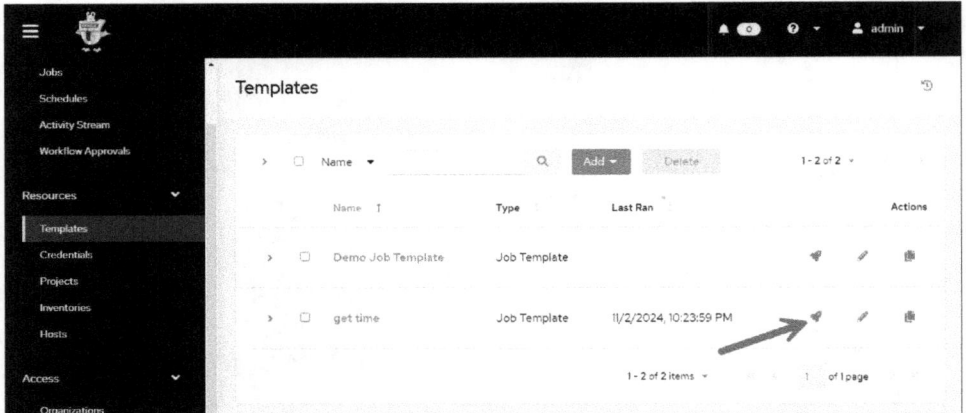

Figure 18-46   User's View

When a user wants to run a template, they click the rocket icon.

Performing Job Analysis

You can see the history of all the jobs that have run in the system. To do this, from the main menu, select **Views > Jobs** to see the history. Failed jobs will show up as red and include Failed in the status (see Figure 18-47).

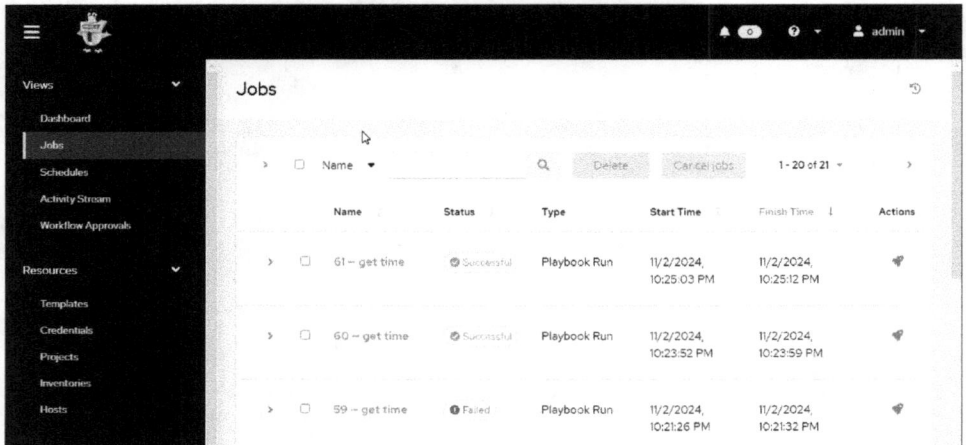

Figure 18-47   Job History

To get more information about the failed job, you can select the job to see the output, as shown in Figure 18-48.

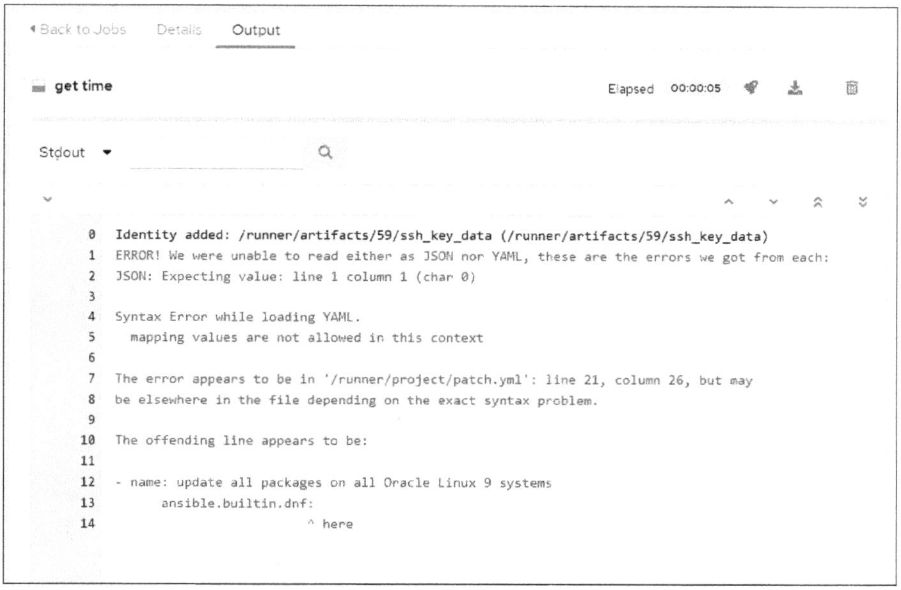

Figure 18-48   Job Output

This job output page shows the details, and often this information is enough to troubleshoot the failure. You can always run the failed job again, after increasing the verbosity up to level 4, but it's not recommended to always run with this level of detail.

Summary

In this chapter, you learned how to set up the OLAM environment that will enable you to create all the resources required to allow your users to securely run playbooks, based on their roles, and limited to a specific subset of servers. You set up users, team inventories, projects, and templates with control over what roles the team members have to run and manage the playbooks. This chapter provided a solid foundation for learning OLAM and how you can enable self-service and full stack automation for all of your staff. The next chapter will switch to using Terraform for automation.

19

Infrastructure as Code

As cloud computing grew in popularity and usage, scaling became an issue.

Managing IT infrastructure is difficult enough, but as the adoption of cloud computing exploded, these infrastructures became difficult to manage and brought to light three challenges in cloud infrastructure management: speed, scalability, and consistency. Speed and scalability are tied closely to each other. With it being extremely easy to provision cloud resources, the ability to keep up with demand becomes increasingly difficult.

In a typical IT enterprise, there can be multiple levels of automation:

- **Source Code:** Tools such as Jenkins or OCI DevOps can be used to check out code from source code repositories such as GitHub or Bitbucket, where they are built and deployed to a target environment. Chapter 9, "OCI DevOps Service," covers OCI DevOps in detail.
- **Container:** A container can be built and configured using tools such as Chef, Puppet, Docker, or OCI DevOps. For example, Oracle Kubernetes clusters can be created and configured through OCI DevOps by checking out a container image from Container Registry, which is a private Docker registry for OKE deployments. Chapter 9 covers OCI DevOps in more detail.
- **Environment:** Setting up a cloud infrastructure involves multiple provisioning steps, including VCNs, subnets, route tables, security rules, and so on. Automating this setup helps ensure that your development, testing, and production environments in OCI are identically configured. This is where the concept of *Infrastructure as Code*, or *IaC*, fits in.

Software developers have always had the benefit of maintaining their code in a version-controlled repository and applying repeatable and consistent deployment processes. Why couldn't the same be done for infrastructure? Being able to treat infrastructure "as code" and deploying said infrastructure in a repeatable, consistent, and rapid fashion follows similar best practices that developers employ when deploying their code. IaC manages the IT infrastructure using configuration files.

IaC follows the DevOps model of continuous integration and continuous deployment. Infrastructure provisioning can go through a CI/CD pipeline, similar to what developers use for code deployment, following similar processes for version control, essentially versioning all infrastructure configuration.

The Problem That IaC Solves

Generally speaking, supporting the deployment of an application, such as a web application, involves a number of activities:

1. A cloud administrator would set up and create the cloud infrastructure, including all aspects of security, compute, storage, and load balancers.
2. The web, application, and database servers may need to be installed and configured.
3. Developers follow standard DevSecOps approaches to deploy and promote their code across the environments, after which it is released and live.

IaC is designed for infrastructure provisioning, specifically step 1 here (not for steps 2 or 3). IaC is not only intended for provisioning but is also used for configuring and tracking changes in your infrastructure.

Even small infrastructure footprints with limited changes can benefit from IaC. It is difficult to manage and maintain hundreds, if not thousands or even tens of thousands, of individual configuration settings in your infrastructure.

Introducing Terraform as an IaC Tool

HashiCorp is a software company that offers a number of open-source and commercial products and was acquired by IBM in February 2025. One of these products is *Terraform*, an open-source IaC software tool created in 2014. It is used as an infrastructure provisioning tool and is the focus of this and the next few chapters.

Terraform uses a proprietary language called *HashiCorp Configuration Language*, or *HCL*. The Terraform configuration is stored in files with a .tf extension. Though alternatives such as JSON and YAML can be used for writing this configuration, this book focuses on the more widely adopted HCL syntax. It is human-readable and makes it easy to quickly write code. While JSON's key-value format enhances readability, it does not support comments like HCL does. Using the JSON syntax, files end with a .tf. json extension. YAML, on the other hand, is whitespace-sensitive, meaning that proper indentation is critical, which can make troubleshooting difficult. You can find more information at http://terraform.io.

Because Terraform infrastructure configuration is versioned, configurations and their changes are documented. Terraform also enables the automation of tasks to manage infrastructure. It can be used to create, change, and destroy virtual infrastructure in an automated fashion across all major cloud providers.

Furthermore, Terraform is a declarative IaC tool as opposed to imperative. Imperative methods require documenting all steps required to achieve the desired end state. Chef, for example, is an imperative tool. Declarative methods, in contrast, simply define what the desired end state should look like, and the tool, in this case Terraform, does all the work. The concept of Terraform, and essentially IaC, is quite simple, as you can observe in Figure 19-1. Terraform executes from some location and uses a Terraform provider (to be discussed later) to create and manage resources on a cloud service provider through the API. Knowledge of the target API or its specifics is unnecessary, and all the hard work is performed by Terraform, since all Terraform needs is the configuration of the end state.

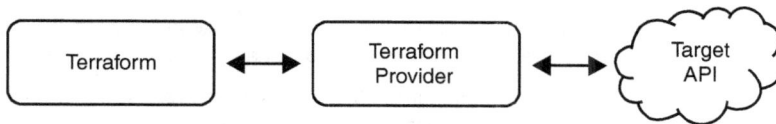

Figure 19-1   How Terraform Works

Terraform as a tool offers numerous advantages and benefits, some of which include

- **Reusability:** Configuration templates can be variabilized and reused.
- **Support for Many Providers:** An incredible number of plug-ins are available to interact with cloud providers, cloud services, and APIs. You can find a list of providers at https://registry.terraform.io/browse/providers.
- **Declarative Nature:** Writing Terraform configurations is easy. Terraform does all the work in most cases.
- **Pipeline Integration:** Terraform can be triggered from CI/CD tools such as OCI DevOps or GitHub Actions.

IaC helps eliminate configuration drift and ensure environments are consistent, provision resources easily and quickly for rapid deployments, and reduce risk and human error for its ability to automate and reuse.

Chapter 15 introduced Ansible. It is an open-source automation tool that can be used to manage applications, systems, and infrastructure. Both Ansible and Terraform are considered IaC tools, though there are differences. In summary, Terraform excels at infrastructure provisioning and lifecycle management of the infrastructure. Ansible's strengths lie in its configuration management capabilities, such as the configuration of provisioned infrastructure. For example, after the infrastructure is provisioned, it can install software, update configuration files, or configure runtime environments.

Terraform Concepts and Terminology

It is important to understand some concepts and terminology of Terraform, documented in Table 19-1, all of which will become clearer as you delve into the hands-on exercises in later chapters.

Table 19-1   Basic Terraform Concepts

Term	Explanation
Terraform	This open-source IaC tool was originally developed by HashiCorp in 2014 and primarily used for infrastructure provisioning.
Resources	Distinct objects or resources, such as a compute instance, VNC, or block storage, are used to create the infrastructure. A resource can be created, retrieved, changed, or destroyed.
Modules	These collections of resources are used together and include their respective configuration definitions. Each module is a folder.
Providers	This is a Terraform plug-in that interacts with various cloud service providers, SaaS services, or APIs. OCI is an example of a provider.
State	The state consists of the persisted state of the infrastructure managed by Terraform.
Configuration Files	These files take the extension .tf and describe the end state of the infrastructure. They are typically written in HCL.
Input Variables	These parameters take the form of key-value pairs for Terraform modules.
Output Variables	These responses are returned by a module and can be further passed to other configurations if necessary.
Data Sources	The sources are used in a module and are simply a read-only operation that returns information on objects external to Terraform.

Figure 19-2 shows how many of these components relate to each other. The administrator creates a series of configuration files. When executed, this configuration is processed by *Terraform Core* (that is, the Terraform binaries). When the configuration is finally applied to the target provider, a Terraform state file is created that matches the target provider.

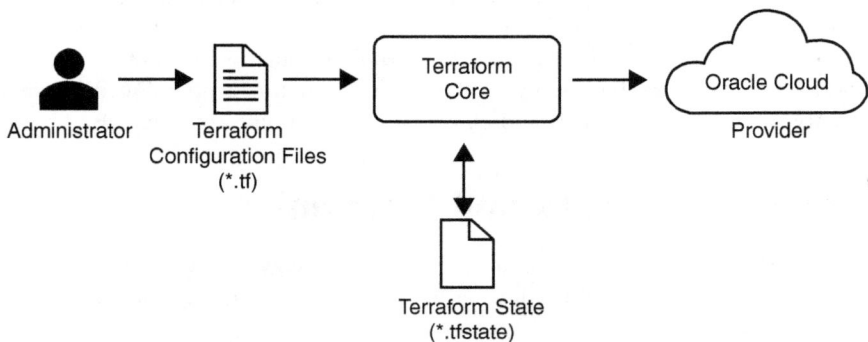

Figure 19-2   How Terraform Components Come Together

Basic Terraform commands are described in Table 19-2. The commands follow an "init → plan → apply" approach to Terraform provisioning or application of changes. Chapter 20, "Transform API with Examples," will walk through examples explaining how to prepare and run each of these commands.

Table 19-2   Basic Terraform Commands

Term	Explanation
terraform init	Initializes the working directory, to include actions such as loading the remote state and downloading any plug-ins required, and consists of all configuration files to be used.
terraform validate	Validates the configuration files by checking syntax and data.
terraform plan	Creates an execution plan that determines what needs to be created, changed, or destroyed. Running this command shows the execution plan without executing it, allowing you to review what will happen.
terraform apply	Applies the actual changes to the target environment.
terraform destroy	Destroys the infrastructure (and its resources) defined.

Declarative Approach

As mentioned earlier, step-by-step instructions to create resources ae not required because Terraform is not imperative. Terraform configuration files are declarative. This means that you only need to define the end state of your infrastructure in your configuration files.

State File

A state file is created after the **terraform apply** command is executed. This file is called terraform.tfstate. It is the source of truth of your provisioned infrastructure that Terraform manages. When the plan is applied, Terraform cross-references your changes (from the .tf file) with the state (the terraform.tfstate file) to determine which part of your configuration has already been created. Thus, Terraform is able to determine the changes needed.

Immutable Infrastructure

Another unique approach to Terraform is that it provisions an *immutable infrastructure*. For example, if you are going through a multi-step infrastructure provisioning plan, and if one of the steps in the middle fails, you can safely rerun it because Terraform is aware of the state and will continue to apply changes from the point it last failed.

Immutable infrastructures do have their disadvantages though. A configuration change may have been applied, but depending on the resource, it may not take effect until you run the image. Furthermore, simple changes on large setups can take a long time as the plan is executed in its entirety.

Plug-ins

Terraform *plug-ins* are called *providers* or *provider plug-ins*. They interact with APIs of various platforms and services to create, update, and delete resources. An incredible number of plug-ins are available to interact with cloud providers, cloud services, and APIs.

Both HashiCorp and the Terraform community have written thousands of plug-ins that are published and freely available to download at https://registry.terraform.io/browse/providers (see Figure 19-3). Plug-ins for cloud providers such as OCI, AWS, Azure, and Google Cloud Platform are available. Plug-ins for other cloud or PaaS services are also available. Examples include plug-ins to Citrix, CloudFlare, BigIP, GitHub, NetApp, Snowflake, Splunk, and many more. For example, the Salesforce plug-in can be used to associate users with profiles and create role hierarchies within Salesforce as part of an environment provisioning process. In fact, to date there are a total of 2,919 plug-ins. Alternatively, you can write a plug-in of your own as well.

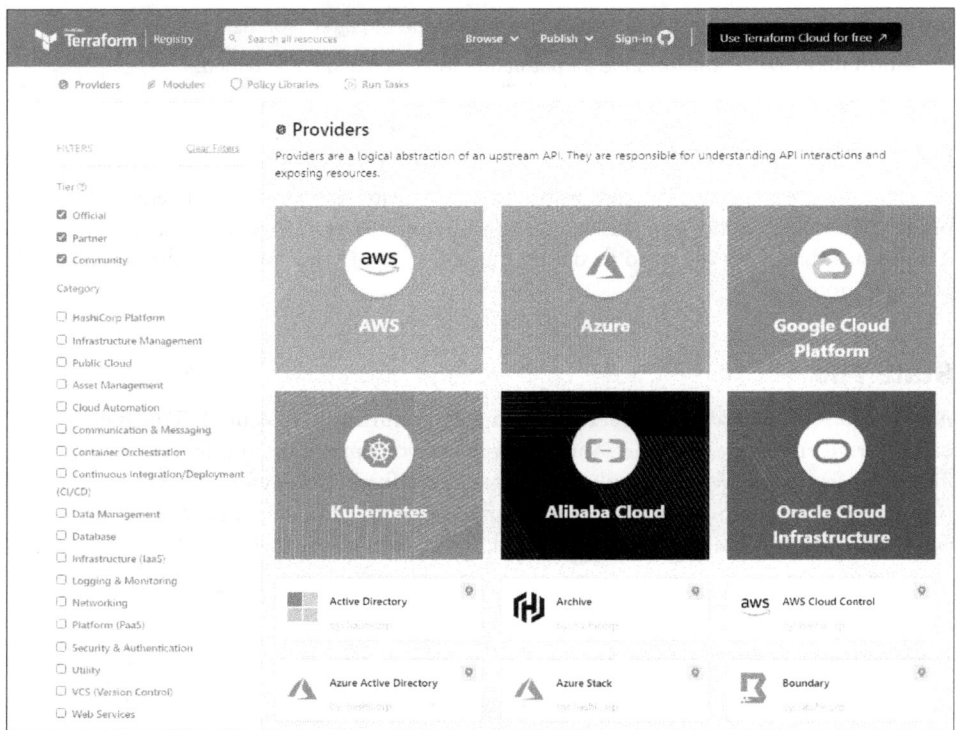

Figure 19-3   The Terraform Registry Web Page to View and Download Plug-ins

For the most part, you do not have to worry about downloading plug-ins. In Chapter 20 as you go through the exercises, you will learn that by simply running the **terraform init** command, the OCI provider plug-in is automatically downloaded for you.

Terraform and OCI

On the OCI console, after navigating to Developer Services, you will observe a Terraform option under Developer Resources, as shown in Figure 19-4. There is no Terraform service. In fact, all links under Developer Resources merely direct you to existing documentation.

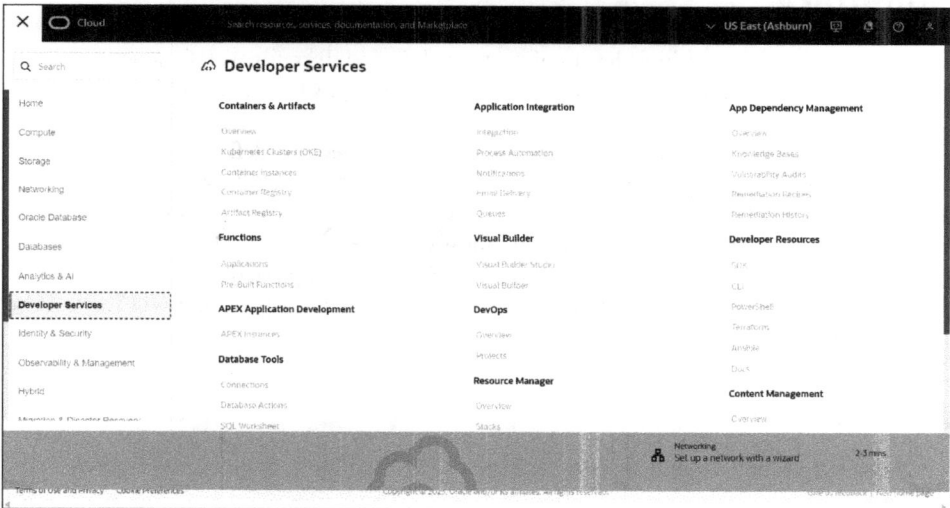

Figure 19-4   Terraform Menu Option in the OCI Console

The OCI Terraform provider plug-in is used to manage your OCI resources. Terraform can be installed on your workstation or server or can run in Terraform Cloud or OCI Resource Manager. Resource Manager is an OCI service that is based on Terraform. You can find the documentation for it at https://docs.oracle.com/en-us/iaas/Content/ResourceManager.

Terraform Best Practices

There are many best practices when working with Terraform. They will make more sense as you progress in your Terraform journey over the next few chapters. Some of them include

- Check all Terraform code into a code repository such as OCI DevOps or GitHub.
- Do not hard-code resources in your Terraform code.
- Back up your state files.
- Validate your Terraform code.
- Use modules.

- Generate a README for each module with input and output variables.
- Do not store credentials in Terraform code.
- Autoformat Terraform files.
- Do not manually manipulate Terraform state unless through Terraform commands.

Summary

This chapter summarized high-level concepts on IaC and Terraform. IaC is designed for infrastructure tracking, configuration, and provisioning. One such tool for this is Terraform.

Terraform is declarative in nature, meaning you only need to define the end state of your infrastructure, and Terraform takes care of the rest. An OCI provider plug-in is available on the Terraform registry and can be used to create, update, and delete OCI resources. Terraform can be executed locally, from Terraform Cloud or directly from OCI Resource Manager, which is the recommended approach when exclusively managing OCI infrastructure and environments. In the next chapter, you will learn more about Terraform APIs.

## 20

Terraform API with Examples

In Chapter 19, "Infrastructure as Code," you learned about IaC and Terraform concepts. This chapter will put in practice those concepts. Oracle provides excellent tutorials that walk you through the initial setup of Terraform to work with OCI, but here we will describe and explain in detail each step of the process to give you a full understanding of how the end-to-end process works.

The best approach to getting started with Terraform is to just dive into it.

Setting Up Terraform in OCI

In this chapter, we will set up Terraform on a Red Hat Enterprise Linux host. This host will become your Terraform client host (that is, the master host that is used to run all your Terraform commands from).

Downloading and Installing Terraform

The Terraform binaries should be installed on some host. This can be a local workstation or a server. It does not make a difference where Terraform executes from, because ideally all your Terraform scripts would be checked out and synced with some code repository.

The first step is to download Terraform for your operating system from https://developer.hashicorp.com/terraform/downloads. By navigating to the Hashicorp Terraform download page, as shown in Figure 20-1, you can download the appropriate version and install it directly by executing the **yum** commands shown.

Figure 20-1 displays the commands needed to download and install Terraform onto a Red Hat Enterprise Linux operating system. Simply run **terraform -v** afterward to confirm that the installation was successful. Alternatively, you can download a zip file of the binaries and install it manually. For Red Hat Enterprise Linux, the manual installation simply involves unzipping the contents of the file and moving it to /usr/local/bin.

As depicted in Figure 20-2, the root user was used to install the Terraform binaries, and the installation was validated with the **terraform -v** command.

Figure 20-1   Downloading Terraform from Hashicorp

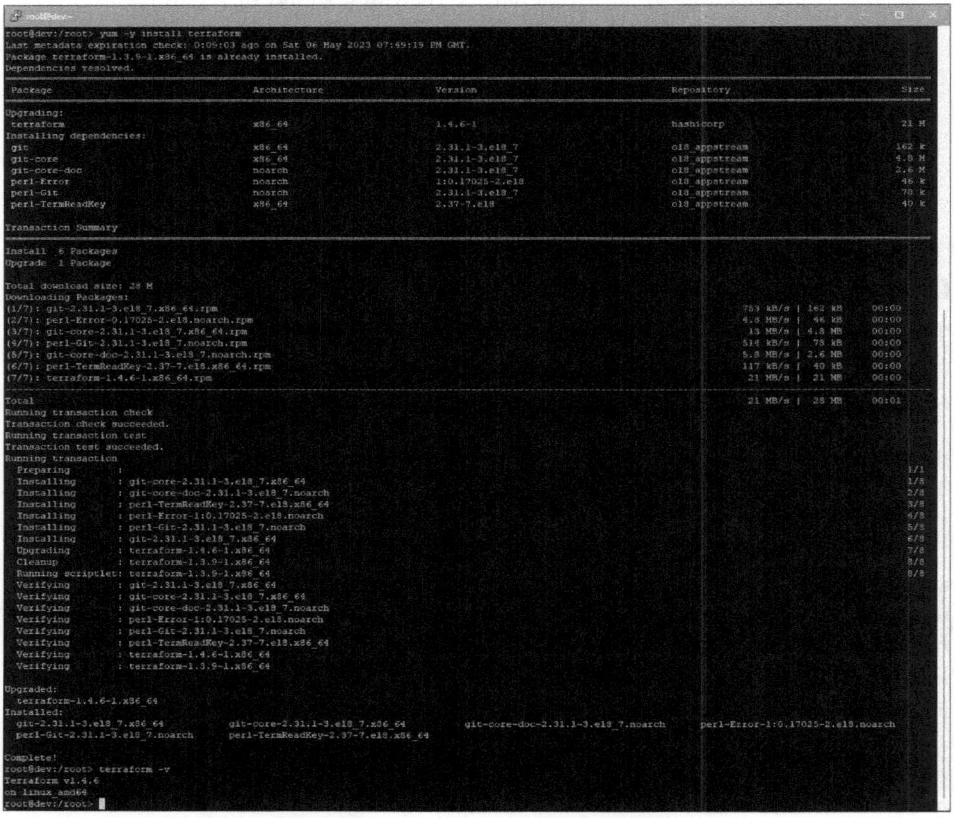

Figure 20-2   Installing Terraform as root

Creating RSA Keys Required for API Signing

An RSA key is required for API signing. This is the key that allows Terraform to authenticate against OCI to provision your services. Since the API key is associated with an OCI user, when you execute the Terraform scripts, it will only be able to provision services that the OCI user is granted permission to do.

Create a public/private key pair on the Terraform client host by running the commands listed in Example 20-1. These commands will create the key pair needed. Though the Terraform binaries were installed as root (see the previous section), Terraform can be executed under any other user.

Example 20-1   Creating a Public/Private Key Pair

```
# Create a directory to store your RSA keys
mkdir $HOME/.oci
cd $HOME/.oci

# Generate a 2048-bit private key (in PEM format)
openssl genrsa -out orakey.pem 2048

# Change permissions to restrict read/write
chmod 600 orakey.pem

# Generate the public key from the private key
openssl rsa -pubout -in orakey.pem -out orakey_public.pem

# Copy the contents of the public key (to be added to your OCI account)
cat orakey_public.pem
```

Now that the RSA keys are created and the contents of the public key have been copied, it is time to add them to the OCI user account:

Step 1. Navigate to the OCI console menu and click **Identity & Security > Users**.

Step 2. Click the username of the OCI user to associate this RSA key with.

Step 3. Click **API Keys** on the left menu.

Step 4. Click **Add API Key**.

Note

There is a limit of three API keys for each OCI user.

Step 5. Select **Paste Public Key**. Then paste the contents of the orakey_public.pem file that was copied in the last command shown in Example 20-1 and click **Add** (see Figure 20-3).

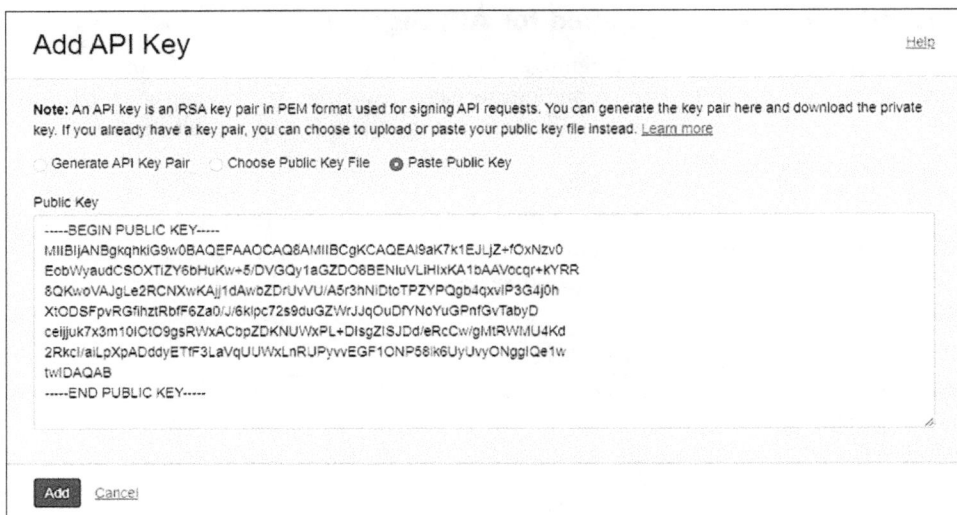

Figure 20-3   Adding a Public Key to the OCI User Account

After the key is added, a window will be displayed, as shown in Figure 20-4.

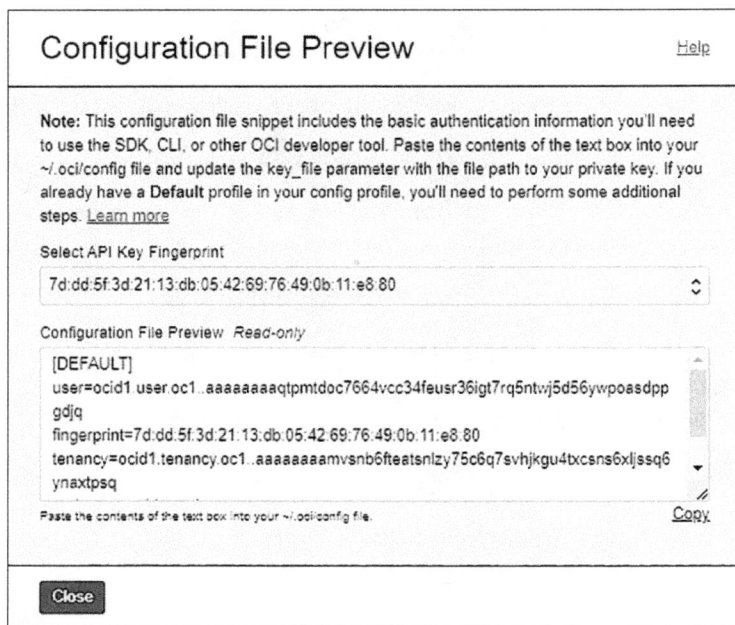

Figure 20-4   Configuration Window After Adding the Public Key

From this window, make note of and copy the tenancy OCID, user OCID, fingerprint, and region identifier. These details can also be obtained from the OCI console at any time using the steps listed in Table 20-1. This information is required for the Terraform scripts to authenticate.

Furthermore, the fully qualified path of the private key on your Terraform client host is needed (also see Table 20-1).

Note that although the region name may be US East (Ashburn), its identifier is us-ashburn-1. Once again, see Table 20-1 on where to obtain this information.

Table 20-1   Required Information for Terraform Authentication

Value	Where to Get It from the OCI Console
Tenancy OCID	Navigate to the user icon on the top right and click the tenancy name. Copy the OCID.
User OCI	Navigate to **Identity & Security** and click **Users**. Click the username and copy the OCID.
Fingerprint	On the same page of the user, click **API Keys** on the leftmost menu. Copy the fingerprint that was just created.
Region Identifier	On the top right of the navigation bar on the OCI console, the region is displayed [such as US East (Ashburn)]. Immediately below it, click **Manage Regions** and obtain the region identifier for your region.
Private Key Path	This value is not retrieved on the OCI console, but rather on the host where Terraform was installed. For example, the path may be /home/oracle/.oci/orakey.pem.

Adding a Policy for the User to Read OCI Resources

Because the API key is associated with an OCI user, the Terraform scripts will only execute commands that are allowed by the OCI user. In the following steps, we add a policy to grant the user to "read all resources" in the tenancy as a prerequisite step:

Step 1. Navigate to the OCI console menu; click **Identity & Security > Users**.

Step 2. Click the OCI user and scroll down to identify which group this user is associated with to add a policy to.

Step 3. Click the username and scroll down to identify the groups that this user has. The subsequent steps will add a new policy to one of these groups.

Step 4. Navigate to the OCI console menu; click **Identity & Security > Policies**.

Step 5. Select the compartment from the drop-down on the left, if it is not already selected.

Step 6. Click **Create Policy**.

Step 7. Enter a name (such as terraform-read-resources), enter a description, and make sure the correct compartment is selected.

Step 8. Switch the toggle button **Show Manual Editor** to enter a manual policy.

Step 9. Enter the policy:

```
allow group <group> to read all-resources in tenancy
```

Step 10. Click **Create**.

The group associated with your OCI user now has a new policy associated with it. These steps are irrelevant if the OCI user is already in the Administrators group.

Exercise 1: Running Terraform for the First Time

Now that the prerequisites are completed, in this section, we will set up Terraform to authenticate and list the availability domains in the OCI tenancy. This does not perform any changes on the OCI infrastructure because it is merely a read operation.

Creating a Working Directory

In this exercise, the entire Terraform configuration will be in a single file: my-list-ads.tf. It will authenticate via the provider configuration, it will read data from the compartment (or tenancy), and it will print the output.

First, run the commands in Example 20-2 to create a folder to host the Terraform scripts.

Example 20-2   Creating a Working Directory

```
# Create a directory to store your Terraform scripts
cd /home/oracle
mkdir tf-provider
cd tf-provider
```

Creating an Initial Terraform Script

Afterward, create the Terraform configuration file my-list-ads.tf in this newly created folder and paste into it the contents of Example 20-3. This file can have any name actually. This file will have three sections:

- **Provider:** Indicates the information required to connect to the OCI cloud service provider
- **Data:** Retrieves data but does not display it
- **Output:** Displays the output retrieved in the data block

Replace the values in the provider and data blocks with those obtained from the previous section.

Example 20-3   Contents of the custom my-list-ads.tf File

```
# Configuration for the OCI provider
provider "oci" {
  tenancy_ocid="ocid1.tenancy.oc1..aaaaaaaamvsnb6fteatsnlzy75c6q7…"
  user_ocid="ocid1.user.oc1..aaaaaaaaqtpmtdoc7664vcc34feusr36igt7…"
  fingerprint="7d:dd:5f:3d:21:13:db:05:42:69:76:49:0b:11:e8:80"
  region="us-ashburn-1"
  private_key_path="/home/oracle/.oci/orakey.pem"
}

# Retrieve the list of OCI availability domains
data "oci_identity_availability_domains" "ads" {
  compartment_id = "ocid1.tenancy.oc1..aaaaaaaamvsnb6fteatsnlz…"
}

# Output the result
output "list-my-ads " {
  value = "${data.oci_identity_availability_domains.ads.availability_domains}"
}
```

Note

All string values in the Terraform configuration .tf files should be surrounded by double or single quotes, and commented lines start with the # sign.

Running Terraform Initialize for the First Time

Now you are ready to run the Terraform initialization for the first time. When you execute the steps in Example 20-4, a local working directory is created, and the initialization command will automatically download the OCI plug-in. To begin, run the commands in Example 20-4.

Example 20-4   Running the **terraform init** Command

```
# Initializes the working directory
cd /home/oracle/tf-provider
terraform init
```

If there are any issues with the Terraform configuration in the scripts, an error is displayed (for example, "Invalid attribute name," "Missing name for data," or "Reference to undeclared resource") with reference to the line number and a brief description of the error. Figure 20-5 shows the successful execution of the **terraform init** command.

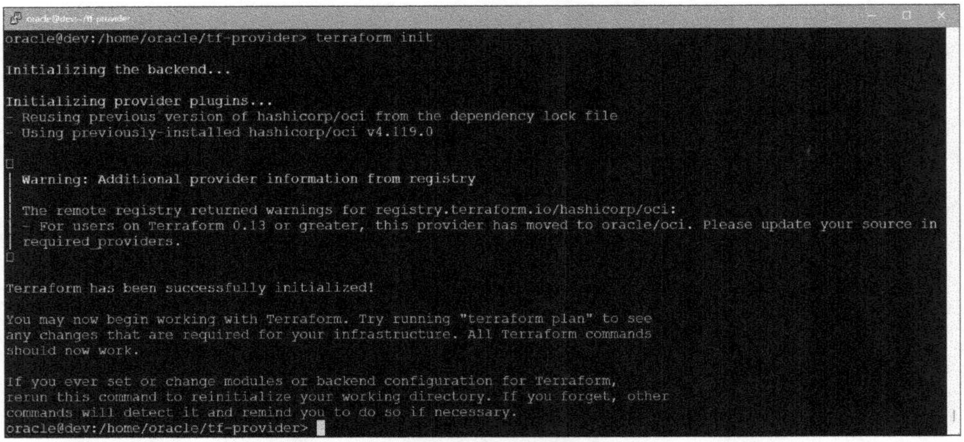

Figure 20-5   Output of the **terraform init** Command

Note that the Terraform initialization does not connect to or authenticate against OCI. After the initialization is successful and completed, a hidden lock file named .terraform.lock.hcl is created. This file should be checked in to your source control. A hidden folder named .terraform is also created; it includes the plug-ins for the OCI provider. An example of this is shown in Figure 20-6.

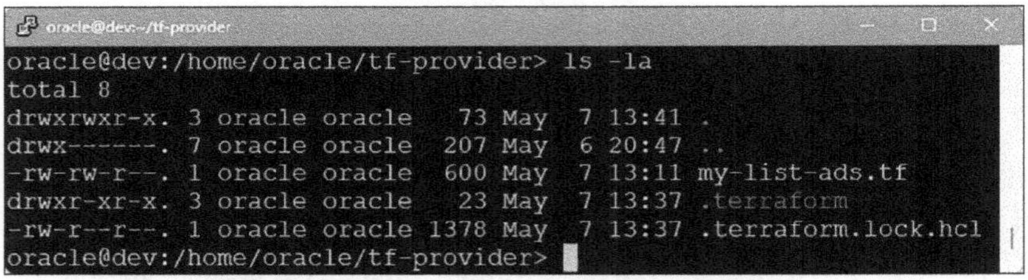

Figure 20-6   Creation of a New .terraform Folder After Initialization

Running terraform plan for the First Time

Running **terraform plan** also does not make any changes to OCI. The output displayed is a sample run-through based on your configuration, allowing you to verify whether it matches what was intended. Run the command in Example 20-5 to execute the plan stage. Figure 20-7 shows the output of a successful plan stage with no errors.

Example 20-5   Running the **terraform plan** Command

```
# Creates a non-intrusive execution plan
terraform plan
```

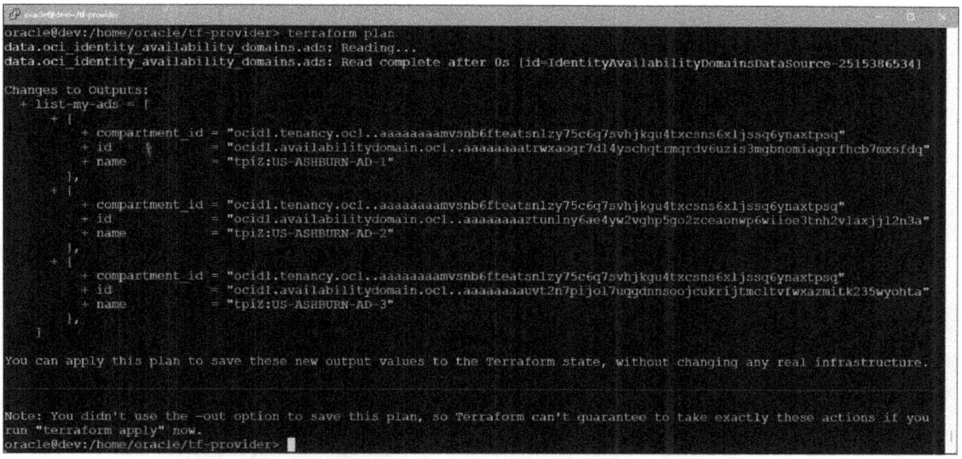

Figure 20-7 Output of the **terraform plan** Command

The Terraform plan stage performs an actual authentication to OCI. If there is an authentication issue or misconfiguration, an error will appear. Figure 20-8 demonstrates an unsuccessful plan attempt due to an invalid user OCID.

Figure 20-8 Authentication Failure Due to an Invalid User OCID

Running terraform apply for the First Time

Running **terraform apply** performs the actual execution of your plan (see Example 20-6). This first exercise merely lists the availability domains in your tenancy, so no creation or updating of resources is performed.

Example 20-6   Running the **terraform apply** Command

```
# Enter 'yes' to apply
terraform apply
```

In the output of the **terraform apply** command in Figure 20-9, you will notice a few things. First, under the Changes to Outputs section, it lists the planned changes. Shortly after, you are prompted to enter "yes" to confirm whether to apply the actions. Finally, the Outputs section lists the output as defined in your .tf configuration file.

Figure 20-9   Output of the **terraform apply** Command

A terraform.tfstate file is created in this directory, which includes information on the state of your OCI infrastructure as Terraform knows it. It is the source of truth of your provisioned infrastructure that Terraform manages. When the execution plan is applied, Terraform cross-references your changes (from the .tf file) with the state (the terraform. tfstate file) to determine which part of your configuration has already been created. This is how Terraform is able to determine the changes needed.

Exercise 2: Parameterizing Terraform Configuration

In Exercise 1, we used a single Terraform configuration file. Separating the code and configuration into separate files is not necessary but helps modularize it for the sake of organization. Furthermore, adding variables provides another level of abstraction.

We'll now split the single Terraform configuration file used in the previous exercise into five separate files. The contents of these files are listed in Examples 20-7 through 20-11 and specifically include

- **providers.tf:** Configuration of the provider (that is, connection and authentication information to OCI); it can include other providers too.
- **my-list-ads.tf:** The actions to be applied. This can include multiple actions, or it can be further split into multiple .tf files. The filename is unimportant.
- **outputs.tf:** The output of the results. The filename is unimportant.
- **variables.tf:** A definition of all variables. The filename is unimportant.
- **terraform.tfvars:** The value of the variables.

Example 20-7   Contents of the providers.tf File

```
# Configuration for the OCI provider
provider "oci" {
  tenancy_ocid="${var.my_oci_tenancy}"
  user_ocid="${var.my_oci_user}"
  fingerprint="${var.my_oci_fingerprint}"
  region="${var.my_oci_region}"
  private_key_path="${var.my_oci_privatekey}"
}
```

Example 20-8   Contents of the my-list-ads.tf File

```
# Retrieve the list of OCI availability domains
data "oci_identity_availability_domains" "ads" {
  compartment_id="${var.my_oci_tenancy}"
}
```

Example 20-9   Contents of the outputs.tf File

```
# Output the result
output "list_my_ads" {
value="${data.oci_identity_availability_domains.ads.availability_domains}"
}
```

Example 20-10   Contents of the variables.tf File

```
# Definition of variables to be used in the configuration files
variable "my_oci_tenancy" {
  type=string
  description="OCI Tenancy OCI"
}
variable "my_oci_user" {
  type=string
  description="OCI User OCID"
}
variable "my_oci_fingerprint" {
  type=string
  description="Oracle Cloud Fingerprint for the key pair"
}
variable "my_oci_privatekey" {
  type=string
  description="OCI API Private Key"
}
variable "my_oci_region" {
  type=string
  description="OCI Region"
}
variable "my_oci_Compartment" {
  type=string
  description="OCI Compartment OCID"
}
```

Example 20-11   Contents of the terraform.tfvars File

```
# Value of the variables
my_oci_tenancy = "ocid1.tenancy.oc1..
   aaaaaaaamvsnb6fteatsnlzy75c6q7svhjkgu4txcsns6xljssq6ynaxtpsq"
my_oci_user = "ocid1.user.oc1..
   aaaaaaaaqtpmtdoc7664vcc34feusr36igt7rq5ntwj5d56ywpoasdppgdjq"
my_oci_fingerprint = "7d:dd:5f:3d:21:13:db:05:42:69:76:49:0b:11:e8:80"
my_oci_privatekey = "/home/oracle/.oci/orakey.pem"
my_oci_region = "us-ashburn-1"
my_oci_compartment = "ocid1.tenancy.oc1..
   aaaaaaaamvsnb6fteatsnlzy75c6q7svhjkgu4txcsns6xljssq6ynaxtpsq"
```

There is no concept of ordering of files in Terraform. During the plan and apply stages, Terraform parses through all files to replace variables and understand the end-state of your infrastructure configuration.

Now that the five new files are created, let's wipe out what we had set up before and rerun the commands from the beginning. The Linux commands to do so are provided in Example 20-12.

Example 20-12 Rerunning the Terraform Scripts After Separating Them

```
# Delete previous setup completely
cd /home/oracle/tf-provider
rm terraform.tfstate
rm .terraform.lock.hcl
rm -rf /home/oracle/tf-provider/.terraform

# Rerun the init, plan and apply stages
terraform init
terraform plan
terraform apply
```

The output will be exactly identical to Figure 20-9.

Exercise 3: Understanding the Terraform OCI Documentation

The Terraform documentation for the Oracle Cloud Infrastructure Provider is the go-to guide for all information as it pertains to Terraform and OCI. Instructions for installing and configuring Terraform for OCI (sometimes referred to as "install the provider" or "configure the provider"), including examples and reference documentation, are all included here. This information can be accessed at https://registry.terraform.io/providers/oracle/oci/latest/docs, and a snippet of this page is shown in Figure 20-10.

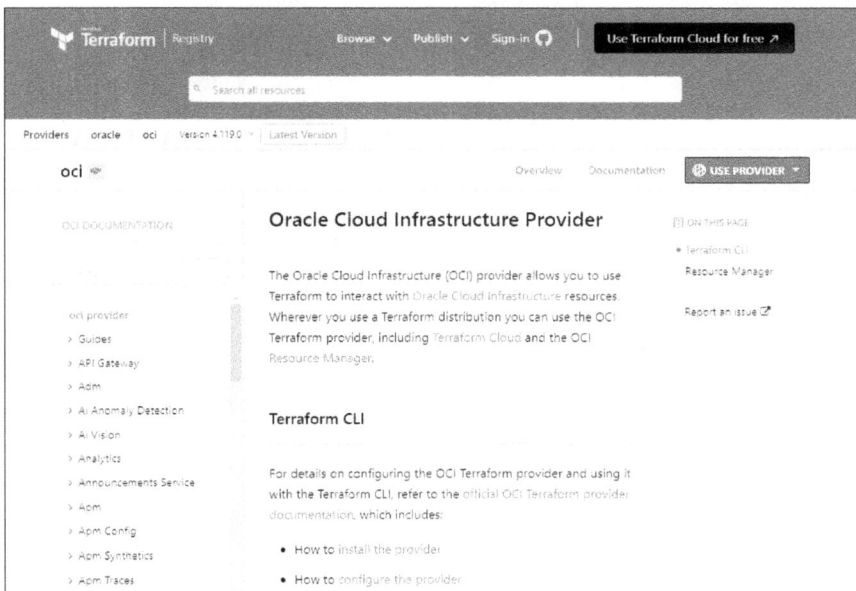

Figure 20-10 The Terraform Documentation for the OCI Provider

It is important to spend a little bit of time to understand how to interpret the documentation because it is critical to setting up your Terraform configuration files. On the left-hand pane are all the supported *resources* and *data sources* for the OCI provider.

A Terraform resource is represented in a resource block in the Terraform configuration and consists of the infrastructure objects (such as compute instances or block volumes) that will be created. A resource takes the following format:

```
<resource_type>.<name>.<attribute>
```

When you run **terraform apply**, the objects defined in the resource blocks are created.

A Terraform data source refers to a resource external to your Terraform configuration. For example, these may be resources already created and are included in the configuration for reference purposes. These are represented with the **data** reserved word. Example 20-8 shows a sample data source:

```
data "oci_identity_availability_domains"
```

This is not an object that was created by our own Terraform configuration, but merely a reference to an existing object in OCI.

A Terraform provider is a plug-in that interacts with the target system's APIs. Our target system here is OCI and is shown in Example 20-7 as follows:

```
provider "oci"
```

The beauty of Terraform is that the connection information to your provider (in this case, the OCI provider) is all that is needed. The details on how to use the underlying APIs provided by OCI are shielded from us.

Updating Terraform Configuration from the Terraform OCI Documentation

In the Terraform OCI documentation, search for "core_volume" on the left-hand pane. The output is shown in Figure 20-11. Here, the top-level menu is Core. You can see that oci_core_volume is shown twice, both under Resources and under Data Sources. The documentation under Resources is for the creation of a new volume and under Data Source is for listing details of the block volumes.

Click **oci_core_volume** under Resources, shown in Figure 20-11. The resulting page includes a brief description of the reference, example usage, argument reference, attributes reference, and any other relevant information. Figure 20-12 displays a snippet of the example usage from this page. This is used to form the basis of a new Terraform configuration file that we will create called my-blocks-volume.tf (see Example 20-13).

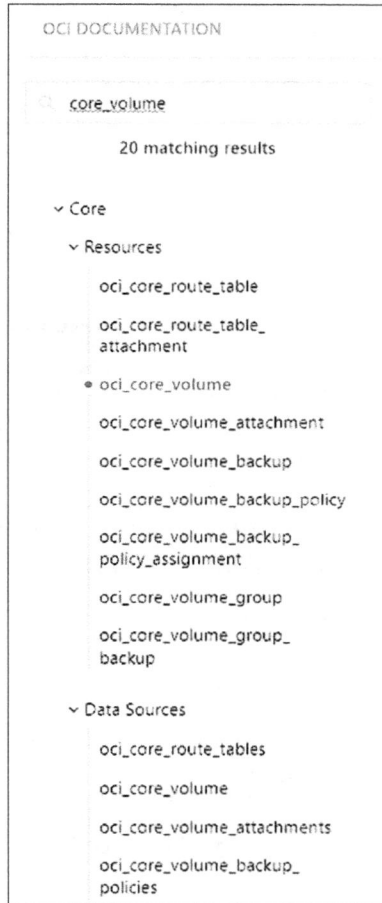

OCI DOCUMENTATION

core_volume

20 matching results

∨ Core

  ∨ Resources

    oci_core_route_table

    oci_core_route_table_
    attachment

    • oci_core_volume

    oci_core_volume_attachment

    oci_core_volume_backup

    oci_core_volume_backup_policy

    oci_core_volume_backup_
    policy_assignment

    oci_core_volume_group

    oci_core_volume_group_
    backup

  ∨ Data Sources

    oci_core_route_tables

    oci_core_volume

    oci_core_volume_attachments

    oci_core_volume_backup_
    policies

Figure 20-11   Reference to Block Volumes in the Terraform Documentation for OCI

The resource named oci_core_volume in Example 20-13 is a reserved word and is the same name as the reference in the Terraform OCI documentation. Other required arguments of this resource such as compartment_id and availability_domain are added. When we eventually apply the Terraform configuration, if this volume is not created, it will be. Note that the availability_domain argument was obtained from the output shown in Figure 20-9. Here, the name of the availability domain is tpiZ:US-ASHBURN-AD-1.

```
Example Usage

resource "oci_core_volume" "test_volume" {
    #Required
    compartment_id = var.compartment_id

    #Optional
    autotune_policies {
        #Required
        autotune_type = var.volume_autotune_policies_autotune_type

        #Optional
        max_vpus_per_gb = var.volume_autotune_policies_max_vpus_per_gb
    }
    availability_domain = var.volume_availability_domain
    backup_policy_id = data.oci_core_volume_backup_policies.test_volume_backup_polic
    block_volume_replicas {
        #Required
        availability_domain = var.volume_block_volume_replicas_availability_domain

        #Optional
        display_name = var.volume_block_volume_replicas_display_name
    }
    defined_tags = {"Operations.CostCenter"= "42"}
    display_name = var.volume_display_name
    freeform_tags = {"Department"= "Finance"}
    is_auto_tune_enabled = var.volume_is_auto_tune_enabled
    kms_key_id = oci_kms_key.test_key.id
    size_in_gbs = var.volume_size_in_gbs
    size_in_mbs = var.volume_size_in_mbs
    source_details {
        #Required
        id = var.volume_source_details_id
        type = var.volume_source_details_type
    }
    vpus_per_gb = var.volume_vpus_per_gb
    block_volume_replicas_deletion = true
}
```

Figure 20-12   Example Usage of the oci_core_volume Resource

Example 20-13   Contents of the my-block-volumes.tf File

```
# Creates a block volume
resource "oci_core_volume" "my_volume_1" {
  # Required argument
  compartment_id="${var.my_oci_tenancy}"
  # This value was obtained from the output in Figure 20-9
  availability_domain="tpiZ:US-ASHBURN-AD-1"
  display_name="My Volume 1"
  size_in_gbs="50"
}
```

Now click **oci_core_volume** under Data on the left-hand navigation pane of the Terraform documentation. A page with this documentation is displayed, a portion of it shown in Figure 20-13.

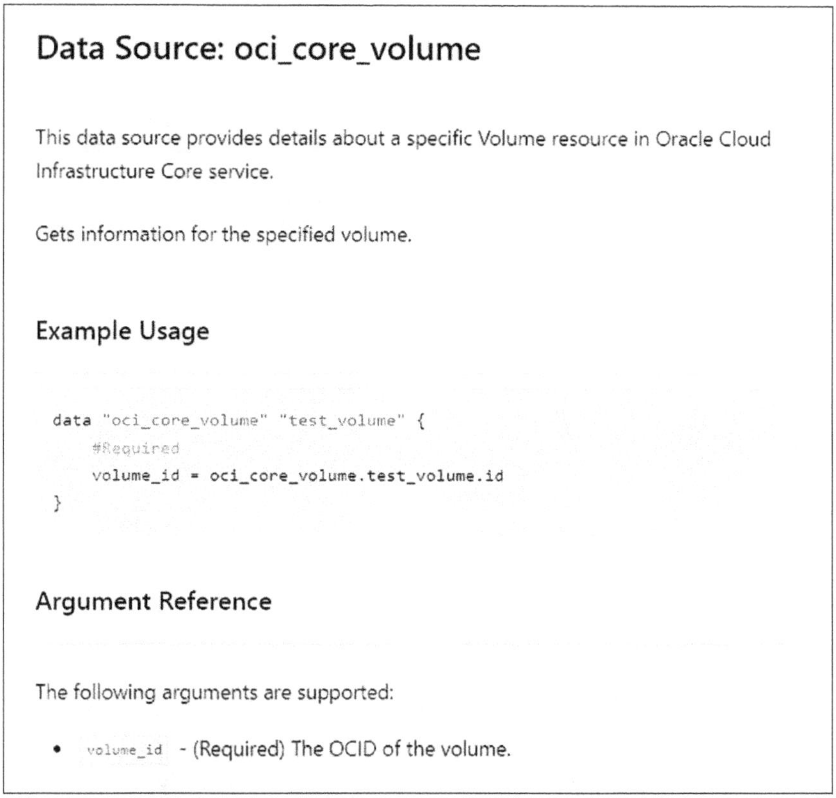

Data Source: oci_core_volume

This data source provides details about a specific Volume resource in Oracle Cloud Infrastructure Core service.

Gets information for the specified volume.

Example Usage

```
data "oci_core_volume" "test_volume" {
    #Required
    volume_id = oci_core_volume.test_volume.id
}
```

Argument Reference

The following arguments are supported:

- volume_id - (Required) The OCID of the volume.

Figure 20-13   Documentation of the oci_core_volume Data Source

Once again, a data source is akin to a read operation. It does not perform any creation or update. After reviewing the syntax in the Example Usage and Argument Reference sections on this page, add a data block to the bottom of the same existing my-blockvolumes.tf file that was just created. The existing my-block-volumes.tf file, shown in Example 20-14, should now include two blocks: one resource block and one data block. The resource block will create the volume, and the data block will read its details.

Example 20-14   Updated Contents of the my-block-volumes.tf File

```
# Creates a block volume
resource "oci_core_volume" "my_volume_1" {
  # Required argument
  compartment_id="${var.my_oci_tenancy}"
```

```
  # This value was obtained from the output in Figure 20-9
  availability_domain="tpiZ:US-ASHBURN-AD-1"
  display_name="My Volume 1"
  size_in_gbs="50"
}
data "oci_core_volume" "my_volume_1" {
  # Required
  volume_id=oci_core_volume.my_volume_1.id
}
```

Finally, update the contents of the outputs.tf file, as shown in Example 20-15. A new output block—list-my-volume—is added that references the data element in the data block shown in Example 20-14. This enables you to display the data that was read in the data block.

Example 20-15   Updated Contents of the outputs.tf File

```
# Output the result
output "list_my_ads" {
value="${data.oci_identity_availability_domains.ads.availability_domains}"
}
output "list-my-volume" {
  value="${data.oci_core_volume.my_volume_1.id}"
}
```

Running the Terraform Script to Create and List a Block Volume

Now that the Terraform scripts are updated to reflect the intent to create my_volume_1 and list the details of the my_volume_1 block volume, they are ready for execution. Recall that Terraform is not about executing the configuration files in a sequenced manner, but rather the entire configuration set is designed to represent the final state of your infrastructure configuration.

In the new set of scripts just updated, the first and only change is the block volume. Any other resource that currently exists in the OCI compartment is untouched (and unknown in the Terraform state file).

Run the commands as shown in Example 20-16.

Example 20-16   Rerunning the Terraform Scripts

```
terraform plan
terraform apply
```

Figure 20-14 shows a snippet of the output of the **terraform plan** command. Recall that this does not apply anything and merely attempts to preview the actions Terraform would make when applying the configuration.

```
oracle@dev:~/tf-provider                                    —   □   X

oracle@dev:/home/oracle/tf-provider> terraform plan
data.oci_identity_availability_domains.ads: Reading...
data.oci_identity_availability_domains.ads: Read complete after 0s [id=IdentityA

Terraform used the selected providers to generate the following execution plan.
symbols:
  + create
 <= read (data resources)

Terraform will perform the following actions:

  # data.oci_core_volume.my_volume_1 will be read during apply
  # (config refers to values not yet known)
 <= data "oci_core_volume" "my_volume_1" {
      + auto_tuned_vpus_per_gb              = (known after apply)
      + autotune_policies                   = (known after apply)
      + availability_domain                 = (known after apply)
      + backup_policy_id                    = (known after apply)
      + block_volume_replicas               = (known after apply)
      + block_volume_replicas_deletion      = (known after apply)
      + compartment_id                      = (known after apply)
      + defined_tags                        = (known after apply)
      + display_name                        = (known after apply)
      + freeform_tags                       = (known after apply)
      + id                                  = (known after apply)
      + is_auto_tune_enabled                = (known after apply)
      + is_hydrated                         = (known after apply)
      + kms_key_id                          = (known after apply)
      + size_in_gbs                         = (known after apply)
      + size_in_mbs                         = (known after apply)
      + source_details                      = (known after apply)
      + state                               = (known after apply)
      + system_tags                         = (known after apply)
      + time_created                        = (known after apply)
      + volume_backup_id                    = (known after apply)
      + volume_group_id                     = (known after apply)
      + volume_id                           = (known after apply)
      + vpus_per_gb                         = (known after apply)
    }

  # oci_core_volume.my_volume_1 will be created
  + resource "oci_core_volume" "my_volume_1" {
      + auto_tuned_vpus_per_gb = (known after apply)
      + availability_domain    = "tpiZ:US-ASHBURN-AD-1"
      + backup_policy_id       = (known after apply)
      + compartment_id         = "ocid1.tenancy.oci..aaaaaaamvsnb6fteatsn1zy75c
      + defined_tags           = (known after apply)
      + display_name           = "My Volume 1"
      + freeform_tags          = (known after apply)
      + id                     = (known after apply)
      + is_auto_tune_enabled   = (known after apply)
      + is_hydrated            = (known after apply)
      + kms_key_id             = (known after apply)
      + size_in_gbs            = "50"
      + size_in_mbs            = (known after apply)
      + state                  = (known after apply)
      + system_tags            = (known after apply)
      + time_created           = (known after apply)
      + volume_backup_id       = (known after apply)
      + volume_group_id        = (known after apply)
      + vpus_per_gb            = (known after apply)
    }

Plan: 1 to add, 0 to change, 0 to destroy.

Changes to Outputs:
  + list-my-ads    = [
```

Figure 20-14   Output of the **terraform plan** Command

Worth noting in this figure are a few items. First, two blocks are shown: the data block and the resource block. The data block would display the details of the referenced volume. As shown in the figure, it "will be read during apply" and the values will only be "known after apply."

Following the data block is the resource block, which depicts the volume we wish to see in our final configuration. The plan phase here identified that the volume does not exist in the target OCI environment, hence, the statement toward the bottom, which is that it is expected that one addition is made:

```
Plan: 1 to add, 0 to change, 0 to destroy
```

Figure 20-15 displays the last snippets of the output of the **terraform apply** command. One resource (in green) was added as shown. The output for list-my-ads and list-my-volumes is also displayed, as expected. The data blocks retrieve the data, and the output blocks display the data.

```
oracle@dev:~/tf-provider                                          —    □    ✕
Do you want to perform these actions?
  Terraform will perform the actions described above.
  Only 'yes' will be accepted to approve.

  Enter a value: yes

oci_core_volume.my_volume_1: Creating...
oci_core_volume.my_volume_1: Still creating... [10s elapsed]
oci_core_volume.my_volume_1: Creation complete after 13s [id=ocid1.volume.ocl.ia
data.oci_core_volume.my_volume_1: Reading...
data.oci_core_volume.my_volume_1: Read complete after 0s [id=ocid1.volume.ocl.ia

Apply complete! Resources: 1 added, 0 changed, 0 destroyed.

Outputs:

list-my-ads = tolist([
  {
    "compartment_id" = "ocid1.tenancy.ocl..aaaaaaaamvsnb6fteatsnlzy75c6q7svhjkgu
    "id" = "ocid1.availabilitydomain.ocl..aaaaaaaatrwxaogr7dl4yschqtrmqrdv6uzis3
    "name" = "tpiZ:US-ASHBURN-AD-1"
  },
  {
    "compartment_id" = "ocid1.tenancy.ocl..aaaaaaaamvsnb6fteatsnlzy75c6q7svhjkgu
    "id" = "ocid1.availabilitydomain.ocl..aaaaaaaaztunlny6ae4yw2vghp5go2zceaonwp
    "name" = "tpiZ:US-ASHBURN-AD-2"
  },
  {
    "compartment_id" = "ocid1.tenancy.ocl..aaaaaaaamvsnb6fteatsnlzy75c6q7svhjkgu
    "id" = "ocid1.availabilitydomain.ocl..aaaaaaaauvt2n7pijol7uqgdnnsoojcukrijtm
    "name" = "tpiZ:US-ASHBURN-AD-3"
  },
])
list-my-volume = "ocid1.volume.ocl.iad.abuwcljt5dzpn5za4uq53okspp6qflusy5vrxuaql
oracle@dev:/home/oracle/tf-provider>
```

Figure 20-15   Output of the **terraform apply** Command

If you navigate to the OCI console under Block Storage, you can confirm that the volume was created, as depicted in Figure 20-16.

Figure 20-16   Confirming the Creation of the Block Volume in the OCI Console

If you rerun the **terraform apply** command, the comments in green shown in Figure 20-17 are self-explanatory. No changes made since the configuration of the environment in our local Terraform state file match what exists in OCI.

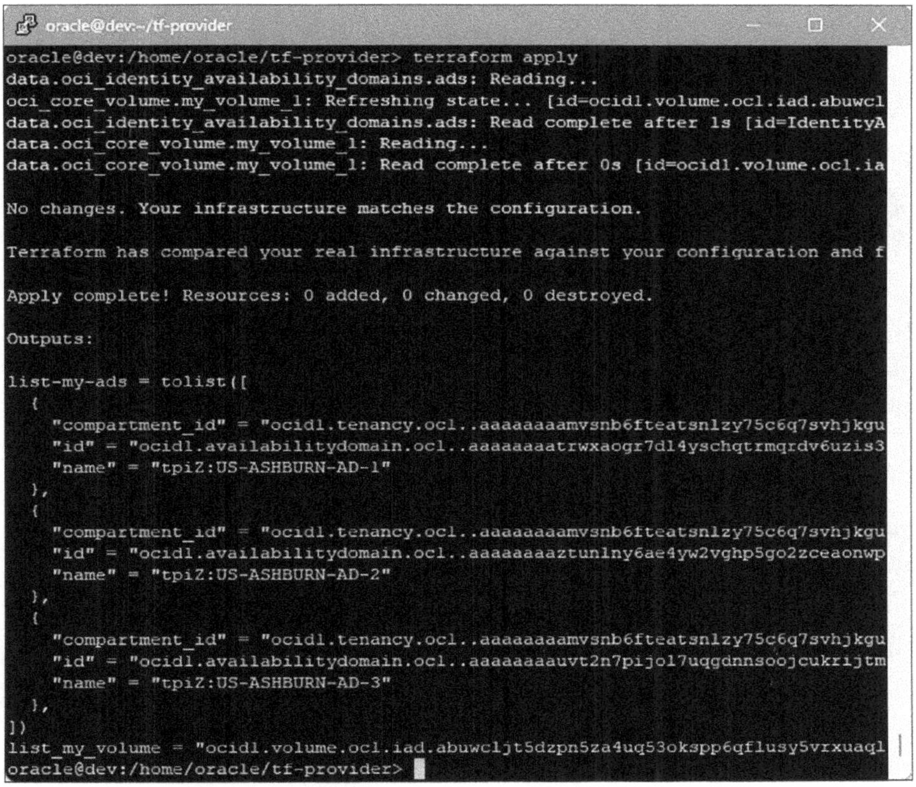

Figure 20-17   Output of the **terraform apply** Command a Second Time

Updating a Resource

Now let's navigate back to the oci_core_volume resource documentation at https:// registry.terraform.io/providers/oracle/oci/latest/docs/resources/core_volume. Scrolling down to the Argument Reference section and noting the documentation of the display_ name argument, between parentheses it says "(Updatable)" (see Figure 20-18). This means that if this particular argument is changed in the Terraform configuration, when the configuration is applied again, it will be updated in OCI.

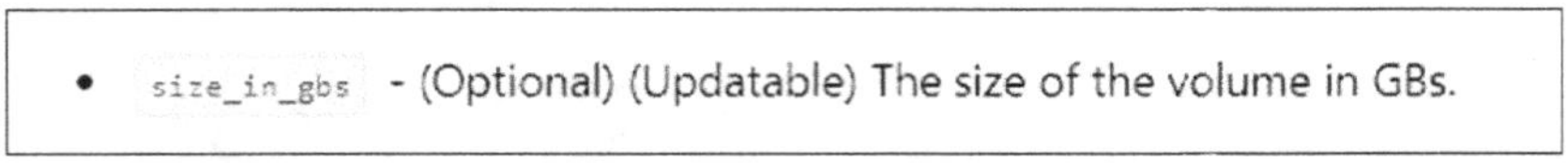

- `size_in_gbs` - (Optional) (Updatable) The size of the volume in GBs.

Figure 20-18　Displaying the display_name Argument of oci_core_volume

Refer to Example 20-14 and update the configuration file my-block-volumes.tf and change this setting, increasing it from 50 to 52. You can run **terraform plan** to preview the change or immediately run **terraform apply** to propagate this change to OCI without verifying it first. Now observe the screenshot in Figure 20-19, which shows a snippet of the apply phase. Prior to confirming the action to apply and toward the top, it recognizes that there is a change in the size_in_gbs argument, increasing it from 50 to 52. In green at the bottom of the same screenshot, it confirms that one resource was changed. Navigating to the OCI console will also reflect this change.

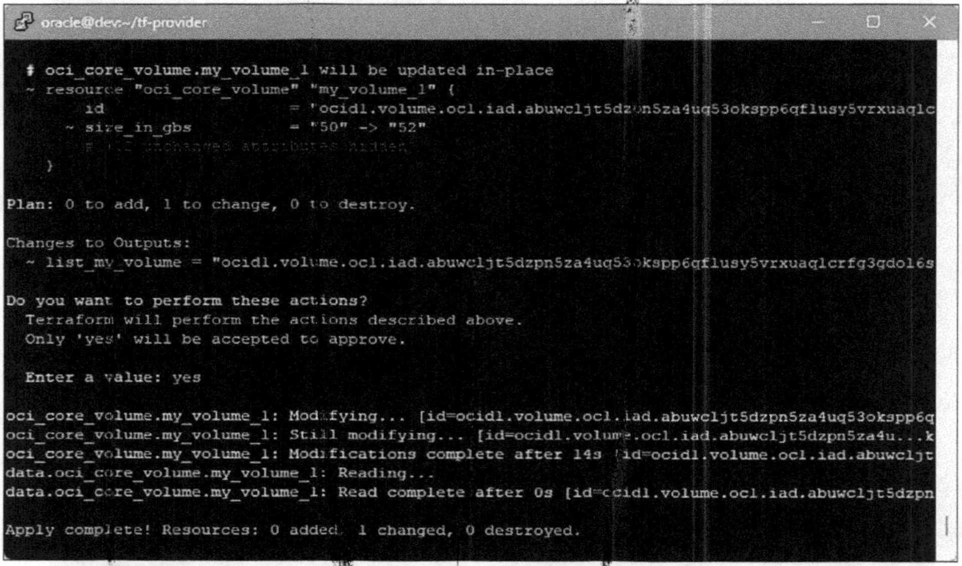

Figure 20-19　Snippet of the **terraform apply** Command After an Update

Parameterizing from Other Output

Earlier in the exercise, we created a my-list-ads.tf file, which reads the list of availability domains in the tenancy (see Example 20-8). There were three availability domains in total. These availability domains were output in the outputs.tf file (refer to Example 20-15). In the my-block-volumes.tf file, the value used for availability_domain was hard-coded to the value tpiZ:US-ASHBURN-AD-1, which we manually copied from this output.

Since the list of availability domains was retrieved in the data block, we can reference this value in my-block-volumes.tf instead of hard-coding it. See Example 20-17. Comment out the line that includes the hard-coded value for availability_domain and add a new one immediately below it as shown in the example.

Example 20-17   Updated Contents of the my-block-volumes.tf File

```
# Creates a block volume
resource "oci_core_volume" "my_volume_1" {
  # Required argument
  compartment_id="${var.my_oci_tenancy}"
  # Use the value from the data block instead
  # availability_domain="tpiZ:US-ASHBURN-AD-1"
  availability_domain="${data.oci_identity_availability_domains.ads.availability_
  domains.0.name}"
  display_name="My Volume 1"
  size_in_gbs="52"
}
data "oci_core_volume" "my_volume_1" {
  # Required
  volume_id=oci_core_volume.my_volume_1.id
}
```

Running **terraform apply** will yield the same exact response. The logic was not changed, and all that was done was remove the hard-coded reference.

Let's break down the value for **${data.oci_identity_availability_domains.ads. availability_domains.0.name}** to understand where each of the subelements that comprise this long string comes from. Table 20-2 breaks down the subelements of the string and explains how it is compiled.

Table 20-2   Understanding the availability_domain Argument Value

Subelement	Source
data	This reserved word references the data block. An example of this is seen in Example 20-8.
oci_identity_availability_ domains	This is an actual resource found in the Terraform OCI documentation and also referenced in Example 20-8. This particular resource is documented at https://registry.terraform.io/providers/oracle/oci/ latest/docs/data-sources/identity_availability_domains.

Subelement	Source
ads	This is a custom name we provide for the resource in the data block of my-list-ads.tf. This is a custom string and is also first referenced in Example 20-8.
availability_domains	The oci_identify_availability_domains retrieves information from OCI. The list of the availability domains is exported to this argument called availability_domains. This is also documented in the Terraform OCI documentation at https://registry.terraform.io/providers/oracle/oci/latest/docs/data-sources/identity_availability_domains.
0	This denotes the array reference. Since the list returned is composed of three rows, the value of 0 refers to the first one.
name	As shown in the output in Figure 20-9 as well as in the Terraform OCI documentation at https://registry.terraform.io/providers/oracle/oci/latest/docs/data-sources/identity_availability_domains, three attributes are exported for each availability domain: compartment_id, id, and name.

Debugging Errors

Undoubtedly, you will run into errors, whether they are typos or syntax errors. Some of them can be easy to resolve, such as that shown in Figure 20-20. Here, it clearly states that a volume size cannot be 1 GB and must have a minimum value of 50 GB. Worth noting in this same screenshot are direct URL links to Terraform OCI documentation for the resource in question, a link to the OCI API reference, as well as the actual REST API that Terraform uses.

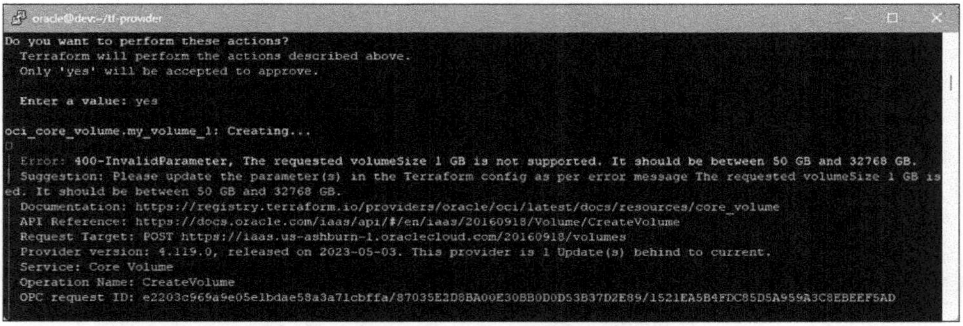

Figure 20-20   Error During **terraform apply**

In many cases though, the errors might not be as straightforward to troubleshoot. Additional debug logs may be helpful. Example 20-18 shows how to disable and enable debugging.

Example 20-18   Disabling and Enabling Debugging in Terraform

```
# Disable debugging
export TF_LOG=""
# Enable debugging
export TF_LOG="DEBUG"
# Setting a path to a log (optional)
export TF_LOG_PATH="/home/oracle/tf-provider/debug.log"
```

A significant amount of logging is displayed (or written to a log file if the TF_LOG_ PATH variable is set). Valid arguments to TF_LOG include, in order of verbosity, ERROR, WARN, INFO, DEBUG, and TRACE. Figure 20-21 lists some of the contents of a debug log file.

Figure 20-21   Contents of the Debug Log File

Summary

In this chapter, you learned that there are a lot of reasons why you should consider Terraform for your infrastructure provisioning, many already discussed in Chapter 19. But focusing solely on the exercises in this chapter, we can identify significant benefits that include

- **No need to learn complicated OCI APIs:** Terraform merely requires defining the end state and not having to worry about authentication or parsing of output of the OCI APIs.
- **Fully automated:** There is no longer a need to manually create or update services and resources through the OCI console.

- **Safe to rerun:** Rerunning **terraform apply** multiple times will not re-create or duplicate your setup. It is only when you explicitly add, update, or remove resources in your Terraform configuration that only those specific changes will be propagated to your OCI environment.
- **Guarantees environment consistency:** When you run centrally managed, versioned controlled scripts, environment consistency is achieved. Environment consistency and the prevention of configuration drift are general themes of IaC.

This chapter covered a range of topics, all intended to provide a hands-on experience in getting started using Terraform. A one-time initial installation and setup of the OCI provider are necessary.

Examples of the three phases—initialize, plan, and apply—were demonstrated. The initialize phase verifies the configuration and downloads the necessary Terraform plug-ins for OCI. There is no need to rerun this unless a new configuration is written. The plan phase provides a preview of what the apply phase plans on executing. The first exercise walked through and explained each of these phases.

The second exercise took that same example and introduced the concept of variables while separating the single configuration file into multiple and more meaningful names.

But the crux of writing Terraform scripts requires an understanding of the Terraform OCI documentation and how to reference it. This was covered in a final detailed exercise. This chapter delved deeper into resources and data sources and their differences. In the next chapter, you will go through an actual Terraform sample use case.

## 21

Terraform Sample Use Case

The previous chapters introduced you to a number of Terraform concepts and examples. Through them, we hope you have obtained a comfortable understanding and usage of Terraform. This chapter will exclusively focus on setting up an entire basic OCI infrastructure from scratch.

After reconfirming the identity and access management (IAM) policies so that the appropriate permissions are set up on the OCI console and ensuring that the one-time setup of the Terraform software and connectivity is complete, this chapter will walk you through the following:

1. Creating a new compartment
2. Creating two virtual cloud networks (VCNs) in this compartment
3. Creating a compute instance in the public VCN
4. Creating an autonomous database in the private VCN

Afterward, we will show you how to reuse the Terraform scripts used to create this compartment, VCNs, compute instance, and database instance to create a completely new and identically configured production environment.

Figure 21-1 depicts the topology of the final architecture. Two environments—a development environment and a production environment—will be created identically. In each, a private and public subnet will exist in the two separated and isolated compartments that will host a compute and autonomous database instances.

The end-to-end sample use case in this chapter will demonstrate how this entire infrastructure can be provisioned in a matter of minutes while ensuring that the production environment is an exact replica of the development one.

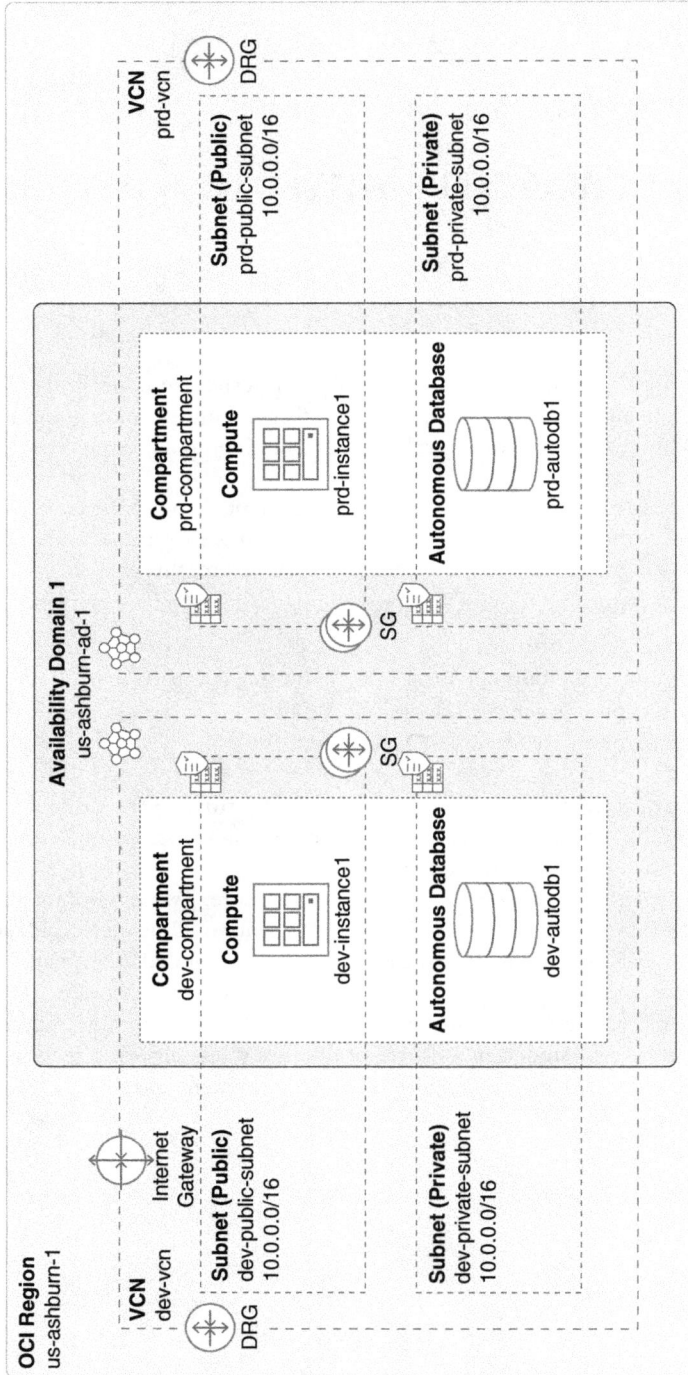

Figure 21-1   The Architecture of the Use Case

Confirming IAM Policies

Chapter 20, "Terraform API with Examples," described how to add a public key to the OCI user account. If this user account is in the Administrators group, then there is no need to configure policies, because the user has full authorization to create and manage resources through Terraform as a result. In a production environment, configuring policies this way is not a good idea. In fact, the *manage all-resources* permission should be granted to a user with caution because the user would have the ability to create and delete resources regardless of whether they are actively being used or are hosting data. There is no undo operation when it comes to deleting cloud resources.

The following steps describe how to create the policy needed on the OCI console, in the event that the user is not in the Administrators group:

Step 1. Navigate to the OCI console menu; click **Identity & Security > Users**.

Step 2. Click the OCI user and scroll down to identify which group this user is associated with to add a policy to.

Step 3. Click the username and scroll down to identify the groups that this user has. The subsequent steps will add a new policy to one of these groups.

Step 4. Navigate to the OCI console menu; click **Identity & Security > Policies**.

Step 5. Select the compartment from the drop-down on the left, if not already selected.

Step 6. Click **Create Policy**.

Step 7. Enter a name (such as terraform-manage-resources), enter a description, and make sure the correct compartment is selected.

Step 8. Switch the toggle button **Show Manual Editor** to enter a manual policy.

Step 9. Add the permissions shown in Example 21-1 to provide the policies necessary for the exercises in this chapter.

Step 10. Click **Create**.

Example 21-1 Granting Permission to Create Compartments and Resources

```
allow group <group> to manage compartments in tenancy
allow group <group> to manage all-resources in compartment <compartment>
```

Setting Up Terraform

Now that the OCI user that Terraform is going to use has the appropriate permissions, it is time to set up the Terraform software on some host. Chapter 20 covered the setup of Terraform on what is referred to as the *Terraform client host*. It is from this host that all Terraform commands will be executed.

Step 1. Download and install Terraform (see "Downloading and Installing Terraform" in Chapter 20).

Step 2. Create a Terraform working directory (see "Creating a Working Directory" in Chapter 20).

Step 3. Create the providers.tf file in the working directory (see Example 20-7).

Step 4. Create the variables.tf file in the working directory (see Example 20-10).

Step 5. Create the terraform.tfvars file in the working directory (see Example 20-11).

Applying the Changes

At this point, the Terraform client is set up to connect to your OCI user account. Now, you can run the commands in Example 21-2 to initialize Terraform for the first time. As a reminder, when you're running **terraform init** for the first time, the .terraform hidden directory is created where the provider plug is initialized. A .terraform.lock. hcl file is also created in the working directory. This lock file tracks dependencies and other changes. Running **terraform plan** will confirm that there are no changes to apply. Thus, running **terraform apply** will actually not do anything on the target OCI environment and only confirms the correct syntax and updates changes. However, a terraform.state file is created locally; it maps the local Terraform configuration to what exists in the OCI infrastructure. These steps are meant to confirm end-to-end connectivity and authentication to OCI.

Example 21-2   Running the Terraform Scripts, Which Will Not Make Any Changes

```
terraform init
terraform plan
terraform apply
```

Now that the Terraform client host is configured, in the next sections, you will perform all OCI infrastructure resource creation and setup. Once you begin using Terraform for your infrastructure management, you should continue using it to manage the Terraform-created resources. If you want to make a change to an existing OCI resource, it is preferred not to make changes directly on the OCI console but rather to make the changes on the Terraform configuration scripts and reapply them. Later in this chapter, we will cover both cases to explain how they work. The local Terraform configuration will continue to remain in sync with the actual setup of your resources and infrastructure in OCI. Therefore, it is important to save and commit the terraform. tfstate file to your source control system frequently (such as SVN or GitHub) because it represents the actual state of your OCI infrastructure.

Creating a New Compartment

Now that the Terraform is set up and can authenticate against OCI, you can create the two files dev_compartments.tf and dev_outputs.tf, respectively, shown in Example 21-3 and Example 21-4. This will create the compartment for the development environment. The output file will merely display the output you define in it.

Example 21-3   Contents of the dev_compartment.tf File

```
resource "oci_identity_compartment" "dev_compartment" {
  # This should be the compartment OCID for the root compartment
  compartment_id="${var.my_oci_tenancy}"
  description="Compartment for development resources"
  name="dev-compartment"
}
```

Example 21-4   Contents of the dev_outputs.tf File

```
# ------------------------------------------
# Outputs for compartment
# ------------------------------------------
output "compartment-name" {
  value=oci_identity_compartment.dev_compartment.name
}
output "compartment-OCID" {
  value=oci_identity_compartment.dev_compartment.id
}
```

Applying the Changes

Now it's time to run the Terraform **plan** and **apply** commands (similar to the two last commands shown in Example 21-2) to first identify the changes that will be implemented and apply them as shown. Figure 21-2 shows some of the output of these commands.

The output in Figure 21-2 outputs both the compartment name and compartment OCID, as defined in the dev_outputs.tf file. The compartment is now created as a child compartment to the root compartment in the OCI console, as can be seen in Figure 21-3. Now a compartment is created which will house the resources that will be created in the next few sections.

Rerunning Terraform Apply with No Changes

Rerunning the **terraform apply** command will do nothing, as confirmed in Figure 21-4, because the state of the configuration in the local Terraform state file already matches that in OCI. The figure shows that 0 resources are added, 0 resources are changed, and 0 resources are destroyed. When applying changes, Terraform will always compare the configuration in OCI against the state file to see if there are any differences. Thus, if no changes are made, there is no risk in reapplying.

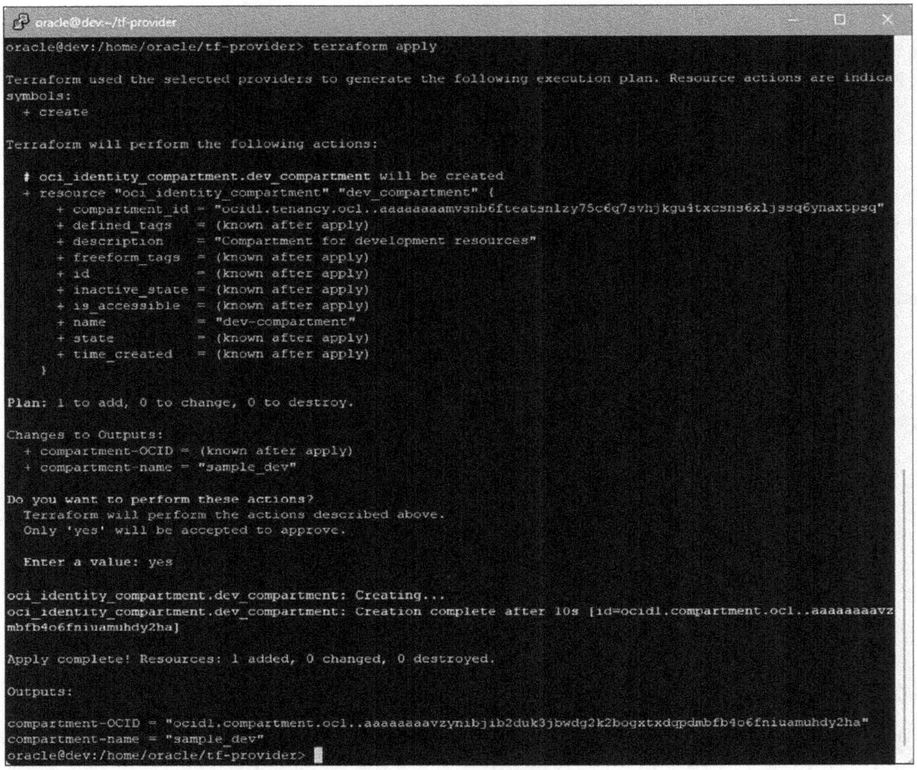

Figure 21-2   Creating a Compartment Using Terraform

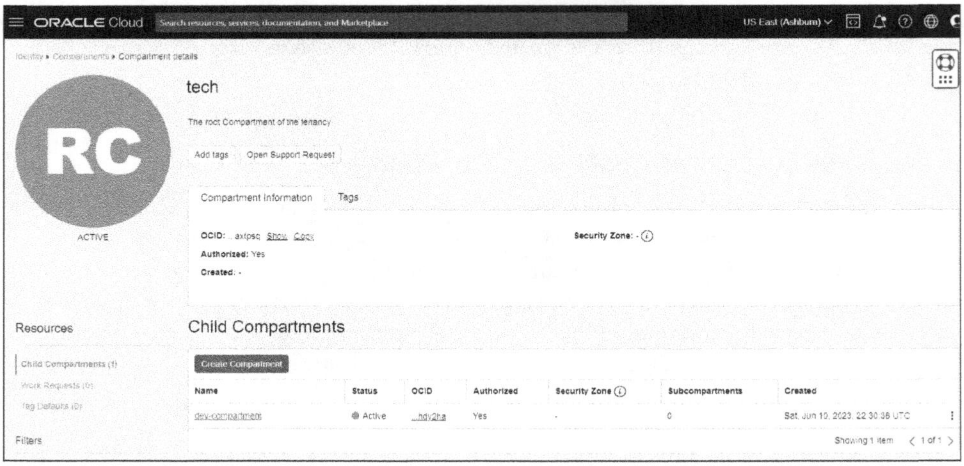

Figure 21-3   Confirming Creation of the Child Compartment

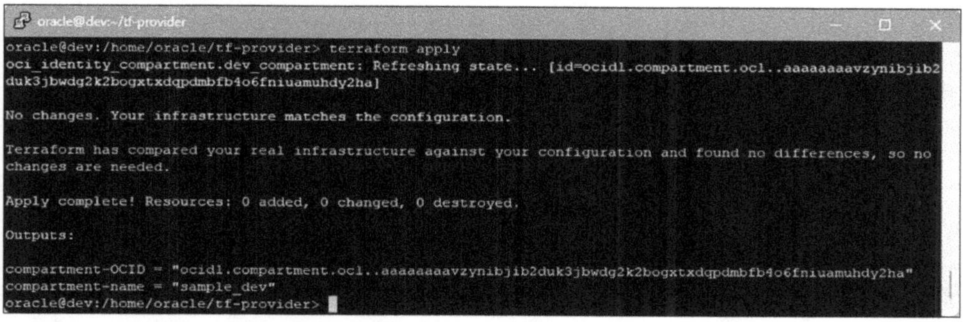

Figure 21-4   Rerunning the Terraform Compartment Creation

This example demonstrates *idempotency*, which means that applying the operation multiple times has the same effect as applying it once. If you have hundreds of cloud resources and make a change to a single one, only the single change is applied, but the remaining unchanged resources are untouched. Idempotency allows for consistent builds and safe rollbacks.

Rerunning Terraform Apply After a Change in Terraform Configuration

We have demonstrated that rerunning the **terraform apply** command will do nothing if no changes have been made, as shown in Figure 21-4. Now you can update the dev_compartments.tf file, changing the description from "Compartment for development resources" to "Compartment for development resources v2." Rerunning **terraform apply** now will deploy this change to OCI. Figure 21-5 confirms that 0 resources were added, 0 resources were destroyed, but 1 resource was changed, specifically the description of the compartment because that was the only change made.

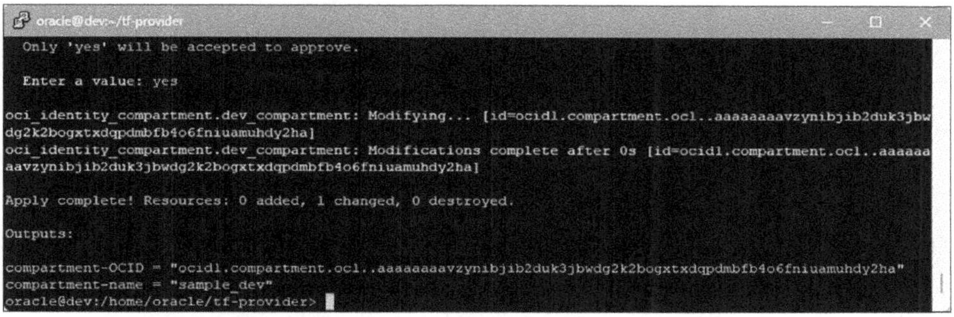

Figure 21-5   Updating the Compartment Description

Rerunning Terraform Apply After a Change on the OCI Console

If the description of the compartment was changed manually on the OCI console, then there is a mismatch between OCI and the local Terraform state file. Running **terraform apply** again will actually update (that is, overwrite) OCI with the local description in dev_compartments.tf, resulting in the same output shown in Figure 21-5. This is why for Terraform-created resources, it is recommended that you continue using Terraform to manage them.

Creating a Virtual Cloud Network

Now that a new child compartment has been created, we will create a VCN where our resources will eventually reside. This step is a prerequisite to the subsequent sections, which will create the compute and database instances.

Though it might seem intimidating to set up a basic network at first, given the need to understand certain cloud networking concepts, refer to Chapter 5, "Oracle IaaS— Network," to review previously discussed networking concepts that included VCNs, CIDRs, subnets, ingress and egress security rules, and security lists. The Terraform configuration for setting up the network in this section can be used as is with minimal changes as a starting point. Many of the settings noted in the remainder of this chapter are prefixed with **dev_** for resource names and **dev-** for display names. This naming convention will help identify what can be customized when the production environment is created later.

In our use case, we will create two subnets: a private subnet and a public subnet. This will allow our services to reach out to the public Internet and likely connect from the public Internet to these services. For example, you will be able to connect via SSH to the compute instance created in the next section from the public Internet. This will require setting up a security list, ingress rules, and egress rules. Thus, a total of five Terraform configuration files will be created:

1. VCN module (see Example 21-5)
2. Private security list with ingress and egress rules (see Example 21-6)
3. Public security list with ingress and egress rules (see Example 21-7)
4. Private subnet (see Example 21-8)
5. Public subnet (see Example 21-9)

Defining a VCN Module

In previous chapters, we introduced the concept of resources and data sources in Terraform. For example, a resource is identified using the **resource** tag in the Terraform configuration files. A module is a concept that groups together resources related to each other. In Example 21-5, a module is defined for what will be a newly created VCN. This VCN module, after creation, will have a VCN OCID, defined as module.dev_vcn. vcn_id. This VCN OCID will be referenced in the subsequent files.

Example 21-5   Contents of the dev_vcn_module.tf File

```
module "dev_vcn" {
  source="oracle-terraform-modules/vcn/oci"
  version="3.1.0"

  # Required; obtain this from the output of previous section
  compartment_id=oci_identity_compartment.dev_compartment.id

  # Required; Chapter 20 describes how to get the region identifier
  region="us-ashburn-1"

  # Required; set to null for now
  internet_gateway_route_rules = null
  local_peering_gateways = null
  nat_gateway_route_rules = null

  # Optional
  vcn_name="dev-vcn-module"
  vcn_dns_label="vcnmodule"
  vcn_cidrs=["10.0.0.0/16"]
  create_internet_gateway=true
  create_nat_gateway=true
  create_service_gateway=true
}
```

There are five required parameters for the VCN shown in Example 21-5. The optional parameters are recommended. When this VCN is created, the DNS domain name takes the format of *<vcn_dns_label>.oraclevcn.com*. We will not apply the changes yet until all the network-related Terraform configuration is defined.

Defining Security Lists and Ingress/Egress Rules

Security lists and their respective ingress and egress rules need to be defined for each of the private and public subnets. To define them, create the files shown in Example 21-6 and Example 21-7.

Example 21-6   Contents of the dev_vcn_private_securitylist.tf File

```
resource "oci_core_security_list" "dev_private_security_list"{

  # Required
  compartment_id=oci_identity_compartment.dev_compartment.id
  vcn_id=module.dev_vcn.vcn_id

  # Optional
  display_name="dev-private-subnet-security-list"
```

```
# Egress security rules
egress_security_rules {
  stateless=false
  destination="0.0.0.0/0"
  destination_type="CIDR_BLOCK"
  protocol="all"
}

# Ingress security rules (TCP)
ingress_security_rules {
  stateless=false
  source="10.0.0.0/16"
  source_type="CIDR_BLOCK"
  protocol="6"
  tcp_options {
    min=22
    max=22
  }
}
# Ingress security rules (ICMP)
ingress_security_rules {
  stateless=false
  source="0.0.0.0/0"
  source_type="CIDR_BLOCK"
  protocol="1"
  icmp_options {
    type=3
    code=4
  }
}
ingress_security_rules {
  stateless=false
  source="10.0.0.0/16"
  source_type="CIDR_BLOCK"
  protocol="1"
  icmp_options {
    type=3
  }
}
}
```

Any number of ingress and egress rules can be added, including other protocols. In these files, the protocol values of 6 and 1 are configured, referencing the TCP and UDP protocols, respectively. Other protocols are supported, and the first link in Table 21-1 contains the standard protocols supported. The second link in the table lists all ICMP parameters that can be used if required (usually it is not).

Table 21-1   Location of Internet Protocol Numbers and ICMP Parameters

Information	URL
Protocol Numbers	https://www.iana.org/assignments/protocol-numbers/protocol-numbers.xhtml
ICMP Parameters	https://www.iana.org/assignments/icmp-parameters/icmp-parameters.xhtml

Example 21-7   Contents of the dev_vcn_public_securitylist.tf File

```
resource "oci_core_security_list" "dev_public_security_list"{

  # Required
  compartment_id=oci_identity_compartment.dev_compartment.id
  vcn_id=module.dev_vcn.vcn_id

  # Optional
  display_name="dev-public-subnet-security-list"

  # Egress security rules
  egress_security_rules {
    stateless=false
    destination="0.0.0.0/0"
    destination_type="CIDR_BLOCK"
    protocol="all"
  }

  # Ingress security rules (TCP)
  # TCP
  ingress_security_rules {
    stateless=false
    source="0.0.0.0/0"
    source_type="CIDR_BLOCK"
    protocol="6"
    tcp_options {
        min=22
        max=22
    }
  }

  # Ingress security rules (ICMP)
  ingress_security_rules {
    stateless=false
    source="0.0.0.0/0"
    source_type="CIDR_BLOCK"
    protocol="1"
```

```
    icmp_options {
      type=3
      code=4
    }
  }
  ingress_security_rules {
    stateless=false
    source="10.0.0.0/16"
    source_type="CIDR_BLOCK"
    protocol="1"
    icmp_options {
      type=3
    }
  }
}
```

Defining the Private and Public Subnets

Now you can create the files shown in Example 21-8 and Example 21-9. These will
eventually create the private and public subnets under the VCN defined earlier. These
subnets also reference their respective security lists defined in the previous section.

Example 21-8   Contents of the dev_vcn_private_subnet.tf File

```
resource "oci_core_subnet" "dev_vcn_private_subnet" {

  # Required
  compartment_id=oci_identity_compartment.dev_compartment.id
  vcn_id=module.dev_vcn.vcn_id
  cidr_block="10.0.1.0/24"

  # Optional
  route_table_id=module.dev_vcn.nat_route_id
  security_list_ids=[oci_core_security_list.dev_private_security_list.id]
  display_name="dev-private-subnet"
  # Required for the Autonomous Database later
  dns_label="vncprivsubnet"
}
```

Example 21-9   Contents of the dev_vcn_public_subnet.tf File

```
resource "oci_core_subnet" "dev_vcn_public_subnet" {

  # Required
  compartment_id=oci_identity_compartment.dev_compartment.id
```

```
vcn_id=module.dev_vcn.vcn_id
cidr_block = "10.0.0.0/24"

# Optional
route_table_id=module.dev_vcn.ig_route_id
security_list_ids=[oci_core_security_list.dev_public_security_list.id]
display_name="dev-public-subnet"
}
```

Updating the Outputs File

This final step, though optional, is highly recommended. This step defines the output we want to display after applying the Terraform configuration.

The setup of a basic network includes multiple pieces, including the following:

- VCN, which also includes an Internet gateway, NAT gateway, and service gateway
- Private and public security lists
- Private and public subnets

Each of these has its own name and its own OCID. The output defined in Example 21-10 will list this information after creation. A dev_outputs.tf file should already exist (see Example 21-4). Add to it the contents shown in Example 21-10, so that it now will include the output for both the compartment and VCN-related setup.

Example 21-10   Additional Output for the dev_outputs.tf File

```
# -------------------------------------
# Outputs for vcn
# -------------------------------------
output "vcn-id" {
  value=module.dev_vcn.vcn_id
}
output "internet-gateway-route-table-id" {
  value=module.dev_vcn.ig_route_id
}
output "nat-gateway-id" {
  value=module.dev_vcn.nat_gateway_id
}
output "nat-gateway-route-table-id" {
  value=module.dev_vcn.nat_route_id
}


# -------------------------------------
# Outputs for private security list
# -------------------------------------
```

```
output "private-security-list-name" {
  value=oci_core_security_list.dev_private_security_list.display_name
}
output "private-security-list-OCID" {
  value=oci_core_security_list.dev_private_security_list.id
}


# ----------------------------------------
# Outputs for public security list
# ----------------------------------------
output "public-security-list-name" {
  value=oci_core_security_list.dev_public_security_list.display_name
}
output "public-security-list-OCID" {
  value=oci_core_security_list.dev_public_security_list.id
}


# ----------------------------------------
# Outputs for private subnet
# ----------------------------------------
output "private-subnet-name" {
  value=oci_core_subnet.dev_vcn_private_subnet.display_name
}
output "private-subnet-OCID" {
  value=oci_core_subnet.dev_vcn_private_subnet.id
}


# ----------------------------------------
# Outputs for public subnet
# ----------------------------------------
output "public-subnet-name" {
  value=oci_core_subnet.dev_vcn_public_subnet.display_name
}
output "public-subnet-OCID" {
  value=oci_core_subnet.dev_vcn_public_subnet.id
}
```

Applying the Changes

Next, it's time to execute the **plan** and **apply** commands, as shown in Example 21-11.
Correct any errors that may appear during the plan phase, such as typos or other
accidental misconfigurations. Rerun the **plan** command as many times as needed until
no errors are shown.

Example 21-11   Applying the Changes for the VCN-Related Setup

```
terraform plan
terraform apply
```

After you have applied the configuration successfully, the output defined in Example 21-10 is shown. See Figure 21-6 for an example of this output. Here you can see that 11 resources were added.

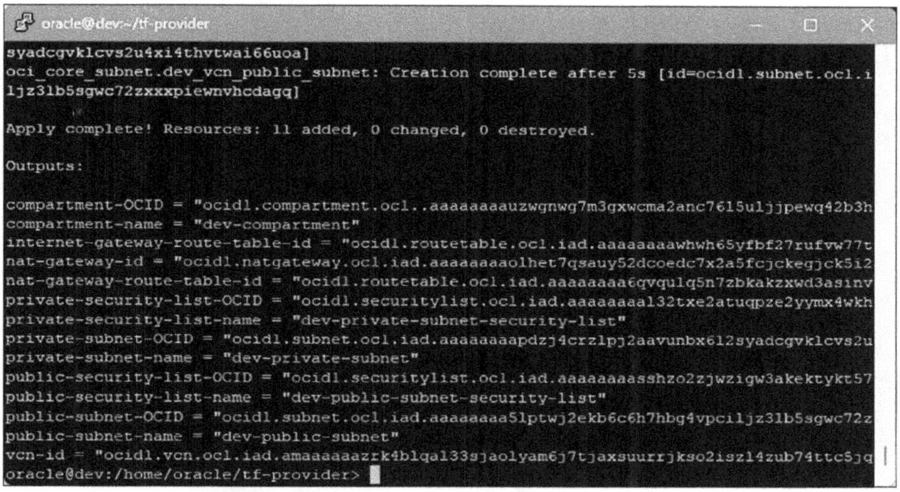

Figure 21-6   Output of the VCN and Related Creation

On the OCI console, navigating to **Networking > Virtual Cloud Networks > dev-vcn-module** will display output identical to what is shown in Figure 21-7. From this figure, you can see that the VCN **dev-vcn-module** was created under the **dev-compartment** compartment, and the route tables, security lists, NAT gateway, and service gateway are also all defined. Some of the other resources, such as DHCP options and a third security list, which do not exist in the configuration in Example 21-10, are created by default.

A basic virtual cloud network now exists where any of our other resources, such as compute, storage, database, or others, can reside. Once again, rerunning **terraform apply** any number of times at this point will not make any changes, since the local Terraform configuration already matches the OCI setup.

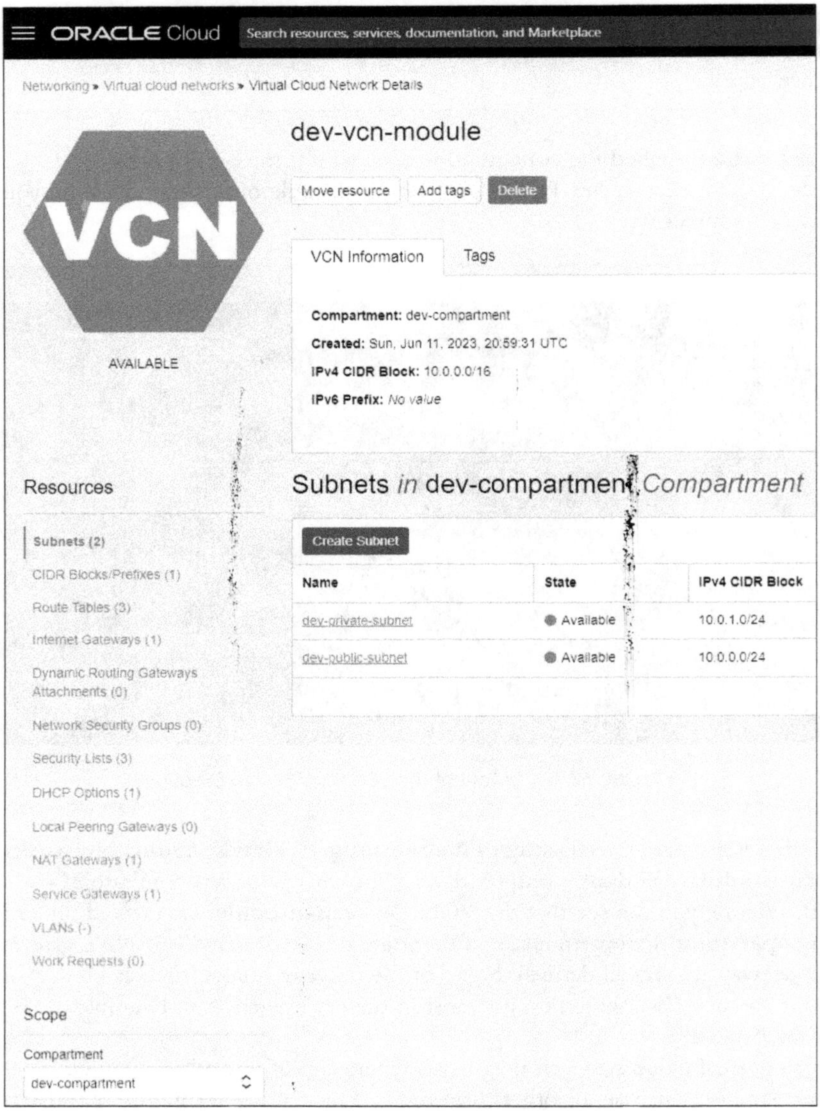

Figure 21-7   Confirming the Creation of VCN

Creating a Compute Instance

Among the many parameters required when creating a compute instance, the compartment and availability domain in which this compute instance will reside are required. The compartment was already created in a previous step. Instead of hard-coding the availability domain, you can dynamically retrieve it. Chapter 20 gives an example of how to fetch and list all the availability domains. In the sample user case in this chapter, we will explicitly set the availability domain because we want to control which one it would be created in, specifically the first one.

To do so, create the file dev_compute.tf, as shown in Example 21-12. Example 21-12 requires a number of parameters to create a compute instance, similar to what is normally required when creating one on the OCI console. This includes the availability domain, shape, image, and also the public SSH key for the default *opc* user on the instance. This is the same public key that would have been pasted or imported on the OCI console. The contents of the key itself can be pasted as shown in the example, or a file reference that exists on the Terraform client host can alternatively be provided.

As a reference, you can locate all options available for the compute instance creation at https://registry.terraform.io/providers/oracle/oci/latest/docs/resources/core. In this sample use case, a single **dev_instance1** compute instance will be created. If desired, you can create several all at once by listing multiple compute instances in this file.

Example 21-12   Contents of the dev_compute.tf File

```
resource "oci_core_instance" "dev_instance1" {
  # Required
  availability_domain="tpiZ:US-ASHBURN-AD-1"
  compartment_id=oci_identity_compartment.dev_compartment.id
  # See https://docs.oracle.com/en-us/iaas/Content/Compute/References/
  computeshapes.htm#vmshapes__vm-standard
  shape="VM.Standard2.1"
  # See https://docs.oracle.com/en-us/iaas/images/ for image OCIDs
  source_details {
    # OCID for Oracle Linux 8 image in us-ashburn-1
    source_id=" ocid1.image.oc1.iad.
  aaaaaaaautmrqednxxohclxwgvawc42o2q62261rbyte7nbe7hge6evbz7oq"
    source_type="image"
  }
  # Does not preserve the boot volume when the instance is terminated
  preserve_boot_volume=false
  # Display name
  display_name="dev-instance1"
  # Virtual network interface card
  create_vnic_details {
    assign_public_ip=true
    subnet_id=oci_core_subnet.dev_vcn_public_subnet.id
  }
  # Include public SSH key for the default opc user on the instance
  metadata = {
    ssh_authorized_keys="ssh-rsa AAAQAAA…H1ISJw== oracloud-key-2023"
    # Use this if referencing a local file
    # ssh_authorized_keys=file("/home/oracle/opc_public.pub")
  }
}
```

Worth noting in Example 21-12 are the **shape** and **source_details** arguments. The list of available shapes can be found at https://docs.oracle.com/en-us/iaas/Content/Compute/References/computeshapes.htm#vmshapes__vm-standard.

The list of available operating system images can be found at https://docs.oracle.com/en-us/iaas/images/. You must drill down to the operating system of choice (such as Oracle-Linux-8.7-2021-05.21-0) and locate the OCID in your region. This is the image OCID that must be used in the **source_details** argument. Not every shape is compatible with every image. When in doubt, try creating one through the OCI console or test the combinations in Terraform first. For example, the VM.Standard2.1 shape is not compatible with the Oracle-Linux-9.1-2021-05.21-0 image.

Also in Example 21-12 is the reference to the public SSH key. The entire public key can be pasted in the **ssh_authorized_keys** argument as a string as shown, or the public SSH key can reside in a local file on your local Terraform client host and referenced in the **ssh_authorized_keys** with the **file()** sub-argument, which is commented out in the example.

Add the contents in Example 21-13 to the existing dev_outputs.tf file to output the compute-related details. Much more information on the compute instance beyond what is shown here can be output if desired, and it is listed in the documentation.

Example 21-13   Additional Output for the dev_outputs.tf File

```
# ---------------------------------------
# Outputs for compute
# ---------------------------------------
output "compute-instance-public-ip" {
  value=oci_core_instance.dev_instance1.public_ip
}
output "compute-instance-name" {
  value=oci_core_instance.dev_instance1.display_name
}
output "compute-instance-OCID" {
  value=oci_core_instance.dev_instance1.id
}
output "compute-instance-state" {
  value=oci_core_instance.dev_instance1.state
}
```

Applying the Changes

The next step is to execute the **plan** and **apply** commands, as shown in Example 21-11. After you have applied the changes successfully, the output variables defined in Example 21-13 are shown. A compute instance dev_instance1 is now created and resides in the subnet dev_vcn_public_subnet of our compartment dev_compartment.

Creating an Autonomous Database

The Terraform OCI documentation for creating an autonomous database resource can be found at https://registry.terraform.io/providers/oracle/oci/latest/docs/resources/database_autonomous_database. Quite a few arguments are supported, and in this section we will create a basic autonomous database.

First, create the file dev_autonomousdatabase.tf, as shown in Example 21-14.

Example 21-14   Contents of the dev_autonomousdatabase.tf File

```
resource "oci_database_autonomous_database" "devautonomousdatabase1" {
    # Required
    db_name="devautonomousdatabase1"
    compartment_id=oci_identity_compartment.dev_compartment.id
    # Optional
    admin_password="ComplexPassword_123"
    data_storage_size_in_tbs=1
    db_version="19c"
    db_workload="OLTP"
    display_name="dev-autonomousdatabase1"
    is_free_tier=false
    cpu_core_count=2
    subnet_id=oci_core_subnet.dev_vcn_private_subnet.id
    license_model="LICENSE_INCLUDED"
}
```

Unfortunately, there may be a considerable amount of trial and error when creating an autonomous database the first time through Terraform. For example, you may learn that **db_name** cannot contain special characters, the **admin_password** must be at least 12 characters long, or that you cannot specify both **cpu_core_count** and **ocpu_count** at the same time. These errors are only discovered when you apply the configuration, and in some cases, the message is not always clear. The error "Error: 409-IncorrectState, You are attempting to use a feature that's not currently enabled for this tenancy" is not entirely descriptive, and neither is the documentation clear on what combination of arguments do not work with each other. It is always best to perform a test run first to identify the working arguments necessary for your infrastructure.

Typically, creating a database is a one-time operation. Once the autonomous database is created, reapplying multiple times will not do anything. The same Terraform scripts used to create the database for your development environment can then be used for your higher environments as well, ensuring consistency across all tiers. Configuration changes should ideally be propagated through Terraform as well (such as memory changes) so that these changes are tracked, version controlled, and applied identically to the higher environments.

Add the contents in Example 21-15 to the existing dev_outputs.tf files to output the autonomous database–related details. The Terraform data source documentation, which lists the various output options, can be found at https://registry.terraform.io/providers/oracle/oci/latest/docs/data-sources/database_autonomous_database.

Example 21-15   Additional Output for the dev_outputs.tf File

```
# ---------------------------------------
# Outputs for autonomous database
# ---------------------------------------
output "autonomousdatabase-OCID" {
  value=oci_database_autonomous_database.devautonomousdatabase1.id
}
output "autonomousdatabase-connection-strings" {
  value=oci_database_autonomous_database.devautonomousdatabase1.connection_strings
}
output "autonomousdatabase-private-endpoint-ip" {
  value=oci_database_autonomous_database.devautonomousdatabase1.
  private_endpoint_ip
output "autonomousdatabase-private-endpoint-ip" {
  value=oci_database_autonomous_database.devautonomousdatabase1.state
}
```

Applying the Changes

Next, you need to execute the **plan** and **apply** commands, similar to what is shown in Example 21-11. The time required to create the database may be lengthy, depending on the size and settings selected, and could range anywhere from 5 minutes to 1 hour.

Figure 21-8 displays a snippet of the output from the creation of the autonomous database that resides in the private subnet.

Figure 21-8   Output of the Autonomous Database Creation

The entire development infrastructure, which is the left half of the logical architecture shown in Figure 21-1, is now created and operational.

Replicating to a Production Environment

The use case in this chapter sets up an end-to-end development environment that hosts a compute instance and an autonomous database.

This section will describe how you can reuse the previous scripts to create an entirely identical replica for a production environment. One such approach is to merely copy the existing scripts to an alternate folder and customize them. All settings and display names for all resources were prefixed with **dev_** and **dev-**, respectively, with the exception of the autonomous database, which may simply have a **dev** prefix. These resources reside in a compartment named dev-compartment.

Example 21-16 shows how to create a copy of only the required .tf and .tfvars files from the ~/tf-providers directory to a newly created ~/tf-providers-prod directory. You do not want to copy the ~/tf-providers folder in its entirety because the state file and other hidden folders are not applicable.

Example 21-16   Copying the dev Scripts to a Newly Created prod Working Directory

```
# Create a new working directory
mkdir /home/oracle/tf-providers-prod

# Copy all scripts to the new working directory
cd /home/oracle/tf-providers
cp *.tf ../tf-provider-prod/
cp *.tfvars ../tf-provider-prod/

# Rename all scripts from dev to prod
cd /home/oracle/tf-providers-prod
mv dev_autonomousdatabase.tf        prod_autonomousdatabase.tf
mv dev_compartment.tf               prod_compartment.tf
mv dev_compute.tf                   prod_compute.tf
mv dev_outputs.tf                   prod_outputs.tf
mv dev_vcn_module.tf                prod_vcn_module.tf
mv dev_vcn_private_securitylist.tf  prod_vcn_private_securitylist.tf
mv dev_vcn_private_subnet.tf        prod_vcn_private_subnet.tf
mv dev_vcn_public_securitylist.tf   prod_vcn_public_securitylist.tf
mv dev_vcn_public_subnet.tf         prod_vcn_public_subnet.tf
```

Now that all files are copied over and renamed, you can edit each of the prod files and replace all references of **dev** with **prod**. Then run the **init**, **plan**, and **apply** commands, as shown in Example 21-2. In a matter of minutes, the entire production environment will be set up under the newly created prod-compartment.

It is possible to manage both development and production environment configurations from a single working directory.

Using Other Terraform Commands

A number of Terraform commands can be used to help format, view, and list the Terraform configuration, some of which will be described here.

Formatting Terraform Configuration

The **terraform fmt** command does just what its name implies: it formats the configuration. As you can see in the output in Figure 21-9, the format command only lists the files that were formatted. If the file is already formatted correctly, it will not be listed in the output of the command. This command can be safely rerun any number of times and makes no changes to your OCI infrastructure.

Figure 21-9   Formatting Terraform Configuration

Validating Terraform Configuration

The **terraform validate** command confirms the syntax of the configuration. For example, in Figure 21-10, an invalid argument **xavailability_domain** is specified in the dev_compute.tf configuration file. After you correct and rerun the command, a confirmation is returned that the configuration is valid. This command can be safely rerun any number of times and makes no changes to your OCI infrastructure.

Listing All Resources in the Terraform State

The **terraform state list** command lists the resources. The state command also has other arguments (run **terraform state** to view them all). Figure 21-11 shows the output of the state list, which is a list of all resources in the Terraform state file. This command can be safely rerun any number of times and makes no changes to your OCI infrastructure.

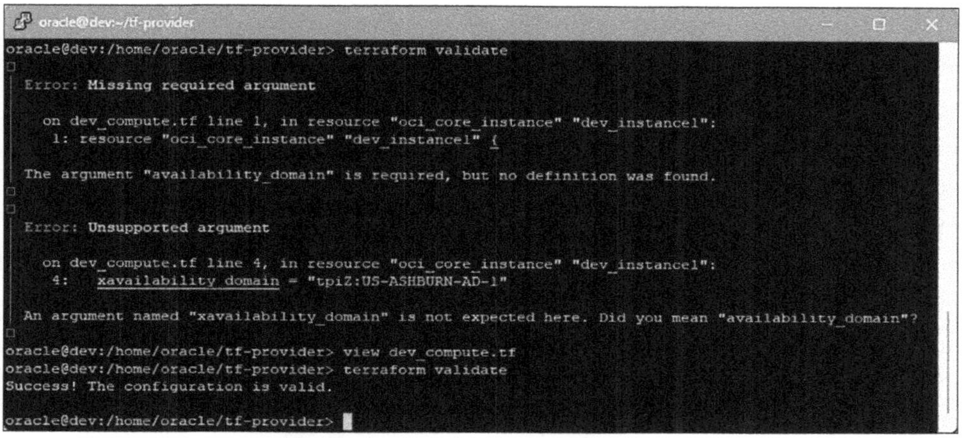

Figure 21-10   Validating Terraform Configuration

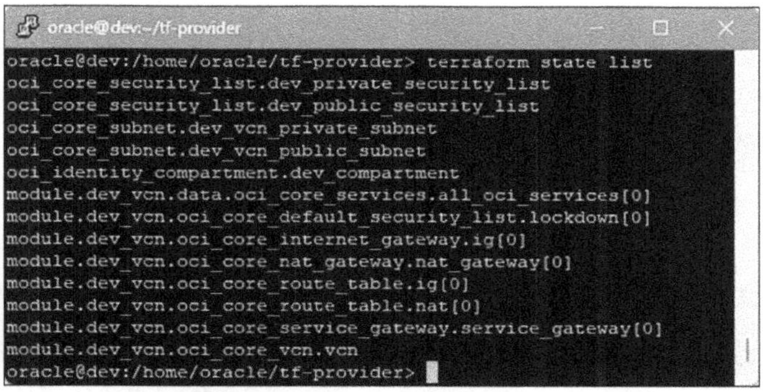

Figure 21-11   Inspecting Terraform State

Displaying Details of All Resources from the Terraform State

The **terraform show** command lists out the contents of the terraform.tfstate file. This file is updated every time you apply Terraform changes via the **terraform apply** command. This file is the local state of your infrastructure and includes the IDs and properties of each resource managed by Terraform. For example, you can run the **show** command to retrieve certain OCIDs for reference purposes.

As mentioned in earlier chapters, the terraform.tfstate file is important and critical, and contains sensitive information, and thus should be saved frequently (such as in source control). Figure 21-12 shows the output of this command, and it may be rather lengthy depending on how many resources are managed. This command can be safely rerun any number of times and makes no changes to your OCI infrastructure.

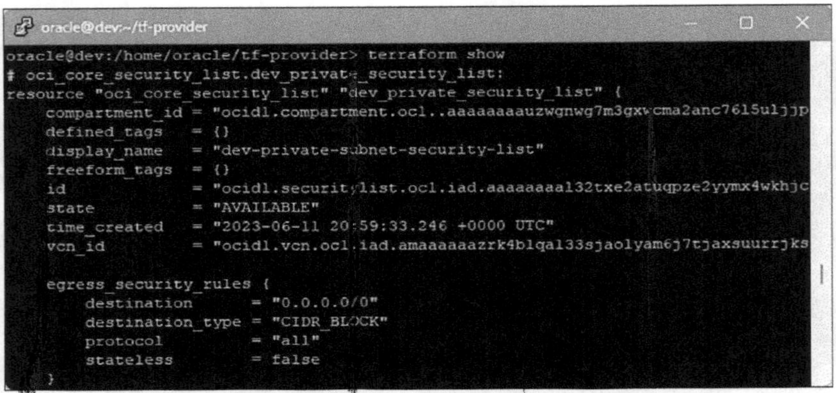

Figure 21-12   Showing Terraform State

Viewing the Terraform Output

The **terraform output** command extracts the values of the output variables, not from OCI, but from the local state file (that is, terraform.tfstate). How this differs from the **terraform show** command is that only the contents defined in the output, via dev_outputs.tf, are shown here, not the details of all resources. Figure 21-13 shows the execution of this command. This command can be safely rerun any number of times and makes no changes to your OCI infrastructure.

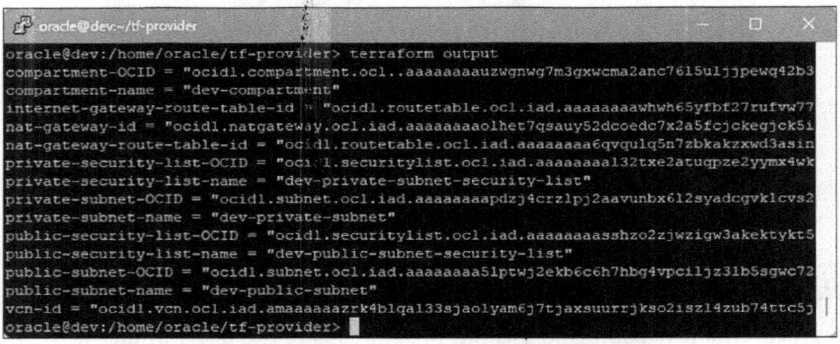

Figure 21-13   Viewing Terraform Output

Destroying Resources

Deleting, or "destroying" as it is referred to in the Terraform world, is the process of irrecoverably deleting a resource. Either a single resource, multiple resources, or the entire infrastructure can be deleted, which is why it is important to reemphasize the danger of granting the manage all-resources permission.

Destroying the Entire Infrastructure

Destroying the entire infrastructure is extremely easy...and dangerous. Through a single command, the entire infrastructure consisting of the autonomous database, compute instance, VCNs, security lists, gateways, and compartment can be deleted. To do so, run the **terraform destroy** command.

The **terraform destroy** command takes the current local Terraform configuration and deletes it all from OCI. It is essentially the opposite of the **apply** command. Running the **terraform destroy** command will delete all the currently defined resources. That is why it is extremely important to limit Terraform configuration to administrators who already have permissions to perform these actions on the OCI console.

Running the **destroy** command will delete all resources, with the exception of the compartment (even though it may indicate that it has been deleted in the output).

Running **terraform apply** will re-create them all again, assigning new OCIDs to each one. Whatever user data that may have existed will be permanently gone.

Destroying a Single Terraform Resource

In most cases, you might need to destroy only a single resource. Let's assume that you no longer want the autonomous database that was created earlier. You can destroy this single resource through Terraform. Destroying is still a dangerous operation because the database may contain data; caution should be exercised because the destroy action cannot be undone.

To destroy only the autonomous database resource, follow these steps:

Step 1. Delete the dev_autonomousdatabase.tf file from the working directory.
Step 2. Remove all references to the autonomous database from dev_outputs.tf.
Step 3. Run the **terraform apply** command.

Terraform is intelligent enough to understand that this resource exists in the state file, but not in the configuration, and therefore will destroy it.

Stopping/Starting Instances with Terraform

So far, you have seen how to create and how to destroy OCI resources through Terraform. It is possible to start and stop OCI resources through Terraform too.

For example, to stop the compute instance, follow these steps:

Step 1. Edit the dev_compute.tf file.
Step 2. Add the line **state="STOPPED"**.
Step 3. Save the file and run **terraform apply**.
Step 4. Run **terraform show** and confirm the state of the compute instance, which should now be stopped (see Figure 21-14). This can also be confirmed from the OCI console.

Figure 21-14   Viewing the Compute Instance State Through Terraform State

Step 5. Repeat steps 1–4 but change the value to **state="RUNNING"** to restart the instance.

Summary

In this chapter, you learned that using Terraform is incredibly easy, particularly after the initial setups are in place. But knowledge of OCI administration is a prerequisite, because Terraform is merely a command-line-based approach to provisioning (or destroying) cloud resources. It is intended for administrators and those with sufficient knowledge and permissions to create and manage OCI resources.

In this chapter, we provided an end-to-end sample use case of setting up an entire OCI infrastructure from scratch, from creating a compartment to a basic network to resources within them. After confirming that your OCI user has the appropriate permissions, you performed the following:

- **Created a compartment:** You created a child compartment to the root compartment. We walked through rerunning the **terraform apply** command multiple times to demonstrate its safety if no changes are made.
- **Created a VCN:** Creating a VCN requires more effort because security lists, security rules, and subnets are required.
- **Created a compute instance:** The process of creating a compute instance, or several, is extremely easy and straightforward, mimicking the options conveyed on the OCI console.
- **Created an autonomous database:** A database is one of many types of OCI resources that can be created.

After completing the exercise of provisioning this entire development environment, you created an entire duplicate production environment with little additional effort. This is one of the many advantages of Terraform, because this production environment is an exact replica of the development environment.

Finally, we demonstrated other Terraform commands that may come in handy, such as **format**, **validate**, **show**, **list**, and **output**. We also described how to destroy, stop, and start OCI resources.

Now that you have an understanding of how to set up Terraform, define resource configurations, define variables, parameterize from other output, and validate and debug, you can begin your journey setting up your first OCI infrastructure with Terraform. In the next chapter, you will learn more about Enterprise Manager Cloud Control.

## 22

Enterprise Manager Cloud Control Installation

Oracle Enterprise Manager Cloud Control, commonly called Oracle Enterprise Manager, is a comprehensive management tool for Oracle software as well as some non-Oracle software lifecycle management. It also works for Oracle cloud deployments, making it a single-point management tool.

At the time of writing, the latest version of Oracle Enterprise Manager is 13.5. One of the major changes from 13.4 is that Oracle Analytics Server has replaced the Business Intelligence (BI) Publisher reporting engine. Best practice is to install the Oracle Enterprise Manager repository database, Oracle Management Service (OMS), and Oracle Analytics Server (OAS) on separate servers.

The Oracle Enterprise Manager architecture includes different core components:

- **Oracle Management Repository (OMR):** OMR is an Oracle Database hosting metadata and data collected by Oracle Management Agent. During the installation, the process will create SYSMAN as a repository user in the database. This user contains different objects such as tables, procedures, and views. These objects are pulled into the Oracle Enterprise Manager cloud console for viewing.
- **Oracle Management Service (OMS):** OMS is a web-based application deployed on the middleware component WebLogic Server. This middleware deployment home also includes software components called Oracle Common, that includes most of the subsystems like the Job System and Event System. The OMS also includes its own Java Development Kit (JDK). OMS also provides the Oracle Enterprise Manager Cloud Control GUI.
- **Oracle Analytics Server (OAS):** OAS is a modern tool including cloud compatibilities to digest, analyze, and report data in easy-to-understand forms. It also includes AI-powered and self-service analytics capabilities for data processing and reporting. Starting with Oracle Enterprise Manager 13.5, Oracle BI Publisher is replaced by OAS for reporting. OAS is an independent component, meaning you install it as a stand-alone configuration and then perform additional configuration to integrate with OMS.
- **Plug-ins:** Plug-ins enable you to discover special types of targets such as engineered systems or fusion middleware targets. Plug-ins are installed on OMS

and Oracle Management Agents. OMS installation will install the default plug-ins Oracle Database, Oracle Fusion Middleware, Oracle Exadata, Oracle Cloud Framework, and System Infrastructure. You can select optional plug-ins as well based on your needs.

- **Oracle Management Agent (OMA):** OMA is Java-based software that helps monitor the host and all other targets on it. It also works with plug-ins to monitor appropriate targets on this manager host. First, OMA is installed on the OMS during the OMS installation and configuration. This agent is called the *central agent*. The agent will need to be installed on all the hosts that you want to monitor using OMS.
- **Enterprise Manager Cloud Control Console:** This console is a graphical user interface that allows you to monitor and manage your complete environment, including hosts, databases, and middleware.

Oracle Enterprise Manager can be deployed on a single node, in a multinode setup, or in a high-availability setup. The single-node setup is recommended for development or test environments. All major components like the Oracle Management Repository database, Oracle Management Server, and Oracle Analytics Server are installed on the same server; therefore, if the server is not configured appropriately, performance issues will arise frequently.

Another option is to install OMR, OMS, and OAS separately on their own nodes. This approach is recommended for production environments. Each of these components has different access-level requirements, so it also becomes easier to control inter-node access and access from the outside world for each node.

Oracle Enterprise Manager can also be configured for a high-availability scenario. Each of the Oracle Enterprise Manager components can be configured to have overall maximum availability with minimum downtime on the Oracle Enterprise Manager. Oracle Enterprise Manager can be configured as active/active or active/passive, depending on the business need. Most common high-availability setups include a physical standby database for a repository database and an active/passive setup for OMS; they are created by installing binaries on shared storage and creating a virtual hostname/ IP address that can be resolved by all underlying nodes.

Oracle Enterprise Manager is free when you purchase any Oracle software license. In other words, if you own an Oracle Database license, then Oracle Enterprise Manager is free to use. It also comes with a restricted license for Oracle Database Enterprise Edition, Oracle WebLogic Server, Oracle WebLogic clustering, Oracle Analytics Server, and Oracle Analytics Server for mobile web to be used only for the Oracle Enterprise Manager. You can also purchase full licenses for this software and/or additional options, management packs, management plug-ins, and other products to get more functionality out of Oracle Enterprise Manager.

Note

Although Oracle Enterprise Manager is free, it may require management packs for additional features. You can find more details on these packs by logging on to the Oracle Enterprise Manager console and navigating to **Setup > Management Packs**.

In this chapter, we will cover the advanced installation process of a medium-size Oracle Enterprise Manager using the silent installation method.

Installing and Configuring the Repository Database

In this chapter, we will install and configure Oracle Grid Infrastructure (GI) 19c and Oracle Database (DB) 19c on the repository database server. Automatic Storage Management (ASM) is recommended to simplify storage management. ASM combines volume manager and file systems capabilities to provide alternative solutions to traditional volumes, file systems, and raw devices. ASM represents a disk or group of disks as a disk group. A disk group can be added or removed dynamically without impacting the overall availability. ASM also distributes and redistributes the file content to provide better performance. In addition, it offers normal, high, and external redundancy options for different types of mirroring options.

Configuration for the Oracle Database server emcc135omr is as follows. Use this as a minimum configuration reference for your environments. For your environments, especially production, pay careful attention to the server configuration.

- Oracle Linux 8.7
- 4 OCPUs
- 8 GB RAM
- 100 GB /u01
- 200 GB for ASM

Download DB and GI 19c software with the latest Release Updates (RUs) from Oracle Support. For this example, download the following software and patches:

- **DB Software:** LINUX.X64_193000_db_home.zip
- **GI Software:** LINUX.X64_193000_grid_home.zip
- **Latest OPatch:** p6880880_122010_Linux-x86-64.zip
- **Latest GI and DB Release Update:** p34762026_190000_Linux-x86-64.zip

All GI 19c prerequisites for operating system settings, packages, kernel parameters, and so on are verified on the server. You can find more details on these prerequisites in the Oracle documentation. For GI and DB, the oracle user will be the owner of these software installations. You have an option to create separate ownerships for both DB and GI home directories.

Oracle provides the oracle-database-preinstall-19c package to perform all the prerequisites for Oracle database installation. It will install required packages and create users and groups. To install the oracle-database-preinstall-19c package and create necessary users for ASM installations and unzip the GI software, enter the script shown in Example 22-1.

Example 22-1   Prerequisites

```
# dnf install oracle-database-preinstall-19c -y
# groupadd asmdba
# groupadd asmoper
# groupadd asmadmin
# mkdir /u01
# chown -R oracle:oinstall /u01
# su - oracle
$ mkdir /u01/app/grid
$ mkdir -p /u01/app/19.0.0.0/grid
$ unzip /u01/sw/LINUX.X64_193000_grid_home.zip -d /u01/app/19.0.0.0/grid/
```

> **Note**
>
> If you're running Red Hat Linux, you will have to perform all prerequisite tasks manually unless you have Oracle Linux Support for your organization.

The physical raw disk (200 GB) is labeled /dev/sdb on this server. You can present it for ASM by using the **asmcmd** command, as shown in Example 22-2. You can use the ASM Filter Driver (ASMFD) for ASM configuration. ASMFD is a kernel module that uses the filter driver to validate write I/O requests to ASM disks. Once the disk is labeled, it will be presented as a candidate disk during the ASM configuration process.

Example 22-2   ASM Disk Prerequisite

```
# dnf install /u01/app/19.0.0.0/grid/cv/rpm/cvuqdisk-1.0.10-1.rpm
# export ORACLE_HOME=/u01/app/19.0.0.0/grid
# export ORACLE_BASE=/tmp
# ./asmcmd afd_label DATA /dev/sdb --init
# ./asmcmd afd_lslbl /dev/sdb
```

Now you are ready for the GI installation, configuration, and patching process. At the time of writing, the latest available GI Release Update was 19.18.0.0.230117 (patch 34762026). You can enter the **GridSetup.sh** command to run the installation process. This command will run with the argument **–applyRU**. This will patch the GI home first and then start the installation process. It is recommended that you patch the GI home first. This way, when you run the installation, all the bugs that can potentially cause issues during the installation will be fixed.

Now you're ready to install the latest OPatch version, create a response file with all the required parameters, run the **GridSetup.sh** command, and perform all the post-install actions asked by the installation process, as shown in Example 22-3. Modify all response file variables per your environment setup.

Example 22-3   Grid Infrastructure Installation and Configuration

```
$ cd /u01/app/19.0.0.0/grid
$ mv OPatch/ OPatch-old/
$ cp /u01/sw/p6880880_122010_Linux-x86-64.zip .
$ unzip p6880880_122010_Linux-x86-64.zip
$ cat /home/oracle/grid.rsp | grep -v "#"
oracle.install.responseFileVersion=/oracle/install/rspfmt_crsinstall_response_
  schema_v19.0.0
INVENTORY_LOCATION=/u01/app/oraInventory
oracle.install.option=HA_CONFIG
ORACLE_BASE=/u01/app/oracle
oracle.install.asm.OSDBA=asmdba
oracle.install.asm.OSOPER=asmoper
oracle.install.asm.OSASM=asmadmin
oracle.install.crs.config.scanType=LOCAL_SCAN
oracle.install.crs.config.ClusterConfiguration=STANDALONE
oracle.install.crs.config.configureAsExtendedCluster=false
oracle.install.crs.config.gpnp.configureGNS=false
oracle.install.crs.config.autoConfigureClusterNodeVIP=false
oracle.install.crs.config.gpnp.gnsOption=CREATE_NEW_GNS
oracle.install.crs.configureGIMR=false
oracle.install.asm.configureGIMRDataDG=false
oracle.install.crs.config.useIPMI=false
oracle.install.asm.SYSASMPassword=Welcome_1
oracle.install.asm.diskGroup.name=DATA
oracle.install.asm.diskGroup.redundancy=EXTERNAL
oracle.install.asm.diskGroup.AUSize=4
oracle.install.asm.diskGroup.disksWithFailureGroupNames=/dev/sdb,
oracle.install.asm.diskGroup.disks=/dev/sdb
oracle.install.asm.diskGroup.diskDiscoveryString=/dev/sd*
oracle.install.asm.monitorPassword=Welcome_1
oracle.install.asm.gimrDG.AUSize=1
oracle.install.asm.configureAFD=true
oracle.install.crs.configureRHPS=false
oracle.install.crs.config.ignoreDownNodes=false
oracle.install.config.managementOption=NONE
oracle.install.config.omsPort=0
oracle.install.crs.rootconfig.executeRootScript=false
$ ./gridSetup.sh -applyRU /u01/sw/34762026 -silent -responseFile /home/oracle/
  grid.rsp
# /u01/app/oraInventory/orainstRoot.sh
# /u01/app/19.0.0.0/grid/root.sh
$ /u01/app/19.0.0.0/grid/gridSetup.sh -executeConfigTools -responseFile /home/
  oracle/grid.rsp -silent
```

At this point, ASM is configured and ready to be referenced by the database. Now you can install and configure the database. To do so, unzip the database software, create a response file, and run the **runInstaller** command to install the database software, as shown in Example 22-4.

Example 22-4   Database Installation and Configuration

```
$ mkdir -p /u01/app/oracle/product/19.0.0/dbhome_1
$ unzip -o /u01/sw/LINUX.X64_193000_db_home.zip -d /u01/app/oracle/product/19.0.0/
  dbhome_1
$ cat /home/oracle/db_sw_install.rsp | grep -v "#"
oracle.install.responseFileVersion=/oracle/install/rspfmt_dbinstall_response_
  schema_v19.0.0
oracle.install.option=INSTALL_DB_SWONLY
UNIX_GROUP_NAME=oinstall
INVENTORY_LOCATION=/u01/app/oraInventory
ORACLE_HOME=/u01/app/oracle/product/19.0.0/dbhome_1
ORACLE_BASE=/u01/app/oracle
oracle.install.db.InstallEdition=EE
oracle.install.db.OSDBA_GROUP=dba
oracle.install.db.OSOPER_GROUP=oinstall
oracle.install.db.OSBACKUPDBA_GROUP=oinstall
oracle.install.db.OSDGDBA_GROUP=oinstall
oracle.install.db.OSKMDBA_GROUP=oinstall
oracle.install.db.OSRACDBA_GROUP=dba
SECURITY_UPDATES_VIA_MYORACLESUPPORT=false
DECLINE_SECURITY_UPDATES=true
oracle.installer.autoupdates.option=SKIP_UPDATES
$ export CV_ASSUME_DISTID=OEL7.8
$ cd /u01/app/oracle/product/19.0.0/dbhome_1
$ ./runInstaller -silent -responseFile /home/oracle/dw_sw_install.rsp -noconfig
  -ignorePrereqFailure
```

The listener is created during the GI installation and configuration. If you did not install GI, make sure to create the listener. Then you can move forward with applying the latest DB Release Update. Follow the README document for the patch for more details. Now patch the database software, as shown in Example 22-5.

Example 22-5   Database Software Patching

```
$ cd /u01/sw/34762026 /34765931/
$ /u01/app/oracle/product/19.0.0/dbhome_1/OPatch/opatch prereq
  CheckConflictAgainstOHWithDetail -ph ./
$ /u01/app/oracle/product/19.0.0/dbhome_1/OPatch/opatch apply
```

Next, you can create the Oracle Enterprise Manager repository database. One of the pluggable databases will host the Oracle Enterprise Manager repository data. Create a response file with all required parameters and enter the **run dbca** command to create the database, as shown in Example 22-6. Modify these parameters per your environment setup.

Example 22-6   Create Repository Database

```
$ cat /home/oracle/create_db.rsp | grep -v "#"
responseFileVersion=/oracle/assistants/rspfmt_dbca_response_schema_v12.2.0
gdbName=emccdb.dj.local
sid=emccdb
databaseConfigType=SI
policyManaged=false
createServerPool=false
force=false
createAsContainerDatabase=true
numberOfPDBs=3
pdbName=emccpdb
useLocalUndoForPDBs=true
pdbAdminPassword=Welcome1!
templateName=/u01/app/oracle/product/19.0.0/dbhome_1/assistants/dbca/templates/
   General_Purpose.dbc
sysPassword=Welcome1!
systemPassword= Welcome1!
runCVUChecks=FALSE
dbsnmpPassword=Welcome1!
olsConfiguration=false
datafileJarLocation={ORACLE_HOME}/assistants/dbca/templates/
datafileDestination=+DATA/{DB_UNIQUE_NAME}/
recoveryAreaDestination=+DATA
storageType=ASM
diskGroupName=+DATA/{DB_UNIQUE_NAME}/
asmsnmpPassword=Welcome_1
recoveryGroupName=+DATA
characterSet=AL32UTF8
nationalCharacterSet=AL16UTF16
registerWithDirService=false
listeners=LISTENER
skipListenerRegistration=false
variables=ORACLE_BASE_HOME=/u01/app/oracle/product/19.0.0/dbhome_1,DB_UNIQUE_
   NAME=emccdb,ORACLE_BASE=/u01/app/oracle,PDB_NAME=,DB_NAME=emccdb,ORACLE_HOME=/
   u01/app/oracle/product/19.0.0/dbhome_1,SID=emccdb
initParams=undo_tablespace=UNDOTBS1,sga_target=1092MB,db_block_size=8192BYTES,nls_
   language=AMERICAN,dispatchers=(PROTOCOL=TCP) (SERVICE=emccdbXDB),diagnostic_
   dest={ORACLE_BASE},remote_login_passwordfile=EXCLUSIVE,db_create_file_
   dest=+DATA/{DB_UNIQUE_NAME}/,audit_file_dest={ORACLE_BASE}/admin/
   {DB_UNIQUE_NAME}/adump,processes=300,pga_aggregate_target=364MB,nls_
   territory=AMERICA,local_listener=LISTENER_EMCCDB,db_recovery_file_dest_
   size=17208MB,open_cursors=300,log_archive_format=%t_%s_%r.dbf,db_domain=dj.
   local,compatible=19.0.0,db_name=emccdb,db_recovery_file_dest=+DATA,audit_
   trail=db
sampleSchema=false
memoryPercentage=40
databaseType=MULTIPURPOSE
automaticMemoryManagement=false
totalMemory=0
```

```
$ export ORACLE_HOME=/u01/app/oracle/product/19.0.0/dbhome_1
$ cd /u01/app/oracle/product/19.0.0/dbhome_1/bin
$ ./dbca -silent -createDatabase -responseFile /home/oracle/create_db.rsp
```

Note

All passwords are for demonstration purposes only.

The repository database is now ready to be referenced by the Oracle Enterprise Manager installation process. It is recommended that you enable archiving and configure auto-restart of the GI components, listener, database, and so on after a server reboot.

Installing and Configuring Oracle Management Service

The next step is to install and configure Oracle Management Service (OMS). In this section, we will also cover how to patch OMS components to the latest available patches at the time of writing this book. For this sample scenario, the server configuration is as follows. It is assumed that the server has all the necessary prerequisites such as packages and OS settings implemented already.

- Oracle Linux 8.7
- 6 vCPU
- 12 GB RAM
- 100 GB disk space

You will need to run prechecks before installing OMS, as shown in Example 22-7. This script will run through all prechecks and provide the report. Anything reported as a fail should be investigated and resolved before beginning the installation process.

Example 22-7   OMS Prechecks

```
$ ./em13500_linux64.bin -prereqchecker -entryPoint "oracle.sysman.top.oms_Core"
  -silent
```

You can either create a response file or extract different response files from the zipped software file. Once it is extracted, you can modify the file with the appropriate parameters. For this example, extract the response files and modify it, as shown in Example 22-8.

Example 22-8   Creating a Response File

```
$ ./em13500_linux64.bin -getResponseFileTemplates -outputLoc /u01
$ grep -v "#"  softwareOnlyWithPlugins_install.rsp
RESPONSEFILE_VERSION=2.2.1.0.0
UNIX_GROUP_NAME=oinstall
INSTALL_UPDATES_SELECTION=skip
STAGE_LOCATION=
MYORACLESUPPORT_USERNAME_FOR_SOFTWAREUPDATES=
MYORACLESUPPORT_PASSWORD_FOR_SOFTWAREUPDATES=
ORACLE_MIDDLEWARE_HOME_LOCATION=/u01/app/oracle/mw_home
AGENT_BASE_DIR=/u01/app/oracle/agent_home
ORACLE_HOSTNAME=emcc135oms.tam.local
PLUGIN_SELECTION={}
b_upgrade=false
EM_INSTALL_TYPE=NOSEED
CONFIGURATION_TYPE=LATER
```

Now, you can install software binaries first and then configure OMS. To do so, execute the commands shown in Example 22-9 to perform a software-only install and run post-install commands.

Example 22-9   OMS Installation

```
$ ./em13500_linux64.bin -silent -responseFile /u01/softwareOnlyWithPlugins_
  install.rsp
# /u01/app/oraInventory/orainstRoot.sh
# /u01/app/oracle/mw_home/allroot.sh
```

It's time to do some preparation on the database side before OMS configuration. Make sure firewall rules are in place to allow OMS to communicate with the database server. Set the required database parameters, as shown in Example 22-10, and reboot the database.

Example 22-10   Database Parameters

```
SQL> alter system set processes=600 scope=spfile;
SQL> alter system set pga_aggregate_target=1500M;
SQL> alter system set session_cached_cursors=300 scope=spfile;
SQL> alter system set sga_target=5G scope=spfile;
SQL> alter system set sga_max_size=6G scope=spfile;
SQL> alter system set shared_pool_size=600M;
SQL> alter system set "_allow_insert_with_update_check"=TRUE scope=spfile;
```

Next, create the response file and perform OMS configuration, as shown in Example 22-11. Oracle Enterprise Manager configuration will run for few minutes and leave OMS running at the end of it.

Example 22-11   OMS Configuration

```
$ grep -v "#" /u01/new_install.rsp
RESPONSEFILE_VERSION=2.2.1.0.0
UNIX_GROUP_NAME=oinstall
INVENTORY_LOCATION=/u01/app/oraInventory
INSTALL_UPDATES_SELECTION=skip
STAGE_LOCATION=
MYORACLESUPPORT_USERNAME_FOR_SOFTWAREUPDATES=
MYORACLESUPPORT_PASSWORD_FOR_SOFTWAREUPDATES=
PROXY_USER=
PROXY_PWD=
PROXY_HOST=
PROXY_PORT=
ORACLE_MIDDLEWARE_HOME_LOCATION=/u01/app/oracle/mw_home
ORACLE_HOSTNAME=emcc135oms.tam.local
AGENT_BASE_DIR=/u01/app/oracle/agent_home
WLS_ADMIN_SERVER_USERNAME=weblogic
WLS_ADMIN_SERVER_PASSWORD=Welcome_1
WLS_ADMIN_SERVER_CONFIRM_PASSWORD=Welcome_1
NODE_MANAGER_PASSWORD=Welcome_1
NODE_MANAGER_CONFIRM_PASSWORD=Welcome_1
ORACLE_INSTANCE_HOME_LOCATION=/u01/app/oracle/gc_inst
CONFIGURE_ORACLE_SOFTWARE_LIBRARY=true
SOFTWARE_LIBRARY_LOCATION=/u01/app/oracle/sw_lib
DATABASE_HOSTNAME=emcc135omr.tam.local
LISTENER_PORT=1522
SERVICENAME_OR_SID=emccpdb1
SYS_PASSWORD=Welcome1!
SYSMAN_PASSWORD=Welcome_1
SYSMAN_CONFIRM_PASSWORD=Welcome_1
DEPLOYMENT_SIZE=MEDIUM
MANAGEMENT_TABLESPACE_LOCATION=+DATA/EMCCDB/
163290B32AD5CFDE0550A00276CACE8/DATAFILE/mgmt.dbf
CONFIGURATION_DATA_TABLESPACE_LOCATION=+DATA/EMCCDB/
163290B32AD5CFDE0550A00276CACE8/DATAFILE /mgmt_ecm_depot1.dbf
JVM_DIAGNOSTICS_TABLESPACE_LOCATION=+DATA/EMCCDB/
163290B32AD5CFDE0550A00276CACE8/DATAFILE /mgmt_deepdive.dbf
EMPREREQ_AUTO_CORRECTION=false
Is_oneWaySSL=
TRUSTSTORE_LOCATION=
TRUSTSTORE_PASSWORD=
Is_twoWaySSL=
KEYSTORE_LOCATION=
KEYSTORE_PASSWORD=
AGENT_REGISTRATION_PASSWORD=Welcome1!
AGENT_REGISTRATION_CONFIRM_PASSWORD=Welcome1!
STATIC_PORTS_FILE=
PLUGIN_SELECTION={}
b_upgrade=false
```

```
EM_INSTALL_TYPE=NOSEED
CONFIGURATION_TYPE=ADVANCED
$ /u01/app/oracle/mw_home/sysman/install/ConfigureGC.sh -silent -responseFile
  /u01/new_install.rsp
```

Oracle Enterprise Manager will then be accessible at https://emcc135oms.
dj.local:7803/em.

Now let's patch all Oracle Enterprise Manager components, including the WebLogic
Server and JDK. Refer to the Oracle Support document titled "Overview of the
Enterprise Manager Proactive Patch Program" (Doc ID 822485.1).

First, let's review all the components and their relevant patches that need to be
applied. Although these should give you enough information to patch all components,
it is important that you refer to the README file of every single patch. Mainly, you
will need Release Update patches for OMS and the agent. You will find a list of other
one-off patches and patches for individual components like Fusion Middleware (FMW)
components as well in the list. These patches will depend on your existing installation.

Now, run the command shown in Example 22-12 to list the current patch level of OMS.

Example 22-12   Current OMS Patch Level

```
$ /u01/app/oracle/mw_home/OPatch/opatch lspatches
33424205;Oracle Enterprise Manager for Systems Infrastructure 13c Release 5
  Plug-in Update 3 (13.5.1.3) for Oracle Management Service
33424193;Oracle Enterprise Manager for Exadata 13c Release 5 Plug-in Update 3
  (13.5.1.3) for Oracle Management Service
33424169;Oracle Enterprise Manager for Oracle Database 13c Release 5 Plug-in
  Update 3 (13.5.1.3) for Oracle Management Service
33424166;Oracle Enterprise Manager for Fusion Middleware 13c Release 5 Plug-in
  Update 3 (13.5.1.3) for Oracle Management Service
33424163;Oracle Enterprise Manager 13c Release 5 Platform Update 3 (13.5.0.3) for
  Oracle Management Service
32941631;Oracle Enterprise Manager for Cloud Framework 13c Release 5 Plug-in
  Update 1 (13.5.1.1) for Oracle Management Service
32880070;One-off
33093748;One-off
31544353;One-off
1221410;Bundle patch for Oracle Coherence Version 12.2.1.4.10
33084721;ADF BUNDLE PATCH 12.2.1.4.210706
32575741;OSS BUNDLE PATCH 12.2.1.4.210302
32784652;OPSS Bundle Patch 12.2.1.4.210418
32673423;OHS (NATIVE) BUNDLE PATCH 12.2.1.4.210324
33059296;WLS PATCH SET UPDATE 12.2.1.4.210629
31818221;One-off
31708760;One-off
30152128;One-off
26626168;One-off
```

Now it's time to begin the patching.

OPatch

At this point, you need to upgrade the OPatch version to the minimum version required for the rest of the patching process. Best practice is to upgrade it to the latest version available. To start, download 28186730 from Oracle Support and move it to the OMS server. Unzip the patch, stop the OMS, install the patch, and verify the version, as shown in Example 22-13.

Example 22-13   OPatch Version Upgrade

```
$ unzip p28186730_1394211_Generic.zip
$ export ORACLE_HOME=/u01/app/oracle/mw_home
$ export PATH=$ORACLE_HOME/OPatch:$ORACLE_HOME/bin:$PATH
$ emctl stop oms -all
$ /u01/app/oracle/mw_home/oracle_common/jdk/bin/java -jar /u01/patches/6880880/
  opatch_generic.jar -silent oracle_home=/u01/app/oracle/mw_home
$ opatch version
```

Oracle Enterprise Manager 13c Update 12 for OMS

OMSPatcher is used to patch the OMS. So just like you upgraded the OPatch, you will need to upgrade OMSPatcher to the latest version available. To do so, download OMSPatcher patch 19999993 for Oracle Enterprise Manager version 13.5 from Oracle Support and move it to the OMS server. Next, move the patch zip file to the OMS home, unzip it, and install the patch, as shown in Example 22-14.

Example 22-14   OMSPatcher

```
$ mv /u01/patches/p19999993_135000_Generic.zip /u01/app/oracle/mw_home/
$ cd /u01/app/oracle/mw_home/
$ mv OMSPatcher/ OMSPatcher-old/
$ unzip p19999993_135000_Generic.zip
$ omspatcher version
```

Now you're ready to patch OMS. When you run the **omspatcher** command, you will be asked to enter the OMS Weblogic admin server URL, admin username, admin password, and repository database SYS user password. Before proceeding, make sure that the **analyze** command will succeed without any errors. To do so, unzip the patch, run **analyze**, and apply the patch if no conflict is found, as shown in Example 22-15.

Example 22-15   Oracle Enterprise Manager Update 12 Patching

```
$ unzip p34795383_135000_Generic.zip
$ export ORACLE_HOME=/u01/app/oracle/mw_home
$ export PATH=$ORACLE_HOME/OMSPatcher: $ORACLE_HOME/OPatcher:$ORACLE_HOME/
  bin:$PATH
```

```
$ cd /u01/patches/34795383/
$ omspatcher apply -analyze
$ emctl stop oms
$ omspatcher apply
$ /u01/app/oracle/mw_home/OPatch/opatch lspatches
34706749;Oracle Enterprise Manager for Exadata 13c Release 5 Plug-in Update 12
   (13.5.1.12) for Oracle Management Service
34706727;Oracle Enterprise Manager for Fusion Middleware 13c Release 5 Plug-in
   Update 12 (13.5.1.12) for Oracle Management Service
34706723;Oracle Enterprise Manager for Oracle Database 13c Release 5 Plug-in
   Update 12 (13.5.1.12) for Oracle Management Service
34706719;Oracle Enterprise Manager 13c Release 5 Platform Update 12 (13.5.0.12)
   for Oracle Management Service
34601404;Oracle Enterprise Manager for Cloud Framework 13c Release 5 Plug-in
   Update 11 (13.5.1.11) for Oracle Management Service
34601397;Oracle Enterprise Manager for Systems Infrastructure 13c Release 5
   Plug-in Update 11 (13.5.1.11) for Oracle Management Service
32458315;ADF BUNDLE PATCH 12.2.1.4.210203
32412974;One-off
31818221;One-off
31808404;OHS (NATIVE) BUNDLE PATCH 12.2.1.4.200826
31708760;One-off
31666198;OPSS Bundle Patch 12.2.1.4.200724
30152128;One-off
26626168;One-off
122146;Bundle patch for Oracle Coherence Version 12.2.1.4.6
32253037;WLS PATCH SET UPDATE 12.2.1.4.201209
```

Note

OMSPatcher will fail if the SYS password has any special characters in it. Therefore, you will need to change the SYS password to something simple temporarily, and after the patching, you can change it back to how you need it to be.

Oracle Enterprise Manager 13c Release 5 Update 12 for Oracle Management Agent

AgentPatcher is used to patch the Oracle Enterprise Manager Agent. If you're patching the new OMS environment, like we're doing here, then you will not find it under the agent home. But for future patching sessions, you will need to back up the existing agentpatcher directory and then install the new version. Best practice is to upgrade it to the latest version available.

For this sample scenario, download patch 33355570 and move it to the OMS server. Next, move the patch zip to the agent home directory and unzip it to install the AgentPatcher command, as shown in Example 22-16.

Example 22-16   AgentPatcher Upgrade

```
$ cp /u01/app/patches/p33355570_13500_Generic.zip /u01/app/oracle/agent_home/
  agent_13.5.0.0.0/
$ cd /u01/app/oracle/agent_home/agent_13.5.0.0.0/
$ unzip p33355570_13500_Generic.zip
$ cd AgentPatcher
$ ./agentpatcher version
```

Now you are ready to patch the Oracle Enterprise Manager Agent. Download patch 34795397 and move it to the server. Unzip the patch, run **analyze** to check for any conflict, and then apply the patch, as shown in Example 22-17.

Example 22-17   Oracle Enterprise Manager Agent Bundle Patch

```
$ cd /u01/app/patches
$ unzip p34795397_135000_Generic.zip
$ export ORACLE_HOME=/u01/app/oracle/agent_home/agent_13.5.0.0.0
$ export PATH=$ORACLE_HOME/AgentPatcher:$ORACLE_HOME/OPatch:$PATH
$ cd /home/oracle/34795397/
$ agentpatcher apply -analyze
$ agentpatcher apply
$ opatch lspatches
34820977;Oracle Enterprise Manager for Fusion Middleware 13c Release 5 Plug-in
  Update 12 (13.5.1.12) for Oracle Management Agent
34795235;Oracle Enterprise Manager for Oracle Database 13c Release 5 Plug-in
  Update 12 (13.5.1.12) for Oracle Management Agent (Discovery)
34795111;Oracle Enterprise Manager 13c Release 5 Platform Update 12 (13.5.0.12)
  for Oracle Management Agent
34706830;Oracle Enterprise Manager for Exadata 13c Release 5 Plug-in Update 11
  (13.5.1.11) for Oracle Management Agent (Discovery)
34611829;Oracle Enterprise Manager for Fusion Middleware 13c Release 5 Plug-in
  Update 10 (13.5.1.10) for Oracle Management Agent (Discovery)
34471145;Oracle Enterprise Manager for Oracle Home 13c Release 5 Plug-in Update 9
  (13.5.0.9) for Oracle Management Agent
34158793;Oracle Enterprise Manager for EMREP 13c Release 5 Plug-in Update 8
  (13.5.0.8) for Oracle Management Agent
33869752;Tracking bug to repackage JDBC patch from 32752229 as 13.5 EM Agent patch
33737099;Oracle Enterprise Manager for Systems Infrastructure 13c Release 5
  Plug-in Update 4 (13.5.1.4) for Oracle Management Agent (Discovery)
32574981;
32313251;
32302527;
```

At this point, you can start the OMS services by using the **emctl** command if they are not already started. The commands are shown in Example 22-18.

Example 22-18 `emctl` Commands

```
$ /u01/app/oracle/mw_home/bin/emctl status oms
$ /u01/app/oracle/mw_home/bin/emctl start oms
$ /u01/app/oracle/mw_home/bin/emctl stop oms
```

Installing and Configuring Oracle Analytics Server

In Oracle Enterprise Manager 13.5, BI Publisher Report is replaced by Oracle Analytics Server (OAS). So, you need to install a stand-alone instance of Oracle Analytics Server 5.5 or higher. For this sample scenario, the server configuration is as follows. It is assumed that the server has all the necessary prerequisites such as packages and OS settings implemented already.

- Oracle Linux 8.7
- 2 OCPUs
- 8 GB RAM
- 100 GB disk space

OAS installation is composed of the following steps:

- Install JDK8 U251 or higher.
- Install the Fusion Middleware (FMW) infrastructure with required one-off patch 31438318.
- Install OAS 5.5 or higher with bundle patches.
- Configure OAS.

You can download OAS and FMW Infrastructure software from https://edelivery. oracle.com. It also includes mandatory patches for the FMW Infrastructure, so be sure to download that too.

Installing JDK

Download the latest JDK8 from https://www.oracle.com/java/technologies/javase/ javase-jdk8-downloads.html. After you download the tar file, just unzip it at the desired location. Then run all the commands shown in Example 22-19 as the oracle user.

Example 22-19 Installing JDK8 U301

```
$ mkdir /u01/app/java
$ cd /u01/app/java
$ export JAVA_HOME=/u01/java/jdk1.8.0_301
$ tar xzf /home/oracle/jdk-8u301-linux-x64.tar.gz
$ export PATH=$JAVA_HOME/bin:$PATH
```

Note

A limited-use JAVA license is included just to run FMW. Any other use requires that you pay for the license.

Installing FMW Infrastructure

FMW Infrastructure provides different middleware products and features such as WebLogic and Coherence. FMW will always be a software-only install. For this setup, you can use Fusion Middleware Infrastructure 12.2.1.4. As a part of the installation process, unzip the software, create a response file, create the oraInst.loc file, and install the software as the oracle user, as shown in Example 22-20.

Example 22-20   FMW Infrastructure Installation

```
$ unzip V983368-01.zip
$ cat fmw_infrastructure.rsp
[ENGINE]
Response File Version=1.0.0.0.0
[GENERIC]
DECLINE_AUTO_UPDATES=true
MOS_USERNAME=
MOS_PASSWORD=
AUTO_UPDATES_LOCATION=
SOFTWARE_UPDATES_PROXY_SERVER=
SOFTWARE_UPDATES_PROXY_PORT=
SOFTWARE_UPDATES_PROXY_USER=
SOFTWARE_UPDATES_PROXY_PASSWORD=
ORACLE_HOME=/u01/app/middleware/OASMW
FEDERATED_ORACLE_HOMES=
INSTALL_TYPE=Fusion Middleware Infrastructure
$ mkdir /u01/app/oraInventory
$ chmod 775 /u01/app/oraInventory
$ cat /u01/app/oraInventory/oraInst.loc
inventory_loc=/u01/app/oraInventory
inst_group=oinstall
$ /u01/app/java/jdk1.8.0_301/java -jar /home/oracle/fmw_12.2.1.4.0_infrastructure.
  jar -silent -responseFile /u01/fmw_infrastructure.rsp -invPtrLoc /u01/app/
  oraInventory/oraInst.loc
```

Now apply a mandatory one-off patch for FMW Infrastructure 3065799. Refer to the README document for prerequisite, installation, and post-installation details. Refer to Example 22-21 for how to apply the patch.

Example 22-21   FMW Infrastructure One-Off Patch

```
$ unzip V988922-01.zip
$ export MW_HOME=/u01/app/middleware/OASMW
$ export ORACLE_HOME=$MW_HOME
$ export PATH=$ORACLE_HOME/OPatch:$PATH
$ cd 30657796/
$ opatch apply
$ opatch lspatches
```

Installing OAS

For setup, we will use Fusion Middleware Infrastructure 5.9.0 in which to run OAS. OAS is deployed as an application in the middleware software stack.

OAS 5.9 is certified for OL8, and OL8 does not include compat-libcap1-1.10 and compat-libstdc++-33-3.2.3-x86_64 packages, which are required by OAS. OAS 5.9 has no dependency on these packages, but the installation process checks for these packages as a part of a precheck process. To work around this issue, add the **-ignoreSysPrereqs** argument to the installation command, as shown in Example 22-22.

Example 22-22   OAS Installation

```
# yum install binutils gcc gcc-c++ glibc glibc-devel libaio libgcc libstdc++
  libstdc++-devel make sysstat -y
$ unzip V988574-01.zip
$ cat /u01/oas.rsp | grep -v "#"
[ENGINE]
Response File Version=1.0.0.0.0
[GENERIC]
DECLINE_AUTO_UPDATES=true
MOS_USERNAME=
MOS_PASSWORD=
AUTO_UPDATES_LOCATION=
SOFTWARE_UPDATES_PROXY_SERVER=
SOFTWARE_UPDATES_PROXY_PORT=
SOFTWARE_UPDATES_PROXY_USER=
SOFTWARE_UPDATES_PROXY_PASSWORD=
ORACLE_HOME=/u01/app/middleware/OASMW
FEDERATED_ORACLE_HOMES=
$ java -jar /home/oracle/Oracle_Analytics_Server_5.5.0.jar -silent -responseFile /
  u01/oas.rsp -invPtrLoc /u01/app/oraInventory/oraInst.loc -ignoreSysPrereqs
```

Next, you can upgrade the OPatch version to the latest available version. The minimum version required for OPatch is 13.9.4.2.5. For this sample scenario, download patch 28186730 with the latest version of OPatch available from the Oracle Support site. Unzip the software and upgrade the OPatch, as shown in Example 22-23.

Example 22-23   OPatch Upgrade

```
$ cd /u01/app/patches
$ unzip p28186730_1394211_Generic.zip
$ export MW_HOME=/u01/app/oracle/mw_home/OASMW
$ export ORACLE_HOME=$MW_HOME
$ export PATH=$ORACLE_HOME/OPatch: /u01/app/java/jdk1.8.0_361/bin:$PATH
$ java -jar /u01/app/patches/6880880/opatch_generic.jar -silent oracle_home=/u01/
  app/oracle/mw_home/OASMW
```

Next, apply the latest bundle patch to OAS. Here, you can use OAS Stack Patch Bundle (SPB) 5.9.0.0.230113. SPB makes patching the different components of OAS easy. Another option would be to patch these components separately. Here, you can apply SPB, as shown in Example 22-24.

Example 22-24   OAS Stack Patch Bundle

```
$ cd /u01/app/patches
$ unzip p34976621_59000_Linux-x86-64.zip
$ cd OAS_SPB_5.9.0.0.230113/tools/spbat/generic/SPBAT/
$ export MW_HOME=/u01/app/oracle/mw_home/OASMW
$ export ORACLE_HOME=$MW_HOME
$ export PATH=$ORACLE_HOME/OPatch: /u01/app/java/jdk1.8.0_361/bin:$PATH
$ ./spbat.sh -phase precheck -oracle_home /u01/app/oracle/mw_home/OASMW
$ ./spbat.sh -phase apply -oracle_home /u01/app/oracle/mw_home/OASMW
$ opatch lspatches
34976720;OAS STACK PATCH BUNDLE 5.9.0.0.230113 (Patch 34976621)
34920573;OAS BUNDLE PATCH 5.9.0.0.221222
34883826;WLS PATCH SET UPDATE 12.2.1.4.221210
34801809;RDA release 23.1-20230117 for OFM 12.2.1.4 SPB
34542329;One-off
34065178;One-off
33639718;33639718 - ADR FOR WEBLOGIC SERVER 12.2.1.4.0 JUL CPU 2022
33093748;One-off
32720458;JDBC 19.3.0.0 FOR CPUJAN2022 (WLS 12.2.1.4, WLS 14.1.1)
1221416;Coherence Cumulative Patch 12.2.1.4.16
31555397;One-off
31032676;One-off
30657796;One-off
```

Configuring OAS

Now you are ready to configure OAS. To do so, create a response file and run the **config.sh** command, as shown in Example 22-25. The configuration process will create database schemas, create system components with standards topology, and start the application server at the end.

Example 22-25   OAS Configuration

```
$ export MW_HOME=/u01/app/oracle/mw_home/OASMW
$ export ORACLE_HOME=$MW_HOME
$ grep -v "#" oas_config.rsp
[ENGINE]
Response File Version=1.0.0.0.0
[GENERIC]
PERFORM_BI_STARTUP=true
SERVICE_INSTANCE_LIMIT=2
LOGOUT_URL=
CONFIGURE_BIEE=false
CONFIGURE_BIP=true
INSTALL_EXALYTICS_IN_MEMORY_SOFTWARE=false
SERVICE_INSTANCE_MODE=SINGLE
DOMAIN_NAME=bi
DOMAINS_DIR=/u01/app/oracle/mw_home/OASMW/user_projects/domains
ADMIN_USER_NAME=weblogic
ADMIN_PASSWORD=Welcome_1
ADMIN_CONFIRM_PASSWORD=Welcome_1
DOMAIN_WORK=LOCAL
SCHEMA_TYPE=SCHEMA_TYPE_NEW
EXISTING_DATABASE_TYPE=ORACLE
CONNECT_STRING=emcc135omr.dj.local:1521:emccpdb3.dj.local
FAN_CONNECT_STRING=
DATABASE_TYPE=ORACLE
NEW_DB_ADMIN_USERNAME=sys
NEW_DB_PASSWORD=welcome1
NEW_DB_SCHEMA_PREFIX=oas
NEW_DB_SCHEMA_PASSWORD=Welcome_1
NEW_DB_CONFIRM_SCHEMA_PASSWORD=Welcome_1
EXISTING_DB_PREFIX=
EXISTING_DB_PASSWORD=
PORT_RANGE_START=9500
PORT_RANGE_END=9999
STATIC_PORTS_FILE=
APPLICATION_TYPE=APPLICATION_TYPE_EMPTY
BI_BUNDLE_FILE=
BI_BUNDLE_PASSWORD=
BI_APP_LITE_PASSWORD=
BI_DEFAULT_SERVICE_INSTANCE_KEY=ssi
$ cd /u01/app/oracle/mw_home/OASMW/bi/bin
$ ./config.sh -silent -responseFile /home/oracle/oas_config.rsp
```

You can use the following URLs to access the GUI console:

- **OAS:** http://emcc135oas.tam.local:9500/console
- **OAS Fusion Middleware Console for Oracle Enterprise Manager:**
  http://emcc135oas.tam.local:9500/em
- **OAS WebLogic Console:** http://emcc135oas.tam.local:9502/xmlpserver

You should be able to access these URLs now. If, for some reason, OAS is not online, you can start the services using the commands shown in Example 22-26. Make sure to restart these services after reboot as well.

Example 22-26   OAS Services Startup

```
$ cd /u01/app/oracle/mw_home/OASMW/user_projects/domains/bi/bitools/bin
$ ./start.sh
$ ./status.sh
$ ./stop.sh
```

Integrating OAS with Oracle Enterprise Manager

Up to this point, you have configured stand-alone OAS. Now you're going to perform some additional configuration on the OAS end to integrate it with Oracle Enterprise Manager.

You will be logging on to the OAS WebLogic console to configure the security infrastructure and data source. Then you will need to log on to the Fusion Middleware console to manage application roles.

Configuring Security Infrastructure

To begin, you will enable a local superuser to perform all the steps for OAS. You can disable this account at the end of the configuration.

Step 1. Log on to the OAS WebLogic console as the weblogic user, as shown in Figure 22-1.

Step 2. Click the **My Profile** icon at the top-right corner and then click **Administration**, as shown in Figure 22-2.

Step 3. From the main menu, select **Security Center > Security Configuration**, as shown in Figure 22-3.

Step 4. On the Security Configuration tab, select the **Enable Local Superuser** check box and provide a username and password, as shown in Figure 22-4. In the Authorization section, for Security Model, select **Oracle Fusion Middleware**, as shown in Figure 22-5. Then click **Apply**.

ORACLE· Analytics

Sign In

Please enter username and password

Username

weblogic

Password

••••••••••

Accessibility Mode ☐

Sign In

English (United States)   ▼

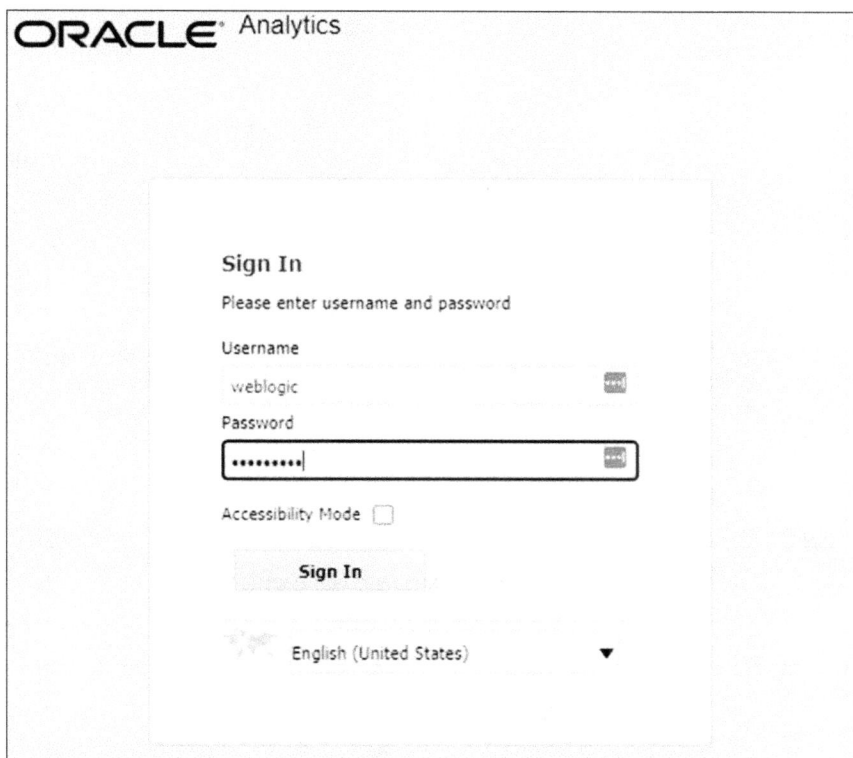

Figure 22-1   OAS WebLogic Console

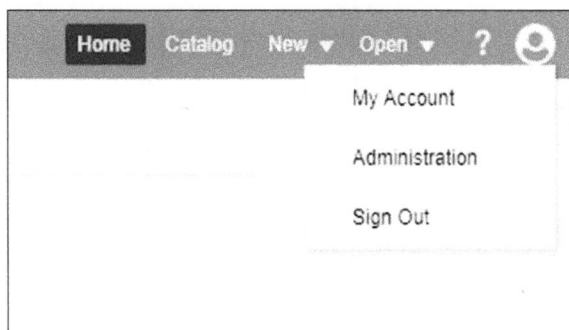

| Home | Catalog | New ▼ | Open ▼ | ? | ☺ |

My Account

Administration

Sign Out

Figure 22-2   My Profile Menu

Data Sources

JDBC Connection
JNDI Connection
File
LDAP Connection
OLAP Connection
Web Service Connection
HTTP Connection
Content Server

Security Center

Security Configuration
Roles and Permissions
Digital Signature

Delivery

System Mai

Server Confi
Scheduler C
Scheduler D
Report Viewe
Manage Cac
Manage Job

Runtime Co

Properties
Font Mappin
Currency Fo

Integration

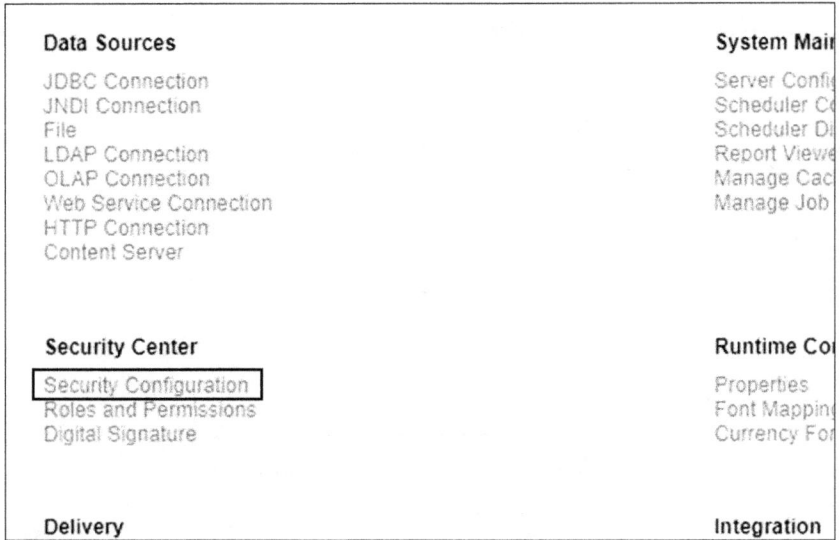

Figure 22-3 Administration Page

Security Configuration   Roles and Permissions   Digital Signature

TIP Any changes will only take effect after the application is restarted.

Apply   Cancel

Local Superuser

Local superuser can log in to the system independent from the selected security model.
☑ Enable Local Superuser

Superuser name   SuperUser
Password   ••••••••

Guest Access

Figure 23-4 Local Superuser

Attribute used for user matching with authorization system

(Example: orclguid)

Authorization

Security Model   Oracle Fusion Middleware ▼

Fusion Apps Security   ☐

Figure 22-5 Authorization

Configuring the Required OAS Datasource

An OAS datasource is necessary to run either out-of-the-box reports or any other customized reports. You can run out-of-the-box reports for the use case here. You can create multiple data sources per your requirements.

Step 1. Log on to the OMS server to change the MGMT_VIEW user password, as shown in Example 22-27.

Example 22-27   MGMT_VIEW User Password Reset

```
$ /u01/app/oracle/mw_home/bin/emctl status oms
$ /u01/app/oracle/mw_home/bin/emctl config oms -change_view_user_pwd
$ /u01/app/oracle/mw_home/bin/emctl stop oms -all
$ /u01/app/oracle/mw_home/bin/emctl start oms
```

Step 2. Log on to the OAS WebLogic console and go to the Administration page, as shown previously in Figure 22-2. Then, on the Administration page, click **Data Sources > JDBC Connection,** as shown in Figure 22-6.

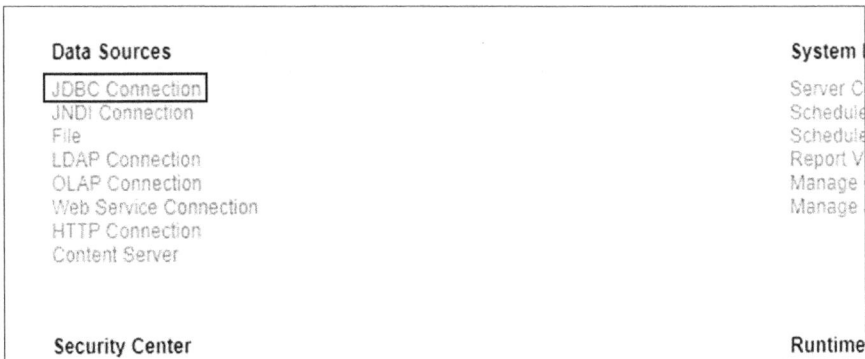

Figure 22-6   Administration Page

Step 3. Click **Add Data Source**, as shown in Figure 22-7.

Figure 22-7   JDBC Data Source

Step 4. Provide connection information for the Oracle Enterprise Manager repository database and click **Test Connection**, as shown in Figure 22-8.

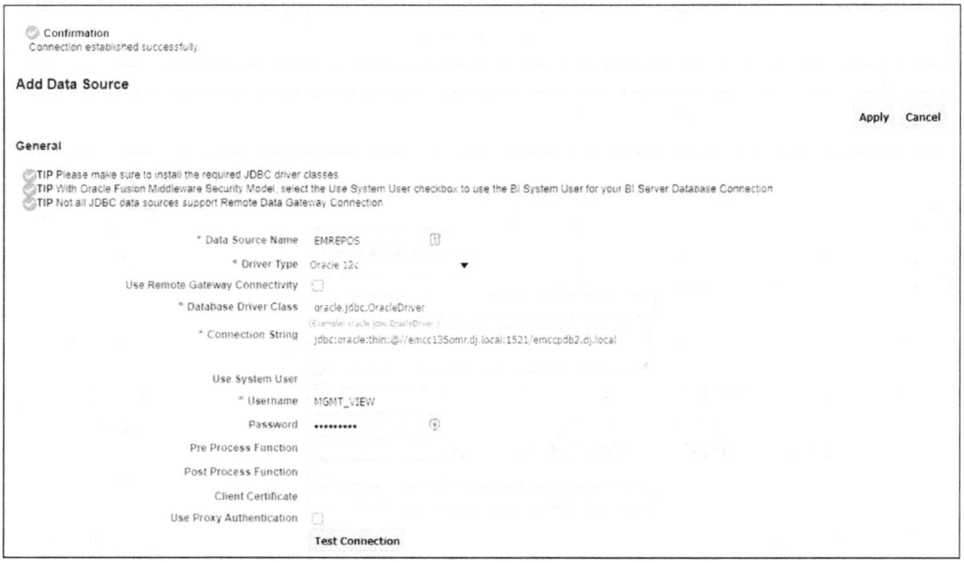

Figure 22-8   Add Data Source

Step 5. On the same page under the Security section, move all **Available Roles** to **Allowed Roles**, as shown in Figure 22-9, and click **Apply**.

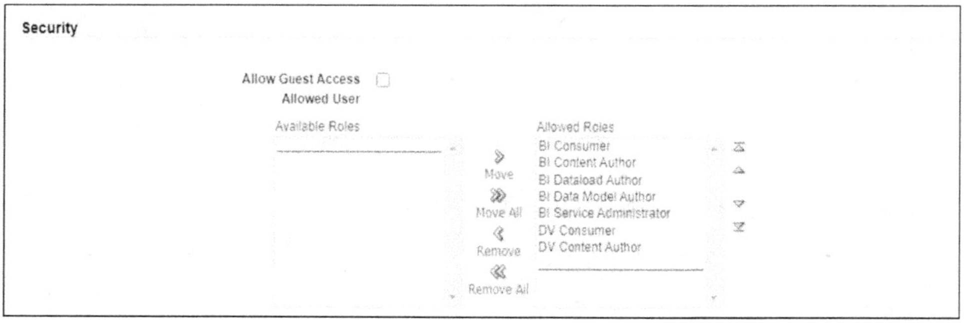

Figure 22-9   Security Roles

Setting OAS Support for Oracle Enterprise Manager-Provided Reports

Oracle Enterprise Manager includes many built-in reports, originally created for Oracle's Business Intelligence Publisher (BIP) system. With the move to OAS, you still have access to the Oracle Enterprise Manager BIP (also shortened to Enterprise Manager BIP [EMBIP]). To use these you must first create necessary EMBIP* roles and map them with the base OAS roles. These roles will then need to be granted to other administrators and/or users so that they can execute Oracle-provided reports.

Step 1. Log on to the OAS Fusion Middleware Control for Oracle Enterprise Manager with the weblogic user, as shown in Figure 22-10.

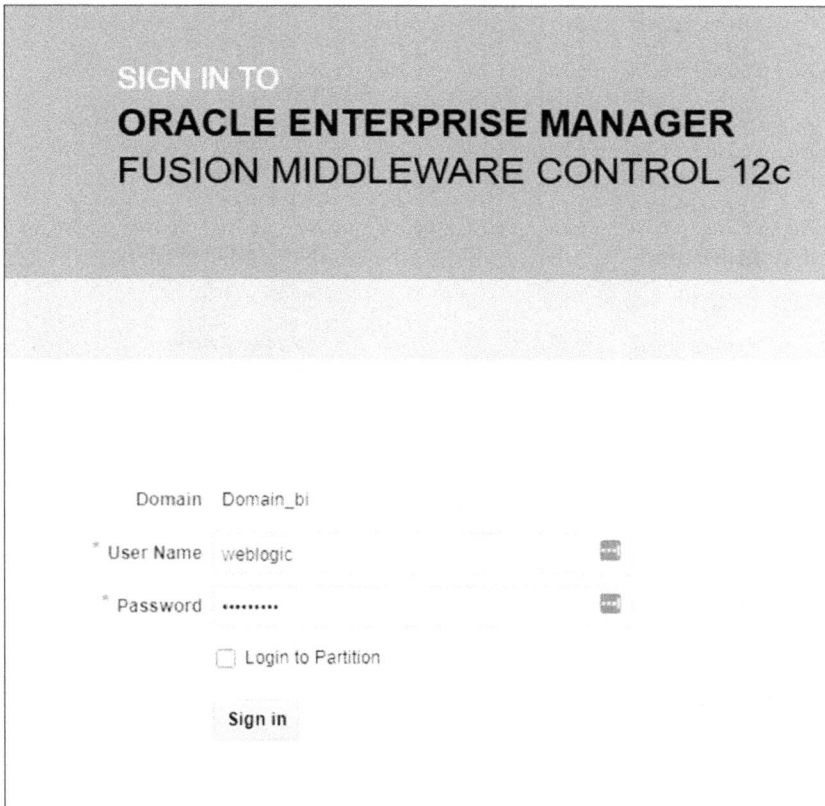

SIGN IN TO
ORACLE ENTERPRISE MANAGER
FUSION MIDDLEWARE CONTROL 12c

Domain	Domain_bi
* User Name	weblogic
* Password	··········

☐ Login to Partition

Sign in

Figure 22-10   OAS Fusion Middleware Control Login

Step 2. Click **WebLogic Domain > Security > Application Roles**, as shown in Figure 22-11.

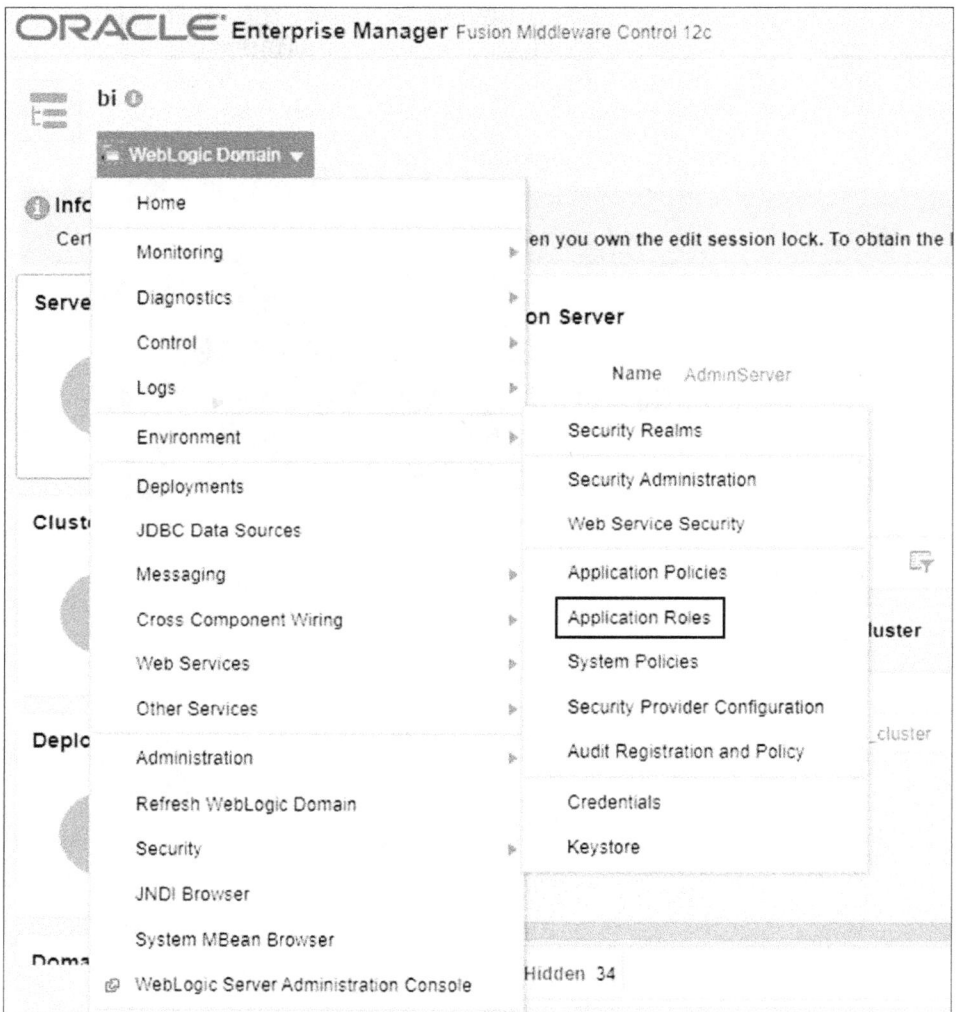

Figure 22-11   WebLogic Domain Menu

Step 3. On the following page, for Application Stripe, select **obi**, and search for the roles. All roles will be displayed, as shown in Figure 22–12. For this example, select the **BIServiceAdministrator** role and click **Create Like**.

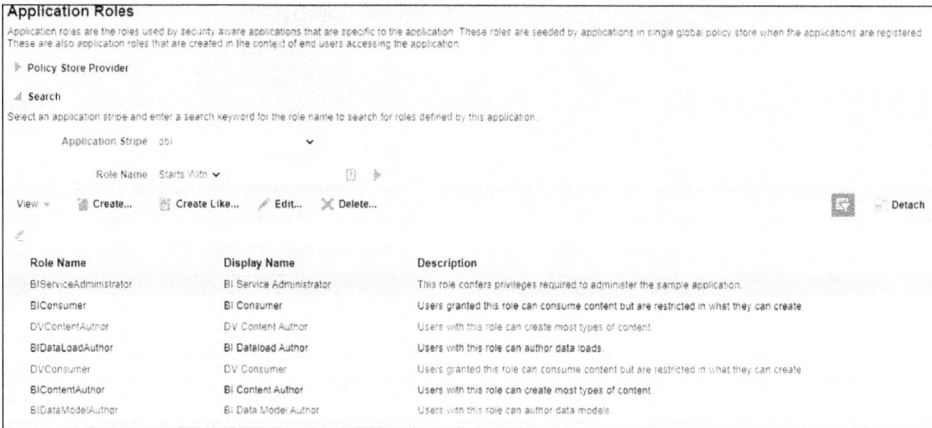

Figure 22-12   Application Roles

Step 4. On the next page, create the EMBIPADMINISTRATOR role and click
OK, as shown in Figure 22-13.

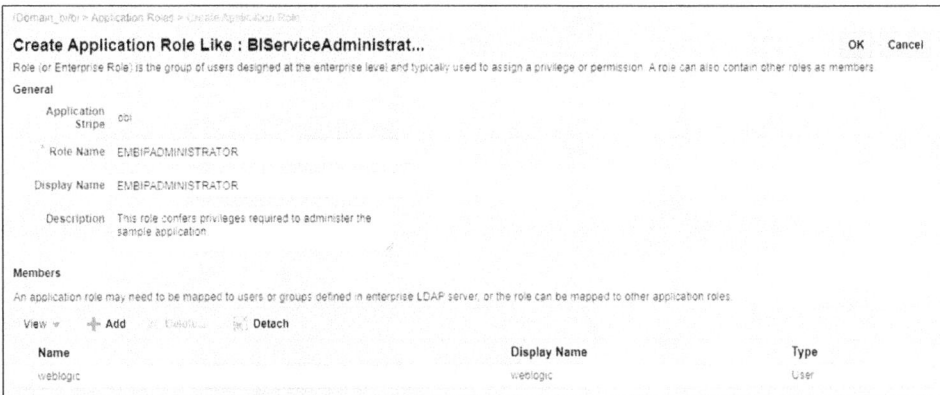

Figure 22-13   Create Application Role

Step 5. Follow the same process to create application roles for EMBIPAUTHOR,
EMBIPSCHEDULER, and EMBIPVIEWER. After these roles are created,
you should see the outcome, as shown in Figure 22-14.

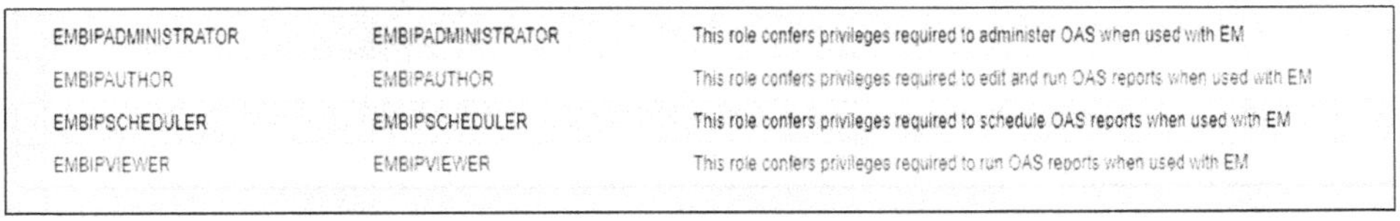

EMBIPADMINISTRATOR	EMBIPADMINISTRATOR	This role confers privileges required to administer OAS when used with EM
EMBIPAUTHOR	EMBIPAUTHOR	This role confers privileges required to edit and run OAS reports when used with EM
EMBIPSCHEDULER	EMBIPSCHEDULER	This role confers privileges required to schedule OAS reports when used with EM
EMBIPVIEWER	EMBIPVIEWER	This role confers privileges required to run OAS reports when used with EM

Figure 22-14   Application Roles

Step 6. Create a mapping of these EMBIP★ roles to the base OAS roles. First, add the EMBIPADMINISTRATOR role as a member of the BIServiceAdministrator role. Select the **BIServiceAdministrator** role and click **Edit**. Then, add the EMBIPADMINISTRATOR role as a member and click **OK**, as shown in Figure 22-15.

/Domain_bi/bi > Application Roles > Edit Application Role

Edit Application Role : BIServiceAdministrat...   OK   Cancel

Role (or Enterprise Role) is the group of users designed at the enterprise level and typically used to assign a privilege or permission. A role can also contain other roles as members

General

Application Stripe	obi
Role Name	BIServiceAdministrator
Display Name	BI Service Administrator
Description	This role confers privileges required to administer the sample application

Members

An application role may need to be mapped to users or groups defined in enterprise LDAP server, or the role can be mapped to other application roles.

View ▾   ➕ Add   ✖ Delete   🔲 Detach

Name	Display Name	Type
weblogic	weblogic	User
EMBIPADMINISTRATOR	EMBIPADMINISTRATOR	Application Role

Figure 22-15   Edit Application Role

Step 7. Add EMBIPVIEWER as a member of the BIConsumer role and EMBIPAUTHOR as a member of the BIContentAuthor role. Next, create a role hierarchy for the OAS roles and EM roles by adding EMBIPADMINISTRATOR as a member of the EMBIPAUTHOR and EMBIPSCHEDULER roles and EMBIPAUTHOR as a member of the EMBIPVIEWER role.

At this point, you can upload Oracle Enterprise Manager out-of-the-box reports and/or create new reports in OAS.

Let's examine a sample out-of-the-box report. These reports for the base framework are in the OMS middleware home and named Enterprise Manager Cloud Control.xdrz. Run the command shown in Example 22-28 to identify these reports. Copy all these reports to the OAS server or to your desktop, where you can upload them to OAS.

Example 22-28   Find Out-of-the-Box Reports

```
[oracle@emcc135oms ~]$ cd /u01/app/oracle/mw_home/
[oracle@emcc135oms mw_home]$ find . -name 'Enterprise Manager Cloud Control.xdrz'
./sysman/jlib/Enterprise Manager Cloud Control.xdrz
./plugins/oracle.sysman.cfw.oms.plugin_13.5.1.0.0/metadata/bipublisherreport/
  emreports/Enterprise Manager Cloud Control.xdrz
./plugins/oracle.sysman.db.oms.plugin_13.5.1.0.0/metadata/bipublisherreport/
  emreports/Enterprise Manager Cloud Control.xdrz
```

```
./plugins/oracle.sysman.xa.oms.plugin_13.5.1.0.0/metadata/bipublisherreport/
  emreports/Enterprise Manager Cloud Control.xdrz
./plugins/oracle.sysman.emas.oms.plugin_13.5.1.0.0/metadata/bipublisherreport/
  emreports/Enterprise Manager Cloud Control.xdrz
./plugins/oracle.sysman.emct.oms.plugin_13.5.1.0.0/metadata/bipublisherreport/
  emreports/Enterprise Manager Cloud Control.xdrz
```

All of these reports can be uploaded to OAS. Let's go over the upload process for one of these files: /.sysmane/jlib/Enterprise Manager Cloud Control.xdrz.

Step 1. Log into the OAS console with the sysman user, as shown earlier in Figure 22-1.

Step 2. Go to the home page and click **Browse/Manage > Catalog Folders**, as shown in Figure 22-16.

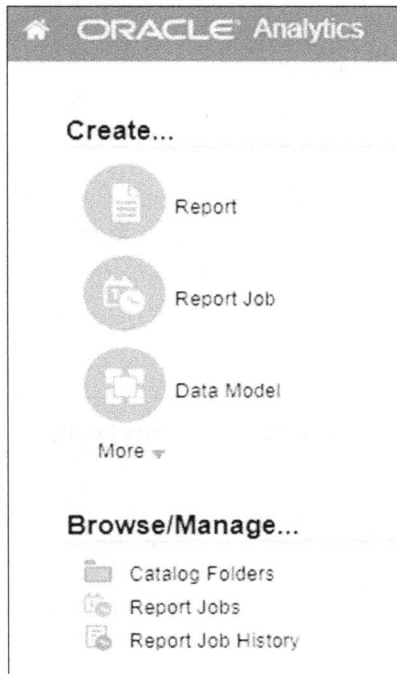

Figure 22-16   OAS Home Page

Step 3. Upload all the reports copied from the OMS server under Shared Folders. To do so, select **Shared Folders** and click **Upload**, as shown in Figure 22-17.

Step 4. Upload all Enterprise Manager Cloud Control.xdrz files one by one. Select **Overwrite Existing File** for every upload, as shown in Figure 22-18.

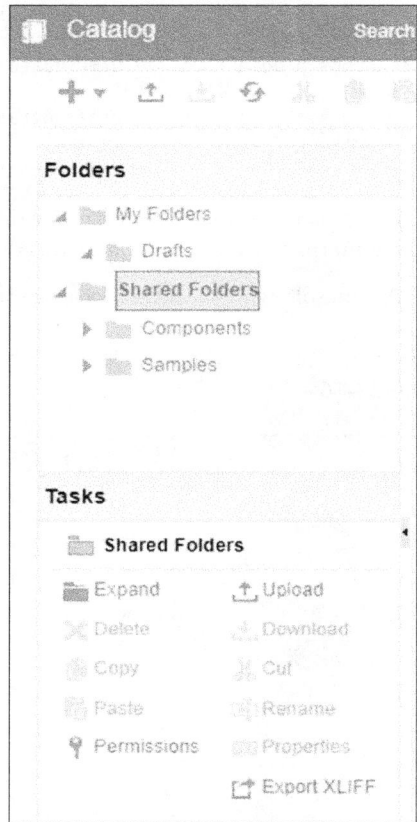

Figure 22-17   Reports Catalog

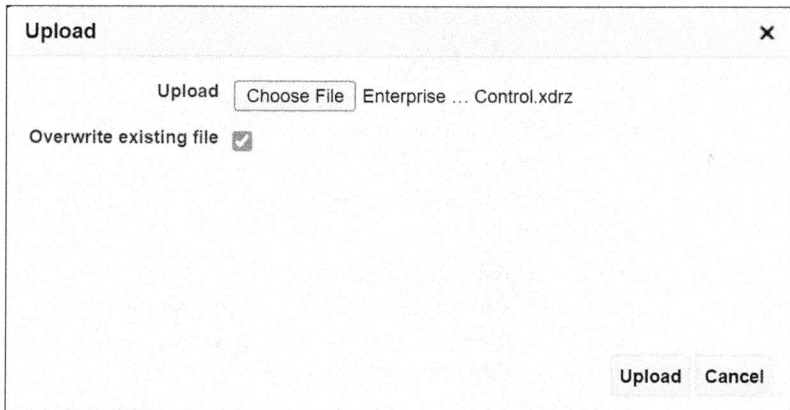

Figure 22-18   Upload Reports

After all the reports are uploaded, you will see the Enterprise Manager Cloud Control directory and all out-of-the-box reports under it, as shown in Figure 22-19.

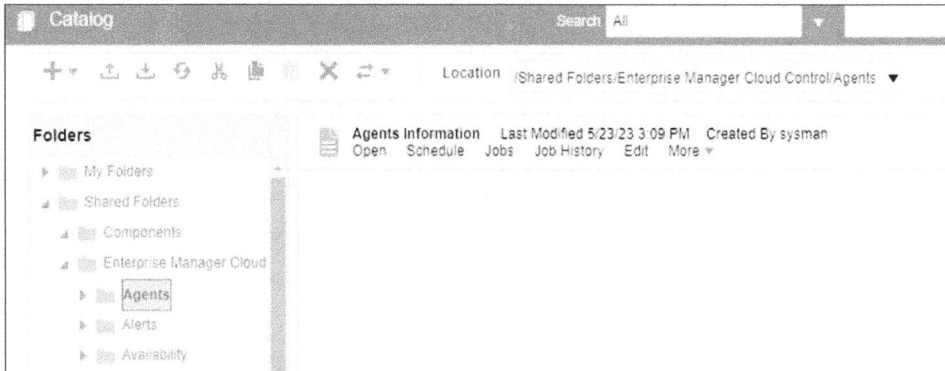

Figure 22-19   Report Navigation

We ran Agents Information reports for the example here. This report will display all agents with some basic system-level information such as OS and CPU usage, as shown in Figure 22-20. You can pick any other reports from the list and run them.

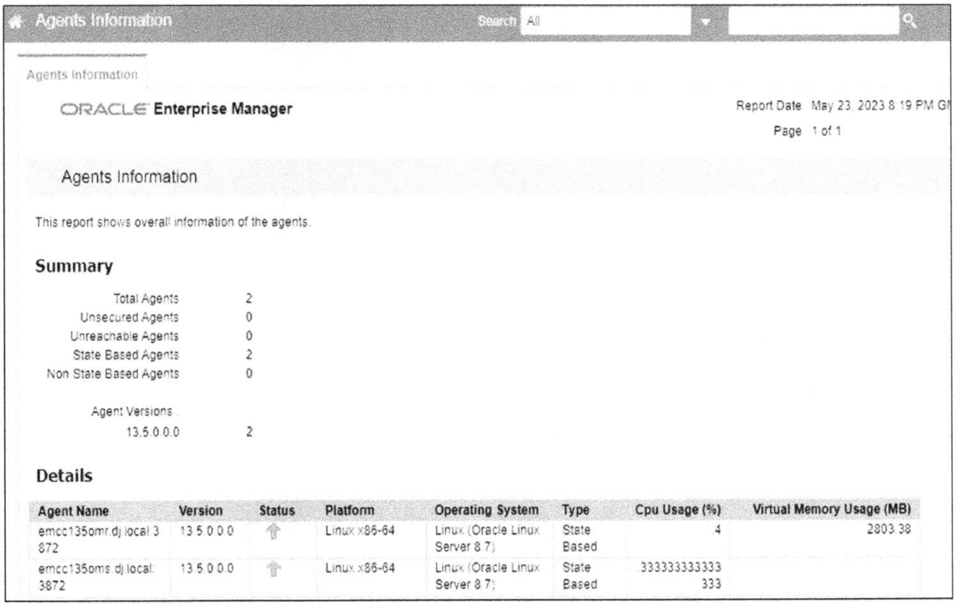

Figure 22-20   Agent Information Report

This simple example illustrated how to run out-of-the-box reports from OAS. You can create custom reports—either simple or complex ones—based on your needs.

Summary

In this chapter, we described the complete end-to-end process of how to set up Oracle Enterprise Manager Cloud Control 13.5 and Oracle Analytics Server (OAS). Most of these processes require a one-time setup, but patching is a recurring process. You should patch your systems with the latest bundle patches at your earliest convenience. In the next chapter, we will go over most common usage and best practices of using Oracle Enterprise Manager Cloud Control.

Using Oracle Enterprise Manager Cloud Control

In this chapter, we will explore how to use Oracle Enterprise Manager Cloud Control to create administrators and monitor OCI resources. Before we dive in, let's review scenarios where you want to use Oracle Enterprise Manager to monitor OCI resources and not just on-premises resources.

Oracle Enterprise Manager can be deployed on-premises and in the cloud. Oracle Enterprise Manager is technically a free management tool for you to use as long as you have the appropriate license for the target managed by Oracle Enterprise Manager—that is, Database, E-Business Suite, WebLogic, and so on. OCI also provides the Observability and Monitoring (O&M) Platform, which consists of various tools such as Application Performance Monitoring, Logging, and Notifications. O&M is a great tool with some cost associated with it, but Oracle Enterprise Manager supports a wider range of technologies with more functionalities, such as e-business patching.

You will need to patch Oracle Enterprise Manager on a regular basis. Oracle releases bug fixes and enhancements regularly. Ideally, you should keep your production's Oracle Enterprise Manager up-to-date with the latest available patches. Oracle moved from distributing major releases—such as 13.2, 13.3, 13.4—every few years to a model more like CI/CD by distributing Release Updates (RUs) more often with new features and bug fixes. At the time of writing, the latest available Release Update is Oracle Enterprise Manager 13.5 RU16. This RU includes OMS patches, OMS side plug-ins, Agent patches, and/or Agent side patches.

To better understand how this Release Update works, let's review some of the last few RUs and features added to it:

- Oracle Enterprise 13.5 Release Update 16
  - User-defined compression policies can be exported and imported.
  - Simple Network Management Protocol (SNMP) trap notifications are supported with third-party tools.
  - New events can be added to Automatic Database Diagnostic Monitor (ADDM) Spotlight to correlate events for better analysis.
  - Widgets support input parameters to custom SQL queries.

- Predefined queries used for out-of-the-box widgets can be modified.
- Heat Map and Automatic Data Optimization (ADO) features are available for pluggable database (PDB) targets.
- A new Fleet Maintenance Hub was introduced to manage database assets to subscribe to gold images, view vulnerabilities, patch databases, and so on. Fleet Maintenance is focused on on-premises management, an example of which are golden images, which are preconfigured images to rapidly install or patch the Oracle database.
- The new metric category Data Guard Fast-Start Failover Observers is available. It collects and monitors the status of fast-start failover observers.
- And more…

- Oracle Enterprise 13.5 Release Update 15
  - Database targets support the High Availability Role property, that is, primary and standby.
  - Oracle Enterprise Manager generic webhooks allow you to send events and incidents to third-party applications such as Slack.
  - An Agent-preferred connection string from the database can be a service name.
  - During the Oracle Enterprise Manager installation process, a non-SYS user can be provided to perform database-related installations or configurations.
  - The Performance Hub now includes a Workload tab to monitor the database workload.
  - The Automatic Database Diagnostic Monitor (ADDM) Spotlight interface has new enhancements. It uses ADDM data to report performance impacts, its recommendations, database parameters, and changes to them during that period.
  - A new Runbooks feature has been added (that is, Oracle-provided runbooks). There is a new OS command step to run commands or scripts.
  - The Oracle Enterprise Manager app Grafana 4.0.0 introduces new dashboards: Exadata Capacity Planning Report and Exadata Cloud Capacity Planning Report.
  - And more…

- Oracle Enterprise 13.5 Release Update 14
  - Oracle Database targets can be discovered and monitored by non-DBSNMP users now.
  - A custom dashboard can be created with Oracle-defined widgets.
  - Privileged Access Management (PAM) solutions can be integrated with Oracle Enterprise Manager to perform management tasks.
  - Fleet patching and provisioning are now integrated with Oracle Enterprise Manager.
  - The EMCLI verb **resync_target** was added.
  - The Exadata Database Service on Dedicated Infrastructure targets discovery process was added as a guided discovery process.
  - And more…

Currently, most organizations run hybrid and multicloud solutions for their environments. They choose all cloud providers according to their expertise. For example, it is common for organizations to choose Azure for their Active Directory and .Net application requirements, and OCI for their database requirements. Oracle and Microsoft have teamed up to integrate their data centers to provide the best performance possible when cloud resources communicate between OCI and Azure. Customers can also choose to run on-premises Oracle Enterprise Manager and cloud Oracle Enterprise Manager separately. In this case, you can use Oracle Enterprise Manager Federation to consolidate the view of all Oracle Enterprise Manager sites in one place.

As we stated previously, Oracle Enterprise Manager is a comprehensive management tool for databases. It provides capabilities for provisioning, patching, upgrading, monitoring, and alerting.

OCI and Oracle Enterprise Manager provide unique functionalities in certain areas. OCI provides logging analytics for application and infrastructure log data, operation insights for capacity planning of databases and hosts, and more. Oracle Enterprise Manager provides various database and host metrics to monitor and report notifications and more. An Audit Analysis is shown in Figure 23-1.

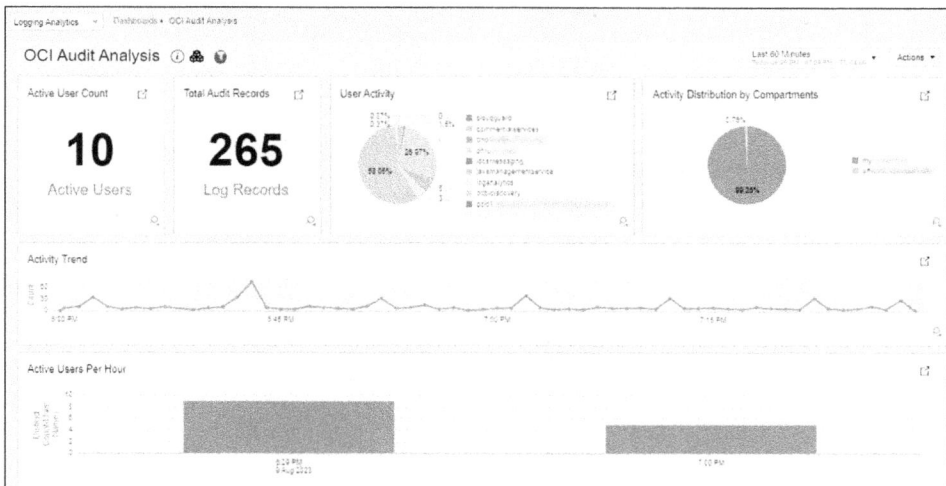

Figure 23-1   OCI Logging Analytics

An OCI Audit Analysis shows active user count, total audit records, user activity by user/OCI services, and activity distribution by compartments at the top of the page. You will find different statistics presented in graph form, including activity trends, active users per hour, and user and activity correlation, all of which is useful information.

Oracle Enterprise Manager provides more metrics capabilities compared to OCI for targets. To see how, let's look at a host target. OCI only provides major metrics such as CPU, memory, disk, and network performance. Oracle Enterprise Manager provides more details on these resources, as you can see in the list shown in Figure 23-2.

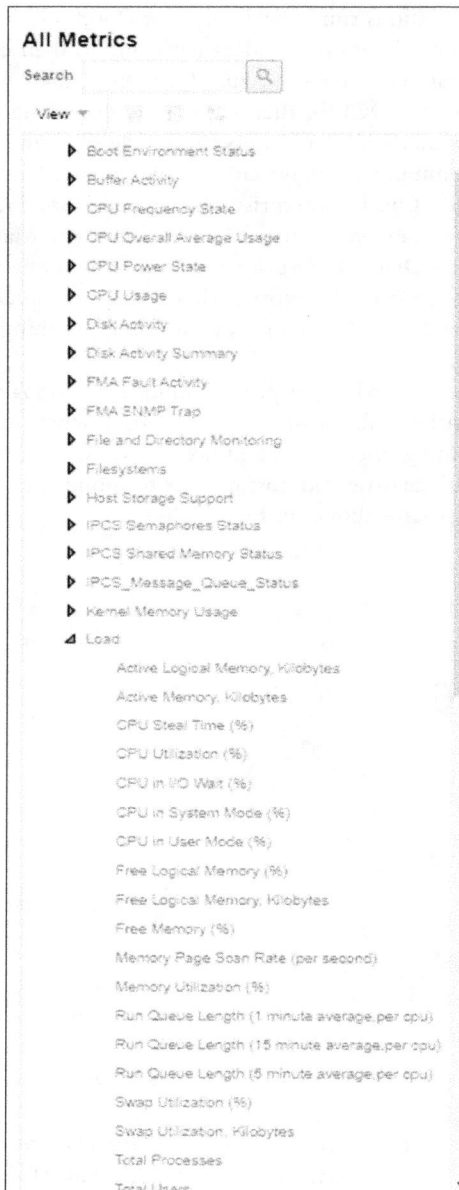

Figure 23-2   Oracle Enterprise Manager Host Metrics

These metrics cover many aspects of the target, which can be useful for analysis. These metrics also make it easier to troubleshoot any performance or other issues. In OCI, you get limited metrics like CPU and memory utilization, whereas Oracle Enterprise Manager provides more than just utilization. As you can see in Figure 23-2, Oracle Enterprise Manager gives you CPU wait time, memory scan rate, swap utilization, and more.

This leads us into the integration of Oracle Enterprise Manager with OCI. You can export data from Oracle Enterprise Manager and import it into OCI to use it with operation insights and logging analytics. We will cover the process of implementing this later in the chapter.

Setting Up Administrators and Users

By default, SYSMAN is the super user for Oracle Enterprise Manager. You can create other administrators and users by assigning appropriate roles to them. It is a good practice to create individual users for all Oracle Enterprise Manager administrators regardless of whether you have one or more admins. You can create users with read-only privileges and admins with limited access to modify database targets only, for example.

Let's go over the process to create an Oracle Enterprise Manager administrator:

Step 1. Log on to the Oracle Enterprise Manager console and click the main menu, then select **Setup > Security > Administrators**, as shown in Figure 23-3.

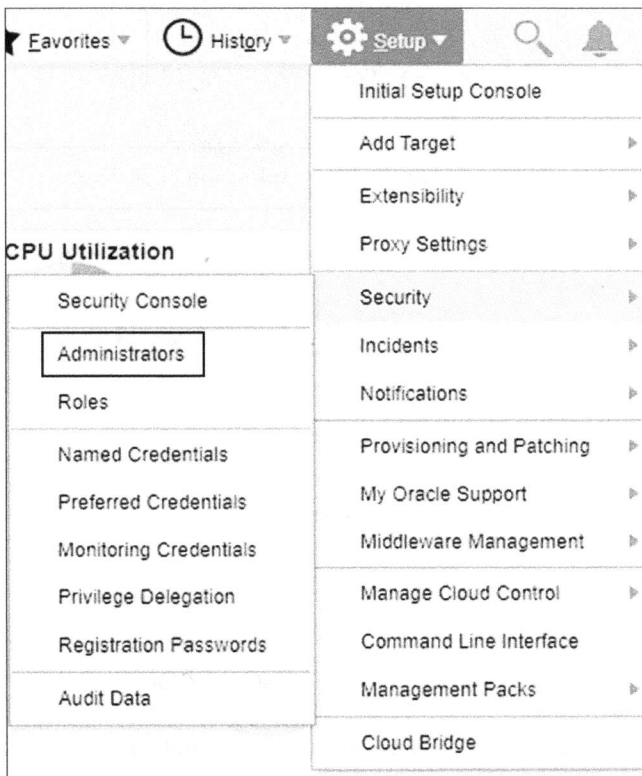

Figure 23-3   Security Menu

Step 2. Enter the username, password, email address, and other optional information, as shown in Figure 23-4. Optional information includes phone number; department, location, and line of business to identify the user from an organization perspective; cost center; description; and if the user is a super administrator (be very careful with this one!).

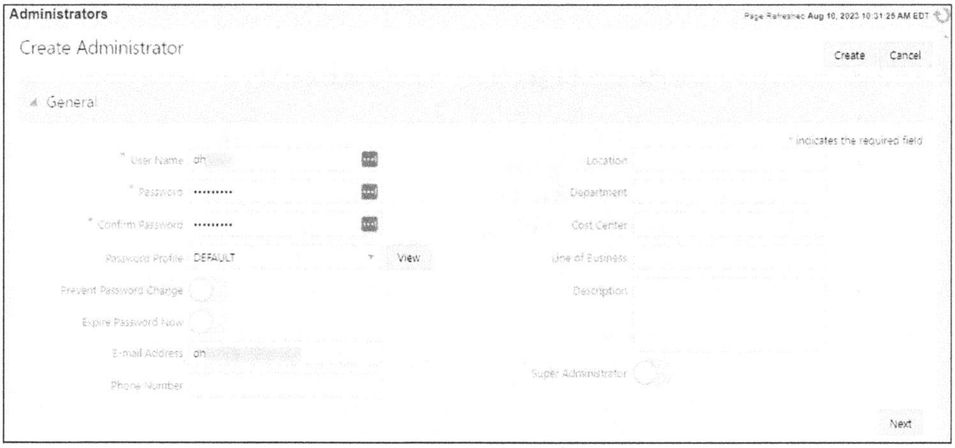

Figure 23-4   Create Administrator Page

Step 3. Assign desired roles to this administrator. For this use case, select the administrator role, a couple of other roles, and click **Next**, as shown in Figure 23-5.

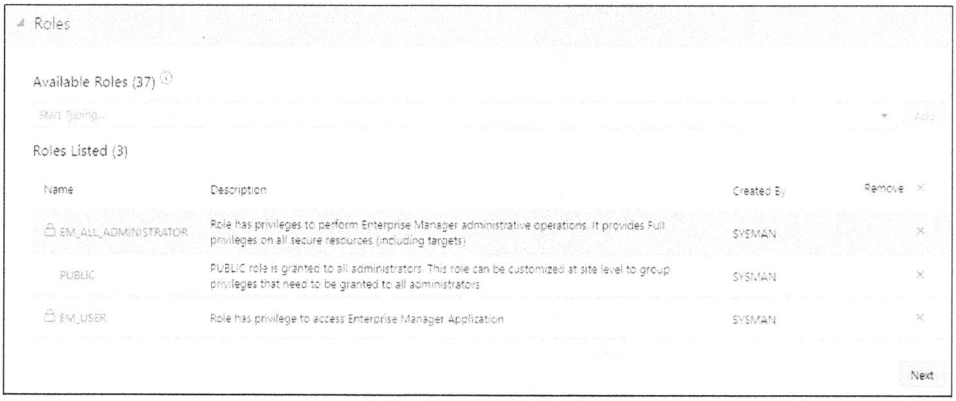

Figure 23-5   Role Assignment Page

Step 4. For target privileges, click **Select Instances** and select all privileges, as shown in Figure 23-6. Here, you can select some or all targets that the administrator can manage.

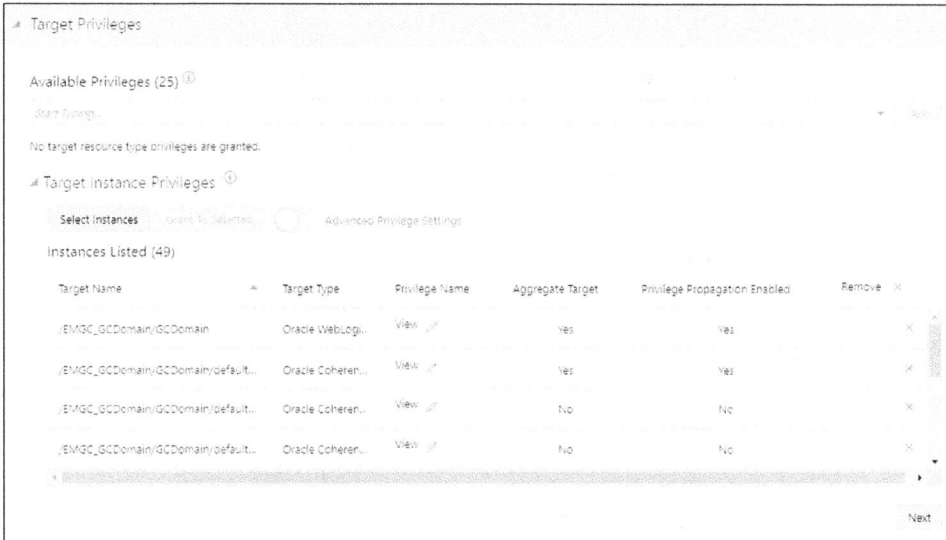

Figure 23-6 Target Privileges

Step 5. Add other resource privileges as needed and click **Create**, as shown in Figure 23-7.

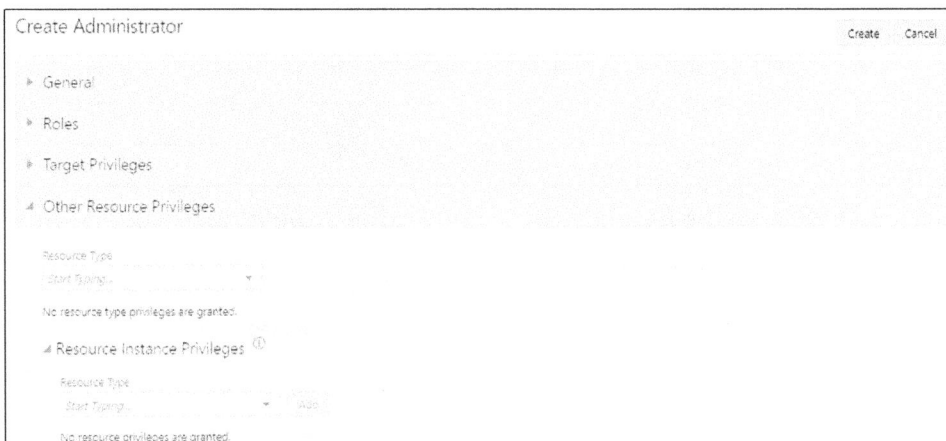

Figure 23-7 Other Privileges Page

Be very careful while creating the super administrator, administrator, or user. You do not want to give a regular user the ability to stop or drop the database.

Monitoring OCI Environments

Oracle Enterprise Manager can monitor both on-premises and OCI environments, giving you a single pane of glass to view your complete environment. In the following sections, we will go over a couple of scenarios illustrating how to discover the OCI compute instance and OCI Autonomous Database.

Monitoring OCI Compute Instance

First, let's discover an OCI compute instance target. This process is similar to discovering any host target. The major difference is network and/or firewall modifications for the Oracle Enterprise Manager server and compute instance to communicate with each other.

Step 1. Log on to the Oracle Enterprise Manager console. Click **Setup > Add Target > Add Targets Manually,** as shown in Figure 23-8.

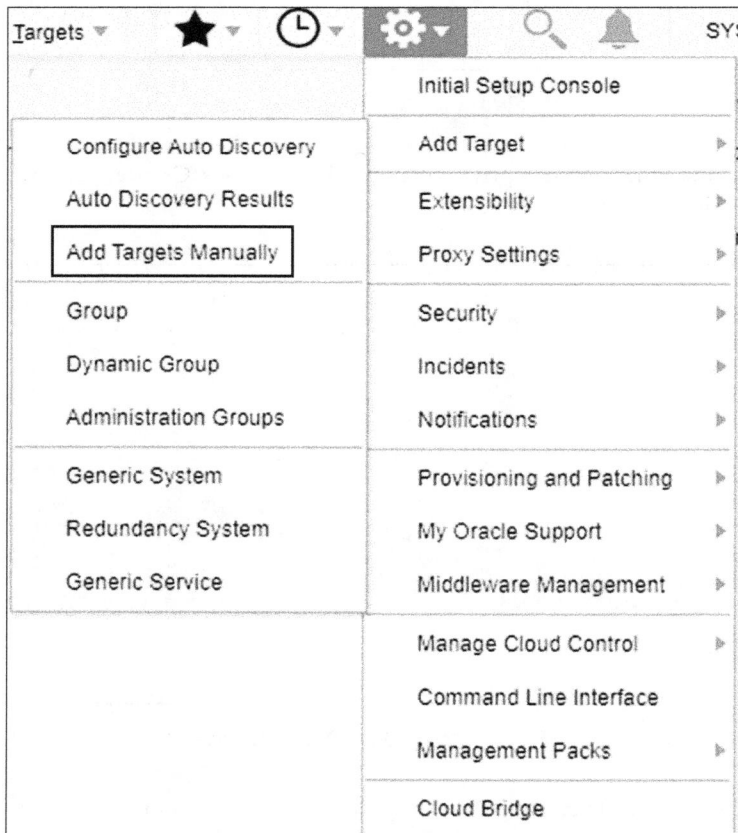

Figure 23-8   Setup Menu

Step 2. Click **Install Agent on Host,** as shown in Figure 23-9.

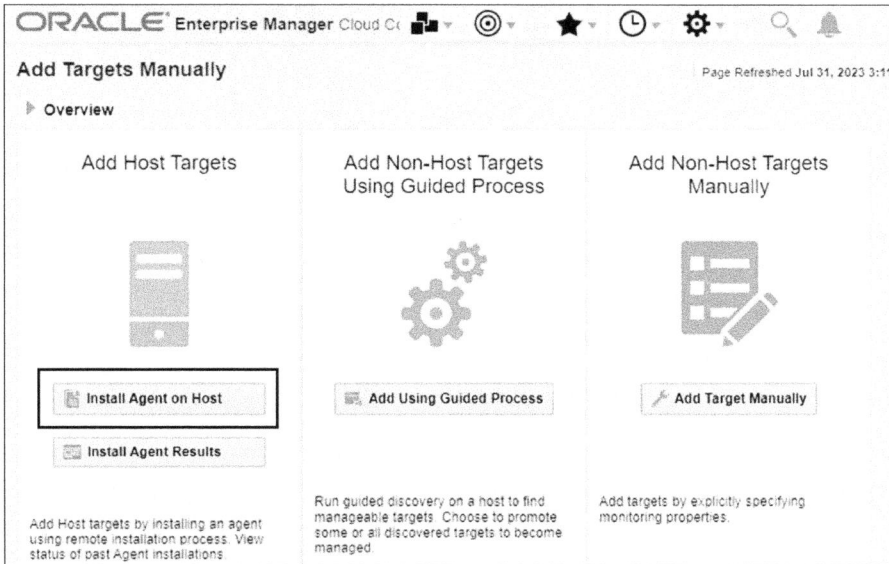

Figure 23-9   Add Targets Options

Step 3. Enter the host name, select an appropriate platform, and click **Next,** as shown in Figure 23-10. Make sure that the Oracle Enterprise Manager server can resolve the compute instance hostname and has a route to reach to the instance. You will need to update route tables, security rules, and other configurations at the VNC level in OCI. Oracle Enterprise Manager must have network access to the targets being monitored.

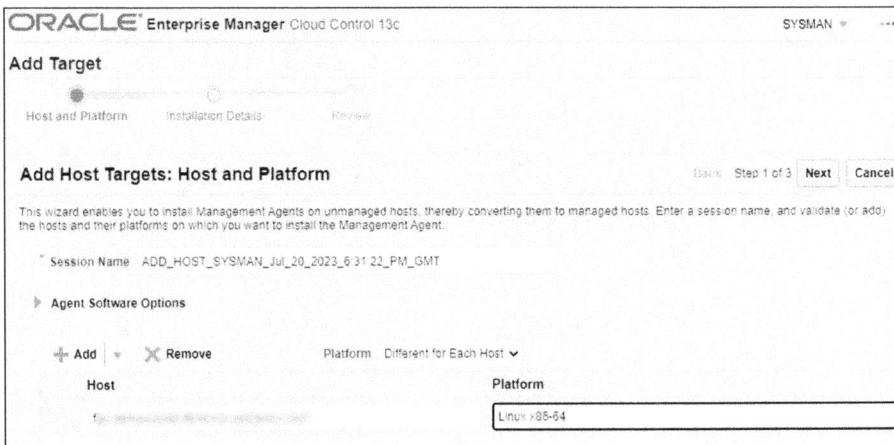

Figure 23-10   Host and Platform

Step 4. Provide an installation base directory, named credential, port, and other settings and click **Next**, as shown in Figure 23-11. For a named credential, use the opc user by providing the appropriate private key.

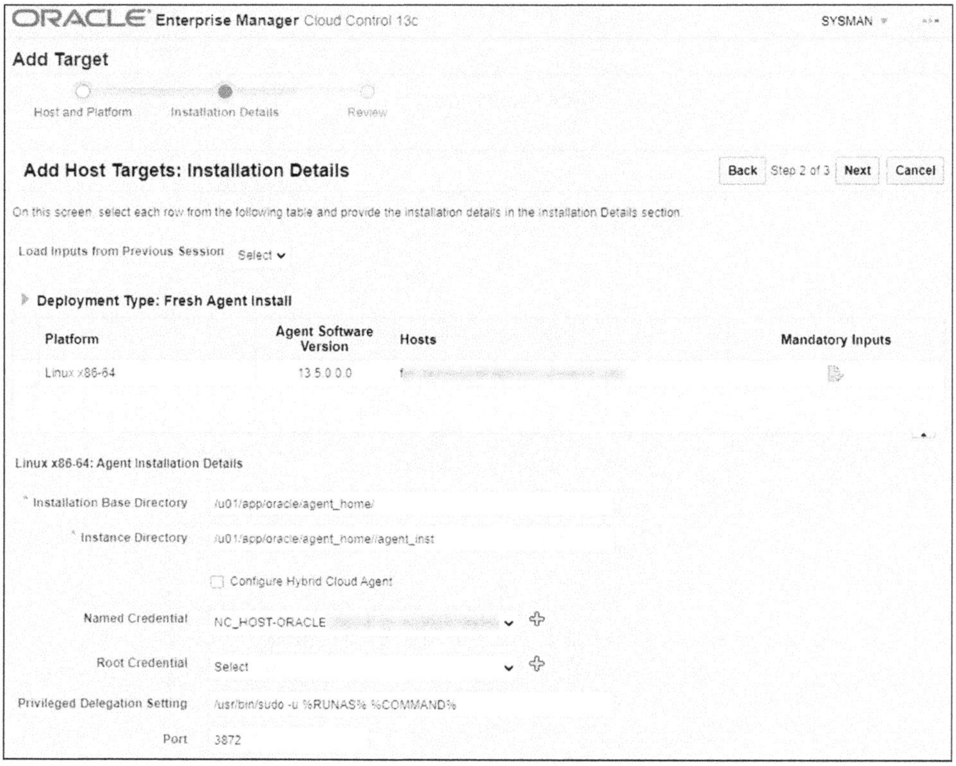

Figure 23-11   Installation Details

Step 5. Review all the information entered so far and click **Deploy Agent**, as shown in Figure 23-12.

It will take a few minutes to deploy the agent. Once the process has completed successfully, you will get a summary page with more details, as shown in Figure 23-13.

Step 6. Check the monitoring status of the newly added host target, as shown in Figure 23-14.

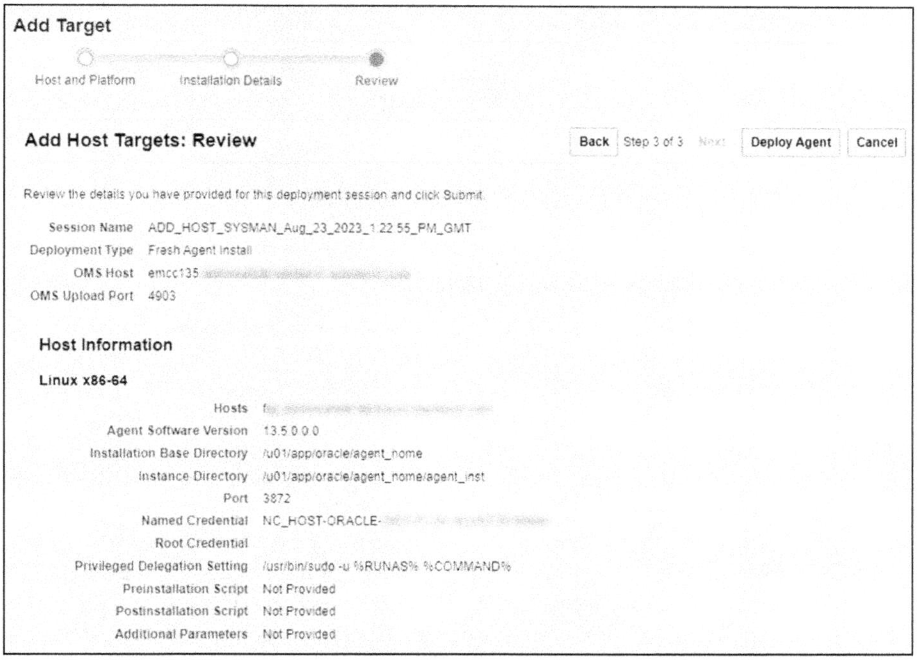

Add Target

Host and Platform   Installation Details   Review

Add Host Targets: Review   Back Step 3 of 3 Next Deploy Agent Cancel

Review the details you have provided for this deployment session and click Submit.

Session Name   ADD_HOST_SYSMAN_Aug_23_2023_1.22.55_PM_GMT
Deployment Type Fresh Agent Install
OMS Host   emcc135
OMS Upload Port 4903

Host Information

Linux x86-64

Hosts   f
Agent Software Version   13.5.0.0.0
Installation Base Directory   /u01/app/oracle/agent_home
Instance Directory   /u01/app/oracle/agent_home/agent_inst
Port   3872
Named Credential   NC_HOST-ORACLE-
Root Credential
Privileged Delegation Setting   /usr/bin/sudo -u %RUNAS% %COMMAND%
Preinstallation Script   Not Provided
Postinstallation Script   Not Provided
Additional Parameters   Not Provided

Figure 23-12 Deploy Agent

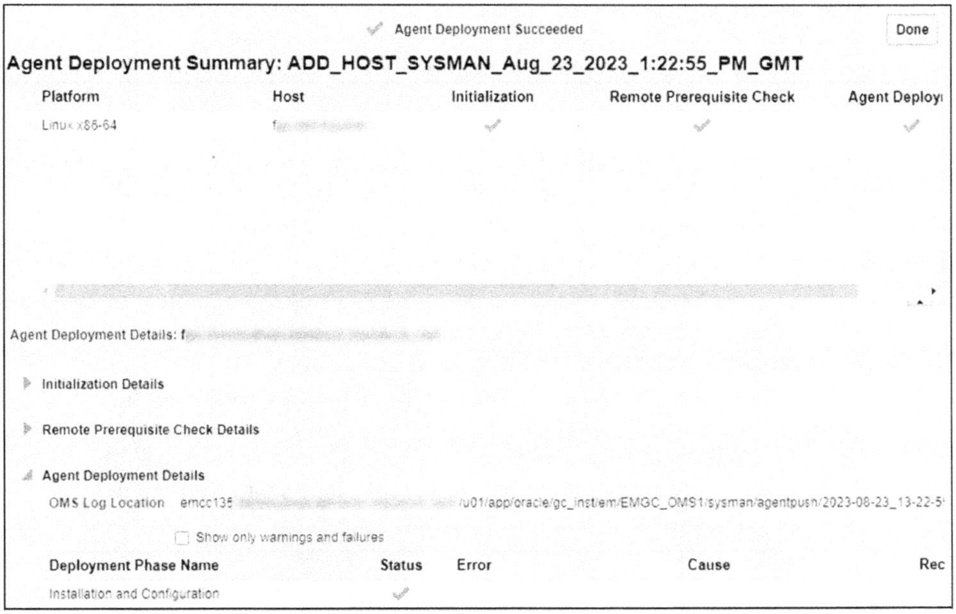

Agent Deployment Succeeded   Done

Agent Deployment Summary: ADD_HOST_SYSMAN_Aug_23_2023_1:22:55_PM_GMT

Platform	Host	Initialization	Remote Prerequisite Check	Agent Deploy
Linux x86-64	f	✓	✓	✓

Agent Deployment Details: f

▷ Initialization Details

▷ Remote Prerequisite Check Details

◢ Agent Deployment Details

OMS Log Location   emcc135 /u01/app/oracle/gc_inst/em/EMGC_OMS1/sysman/agentpush/2023-08-23_13-22-5

☐ Show only warnings and failures

Deployment Phase Name	Status	Error	Cause	Rec
Installation and Configuration	✓			

Figure 23-13 Agent Deployment Summary

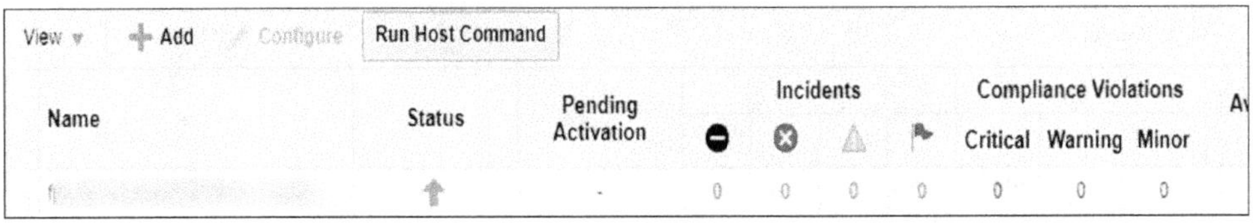

Figure 23-14   Host Target Status

Monitoring OCI Autonomous Database

For the next use case, let's discover OCI Autonomous Database—Serverless in Oracle Enterprise Manager. For this example, you will need to install Oracle Enterprise Manager 13.5 Release Update 16 for Oracle Enterprise Manager and Agent for this discovery to work at minimum. Make sure to install the latest available Release Update for Oracle Enterprise Manager and Agent.

Oracle Enterprise Manager can discover the Serverless Autonomous Database by using a private endpoint or service gateway. A private endpoint assigns a private IP address and FQDN to the Autonomous Database within the Virtual Cloud Network (VCN). It acts like a virtual network interface card (VNIC), so access can also be controlled the same way using security rules, Network Service Group (NSG), and so on. It also prevents traffic to and from the Autonomous Database going over the Internet.

A service gateway allows private access OCI resources like Autonomous Database from other OCI resources and/or on-premises resources. It also prevents traffic from going over the public Internet. To use the service gateway, you add a route with a target as the service gateway in a route table. Further, you can use a security rule to control access through the service gateway. If you have more than one Autonomous Database, a service gateway may be a better choice. If you use a private endpoint, it will create a private IP for each Autonomous Database, and then you will have managed the access for each one separately.

For this use case, let's use a private endpoint. Autonomous Database (ADB) is already created to allow secure access from everywhere. So, you will have to modify it to use private endpoint access only. Let's go through some steps that need to be performed before you can begin the Oracle Enterprise Manager discovery:

Step 1. Log on to the OCI console and go to the ADB database home page, as shown in Figure 23-15. Click **Database Connection** to download the client credentials wallet.

Step 2. Select **Instance Wallet** as the wallet type and click **Download Wallet**, as shown in Figure 23-16.

The ADBSNMP monitoring user is created out-of-the-box when the Autonomous Database is created. It is locked by default. You can use the ADMIN super user for monitoring, but it is recommended that you use the ADBSNMP user instead. For this use case, use the ADBSNMP user. Later, you will use SQL Developer to test the wallet you downloaded and log on to the database.

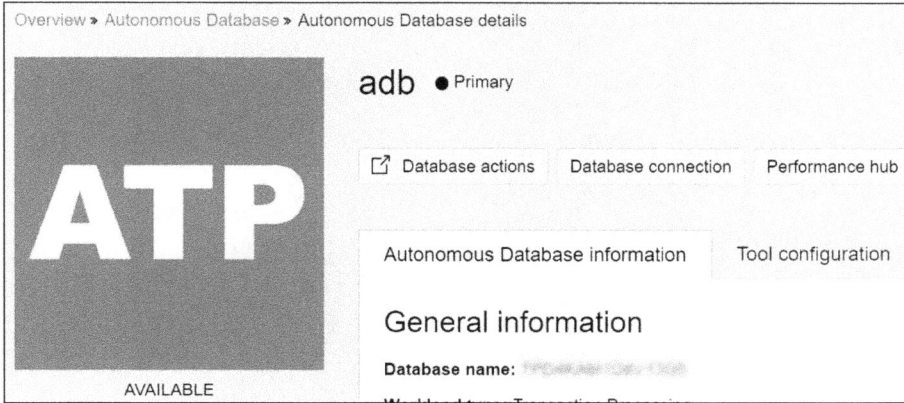

Figure 23-15   Autonomous Database Home Page

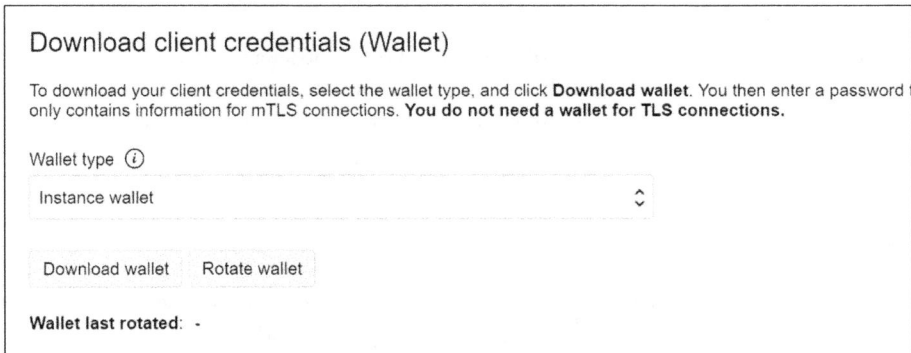

Figure 23-16   Download Wallet

Step 3. To connect to the Autonomous Database, create a new connection with Cloud Wallet as the connection type and provide the wallet you downloaded earlier, along with ADMIN user credentials.

The ADBSNMP user will need to be unlocked with the password and require some privileges to use Oracle Enterprise Manager. These commands are shown in Example 23-1.

Example 23-1   ADBSNMP User

```
Alter user adbsnmp identified by "<password>" account unlock;
Grant create session, select any dictionary, select_catalog_role to adb_monitor;
Alter user adbsnmp default role all;
```

Step 4. Go back to the ADB database home page and click **More Actions > Update Network Access**, as shown in Figure 23-17.

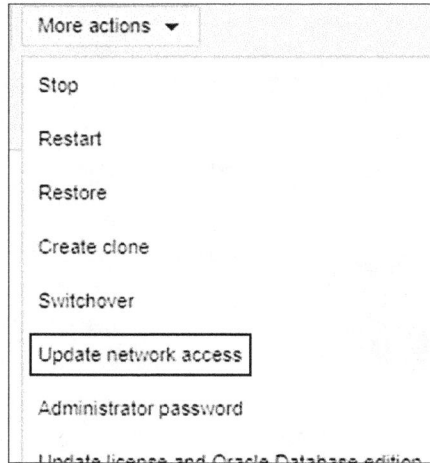

Figure 23-17   Autonomous Database Menu

Step 5. Select the **Private Endpoint Access Only** option and click **Update**, as shown in Figure 23-18. It will take a few minutes to update the configuration. Wait until the update is complete before moving to the next step.

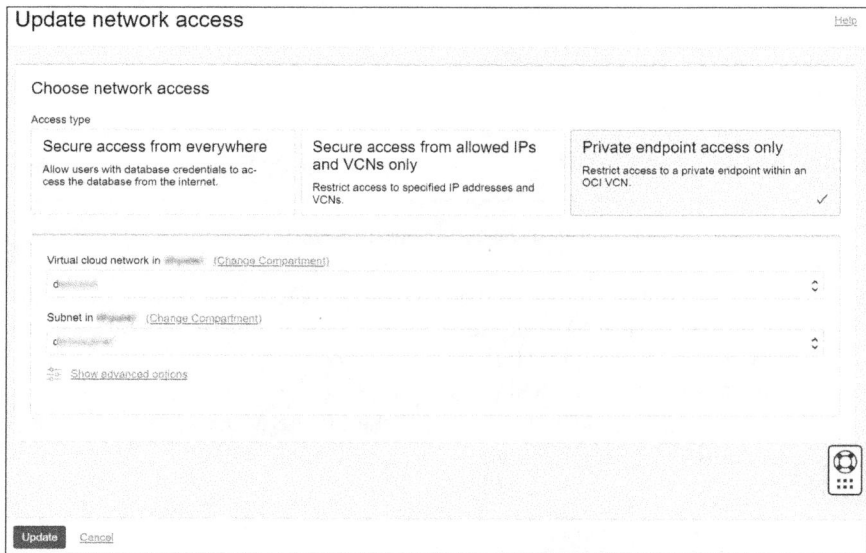

Figure 23-18   Autonomous Database Configuration

Step 6. Find the private endpoint URL assigned to ADB. You will need this during the Oracle Enterprise Manager discovery steps. Then go to the ADB database home page and copy the private endpoint URL from the Network section, as shown in Figure 23-19.

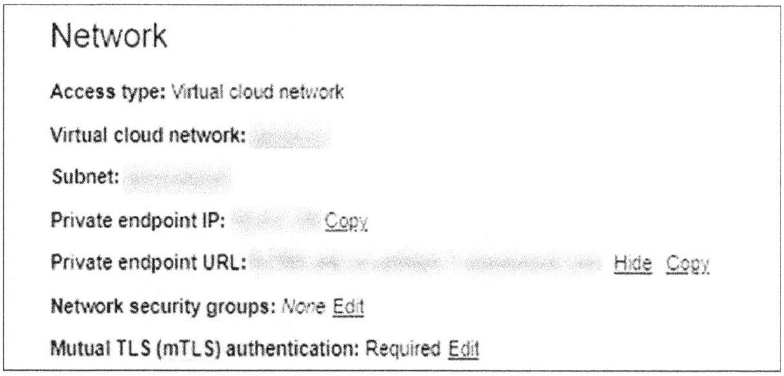

Figure 23-19   Autonomous Database Network Configuration

Step 7. Log on to the Oracle Enterprise Manager console now and click **Setup > Add Target > Add Targets Manually**, as shown in Figure 23-20.

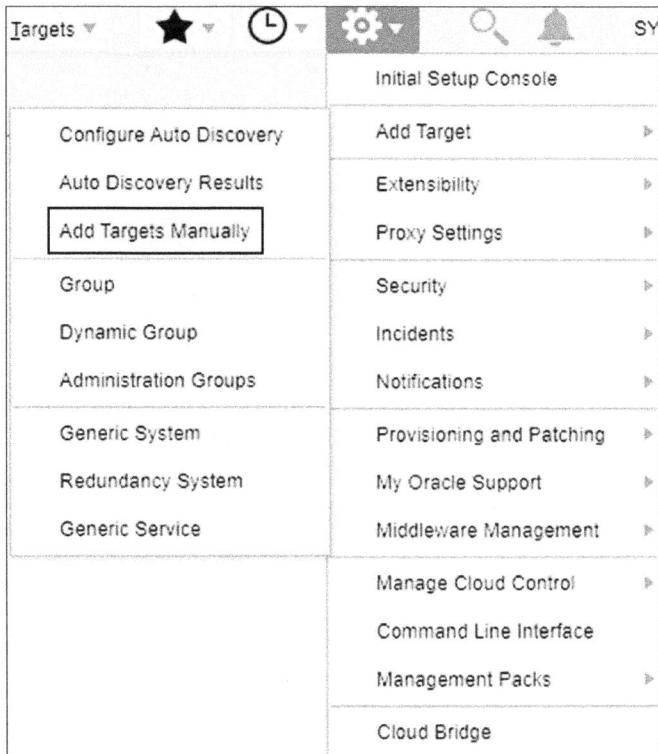

Figure 23-20   Add Target Manually

Step 8. Select **Add Target Manually**, as shown in Figure 23-21.

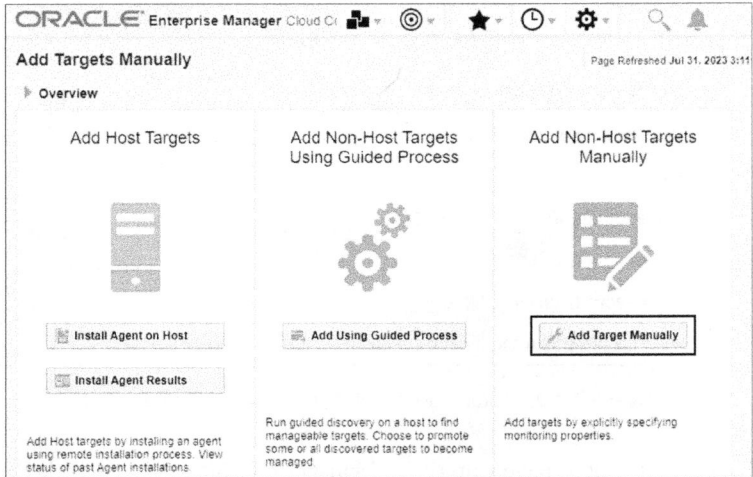

Figure 23-21   Add Host Targets Options

Step 9. Select the agent that will be used to monitor the Autonomous Database. For this use case, you will use the agent installed on the Oracle Enterprise Manager server. First, select the Oracle Enterprise Manager agent; for Target Type, select **Autonomous Transaction Processing** and then click **Add**, as shown in Figure 23-22.

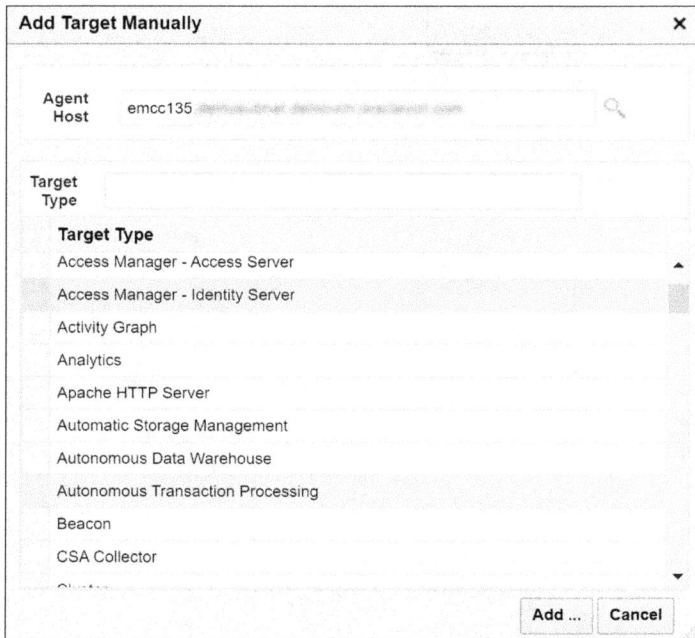

Figure 23-22   Agent Host and Target Type

Step 10. Provide the private endpoint URL as the target name, the password for the Client Credential wallet zip downloaded earlier, the ADBSNMP user password, and click **Next**, as shown in Figure 23-23.

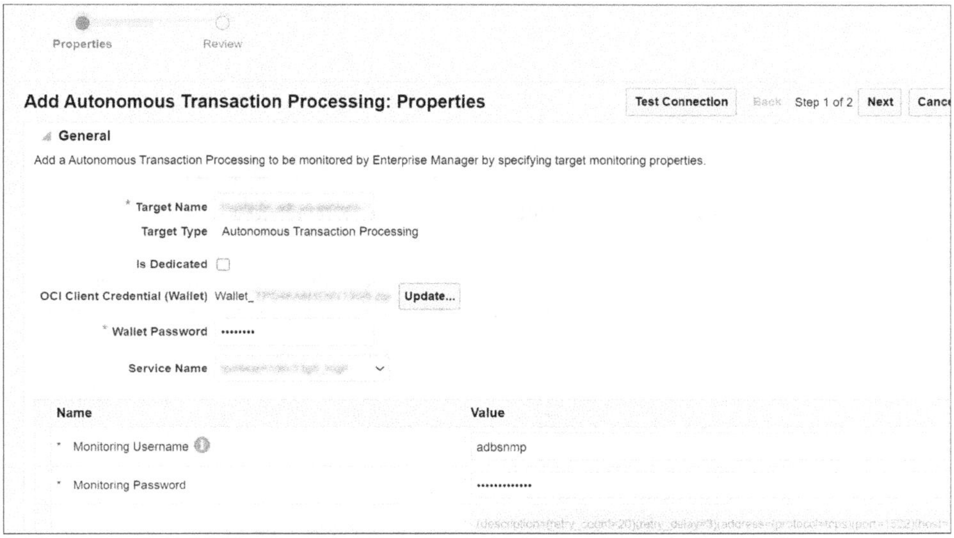

Figure 23-23 Autonomous Database Connection Information

Step 11. You might get the informational message shown in Figure 23-24 if the network is slow. Click **Continue** to proceed with the discovery.

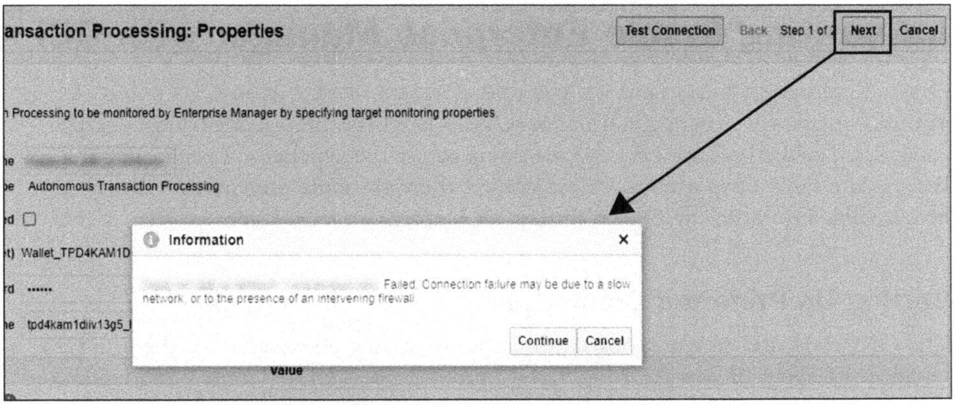

Figure 23-24 Informational Message

Step 12. Review all the information entered and click **Submit**, as shown in Figure 23-25.

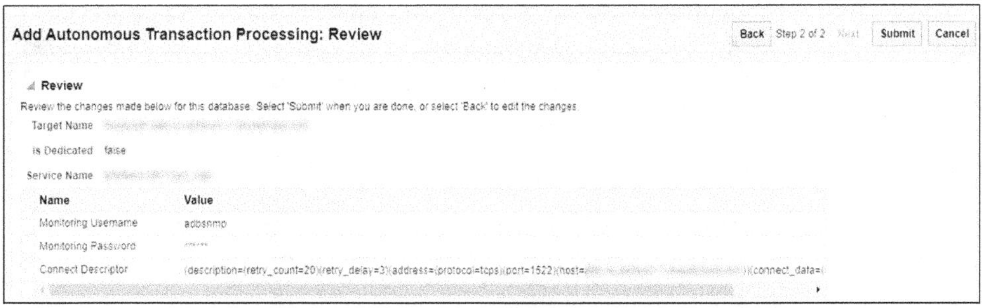

Figure 23-25   Review Autonomous Database Connection Information

Once the discovery process is complete, you will see the online status for the discovered Autonomous Database on the database target page, as shown in Figure 23-26.

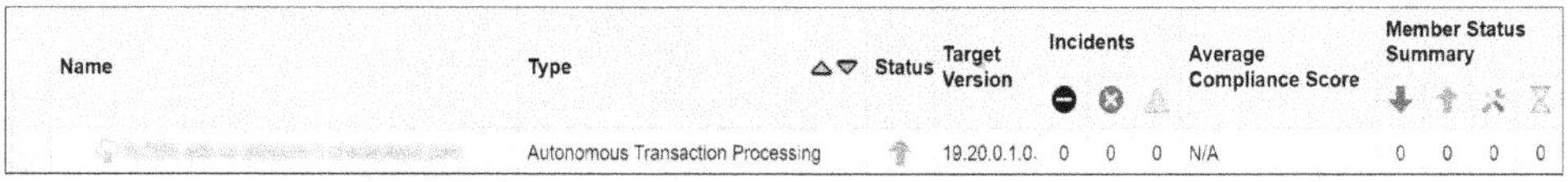

Figure 23-26   Target Autonomous Database Status

Now you can monitor Autonomous Database performance, run ADDM/AWR reports, perform administration tasks, and more. Oracle Enterprise Manager provides many different metrics to measure the performance and create alerts for it.

Integrating Oracle Enterprise Manager with OCI

Oracle Enterprise Manager enables you to export repository data to OCI object storage. You can import this data to OCI native services like Operation Insight and Logging Analytics. For the use case here, we are going to use the Operation Insight service. Before data can be exported to object storage, there are some prerequisites that need to be completed on both the Oracle Enterprise Manager and OCI side. Let's go over them.

Setting Up Preferred Credentials

The OMS host and all target hosts must have preferred credentials set to the user who installed the agent. If you are using SUDO privileges to perform some or all tasks, you will also need to set up privilege delegation. To do so, follow these steps:

Step 1. Log on to the Oracle Enterprise Manager console and click the main menu and select **Setup icon > Security > Privilege Delegation**, as shown in Figure 23-27.

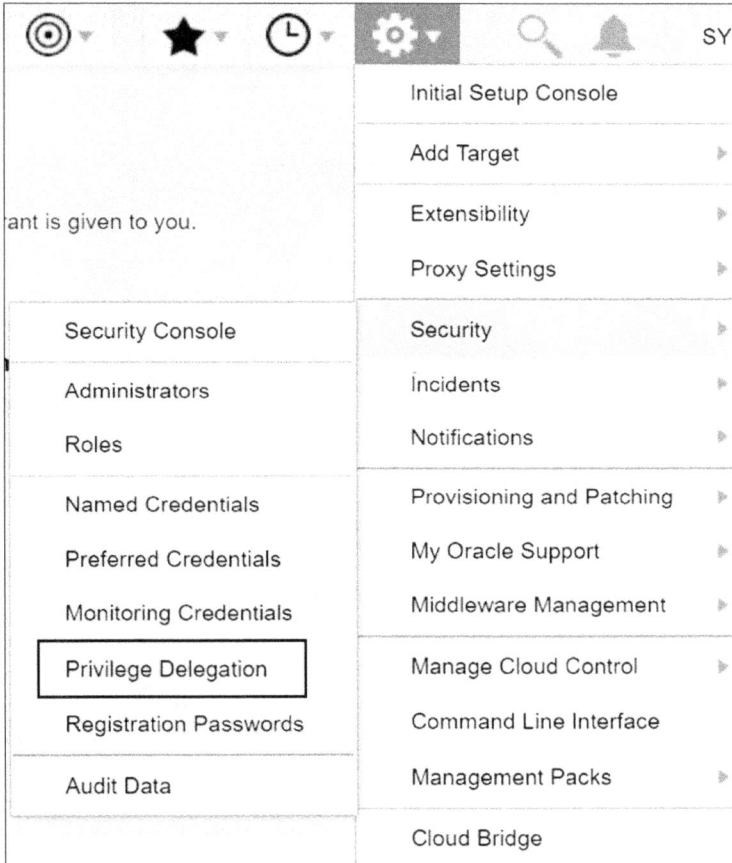

Figure 23-27   Oracle Enterprise Manager Setting Menu

Step 2. Click the host for which privilege delegation needs to be set, as shown in Figure 23–28.

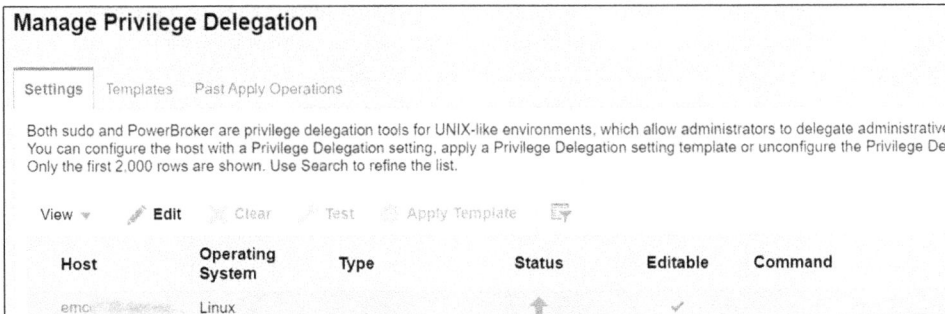

Figure 23-28   Privilege Delegation

Step 3. For the Type, select **Sudo**; for Sudo Command, enter **/usr/bin/sudo -u %RUNAS% %COMMAND%**, and click **Save**, as shown in Figure 23-29.

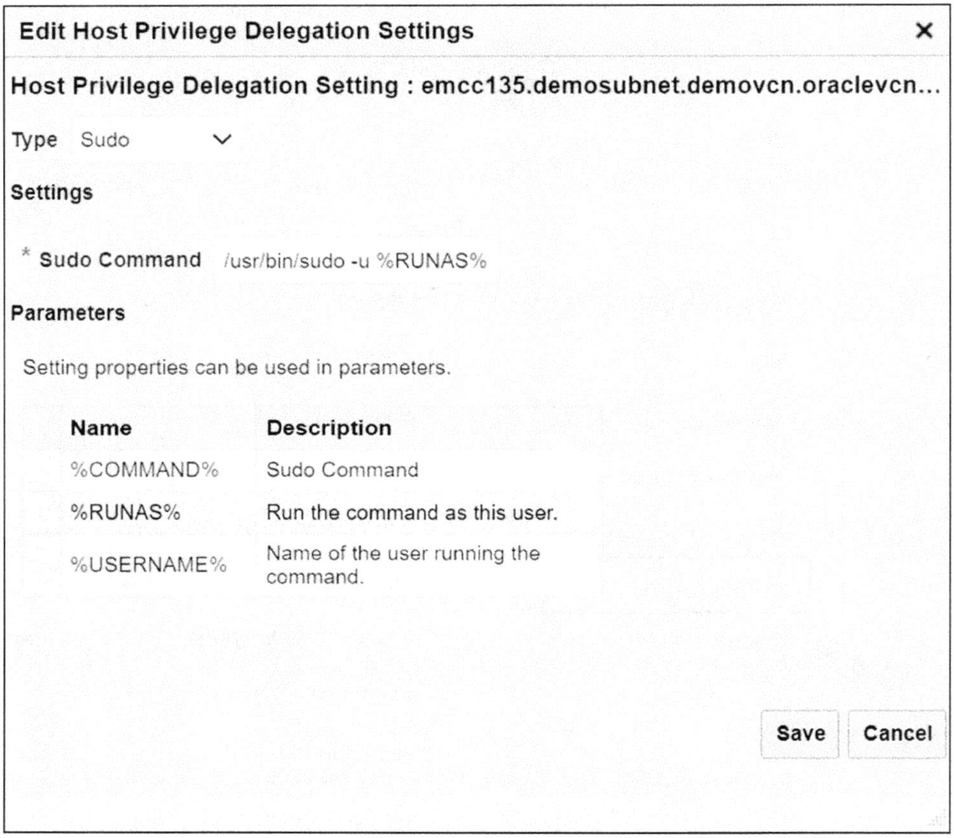

Edit Host Privilege Delegation Settings   ✕

Host Privilege Delegation Setting : emcc135.demosubnet.demovcn.oraclevcn...

Type   Sudo   ⌄

Settings

* **Sudo Command**   /usr/bin/sudo -u %RUNAS%

Parameters

Setting properties can be used in parameters.

Name	Description
%COMMAND%	Sudo Command
%RUNAS%	Run the command as this user.
%USERNAME%	Name of the user running the command.

Save   **Cancel**

Figure 23-29   Privilege Delegation Setup

Step 4. Now you need to set preferred credentials for all targets. Go to **Setup > Security > Preferred Credentials**. For the target type, select a host and then click **Manage Preferred Credentials**, as shown in Figure 23-30.

Step 5. Select one of the host targets and click **Set**, as shown in Figure 23-31. Follow this process for each of the hosts.

Step 6. Named credentials are already created for all hosts during the discovery phase, so you can select an appropriate existing one. Select this named credential and click the **Test and Save** button, as shown in Figure 23-32.

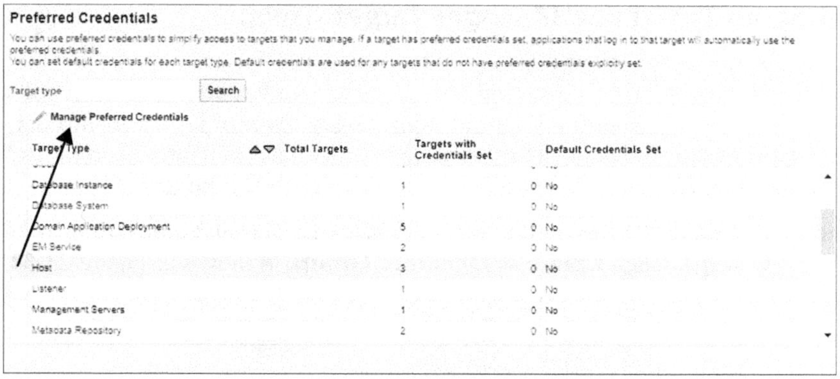

Figure 23-30   Preferred Credentials

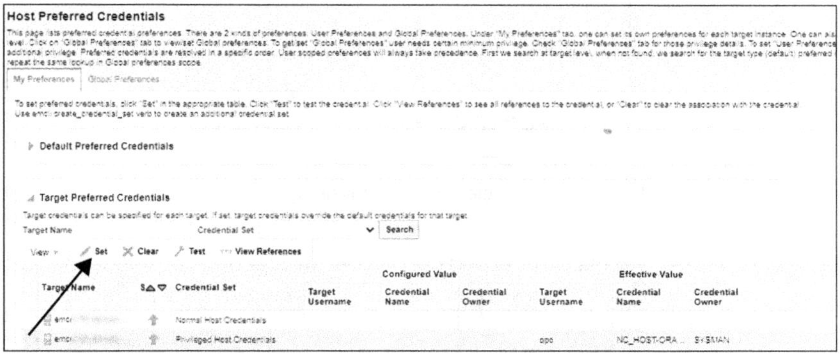

Figure 23-31   Host Preferred Credentials

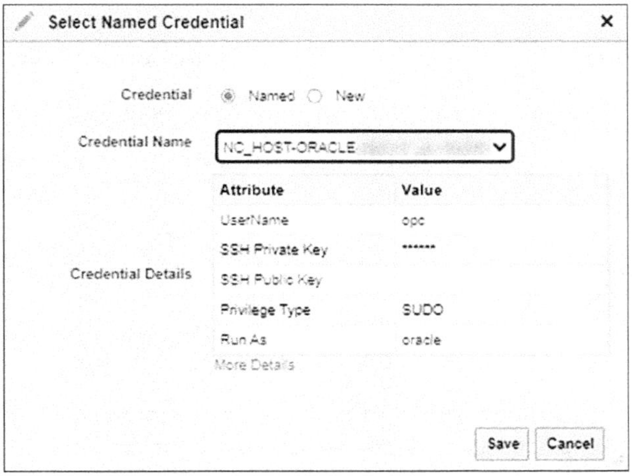

Figure 23-32   Named Credential

Creating an Enterprise Manager Target Group

Next, let's create a separate target group with all hosts and databases as members that you will need to move to OCI. During the OCI Data Service Export step later, it will ask you to provide a group name and not individual targets. Therefore, it is mandatory to create a target group containing all relevant targets that need to be exported to OCI. For the example here, let's create a dynamic group with all database targets:

Step 1. Log on to the Oracle Enterprise Manager console and go to **Targets > Groups**. Click **Create > Dynamic Group**, as shown in Figure 23-33.

Figure 23-33   Oracle Enterprise Manager Group Menu

Step 2. Define the membership criteria, as shown in Figure 23-34. For this example, you can include all hosts and databases discovered in Oracle Enterprise Manager as a target.

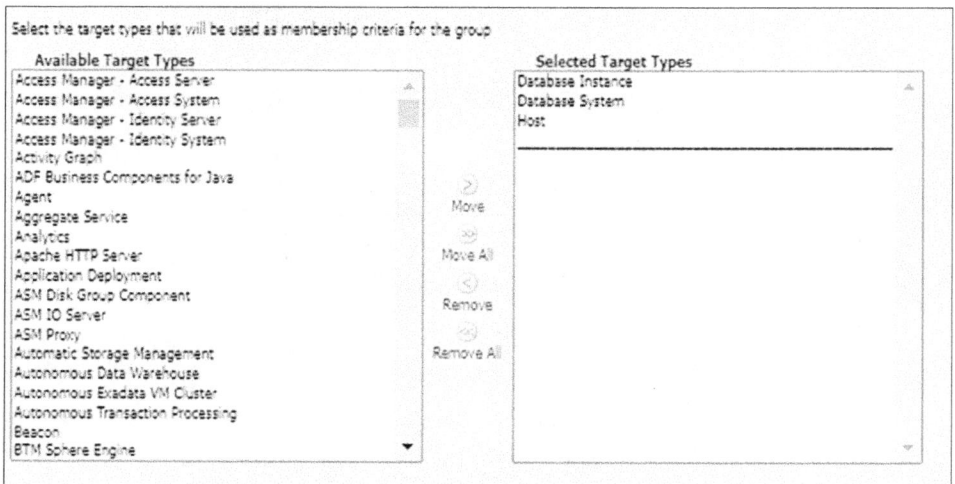

Figure 23-34   Dynamic Group Criteria

Once a group is created, you should see all members registered with this group, as shown in Figure 23-35.

Name	△▽	Group Type	Members
oci-group			Pluggable Database (4), Host (3), Database Instance (1), Database System (1), Oracle Home (1), More...

Figure 23-35   Dynamic Group Details

Creating an Oracle Enterprise Manager Super Administrator

An Oracle Enterprise Manager super administrator is required to export Oracle Enterprise Manager data to designated object storage. It is recommended that you create a separate administrator for this task. To do so, log on to the Oracle Enterprise Manager console and go to **Setup > Security > Administrators**. Enter a username and password and select **Super Administrator**, as shown in Figure 23-36.

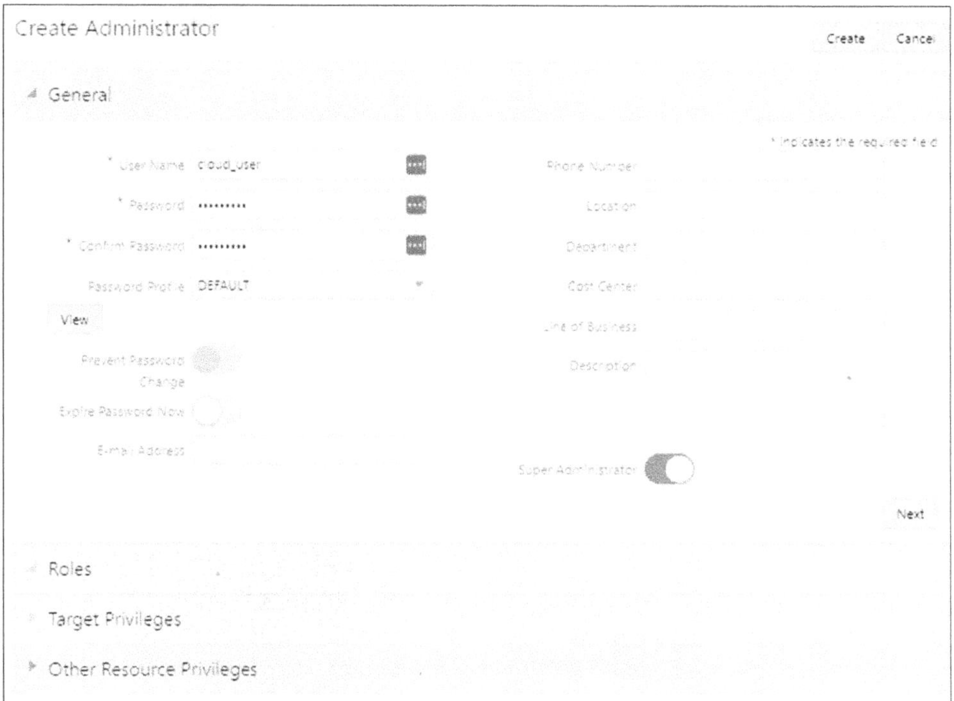

Figure 23-36   Oracle Enterprise Manager Super Administrator

Creating a Global Named Credential

You also can create a global named credential in Oracle Enterprise Manager that will be used to log on to OCI. It is recommended that you not use an individual account but instead create a separate account just for this purpose. A global credential will make it available for all targets. This credential allows Oracle Enterprise Manager to move data to OCI.

Step 1. Log on to the Oracle Enterprise Manager console, go to **Setup > Security > Named Credentials**, and click **Create**.

Step 2. Enter a credential name and the following field details (see Figure 23-37):

    a. For Authenticating Target Type, select **Oracle Cloud Infrastructure**.

    b. For Scope, select **Global**.

    c. Enter a **Tenancy OCID**.

    d. Enter a **User OCID**.

    e. Enter a **Public Key Fingerprint**.

    f. Enter a **Private Key**.

    g. Enter a **Private Key Passphrase**.

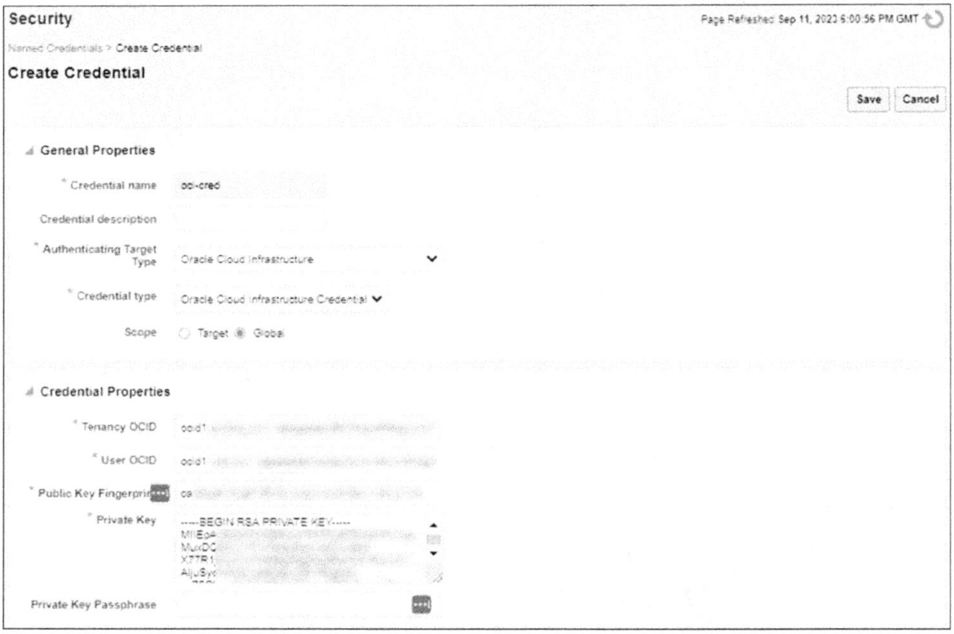

Figure 23-37   Global Named Credential

Now you have all the necessary pieces in place to create the OCI service connectivity. For this, you need to configure Cloud Bridge. Cloud Bridge contains the necessary connection information to move data from Oracle Enterprise Manager to an object storage bucket in OCI. Let's begin:

Step 1. Log on to the Oracle Enterprise Manager console and click **Setup > Cloud Bridge**, as shown in Figure 23-38.

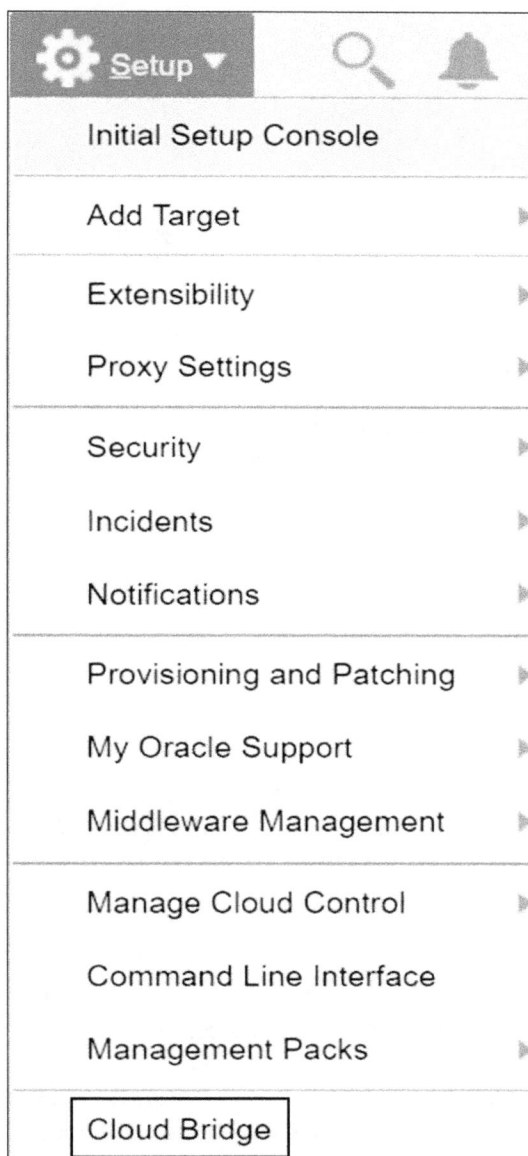

Figure 23-38 Oracle Enterprise Manager Setup Menu

Step 2. Click **Manage OCI Connectivity**, as shown in Figure 23-39. First, you can set up the connectivity and then go over how to export the data.

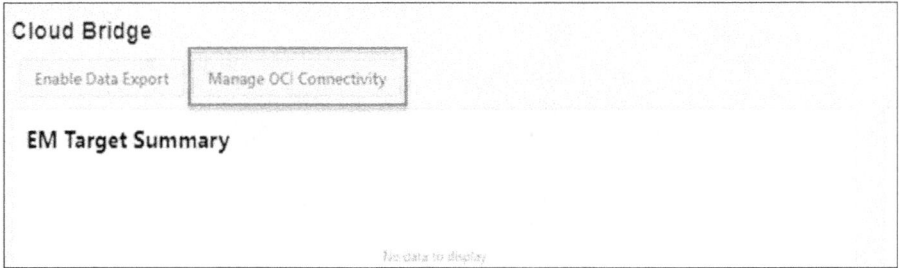

Figure 23-39   Cloud Bridge Page

Step 3. Within the Manage OCI Connectivity window, enter the OCI Credential name that was created as a part of one of the prerequisites, along with the Base URL, Bucket name, and OCI Bridge name. Then click **Test** to verify, and once successful, click **Create**, as shown in Figure 23-40. The Base URL format is https://objectstorage.<region>.<domain>, so if you are using another region, change it accordingly.

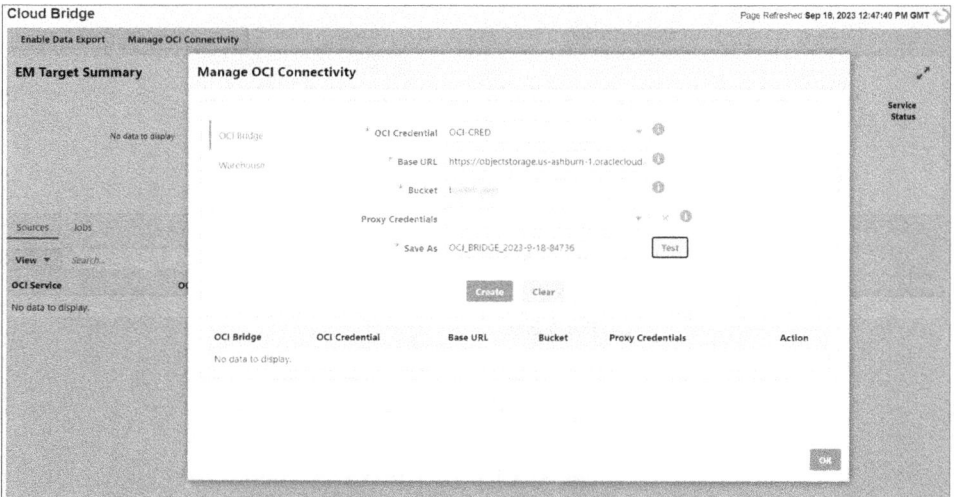

Figure 23-40   Manage OCI Connectivity

Step 4. Now it's time to export the data to object storage in OCI. To do so, click **Enable Data Export** on the Cloud Bridge home page, as shown in Figure 23-41.

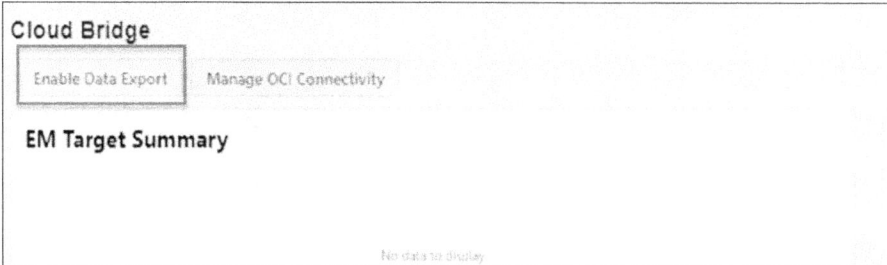

Figure 23-41   Cloud Bridge Home Page

Step 5. Within the OCI Service Data Export window, select **Operation Insights: Capacity Planning and SQL WH**. For the source, enter the EM target group **oci_group** created during "Creating an Enterprise Manager Target Group" section earlier in this chapter, along with the OCI Bridge name provided in Step 3. Then click **Submit**, as shown in Figure 23-42. You have other choices for the OCI Service field, such as Logging Analytics, Operation Insights: Exadata Warehouse, and Operation Insights: EM Warehouse.

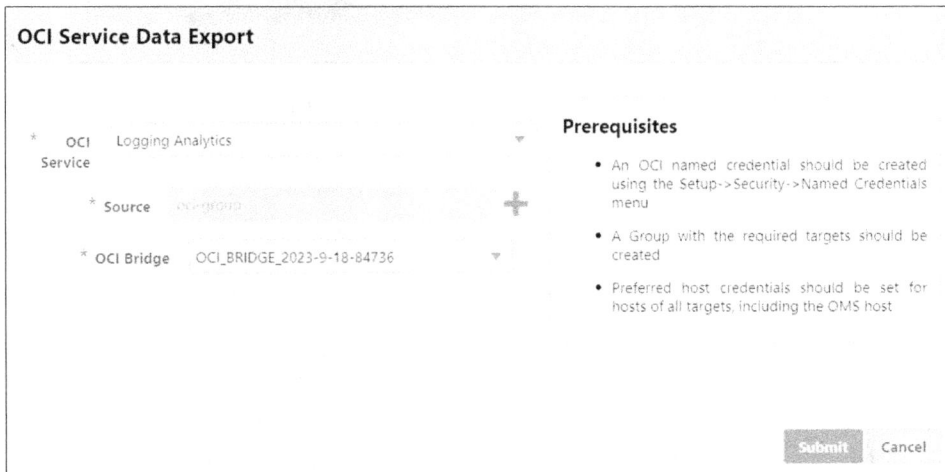

Figure 23-42   OCI Service Data Export

The Cloud Bridge dashboard, as shown in Figure 23-43, will show the data export status.

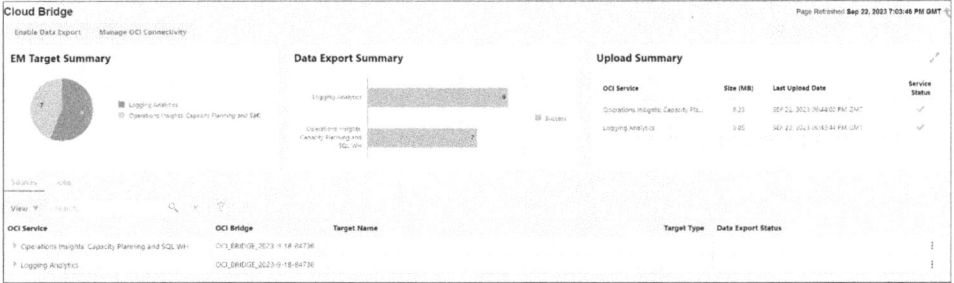

Figure 23-43   Cloud Bridge Dashboard

Now let's move over to OCI and go over how to utilize this information. You can use the Operation Insights service for this task:

Step 1. Log on to the OCI tenancy, click the main menu, and click **Observability & Management > Administration** under Operations Insights, as shown in Figure 23-44.

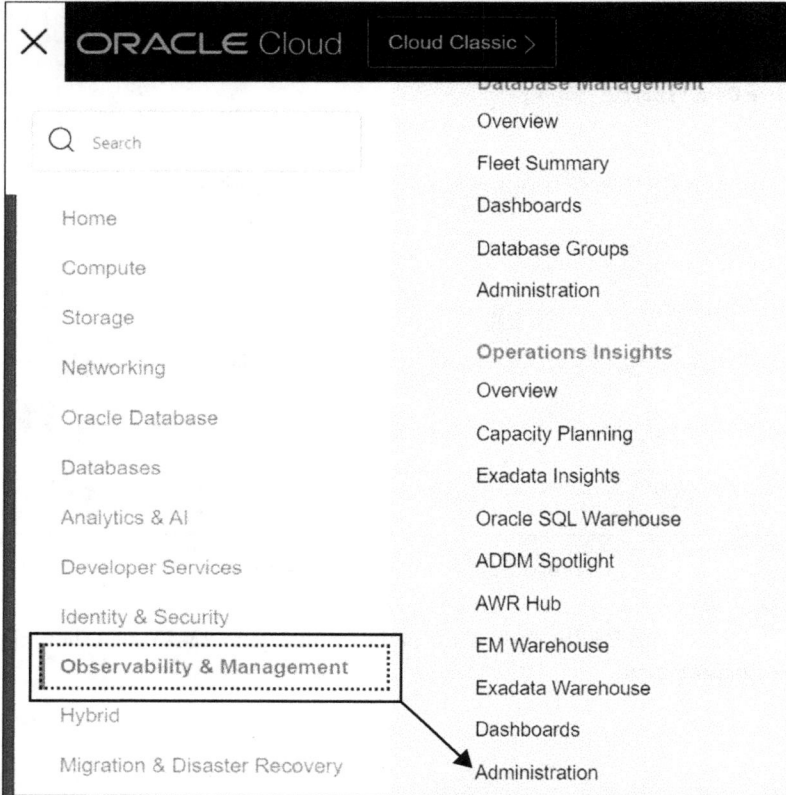

Figure 23-44   OCI Menu

Step 2. On the Operations Insights home page, click **Administration > EM Bridges** on the left panel, as shown in Figure 23-45.

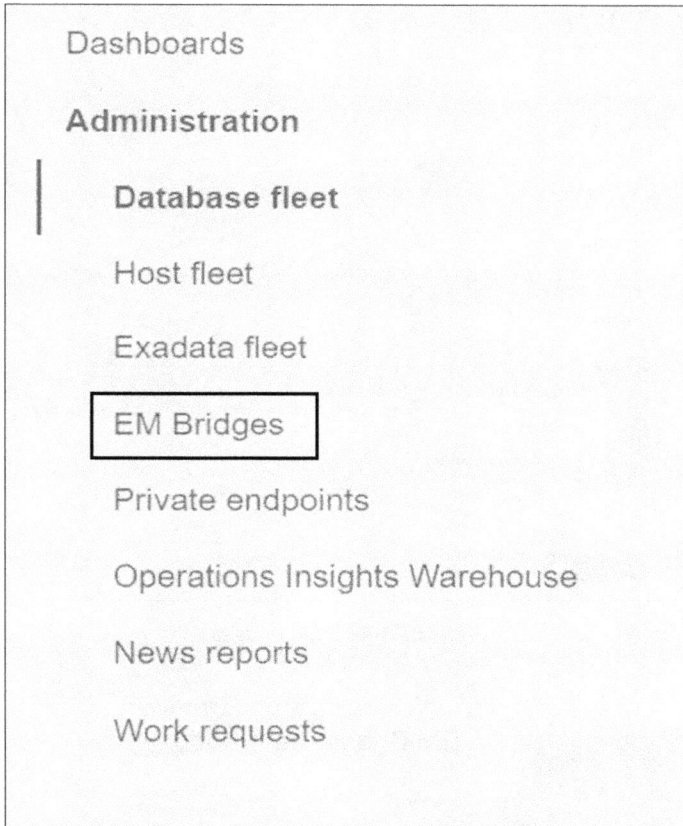

Dashboards

Administration

Database fleet

Host fleet

Exadata fleet

EM Bridges

Private endpoints

Operations Insights Warehouse

News reports

Work requests

Figure 23-45   Operations Insights Menu

Step 3. Click **Create Bridge** and enter a bridge name, compartment, bridge description, and object storage having Oracle Enterprise Manager data; then click **Create Bridge**, as shown in Figure 23-46.

Step 4. Once the EM bridge is created, click **Add Databases** on the home page, as shown in Figure 23-47.

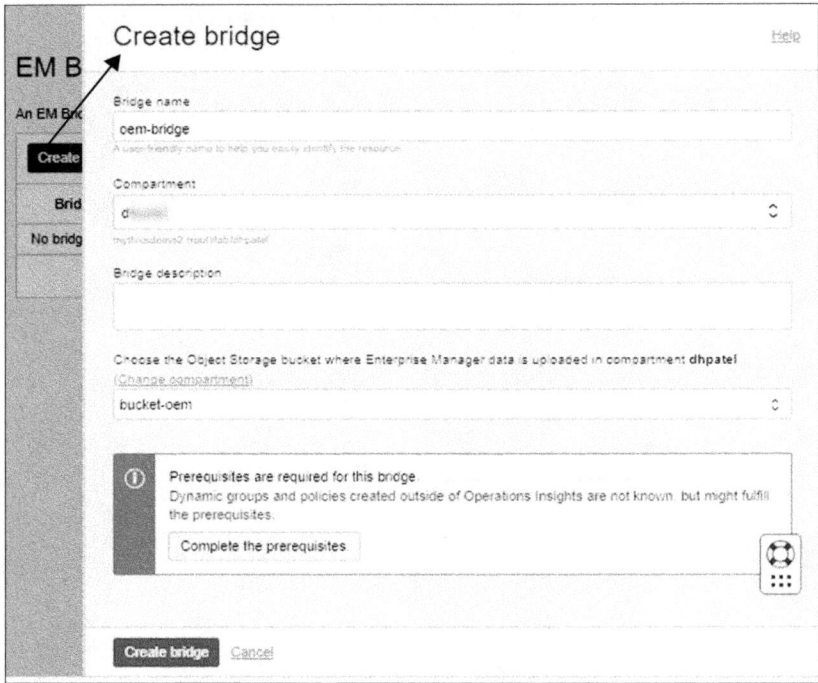

Figure 23-46   EM Bridges

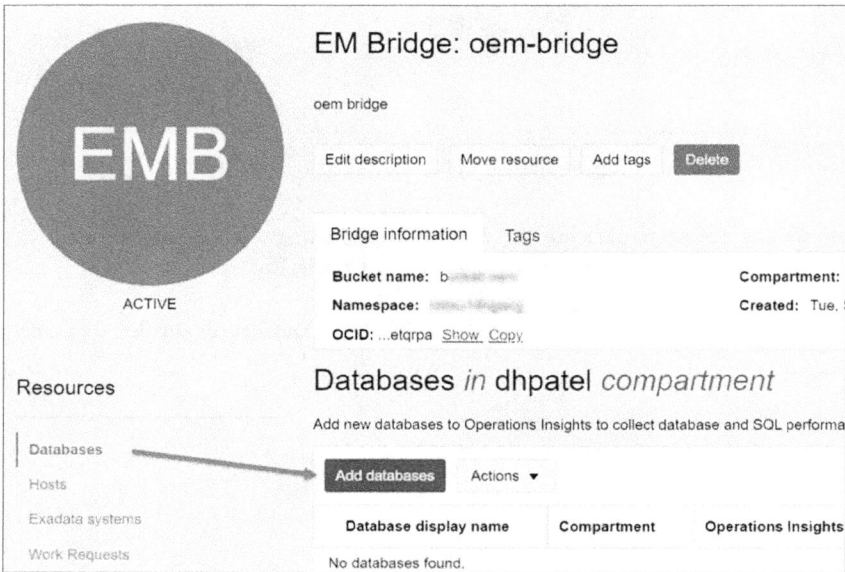

Figure 23-47   EM Bridge Home Page

The OCI service will list all databases that had data exported from Oracle Enterprise Manager to object storage.

Step 5. Click to select all the databases and click **Add Databases**, as shown in Figure 23-48.

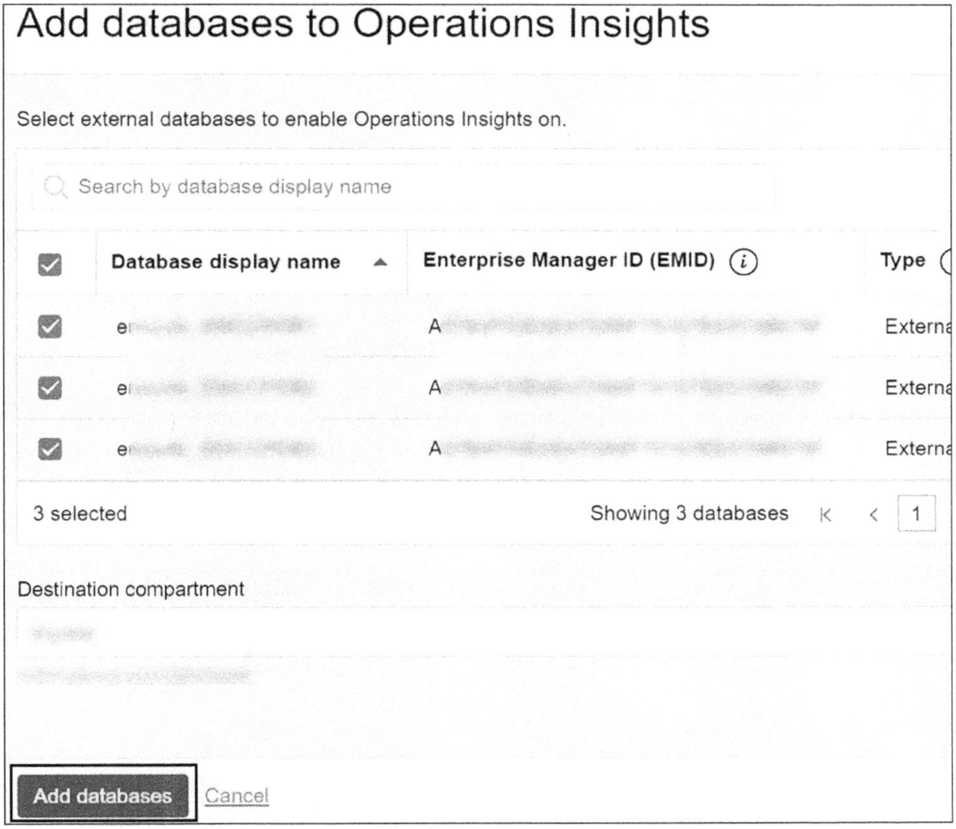

Add databases to Operations Insights

Select external databases to enable Operations Insights on.

> Search by database display name

☑	Database display name ▲	Enterprise Manager ID (EMID) ⓘ	Type ⓘ
☑	e⋯	A⋯	Externa
☑	e⋯	A⋯	Externa
☑	e⋯	A⋯	Externa

3 selected   Showing 3 databases |< < 1

Destination compartment

[Add databases] Cancel

Figure 23-48   Add Databases to Operations Insights

Step 6. Go back to the Operations Insights home page and click **Capacity Planning**, as shown in Figure 23-49. By default, the Database Capacity Planning page should open. It will show overall stats for all databases, including CPU, storage, and memory.
You can view detailed insights for CPU, storage, memory, IO, and so on for each database.

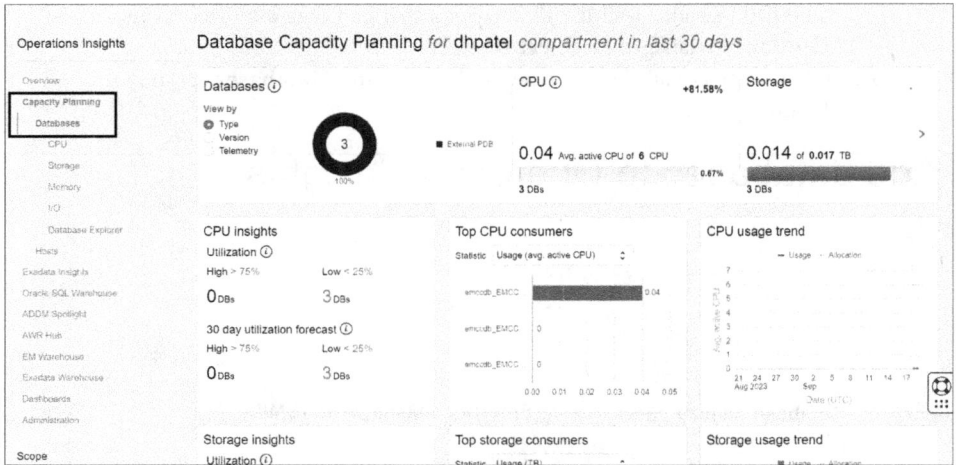

Figure 23-49   Capacity Planning Dashboard

Step 7. Click **Storage** for this use case, as shown in Figure 23-50. Here, the first database in the list has been selected with the Tablespace breakdown option. You can see the Trend & Forecast for each tablespace within the database represented as dotted lines in the chart.

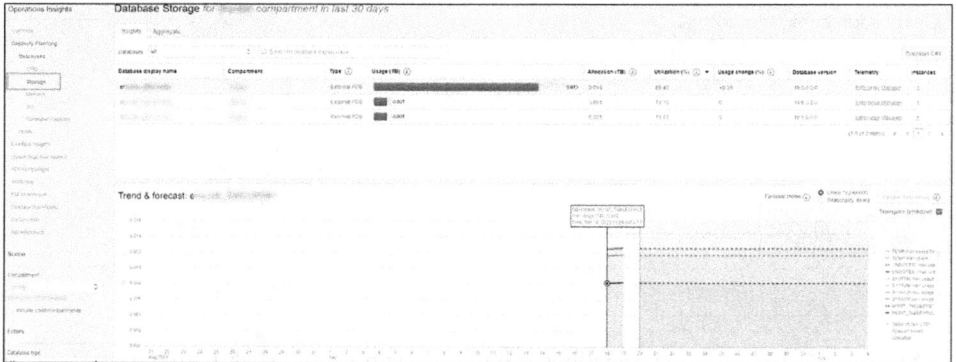

Figure 23-50   Operations Insights Storage Dashboard

Incorporating Best Practices

Finally, let's review some of the basic but important security and operational best practices for Oracle Cloud Control.

Monitoring Database Security

Security is one of the most critical aspects of Oracle Enterprise Manager. To discover, monitor, and administer different target types, user security should be very restrictive. You do not want to provide too many privileges to any user or administrator. Follow the process shown earlier in this chapter to create administrators and users. During the process, be sure to assign the roles and privileges appropriately for each user. Oracle provides out-of-the-box roles to make this process easier. One of the most common requirements for an organization is to have limited privileges for all database administrators, for example. Based on the job role—database administrator, application administrator, data guard administrator, and so on—the correct roles, target privileges, and resource privileges should be assigned.

Database targets can be monitored by non-DBSNMP users starting from Oracle Enterprise Manager 13.5 RU4. This monitoring user will need similar privileges to the DBSNMP user. When you have more than one Oracle Enterprise Manager environment, this capability is very useful because now you can distinguish where any database action was triggered from by looking at the logs.

Standby databases can be monitored by user with the SYSDG privilege starting from Oracle Enterprise Manager 13.5 RU6. In most cases, the user with the SYSDBA privilege is used to monitor standby databases. SYSDBA is a powerful privilege; this new enhancement allows organizations to use lesser privileged users in this scenario.

Oracle Enterprise Manager supports Kerberos and RADIUS authentication from Oracle Enterprise Manager 13.5 RU6. You can use these authentication methods as the preferred credential, to perform basic management operations, execute SQL/SQL script jobs, and so on. More capabilities are added with every Release Update, which is one reason why Oracle Enterprise Manager should be patched often.

Patching Oracle Enterprise Manager

Oracle Enterprise Manager should be patched on an ongoing basis as Oracle releases updates. We already went over how these Release Updates include not just bug fixes but also new features, security fixes, and so on.

Patches can be applied using the traditional method or the Rapid Platform Update method. Rapid Platform Update was introduced with Oracle Enterprise Manager 13.5 RU5. It minimizes the downtime required for patching. In traditional patching, OMS needs to be shut down for the entire patching activity. Rapid Platform Update breaks down the patching activity into two phases: deploy and update operations. The deploy operation is performed while OMS is online. The update operation is performed during the maintenance window when OMS can be offline. The deploy operation creates a clone of the existing Middleware home and creates a new version for this clone in the repository database. Now these new clones and new versions of the data get patched while keeping OMS active and the repository data untouched. The update operation runs during the downtime window; it applies changes to the active OMS home and switches the new version created in the repository database during the deploy operation to the active version.

Let's go over the process of applying Oracle Enterprise Manager 13 Release Update 16 here using the Rapid Platform Update method. The Oracle Support article titled "Enterprise 13.5 Main Release Update List (Includes Plug-ins)" (Doc ID 2760230.2) is a great source of information for Oracle Enterprise Manager 13c RUs. To apply RU16 (as shown in Examples 23-2 and 23-3), download OMS Release Update 16 Patch 35437906 and Agent Release Update 16 Patch 35437910. Both patches include all required plug-in patches. It is a best practice to read the README file for each of these patches before applying.

Some of the most common prerequisites for OMS/Agent patching are as follows (refer to the README file for a complete list):

- Apply required patches to the repository database.
- Download the latest version of OMSPatcher.
- Apply required patches to OMS to use Rapid Platform Update.
- Download the latest AgentPatcher version.

Example 23-2   OMS Patching

```
Pre-downtime patching command,
$ cd   <PATH_DIR>/35437906
$ omspatcher deploy
Downtime patching command,
$ <OMS_HOME>/bin/emctl stop oms
$ omspatcher update
```

Example 23-3   Agent Patching

```
$ cd   <PATH_DIR>/35437910
$ <AGENT_HOME>bin/emctl stop agent
$ agentpatcher apply
$ <AGENT_HOME>bin/emctl start agent
```

Oracle keeps adding security features and fixing known bugs to every patch set release, so it is recommended that you keep Oracle Enterprise Manager patched to the latest available RU if possible.

Sizing Oracle Enterprise Manager

Oracle Enterprise Manager deployment sizing is critical for Oracle Enterprise Manager to function properly. Oracle Enterprise Manager sizing mainly depends on a number of targets, but server configuration (virtualized or physical) also plays an important part. Oracle Enterprise Manager supports high availability configuration. For the discussion here, let's focus on the minimum configuration requirements for a stand-alone Oracle Enterprise Manager deployment shown in Table 23-1.

Table 23-1 Oracle Enterprise Manager Minimum Server Configuration by Size

Size	Target Count	Server Configuration			Database Storage (GB)	
		Cores	Memory (GB)	Storage (GB)	Data	Temporary
Eval	<100	2	10	24	20	5
Small	<1000	4	10	24	150	15
Medium	>=1000, <10,000	6	12	24	350	20
Large	>=10,000	12	24	24	500	40
Extra Large	>=50,000	24	32	24	700	80

Table 23-1 shows an optimal configuration required for an Oracle Enterprise Manager server depending on the deployment size. For target count <=1000 and <10,000, use a medium deployment size. It requires a server with at least six cores, 12 GB RAM, and 24 GB of storage, and a database server with 350 GB for data tablespaces and 20 GB for temp tablespaces. It is a good idea to configure your server and database with a little more than the configuration recommended here. For the database tier, you can use two or more Real Application Cluster (RAC) nodes for medium and above deployment size. In this case, you should replicate the same server configuration to all servers.

When you are in the planning phase, also consider the near future that can impact the target count so that you are sizing your configuration correctly for the long term.

Summary

In this chapter, you learned that Oracle Enterprise Manager is a useful management tool for on-premises and cloud environments, as you have seen here with some examples. Oracle Enterprise Manager integrates security at every phase of lifecycle management, which makes it an important tool in the DevSecOps world.

In this book you have learned the basics about Oracle Cloud Infrastructure (OCI) and its more common services. You have learned how to overcome the challenge of learning new technology by embracing many of the services OCI offers unrelated to Oracle's database. You have learned a few ways of enabling automation, with security being an included aspect of the deployment. This should help your teams deploy secure applications as their journey into the cloud with OCI starts.

Index

A

A1 compute, 145–147
access control policy, 55–59
administrator user
  Oracle Data Safe
    creating, 247
    privileges, 249–250
  Oracle Enterprise Manager, creating, 551–553
AgentPatcher, upgrading, 527–529
Agile, 207
alert/s
  marking, 330–331
  policies, 243–244
  remediation, 329–330
  reports, 244
AMD Epyc CPU, 145–147
Ampere Altra CPU, 145–146
AmpereOne CPU, 145–146
analyze command, 526–527
Ansible, 4, 420–421, 455
  agentless approach, 345
  collections, 345, 354
    Galaxy, installation, 356
    OCI, installation, 354–355
  modules, 345, 354
  playbooks, 356, 363, 383
    advanced features, 369
    assigning a user to a group, 376–377
    attaching a block volume to an instance, 381
    best practices, 374
    blocks, 371
    conditional statements, 367–368
    creating a block volume, 380
    creating a policy, 376
    creating a routing table, 378
    creating a user, 376
    creating a VCN, 377–378
    creating an instance, 381
    creating an Internet gateway, 378
    creating an NSG, 378
    creating file storage, 380
    creating groups, 375–376
    debugging, 372–373
    deleting an instance, 382
    errors, 358–359
    getting object storage namespace, 379
    handlers, 369–370
    ignore_errors, 371–372
    key components, 364
    keywords, 366
    listing all objects from buckets, 379–380
    logical operators, 367
    loops, 366–367
    Nginx sample, 364
    output, 357–358
    plays, 357, 363
    rescue option, 372
    resetting an instance, 382
    retrieving a list of availability domains, 375
    roles, 369
    setting a user's password, 377
    stopping an instance, 382
    structure, 363–364
    tags, 370–371
    testing, 373
    variables, 364–365
  setting up the CLI configuration file, 355–356
  WinRM (Windows Remote Management) protocol, 345–346
  YAML, 345
ansible-galaxy command, 354
ansible-playbook command, 358
API key, 99–100, 263–269, 350–352
application/s, 91. *See also* Functions
  cloud-native, 89–90

creating, 92–95
    OLAM (Oracle Linux Automation Manager),
        420
apply command, 295
archive storage, 165, 179
ARM architecture, 145–146
Artifacts Registry, 213
    creating, 216
    uploading deploy_apache.sh script to, 216–217
ASM (Automatic Storage Management), 517
Audit, 84–86
audit
    logs, 306–307
    policies, 241–242
    profile, 241
    reports, 242–243
    trail, 242
authentication. *See also* IAM (identity and access
    management)
    API keys, 263–269
    credentials, 399–401. *See also* credentials
    database passwords, 258–263
    OCI, 350
        adding the OLAM credential, 353
        getting the OCI information, 350–353
    Terraform, 463–465
automation. *See also* Ansible
    alert remediation, 329–330
    CI/CD (continuous integration and continuous
        delivery), 4, 207
    deployment pipeline. *See also* sample DevOps
        project, creating
            creating, 222
            running a deployment pipeline, 222–224
    DevSecOps, 4–5
    IaC (Infrastructure as Code), 4
    in an IT enterprise, 453
    OCI (Oracle Cloud Infrastructure), 2
    scripts, 213–215
autonomous database
    creating, 505–506
    discovering, 558–564
Autonomous Database Service, 187–189
    client credentials wallets, 188
    compute, 187
    dedicated Exadata infrastructure, 189
    free trial, 188
    OCPU/ECPU pools, 188
    Oracle Database 23ai, 187–188
    provisioning, 196–199

    registering to Oracle Data Safe, 245–247
    shared Exadata infrastructure, 188–189
Autonomous Linux, 296
    plug-in, 296–297
    selecting an image, 296
    viewing a scheduled job, 298
AWS (Amazon Web Service), cost of service
    offerings, 7–8

B

backup
    block volume, restoring, 173–174
    policy, 172–173
bandwidth, OCI (Oracle Cloud Infrastructure), 8
bastions, 38–39, 44
    managed SSH sessions, 44–49
    setting up, 44
benefits
    of cloud-native design, 89–90
    of DevSecOps automation, 5
    of OCI (Oracle Cloud Infrastructure), 7
    of Terraform, 455
Billing and Cost Management tool, 26–27
    budgets, 30–32
    Cost Analysis system, 27–29
    Cost and Usage Reports, 27
Block Storage Auto-Tiering, 25
block volume, 165–167
    attaching to an instance, 167–169, 381
    cloning, 175
    configuring performance, 169
    creating, 167, 380, 478–481
    performance monitoring, 171
    performing a backup, 172–173
    restoring a backup, 173–174
    security, 179–180
    UHP (ultra high performance), 170–171
    volume groups, 174–175
blocks, 371
blue-green deployment strategy, 210
buckets
    creating, 110–111
    uploading files to, 175–176
budget, creating, 30–32
building a VM
    boot options, 142
    image and shape, 141–142
    image networking, 142
    image placement, 140–141

image SSH keys, 142
instance configuration, 140
BYOL (Bring Your Own License), 184

C

canary deployment strategy, 211
Chef, 454–455
child tenancy, creating, 16–19
chmod command, 101
CI/CD (continuous integration and continuous
    delivery), 4, 207
CIDR (Classless Inter-Domain Routing), 122
claim issuance policy, 284–292
CLI, OCI (Oracle Cloud Infrastructure)
    installation, 263
    setup, 263–265
    uploading a document, 175–176
client host configuration, Terraform, 489–490
cloning
    recipes, 334–335
    volume, 175
Cloud Advisor, 21–22
    cost management summary, 22–23
    HA (high availability) summary, 25
    performance summary, 24–25
Cloud Guard, 321
    alerts
        marking, 330–331
        remediation, 329–330
    detectors, 325–327
    initial configuration, 322–329
    integration with other OCI services, 321
    integration with Threat Intelligence Service,
        52–53
    key features, 321–322
    policies, 323–324
    recipe/s
        accessing, 332–333
        cloning, 334
        detector, 331–332, 3334
        management, 331
        responder, 332, 334–338
        rules, 335–337
    security zones, 338–340
cloud/cloud computing
    compute. See also compute
        AMD Epyc CPU, 145
        ARM architecture, 145
        Intel X64 architecture, 145

DBaaS (Database as a Service). See DBaaS
    (Database as a Service)
hybrid, 187
IaaS (Infrastructure as a Service), 37. See also
    IaaS (Infrastructure as a Service)
incorrectly sized resources, 1
security, 20–21
shared responsibility model, 2
sprawl, 21
cloud-native, 89–90
    Events, 108, 110
        creating a bucket, 110–111
        rules, 110–112
        security policy, 108–109
    Functions, 90–91, 104–107
        deployment using a Linux server, 91–107
        open-source, 90
        policies, 92–93
    OKE (Oracle Kubernetes Engine),
        112–114
        authentication and authorization, 114
        control plane nodes, 113
        managed nodes, 113
        self-managed nodes, 113
        virtual nodes, 113
        worker nodes, 114
    Streams, 107–108
cluster
    Heatwave, 190
    Kubernetes, creating, 115–119
code
    infrastructure as. See IaC (Infrastructure as
        Code)
    whitespace-sensitive, 454
code repository, 213
collaboration, DevSecOps team member, 7
collections, 345, 354
    Galaxy, installation, 356
    OCI, installation, 354–355
command/s. See also CLI
    analyze, 526–527
    ansible-galaxy, 354
    ansible-playbook, 358
    apply, 295
    chmod, 101
    config, 264–265
    config.sh, 532–533
    curl, 355
    dnf, 387
    Docker login, 103

Docker version, 98
emctl, 529
fn deploy, 104
fn init, 104
fn invoke, 104
GridSetup.sh, 518
iscsiadm, 168–169
Ksplice management, 294–295
kubectl, 119
lsblk, 170
omspatcher, 526–527
runInstaller, 519–520
running, 404–407
ssh, 47
sudo, 96–97, 178, 215, 354–355
systemctl status postgresql, 387
Terraform, 457
terraform apply, 469–470, 474, 480–483,
    490–491, 500–501
    rerunning after a change in Terraform
        configuration, 493
    rerunning after a change on the OCI
        console, 494
    rerunning with no changes, 491–493
terraform destroy, 511
terraform fmt, 508
terraform init, 467–468, 490
terraform output, 510
terraform plan, 468–469, 478–479, 482,
    490–491, 500–501
terraform show, 509–510
terraform state list, 508–509
terraform -v, 461
terraform validate, 508
yum, 461
compartments, 11, 15, 38, 257
policies, 276–277
quotas, 16
compliance
officer, DevSecOps, 6
regulatory, 5, 114
software development, 4–5
compute, 139, 349
Autonomous Database Service, 187
building a VM
    boot options, 142
    image and shape, 141–142
    image networking, 142
    image placement, 140–141
    image SSH keys, 142
    instance configuration, 140

CPU
AMD Epyc, 145
Ampere Altra, 145–146
AmpereOne, 145–146
ARM architecture, 145–146
Intel X64 architecture, 145
performance, 146–147
instance
    creating, 296, 381, 502–504
    deleting, 382
    discovering, 554–558
    resetting, 382
    stopping, 382
OCPU (Oracle Compute Processing Unit),
    146, 186
Compute Instance Run Command plug-in,
    215–216
conditional policies, 275–276
conditional statements, 367–368
config command, 264–265
config.sh command, 532–533
configuration drift, 455
configuration file
CLI, setting up in Ansible, 355–356
replicating to a production environment, 507
Terraform, 456
    creating, 466–467
    dev_compute.tf, 503
    dev_outputs.tf, 499–500, 504
    dev_vcn_private_subnet.tf, 498–499
    dev_vcn_public_securitylist.tf, 497–498
    parameterizing, 471–473, 483–484
    running, 478–481
    updating, 474–478
YAML, 360
consumer, 107
Container Registry, 213
containers, 112–113, 387
control plane nodes, 113
cost, OCI (Oracle Cloud Infrastructure), 7–9
Cost Analysis system, 27
cost analysis section, 29
details section, 29–30
settings, 28–29
Cost and Usage Reports option, Billing and Cost
    Management tool, 26–27
cost management summary, Cloud Advisor, 22–23
CPU, 8–9
AMD Epyc, 145
Ampere Altra, 145–146
AmpereOne, 145–146

ARM architecture, 145–146
Flex shapes, 148–153
Intel X64 architecture, 145
OLAM requirements, 349
performance, 146–147
shape, 147–148
thread, 9
creating. *See also* provisioning
API key, 99–100, 350–352
applications, 92–95
Artifacts Registry, 216
autonomous database, 505–506
block volume, 167, 380, 478–481
buckets, 110–111
budget, 30–32
compartments, 490–491
compute instance, 296, 502–504
credentials, 430–436
custom logs, 311–313
custom recipes, 42
dashboards, 33
data masking policy, 237–240
deployment pipeline, 222
DevOps project, 218. *See also* sample DevOps
    project, creating
dynamic groups, 270–273
file storage, 380
file system, 176–177
flow logs, 132–133
global credential, 570–578
groups, 375–376
Internet gateway, 378
job template, 446–450
Kubernetes cluster, 115–119
master encryption key, 83
Network Firewall policy, 67–74
NSG (network security group), 130, 378
Oracle Enterprise Manager administrators and
    users, 551–553
policies, 376
projects, 436–439
routing table, 378
RSA key pair, 463–465
scan recipe, 299–301
security zones, 39–42
subnet, 125–126
teams, 426–430
tenancy, 14–15
    child, 16–19
    new, 19–20

Terraform script, 466–467
users, 376, 423–426
VCN (virtual cloud network), 124–125,
    377–378, 494
    applying changes, 500–501
    defining a VCN module, 494–495
    defining private and public subnets,
        498–499
    defining security lists and ingress/egress
        rules, 495–498
    updating the outputs file, 499–500
WAF policy, 64–65
credentials
    creating, 430–436
    custom types, 416
    global, creating, 570–578
    OLAM (Oracle Linux Automation Manager),
        399–401
CSI (Customer Support Identifier), 16
CSPs
    compute offerings, 147–148
    cost of service offerings, 7–9
    IOPS (input/output operations per second), 7–8
    SLA (service-level agreement), 8
    vCPU metric, 9
curl command, 355
cursor, 107
custom credential types, 416
custom logs, 307, 311–313
custom OS images, creating, 160–162
custom recipes, creating, 42
CVE (Common Vulnerabilities and Exposures), 298

D

dashboard, 32, 34–36
    Cloud Guard, 322
    creating, 33
    widgets, 33–34
data
    masking, 237–240
    sensitive type, 230
        category, creating, 231
        creating a data model, 231–235
        discovering, 231
data source, 474. *See also* resources
    oci_core_volume, 477
    Terraform, 474
Data Transfer Appliance, 165–166
database. *See also* DBaaS (Database as a Service);
    Oracle Data Safe; Oracle Database

audit profile, 241
autonomous, creating, 505–506
passwords, 258–263
PostgreSQL, setting up, 385–387
security, 579
threat indicator, 49–51
DBaaS (Database as a Service), 183
Autonomous Database Service,
187–189
client credentials wallets, 188
compute, 187
dedicated Exadata infrastructure, 189
free trial, 188
OCPU/ECPU pools, 188
Oracle Database 23ai, 187–188
provisioning, 196–199
shared Exadata infrastructure, 188–189
Exadata, 186–187
Exadata Cloud@Customer, 187
MySQL database service, 189, 199–203
MySQL Heatwave, 189–190
NoSQL database service, 189–190, 204–205
Oracle Base Database Service, 186, 191–196
debugging
playbooks, 372–373
Terraform errors, 484–485
dedicated Exadata infrastructure, 189
deleting an instance, 382
deploy_apache.sh script, 216–217
deployment pipeline, 211. *See also* sample DevOps
project, creating
creating, 222
running, 222–224
destroying resources, 510–511
detectors. *See also* alert/s
Cloud Guard, 325–327
recipe, 321–322, 331–332, 3334
dev_compute.tf, 503
dev_outputs.tf, 499–500, 504
dev_vcn_private_subnet.tf, 498–499
dev_vcn_public_securitylist.tf, 497–498
DevOps
CI/CD (continuous integration and continuous
delivery), 207
life cycle, 2
security practices, 4
DevSecOps, 1
automation, 4
CI/CD, 4
IaC (Infrastructure as Code), 4
benefits of, 5
compliance officer, 6

engineer, 6
lifecycle phases, 2
operations engineer, 6
product owner, 6
security engineer, 6
shared responsibility model, 4–5
software developer, 6
team, 6–7, 420–421
test engineer, 6
diagram, network architecture, 122–124
discovering
OCI Autonomous Database, 558–564
OCI compute instance, 554–558
sensitive type data, 231
disk group, 517
dnf command, 387
Docker, 113
Docker login command, 103
Docker version command, 98
documentation, Terraform, 473–478
downloading
Logging Analytics Management Agent,
317–319
Terraform, 461
DRG (dynamic routing gateway), 129, 136
dynamic groups, 38, 269–273
creating, 270–273
matching rules, 269–270

E
ECPU, 9, 188
EMCC (Enterprise Manager Cloud Control).
See Oracle Enterprise Manager
emctl commands, 529
encryption keys, 80
enforcement point, WAF policy, 63
engineer, DevSecOps, 6
environment, creating for DevOps project,
218–219
ephemeral principal, 269
Epyc CPU, 145
errors
ignore_, 371–372
playbook, 358–359
Terraform, debugging, 484–485
event logs, searching, 85–86
Events, 108, 110
creating a bucket, 110–111
rules, 110–112
security policy, 108–109
Exadata Cloud@Customer, 187

Exadata Database service, 186–187
execution environments, 420–421

F

family resource types, 274
federation, 39, 277–292
file storage, 165
    creating, 380
    file system
        creating, 176–177
        mounting, 178
FinOps, 21
firewall. *See also* Network Firewall service; WAF
    (Web Application Firewall)
    network
        creating, 74–77
        OCI network resources, 65–66
        policies, creating, 67–74
        route table configuration, 77–79
        setting up, 66
Flex shapes, 148–153, 186
flexibility, OCI (Oracle Cloud Infrastructure), 1
flow logs, creating, 132–133
FMW infrastructure, installation, 530–531
fn deploy command, 104
fn init command, 104
fn invoke command, 104
FNP project, 90
formatting, YAML, 360–362
free services
    Cloud Advisor, 21–22
    OCI (Oracle Cloud Infrastructure), 9–10
free trial
    Autonomous Database Service, 188
    starting, 12–15
Functions, 90–91, 104–107
    deployment using a Linux server
        creating and running a function, 104–107
        creating the application, 92–95
        setting up the Linux host, 95–104
        setting up the tenancy, 91–93
    open-source, 90
    policies, 92–93

G

gateways, 136
global credential, creating, 570–578
global namespace, 11
GridSetup.sh command, 518
group/s, 38, 269

assigning a user to a, 376–377
creating, 375–376
dynamic, 38, 269–270
    creating, 270–273
    matching rules, 269–270
log, 307

H

handlers, 369–370
HashiCorp, 454. *See also* Terraform
HCL (HashiCorp Configuration Language), 454
high-availability
    Oracle Enterprise Manager, 516
    summary, Cloud Advisor, 25
hosts, OLAM (Oracle Linux Automation Manager),
    408–409
HSM (hardware security module), 80
hybrid cloud, 187

I

IaaS (Infrastructure as a Service), 37. *See also* cloud-
    native; security
    cloud-native, 89–90
    compute, 139. *See also* compute
    network/ing, 121. *See also* network/ing
        CIDR (Classless Inter-Domain Routing),
            122
        creating a subnet, 125–126
        creating flow logs, 132–133
        creating NSGs, 130
        diagram, 122–124
        establishing peering between VCNs,
            128–129
        gateways, 136
        icons, 123
        Internet gateway, 122
        LPG (local peering gateway), 127–128
        private IP address, 122
        route table, 122
        security, 136
        security list, 122
        security rules, 122
        subnet, 122–123
        updating the security list, 126–127
        VCN (virtual cloud network), 122
        VNIC (virtual network interface card), 122
    security. *See* security
    security zones, 39
    storage. *See also* storage
        archive, 165

block volume, 165–174
  file, 165
  object, 165
  Streams, 107–108
IaC (Infrastructure as Code), 4, 215, 453–455.
  See also Terraform
IAM (identity and access management), 37, 257.
  See also policy/ies
  authentication settings, 258
    API keys, 263–269
    database passwords, 258–263
  federation, setting up, 277–292
  groups, 38, 269
    dynamic, 38, 269–270
    dynamic, creating, 270–273
  managed resources, 38–39
  policy/ies
    claim issuance, 284–292
    conditional, 275–276
    confirming, 489
    effect on compartments, 276–277
    statements, 273
    verbs, 273
  users
    local, 258
    Oracle Data Safe administrator, creating, 247
    Oracle Data Safe administrator, privileges, 249–250
    risk assessment, 228–230
icons, networking, 123
IDaaS (Identity as a Service), 258
IDCS (Oracle Identity Cloud Service), 258
idempotency, 493
IdP (identity provider), 277
ignore_errors, 371–372
immutable infrastructure, 457
imperative tools, 454–455
infrastructure
  destroying, 511
  immutable, 457
infrastructure principal, 269
installation
  FMW infrastructure, 530–531
  JDK8, 529–530
  Logging Analytics Management Agent, 317–319
  OAS (Oracle Analytics Server), 531–532
  OCI CLI, 263
  OLAM (Oracle Linux Automation Manager), 383, 391–392
    cleaning up the Receptor, 390

configuring Nginx, 388–389
configuring Redis, 387
configuring the database connection, 388
creating the initial OLAM configuration, 388
installing the container using podman, 388
installing the software, 387
preparing Linux, 383–385
provisioning the OLAM instance, 390
setting up PostgreSQL, 385–387
OMR (Oracle Management Repository), 517
  ASM disk prerequisite, 518
  create repository database, 520–522
  database installation and configuration, 519–520
  database software patching, 520
  grid infrastructure installation and configuration, 519
  prerequisites, 517–518
OMS (Oracle Management Service), 522–523
  configuration, 523–525
  creating a response file, 522–523
  current OMS patch level, 525
  database parameters, 523
  prechecks, 522
Unified Monitoring Agent, 311–312
instance, 108
  creating, 381, 502–504
  deleting, 382
  groups, 220–221, 420
  resetting, 382
  starting/stopping, 511–512
  stopping, 382
integrated services, OCI (Oracle Cloud Infrastructure), 2
Intel X64 architecture, 145–147
Internet gateway, 122, 378
inventory, 403–408, 439–446
inviting an existing tenancy into an organization, 16–19
IOPS (input/output operations per second), 7–8, 168, 349
iscsiadm commands, 168–169

J

JDK8, installation, 529–530
job
  analysis, 450–451
  template, creating, 446–450
JSON, 85, 303–305, 454

K

K8s, 114
key, 108
keywords, playbook, 366
Ksplice, 293–294
    key commands for managing, 294–295
    viewing available kernel updates, 295–296
kubectl command, 119
Kubernetes, 112, 115–119

L

licensing, Oracle Enterprise Manager,
    516, 547
lifecycle
    DevOps, 2
    DevSecOps, 2
Lint, 373
Linux. *See also* Autonomous Linux; Ksplice
    ARM architecture, 146
    Functions, hosting
        creating and running a function, 104–107
        creating the application, 92–95
        setting up the Linux host, 95–104
        setting up the tenancy, 91–93
    repo, 96
    sudo command, 96–97, 178, 215, 354–355
    viewing attached volumes, 170
local users, 258
log/s, 303. *See also* OCI (Oracle Cloud
Infrastructure), Logging Service; Oracle Cloud
Logging Analytics
    audit, 306–307
    custom, 307, 311–313
    event, 84
    flow, creating, 132–133
    groups, 307
    service, 305
    unit, 319
    VCN subnet service, 307–311
loops, playbook, 366–367
LPG (local peering gateway), 127–128, 136
lsblk command, 170

M

manage all-resources permission, 489
managed cluster, 114
management jobs, OLAM (Oracle Linux
    Automation Manager), 418–419
Marketplace, 153–155

custom OS images, 160–162
    launching a stack, 156–160
marking, alerts, 330–331
master encryption key, creating, 83
matching rules, 269–270
memory
    Flex shapes, 148–153
    OLAM requirements, 348–349
    shape, 147–148
messages, 107–108
module/s, 345
    Ansible, 354
    VCN, 494–495
Molecule, 373
monitoring
    database security, 579
    OCI Autonomous Database, 558–564
    OCI compute instance, 554–558
mounting a file system, 178
MySQL database service, 189
MySQL Heatwave, 189–190

N

namespace, object storage, 379
NAT (Network Address Translation), gateway, 136
navigation menu, OLAM (Oracle Linux
    Automation Manager), 392–394
Network Firewall service, 65–66
    creating a network firewall, 74–77
    OCI network resources, 65–66
    policies, creating, 67–74
    route table configuration, 77–79
    setting up, 66
network/ing, 121
    CIDR (Classless Inter-Domain Routing), 122
    diagram, 122–124
    flow logs, creating, 132–133
    gateways, 136
    icons, 123
    Internet gateway, 122
    NSG (network security group)
        attaching the VNIC, 131–132
        creating, 130
    private IP address, 122
    route table, 122
    security, 136
    security list, 122, 126–127
    security rules, 122
    source, 38

subnet, 122–123, 125–126
VCN (virtual cloud network), 122
    adding a route rule to the route table,
        129–130
    creating, 124–125, 494
    defining a VCN module, 494–495
    defining security lists and ingress/egress
        rules, 495–498
    LPG (local peering gateway), 127–128
    peering, 128–129
    subnet service log, enabling, 307–311
VNIC (virtual network interface card), 122
NFS (network file system)
    creating, 176–177
    mounting, 178
NoSQL database service, 189–190, 204–205
notifications, OLAM (Oracle Linux Automation
Manager), 417–418. *See also* alert/s
NPA (Network Path Analyzer), 133–135
NSG (network security group), 128
    attaching the VNIC, 131–132
    creating, 130, 378

O

OAS (Oracle Analytics Server)
    configuration, 532–534
    installation, 529, 531–532
    integrating with Oracle Enterprise Manager, 534
        configuring security infrastructure, 534–536
        configuring the required OAS datasource,
            537–538
        setting OAS support for Oracle Enterprise
            Manager-provided reports, 538–546
    setting up support for Oracle Enterprise
        Manager-provided reports, 538–546
object storage, 165, 175
    buckets, 175–176
    listing all objects from buckets, 379–380
    namespace, 379
    uploading objects, 175
Observability and Manageability services, 2, 547
OCI (Oracle Cloud Infrastructure), 4. *See also*
DBaaS (Database as a Service); IaaS (Infrastructure
as a Service)
    A1 compute, 145–147
    Audit, 84–86
    authentication, 350
        adding the OLAM credential, 353
        getting the OCI information, 350–353
    automation, 2

bandwidth, 8
bastions, 44
    creating a managed SSH session, 44–49
    managed SSH session, 44
    setting up, 44
benefits of, 7
building a VM
    boot options, 142
    image and shape, 141–142
    image networking, 142
    image placement, 140–141
    image SSH keys, 142
    instance configuration, 140
CLI
    installation, 263
    setup, 263–265
    uploading a document, 175–176
Cloud Guard integration, 321. *See also* Cloud
Guard
Compute menu, 139–140
cost of service offerings, 7–9
DevOps, 208–209
    blue-green deployment strategy, 210
    canary deployment strategy, 211
    creating a sample project. *See* sample
        DevOps project, creating
    deployment environments, 210
    deployment pipeline, 211
    DevOps project, 208
    project resources, 213
    scripts, 213–215
ECPU metric, 9
Events, 108, 110
    creating a bucket, 110–111
    rules, 110–112
    security policy, 108–109
federation support, 277–292
Flex shapes, 148–153
free services, 9–10
Functions, 90–91
    creating the application, 92–95
    deployment using a Linux server, 91–107
    open-source, 90
    policies, 92–93
global namespace, 11
IAM (identity and access management),
    37–39, 257
integrated services, 2
integrating with Oracle Enterprise Manager, 564
    creating a global named credential, 570–578

creating an Enterprise Manager target group, 568–569
setting up preferred credentials, 564–567
Logging Service, 303–305
 audit logs, 306–307
 custom logs, 307, 311–313
 enabling a VCN subnet service log, 307–311
 JSON format, 303–305
 log categories, 305–306
 log groups, 307
 logging and monitoring plug-in, 311
 service logs, 305
 Unified Monitoring Agent, installing, 311–312
Marketplace, 153
 custom OS images, 160–162
 launching a stack, 156–160
 searching, 154–155
Network Firewall service, 65
 creating a network firewall, 74–77
 network resources, 65–66
 policies, creating, 67–74
 route table configuration, 77–79
 setting up, 66
network/ing, 121. *See also* network/ing
 CIDR (Classless Inter-Domain Routing), 122
 creating a subnet, 125–126
 creating flow logs, 132–133
 creating NSGs, 130
 diagram, 122–124
 establishing peering between VCNs, 128–129
 gateways, 136
 icons, 123
 Internet gateway, 122
 LPG (local peering gateway), 127–128
 private IP address, 122
 resources, 65–66
 route table, 122
 security, 136
 security list, 122, 126–127
 security rules, 122
 subnet, 122–123
 updating the security list, 126–127
 VCN (virtual cloud network), 122
 VNIC (virtual network interface card), 122
Observability and Manageability services, 2, 547
OCPU metric, 9

and Oracle Enterprise Manager, 549–551
OKE (Oracle Kubernetes Engine), 112–114
 authentication and authorization, 114
 control plane nodes, 113
 creating a cluster, 115–119
 managed nodes, 113
 self-managed nodes, 113
 virtual nodes, 113
 worker nodes, 114
Oracle Database editions, 183–184
parent tenancy unit, 11
region, 11
scalability and flexibility, 1
security zones, 39
 adding, 340–343
 creating, 39–42
 policies, 338–340
 recipe, 339
storage. *See also* storage
 archive, 165
 block volume, 165–174
 file, 165
 object, 165
Streams, 107–108
tenancy
 compartments, 11, 15
 creating, 14–15
 Details page, 16–17
 inviting into an organization, 16–19
Terraform documentation, 473–478
Terraform menu option, 459
Threat Intelligence Service, 49
 Cloud Guard integration, 52–53
 threat indicator database, 49–51
Vault
 accessing, 80–82
 creating a secret, 83–84
 creating the master encryption key, 83
VSS (Vulnerability Scanning Service), 298–301
WAF (Web Application Firewall), 54
 policies, 54–65
oci_core_volume data source, 477
OCID (Oracle Cloud Identifier), 16, 19
 child tenancy, 16–17
 obtaining, 350–353
OCPU (Oracle Compute Processing Unit), 9, 146, 186

Flex shapes, 148–153
    pool, 188
offset, 108
OKE (Oracle Kubernetes Engine), 112–114
    authentication and authorization, 114
    control plane nodes, 113
    creating a cluster, 115–119
    managed nodes, 113
    self-managed nodes, 113
    virtual nodes, 113
    worker nodes, 114
OLAM (Oracle Linux Automation Manager), 346, 383
    access management, 410
    administrative options, 416
    applications, 420
    credentials, 399–401, 430–436
    features and packs, 346
    hosts, 408–409
    installation, 383, 391–392
        cleaning up the Receptor, 390
        configuring Nginx, 388–389
        configuring Redis, 387
        configuring the database connection, 388
        creating the initial OLAM configuration, 388
        installing the container using podman, 388
        installing the software, 387
        preparing Linux, 383–385
        provisioning the OLAM instance, 390
        setting up PostgreSQL, 385–387
    instance groups, 420
    inventory, 403–408, 439–446
    job analysis, 450–451
    job template, creating, 446–450
    management jobs, 418–419
    navigation menu, 392–394
    notifications, 417–418
    OCI authentication, 350
        adding the OLAM credential, 353
        getting the OCI information, 350–353
    organizations, 410–411
    projects, 401–403, 436–439
    releases, 346–347
    resource management, 394–395
    service mesh, 346–348
        Enterprise, 347–348
        supported node types, 347
    sizing the deployment, 348–349
        CPU, 349

        database disk space, 349
        memory, 348–349
    teams, 414–416, 426–430
    templates, 395
        Access tab, 397
        Details tab, 395–397
        Job tab, 398–399
        Notifications tab, 397
        Schedules tab, 398
        Survey tab, 399
    users, 412–414, 423–426
OMR (Oracle Management Repository), installation, 517
    ASM disk prerequisite, 518
    create repository database, 520–522
    database installation and configuration, 519–520
    database software patching, 520
    grid infrastructure installation and configuration, 519
    prerequisites, 517–518
OMS (Oracle Management Service), installation and configuration, 522–525
    creating a response file, 522–523
    current OMS patch level, 525
    database parameters, 523
    prechecks, 522
    updating OMSPatcher, 526–527
    upgrading the OPatch version, 526
OMSPatcher, updating, 526–527
omspatcher command, 526–527
open-source, Functions, 90. *See also* Ansible
operations engineer, DevSecOps, 6
Oracle Autonomous Linux. *See* Autonomous Linux
Oracle Base Database Service, 186
    provisioning, 191–196
    registering to Oracle Data Safe, 247–253
Oracle Cloud Guard. *See* Cloud Guard
Oracle Cloud Logging Analytics, 313
    clearing and resetting, 320
    disabling, 320
    downloading and installing the Management Agent, 317–319
    setting up logging analytics for the first time, 313–317
    unit, 319
Oracle Data Safe, 225
    Activity Auditing, 241
        audit policies, 241–242
        audit profile, 241
        audit reports, 242–243
        audit trails, 242

alert policies, 243–244
alert reports, 244
creating an administrator user, 247
Data Discovery
    creating a report, 235–236
    creating a sensitive data model, 231–235
    creating a sensitive type category, 231
    discovering sensitive data, 231
    sensitive type data, 230
Data Masking, 236–237
    creating a masking policy, 237–240
    creating a report, 240
    main page, 237
registration
    autonomous database, 245–247
    Oracle Base Database, 247–253
    on-premises database, 253–255
Security Assessment, 225–226
    details, 227
    history, 226
    recommendations, 226
    report, 227–228
User Assessment, 228
    details, 229–230
    history, 228–229
Oracle Database
Autonomous Database Service,
    187–189
    client credentials wallets, 188
    compute, 187
    dedicated Exadata infrastructure, 189
    free trial, 188
    OCPU/ECPU pools, 188
    Oracle Database 23ai, 187–188
    provisioning, 196–199
    shared Exadata infrastructure, 188–189
Base Database Service, 186, 191–196
editions, 183–184
Exadata Cloud@Customer, 187
Exadata Database service, 186–187
features and packs, 184–185
MySQL database service, 189, 199–203
MySQL Heatwave, 189–190
NoSQL database service, 189–190, 204–205
Oracle Enterprise Manager, 515
administrators and users, creating, 551–553
AgentPatcher upgrade, 527–529
core components, 515–516
FMW infrastructure, installation, 530–531
high-availability setups, 516

integrating with OCI, 564
    creating a global named credential, 570–578
    creating an Enterprise Manager target
        group, 568–569
    setting up preferred credentials, 564–567
JDK8, installation, 529–530
licensing, 516
monitoring database security, 579
monitoring OCI environments, 554
    OCI Autonomous Database, 558–564
    OCI compute instance, 554–558
OAS (Oracle Analytics Server)
    configuration, 532–534
    configuring security infrastructure, 534–536
    configuring the required OAS datasource,
        537–538
    installation, 529, 531–532
    integrating with Oracle Enterprise
        Manager, 534
    setting OAS support for Oracle Enterprise
        Manager-provided reports, 538–546
and OCI (Oracle Cloud Infrastructure), 549–551
OMR (Oracle Management Repository),
    installation
    ASM disk prerequisite, 518
    create repository database, 520–522
    database installation and configuration,
        519–520
    database software patching, 520
    grid infrastructure installation and configu-
        ration, 519
    prerequisites, 517–518
OMS (Oracle Management Service), installa-
    tion, 522–523
    configuration, 523–525
    creating a response file, 522–523
    current OMS patch level, 525
    database parameters, 523
    prechecks, 522
    updating OMSPatcher, 526–527
    upgrading the OPatch version, 526
patching, 547, 579–580
Rapid Platform Update, 579
release updates, 547–548
reports, configuring OAS support, 538–546
single-node setup, 516
sizing, 580–581
Oracle Ksplice. *See* Ksplice
Oracle Support Rewards Program, 185
organizational governance
    creating a new tenancy, 16–19

inviting an existing tenancy into, 16–19
organizations, 410–411
OS (operating system), creating a custom image, 160–162

P

packs, Oracle Database, 184–185
Palo Alto Networks, 65
parent tenancy unit, 11
partitions, 107
passwords. *See also* authentication
    assigning to a user, 377
    database, 258–263
patching, Oracle Enterprise Manager, 579–580. *See also* updating
peering, 128–129
performance
    block volume, 169
    CPU, 146–147
    IOPS (input/output operations per second), 168
    summary, Cloud Advisor, 24–25
playbook/s, 345, 356, 363, 383
    advanced features, 369
    best practices, 374
    blocks, 371
    conditional statements, 367–368
    debugging, 372–373
    errors, 358–359
    handlers, 369–370
    ignore_errors, 371–372
    key components, 364
    keywords, 366
    logical operators, 367
    loops, 366–367
    Nginx sample, 364
    output, 357–358
    plays, 357, 363
    rescue option, 372
    roles, 369
    structure, 363–364
    tags, 370–371
    tasks
        assigning a user to a group, 376–377
        attaching a block volume to an instance, 381
        creating a block volume, 380
        creating a policy, 376
        creating a routing table, 378

creating a user, 376
creating a VCN, 377–378
creating an instance, 381
creating an Internet gateway, 378
creating an NSG, 378
creating file storage, 380
creating groups, 375–376
deleting an instance, 382
getting object storage namespace, 379
listing all objects from buckets, 379–380
resetting an instance, 382
retrieving a list of availability domains, 375
setting a user's password, 377
stopping an instance, 382
    testing, 373
    variables, 364–365
plug-ins
    Autonomous Linux, 296–297
    Logging Analytics, 319
    logging and monitoring, 311
    Oracle Enterprise Manager, 515–516
    Terraform, 458
policy/ies, 38, 273
    alert, 243–244
    audit, 241–242
    backup, 172–173
    claim issuance, 284–292
    Cloud Guard, 323–324
    conditional, 275–276
    creating, 376
    data masking, 237–240
    effect on compartments, 276–277
    Events, 108–109
    Network Firewall service, creating, 67–74
    OCI Function, 92–93
    "read all resources", 465–466
    recipe, 39
        creating, 42
        threat detector, 52–53
    security zone, 338–340
    statements, 273
    storage security, 179–180
    template, 274–275
    verbs, 273
    WAF (Web Application Firewall), 54
        access control, 55–59
        creating, 64–65
        enforcement point, 63
        protection rules, 60–63
        rate limiting, 59–60

PowerShell, 345–346
on-premises database, registering to Oracle Data
    Safe, 253–255
pricing
    AWS (Amazon Web Service), 7–8
    Logging Analytics, 319
principal, 269
private endpoint, 558
private IP address, 122
privilege/s. *See also* administrator user; credentials;
    user/s
    delegation, 564–567
    Oracle Data Safe administrator, 249–250
producer, 108
product owner, DevSecOps, 6
projects
    creating, 436–439
    OLAM (Oracle Linux Automation Manager),
        401–403. *See also* playbooks
protection rules, WAF policy, 60–63
provisioning
    Autonomous Database Service, 196–199
    infrastructure, 454. *See also* IaC (Infrastructure
        as Code)
    MySQL database service, 199–203
    Oracle Base Database Service, 191–196

Q-R

quotas, 16
RAM
    Flex shapes, 148–153
    OLAM requirements, 348–349
Rapid Platform Update, 579
rate limiting policy, 59–60
"read all resources" policy, granting to Terraform
    user, 465–466
recipe/s, 39. *See also* Cloud Guard
    accessing, 332–333
    cloning, 334–335
    creating, 42
    detector, 321–322, 331–332, 3334
    management, 331
    responder, 322, 332, 334–338
    rules, 335–337
    scan, creating, 299–301
    security zone, 339
    threat detector, 52–53
Redis (Remote Dictionary Server), configuring,
    387
region, 11

registration, Oracle Data Safe
    autonomous database, 245–247
    Oracle Base Database, 247–253
    on-premises database, 253–255
regulatory compliance, 5, 114
remediation, alert, 329–330
replicating a production environment, 507
repo, 96
reports
    alert, 244
    audit, 242–243
    cost analysis, 28–30
    data masking, 240
    Oracle Enterprise Manager, configuring OAS
        support, 538–546
    Security Assessment, 227–228
    sensitive data model, 235–236
rescue option, playbooks, 372
resetting an instance, 382
resources
    compartment, 11, 15, 38, 257
        creating, 490–491
        quotas, 16
    destroying, 510
    DevOps project, 213
    family, 274
    network, 65–66
    OLAM (Oracle Linux Automation Manager),
        394–395
        access management, 410
        applications, 420
        credentials, 399–401
        hosts, 408–409
        instance groups, 420
        inventory, 403–408
        notifications, 417–418
        organizations, 410–411
        projects, 401–403
        teams, 414–416
        templates, 395–399
        users, 412–414
    principal, 269
    quotas, 16
    Terraform, 474, 511
    updating, 482
responder recipes, 322, 332, 334–338
restoring a backup volume, 173–174
roles
    DevSecOps
        compliance officer, 6

engineer, 6
operations engineer, 6
product owner, 6
security engineer, 6
software developer, 6
test engineer, 6
playbook, 369
routing table, 122
adding a route rule, 129–130
creating, 378
RPC (remote peering connection), 129, 136
RSA key pair, creating, 463–465
rules
Events, 110–112
matching, 269–270
recipe, 335–337
runInstaller command, 519–520
running a command, 404–407
running a deployment pipeline, 222–224

S

sample DevOps project, creating, 213–214
adding an artifact from the Artifact Registry,
219–220
adding an instance group deployment
configuration artifact, 220–221
create an Artifact Registry to host artifacts, 216
creating a deployment pipeline, 222
creating a DevOps project, 218
creating a notification topic, 218
creating an environment, 218–219
creating compute instances to deploy to, 215
grant permissions to Compute Instance Run
Command plug-in, 215–216
running the deployment pipeline, 222–224
uploading a script to the Artifact Registry,
216–217
scalability, OCI (Oracle Cloud Infrastructure), 1
scan recipe, creating, 299–301
scanning, vulnerability, 2
schedules, template, 398
script/s. See also configuration file
deploy_apache.sh, 216–217
OCI DevOps, 214
playbooks, 345
Terraform
creating, 466–467
replicating to a production environment, 507
running, 477
uploading to Artifact Registry, 216

SDLC (software development lifecycle), 4
searching
event logs, 85–86
OCI Marketplace, 154–155
threat indicator database, 50–51
secrets, 80, 83–84
security. See also Cloud Guard; firewall; IAM
(identity and access management); Oracle Data
Safe; Threat Intelligence Service
bastions, 38–39, 44
managed SSH sessions, 44
managed SSH sessions, creating, 44–49
setting up, 44
DevOps, 4
IAM (identity and access management), 38–39
list, 122, 126–127, 495–498
network, 136
OCID (Oracle Cloud Identifier), 19
rules, 122
shared responsibility model, 2, 4–5
storage, 179–180
Vault, 80
accessing, 80–82
creating a secret, 83–84
creating the master encryption key, 83
WAF (Web Application Firewall), 54
access control policies, 55–59
policies, 54
policies, creating, 64–65
policies, enforcement point, 63
policies, protection rules, 60–63
rate limiting policies, 59–60
zones, 39, 322, 338–340
adding, 340–343
creating, 39–42
policies, 338–340
recipe, 339
security engineer, DevSecOps, 6
sensitive type data, 230
category, creating, 231
creating a data model, 231–235
creating a report, 235–236
discovering, 231
serverless Kubernetes, 113
service gateway, 136, 558
service mesh, 346–348
setting up
federation, 277–292
inventory, 439–446
Network Firewall service, 66

OCI CLI, 263–265
VSS (Vulnerability Scanning Service), 299
settings
   Cost Analysis system, 28–29
   IAM (identity and access management), 258
      API keys, 263–269
      database passwords, 258–263
shape, 147–148. *See also* Flex shapes
shared Exadata infrastructure, 188–189
shared responsibility model, 2, 4–5
shielded instance, 152
sizing
   OLAM (Oracle Linux Automation Manager),
   348–349
      CPU, 349
      database disk space, 349
      memory, 348–349
   Oracle Enterprise Manager, 580–581
SLA (service-level agreement), 8
Smart Scan technology, 186
software development, 6, 207. *See also* DevOps;
  DevSecOps
SSH (Secure Shell)
   port forwarding, 44
   using with Ansible, 345
ssh command, 47
stacked principal, 269
starting/stopping instances with Terraform,
  511–512
state file, 457
statements
   conditional, 367–368
   policy, 273
stopping an instance, 382
storage
   archive, 165, 179
   artifact, 213
   block volume, 165–167
      attaching to an instance, 167–169, 381
      cloning, 175
      configuring performance, 169
      creating, 167, 380, 478–481
      performance monitoring, 171
      performing a backup, 172–173
      restoring a backup, 173–174
      UHP (ultra high performance), 170–171
      volume groups, 174–175
   file, 165
      creating, 380
      creating a file system, 176–177
      mounting the file system, 178

object, 165, 175
   buckets, 175–176
   listing all objects from buckets, 379–380
   namespace, 379
   uploading objects, 175
   securing, 179–180
Streams, 107–108
structure, playbooks, 363–364
subnet, 122–123
   creating, 125–126
   service log, 307–311
sudo command, 96–97, 178, 215, 354–355
survey, template, 399
sysbench, 146–147
systemctl status postgresql command, 387

T

tags, 370–371
target, scan recipe, 299
teams, 410, 414–416
   creating, 426–430
   credentials, creating, 430–436
   DevSecOps, 6–7
template/s
   job, creating, 446–450
   OLAM (Oracle Linux Automation Manager),
   395–399
   policy, 274–275
   schedules, 398
tenancy
   compartment, 11, 15, 38, 257, 490–491
   creating, 14–15, 19–20
   CSI (Customer Support Identifier), 16
   Details page, 16–17
   inviting into an organization, 16–19
   OCID (Oracle Cloud Identifier), 16, 19
      child tenancy, 16–17
      obtaining, 350–353
   quotas, 16
   setting up to run functions, 91–93
Terraform, 4, 454
   adding "read all resources" policy, 465–466
   basic concepts, 456
   benefits, 455
   best practices, 459–460
   client host configuration, 489–490
   commands, 457
   configuration file, 456
      creating, 466–467

dev_compute.tf, 503
dev_outputs.tf, 499–500, 504
dev_vcn_private_subnet.tf, 498–499
dev_vcn_public_securitylist.tf, 497–498
parameterizing, 471–473, 483–484
running, 477
updating, 474–478
creating a compartment, 490–491
creating a compute instance, 502–504
creating a VCN, 494
applying the changes, 500–501
defining a VCN module, 494–495
defining private and public subnets, 498–499
defining security lists and ingress/egress rules, 495–498
updating the outputs file, 499–500
creating a working directory, 466
creating RSA keys required for API signing, 463–465
data source, 474
debugging errors, 484–485
destroying resources, 510
destroying the entire infrastructure, 511
downloading, 461
granting permission to create and manage resources, 489
HCL (HashiCorp Configuration Language), 454
immutable infrastructure, 457
initialization, 467–468
and OCI, 459
OCI documentation, 473–474
plug-ins, 458
provider, 474
replicating a production environment, 507
script, creating, 466–467
starting/stopping instances, 511–512
state file, 457
terraform apply command, 469–470, 474, 480–483, 490–491, 500–501
rerunning after a change in Terraform configuration, 493
rerunning after a change on the OCI console, 494
rerunning with no changes, 491–493
terraform destroy command, 511
terraform fmt command, 508
terraform init command, 467–468, 490
terraform output command, 510

terraform plan command, 468–469, 478–479, 482, 490–491, 500–501
terraform show command, 509–510
terraform state list command, 508–509
terraform -v command, 461
terraform validate command, 508
test engineer, DevSecOps, 6
testing, playbooks, 373
thread, 9
threat detector recipe, 52–53
Threat Intelligence Service, 49
Cloud Guard integration, 52–53
threat indicator database, 49–50
searching, 50–51
tools. See also Ansible
Billing and Cost Management, 26–27
budgets, 30–32
Cost Analysis system, 27–30
Cost and Usage Reports, 26–27
IaC (Infrastructure as Code). See Ansible; Terraform
imperative, 454–455
NPA (Network Path Analyzer), 133–135
sysbench, 146–147

U

UHP (ultra high performance) volume, 170–171
updating
OMSPatcher, 526–527
resources, 482
security list, 126–127
Terraform configuration, 474–478
upgrading
AgentPatcher, 527–529
OPatch, 526
user/s, 38, 269–273, 410. See also IAM (identity and access management)
assigning to a group, 376–377
creating, 376, 423–426
database, monitoring, 579
groups, 38, 269
dynamic, 38, 269–273
dynamic, creating, 270–273
local, 258
OLAM (Oracle Linux Automation Manager), 412–414
Oracle Data Safe administrator
creating, 247
privileges, 249–250

risk assessment, 228–230
Terraform, granting permission to create and manage resources, 489
Oracle Enterprise Manager, creating, 551–553

V

variables, playbook, 364–365
Vault, 80
    accessing, 80–82
    creating a secret, 83–84
    creating the master encryption key, 83
VCN (virtual cloud network), 122
    adding a route rule to the route table, 129–130
    creating, 124–125, 377–378, 494
        applying changes, 500–501
        defining a VCN module, 494–495
        defining private and public subnets, 498–499
        defining security lists and ingress/egress rules, 495–498
        updating the outputs file, 499–500
    creating an NSG, 130
    LPG (local peering gateway), 127–128
    peering, 128–129
    subnet service log, enabling, 307–311
verbs, 273
virtual cluster, 114
virtual nodes, 113
VM (virtual machine)
    building
        boot options, 142
        image and shape, 141–142
        image networking, 142
        image placement, 140–141
        image SSH keys, 142
        instance configuration, 140
    Flex shapes, 148–153
    shape, 147–148

shielded instance, 152
VNIC (virtual network interface card), 122
    attaching to NSG, 131–132
    flow logs, 132–133
volume groups, 174–175
VPU (volume performance unit), 169
VSS (Vulnerability Scanning Service), 298
    creating a scan recipe, 299–301
    setting up, 299
vulnerabilities, 2

W

WAF (Web Application Firewall), 54
    policies, 54
        access control, 55–59
        creating, 64–65
        enforcement point, 63
        protection rules, 60–63
        rate limiting, 59–60
web interface, creating a tenancy, 12–15
whitespace-sensitive, 454
widgets, 33–34
Windows, PowerShell, 345–346
WinRM (Windows Remote Management) protocol, 345–346
wizard
    Cloud Guard, 322–327
    Logging Analytics, 313–317
worker nodes, 114

X-Y-Z

YAML, 345, 359–360. *See also* playbooks
    files, 360
    formatting, 360–362
    key features, 360
    whitespace-sensitive, 454
yum commands, 461

ORACLE

Beta Test Oracle Software

Get a first look at Oracle's latest products, features, and cloud services – and help perfect them! Work closely with Oracle's product development teams to share your feedback and suggestions for product improvements.

To view and apply for beta program participation, check out the Oracle Beta Testing Opportunities site:

https://pdpm.oracle.com/pls/apex/f?p=102:250